PUBLIC AND PRIVATE
IN THOUGHT AND PRACTICE

❏

Morality and Society

A series edited by

Alan Wolfe

❏

Jeff Weintraub & Krishan Kumar

editors

❏

PUBLIC AND PRIVATE IN THOUGHT AND PRACTICE

Perspectives on a Grand Dichotomy

❏

The University of Chicago Press

Chicago & London

JEFF WEINTRAUB teaches political and social theory at Williams College.
KRISHAN KUMAR is professor of sociology at the University of Virginia.

The University of Chicago Press, Chicago 60637
The University of Chicago Press, Ltd., London

© 1997 by The University of Chicago
All rights reserved. Published 1997
Printed in the United States of America

06 05 04 03 02 01 00 99 98 97   1 2 3 4 5

ISBN 0-226-88623-9 (cloth)
     0-226-88624-7 (paper)

Library of Congress Cataloging-in-Publication Data

Public and private in thought and practice: perspectives on a grand
   dichotomy / edited by Jeff Weintraub and Krishan Kumar.
      p.   cm. — (Morality and society)
   Includes bibliographical references and index.
      ISBN 0–226–88623–9 (alk. paper). — ISBN 0–226–88624–7 (pbk.: alk.
paper)
      1. Privacy, Right of.   2. Community.   3. Public interest.
I. Weintraub, Jeff Alan.   II. Kumar, Krishan.   III. Series.
JC596.P83   1997
323.44′8—dc20   96-8506
                                                                 CIP

Contents

About the Contributors vii

Preface xi

1 *Jeff Weintraub* The Theory and Politics of the
Public/Private Distinction 1

2 *Allan Silver* "Two Different Sorts of Commerce"—
Friendship and Strangership
in Civil Society 43

3 *Craig Calhoun* Nationalism and the Public Sphere 75

4 *Daniela Gobetti* Humankind as a System: Private and
Public Agency at the Origins
of Modern Liberalism 103

5 *Jean L. Cohen* Rethinking Privacy: Autonomy, Identity,
and the Abortion Controversy 133

6 *Jean Bethke Elshtain* The Displacement of Politics 166

7 *Alan Wolfe* Public and Private in Theory and Practice:
Some Implications of an Uncertain
Boundary 182

8 *Krishan Kumar* Home: The Promise and Predicament
of Private Life at the End of the
Twentieth Century 204

v

Contents

9 *David Brain*   From Public Housing to Private
Communities: The Discipline of Design
and the Materialization of the
Public/Private Distinction in the
Built Environment   237

10 *Karen V. Hansen*   Rediscovering the Social: Visiting Practices
in Antebellum New England and the
Limits of the Public/Private Dichotomy   268

11 *Marc Garcelon*   The Shadow of the Leviathan: Public and
Private in Communist and Post-
Communist Society   303

12 *Oleg Kharkhordin*   Reveal and Dissimulate: A Genealogy of
Private Life in Soviet Russia   333

    Index   365

JEFF WEINTRAUB (editor) is a social and political theorist who has taught at Harvard, the University of California at San Diego, and Williams College; during 1991– 92 he was a Jean Monnet Fellow at the European University Institute in Florence. Publications include the forthcoming *Freedom and Community: The Republican Virtue Tradition and the Sociology of Liberty,* which attempts both a reinterpretation of the social-philosophical roots of modern social theory and a reassessment of the nature and conditions of democratic citizenship. He is at work on an exploration of the interplay between citizenship, nationalism, and revolution in the modern era, from 1776 and 1789 through 1989 (and beyond).

KRISHAN KUMAR (editor) is professor of sociology at the University of Virginia and was previously professor of social and political thought at the University of Kent at Canterbury. He has also been a producer of talks and documentaries for the BBC; a visiting scholar in the Sociology Department at Harvard University; a visiting professor of sociology at the University of Colorado at Boulder; and, more recently, a visiting professor at the Central European University in Prague. His books include *Prophecy and Progress: The Sociology of Industrial and Post-Industrial Society* (1978); *Utopia and Anti-Utopia in Modern Times* (1987); *The Rise of Modern Society* (1988); *Utopianism* (1991); and *From Post-Industrial to Post-Modern Society* (1995).

DAVID BRAIN is a sociologist who currently teaches at New College of the University of South Florida. He has published articles dealing with cultures of production and the production of culture, and is finishing a book, *The Discipline of Design,* on the formation of the architectural profession in the United States. His current research interests focus on the ways that patterns of social relations, especially forms of cultural authority, are inscribed in material artifacts and built into the spatial organization of social life.

CRAIG CALHOUN is professor of sociology and history at the University of North Carolina at Chapel Hill, where he is also director of the University Center for International Studies and of the Program in Social Theory and Cross-Cultural Studies. Calhoun has edited *Habermas and the Public Sphere* (1992) and *Social Theory and the Politics of Identity* (1994); his other books include *The Question of Class Struggle: Popular Protest in Industrializing England* (1982), *Neither Gods Nor*

Emperors: Students and the Struggle for Democracy in China (1994), and *Critical Social Theory* (1995).

JEAN L. COHEN is associate professor of political science at Columbia University and has published extensively in the fields of contemporary political and social theory. She is the author of *Class and Civil Society: The Limits of Marxian Critical Theory* (1982) and coauthor of *Civil Society and Political Theory* (with Andrew Arato, 1992), and is now working on a book on gender and the law, focusing on privacy and privacy rights.

JEAN BETHKE ELSHTAIN is the Laura Spelman Rockefeller Professor of Social and Political Ethics at the University of Chicago. Her books include *Public Man, Private Woman: Women in Social and Political Thought* (1981); *Meditations on Modern Political Thought* (1986); *Women and War* (1987); *Power Trips and Other Journeys* (1990); and *Democracy on Trial* (1995). She is editor of *The Family in Political Thought* (1982); co-editor of *Women, Militarism, and War* (1990); co-author of *But Was It Just?: Reflections on the Morality of the Persian Gulf War* (1992); and the author of some two hundred articles and essays in scholarly journals and journals of civic opinion.

MARC GARCELON is currently a lecturer in sociology at the University of California at Berkeley and was previously a fellow at the Kennan Institute for Advanced Russian Studies in Washington, DC. He received his Ph.D. in sociology from the University of California at Berkeley in 1995 and is revising for publication his dissertation, "Democrats and Apparatchiks: The Democratic Russia Movement and the Specialist Rebellion in Moscow, 1989–1991."

DANIELA GOBETTI is a political theorist interested in problems of political participation and changes in the use of the language of rights. Publications include *Private and Public: Individuals, Households, and Body Politic in Locke and Hutcheson* (Routledge, 1992) and articles in Italian and English on seventeenth- and eighteenth-century Natural Law theorists.

KAREN V. HANSEN is associate professor of sociology at Brandeis University. She is the author of *A Very Social Time: Crafting Community in Antebellum New England* (1994) and co-editor of *Women, Class, and the Feminist Imagination* (1990). She is co-editing (with Anita Garey) a forthcoming volume on *Families, Kinship, and Domestic Politics in the United States: Critical Feminist Perspectives.*

OLEG KHARKHORDIN is a Russian scholar of diverse interests, whose recent articles have appeared in such journals as *Europe-Asia Studies* and *International Sociology*. He has been a lecturer in political theory at the European University in St. Petersburg, Russia, and is currently an Academy Scholar at the Center for International Affairs at Harvard University. He recently received his Ph.D. in political science from the University of California at Berkeley, for which he wrote a dissertation on the historical formation of the individual and the collective in Soviet society.

ALLAN SILVER is professor of sociology at Columbia University. He has published studies of British, American, and French politics; the political sociology of military and police institutions; sociological theory; and, more recently, the historical sociology of friendship and trust.

ALAN WOLFE has interests in the sociology of moral issues, which he explores in both the scholarly and quasi-scholarly press. His current position is University Professor and professor of sociology at Boston University, and his most recent books are *Whose Keeper? Social Science and Moral Obligation* (1989), *America at Century's End* (an edited volume, 1991), and *The Human Difference: Animals, Computers, and the Necessity of Social Science* (1993).

This book brings together a set of original essays, both theoretical and empirical, that focus on the public/private distinction in social life and social thought, exploring different dimensions of, and approaches to, this grand dichotomy. The aim of the collection is to bring out the significance of this overarching theme for a wide range of issues and debates and, at the same time, to confront directly the complexity and ambiguity of the public/private distinction itself, both theoretically and sociohistorically.

Drawing the lines between public and private—both practically and theoretically—has been a central preoccupation of Western thought since classical antiquity; and "public" and "private" have long served as key organizing categories in social and political analysis, in legal practice and jurisprudence, and in moral and political debates. We encounter this distinction in contexts that run from the most abstract theorizing to the most practical and immediate arenas of everyday life. In recent decades, different versions of the public/private distinction have become even more salient in a striking range of disciplines and areas of inquiry, from "public choice" economics to social history and feminist scholarship. While the relationship between the "public sector" and "privatization" has become a prominent issue of economic policy and political debate, there has also been an intensified interest in the history and transformations of "private life"—meaning, in this case, not corporations or entrepreneurship but changing modes of intimacy, sexuality, family, and friendship. An expanding "public choice" literature, rooted in neoclassical economics, coexists with a wave of concern for the "public sphere" of discussion and political action delineated by Jürgen Habermas or Hannah Arendt and for the "public life" of sociability charted by Philippe Ariès, Jane Jacobs, or Richard Sennett. While some wonder whether the social impact of new communications technologies is shifting (and perhaps eroding) the boundaries between "publicity" and "privacy" in fundamental ways, "privacy" has become a central concept in the controversy over abortion rights. In these and many other areas, the public/private distinction is more than ever a lively, even a burning, subject.

However, much of this discussion is weakened by two interconnected limitations: The enormous bodies of discourse that use "public" and "private" as organizing categories are not always informed by a careful consideration of the meanings and implications of the concepts themselves. And, even when the discussions are more conceptually self-reflective, those who draw on one or another version of the public/private distinction often do so without systematic attention to, or even clear awareness of, the wider range of alternative frameworks within which it is employed. Aside from fragmenting the different fields of discussion, the result is that people operating within these different perspectives are often not fully aware of the undercurrents of assumption and implication bound up in their own conceptual vocabularies. People not only talk past each other, or operate in mutual isolation, but confuse themselves as well. Therefore, the prevailing situation is too often one of conceptual confusion rather than fruitful cross-fertilization and reasoned contestation. By contrast, the present collection builds on the recognition that the public/private distinction is not unitary, but protean. It comprises, not a single paired opposition, but a complex family of them, neither mutually reducible nor wholly unrelated.

This is especially the thrust of the first essay by Jeff Weintraub, which offers a critical overview of the major uses of the notions of "public" and "private," seeking to elucidate their theoretical and sociohistorical roots and to bring some intelligible order to the confusing multiplicity of ways that they are employed. Weintraub delineates, in particular, four broad fields of discourse in which different notions of "public" and "private" currently play important roles: (1) the liberal-economistic model, dominant in most "public policy" analysis and in a great deal of everyday legal and political debate, which sees the public/private distinction primarily in terms of the distinction between state administration and the market economy; (2) the civic perspective, which sees the "public" realm (or "public sphere") in terms of political community and citizenship, analytically distinct from *both* the market and the administrative state; (3) the approach, exemplified in different ways by the work of Ariès and Jane Jacobs (and other figures in social history and anthropology), which sees the "public" realm as a sphere of fluid and polymorphous sociability, distinct from both the structures of formal organization and the "private" domains of intimacy and domesticity; and (4) those tendencies in feminist scholarship (and related areas) that conceive of the distinction between "private" and "public" in terms of the distinction between the family and the larger economic and political order—with the market economy often becoming the paradigmatic "public" realm. A central theme of Weintraub's discussion is the inadequacy of any single or dichotomous model of the public/private distinction to capture the institutional and cultural complexity of modern societies. By mapping out and explicating the different forms, variants, and dimensions of the public/private distinction, his essay also attempts to provide an orienting conceptual framework for the issues addressed in the remainder of the volume.

The next three essays, while pursuing their own specific agendas, also address the historical emergence of key dimensions of the public/private distinction as it has come to be understood and institutionalized in modern societies. One distinctive aspect of Western modernity, and especially of liberal thought and practice, has been its emphasis on demarcating the "public" domain of state power from the "private" domain of the market and civil society. But modern society has also been marked by an increasingly sharp polarization between a "private" domain of "personal life," understood as the special preserve of intimacy, affection, trust, and elective affinity, and the larger world of impersonal and instrumental relations epitomized by the market *and* the modern state. Allan Silver's essay addresses this second division. As he points out, in modern sensibility the domain of personal relations—of friendship, the family, romantic love, and so on—is often understood as a precarious historical survival in tension with, and indeed threatened by, the abstract and impersonal structures of modern society. However, Silver argues, this realm of anti-instrumental private life is in fact a distinctive creation of modernity; and its existence requires the very impersonality of the new "public" world of bureaucratic administration, contractualism, and monetized exchange against which it is culturally distinguished. Sympathetically reconstructing the analysis developed by the Scottish Enlightenment of the eighteenth century, which forms the basis for his own argument, Silver contends that it continues to offer a powerful theoretical contribution to addressing contemporary concerns.

Craig Calhoun's essay addresses a different dimension of the ways that the public/private distinction has figured in the historical sociology of modernity. Calhoun analyzes the changing historical meanings of "public," "nation," and "people" as different modes of conceiving of an inclusive community, and links these notions to the emergence of the modern state and of new forms of large-scale social integration. The discourse of nationalism—in complex interplay with currents of liberalism, republicanism, and religion—has furnished one answer to the problem of forming and recognizing modern political communities, and for this reason has played a significant role in the history of democracy. Yet it also has dangerous implications because of its tendency to conceive of the public realm in a monolithic and undifferentiated way. Drawing on a critical appropriation of Habermas's treatment of the "public sphere," Calhoun argues that one of the crucial questions of the modern era is to understand the conditions under which meaningful and efficacious public discourse, involving neither fragmentation nor repression of difference, can be achieved.

Daniela Gobetti's essay reconstructs and examines some key aspects of the historical elaboration of the liberal distinction between private and public. Her starting point is the pervasive influence of the classical model, later embedded in Roman law, for which distinction between private and public corresponded to a division between the domains of the household and the body politic. This was gradually displaced by a model for which the "private" corresponded to the individual, or to civil society centered on market relations. Feminist thinkers have argued that, where women are concerned, liberal thought and practice superimposed this newer model on the older one, maintaining the family/household as a "natural" realm of subordination while excluding women from full participation in both civil society and the body politic. Gobetti argues that such readings, while illuminating, have been incomplete and thus potentially misleading. Rather, early modern natural law theorists—from Pufendorf to Locke and Hutcheson—were led to revise the dominant models of both the household *and* the political domain in profound ways, and in the process to plant the seeds for a more universalist egalitarianism than they themselves were willing to accept. At the same time, they helped lay the groundwork for continuing problems in our understandings of political judgment.

All these essays link their historical analysis to current theoretical and practical concerns. Such concerns are the central focus of the next set of essays. Once the public/private distinction has been shown to be ambiguous and sociohistorically variable rather than "natural" or straightforward, one response may be that we should simply dispense with it as misleading or ideologically oppressive. In different ways, the essays by Jean Cohen, Jean Elshtain, and Alan Wolfe all argue against such a move. Jean Cohen, taking as her starting point the U.S. Supreme Court's decision to base a woman's right to choose abortion on a constitutionally protected right to privacy, defends the discourse of privacy and privacy rights against criticisms by both feminist legal scholars and "communitarians." Undertaking to "redescribe the good that privacy protects" in nonatomistic and nonpatriarchal terms, Cohen argues that a legally safeguarded right to privacy—the protection of the "territories of the self"—is essential to any serious modern conception of freedom. Jean Elshtain, in a parallel argument, warns against the dangers of current forms of "identity politics" that attempt, in effect, to eclipse altogether the distinction between public and private by collapsing the personal into the political. And Alan Wolfe argues that, while some forms of the public/private distinction are necessary for both understanding and improving modern societies, a unitary and dichotomous public/private framework is inadequate to address key issues in both social theory and political practice. All three of these contributors argue, in effect, that the proper response is not simplification but complexification.

The essays of Cohen and Wolfe both point to a critical ambiguity of the "private" as comprising either the individual or the family. Krishan Kumar turns his attention to this second face of the "private sphere": the one that identifies it with the social space and the intimate life of the home. Drawing on the thinking of Philippe Ariès and Hannah Arendt, he argues that contemporary celebrations of the home and family are often misguided appeals to a sphere that has already been severely weakened over the past century, and one that is dangerously vulnerable to the incursions of politics, commerce, and individualism. In a complementary vein, David Brain, charting the transformations in the theory and practice of architecture and urban design in the United States from the heyday of "modernism" to the "postmodernist" reaction against the modernist project, questions the extent to which the "new urbanism" and the "planned communities" of the 1980s and 1990s have overcome the tendencies toward alienation, isolation, and the degradation of "public space" attributed to the practices of modernist architecture. Rather than a revitalization of public space, community, and urban sociability, the results are more often to foster consumerism, the hardening of social boundaries, and a combination of pseudocommunity and privatization. Furthermore, critical discussions of these issues tend to be handicapped by inadequate and misleading understandings both of the social dynamics of public space and of the processes by which the public/private distinction is given concrete form in the built environment.

Karen Hansen, in a historical study of working-class life in antebellum New England based on the analysis of personal narratives, questions the prevailing historical understanding of social life in nineteenth-century America as sharply dichotomized between public and private spheres, with women largely confined to the latter. Her findings undermine both the assumption of a rigid separation between these two domains and the related picture of gender-segregated lifeworlds based on the nineteenth-century doctrine of "separate spheres" for men and women. The larger implications of this analysis point to the problematic character of the public/private dichotomy itself as an analytic framework in history and the social sciences. When used as a binary model of social structure, Hansen argues, the public/private dichotomy obscures the depth, breadth, and importance of informal sociability in everyday life as a distinctive field of practices—with a cultural logic not reducible to those of the market, the state, or the domestic sphere—that can help to sustain communities and weave these different realms together.

The last two essays, by Marc Garcelon and Oleg Kharkhordin, provide a different kind of historical and comparative perspective by examining the distinctive configurations of public and private as they developed in Soviet-type societies, particularly the Soviet Union itself. As both of them note, the Russian language has no satisfactory equivalents for "public" and "private" as these terms appear in Western European languages, nor had Russian thought generated a tradition of theoretical reflection centering on this pair of concepts. In some ways, these linguistic and conceptual "translation problems" pose interpretive difficulties, but they also open up some useful possibilities, since many of the concepts that are fused together in the public/private dichotomy are captured by distinct terms in Russian. Garcelon's essay, which is grounded in a systematic contrast of the historical experiences of Western and Soviet-type societies, makes it clear that such notions as "public," "private," "public sphere," and "civil society"—which are complex enough in a Western context—cannot simply be applied to Communist and post-Communist societies without careful refinement and specification. Communism spawned a hyper-trophied public realm in the sense of state sovereignty and officialdom, but an atrophied public realm in the sense of republican citizenship and political society. And, on the other hand, Soviet-type societies experienced a general tendency toward "privatization," but this involved neither the "civil particularism" of the market nor an individualized private realm based on recognized privacy and elective affinities. Instead, it took the form of a pervasive web of patron-client ties and other instrumental-personal relationships, and a distorted form of familial privatism in the domestic sphere. Kharkhordin examines, in a more focused way, the paradoxical outcome of the Bolshevik project of creating a new, morally redeemed individual, through a radical transformation of everyday life that simultaneously demanded a new "personal life" based on internalized commitment and rejected privacy and private interests as illegitimate. The ultimate result was neither saintly zeal nor legitimate privacy, but a society marked by pervasive and cynical dissimulation, with a hidden underside of carefully guarded secrecy.

A persistent challenge in assembling edited collections is to combine breadth and variety with a reasonable degree of thematic and conceptual coherence. We did not select contributors with an eye to pushing a single perspective, nor did we try to impose a particular framework on their discussions.

What we did ask was that, whatever the substantive focus of their essays, they should also be consciously attentive to the complex, contested, and multivalent character of the concepts themselves. An early version of Weintraub's essay was made available to the other contributors, and they were invited to draw from, modify, or react against its conceptual framework if that seemed useful. A number of the contributors have done so, to a greater or lesser extent, and some of them have drawn on essays by other contributors as well. Partly for these reasons, it seems to us that the volume as a whole hangs together fairly coherently, and that the arguments of these essays interconnect in a number of significant and illuminating ways, for all their differences in outlook and subject matter. Taken together, they add up to a sustained reflection on one of the central organizing principles of social thought and social life, particularly (but not exclusively) in Western societies.

Several of the contributors deserve thanks for more than their essays—which would have been quite enough. Allan Silver provided extremely valuable advice, both intellectual and practical, from an early stage of this project. We should also like to thank Alan Wolfe, as the editor of the series in which this book appears, for his assistance and encouragement. We are indebted to the encouragement, enthusiasm, and good judgment of Doug Mitchell, our editor at the University of Chicago Press, a genuine intellectual with whom it is always a pleasure to work. Kathryn Kraynik, our manuscript editor, shepherded the book through its final stages with a mixture of skilled professionalism and unfailing good humor that was sometimes tested and much appreciated. And we are also grateful to Doug and to some of the contributors for their patience in the face of what proved to be this book's unexpectedly long period of gestation. We hope they feel it was worth the wait.

O N E

The Theory and Politics
of the Public/Private Distinction

Jeff Weintraub

> Binary distinctions are an analytic procedure, but their usefulness does
> not guarantee that existence divides like that. We should look with sus-
> picion on anyone who declared that there are two kinds of people, or
> two kinds of reality or process.
> —Mary Douglas, "Judgements on James Frazier" [1]

THE DISTINCTION BETWEEN "public" and "private" has been a central and
characteristic preoccupation of Western thought since classical antiquity, and
has long served as a point of entry into many of the key issues of social
and political analysis, of moral and political debate, and of the ordering of
everyday life. In Norberto Bobbio's useful phrase, the public/private distinction stands out as one of the "grand dichotomies" of Western thought, in the
sense of a binary opposition that is used to subsume a wide range of other
important distinctions and that attempts (more or less successfully) to dichoto-
mize the social universe in a comprehensive and sharply demarcated way.[2] In
recent decades, different versions of this distinction have attained new or renewed prominence in a wide range of disciplines and areas of inquiry, from
"public choice" economics to social history and feminist scholarship.

However, the use of the conceptual vocabulary of "public" and "private"
often generates as much confusion as illumination, not least because different
sets of people who employ these concepts mean very different things by

This essay took its first written form as a paper presented at the 1990 annual meeting
of the American Political Science Association for a session organized by Jean Cohen, and
its prehistory goes back to an invited lecture for a course offered by Paul Starr, so I owe
them thanks for helping provoke me to focus my thoughts on this subject. During the
essay's gestation I have benefitted from discussions on relevant issues with more people than
I can acknowledge here, including Philip Kasinitz, my co-editor Krishan Kumar, and the
other contributors to this volume.

1. *Daedalus* 107, no. 4 (fall 1978): 161. I am indebted for this quotation to José Casanova's *Public Religions in the Modern World* (1994), which in turn draws in valuable ways on
the argument of the present essay: see in particular chapter 2, "Private and Public Religions."

2. Norberto Bobbio, "The Great Dichotomy: Public/Private," in *Democracy and Dicta-*
torship.

them—and sometimes, without quite realizing it, mean several things at once. The expanding literature on the problem of "public goods," which takes its lead from neoclassical economics, is addressing quite a different subject from the "public sphere" of discussion and political action delineated by Jürgen Habermas or Hannah Arendt, not to mention the "public life" of sociability charted by Philippe Ariès or Richard Sennett. What do the current debates over "privatization," largely concerning whether governmental functions should be taken over by corporations, have to do with the world explored by Ariès and Duby's multivolume *History of Private Life*[3]—families, sexuality, modes of intimacy and obligation—or with the way that "privacy" has emerged as a central concept in the controversy over abortion rights?

Unfortunately, the widespread invocation of "public" and "private" as organizing categories is not usually informed by a careful consideration of the meaning and implications of the concepts themselves. And, even where there is sensitivity to these issues, those who draw on one or another version of the public/private distinction are rarely attentive to, or even clearly aware of, the wider range of alternative frameworks within which it is employed. For example, many discussions take for granted that distinguishing "public" from "private" is equivalent to establishing the boundary of the political[4]—though, even here, it makes a considerable difference whether the political is conceived in terms of the administrative state or of the "public sphere." But the public/private distinction is also used as a conceptual framework for demarcating other important boundaries: between the "private" worlds of intimacy and the family and the "public" worlds of sociability or the market economy; between the inner privacy of the individual self and the "interaction order" of Erving Goffman's *Relations in Public;* and so on in rich (and overlapping) profusion.

The public/private distinction, in short, is not unitary, but protean. It comprises, not a single paired opposition, but a complex family of them, neither mutually reducible nor wholly unrelated. These different usages do not simply point to different phenomena; often they rest on different underlying images of the social world, are driven by different concerns, generate different problematics, and raise very different issues. It is all too common for these

3. Philippe Ariès and Georges Duby et al., eds., *A History of Private Life,* 5 vols. (1987–91).

4. This assumption is built right into the title of a valuable collection edited by Charles Maier, *Changing Boundaries of the Political: Essays on the Evolving Balance between the State and Society, Public and Private in Europe* (1987); however, a number of the essays in the book make it clear, in various ways, that the picture is actually more complicated.

different fields of discourse to operate in mutual isolation, or to generate confusion (or absurdity) when their categories are casually or unreflectively blended. If the phenomena evoked by these different usages, and the issues they raise, were *entirely* disconnected, then it might not be terribly difficult to sort them out; but matters are not as simple as that, either. Rather, these discourses of public and private cover a variety of subjects that are analytically distinct and, at the same time, subtly—often confusingly—overlapping and intertwined.

These different public/private distinctions emerge, to put it another way, from different (often implicit or only partly conscious) theoretical languages or universes of discourse, each with its own complex historical cargo of assumptions and connotations. While the analysis of public and private can usefully be informed by a number of these approaches, the result is most likely to be fruitful cross-fertilization and reasoned contestation—as opposed to the prevailing conceptual confusion—if we start with a clear grasp of the differences between them. Not only is this essential to avoid missing the point of arguments that employ the categories of public and private; it can also help us reflect with conceptual self-awareness about how far the concerns of these different perspectives can or should be synthesized. Some of these differences simply involve variations in terminology, and could be cleared up (or reconciled) conceptually without requiring any very agonized choices. But to a considerable degree they also reflect deeper differences in both theoretical and ideological commitments, in sociological assumptions, and/or in sociohistorical context. Partly for these reasons, debates about how to cut up the social world between public and private are rarely innocent analytical exercises, since they often carry powerful normative implications—but quite disparate normative implications, depending on context and perspective. In short, any discussion of public and private should begin by recognizing, and trying to clarify, the multiple and ambiguous character of its subject matter. To bring some intelligible order into the discussion, its complexity needs to be acknowledged, and the roots of this complexity need to be elucidated.

This essay will undertake an initial venture in clarification by delineating what I see as four major organizing types of public/private distinction that operate under the surface of current discussion (political as well as scholarly) and by attempting to elucidate the theoretical imageries and presuppositions that inform them. This is not the only possible or useful starting point for such an examination; and, if one wished to minimize the conceptual messiness of the discussion, good cases could be made for pursuing either a more systematically historical analysis or a more purely analytical one. However, I think this approach has advantages for helping to clarify the ways that people customarily talk past each other—and confuse themselves—on these issues and for bringing out the potentially useful and problematic elements in each of these perspectives.[5]

PUBLIC AND PRIVATE: SOME BASIC ORIENTATIONS

WE CAN BEGIN BY reminding ourselves that any notion of "public" or "private" makes sense only as one element in a paired opposition—whether the contrast is being used as an analytical device to address a specific problem or being advanced as a comprehensive model of social structure. To understand what either "public" or "private" means within a given framework, we need to know with what it is being contrasted (explicitly or implicitly) and on what basis the contrast is being drawn.

One reason the criteria involved are irreducibly heterogeneous is that, at the deepest and most general level, lying behind the different forms of public/ private distinction are (at least) *two* fundamental, and analytically quite distinct, kinds of imagery in terms of which "private" can be contrasted with "public":

5. It is worth noting another fairly recent effort along these lines, probably the most systematic and comprehensive I know of. The excellent collection edited by S. I. Benn and G. F. Gaus on *Public and Private in Social Life* (1983) is one of the best books on this topic currently available—and one of the surprisingly few that attempt to elucidate these concepts in addition to using them. In particular, the editors' two introductory essays— "The Public and the Private: Concepts and Action" and "The Liberal Conception of the Public and the Private"—add up to a very useful and intelligent attempt to "map" the various permutations of the public/private distinction and to analyze their conceptual underpinnings.

Without entering into an extensive comparison between their typology and mine, I would like to offer two brief remarks. First, although they specify the analytical elements involved in more detail and profusion than I will undertake here, in the end the range of concrete approaches to the public/private distinction that they effectively address is narrower than those with which this essay will deal. Second, I would say that their analysis is weakened by the fact that they employ the category of "liberal" in an unacceptably broad and unselective way, so that it gradually subsumes (and homogenizes) a whole spectrum of divergent and even conflicting tendencies in Western social and political thought. In fact, in their discussion "liberalism" appears to be more or less equivalent to "modernity." When "the liberal conception of the public and the private" is taken to include Rousseau, Hegel, and Arendt—all engaged, in one way or another, in fundamental *critiques* of liberalism—then it strikes me that some important distinctions are being blurred. (People who have had occasion to read both this essay and the discussion by Benn and Gaus can decide whether these comments seem fair.)

1. What is hidden or withdrawn versus what is open, revealed, or accessible.
2. What is individual, or pertains only to an individual, versus what is collective, or affects the interests of a collectivity of individuals. This individual/collective distinction can, by extension, take the form of a distinction between part and whole (of some social collectivity).[6]

We might refer to these two underlying criteria as "visibility" (audibility being one component) and "collectivity." The two may blur into each other in specific cases, and can also be combined in various ways, but the difference in principle is clear enough. When an individual is described as pursuing his or her private interest rather than the public interest—or a group is described as pursuing a "special interest" rather than the public interest—the implication is not necessarily that they are doing it in secret. The criterion involved is the second one: the private is the particular. One especially pure application of this criterion is perhaps the way in which economists use the term "public good" to mean an indivisible collective benefit—that is, one which is *essentially* collective; the question of "visibility" is irrelevant here. Likewise, the basis for using the term "public" to describe the actions and agents of the state (so that public/private = state/nonstate) lies in the state's claim to be responsible for the general interests and affairs of a politically organized collectivity (or, at least, the state's ability to monopolize them) as opposed to "private"—that is, merely particular—interests. Treating the state as the locus of the "public" *may* be combined with arguments for the openness or "publicity" of state actions; but it has been at least equally common to claim that, in order to advance the public interest, rulers must maintain "state secrets" and have recourse to the *arcana imperii*. If market exchange is considered a "private" act—on the grounds of being, in principle, self-interested, nongovernmental, and unconcerned with collective outcomes—then it does not cease to be private when it is carried out "in public." And, correspondingly, voting in an election does not necessarily cease to be a "public" act if it is carried out "in private" by secret ballot.[7]

6. I was reminded of this refinement by Paul Starr. Starr makes use of some of the ideas I am presenting here in his perceptive essay on "The Meaning of Privatization," in the edited volume by Sheila B. Kamerman and Alfred J. Kahn, *Privatization and the Welfare State* (1989).

7. It is true that John Stuart Mill, while recognizing the force of arguments in favor of the secret ballot, was uneasy about it because it might encourage the voter to think of his or her vote as an expression of purely "private"—that is, individual—interest, preference, or whim (roughly the way it is treated by most social scientific voting studies), divorced from any recognition of civic responsibility or concern for "the public good" that should inform participation in the exercise of collective power (see chapter 10 of Mill's *Representative Government* [1861]). But, on the other hand, a key justification for the secret ballot has been

As for the first criterion, "visibility," its basic thrust is too evident to require much explication. Its specific instances, however, can be sociologically quite subtle and even paradoxical.[8] The use of the term "privacy" usually signals the invocation of this criterion, since it generally concerns things that we are able and/or entitled to keep hidden, sheltered, or withdrawn from others.[9] (There may also be things that we are required to keep hidden from others, such as our "private parts," so that having sex or urinating "in public" is frowned on in many cultures.[10])

There are a number of ways in which each of these underlying criteria can be conceived, and a number of ways in which they can be combined, to produce the various concrete versions of the public/private distinction. The range of permutations is sufficiently formidable that I will not attempt even to begin to list all the ways in which "public" and "private" are used and contrasted in current discourse. But it may be worth reemphasizing the cautionary point that there is no necessary connection between the notions of "public" and "political"; while this should be obvious (as I hope the discussion this far has made clear), it is often overlooked that there are many varieties of public/private distinction which have little or nothing to do—directly, at all events— with politics. For example: when Clifford Geertz insists, as he does frequently,

---

precisely that it enables the voter to perform this "public function" (as Mill terms it) by protecting him or her from "private" pressure, intimidation, or retaliation by employers, landlords, and other powerful individuals—or even by neighbors and relatives.

8. Take, for example, the sociologically fascinating notion of acting "discreetly"—that is, acting in a way that is not really hidden but also not flaunted, so that it is known but not officially "visible"—which every culture develops in its own unique way.

9. Privacy is a rich and complex subject in itself—which, unfortunately, I can address only tangentially in this essay. Several of the other essays in this volume attack various facets of it in a more sustained way, including those by Jean Cohen, Jean Elshtain, Marc Garcelon, Oleg Kharkhordin, Krishan Kumar, and Alan Wolfe. One excellent collection of essays on the subject, deriving mostly—though not quite entirely—from the borderland between (Anglo-Saxon) philosophy and (American) jurisprudence, is Ferdinand David Schoeman's edited collection, *Philosophical Dimensions of Privacy* (1984). Barrington Moore, *Privacy: Studies in Social and Cultural History* (1984), provides a somewhat diffuse but important and often insightful comparative study.

10. In the work of Erving Goffman, practically all activity carried out in the presence of others constitutes "behavior in public places" or "the field of public life"; the domain of the private is restricted to the "backstage" where we prepare to enact our roles in social interaction. "Visibility"—in its many degrees and modulations—is the defining criterion here. For some illustrations, see Erving Goffmann, *Behavior in Public Places: Notes on the Social Organization of Gatherings* (1963), and *Relations in Public: Microstudies of the Public Order* (1971).

"that human thought is both social and public,"[11] he is using the language of post-Wittgensteinian analytical philosophy to express the idea that thought is essentially intersubjective rather than something that happens entirely in the individual head, that it relies on collectively elaborated media such as language and cultural symbolism.[12] This quite significant conception of "public" applies to politics no more than to any other human activity.

I will not pursue this particular example any further, since in one respect it leads away from the main thrust of my discussion. The kind of argument being made here by Geertz is that all human action necessarily has an element that is, in a certain sense, "public." More often, however, "public" and "private" are used, descriptively and/or normatively, to distinguish different *kinds* of human action—and, beyond that, the different realms of social life, or the different physical and social spaces, in which they occur; and these are the sorts of arguments on which I want to focus. The following are, I think, the four major ways in which these distinctions are currently drawn in social and political analysis (I remind the reader that this list is not meant to be exhaustive):

I.   The liberal-economistic model, dominant in most "public policy" analysis and in a great deal of everyday legal and political debate, which sees the public/private distinction primarily in terms of the distinction between state administration and the market economy.

II. The republican-virtue (and classical) approach, which sees the "public" realm in terms of political community and citizenship, analytically distinct from *both* the market and the administrative state.

III. The approach, exemplified for instance by the work of Ariès (and other figures in social history and anthropology), which sees the "public" realm as a sphere of fluid and polymorphous sociability, and seeks to analyze the cultural and dramatic conventions that make it possible. (This approach might almost be called dramaturgic, if that term were not so ambiguous.)

IV. A tendency, which has become important in many branches of feminist analysis, to conceive of the distinction between "private" and "public" in terms of the distinction between the family and the larger economic and political order—with the market economy often becoming the paradigmatic "public" realm.

Now let me elaborate.

11. "The Impact of the Concept of Culture on the Concept of Man," in *The Interpretation of Cultures* (1973), p. 45.

12. Terminology aside, this is of course a crucial Durkheimian insight, partly reinvented by Wittgenstein—as Ernest Gellner was fond of pointing out.

I. LIBERALISM: THE MARKET AND THE STATE

THIS IS THE FRAMEWORK into which such terms as "public sector" and "private sector" usually fit, and which structures the great bulk of what is called "public policy" debate. The assumptions of neoclassical economics tend to dominate,[13] which is to say—putting the matter into a grander theoretical perspective—the assumptions of utilitarian liberalism.[14] They are embodied in a characteristic, if not always explicit, image of social reality (which, like most such images, has both descriptive and normative dimensions): that what exists in society are individuals pursuing their self-interest more or less efficiently (that is, "rationally," in the peculiar sense in which this term is used in utilitarian liberalism); voluntary (particularly contractual) relations between individuals; and the state. Thus, in practice the distinction between public and private—between the "public sector" and the "private sector"—usually means the distinction between "governmental" and "nongovernmental," with the implication that this distinction should be as clearly and sharply dichotomous as possible. The field of the nongovernmental is conceived essentially in terms of the market. It is therefore not surprising that the use of the public/private distinction within this framework has characteristically involved a preoccupation with questions of *jurisdiction,* and especially with demarcating the sphere of the "public" authority of the state from the sphere of formally voluntary relations between "private" individuals. These questions of jurisdiction tend predominantly to boil down to disputes about whether particular activities or services should be left to the market or be subject to government "intervention," usually conceived in terms of administrative regulation backed by coercive force.

To put it another way, this orientation defines public/private issues as having to do with striking the balance between individuals and contractually created organizations, on the one hand, and state action, on the other. The fact that these disputes may often be quite bitter should not conceal the fact that both sides are operating within a common universe of discourse, drawing different conclusions from the same premises. They are simply replicating the two classic answers to the problem of social order as posed by utilitarian liberal-

13. This fact and some of its implications are brought out well by Robert Bell in *The Culture of Policy Deliberations* (1985).

14. "Liberalism" is another contested and ambiguous term; any usage is potentially controversial, and this is not the place for a lengthy justification of the one employed here. Let me just note that I have specified "utilitarian liberalism" to make it clear that I am not addressing the Kantian strain in liberalism, whose approach to the public/private distinction is somewhat different—in ways that would merit a separate discussion.

ism.[15] Locke and Adam Smith on the one hand, Hobbes and Bentham on the other, might be taken as the most distinguished representatives of the two poles within this universe of discourse: the side that leans toward a "natural" harmonization of selfish interests, whose grand theoretical achievement is the theory of the market; and the more technocratic, social-engineering side, which posits the need for a coercive agency standing above society (epitomized by Hobbes's *Leviathan*) that maintains order by manipulating the structure of rewards and punishments within which individuals pursue their "rational" interests. Given the underlying assumptions, the "invisible hand" of the market and what Alfred Chandler calls the "visible hand" of administrative regulation[16] recur as the two key solutions. The pervasiveness of this dichotomous model is brought out by the way it is replicated when the second pole is represented, not by the state, but by the "private government" of the business firm; again, the alternatives, as captured in the title of an influential book by Oliver Williamson, are seen as *Markets and Hierarchies.*[17]

This theoretical tendency is of course highly imperialistic, and its influence extends well beyond its core stronghold in neoclassical economics. Important examples of attempts to generalize this perspective range from Anthony Downs's *Economic Theory of Democracy* to the work of Gary Becker and the "exchange theory" of Peter Blau; and its inroads throughout the social sciences are registered by the alarming vogue of what is currently termed "rational choice theory." [18] (Along the same lines, a good deal of "analytical Marxism" is essentially a branch of utilitarian liberalism, even where the "Marxist" part of the package has not gradually disintegrated—the intellectual trajectory of Jon Elster being instructive here.) Its limitations are brought out, from the

15. I am drawing here on the well-known argument of Elie Halévy in *The Growth of Philosophic Radicalism* [1928], along lines suggested by Parsons in *The Structure of Social Action* [1937]. Decades of criticism and historiographic revisionism—especially work on the Scottish Enlightenment of the eighteenth century—have made clear the need for extensive refinements in the Halévy/Parsons argument; but they have not, I think, refuted this crucial insight.

16. Alfred D. Chandler, Jr., *The Visible Hand: The Managerial Revolution in American Business* (1977).

17. Oliver Williamson, *Markets and Hierarchies* (1975).

18. For examples, see Anthony Downs, *An Economic Theory of Democracy* (1957); Peter Blau, *Exchange and Power in Social Life* (1964); Gary Becker, *The Economic Approach to Human Behavior* (1976); and, most recently, James Coleman, *Foundations of Social Theory* (1990). For an overview of both the multidisciplinary influence of this perspective and some important lines of criticism, see the useful collection edited by Jane Mansbridge, *Beyond Self-Interest* (1990).

inside, by two currently influential writers: the first does it unintentionally, the other quite self-consciously.

The first is Mancur Olson, whose core argument was set out in *The Logic of Collective Action*.[19] Olson argues that "rational" actors will never engage in collective action—due to the "free-rider" problem—unless subjected to coercion and "selective incentives." Workers, for example, submit to coercion by unions for the same reason that Hobbes's individuals in the state of nature submit to the sovereign: it is the only way they can pursue or protect their egoistic interests, which they are incapable of pursuing cooperatively. Actually, what Olson shows is that these premises render many forms of collective action—and particularly collective self-determination—incomprehensible. The premises are too narrow, and the dichotomous framework is too restricted.[20]

A writer who starts within this framework and deliberately works through to its limits is Albert Hirschman, particularly in *Exit, Voice, and Loyalty*.[21] "Exit"—which exercises an indirect pressure on the operation of "firms, organizations, and states"—is the only option of the "rational" individual of liberal theory. But that is inadequate as a mechanism to keep the world going. There is also a role for "voice," which means participation in making (or, at least, influencing) decisions about matters of common concern. And for "voice" to work requires some degree of "loyalty." Within the framework from which Hirschman begins, "voice" is an imported category, and "loyalty" an essentially residual one; thus, both are only thinly fleshed out. But they point the way to the problematic of the next perspective, which focuses on the problem of citizenship.

II. CITIZENSHIP: FROM THE POLIS TO THE "PUBLIC SPHERE"

HERE THE "PUBLIC" REALM is the realm of political community based on citizenship: at the heart of "public" life is a process of active participation in collective decision making, carried out within a framework of fundamental solidarity and equality. The key point is that this whole realm of activity, and the problematic it generates, are essentially invisible within the framework of the first perspective.

19. Mancur Olson, *The Logic of Collective Action* (1971; 1st ed., 1965).

20. For an instructive concrete illustration of this point, see Robert D. Putnam, *Making Democracy Work: Civic Traditions in Modern Italy* (1993), especially chapter 6.

21. See Albert O. Hirschman, *Exit, Voice, and Loyalty: Responses to Decline in Firms, Organizations, and States* (1970); some of the issues raised by this analysis are explored further, with more explicit reference to the terminology of public and private, in Hirschman's *Shifting Involvements: Private Interest and Public Action* (1982).

In a sense, "public" means "political" in both perspectives I and II. But these are very different meanings of "political." For I, "political" or "public" authority means the administrative state. For II, "politics" means a world of discussion, debate, deliberation, collective decision making, and action in concert. This understanding of the political is captured, for example, in Hannah Arendt's powerful conception of "public space" (or the "public realm": *öffentliche Raum*) as a distinctive field of action that can emerge whenever human beings act and deliberate in concert.[22] In this context, it makes sense to speak, not only of "public" jurisdiction and "public interest," but also of "public life."

These two notions of "public" as "political" become clearer if we grasp their historical roots and the social contexts from which they emerged.[23] Both derive originally from classical antiquity. The words "public" and "private" are originally Roman, the concepts Greco-Roman. Their dual register stems in part from the fateful circumstance that the Roman empire took over much of the political language of the Roman republic (including such terms as "public" and even "citizen") but shaded their meanings rather differently. A great deal of the conceptual vocabulary of Western social, political, and moral discourse has thus been shaped by two interconnected but distinctive legacies, those of ancient republicanism and of the Roman empire—the latter being conveyed, above all, by the massive influence of Roman law, not only on jurisprudence but on the categories of more than a thousand years of Western social and political philosophy.

The result is that there are two basic models of the "public" realm drawn from antiquity:

1. The self-governing polis or republic (*res publica,* literally "public thing"), from which we inherit a notion of politics as *citizenship,* in which individuals, in their capacity as citizens, participate in an ongoing process of conscious collective self-determination.

2. The Roman empire, from which we get the notion of *sovereignty:* of a centralized, unified, and omnipotent apparatus of rule which stands above the society and governs it through the enactment and administration of laws. The "public" power of the sovereign rules over, and in principle on behalf of, a society of "private" and politically passive individuals who are bearers of rights granted to them and guaranteed by the sovereign. This

---

22. Her most systematic discussion of these concepts is in *The Human Condition* (1958).

23. I have developed the argument which follows more fully in *Freedom and Community: The Republican Virtue Tradition and the Sociology of Liberty* (forthcoming), particularly chapter 3.

conception of the public/private distinction permeates, for example, Roman (imperial) law.[24]

Many of the ambiguities in our thinking about politics stem from the fact that both of these underlying images have a significant presence in modern thought. As compared to the main patterns of political thought developed in other civilizations, both are distinctive in the sharpness of the line they draw between "public" and "private." In many other respects, however, their presuppositions and implications are profoundly different.

If we examine the origins of systematic political reflection in other civilizations, and in other periods of Western history as well, the most common pattern is for political thought to take one or another form of monarchy as its main point of reference; and the notion of politics centered on the model of sovereignty accords with this general tendency. In such a context, the key issues for discourse and sophisticated theorizing about politics center on the problem of rulership or, to use the more Roman term, domination—its nature, its modes, its justifications, its limits. This kind of theorizing takes for granted, in its underlying premises, the separation between rulers and ruled (whether it takes the side of the rulers or of the ruled). Classical moral and political philosophy, however, was profoundly marked by the fact that it took as its point of departure a fundamentally different, and considerably more exceptional, model of politics, one based on a process of collective decision making by a body of citizens united in a community (albeit, of course, a restricted and exclusive community). Thus, the central image of "political" action as we find it in Aristotle is not domination and compliance (or resistance) but participation in collective self-determination; Aristotle's classic definition of the citizen is one who is capable *both* of ruling and of being ruled. The appropriate sphere for domination is within the private realm of the household, which is structured by relationships of "natural" *in*equality: between master and slave, parent and child, husband and wife.

What separates the problematic of citizenship, in any strong sense of the term, from the conceptual framework of liberal social theory is that the practice of citizenship is inseparable from active participation—direct or mediated—in a decision-making *community* maintained by solidarity and the exercise of (what used to be called) republican virtue. But, since liberalism is too often

24. It is distilled in a crucial formulation which appears, identically worded, in the first chapter of each of the two sections of the *Corpus Juris Civilis,* the great compilation of Roman law issued in the name of the Emperor Justinian in 533–34: "Public law is that which regards the condition of the Roman commonwealth, private, that which pertains to the interests of single individuals." (*"Publicum jus est, quod ad statum rei Romanae spectat, privatum, quod ad singulorum utilitatem pertinet"*: my translation.)

counterposed nowadays to an undifferentiated "communitarianism," it is also important to emphasize that membership in community does not necessarily constitute citizenship. Citizenship entails participation in a particular *kind* of community (which I have elsewhere called "willed community"[25]): one marked by, among other things, fundamental equality and the consideration and resolution of public issues through conscious collective decision making.

Both the notion of citizenship and the notion of sovereignty went into eclipse in the Middle Ages, for reasons which are understandable. For one thing, neither of them is compatible with the feudal system of rule, based on a web of personal dependent ties and the absence of any significant distinction between "public" and "private" authority. The same can be said of the customary communities of medieval gemeinschaft. As has frequently been stressed, a society of this sort really does not have a differentiated public *or* private realm, in either of the senses I have been discussing. In such a context, the distinction does not make sense.

A significant element in the shaping of modernity has involved the gradual rediscovery of these notions and the attempt to realize and institutionalize them—and sometimes, in a move that might have puzzled the ancients, to combine them. Behind this process lie three grand historical transformations, whose complex interconnections need not trouble us here:

1. The development of modern civil society, which is the seedbed of liberalism. "Civil society" is, of course, another historically complex and multivalent term; but I do not want to enter into the relevant controversies at this point, so I will simply state my own position. Following Hegel's guide, I will use "civil society" to refer to the social world of self-interested individualism, competition, impersonality, and contractual relationships—centered on the market—which, as thinkers in the early modern West slowly came to recognize, seemed somehow able to run itself. Liberalism is the philosophy of civil society and, frequently, its apology. Its tendency is to reduce society to civil society (in the case of "rational choice theory," for example, to collapse both politics and community into the market).

2. The recovery of the notion of sovereignty, to complement the notion of the atomistic liberal individual. The rediscovery of sovereignty was obviously connected in its initial stages with the gradual reassertion of royal power, with the multifaceted "recovery" of Roman law which often accompanied it, and particularly with the era of absolutism.[26] To restate a point empha-

25. See *Freedom and Community,* particularly chapters 1 and 2.

26. On this subject, see, for example, Gianfranco Poggi, *The Development of the Modern State* (1978), and Joseph R. Strayer, *On the Medieval Origins of the Modern State* (1970). On the "recovery" or "reception" of Roman law and its significance, the commanding

sized earlier, the liberal conception of the public/private distinction turns fundamentally on the separation between the administrative state and civil society—one dichotomy being mapped onto the other. It has difficulty dealing with other aspects of social life.

3. The recovery of the notion of citizenship. This followed a different route from the rediscovery of sovereignty, beginning with the reemergence of the self-governing city in the later Middle Ages and the rebirth of civic consciousness which this made possible. From this perspective, the "public" realm is above all a realm of participatory self-determination, deliberation, and conscious cooperation among equals, the logic of which is distinct from those of *both* civil society and the administrative state.

The distinctive character of the "public" or "political" realm, understood in this way as the terrain of active citizenship, is captured especially sharply in a passage from *The Old Regime and the French Revolution* where Tocqueville suggests why Roman law was useful for the centralizing projects of early modern absolutist monarchies:

> The Roman [imperial] law carried civil society to perfection, but it invariably degraded political society, because it was the work of a highly civilized and thoroughly enslaved people. Kings naturally embraced it with enthusiasm, and established it wherever they could throughout Europe.[27]

Tocqueville's conception of "political society," Arendt's conception of the "public realm," and Habermas's conception of the "public sphere" represent

---

treatment is still to be found in the work of Otto Gierke; see, for example, the portion of *Das Deutsche Genossenschaftsrecht* [1881] translated by F. W. Maitland as *Political Theories of the Middle Age.*

To avoid any ambiguity on this point: the *word* "sovereign" does not come to us from antiquity. It is of later origin, and its different variants—the Old French *souverein,* the Spanish *soberano,* and so on—appear to be derived from the medieval Latin *superanus* (at least, this is the tentative suggestion of the *Oxford English Dictionary*). But the *concept* is characteristically Roman, and the increasing importance of this terminology, from the later Middle Ages onward, is part of the process which Gierke describes as "the resuscitation and further development of the classical idea of Sovereignty" (*Political Theories of the Middle Age,* p. 92). To employ one of Gierke's favorite formulations, sovereignty is a quintessentially "ancient-modern" concept, as opposed to a "properly mediaeval" one.

27. See Alexis de Tocqueville, *The Old Regime and the French Revolution* [1856], endnote 1, p. 223. Tocqueville's most extensive analyses of the dynamics of political society and their significance for the vitality of political liberty (or "public liberty") are of course developed throughout *Democracy in America* [1835, 1840].

some of the more significant efforts to characterize and theorize this sphere of social life.[28] Without minimizing the significant differences between their analyses, it is worth emphasizing one larger implication that emerges from all three: attempts to use the public/private distinction as a dichotomous model to capture the overall pattern of social life in a society—as opposed to using one or another version for specific and carefully defined purposes—are always likely to be inherently misleading, because the procrustean dualism of their categories will tend to blank out important phenomena. Thus, just as the "public" realm (and politics) cannot be reduced to the state, the realm of social life outside the state (and its control) cannot simply be identified as "private."[29] The conceptual limitations of the public/private dichotomy in this connection are emphasized by Habermas's deliberately paradoxical formulation that "the bourgeois public sphere may be conceived above all as the sphere of private people [who have] come together as a public" (outside and even against the state) to discuss and debate matters of common concern.[30] Similarly, the fact that "political society," though it coexists with both civil society and the state, is not reducible to either lies behind an

28. For the arguments behind these remarks, see my discussions in "Democracy and the Market: A Marriage of Inconvenience," in Margaret Nugent's *From Leninism to Freedom: The Challenges of Democratization* (1992), and chapters 7 and 8 of *Freedom and Community*. In particular, I spell out why I find the usual state/civil society division—in which "civil society" tends to serve as an undifferentiated residual category—theoretically inadequate, and why a step in the right direction is the tripartite distinction which Tocqueville (I argue) draws between the state, civil society, and political society. (The next step required is to distinguish more carefully and systematically than Tocqueville does between civil society and the truly "private" realm of the family and intimate relationships. More on this below.)

29. The need to move beyond such dichotomous models of modern societies is also a central theme of Jean L. Cohen and Andrew Arato's ambitious exploration of *Civil Society and Political Theory* (1992). (While their conceptual specification of both "civil society" and "political society" differs in various ways from the approach I have sketched out here, I would say that there is considerable accord on the substantive implications.) A recognition of the inadequacy of a dichotomous public/private perspective has also—explicitly or implicitly—informed arguments by neoconservatives (among others) emphasizing the importance of "mediating structures": one instructive example is Peter Berger and Richard Neuhaus, *To Empower People: The Role of Mediating Structures in Public Policy* (1977).

30. Jürgen Habermas, *The Structural Transformation of the Public Sphere: An Inquiry into a Category of Bourgeois Society* (Cambridge, MA: MIT Press, 1989), p. 26. (This was originally published in 1962 as *Strukturwandel der Öffentlichkeit*, but only recently translated into English. A condensed version of the argument can be found in Habermas's 1964 encyclopedia article on "The Public Sphere," reprinted in *New German Critique* 1, no. 3 [fall 1974]: 49–55). Habermas's approach here is influenced by Arendt's explicitly tripartite model of modern society, which I will discuss below.

equally paradoxical observation of Tocqueville's which is really central to his argument in *The Old Regime:* that, precisely as the centralized and bureaucratized French state achieved its apotheosis, *political* life was smothered and suppressed.[31]

In short, these two notions of the "public"—and the two versions of the public/private distinction in which they are embedded—rest on crucially different images of politics and society, and a good deal of modern thought reflects the tension between them. However, they far from exhaust the significant discussion of public and private. For example, although they intersect with it intermittently, they largely bypass the enormous field explored, from different directions, by cultural anthropology and by the sociology of Erving Goffman: the symbolic demarcation of interactional space as a key constitutive feature of social reality. And, more specifically, neither of them captures the alternative vision of public life that links it, neither to the state nor to citizenship, but to sociability.

III. "PUBLIC" LIFE AS SOCIABILITY

FOR A PRELIMINARY sense of the contrasts involved, consider the messages conveyed by these two declarations:

> The better constituted the state, the more public affairs outweigh private ones in the minds of citizens. . . . In a well-conducted city, everyone rushes to the assemblies. Under a bad government, no one cares to take even a step to attend them: no one takes an interest in what is

31. This theme is pervasive in Tocqueville's work, but one especially compact formulation appears in the concluding chapter of *The Old Regime,* on pp. 204–5. Tocqueville's insight is further confirmed by the historical experience of state-socialist regimes, where the hypertrophy of the state (based on "public" control of the economy) was accompanied by the atrophy of public life in the sense of citizenship and participation. Ironically, the Jacobin approach to citizenship, carried on and intensified by Leninism, which aims at having the public entirely submerge the private through the continuous mobilization of civic virtue, ultimately yields the same privatizing result (as Tocqueville also understood). Maoism attempted the most hyper-Jacobin intensification of participation and public virtue—and wound up, perhaps, most thoroughly burning them out. In general, the attempt by these regimes to "politicize" everything in society has led, in the long or short run, to massive depoliticization and a retreat to the privacy of personal relations (when these are not themselves under direct assault, as in periods of "high" totalitarianism like the 1930s in the Soviet Union, the Cultural Revolution in China, or Cambodia under the Khmer Rouge). (At the same time, the forms of "privatization" characteristic of state-socialist societies have been both complex and distinctive: for explorations of this phenomenon, see the essays by Marc Garcelon and Oleg Kharkhordin in this volume.)

done there, since it is predictable that the general will won't prevail, and so finally domestic concerns absorb everything.

—Rousseau, *The Social Contract*[32]

❑

The tolerance, the room for great differences among neighbors—differences that often go far deeper than differences in color—which are possible and normal in intensely urban life, but which are so foreign to suburbs and pseudosuburbs, are possible and normal only when streets of great cities have built-in equipment allowing strangers to dwell in peace together on civilized but essentially dignified and reserved terms. Lowly, unpurposeful and random as they may appear, sidewalk contacts are the small change from which a city's wealth of public life may grow.

—Jane Jacobs, *The Death and Life of Great American Cities*[33]

BOTH OF THESE striking passages are quoted often, but rarely, I think, in the same places. This is a pity, because when taken in juxtaposition they have the advantage of capturing two powerful, influential, yet curiously disparate images of "public life" and of the public space in which it can thrive. Rousseau's is a characteristically extreme formulation of the conception that ties "public" life to the practice of citizenship. The citizens who "rush" to the public space of the assembly do so to engage in self-conscious collective action, deliberation, and decision concerning common—that is, "public"—affairs. When we venture into Jane Jacobs's public space, on the other hand, we enter what Roger Scruton has aptly termed "a sphere of broad and largely unplanned encounter,"[34] of fluid sociability among strangers and near-strangers. The "wealth" of the "public life" to which it contributes lies, not in self-determination or collective action, but in the multistranded liveliness and spontaneity arising from the ongoing intercourse of heterogeneous individuals and groups that can maintain a civilized coexistence. Its function is not so much to express or generate solidarity as, ideally, to "make diversity agreeable"[35]—or, at least,

32. Jean-Jacques Rousseau, *On the Social Contract* [1762] (New York: St. Martin's, 1978), book 3, chapter 5, p. 102 (translation slightly emended).

33. Jane Jacobs, *The Death and Life of Great American Cities* (1961), p. 72.

34. Roger Scruton, "Public Space and the Classical Vernacular," in Nathan Glazer and Mark Lilla's edited volume, *The Public Face of Architecture: Civic Culture and Public Spaces* (1987), p. 13.

35. To borrow another phrase, slightly out of context, from Scruton, "Public Space," p. 23. A remark by Philippe Ariès (in his introduction to volume 3 of *A History of Private Life*) brings out the same implication of this particular meaning of "public": "I am here

manageable. It may be that both these forms, or aspects, of public life are valuable and ought to be encouraged; and some might argue that, in the right circumstances, they can even be complementary. But it is clear that they differ in their defining characteristics, requirements, and implications.

The second notion of "public" is the one we have in mind if we speak of Mediterranean (but not usually American) cities having a rich public life. It is what Philippe Ariès means when he says that, in the society of the old regime, "life . . . was lived in public," and the intense privatization of the family and intimate relations, with their sharp separation from an impersonal "public" realm, had not yet occurred. The essential point is that "public" in this sense has nothing to do, necessarily, with collective decision making (let alone the state). The key to it is not solidarity or obligation, but sociability.

The work of Ariès, beginning with *Centuries of Childhood,*[36] forms an outstanding starting point for the exploration of this world. The significance of Ariès's analysis in this respect is often missed because of the misimpression that he is recounting *simply* an isolated history of the family. Instead, he is developing—admittedly in a discursive and far from analytically rigorous way—a sweeping interpretation of the transformations in the texture of Western society from the old regime to the modern era. In this connection, the emergence of the modern family can be understood only in the context of the changing *relationship* between the family and the broader web of communal ties and sociability. The heart of the story, therefore, really lies in Ariès's reconstruction of the public life of the society of the old regime and its gradual decay. The decay of the older public world and the emergence of the modern family (along with other relationships committed to creating islands of privacy and intense intimacy) form a mutually reinforcing process. The result is a drastic transformation of the relationship between the "public" and "private" realms, and of the character of each. For Ariès (to put words in his mouth), modern civil society represents not the "private" realm but the new "public" realm; the "private" realm is the realm of personal life, above all of domesticity. "The progress of the concept of the family followed the progress of private life, of domesticity."[37] And this "private" realm of domesticity is not, one

---

using the word 'public' as it is used in 'public park' or 'public place,' to denote a place where people who do not know each other can meet and enjoy each other's company" (p. 9).

36. A slightly misleading translation of his title, which is more literally "The Child and Family Life in the Old Régime": Philippe Ariès, *Centuries of Childhood: A Social History of Family Life,* first published in 1960 as *L'Enfant et la vie familiale sous l'Ancien Régime.* The quotation in the previous paragraph is from p. 405.

37. *Centuries of Childhood,* p. 375.

should note, a realm of isolated individuals—nor of individualism, in most senses of that slippery term. On the contrary, the family is (to a greater or lesser extent) a collective unit, constituted by particularistic ties of attachment, affection, and obligation; and the modern family has characteristically been understood—and idealized—precisely as a refuge against the self-interested individualism and impersonality of civil society.

This notion of the "public" realm, then, sees it as a realm of sociability, mediated by conventions that allow diversity and social distance to be maintained despite physical proximity. What emerges from Ariès's historical reconstruction is a picture of a world more disorderly and yet in some ways more stable, less intimate but also less impersonal, than our own (if we happen to be middle-class North Americans and Northwest Europeans). Huizinga is trying to capture some of the same phenomena, but striking a more somber note, when he observes in *The Waning of the Middle Ages* that "all things in life were of a proud and cruel publicity." [38] The great and the small, the rich and the poor, were jumbled together more casually and promiscuously than today; both ostentation and wretchedness were less embarrassed. Ariès's brilliant, though unsystematic, depiction of this world is probably aided by the fact that he was something of a conservative with a real sympathy for the society of the old regime. But the insights to be derived from this conceptual framework do not depend on ideological attitude. For example, Lawrence Stone's book on *The Family, Sex, and Marriage in England, 1500–1800* draws very powerfully on Ariès despite the fact that Stone, unlike Ariès, believes in "progress" (a little excessively for my taste) and is firmly convinced of the relative wretchedness of the past.[39]

I have chosen Ariès as a touchstone for identifying this version of the public/private distinction,[40] but the project of delineating the "public" world

38. Johan Huizinga, *The Waning of the Middle Ages* [1924] (Garden City, NY: Doubleday, 1954), p. 9 ("*een pronkende en gruwelijke openbaarheid,*" or, in the very close German translation, "*einer prunkenden und grausamen Öffentlichkeit*": translation here slightly altered to make it more literal).

39. Lawrence Stone, *The Family, Sex and Marriage in England, 1500–1800* (1979); see also Barbara Laslett, "The Family as a Public and Private Institution: An Historical Perspective," *Journal of Marriage and the Family* 35, no. 3 (1973): 480–92.

40. Quite late in his life, in his introduction to volume 3 of *A History of Private Life*, Ariès observed with charming nonchalance that, until he entered on that collaborative project and discovered with surprise that his colleagues all associated the distinction public/private with the distinction state/nonstate, the idea had barely occurred to him—not for any deeply considered reasons, but because he was profoundly uninterested in "political history" (p. 9). This was one of those fruitful oversights that sometimes help a scholar develop a distinctive vision. (Ariès concedes that his colleagues helped him "to realize that

of sociability and tracing its transformations is not, of course, peculiar to Ariès. It now informs an enormous range of scholarship in the social history and historical sociology of the family—some of it inspired by Ariès, some of it running parallel to, or intersecting with, his work. And many of the issues he is dealing with would be immediately recognizable to readers of anthropological investigations in many non-Western (or even Mediterranean) cultures. Thus, it is not surprising that, if one looks for them, one finds many of the same themes in the work of the better social historians influenced by interpretive anthropology—the treatment of everyday ritual and popular culture by Natalie Davis and Robert Darnton are good examples—as well as those *Annales* historians who have returned to the reconstruction of *mentalités*.

However, it has to be said that people not concerned with these particular lines of historiographic investigation, even if they are aware of these bodies of work, have often failed to address the more general theoretical challenges they raise for social and political analysis. It might help to point out—at least, this is what I would argue—that Ariès, Norbert Elias, and Foucault were all, in different ways, exploring the same broad historico-theoretical terrain: the triumph of privacy and discipline in the modern West. The composite picture of the historical transformation of Western societies that has emerged from these different lines of research emphasizes, albeit in very different ways, the breakdown of the older "public" realm of polymorphous sociability and, with it, the sharpening polarization of social life between an increasingly impersonal "public" realm (of the market, the modern state, and bureaucratic organization) and a "private" realm of increasingly intense intimacy and emotionality (the modern family, romantic love, and so forth). As Elias puts it: "In other words, with the advance of civilization the lives of human beings are increasingly split between an intimate and a public sphere, between secret and public behavior. And this split is taken so much for granted, becomes so compulsive a habit, that it is hardly perceived in consciousness." [41]

In short, one of the most salient forms (or versions, or variants) of the public/private distinction in modern culture (in both thought and practice) is that which demarcates the "private" realm of "personal life" from the "public" realm of gesellschaft (as we have come to call it since Tönnies), epitomized by the market and bureaucratically administered formal organization. The contrast between the "personal," emotionally intense, and intimate domain of family, friendship, and the primary group and the impersonal, severely in-

---

the problem was not as monolithic as I had imagined," and his discussion in the introduction makes a stab at integrating the two approaches; but it would be more accurate to say that he shuttles back and forth between them.)

41. Norbert Elias, *The Civilizing Process* [1939], 1:190.

strumental domain of the market and formal institutions is in fact widely experienced—one need only think about the evidence of popular culture—as one of the great divides of modern life.[42] But historically these two poles emerge together, to a great extent in dialectical tension with each other; and the sharpness of the split between them is one of the defining characteristics of modernity. This perspective can help us to make sense of the emergence of a whole range of different forms of "private" relationship that are distinctive to modern society and that are simultaneously defined in opposition to the logic of gesellschaft: for example, the modern notion of anti-instrumental friendship based exclusively on sympathy and affection; or the ideal of romantic marriage and the emotionally bonded child-centered family with its cult of the economically useless but emotionally "priceless child." [43] Ariès sums up his view of this process with this striking remark: "It is not individualism which has triumphed, but the family. But this family has advanced in proportion as sociability has retreated. It is as if the modern family had sought to take the place of the old social relationships (as these gradually defaulted) in order to preserve mankind from an unbearable moral solitude." [44] A similar vision is expressed, in more general terms, in these formulations by Peter Berger and his coauthors in *The Homeless Mind:*[45]

> *All* the major public institutions of modern society have become "abstract" [p. 183]. . . . There are also discontents specifically derived from the pluralization of social life-worlds. Generally, these discontents can be subsumed under the heading of "homelessness" [p. 184]. . . . Modern society's "solution" to these discontents has been, as we have seen, the creation of the private sphere as a distinctive and largely segregated sector of social life, along with the dichotomization of the individual's societal involvements between the private and the public spheres. The private sphere has served as a kind of balancing mechanism providing meanings and meaningful activities to compensate for the discontents brought about by the large structures of modern society. [pp. 185–86][46]

42. I have borrowed the last phrase from Allan Silver's useful and insightful essay, " 'Two Different Sorts of Commerce'—Friendship and Strangership in Civil Society," in this volume.

43. To borrow the expression of Viviana Zelizer in *Pricing the Priceless Child* (1985).

44. *Centuries of Childhood,* p. 406.

45. Peter Berger, Brigitte Berger, and Hansfried Kellner, *The Homeless Mind: Modernization and Consciousness* (1974).

46. To be precise, among the perspectives that explore this distinctively modern polarization of "private" and "public" life along personal/impersonal lines, there are really *two* broad theoretical currents. One, which might be termed a more "eighteenth-century" ap-

This is not necessarily a happy or secure solution. One implication of this process—and here Ariès's reflections converge in an interesting way with the concerns of Philip Slater, the brilliant outlaw Parsonian sociologist[47]—is the possibility that the emotional "overloading" of the domain of intimate relations will develop in tandem with the increasing emotional emptiness and isolation of an inhospitable "public" domain. Not that many of us would want to abandon the satisfactions of intimate life or the advantages of impersonal institutions: they are, at least potentially, among the benefits of modernity. But if they confront us as sharply dichotomized and exclusive alternatives, they add up to an unsatisfactory prospect. Once again, part of the solution, both theoretical and practical, may lie in complexification—a key element of which would be the existence and vitality of a sphere of public life, in the sense of sociability, that can mediate between the particularistic intimacies of "private" life and the extreme impersonality and instrumentalism of gesell-schaft.

It has often been claimed that this "wealth of public life" is one of the characteristic achievements, at its best, of the successful cosmopolitan city.[48] The analysis of sociability thus ought to be a central concern in thinking about

proach (drawing especially on the Scottish Enlightenment and Georg Simmel), emphasizes the ways in which the impersonal structures of gesellschaft, paradoxically, create a space for and enable the emergence of this new realm of anti-instrumental "private" life (for example, by reducing the need to seek vital resources and physical protection through one's personal ties). This is the position sympathetically reconstructed by Silver in his essay for this volume. Then there is a more "nineteenth-century" approach that emphasizes the ways in which these new forms of personal relations emerge, at least in part, in reaction *against* the world of gesellschaft. This perspective has taken on a range of forms ("left" and "right," conservative, marxisant, romantic, and so forth); contemporary examples would include not only Ariès and Peter Berger but also Christopher Lasch, Richard Sennett, Philip Slater, and Eli Zaretsky. (For Zaretsky, see *Capitalism, the Family, and Personal Life* [1976, 1986]; for Lasch, see *Haven in a Heartless World: The Family Besieged* [1979].) Though the spirit and implications of the two approaches are in many ways quite different, they are probably more complementary than incompatible.

47. See especially *The Glory of Hera: Greek Mythology and the Greek Family* (1968), and *The Pursuit of Loneliness: American Culture at the Breaking Point* (1970). Slater synthesized Parsons with Freud (a Freud closer to the version of the British "object-relations" psychoanalysts than the one Parsons had already ingested) to produce a radical critique of modern society. He is a powerful influence behind the work of Nancy Chodorow and—I assume independently—behind Hannah Pitkin's feminist reading of Machiavelli in *Fortune Is a Woman* (1984), so he can serve to illustrate some of the bridges which connect the concerns of Ariès and Elias with those of feminist scholars I will discuss in the next section.

48. For a range of historical and contemporary explorations of this theme, including my own essay on "Varieties and Vicissitudes of Public Space," see Philip Kasinitz's edited collection, *Metropolis: Center and Symbol of Our Times* (1995).

city life; and, as Jane Jacobs brought home powerfully in her account of the "intricate ballet" of the streets, this form of public life has its own distinctive conditions of vitality and fragility. Of the types we have examined so far, it is probably the most closely and essentially tied to the spatial organization of social life. Its domain lies, after all, in the public space of street, park, and plaza—but also of neighborhood, bar, and café. Its character and possibilities are influenced by the ways that the configurations of physical space facilitate, channel, and block the flow of everyday movement and activity. This aspect of Jacobs's legacy is especially well represented by William H. Whyte's long-term project to investigate the ways that the shape of urban space can enhance the vitality of public life.[49] On the other hand, it is also clear that the requirements of successful public space are never only physical. Two of the most influential and evocative ethnographic accounts of urban sociability, William Foote Whyte's *Street Corner Society* and Herbert Gans's *The Urban Villagers,* dealt with ethnic enclaves whose sense of "neighborhood" was culturally as well as physically based. The context of ethnic community helped to maintain—though by itself it can never guarantee—the background conditions of basic trust, security, predictability, and a sense of shared conventions against which the spontaneity of public life can develop.

These background conditions are even more important if public space is to do its more ambitious work of allowing more diverse individuals and groups "to dwell in peace together on civilized but essentially dignified and reserved terms." The characteristic virtue of this form of public space, which it both requires and reinforces, is civility[50]—which is a matter of codes and conventions, no less important for being largely implicit. Once established as a pattern (and it comes in a variety of sociohistorical forms) civility can be resilient; but it can also begin to unravel if put under excessive strain. Or, if different groups start out with enough mutual fear, hostility, or incomprehension, it is unlikely to emerge in the first place.[51] And this leaves out of account the fact that successful public space relies on a range of political and economic resources—including such mundane matters as policing, trash collection, and street cleaning—which it does not itself provide. Even in its most physically situated form, the public space of sociability emerges from a complex interplay of spatial and social arrangements.

49. See *The Social Life of Small Urban Spaces* (1980), and *City: Rediscovering the Center* (1988).

50. Not that far removed, either etymologically or conceptually, from urbanity.

51. For a powerful and sobering analysis of the ways that a viable public life can fail to establish itself—or can disintegrate—under these conditions, see Elijah Anderson's *Streetwise: Race, Class, and Change in an Urban Community* (1990).

All these qualifications point to a larger reservation. The face-to-face inter-action of the neighborhood—where Jacobs's vision is at its strongest and most illuminating—is not sufficient by itself to tie a city together, to manage the relations between its different groups and interests, and to make it work. But Jacobs and much of the work she has inspired have found it difficult to deal with the processes that connect the world of neighborhood sociability to these larger arenas—which have profound effects on the character and viability of the small-scale arenas themselves. Nor is this only a question of scale. The success or failure of cities—and societies—requires a range of decisions, ac-tions, and policies that cannot emerge from the flow of everyday sociability alone. Their terrain is a different sort of public space, that of the political. If this public space cannot generate and maintain a political community capable of collective decision and collective action, then the crucial tasks will have to be addressed by authority and administration from above—or they may not get done at all. An analysis of public life that cannot effectively deal with the political is necessarily truncated.

Nevertheless, Jacobs's work helps to make it clear why a notion of the "public" sphere of sociability, conceived broadly along the lines developed by Ariès and Elias, is not only of historical interest, but ought to be employed in the analysis of contemporary societies. Doing so would require that this conception of the "public" sphere be more explicitly elaborated and theoreti-cally refined so as to increase its analytical flexibility, and so that its interplay with other forms of public life can be systematically explored. Probably the most ambitious and comprehensive effort along these lines has been that of Richard Sennett, most notably in *The Fall of Public Man*.[52] Sennett insists (though not in precisely this terminology) on the need to link the study of the great cosmopolitan city to a theoretically informed analysis of sociability—one that addresses the interplay between the spatial organization of cities and long-term sociohistorical processes—and further attempts to link the analysis of sociability to a vision of the political. Whether or not the success of Sennett's project has fully matched its ambition, it underlines the need for further efforts to theorize this notion of public space more fully, and to integrate it more systematically into the comprehensive analysis of modern societies.

Sennett, like Ariès, sees in the decay of sociability a threatening dialectic between "dead public space" and a pathological overinvestment in intimate life—with the additional side effect that community comes to be disastrously misconceived as intimacy writ large, which renders it both exclusivistic and

52. *The Fall of Public Man: On the Social Psychology of Capitalism* (1978); these themes are elaborated somewhat unsystematically in Richard Sennett, *The Conscience of the Eye: The Design and Social Life of Cities* (1990).

ultimately unworkable. Here is the way that Ariès sums up some of the key themes we have been considering:[53]

> My central theme will be that when the city (and, earlier, the rural community) deteriorated and lost its vitality, the role of the family expanded like a hypertrophied cell [p. 227]. . . . Thus, the separation of space into work areas and living areas corresponds to the division of life into a public sector and private sector. The family falls within the private sector. [p. 230]
>
> [The family and the café] were the only two exceptions to the modern system of surveillance and order which came to include all social behavior. [p. 232]
>
> In the so-called post-industrial age of the mid twentieth century, the public sector of the nineteenth century collapsed and people thought they could fill the void by extending the private, family, sector. They thus demanded that the family see to all their needs. . . . Although people today often claim that the family is undergoing a crisis, this is not, properly speaking, an accurate description of what is happening. Rather, we are witnessing the inability of the family to fulfill all the many functions with which it has been invested, no doubt temporarily, during the past half-century. [pp. 234–35]

If, as Ariès suggests, the realm of "personal life" cannot fully bear this weight of emotional expectation, then at least part of the answer must lie in a revitalization of the public world—including the complex and subtly textured world of sociability.

The Two Cities

BEFORE LEAVING THE problem of sociability and its sociohistorical transformations, I would like to dwell for a moment on its larger theoretical significance. As I emphasized earlier, one important feature of this version of the public/private distinction is that it entails a very different conception of "public space" from that of the civic perspective (II). (The two *may* be combinable, both in practice and in theory, but they are analytically distinct.) This is a space of heterogeneous coexistence, not of inclusive solidarity or of conscious collective action; a space of symbolic display, of the complex blending of practical motives with interaction ritual and personal ties, of physical proximity coexisting with social distance—and *not* a space (to use a Habermasian formulation) of discourse oriented to achieving rational consensus by communicative

53. From "The Family and the City," in the edited volume by Alice S. Rossi et al., *The Family* (1977).

means to address common concerns. It is worth noting some implications of these differences, which go well beyond issues of face-to-face interaction.

One of the slippery features of discussing the public space of cities, as I have done in this section, is that the city is both an object of theoretical analysis and, simultaneously, the metaphorical source of many of the key concepts of Western social and political theory. So let me turn this difficulty to advantage by drawing on the dual character of the city as both social fact and evocative symbol. If we compare the notions of "the public" of, for example, Hannah Arendt in *The Human Condition* and Philippe Ariès in the passages just quoted, I think one could say that a certain image of the city lies in the background of each. But they are very different cities. Arendt's city is, of course, the polis; it is a self-governing political community whose common affairs are in the hands of its citizens, which both allows and requires that they act together and deliberate explicitly about collective outcomes. (As the Romans would have put it, her city is not just *urbs,* which means a city as physical agglomeration, but *civitas.*) But the Greeks of Aristotle's time were already familiar with an alternative image of the city, and it was "Babylon": the world-city defined by the interconnected facts that it was enormous, heterogeneous, and unfree (that is, not self-governing). Size is not necessarily the essential point. The central point about "Babylon" was that it was *not* a political community; and, since its heterogeneous multitudes were not called upon to be citizens, they could remain in apolitical coexistence, and each could do as he wished without the occasion to deliberate with his neighbors. In short, this is the city, not as polis, but as cosmopolis—I mean "cosmopolis" not in the Stoic or Kantian sense of the ideal unity of mankind, but in the sense of Haroun al-Rashid's Baghdad or of "Paris, the capital of the nineteenth century." [54]

Now, cosmopolis is not the only alternative to the polis as an image of city life, but by its extreme opposition it highlights some of the key issues. Cosmopolis has often been decried, but it has also exercised a certain charm. Its charms are those of diversity, of openness, of "street life," and of the tolerable (though often not happy) coexistence of groups that mingle without joining; but they are not necessarily—are not usually—the charms of active citizenship. Can modern societies combine the advantages of polis and

54. To borrow the phrase, though not the whole argument, from Walter Benjamin's chapter on "Paris, Capital of the Nineteenth Century" in *Reflections.* One of the disconcerting secrets of the history of great cosmopolitan cities, which is brought out nicely by Bonnie Menes Kahn's charming and stimulating book-length essay on *Cosmopolitan Culture,* is that very often they flourish most successfully in a political context of (relatively) benign despotism—Vienna being, perhaps, an especially poignant example.

cosmopolis? Perhaps, but the route to answering that question must lie through developing ways to understand both of the types of "public space" they represent.

IV. FEMINISM: PRIVATE/PUBLIC AS FAMILY/CIVIL SOCIETY

> The dichotomy between the private and the public is central to almost two centuries of feminist writing and political struggle; it is, ultimately, what the feminist movement is about.
> —Carole Pateman, "Feminist Critiques of the Public/Private Dichotomy" [55]

WHILE NOT ALL FEMINISTS would agree with such an emphatic formulation, the split between public and private life has been a central organizing theme in feminist scholarship—as well as semischolarly debates—for the last several decades.[56] As one might expect, the concerns driving this scholarship have led to some sharp reformulations of the terms in which the public/private distinction is considered. This is by now too rich and diverse a field of discourse to characterize in a short space. Rather than attempt anything like a comprehensive overview of feminist treatments of the public/private distinction, therefore, I will focus on delineating a few of the distinctive themes they have introduced to the discussion and their implications for some issues we have already encountered.

Broadly speaking, the characteristic tendency in most branches of feminist scholarship is to treat the family as the paradigmatic "private" realm, so that the formulation "domestic/public" is often used almost interchangeably with "private/public." To that extent, a number of feminist approaches have something in common with the perspective just discussed, and often shade into it in practice, but—and here one has to speak cautiously because of the range of positions in feminist argument—the implications tend to be different. While the "private" sphere tends to be that of the family (sometimes also of intimacy), as with perspective III, the conception of the "public" sphere is

55. In Pateman, *The Disorder of Women: Democracy, Feminism and Political Theory*, p. 119. (This essay originally appeared in 1983 in Benn and Gaus's edited volume, *Public and Private in Social Life*.)

56. For a number of key formulations, see two of the landmark essay collections of the 1970s: Michelle Zimbalist Rosaldo and Louise Lamphere's *Woman, Culture, and Society* (1974), and Rayna R. Reiter's *Toward an Anthropology of Women* (1975). For one illustration of the continuing centrality of this theme—and of both continuities and elaborations in the ways it is now approached—see the essays in Seyla Benhabib and Drucilla Cornell's edited collection, *Feminism as Critique* (1987).

often quite different. The ideological and normative concerns driving the analysis also tend to be different—though they are themselves far from uniform.

One further general point is worth making. I think it is fair to say that, for perspectives I and II, the main conceptual interest is usually in defining the "public" and its boundaries, with the "private" often becoming, to some extent, a residual category. Here, however, the conceptual starting point is the "private" sphere, conceived as the family, and if anything it is the "public" which is often treated as a residual category. In this respect, perspective III is intermediate between I and II, on the one hand, and most feminist approaches, on the other.

The domestic/public framework was first elaborated by a set of writers in the overlapping categories of feminist anthropology and Marxist (or, more broadly, socialist) feminism. One of the earliest influential formulations along these lines appears to have been that of the anthropologist Michelle Zimbalist Rosaldo.[57] Her orienting framework, which opposes the "private" or "domestic" sphere to the "public" sphere of extrafamilial economic and political activity, recurs with remarkable frequency in subsequent work. The central point is that in all known societies (some would say "most") this social division is asymmetric in gender terms—in varying degrees, of course—and the "domestic" sphere is disproportionately (to use a nineteenth-century American phrase) "woman's sphere." While the arguments discussed in the previous section of the essay tend to focus on the ways that many of the characteristically modern forms of public/private division cut through the lives of both men and women, feminists have emphasized the ways that these public/private divisions are gender-linked in terms of both social structure and ideology.

Feminists have tended to make (at least) three overlapping, but not precisely identical, points. One is that the conceptual orientations of much social and political theory have ignored the domestic sphere or treated it as trivial.[58] The second is that the public/private distinction itself is often deeply gendered, and in almost uniformly invidious ways. It very often plays a role in ideologies that purport to assign men and women to different spheres of social life on the basis of their "natural" characteristics, and thus to confine women

57. Michelle Zimbalist Rosaldo, "Woman, Culture, and Society: A Theoretical Overview," in Rosaldo and Lamphere's edited volume, *Woman, Culture, and Society*.

58. The directions in which this complaint is developed are diverse. In this respect, current feminist discussions tend increasingly to waver between those that target the family as a site of isolation, emotional claustrophobia, and patriarchal oppression and those that approach it as the field of certain distinctive values and virtues—of emotional depth, mutual concern, and concrete attachments—that are harmfully devalued by the larger society. Attempts to combine these themes add to the complexity.

to positions of inferiority. The third is that, by classifying institutions like the family as "private"—even when this is done in ostensibly gender-neutral ways—the public/private distinction often serves to shield abuse and domination within these relationships from political scrutiny or legal redress.

This version of the public/private distinction took a wide range of feminist scholarship by storm, since it appeared to speak to a dimension of gender relations that was at once deeply consequential, apparently universal, and highly nuanced. A good many feminist writers treated the public/private distinction as an essential key to understanding women's oppression, and in some cases tended to forget that there were important versions of the public/private distinction that could not be mapped directly onto a female/male opposition.[59] A number of reconsiderations beginning in the 1980s have brought a more troubled and ambivalent attitude toward this use of the public/private distinction as a conceptual tool. Some have argued that to accept that women have indeed always been confined to the "private" realm is to repeat ideologies of male domination rather than criticizing them, and that the reality has almost always been more complex.[60] There has also been an increasing recognition of the complexity of the public/private distinction itself, as well as an increasing diversity in the ways it is approached.

One way or another, one of the significant contributions of feminist treatments of the public/private distinction has been to greatly extend the range of people who are aware of the insights to be gained by linking the "private" to the family—rather than, say, to the market or to the isolated individual. In a sense, however, it is odd that this perspective had to be recovered, since it is, so to speak, the one with which Western social and political theory began. In Aristotle, for example, the distinction between "private" and "public" is fundamentally that between the household (the *oikos*) and the political community—with the household seen as a realm of both particularistic ties and "natural" inequality. The "public" space of the polis, on the other hand, is a sphere of wider engagement and fundamental equality in the practice of

59. Both these characteristics are exemplified by an otherwise quite useful collection of essays by feminist sociologists, edited by Eva Gamarnikow et al., *The Public and the Private* (1983).

60. One important recent collection that focuses on these themes is Dorothy O. Helly and Susan M. Reverby's edited collection, *Gendered Domains: Rethinking Public and Private in Women's History* (1992); also see Karen Hansen's "Rediscovering the Social," in this volume. (In 1980 Michelle Rosaldo wrote a reflective essay reconsidering her original argument, "The Use and Abuse of Anthropology: Reflections on Feminism and Cross-Cultural Understanding." In the end, however, she essentially restates the original domestic/public distinction, while acknowledging the complexity and diversity of the ways it is socially institutionalized.)

citizenship. Men (or, at least, citizens) have the ability to move between these two realms; and one of the bases of the citizen's public, civic personality is his private personality as a head of household. Women (like children and slaves), however, belong "naturally," and exclusively, in private life. Variations on this model have remained influential in political theory for the subsequent 2,500 years.[61] In the last several centuries, however, it has been overlaid and often displaced by the alternative frameworks this essay has been examining.

The road back to family as the "private" realm seems to have had a dual route: one, as noted, from feminist anthropology, the other from "the un-happy marriage of Marxism and feminism."[62] Since many feminist writers and activists had to grapple with Marxism at some point in their intellectual formation, one key question was how to deal with the fact that most formula-tions of the all-important "mode of production" relegated the household (and the women in it) to a minor role. The formulation of the "domestic/public" framework helped provide a theoretical emancipation from the more rigid Marxist frameworks.[63] On the other hand, in relation to the alternative forms of public/private distinction I have been outlining so far, this move also leads back to—and highlights—the analytical difficulties surrounding the treat-ment of civil society in all these discussions. Once one adopts the standpoint of the family and looks out, it seems very peculiar to treat civil society as the "private" sphere; and this recognition ought to raise questions about the whole notion of a dichotomous model of public and private.

Since at first there was not much traffic between feminist writing and "mainstream" political theory (let alone "public choice" economics!), it took some time for this problem to be faced explicitly and systematically. One of the first people to do so was Pateman (who might be said to have had a foot

61. As one of the first prominent figures in post-1960s feminism whose starting point included an active engagement with classical political thought, Jean Elshtain was one of the first to address this legacy and its problematic in *Public Man, Private Woman* (1981).

62. Heidi Hartmann, "The Unhappy Marriage of Marxism and Feminism: Towards a More Progressive Union," in Lydia Sargent's *Women and Revolution: A Discussion of the Unhappy Marriage of Marxism and Feminism* (1981).

63. A second extremely important step in this direction was Gayle Rubin's formulation of the notion of the "sex/gender system" in "The Traffic in Women: Notes on the 'Political Economy' of Sex" (in Reiter, ed., *Toward an Anthropology of Women*). A third influential statement of this sort was Sherry Ortner's "Is Female to Male as Nature Is to Culture?" (in Rosaldo and Lamphere, eds., *Woman, Culture, and Society*); unfortunately, despite raising some thought-provoking questions, Ortner's formulation is considerably more problematic than the other two (since the universal and cross-cultural answer to her central question is *not* uniformly yes).

in each camp). Since "domestic life is . . . paradigmatically private for feminists," she notes, it is civil society that is the "public" realm. The historic liberal formulation of the public/private distinction in terms of the division between state and civil society has the effect of mystifying certain crucial facts about social life. "Precisely because liberalism conceptualizes civil society in abstraction from ascriptive domestic life, the latter remains 'forgotten' in theoretical discussions. The separation between private and public is thus reestablished as a division *within* civil society itself, within the world of men." [64] That is, the supposedly "private" realm of civil society as well as the "public" realm of politics are populated largely by male heads of household (as with Locke) or male wage workers (as with much Marxism), and so on. The truly privatized realm of the family is hidden behind them. Thus, women "disappear" theoretically along with the domestic sphere. This is not, however, a benign neglect. Its result is to exclude women (on the basis of their "naturally" private character) from both of the spheres in which men have increasingly claimed equality and agency in the modern world, as independent actors in civil society and as citizens in the political community. On the other hand, the "private" realm of domesticity to which this ideology confines women continues in practice to be regarded (as Aristotle regarded it) as appropriately a realm of male authority and female subordination.

Breaking the taken-for-granted identification between "civil society" and the "private" side of the public/private dichotomy—indeed, recognizing that law and ideology in modern societies contain "a double separation of the private and public," [65] not a single dichotomy—is therefore a key requirement for a feminist rethinking of a wide range of social and political theory. And overcoming the gendered and invidious separation between the "private" sphere of the family and the rest of social life is a key practical task for women's emancipation. One of the strengths of Pateman's analysis is that it confronts directly the essential ambiguity of the public/private distinction itself—and the importance of this ambiguity. In this respect, however, it remains relatively unusual, despite the broad appeal of Pateman's recent writings. It is striking

64. Pateman, "Feminist Critiques of the Public/Private Dichotomy," pp. 121–22. For some further elaborations and applications of this argument by Pateman, see "The Fraternal Social Contract" and "The Patriarchal Welfare State" (also included in *The Disorder of Women*).

65. Pateman, "The Patriarchal Welfare State," p. 183. In this passage Pateman is commenting on Hegel's picture of modern society; but her larger point is that Hegel's theory remains a more illuminating guide to these questions than much of contemporary political theory.

that most feminist writing (there are important exceptions) continues to treat the public/private dichotomy as a binary opposition—or, rather, as a shifting cluster of binary oppositions.

Once the social world has been split along domestic/public lines, the next question is how the "public" realm is defined. To this question there is no uniform answer; and most of the time, as I noted earlier, the "public" side of the division tends to be an undifferentiated or grab-bag residual category.[66] One move to give the "public" realm a more concrete content involved the convergence, via the influence of Engels's book on *The Family, Private Property, and the State,*[67] of the "domestic/public" framework with a Marxist-feminist discussion stressing the articulation between the "mode of production" and the "mode of reproduction." This approach also suggested a way of understanding the historical specificity of the public/private split as it has developed in modern societies. One effect of the triumph of capitalist commodity production (as people from a number of theoretical perspectives have pointed out) is to sharpen, in many respects, the institutional separation between "work" and home. Only the production of exchange-value (disproportionately by men) in the market economy is considered real "work," as opposed to the production of use-values and emotional management (disproportionately by women) in the home. In the process, both of these realms are transformed—and the domestic realm, it could be argued, is simultaneously feminized and socially marginalized. Eli Zaretsky's synthesizing argument in *Capitalism, the Family, and Personal Life* played a pivotal role in bringing these threads together[68]; but, once this paradigm had crystallized, it was elaborated and applied by a remarkably wide array of writers, in contexts ranging from political controversy to academic historiography—among others.[69] One distinctive feature of this model is worth noting: while in the discus-

66. One nice illustrative example would be Rayna Reiter's (perceptive but analytically diffuse) essay on "Men and Women in the South of France: Public and Private Domains" (in Reiter, ed., *Toward an Anthropology of Women*). The "private" domain is defined by the household and kinship relationships; the "public" domain comprehends the economy, politics, open (versus enclosed) physical spaces—and so on. It would be easy to multiply further examples.

67. Frederick Engels, *The Origin of the Family, Private Property, and the State* [1884].

68. This first appeared as a series of articles in *Socialist Revolution*, nos. 13–15 (January–June 1973), before being published as a book in 1976. The influence of this work on the emerging feminist scholarship of the 1970s was more significant and pervasive than explicit citations alone would lead one to believe.

69. For a brief (and critical) overview of this perspective and its influence, especially in the fields of social history and historical sociology, see Karen Hansen's "Rediscovering the Social," in this volume, particularly pp. 271–73; some of the arguments emerging from this approach are also discussed in Krishan Kumar's essay for this volume, "Home: The

sion of preindustrial societies the "public realm" often remains an undifferentiated residual category, in terms of *modern* society the effective conception of the "public" realm is essentially the market economy. A typical example (of many) would be Karen Sacks's distinction (following Engels) between the "private *domestic* labor of women" and "public or wage labor." [70] At this point the attentive reader will have noticed that, as our discussion of the public/private distinction has moved from the liberal-economistic formulation to the Marxist-feminist formulation, the market economy has migrated from the heart of the "private sector" to the heart of the "public realm."

I have picked out this particular approach, not because it is in any way predominant (nor even as pervasively influential as it once was), but because it constituted the most sharply defined solution within feminism to the problem of formulating a binary public/private dichotomy that included a concrete picture of both poles. However, while this is a solution, it is not an entirely adequate one. Aside from flattening out the complexity of past and present societies, it may be quite misleading as a guide to action. As Jean Elshtain, for example, has pointed out in a series of sharp criticisms beginning in the 1970s, the way in which this literature formulates the public/private distinction has the effect of conflating "public" in the sense of the market economy with "public" in the quite different sense of politics (in the form of citizenship). Thus, while the family has been rescued from theoretical invisibility, the end result is that the civic "public realm" is blanked out as thoroughly as in the utilitarian liberal perspective.

Elshtain has also argued that the same urge for simplification lies behind potentially dangerous tendencies in some varieties of feminist argument to call for eliminating any separation between "public" and "private." [71] (These tendencies, which were once fueled by Maoist fantasies, are now more likely to be informed by "postmodern" deconstruction or by the type of radical feminism represented by Catharine MacKinnon.[72]) Similar arguments have been made by other writers whose viewpoints are in other respects very differ-

Promise and Predicament of Private Life at the End of the Twentieth Century," pp. 211–12.

70. Karen Sacks, "Engels Revisited: Women, the Organization of Production, and Private Property" (in Reiter's *Toward an Anthropology of Women*, p. 232). For a key formulation of this contrast by Engels, see pages 137–38 of *Origin*.

71. See, for example, *Public Man, Private Woman*, especially chapter 5. For a more recent discussion, with new polemical targets, see Elshtain's "The Displacement of Politics," in this volume.

72. See, for example, Catharine A. MacKinnon, "Privacy v. Equality," in *Feminism Unmodified* (1987), and "Abortion: On Public and Private," in *Toward a Feminist Theory of the State* (1989).

ent from Elshtain's; one important example is Nancy Fraser, who is one of the current feminist writers most perceptively sensitive to the complexities of the public/private distinction and to the need—both theoretical and practical—for complexification rather than simplification.[73]

These criticisms and reservations seem to me well taken. But the problem they point to is not merely a problem of Marxist or radical feminism—nor, indeed, of feminism more generally. Rather, as I have already hinted more than once, it reflects the sort of difficulty which any attempt at a dichotomous public/private model will eventually encounter. When used as comprehensive models of social life, such binary frameworks will always prove inadequate—both theoretically and normatively—to the complexity of modern societies.

THE GREAT DIVIDE—AND ITS LIMITS

LET US TAKE STOCK. My primary purpose has been to establish the historical and theoretical complexity of the public/private distinction; to delineate some of the more important of the multiplicity of ways in which this distinction is employed; and to bring out some of the implications of this multiplicity. I hope this task has been accomplished. As a quick reminder of the main outlines of the discussion, I offer below a somewhat simplified illustrative restatement of examples from the four organizing models I have been examining, reshuffled slightly to bring out some salient contrasts. Listed in column 4 are the social forms which provide—explicitly or implicitly—each perspective's key point of reference. As I have been trying to suggest, the "roots" of the different perspectives are sociohistorical as well as theoretical and ideological.

73. See, in particular, "Rethinking the Public Sphere: A Contribution to the Critique of Actually Existing Democracy" (in Craig Calhoun's edited volume, *Habermas and the Public Sphere*), and "What's Critical about Critical Theory?: The Case of Habermas and Gender" (in *Unruly Practices*). Although Fraser's arguments along these lines are particularly cogent, one could cite a growing feminist theoretical literature that is sensitive to these complexities and their normative significance. To pick out just two examples that concentrate on different sides of the public/private dichotomy: Seyla Benhabib, in a recent essay, delineates and contrasts three "Models of Public Space" (in Calhoun's *Habermas and the Public Sphere*) associated, respectively, with Arendt, with neo-Kantian liberalism of a broadly Rawlsian variety, and with Habermas. However, it ought to be noted that all three of these versions of "public space" fall within just one of the categories I have outlined in this essay (namely, category II). For a vigorous antisimplificationist defense of the discourse of privacy and privacy rights against both feminist and "communitarian" critiques, see Jean Cohen's "Rethinking Privacy: Autonomy, Identity, and the Abortion Controversy," in this volume.

	Private	*Public*	*Sociohistorical Point of Reference*
Aristotle	Household (*oikos*)	Political community	Polis
Ariès	Domesticity	Sociability	Old Regime
Marxist feminism	Family	Market economy	Capitalism
Mainstream economics	Market economy	Government (that is, administrative "intervention")	Capitalism

One sociohistorical factor deserves special mention, since it helps to explain the ultimately irreducible complexity of modern treatments of the public/private distinction: For Aristotle, the sphere of the *oikos* comprises *both* the family and "economic" life, since he could regard the household as the main institution regulating production and distribution. With the increasing centrality of the *market* economy, and the whole world of contractual social relations centered on the market, it becomes less plausible to combine family and "economy" in the same category of "private" life. And indeed the market economy, as a large-scale and impersonal system of interdependence, is "private" only in a rather special and ambiguous sense—which explains why some approaches can treat it as the "public" realm. We have been encountering this ambiguity throughout the discussion.

Arendt, of course, faces this difficulty directly, and in response develops an explicitly tripartite model of modern society, introducing the category of "the social" as a realm alternative to both "the private" and "the public," one whose rise is distinctive to modernity. Essentially—to sweep too quickly over some complicated interpretive problems—"the social" is Arendt's characterization of modern civil society, in the sense that I have been using the term in this essay. In this way, despite some very important differences, her typology has a certain family resemblance to another influential tripartite model of modern society, Hegel's framework of family, civil society, and the state. Both examples illustrate the tendency for dichotomous models of modern society to break down when they are thought through seriously and to begin generating intermediate and residual categories, as well as underlining the specific difficulties involved in fitting modern civil society into any dichotomous public/private framework.[74]

74. By denying the attribution of "private" to civil society, transferring it to the domestic sphere, yet continuing to recognize the need to distinguish between civil society and politics, Pateman also moves (not entirely explicitly) to a tripartite model. This parallel between Pateman and Arendt is ironic, since Arendt can hardly be termed a feminist thinker, and her ideal involves precisely the kind of rigid division between the "private" sphere of the household and the "public" realm of political community (along with a devaluation of

These considerations help to explain why the reader should not now expect me to offer a new and comprehensive typology that can resolve the ambiguities and loose ends I have outlined. However, as a more modest and partial step, I do think it is possible to point to two major families of current approaches to the treatment of "public" and "private" and to suggest that they are rooted in attempts to use the public/private distinction to capture (at least) two kinds of institutional divisions that have become increasingly sharp and salient in modern societies (in culture and experience as well as theory). I should emphasize that these broad characterizations are offered as an interpretive supplement to the four central categories I have used in this essay, not as a replacement for them.

On the one hand, a wide range of discussions and debates that draw on the notions of "public" and "private" tend to assume (often implicitly and more or less unreflectively) that the distinction public/private corresponds, one way or another, to the distinction political/nonpolitical. In most of these discussions, the predominant (even paradigmatic) image of the nonpolitical, "private" sphere is that of the market (and/or of the civil society based on the market). The "private" sphere is thus characterized by the centrality of explicit contract, rational exchange, impersonality, instrumental calculation of individual advantage, and so forth.[75] As I emphasized earlier, the character of the "political" is deeply ambiguous in these discussions. If the political is conceived in terms of the administrative state, then the "public" realm is distinguished by the use of legitimate coercion and the authoritative direction of collective outcomes, as opposed to formally voluntary contract and spontaneous order based on market exchange.[76] Or, in certain more "civic" perspectives, the distinctiveness of the "public" realm (or "public sphere") may have more to do with the significance of solidarity, of "public spirit," of participation in a process of active citizenship and collective self-determination, and so on.[77] But, in either case, the "public" realm is commonly defined, above all, in opposition to the "private" realm of the market and civil society. These conceptual mappings, and the problematics that go with them, are of course tied up with historical emergence of the new "private" sphere of civil society and of distinctively modern forms of state and polity.

---

the former) which Pateman would like to overcome. But this convergence brings out the theoretical difficulty to which both are responding.

75. In other fields of discourse, these are all taken to be the characteristics of the "public" realm—which is precisely the point I am trying to emphasize here.

76. Thus, public/private = state/society or state/market.

77. In which case, as we have seen, the "public" realm is something *distinct* from the administrative state.

Then, as we have seen, there is *another* field of discourse (or, rather, several) in which the realm of "private life" is above all the world of personal relationships, particularly those bound up with intimacy, domesticity, and "privacy." The "public" realm to which *this* version of the private is contrasted is either that of sociability or—especially in the context of modernity—the large-scale order of gesellschaft based on impersonality, formal institutions, instrumental relations, and so on. In sociohistorical terms, the new sphere of the private being addressed *here* is exemplified by new types of personal relationships, a key characteristic of which is that, to a great extent, they are defined in direct opposition to the ethos of the (equally new) "public" realm of impersonal relations and institutions, and are valued precisely for that reason. In this connection, a key task is to grasp the way in which the world of "personal" relations has *become* so essentially private—in this particular sense of "private." That is, this version of the public/private distinction is not straightforwardly universal in its applicability—any more than the other versions—but is sociohistorically variable. In this framework, unlike the first one(s) I just outlined, the market is often paradigmatic of the *public* realm.

In two different forms then, what might have appeared as an institutional and experiential continuum in other kinds of society has increasingly appeared as a great divide—which makes the invocation of the grand dichotomy of public/private appear especially appropriate to capture it. However, this comparison also brings out some of the limitations of the public/private dichotomy for these purposes. First, although each of these pictures of polarization captures pervasive and powerful *tendencies,* they are tendencies rather than accomplished outcomes. In neither case have the social mediations between the two poles of the dichotomy actually disappeared, nor are they likely to. Second, it is clear that (at least) two different forms of public/private distinction are involved, raising different sets of issues, which cannot usefully be amalgamated into a single grand dichotomy. Nor could this problem be solved by a quantitative scale of degrees of "publicness" or "privateness," since—as I have just been trying to make clear—the (more or less implicit) defining criteria of "public" and "private" differ between the two cases. It might appear, for example, that we can describe the market economy as more "public" than the nuclear family, while the state is more "public" still. But the basis for this scale is far from self-evident. It seems straightforward to describe the jurisdictions of both city governments and national states as "public," but what makes them more "public" than the market? The comprehensive interdependencies of the market routinely transcend the boundaries of these jurisdictions, and market relations can often be more "open" and "visible" than the activities of government bureaucracies. Part of what makes the market economy "private" is that it is seen as a legitimate field for competitive and self-interested individualism; but, as I noted earlier, a crucial element of what culturally defines the "private life" of friendship, home, and family is precisely that it is valued as a refuge *against* the self-interested individualism of the market. And so on.

Nevertheless, while the public/private distinction is inherently problematic and often treacherous, frequently confusing and potentially misleading, it is also a powerful instrument of social analysis and moral reflection if approached with due caution and conceptual self-awareness. It is, at all events, an inescapable element of the theoretical vocabularies as well as the institutional and cultural landscape of modern societies. Thus, it can neither be conveniently simplified nor usefully avoided. The variability, ambiguity, and difficulty of the public/private distinction need to be recognized and confronted—but also the richness and apparent indispensability of this grand dichotomy.

REFERENCES

Anderson, Elijah. 1990. *Streetwise: Race, Class, and Change in an Urban Community.* Chicago: University of Chicago Press.

Arendt, Hannah. 1958. *The Human Condition.* Chicago: University of Chicago Press.

Ariès, Philippe. 1962. *Centuries of Childhood: A Social History of Family Life.* New York: Vintage. Originally published as *L'Enfant et la vie familiale sous l'Ancien Régime* (Paris: Plon, 1960).

———. 1977. "The Family and the City." In *The Family,* edited by Alice S. Rossi et al. New York: Norton.

Ariès, Philippe, Georges Duby, et al., eds. 1987–91. *A History of Private Life.* 5 vols. Cambridge, MA: Harvard University Press.

Becker, Gary. 1976. *The Economic Approach to Human Behavior.* Chicago: University of Chicago Press.

Bell, Robert. 1985. *The Culture of Policy Deliberations.* New Brunswick, NJ: Rutgers University Press.

Benhabib, Seyla. 1992. "Models of Public Space: Hannah Arendt, the Liberal Tradition, and Jürgen Habermas." In *Habermas and the Public Sphere,* edited by Craig Calhoun. Cambridge, MA: MIT Press.

Benhabib, Seyla, and Drucilla Cornell, eds. 1987. *Feminism as Critique.* Minneapolis: University of Minnesota Press.

Benjamin, Walter. 1978. *Reflections.* New York: Harcourt Brace Jovanovich.

Benn, S. I., and G. F. Gaus, eds. 1983. *Public and Private in Social Life.* London: Croom Helm.

Berger, Peter, Brigitte Berger, and Hansfried Kellner. 1974. *The Homeless Mind: Modernization and Consciousness.* New York: Vintage.

Berger, Peter, and Richard Neuhaus. 1977. *To Empower People: The Role of Mediating Structures in Public Policy.* Washington, DC: American Enterprise Institute.

Blau, Peter. 1964. *Exchange and Power in Social Life.* New York: Wiley.

Bobbio, Norberto. 1989. "The Great Dichotomy: Public/Private." In *Democracy and Dictatorship.* Minneapolis: University of Minnesota Press.

Calhoun, Craig, ed. 1992. *Habermas and the Public Sphere.* Cambridge, MA: MIT Press.

Casanova, José. 1994. *Public Religions in the Modern World.* Chicago: University of Chicago Press.

Chandler, Alfred D., Jr. 1977. *The Visible Hand: The Managerial Revolution in American Business.* Cambridge, MA: Harvard University Press.

Cohen, Jean, and Andrew Arato. 1992. *Civil Society and Political Theory.* Cambridge, MA: MIT Press.

Coleman, James. 1990. *Foundations of Social Theory.* Cambridge, MA: Harvard University Press.

Darnton, Robert. 1985. *The Great Cat Massacre and Other Episodes in French Cultural History.* New York: Vintage.

Davis, Natalie Zemon. 1975. *Society and Culture in Early Modern France.* Stanford, CA: Stanford University Press.

Douglas, Mary. 1978. "Judgements on James Frazier." *Daedalus* 107, no. 4 (fall): 151–64.

Downs, Anthony. 1957. *An Economic Theory of Democracy.* New York: Harper & Row.

Elias, Norbert. [1939] 1978, 1982. *The Civilizing Process.* 2 vols. New York: Pantheon.

Elshtain, Jean Bethke. 1981. *Public Man, Private Woman.* Princeton, NJ: Princeton University Press.

Engels, Frederick. [1884] 1972. *The Origin of the Family, Private Property, and the State.* New York: International Publishers.

Fraser, Nancy. 1992. "Rethinking the Public Sphere: A Contribution to the Critique of Actually Existing Democracy." In *Habermas and the Public Sphere,* edited by Craig Calhoun. Cambridge, MA: MIT Press.

————. 1989. "What's Critical about Critical Theory? The Case of Habermas and Gender." In *Unruly Practices: Power, Discourse, and Gender in Contemporary Social Theory.* Minneapolis: University of Minnesota Press.

Gamarnikow, Eva, et al., eds. 1983. *The Public and the Private.* London: Heinemann.

Gans, Herbert. 1962. *The Urban Villagers: Group and Class in the Life of Italian-Americans.* Glencoe, IL: Free Press.

Geertz, Clifford. 1973. *The Interpretation of Cultures.* New York: Basic.

Gierke, Otto. [1881] 1987. *Political Theories of the Middle Age.* Cambridge: Cambridge University Press.

Glazer, Nathan, and Mark Lilla, eds. 1987. *The Public Face of Architecture: Civic Culture and Public Spaces.* New York: Free Press.

Goffman, Erving. 1963. *Behavior in Public Places: Notes on the Social Organization of Gatherings.* New York: Free Press.

———. 1971. *Relations in Public: Microstudies of the Public Order.* New York: Basic.

Habermas, Jürgen. 1974. "The Public Sphere." *New German Critique* 1, no. 3 (fall): 49–55. Originally published in 1964 as an encyclopedia article in the *Fischer-Lexikon.*

———. 1989. *The Structural Transformation of the Public Sphere: An Inquiry into a Category of Bourgeois Society.* Cambridge, MA: MIT Press. Originally published as *Strukturwandel der Öffentlichkeit: Untersuchungen zu einer Kategorie der bürgerlichen Gesellschaft* (Neuwied: Luchterhand, 1962).

Halévy, Elie. [1928] 1972. *The Growth of Philosophic Radicalism.* Reprint, Clifton: Augustus M. Kelley.

Hartmann, Heidi. 1981. "The Unhappy Marriage of Marxism and Feminism: Towards a More Progressive Union." In *Women and Revolution: A Discussion of the Unhappy Marriage of Marxism and Feminism,* edited by Lydia Sargent. Boston: South End Press.

Helly, Dorothy O., and Susan M. Reverby, eds. 1992. *Gendered Domains: Rethinking Public and Private in Women's History.* Ithaca, NY: Cornell University Press.

Hirschman, Albert O. 1970. *Exit, Voice, and Loyalty: Responses to Decline in Firms, Organizations, and States.* Cambridge, MA: Harvard University Press.

———. 1982. *Shifting Involvements: Private Interest and Public Action.* Princeton, NJ: Princeton University Press.

Huizinga, Johan. [1924] 1954. *The Waning of the Middle Ages.* Garden City, NY: Doubleday.

Jacobs, Jane. 1961. *The Death and Life of Great American Cities.* New York: Vintage.

Lasch, Christopher. 1979. *Haven in a Heartless World: The Family Besieged.* New York: Basic.

Laslett, Barbara. 1973. "The Family as a Public and Private Institution: An Historical Perspective." *Journal of Marriage and the Family* 35(3): 480–92.

Kahn, Bonnie Menes. 1987. *Cosmopolitan Culture: The Gilt-Edged Dream of a Tolerant City.* New York: Atheneum.

MacKinnon, Catharine A. 1987. "Privacy v. Equality." In *Feminism Unmodified.* Cambridge, MA: Harvard University Press.

———. 1989. "Abortion: On Public and Private." In *Toward a Feminist Theory of the State.* Cambridge, MA: Harvard University Press.

Maier, Charles, ed. 1987. *Changing Boundaries of the Political: Essays on the Evolving Balance between the State and Society, Public and Private in Europe.* New York: Cambridge University Press.

Mansbridge, Jane J. 1990. *Beyond Self-Interest.* Chicago: University of Chicago Press.

Mill, John Stuart. [1861] 1975. *Representative Government.* In *Three Essays,* edited by Richard Wollheim. New York: Oxford University Press.

Moore, Barrington. 1984. *Privacy: Studies in Social and Cultural History.* Armonk, NY: M. E. Sharpe.

Olson, Mancur. 1965, 1971. *The Logic of Collective Action.* Cambridge, MA: Harvard University Press.

Ortner, Sherry B. 1974. "Is Female to Male as Nature Is to Culture?" In *Woman, Culture, and Society,* edited by Michelle Zimbalist Rosaldo and Louise Lamphere. Stanford, CA: Stanford University Press.

Parsons, Talcott. [1937] 1968. *The Structure of Social Action.* Reprint, New York: Free Press.

Pateman, Carole. 1989. "Feminist Critiques of the Public/Private Dichotomy." In *The Disorder of Women: Democracy, Feminism and Political Theory.* Stanford, CA: Stanford University Press.

———. 1989a. "The Fraternal Social Contract." In *The Disorder of Women: Democracy, Feminism and Political Theory.* Stanford, CA: Stanford University Press.

———. 1989b. "The Patriarchal Welfare State." In *The Disorder of Women: Democracy, Feminism, and Radical Theory.* Stanford, CA: Stanford University Press.

Pitkin, Hannah Fenichel. 1984. *Fortune Is a Woman: Gender and Politics in the Thought of Niccolò Machiavelli.* Berkeley: University of California Press.

Poggi, Gianfranco. 1978. *The Development of the Modern State: A Sociological Introduction.* Stanford, CA: Stanford University Press.

Putnam, Robert D. 1993. *Making Democracy Work: Civic Traditions in Modern Italy.* Princeton, NJ: Princeton University Press.

Reiter, Rayna R. 1975. "Men and Women in the South of France: Public and Private Domains." In *Toward an Anthropology of Women,* edited by Rayna R. Reiter. New York: Monthly Review Press.

Reiter, Rayna R., ed. 1975. *Toward an Anthropology of Women.* New York: Monthly Review Press.

Rosaldo, Michelle Zimbalist. 1974. "Woman, Culture, and Society: A Theoretical Overview." In *Woman, Culture, and Society,* edited by Michelle Zimbalist Rosaldo and Louise Lamphere. Stanford, CA: Stanford University Press.

———. 1980. "The Use and Abuse of Anthropology: Reflections on Feminism and Cross-Cultural Understanding." *Signs* 5, no. 3 (spring): 389–417.

Rosaldo, Michelle Zimbalist, and Louise Lamphere, eds. 1974. *Woman, Culture, and Society.* Stanford, CA: Stanford University Press.

Rousseau, Jean-Jacques. [1762] 1978. *On the Social Contract.* New York: St. Martin's.

Rubin, Gayle. 1975. "The Traffic in Women: Notes on the 'Political Economy' of Sex." In *Toward an Anthropology of Women,* edited by Rayna R. Reiter. New York: Monthly Review Press.

Sacks, Karen. 1975. "Engels Revisited: Women, the Organization of Production, and Private Property." In *Toward an Anthropology of Women,* edited by Rayne R. Reiter. New York: Monthly Review Press.

Schoeman, Ferdinand David, ed. 1984. *Philosophical Dimensions of Privacy: An Anthology.* Cambridge: Cambridge University Press.

Scruton, Roger. 1963. "Public Space and the Classical Vernacular." In *The Public*

Face of Architecture: Civic Culture and Public Spaces, edited by Nathan Glazer and Mark Lilla. New York: Free Press.

Sennett, Richard. 1978. *The Fall of Public Man: On the Social Psychology of Capitalism.* New York: Vintage.

———. 1990. *The Conscience of the Eye: The Design and Social Life of Cities.* New York: Knopf.

Slater, Philip. 1968. *The Glory of Hera: Greek Mythology and the Greek Family.* Boston: Beacon.

———. 1970. *The Pursuit of Loneliness: American Culture at the Breaking Point.* Boston: Beacon.

Starr, Paul. 1989. "The Meaning of Privatization." In *Privatization and the Welfare State,* edited by Sheila B. Kamerman and Alfred J.Kahn. Princeton, NJ: Princeton University Press.

Stone, Lawrence. 1979. *The Family, Sex and Marriage in England, 1500–1800.* New York: Harper & Row.

Strayer, Joseph R. 1970. *On the Medieval Origins of the Modern State.* Princeton, NJ: Princeton University Press.

Tocqueville, Alexis de. [1835, 1840] 1969. *Democracy in America.* Garden City, NY: Doubleday Anchor.

———. [1856] 1955. *The Old Regime and the French Revolution.* Garden City, NY: Anchor.

Weintraub, Jeff. 1992. "Democracy and the Market: A Marriage of Inconvenience." In *From Leninism to Freedom: The Challenges of Democratization,* edited by Margaret Latus Nugent. Boulder, CO: Westview.

———. 1995. "Varieties and Vicissitudes of Public Space." In *Metropolis: Center and Symbol of Our Times,* edited by Philip Kasinitz. New York: New York University Press; London: Macmillan.

———. Forthcoming. *Freedom and Community: The Republican Virtue Tradition and the Sociology of Liberty.* Berkeley: University of California Press.

Whyte, William Foote. [1943] 1993. *Street Corner Society: The Social Structure of an Italian Slum.* Chicago: University of Chicago Press.

Whyte, William H. 1980. *The Social Life of Small Urban Spaces.* Washington, DC: Conservation Foundation.

———. 1988. *City: Rediscovering the Center.* New York: Doubleday.

Williamson, Oliver. 1975. *Markets and Hierarchies.* New York: Free Press.

Wilson, Thomas, and Andrew S. Skinner. 1976. *The Market and the State: Essays in Honour of Adam Smith.* Oxford: Clarendon Press.

Zaretsky, Eli. 1976, 1986 (rev. and expanded). *Capitalism, the Family, and Personal Life.* New York: Harper & Row. Originally published as a series of articles in *Socialist Revolution,* nos. 13–15 (January–June 1973).

Zelizer, Viviana. 1985. *Pricing the Priceless Child.* New York: Basic.

"Two Different Sorts of Commerce"—
Friendship and Strangership in Civil Society

Allan Silver

PERSONAL IS PRIVATE, IMPERSONAL IS PUBLIC

IN MODERN SENSIBILITY, personal relations are widely understood to inhabit and define a distinctive domain of private life, the special preserve of valuable moral qualities such as intimacy, affection, generosity, and trust. Thus, a discussion of exemptions from the legal requirement to provide testimony about the words and conduct of others argues:

> Although one can imagine [that] . . . individuals might come to trust or love one another without communicating privately . . . [p]rivacy permits people to share intimacies and ideas on their own terms, and thus to establish those mutual reciprocal relinquishments of the self that underlie the relations of love, friendship and trust. Without a reserve of privacy, we would have nothing to share and, hence, nothing to build upon in our human relationships save fear, mistrust and combativeness. The ability to shield ourselves from public view permits the exchange of intimate confidences necessary to establish a secure love or trust. The right to privacy is thus an inseparable aspect of our humanity.[1]

Personal relations are prevailingly defined and experienced as antipodal to the impersonal structures of modern society—the domains of market exchange, legal contract, bureaucracy, the state. Poets and economists, in their separate fashions, have elaborated this great divide of modern life. An interwar poet, Christopher Caudwell, puts the idea in a romantic, quasi-Marxist version of which Tönnies is the classic instance:

> As . . . [commodity] relations produced industrial capitalism and the modern bourgeois State, it sucked the tenderness out of all social rela-

This essay owes much to Jeff Weintraub's exceptional mix of warm empathy, detached acuity, and tireless perseverance. It has also benefitted from a careful reading by Samuel Fleischacker. Unattributed translations from the French are mine.

1. Thomas Krattenmaker, "Interpersonal Testimonial Privileges under the 'Federal Rules of Evidence,'" *Georgetown Law Journal* 64 (1976): 615.

tions . . . [L]ove and economic relations have gathered at two opposite poles. All the unused tenderness of man's instincts gather at one pole and at the other are economic relations, reduced to bare coercive rights, to commodities.[2]

In the late-nineteenth-century's major treatise in neoclassical economics, Alfred Marshall offers a dispassionate variant: " 'Business'. . . includes all provision for the wants of others . . . made in the expectation of payment. . . . It is thus contrasted with . . . those kindly services which are prompted by friendship and family affection." [3] In both culture and theory, "love, friendship and trust," the "tenderness . . . of social relations," and "kindly services . . . prompted by friendship and family affection" are most commonly understood as historical survivals in a modern world dominated by impersonal economic and bureaucratic institutions, survivals whose fragility renders them the more precious. Historical and anthropological scholarship has barely affected this vision's hold not only on many romantics, Marxists, and conservatives both religious and cultural, but on some liberals as well.[4] The idea persists that there is an incompatible tension in modern life, ranging from incongruity to antagonism, between the private domain of the personal and morally generous on the one hand, and the public domain of the impersonal and instrumental on the other—and that the former historically precedes, and is antipodal to, the latter.

This essay argues, instead, that this domain of the private, however suffused by historical imagery, is less a historical survival than a distinctive creation of the impersonal order central to modern economies and polities. The private sphere understood as the ideal arena of love, tenderness, and "kindly services" requires the very impersonality of the public world of bureaucratic administration, contractualism, and monetized exchange against which it is culturally distinguished. This analysis is not new.[5] It dates seminally to the Scottish Enlightenment of the eighteenth century, which proposed that market society

2. Christopher Caudwell, *Studies In a Dying Culture* [1938] (London: Bodley Head, 1948), pp. 153, 156–57.

3. Alfred Marshall, *Principles of Economics* [1890] (London: MacMillan, 1927), p. 291.

4. As in Cooley's influential treatment of the "primary group." See chapters 1 through 5 of Charles Horton Cooley, *Social Organization* [1909]. See also chapters 8 through 11 of Fred Hirsch, *Social Limits to Growth*.

5. For anthropological and historical expressions, see, respectively, Robert Paine, "In Search of Friendship: An Exploratory Analysis in Middle Class Culture"; and Michael Anderson, *Family Structure in Nineteenth Century Lancashire*, and "The Impact on the Family Relationships of the Elderly of Changes Since Victorian Times in Governmental Income Maintenance Provision," in Ethel Shanas and Marvin Sussman's edited volume, *Family, Bureaucracy and the Elderly*.

and the administered polity, far from being in tension with personal relations valued for their anti-instrumental qualities, are key to their essential attributes. The theoretical contribution of the Scots—Adam Smith, David Hume, and others—remains so powerful that to recover it, far from being an antiquarian exercise, bears centrally on current interpretive concerns.

Smith, Hume, and other contemporaries argue that "commercial society" [6] introduces a historically unprecedented distinction between self-interested relations and personal bonds that are normatively free of instrumental and calculative orientations. On this view, market society has constitutive significance for the emergence of a new sphere of the private characterized by new forms of personal relations, the ethos of which is quite distinct from that of market exchange. This newly "private" world of personal relationships is not residual, fragile, fugitive, or interstitial, but is rather made possible by the new "public" world of commerce, contract, and impersonal administration.

In the dominant understanding, cultural tensions between the domains of the personal and private and of the impersonal and public originated in the nineteenth century, when industrialization, urbanization, and commodification broke what Walter Bagehot called the "cake of custom." [7] But while nineteenth-century liberals contested the claims of contemporary socialists, conservatives, and reactionaries, their predecessors engaged an Old Regime very much in place. The paradigmatic shift of liberal theory in analyzing the mutual bearing of personal and impersonal relations is more powerfully displayed in the social theories of the eighteenth than in those of the nineteenth century, which were often derivative, reactive, or sentimental. To grasp the force of the Scots' argument requires recovering their historical account. However, it is necessary first to offer a concept of personal relations appropriate to this

6. "Commercial society" or "commercial countries" are phrases used by Adam Smith and many contemporaries to refer to what is later called market society. These terms emphasize the universal imperative of exchanging, of buying and selling, caused by the pervasive division of labor that it also stimulates. Smith's definition occurs early in *The Wealth of Nations:* "When the division of labor has been once thoroughly established, it is but a very small part of a man's wants which the produce of his own labor can supply. He supplies the far greater part of them by exchanging that surplus of his own labor, which is over and above his own consumption, for such parts of the produce of other men's labor as he has occasion for. Every man thus lives by exchanging, or becomes in some measure a merchant, and the society itself grows to be what is properly a commercial society" (Adam Smith, *An Inquiry into the Nature and Causes of the Wealth of Nations* [1776], p. 37). In contrast, "capitalism," a word Smith never uses, stresses the transformative effects of the movement of investment capital among opportunities for profit. The writers of the Scottish Enlightenment are often concisely called, in context, "the Scots," and are so named in this essay.

7. Walter Bagehot, *Physics and Politics* [1872], p. 29.

task, and for this purpose friendship serves usefully as a prototype of the larger category of personal relations.

THE EXEMPLARY SIGNIFICANCE OF FRIENDSHIP

IN MODERN SOCIETY, kinship, marriage, the family, and erotic relations all inhabit this private domain of personal life. In this respect, romantic marriage and the "routinized romanticism" of the modern friendship ideal are equally distinctive to modern society. Friendship, however, is a prototypically "private" relationship, in the specifically modern sense of this notion.

In modern culture, the essence of the "personal" is understood to inhere, not in formal roles and obligations, but in subjective definitions of the situation. Not normatively constituted by public roles and obligations—indeed, often constituted in distinction from them—friendship is, in principle, the "purest" and most widely available instance of personal relations in this sense. Spouses, lovers, kin, and colleagues are "friends" to the extent that they treat the objective conditions of their bond as collateral or inessential. Friendship, as a continuous creation of personal will and choice, is ungoverned by the structural definitions that bear on family and kinship and, unlike erotic relations, may ignore gender. It is an ideal arena for that individualized conception of personal agency central to modern notions of personal freedom.[8]

Normatively, friendship is grounded in the unique and irreplaceable qualities of partners, defined and valued independently of their place in public systems of kinship, power, utility, and esteem, and of any publicly defined status. The privacy of friendship is not only cultural but formal. No body of law and administrative regulation brings sovereign authority to bear on friendships; correspondingly, friendship is unprotected by law—for example, friends do not enjoy immunity from testifying about each other in court, unlike physicians about patients, clergy about congregants, and spouses about each other.[9] Culturally, others may pass censure or render judgment, but

8. The core idea is well expressed by a modern theologian: "As compared with marriage and the ties of kindred, friendship has no generally recognized rights, and is therefore wholly dependent on its own inherent quality. It is by no means easy to classify friendship sociologically. . . . Marriage, labor, the state and the Church all exist by divine decree. . . . Friendship belongs to the sphere of freedom. . . . Within the sphere of . . . freedom, friendship is by far the rarest and most priceless treasure, for where else does it survive in this world of ours, dominated as it is by the three . . . decrees?" See Dietrich Bonhoeffer's *Letters and Papers from Prison,* pp. 192–93. See also David L. Norton, *Personal Destinies: A Philosophy of Ethical Individualism;* and Ralph Turner, "The Real Self: From Institution to Impulse."

9. In the words of a judicial opinion: "The statements made by Burger to which Spurling testified were not made by Burger in 'professing religious faith, or seeking spiritual comfort' or 'guidance,' but were conversational statements to Spurling who was his friend and frequent companion, of his intent to kill his wife and her lover. The ministerial privilege

friends have the right and capacity to ignore them, for only friends themselves are effectively and normatively competent to judge the extent to which they meet the moral demands of their friendships.[10]

It is not peculiar to modern society that ideals of friendship express some of the "noblest" potentials of human association.[11] But an ideal of friendship so quintessentially "private," so contrary to the forms of association that dominate the "public" domain, is distinctive to our times. Explicit contract, rational exchange, formal division of labor, and impersonal institutions define the public world of the "Great Society"—as Graham Wallas and John Dewey, two quintessential liberals, referred to modern societies no longer understandable as aggregates of personal relations, local communities, and corporate orders.[12] The inverse of the Great Society—its contractualism, monetized exchange, impersonal administration—defines those ideals constituting friendship understood at its morally best. Especially in the urban, educated core of Western society, friendships are judged of high quality precisely to the extent they

---

[of immunity from the requirement to testify] was not applicable" (*Burger v. State,* 238 Georgia (1977), 171, 172, 231 S.E.2d 769, 771)—quoted in an interesting analysis of the general issue by Sanford Levinson, "Testimonial Privileges and the Preferences of Friendship."

10. This account is a selective compound drawn from the literature and my own work. For earlier statements, see my "Friendship and Trust as Moral Ideals: An Historical Approach," and "Friendship in Commercial Society," from which parts of this essay are drawn. See also Graham Allan, *A Sociology of Friendship and Kinship,* and *Friendship: Developing a Sociological Perspective;* Sanford Levinson, "Testimonial Privileges and the Preferences of Friendship"; Kaspar Naegele, "Friendships and Acquaintances: An Exploration of Some Social Distinctions"; Robert Paine, "In Search of Friendship"; Gerald Suttles, "Friendship as a Social Institution," in George McCall, ed., *Social Relationships;* Friedrich H. Tenbruck, "Freundschaft: ein Beitrag zu einer Soziologie der persönlichen Beziehungen"; Ralph Turner, "The Real Self"; and Eric Wolf, "Kinship, Friendship, and Patron-Client Relations in Complex Societies," in Michael Banton, ed., *The Social Anthropology of Complex Societies.* The most seminal sociological writing on friendship is embedded in broader discussions by Georg Simmel; see Kurt Wolff, ed., *The Sociology of Georg Simmel,* pp. 118–28, 307–44. Discussions by contemporary philosophers that address the same themes as the sociologists include Elizabeth Telfer, "Friendship"; Jeffrey Reiman, "Privacy, Intimacy and Personhood"; Lawrence Thomas, "Friendship"; Neera Kapur Badhwaar, "Friends as Ends in Themselves"; and David B. Annis, "The Meaning, Value, and Duties of Friendship."

11. For a survey of medieval and Renaissance friendship ideals as reflected in literature, see Laurens J. Mills, *One Soul in Bodies Twain: Friendship in Tudor Literature and Stuart Drama.* For the classical world, see Gabriel Herman, *Ritual Friendship and the Greek City;* Mary Whitelock Blundell, *Helping Friends and Harming Enemies: A Study in Sophocles and Greek Ethics;* and Horst Hutter, *Politics as Friendship: The Origins of Classical Notions of Politics in the Theory and Practice of Friendship.*

12. Graham Wallas, *The Great Society: A Psychological Analysis* [1914] (London: Macmillan, 1936); and John Dewey, *The Public and Its Problems* (New York: Holt, 1927).

invert the ways of the public domain. They are grounded in open-ended commitments without explicit provision for their termination—unlike contractual relations, prior stipulation of the conditions that legitimately end a friendship cannot be constitutive of friendship. In such an ideal, friendships are diminished in moral quality if terms of exchange are consciously or scrupulously monitored, for this would imply that the utilities derived from friendship are constitutive, as in market relations, rather than valued as expressions of personal intentions and commitments. Friends are normatively oriented to the intentions and subjective meanings that give rise to each others' acts, not the public meaning or import of acts.

Since relations other than friendship are to some extent constituted by public or ascriptive statuses, or legitimately regulated by public authority and agencies, friendship—though not necessarily the most emotionally intense—is the most prototypically personal of relationships. At this point we reach the core of the idea of a "personal relationship." In modern sensibility, the domain of the "personal" is often held to be constituted by emotions and values that set it apart from the impersonal. However, the genotype of the personal, as Simmel has subtly argued, lies not in its emotional content but in the structural attribute of "substitutability." [13] That is, the extent to which the replacement of others is consequential indicates the extent to which a relationship is "personal." In times past, personal ties in this sense were deeply embedded in structures and codes not of the parties' making and inescapably implicated in practical imperatives. Thus, the relationship between lord and serf is structurally more "personal" than that between employer and wage laborer—not because capitalism has diminished "tenderness," to use Christopher Caudwell's term, but because person and station are less separable in premarket and prebureaucratic society.[14] In modern societies, with their unprecedented depersonalization of economy, polity, and administration, concerns for personal safety and the advancement of competitive interests are addressed—to an extent not earlier imaginable—by impersonal means. This degree of impersonality in modern society, which frees us from dependence on particular others for a host of practical needs, is precisely what creates the possibility of personal

13. Georg Simmel, *The Philosophy of Money* [1907] (London: Routledge & Kegan Paul, 1978), pp. 292–303.

14. In a brilliant, but brief and little-noted analysis of this point in the *Grundrisse* (pp. 161–65), Marx surpasses the neoromantic aspects of his earlier, abundantly cited formulations in such writings as the *Economic and Philosophical Manuscripts of 1844* and *The German Ideology*. See also the classic paper of Marcel Mauss, "A Category of the Human Mind: The Notion of Person; the Notion of Self," in the edited volume by Michael Carrithers et al., *The Category of the Person: Anthropology, Philosophy, History.*

relations valued as expressions of inner intention and commitment, apart from practical agendas and formal obligations.

Modern friendship thus has exemplary significance as the prototype of the personal. The historical transformation of friendship illuminates the larger processes that have helped to produce the characteristically modern distinction between the "private" world of personal life and the "public" world of the Great Society.

Friendship in Classical Liberalism

A PASSAGE FROM Hume illustrates the Scottish Enlightenment's awareness of a new distinction between personal and public domains associated with the advent of commercial society:

> Although self-interested commerce . . . begins to dominate in society, it does not abolish the more generous and noble intercourse of friendship and good offices. I may still do services to such persons as I love, and am more particularly acquainted with, without any prospect of advantage. . . . In order to distinguish these two different sorts of commerce, the interested and the disinterested, there is a certain form of words invented for the former, by which we bind ourselves to the performance of any action. This form of words we call a *promise,* which is the sanction of the interested part of mankind.[15]

"Commerce," which now denotes only economic activity, had in the eighteenth century a broader meaning: "to . . . converse, hold communication, associate" *(Oxford English Dictionary).* Similarly, an older meaning of "promise" as formally sanctioned undertaking and contract, Hume's usage, is preserved in legal terminology, but in ordinary use the word now largely applies to personal and informal situations.[16] Thus, the phrase "two different sorts of commerce" points both to the historically prevalent coexistence of practical agendas and personal obligations and also, by contrast, to the sharp distinction

15. David Hume, *A Treatise of Human Nature* [1749], edited by L. Selby-Bigge, revised edition by P. H. Niddich (Oxford: Clarendon, 1978), p. 521.

16. "Promises" are treated in liberal theory as paradigmatic for contractual relations; on promise as contract, see Allan E. Farnsworth, "The Past of Promise: An Historical Introduction to Contract," and references cited in Thomas L. Haskell, "Capitalism and the Origins of Humanitarian Sensibility, Part 2," pp. 553–56. Hume uses "interest" with attention to the historically new clarity with which interests are calculated and perceived in commercial society—what Hirschman calls the "interest paradigm," dating from the late seventeenth and early eighteenth centuries in the most commercially advanced regions of Europe. See Albert O. Hirschman, *The Passions and the Interests: Arguments for Capitalism before Its Triumph,* especially pp. 32–33, 42–56.

between them in commercial society. Hume argues that distinguishing friendship from instrumental concerns creates a distinctive moral domain for personal relations:

> It is remarkable that nothing touches a man of humanity more than any instance of extraordinary delicacy in love or friendship, where a person is attentive to the smallest concerns of his friend, and is willing to sacrifice to them the most considerable interest of his own. . . . Such delicacies . . . [are] the greatest trifles: but they are the more engaging the more minute the concern is, and are a proof of the highest merit in any one . . . capable of them.[17]

On this understanding, the moral quality of friendship is enhanced precisely because it is not implicated in "self-interested commerce."

Adam Smith's study of the moral order, *The Theory of Moral Sentiments*, offers a vivid historical contrast with this sort of friendship:

> The necessity or conveniency of mutual accommodation very frequently produces a friendship not unlike that which takes place among those who are born to live in the same family. Colleagues in office, partners in trade, call one another brothers; and frequently feel towards one another as if they really were so. . . . The Romans expressed this sort of attachment by the word *necessitudo*, which . . . seems to denote that it was imposed by the necessity of the situation.[18]

The displacement of *necessitudo* by commercial society brings with it what Smith regards as a morally superior form of friendship—voluntary, based on "natural sympathy," unconstrained by necessity. It is superior also, Smith argues, because unlike such forms of personal solidarity as fictive kinship and clientage, it is not exclusivistic, but reflects the new universalism of civil society.[19]

Adam Smith does not share the view—dominant in anticapitalist criticisms

17. Hume, *Treatise of Human Nature*, pp. 604–5.

18. Adam Smith, *The Theory of Moral Sentiments* [1759, 1791], edited by D. D. Raphael and A. L. Macfie (Oxford: Clarendon, 1976), pp. 223–24.

19. "Of all attachments to an individual, that which is founded altogether upon the esteem and approbation of his good conduct and behavior . . . is, by far, the most respectable. Such friendships, arising not from a constrained sympathy, not from a sympathy which has . . . [become] habitual for the sake of conveniency and accommodation; but from a natural sympathy, from an involuntary feeling that the persons to whom we attach ourselves are the natural and proper objects of esteem and approbation; can exist only among men of virtue. . . . [They] need not be confined to a single person, but may safely embrace all the wise and virtuous, with whom we have been long and intimately acquainted" (*Moral Sentiments*, pp. 224–25).

of modern society, both radical and conservative, and in contemporary "exchange theories"—that the ethos and principles of market exchange pervade and explain personal relations. As a seminal instance, consider Tönnies's account of "conventional society life" in *gesellschaftliche* society:

> It consists of an exchange of words and courtesies . . . [in which] in reality everyone is thinking of himself, in competition with the others. For everything pleasant which someone does for someone else, he expects, even demands, at least an equivalent. He weighs exactly his services, flatteries, presents, and so on, to determine whether they will bring about the desired result. Formless contracts are made continuously, as it were, and constantly many are pushed aside in the race by the few fortunate and powerful ones.[20]

In contrast, Smith argues that practical imperatives of calculation were more pervasive before commercial society and impersonal administration instituted a sharp normative distinction between self-interested and personal relations. Indeed, attributing calculative exchange in personal relations solely or largely to market society is palpably unhistorical. European notions of what later sociological theory considers "instrumental" exchange were deeply formed by practices and institutions preceding the modern market—for example, deference, clientelism, honor—and were therefore embedded in cultural understandings antipodal to both bureaucracy and commercial society. Norbert Elias's analysis of social interaction at the court of Versailles illustrates aspects of the Old Regime to which the Scots were deeply averse:

> To make the dealings of people . . . calculable . . . an analogous means was used to that by which a work process is made calculable in economic society. . . . [I]t was possible to define exactly the prestige-value of every step in court society, like money-value in capitalist society. The intensive elaboration of etiquette, ceremony, taste, dress, manners and even conversation had the same function. Every detail . . . was an . . . instrument in the prestige struggle. . . . Bourgeois-industrial rationality is generated by the compulsion of the economic mesh; by it power-opportunities founded on private or public capital are made calculable. [In] court rationality . . . people and prestige are made calculable as instruments of power.[21]

Elias's "court rationality" differs from the rationality of modern markets and bureaucracies, in part, because at Versailles calculative conduct legitimately

20. Ferdinand Tönnies, *Community and Society (Gemeinschaft und Gesellschaft)* [1887] (New York: Harper & Row, 1957), p. 78.
21. Norbert Elias, *The Court Society* [1969] (New York: Pantheon, 1983), p. 111.

and necessarily pervades many personal interactions. Smith's thorough rejection of "court rationality" is shared, of course, by other classical liberals. One among many expressions of this aversion frames Smith's celebrated account of the conduct of butchers, brewers, and bakers in terms of "interest" and "self-love." Frequent quotation of these lines has obscured the condemnation that precedes and follows them of the "servile and fawning attentions" by which persons must often induce others "to act according to [their] inclinations" when unable to obtain resources by impersonal market exchange.[22]

Smith's theory of personal relations is based on the dynamics of sympathy, not of self-interested exchange. Sympathy is central to Smith's model of social control in two complementary applications—to the new form of friendship and, equally important, to its logically implied opposite, "strangership." Both are constitutive elements of a new, universalistic sociability. For Smith, sympathy makes possible the creation and coordination of moral action in an individuated society no longer morally governed by princes, clergy, notables, and landlords.[23] It is a procedural mechanism, without intrinsic emotional or moral content.[24] Smith argues that people moderate their behavior to attract others' sympathy, forthcoming only if others "sympathize" with their ideas and conduct—if, to evoke the acoustical metaphor of sympathetic vibration with which Smith introduces the idea, they are sufficiently in tune with others to produce, if not the "unison" impossible in a society of individuals, then that "concord" required for "the harmony of society." [25]

In the Scots' historical vision, the space between friend and enemy was not occupied, prior to commercial society, by mere acquaintances or neutral

22. Smith, *Wealth of Nations*, pp. 26–27.

23. Joseph Cropsey, *Polity and Economy: An Interpretation of the Principles of Adam Smith*, pp. 35–36.

24. "Pity and compassion are words appropriated to signify our fellow-felling with the sorrow of others. Sympathy, though its meaning was, perhaps, originally the same, may now . . . be made use of to denote our fellow-feeling with any passion whatsoever" (Smith, *Moral Sentiments*, p. 10). As a comment by Morrow well summarizes: "To say that Smith's ethics is based upon sympathy does not mean that sympathy is the content of morality, but means rather that sympathy is the principle of communication between individuals which makes possible the moral judgment" (Glenn R. Morrow, *The Ethical and Economic Theories of Adam Smith*, p. 29). See also the excellent discussion by Cropsey in *Polity and Economy*, pp. 11–22. In Cooley and others of the "social control" school, "sympathy" is intrinsically cooperative and mutually enhancing—a quasi-romantic idea, in Cooley's case influenced by Emersonian transcendentalism (Vernon Dibble, "Transcendentalism and Sociology: The Case of Charles Horton Cooley"), quite different from Smith's. For some vicissitudes of "sympathy" in nineteenth-century culture, see Barbara Jane Friedberg, "Sympathetic Imagination as an Intellectual Ideal in Victorian Literature and Controversy."

25. Smith, *Moral Sentiments*, p. 22.

strangers, but was charged with uncertain and menacing possibilities.[26] The new universalism implies, for Smith, a society of indifferent strangers—indifferent not in a rhetorical, but in a technical sense. Unlike the prevailing condition in other settings, strangers in commercial society are not either potential enemies or allies, but authentically indifferent to each other—an indifference that enables all to make contracts with all. In Smith's account, strangers are "impartial spectators" of each others' behavior, with whom persons reflexively interact through a mechanism of universal human nature, that of sympathy.[27] The new "strangership" of commercial society is well described in terms of a

> stranger [who] is not a friend from whom we can expect any special favor and sympathy. But at the same time he is not an enemy from whom we cannot expect any sympathy at all. Everyone in society is as independent of every other as a stranger, and is equal with every other [because] they can [imagine the] exchange [of their] situations. The famous impartial spectator is no one else but the spectator who is indifferent.[28]

These are not the strangers who inhabit modern society as described by Tönnies, Simmel, and many others until the work of Erving Goffman. The exis-

---

26. For a social-scientific account of the tensions associated with strangership in traditional society (though not focused on precommercial Europe), see Julian Pitt-Rivers, "The Stranger, the Guest and the Hostile Host," in J. G. Peristiany's edited volume, *Contributions to Mediterranean Sociology.* On the contrasting texture of acquaintanceship in modern civil society, see Suzanne B. Kurth, "Friendship and Friendly Relations," in George McCall's edited collection, *Social Relationships;* Claire Bidart, *Les semblables, les amis et les autres: Sociabilité et amitié;* and Jean Maisonneuve and Lubomir Lamy, *Psycho-sociologie de l'amitié.*

27. Smith's account of the social psychology involved is subtle and elaborate—this condensed excerpt cannot do it justice: "In order to produce this concord, as nature teaches the spectators to assume the circumstances of the person principally concerned, so she teaches this last in some measure to assume those of the spectators. As they are continually placing themselves in his situation, and thence conceiving emotions similar to what he feels, so he is as constantly placing himself in theirs, and thence conceiving some degree of that coolness about his own fortune, with which he is sensible that they will view it. As they are constantly considering what they themselves would feel, if they actually were the sufferers, so he is as constantly led to imagine in what manner he would be affected if he was only one of the spectators of his own situation. As their sympathy makes them look at it, in some measure, with his eyes, so his sympathy makes him look at it, in some measure, with theirs: . . . and as the reflected passion, which he thus conceives, is much weaker than the original one, it necessarily abates the violence of what he felt . . . before he began to recollect in what manner they would be affected by it" (Smith, *Moral Sentiments,* p. 220).

28. Hiroshi Mizuta, "Moral Philosophy and Civil Society," in Andrew S. Skinner and Thomas Wilson's edited volume, *Essays on Adam Smith,* p. 110.

tence of numerous indifferent strangers does not, for Smith, weaken the moral order but rather helps define it.

This historical transformation of "strangership" is summed up by the changing meanings of "strange" and "stranger" traced in the *Oxford English Dictionary*. These words once predominantly denoted one who is "foreign, alien; of a place . . . other than one's own; who belong[s] to others"; who is "unfriendly . . . distant or cold in demeanour . . . uncomplying, unwilling to accede to a request or desire." An example from Shakespeare illustrates this usage: when Othello is described as "an extravagant and wheeling stranger / Of here and everywhere" (I.i.137–38), the implication is that one who wanders ("extravagant") without attachment to a fixed abode ("wheeling") is permanently a stranger, an outsider whose marriage to a Venetian is anomalous. The *OED* remarks that these meanings, when not obsolete, are "now somewhat rare . . . [replaced by such] recent examples" as: "A new comer who has not *yet* become well acquainted with the place, or . . . one who is not *yet* well known . . . an unknown person whom one has not seen before . . . [and] with whom one is not *yet* well acquainted" (emphases added). These examples nicely capture the status of the modern "stranger" in well-ordered civil society as one who participates in the same society as oneself, who shares common ground in the literal and metaphorical senses of the phrase, and with whom there exists the pervasive possibility of becoming acquainted or allied.

In commercial society, Smith argues, the dynamics of sympathy create the possibility of friendship across the boundaries of social station and the constraints of *necessitudo*.[29] Individuals inhabiting civil society contribute by their natural behavior towards something like a civic fund of good will, a background of routinized benevolence, diminishing the historically prevailing imperative to form exclusivistic personal attachments. No one need suffer, Smith writes, if one's "beneficence" towards another does not elicit commensurate "kindness" or "gratitude": "No benevolent man ever lost the fruits of his benevolence. If he does not gather them from the persons from whom he ought to have gathered them, he seldom fails to gather them, and with a tenfold increase, from other people."[30] Smith applauds the new forms of personal relations not because they abolish royal or mercantile constraints on market exchanges, but for their contribution to a civil society ideally free of exclusivistic and mutually hostile or suspicious personal associations.

In contrast to the categorical distinction between friends or allies or citizens

---

29. T. D. Campbell, *Adam Smith's Science of Morals,* pp. 87–107; Nicholas Phillipson, "Adam Smith as Civic Moralist," in Istvan Hont and Michael Ignatieff's edited collection, *Wealth and Virtue: The Shaping of Political Economy in the Scottish Enlightenment.*

30. Smith, *Moral Sentiments,* p. 225.

on the one hand and strangers and enemies on the other, Smith establishes the moral basis of commercial society in the associations of private individuals meeting in a social space not shaped by institutional constraints. The mutual control of behavior that results, through a complex play of interacting and reflexive mechanisms, is both source and prototype of moral conduct. Sympathy moderates ideas and conduct and distributes fellow-feeling in an essentially democratic spirit. The exclusivistic bonds defined by custom, corporate group, station, and estate are dissolved. Sympathy generates a kind of social lubrication throughout civil society, and is key to a deinstitutionalized moral order no longer authoritatively sustained by religious, economic, and political institutions.

The Scots understand commercial society as limiting instrumental exchange to the newly distinct domain of commercial dealings. On this view, the logic of exchange in personal relations is pervasively compelling before, rather than in, commercial society. Adam Ferguson's critique of personal relations before the rise of commercial society is similar to many later made of capitalist culture by its hostile critics:

> In societies where men are taught to consider themselves as competitors, and every advantage they gain as comparative to that of some other person, the conscientious [man] may be faithful and true to his engagements . . . ; but . . . interested and sordid [men] make no allowance for good or ill offices that neither empty nor fill the pocket.[31]

Such societies do not offer the possibility of disinterested relations, insulated from the clash and calculation of interests; the development of the market does so—in those domains falling outside the market itself, and therefore newly distinguishable from the interplay of interest. Before the ascendancy of impersonal means of administration and exchange, the purpose of friendship, as the Scots see it, was to help friends by means of defeating enemies—indeed, helping friends and hurting enemies were indistinguishable acts.[32] Where vital resources are not created and distributed impersonally by markets and bureaucracies, one has no choice but to be, in Ferguson's disapproving phrase, "inter-

31. Adam Ferguson, *Principles of Moral and Political Science*, 2 vols. (Edinburgh: Creech, 1792), vol. 1: 376.

32. In one of his dialogues, Plato ascribes to an average Athenian citizen this description of prevailing values and practices: "The *aretē* [worth, virtue, success] of a man is to be capable of taking an active part in politics and, while doing so, to be capable of helping one's *philoi* [friends, allies] while harming one's *echtroi* [enemies within the city], while taking care to suffer no harm oneself at their hand" (*Meno*, 71E 2ff; quoted in A. W. H. Adkins, *Moral Values and Political Behavior in Ancient Greece*, p. 131). For a general discussion of this theme in ancient Greece, see Blundell, *Helping Friends and Harming Enemies*.

ested and sordid" in all interactions, concerned only with whether they "empty [or] fill the pocket," because in such settings it is largely by what modern culture and theory consider personal relations that vital resources are obtained. In contrast, the Scots understand commercial society as one in which personal relations can benefit those involved at no cost to others; friendship becomes a private virtue that contributes to the public good of civil society.

BROTHERS TO OTHERS: DOES COMMERCIAL SOCIETY DIMINISH FRIENDSHIP?

A SUGGESTIVE, HISTORICALLY INFORMED discussion of friendship somewhat at odds with that just outlined is offered by Benjamin Nelson.[33] According to Nelson, Enlightenment thinkers, preceded by practical spokesmen for the merchant class in the seventeenth century, attacked strenuously elevated forms of friendship, associated with aristocratic milieux, because these inhibited efficient markets and orderly polities. Noble friendship ideals, centered on honor, glory, and personal loyalties, contributed to feuding, rebellion, and endemic war. Aristocratic allies and friends were also often obligated to stand surety for one another should one need ransom, aid in legal causes, or loans. In standing surety for a friend out of solidaristic obligation and personal honor, rather than in terms of business, the person whose risks are reduced by a friend's surety is encouraged to undertake commercial enterprises on bases other than market rationality; and the chances of one who stands surety falling into ruinous debt, unjustified by rational calculation, are increased. Thus Daniel Defoe's success manual of 1726, *The Complete English Tradesman,* sternly warns merchants against the "frequent ruin" occasioned by " 'striking hands with a stranger,' or one tradesman being bound for another. . . . Would the tradesman [contemplate the dangers] . . . when he is called upon to do the frequently fatal office of being surety for his friend, he would not easily be drawn into any snare on that account." [34] Defoe's oscillation between describing suretyship among merchants as a relationship of "strangers" and of "friends" captures exactly the transitional moment Nelson describes.

According to Nelson, attacks on noble ideals of friendship, promoting the development of rational markets, involved a "lowering of the moral standard," one step in an historic process by which friendship ideals moved from "tribal brotherhood" to the "universal otherhood" of liberal society:

33. Benjamin Nelson, *The Idea of Usury: From Tribal Brotherhood to Universal Otherhood* [1949] (Chicago: University of Chicago Press, 1969), pp. 155–64.

34. Daniel Defoe, *The Complete English Tradesman* [1726] (New York: Franklin, 1970), pp. 85–87.

The road from clan comradeship to universal society is beset with hazards. When two communities merge and two sets of others become one set of brothers, a price is generally paid. The price . . . is an attenuation of the love which had held each set together. It is a tragedy of moral history that the expansion of the moral community has ordinarily been gained through the sacrifice of the intensity of the moral bond, or . . . that all men have been becoming brothers by becoming equally others.[35]

Nelson's analysis permits us to move beyond the simplistically invidious dichotomies inherited from nineteenth-century thought, whether liberal, conservative, or socialist. However, the Scots have a vivid sense of the problematics inherent in "clan comradeship" that escapes Nelson's seductively resonant distinction between brotherhood and otherhood.

Brotherhood

THE SCOTS UNDERSTAND the solidaristic and heroic forms of friendship in precommercial society as inescapably contaminated by calculations of interest, in contrast to the personal and civil friendship possible in commercial society. Here is Adam Ferguson reflecting on these matters:

We are told of a maxim . . . : "Live with your friend as with one who may become an enemy." This maxim is prudent in the occasional cooperations of interest or party. The person who supports me today because it is in his interest to do so, may wish to overthrow me tomorrow, if an opposition of interest should take place. It may be prudent, therefore, not to furnish him as a friend with arms, which he may afterwards turn against me as an enemy. But this maxim, applied to the case of parties united by mutual conviction of unalterable worth, entire affection, and unlimited confidence, would be altogether preposterous, and cannot be adopted without discontinuing the connection of friendship, or stifling the affection in which it consists.[36]

The maxim Ferguson cites derives from the long history of friendship as an essential but troublesome resource in risky undertakings in war, economy, and politics. In these settings, loyal friends were indispensable lest, according to a Tudor document, one "remain as a hoop without a pole, live in obscurity,

35. Nelson, *The Idea of Usury,* p. 136.

36. *Principles of Moral and Political Science* 2:363. In other, better-known writings, especially his *Essay on the History of Civil Society* [1767], Ferguson expresses esteem for the heroic virtues, and reservations about the "polite" manners of commercial society. Ferguson and Francis Hutcheson, unlike Smith and Hume, are not thorough liberals, but this essay focuses on their protoliberal aspects.

and be made a football for every insulting companion to spurn at." However, according to another text of the late sixteenth century:

> These days there is such unsteady friendship among many, that it is hard to find a perfect and trusty friend: for now friendly words are common but when friendship cometh to the touch of proof, the alteration is marvellous: yea, and sometimes so dangerous that of friends in words they will become enemies in deeds.

In 1607, for example, Sir William Wentworth warned in an "Advice" to his son that a friend "may become your enemy, a thing very common in these days"—the very situation addressed by the "maxim" Ferguson finds so distasteful.[37]

Indifferent or benign neutrality was a difficult accomplishment in precommercial societies, certainly not a background condition that could be taken for granted. Necessitous friendships were indispensable to make one's way in the world and guard against dangers, but such friendships—however much they aspired to total mutual confidence—were subject to tensions originating, not in human imperfection or emotional ambivalence, but in the logic of the situation.[38] In ideal and practice, necessitous friendships inextricably fused Hume's "two different sorts of commerce, the interested and the disinterested."

By the eighteenth century, however, the meaning of friendship encompassed both older and modern meanings. The word "could mean a distant or close relation, a patron or a client, an individual to whom one was tied by mutual sponsorship, or someone attached by warm affection."[39] In mid-

---

37. These quotations are drawn from Lacy Baldwin Smith, *Treason in Tudor England*, pp. 46–47; see also Lawrence Stone, *The Family, Sex and Marriage in England, 1500–1800*, pp. 97–99.

38. While modern friendship culture would be offended by explicit stipulations against betrayal, oaths of institutionalized friendship often warn against betrayal and specify punishments for disloyalty, as illustrated by two very disparate instances. The blood-brotherhood oath of the Azande: "If you do me an injury, may you die from the blood. If you commit adultery with our wives . . . may you all perish, your father, your mother's brothers, all your kin will die. . . . If you speak ill of me to the chiefs, may you die" (E. E. Evans-Pritchard, "Zande Blood-Brotherhood," pp. 377–78). And: "A formal contract of friendship between scholars . . . written in Cairo on January 2, 1564 . . . [specifies that] they will lend each other any book they might possess . . . and will never conceal from each other any book they have" (S. D. Goitein, "Formal Friendship in the Medieval Near East," p. 488).

39. Stone, *Family, Sex and Marriage*, p. 97. For a fuller description of eighteenth-century "friends" as "all those who expected or, reciprocally, from whom one could expect, the benefits of patronage," see Harold Perkin, *The Origins of Modern English Society, 1780–1880*, pp. 46–51. An account of the similar system in prerevolutionary America is offered in part 1 of Gordon S. Wood, *The Radicalism of the American Revolution*.

century, Dr. Johnson's dictionary defined a friend as "one who supports you and comforts you while others do not," someone "with whom to compare minds and cherish private virtues." In precommercial society, to treat friends as if they might become enemies—the maxim Ferguson so dislikes—is an unhappy but prudent counsel; but to treat friends thus when political and economic arrangements were becoming unprecedentedly impersonal, and with friendship turning, in Dr. Johnson's terms, on comparing minds and cherishing private virtues, was "preposterous" because this would "[discontinue] the connection of friendship" and "[stifle] the affection in which it consists."

We have seen that the Scots perceive commercial society, far from "contaminating" personal relations with instrumentalism, as "purifying" them by clearly distinguishing friendship from the calculation of utility, and founding friendship on sympathy and affection. While the ties of friendship in liberal society, on this view, lack the noble and sacral character of what Nelson calls "brotherhood," they are free of those intrinsic tensions and suspicions that inevitably derive from the historically prevalent implication of interest and friendship before commercial society.[40]

Otherhood

THESE CLASSICAL LIBERALS ardently desire the new sociability, based on the universalism of sympathy, to dissolve older, intense forms of exclusivistic relationships. This change is driven, not only by the division of labor and commercial exchange, but also by the emergence of impersonal and pervasive political administration. Thus, Smith observes how the stability afforded by efficient and uniform law and police entails the decline of what he calls relations of *necessitudo,* and Nelson calls "clan brotherhood":

40. While the phrase "precommercial society" reflects the Scots' historical vision, we must avoid the impression that, prior to modern commercial society, all friendship patterns were homogeneously "necessitous," constituted by objective obligations rather than inner feelings. For example, some types of friendship based on personal affect appear in ancient Greece and Rome, especially in the context of highly developed civic institutions, despite the continuing importance of clientelism in both cases. On the other hand, even in these cases there is no parallel to the sharply anti-instrumental thrust of the modern friendship ideology. See, for example, David Konstan's analysis of the semantic fields of *philos* and *philia* in "Greek Friendship," his treatment of "the shift in the discourse of friendship between the classical Athenian democracy and the Hellenistic and Roman states" in "Friendship and the State: The Context of Cicero's *De Amicitia,*" and his "Patrons and Friends." Here it is enough to note that the Scots were evidently reacting most strongly to the contrast between practices prevailing in commercial societies and the historical alternatives closest to them—feudalism, aristocratic milieux, court life, and the warrior culture of the Scottish clans.

In pastoral countries . . . [the] association [of families] is frequently necessary for their common defense. . . . Their concord strengthens their necessary association; their discord always weakens, and might destroy it. . . . In commercial countries, where the authority of law is always perfectly sufficient to protect the meanest man in the state . . . [families], having no such motive for keeping together, naturally separate and disperse as interest or inclination may direct . . . [I]n a few generations, they not only lose all care about one another, but all remembrance of their common origin.[41]

The Scots approve this change as one aspect of the movement, to use their vocabulary, from barbarity and rudeness to politeness and polish, indispensable to forming the new civil morality appropriate to commercial society.[42] They do not hold, as does Nelson, that this advance involves the "attenuation" of moral bonds. A more pressing problem, for them, is reconciling the Christian imperative of universal love with the moral social psychology of commercial society.

Christian theology has long addressed the problem of "preferential friendship"—friendship offered to one or some, but not to others or to all—in the light of the Christian obligation to love all humanity according to the demands of agape, and in imitation of divine love. In the classic theological accounts, friendship ought to reflect divine love in a spirit of *imitatio dei,* not social interaction.[43] Francis Hutcheson, however, analyzes friendship in a naturalistic and functional spirit, deploying an elaborated metaphor drawn from the most advanced science of the day, Newtonian physics:

The *universal benevolence* toward all men, we may compare to . . . *gravitation* which . . . increases as the distance is diminished. This increase, on nearer approach, is . . . necessary . . . [f]or a general attraction, equal in all distances, would by the contrariety of such multitudes of equal forces, put an end to all regularity of motion, and perhaps stop it altogether. . . . These different sorts of love to persons according to their nearer approaches to ourselves by their benefits,

41. Smith, *Moral Sentiments,* pp. 224–25.

42. Cropsey, *Polity and Economy;* Hirschman, *The Passions and the Interests;* Mizuta, "Moral Philosophy and Civil Society"; Nicholas Phillipson, "Adam Smith as Civic Moralist."

43. The problematic of "preferential friendship" in Christian doctrine is described, from varying perspectives, by Gilbert C. Meilaender, *Friendship: A Study in Theological Ethics;* Anders Nygren, *Agape and Eros: The Christian Idea of Love and Its Transformation,* passim; and Paul J. Wadell, *Friendship and the Moral Life,* chapter 4. For a brilliant sociological application of agape to social interaction see Luc Boltanski, *L'Amour et la justice comme compétences,* pp. 137–254.

is observable . . . in all the strong ties of friendship, acquaintance, neighbourhood, partnership; which are exceedingly necessary to the order and happiness of human society.[44]

The utopia of universal Christian love, of agape, is rejected as leading to a chaos of "contrariety." Benevolence is distributed preferentially, gradated according to proximity but not withheld from anyone with hostile or suspicious intent. In place of both the utopia of agape and the historically prevalent trichotomy of friend/enemy/stranger, Hutcheson envisions a moral order in which the prospect of what Nelson calls "attenuation" is compensated by local gravitational fields, as it were, of intense benevolence arranged in a manner contributing to "the order and happiness of human society."

Adam Smith's version of Hutcheson's gravitational model was unoriginal in its time and later became a cliché: the individual in the innermost of a series of concentric circles, family and friends at the center, widening in successively weaker circles to include all humanity.[45] Friendship emerges as one of a variety of benign social bonds, like family, neighborhood, and the routine contacts of individuals in civil and commercial society; no longer constituted in terms of station, corporate group, and political and economic imperatives (as in the Romans' *necessitudo,* or Tudor nobles' need for trustworthy allies), it is understood as shaped by propinquity and sympathy, an account adumbrating that offered by modern social psychology.

Thus, for these classical liberals, modern friendship exemplifies the new world of private life and its increasingly sharp distinction from the public domain. They seek to show how personal relations, such as friendship, can no longer be governed by formal codes, whether those of religion or noble concepts of honor. But they are equally concerned to show that private relations of friendship cannot be regulated by those principles of exchange that prevail in the new, public world of commercial relations—that "self-interested commerce . . . [beginning] to dominate in society."

Adam Smith remarks on the formlessness of personal obligations in commercial society and their insusceptibility to precise calculation:

> The general rules which determine what are the offices of prudence,
> of charity, of generosity, of friendship . . . admit of so many exceptions

44. Francis Hutcheson, *An Inquiry into the Original of Our Ideas of Beauty and Virtue. Treatise II: An Inquiry Concerning the Original of Our Ideas of Virtue or Moral Good* [1725, 1738], in D. D. Raphael's *British Moralists, 1650–1800* (Oxford: Clarendon, 1969), 1:290 (emphasis in original).

45. Morrow, *Ethical and Economic Theories of Adam Smith,* pp. 55–56; Smith, *Moral Sentiments,* pp. 219–37.

. . . that it is scarce possible to regulate our conduct entirely by a regard to them. . . . The actions required by friendship, humanity, hospitality, generosity are . . . vague and indeterminate.

Contrary to modern "exchange theorists," Smith rejects the applicability of the exchange model, drawn from the impersonal market, to personal relations:

That as soon as we can we should make a return of equal or superior value to the services we have received, would seem to be a pretty plain rule. . . . Upon the most superficial examination, however, this rule . . . appear[s] in the highest degree loose and inaccurate, and to admit of a thousand exceptions.

The "thousand exceptions" are occasioned by circumstances unique to the varieties of personality and circumstances—in short, to the essentially private nature of friendship:

If your friend lent you money in your distress, ought you to lend him some in his? How much ought you lend him? When ought you lend him? Now, or tomorrow, or next month? And for how long a time? It is evident that no general rule can be laid down, by which a precise answer can be given. . . . The difference between his character and yours, between his circumstances and yours, may be such, that you may be perfectly grateful and yet justly refuse to lend him a half-penny; and on the contrary, you may be willing to lend him ten times the sum which he lent you and yet justly be accused of . . . not having fulfilled the hundredth part of the obligation you lie under.[46]

The emergence of impersonal markets in the economy, far from providing a normative or theoretical model for personal relations, rather clarifies the distinction between the two domains. In Smith's account, market exchange theory cannot address the new forms of personal relations—private, uncodified, informal, idiosyncratic—that commercial society facilitates.

This distinction evokes the so-called Adam Smith problem—namely, the apparent inconsistency between *The Theory of Moral Sentiments* and *The Wealth of Nations* raised by German scholars in the late nineteenth century. It gave rise to an extensive literature taking it as problematic that the author of the seminal classic on market theory also elaborated a morality centered on sympathy and benevolence.[47] What is the conceptual relationship between

46. Smith, *Moral Sentiments*, p. 174.
47. See August Oncken, "The Consistency of Adam Smith," pp. 443–50, for a formulation of the original "problem." Of the abundant literature on it stimulated by the bicentenary of the publication in 1776 of *The Wealth of Nations*, the most relevant for this essay is Richard Teichgraeber III, "Rethinking *Das Adam Smith Problem*," especially pp. 115–23.

Smith's market theory and his moral social psychology? The former is captured in the most famous vignette in social theory:

> It is not from the benevolence of the butcher, the brewer, or the baker, that we expect our dinner, but their regard to their own interest. We address ourselves, not to their humanity, but to their self-love, and we never talk to them of our own necessities but of their own advantages.[48]

The latter, which enjoys no comparably concise expression, is seen at its clearest in the new concept of personal relations developed by Smith and the other Scots. Contrary to the cultural assumptions underlying "the Adam Smith problem," there is no ideological or theoretical tension between the two; on the contrary, they are deeply consistent. In Smith's theory, the moral order is generated by means precisely analogous to the system of market exchange. Persons in commercial society "truck, barter, and exchange" in markets; they thus engage in conduct yielding a result—an increase in the wealth of nations—that individually they do not intend. In the domain of sociability, individuals behave in a precisely comparable manner. Just as the propensity to exchange is a generalized utility-seeking mechanism, so "sympathy denote[s] our fellow-feeling with any passion whatever."[49] Thus, the moral order, like the wealth of nations, is continuously created by an indefinitely large number of acts as individuals encounter each other in a field defined, not by institutions or tradition, but by their own interactions. The causal textures of both branches of Smith's theory, the economic and the social, are identical: desirable aggregate outcomes are the unintended results of an infinity of small-scale interactions by ordinary individuals. In both, the outcome is other and "better" than any they intend. Self-interest in a market system increases the wealth of all; sociability in civil society sustains a universal morality from which all benefit.[50]

Advocates and critics of liberalism have long noted its emphasis on demarcating the "public" domain of state power from the "private" domain of the

48. Smith, *Wealth of Nations,* pp. 26–27.

49. Smith, *Moral Sentiments,* p. 10.

50. This speaks directly to the consistency of Smith's theories of personal and market relations, but only indirectly to the question of why they cannot, in Smith's terms, be unified. On this: "While expressed mainly in terms of friendship, sympathy, and esteem, there is no suggestion [in Smith] that beneficence might not also take the form of material support. Why, then, does not this expression of virtue find a place in Smith's view of the fiscal system? Its absence is explained by the voluntary nature of beneficence, a virtue which will be regarded with sympathy but cannot be enforced." See R. A. Musgrave, "Adam Smith on Public Finance and Distribution," in Thomas Wilson and A. S. Skinner, eds., *The Market and the State: Essays in Honour of Adam Smith,* p. 301.

market and civil society. But liberal thought also celebrates a clear distinction between the domain of "private life," defined by intimacy and personal relations, and the "public" world of impersonal relations epitomized by the market.[51] Optimally, the two domains benignly complement each other. In the ideal liberal commonwealth, the bourgeois polis, the peaceful exchange of equivalent values benefits all; the virtue of exchange is in utility, equivalence, and the creation of new value. Conversely, conditional helpfulness and the explicit exchange of valued services and resources become morally abhorrent in friendship. "If you are right," cries the impulsive Aziz to his friend Fielding in E. M. Forster's *Passage to India*, "there is no point in any friendship; it all comes down to give and take, or give and return, which is disgusting."[52]

As we have seen, aversion to calculative exchange in personal relations is historically based in the transformation of the polity as well as the economy. Indeed, it appears first not as a recoil against commercial society, but rather in the counterculture, so to speak, of the *ancien régime*. The incompatible demands of the *ancien régime*'s personal politics and of personal friendship in the liberal sense emerge in Saint-Evremond's acute analysis of *amitié* at the court of Versailles:

> The usual relationship of kings and their courtiers is a relationship of interest. Courtiers seek fortunes of kings; kings require services from their courtiers. However, sometimes the crush of business, or disgust with splendor, forces Princes to seek in the purity of nature the pleasures they do not have in their *grandeur*. . . . Worn out by suspicions and jealousies, they seek to open a heart that they show to the world as hard. The flatteries of adulators make them wish for the sincerity of a friend, [which] they make of . . . confidants called favorites, persons dear to Princes with whom they relieve the pressures of their secrets; with these, they wish to taste all the pleasures that familiarity of association and freedom of conversation may endow on private friends. But how dangerous are these friendships to a favorite who dreams more of love than of watching his own conduct! Wishing to find his friend, this confidant meets his master; [his] familiarity is punished as the indiscreet freedom of a servant who forgets his place. Courtiers whose conduct is always governed by interest know how to please, and their prudence makes them avoid whatever shocks and displeases. He who truly loves his master does not listen to his [own] heart.[53]

51. Gerald F. Gaus, *The Modern Liberal Theory of Man*, pp. 39–66.
52. E. M. Forster, *A Passage to India*, p. 254.
53. Charles de Saint-Evremond, "Sur l'amitié" [1689], in *Œuvres en prose*, pp. 308–9. Aristocratic circles strenuously created stylized conversational forms avoiding matters of substance in an attempt to create a private domain, distinguished from the pervasive political

Private friendship is no more possible between political friends than, in Tönnies's view, among the bourgeoisie of capitalist society. But, as we have seen, Tönnies's indictment of social interaction in *Gesellschaft*—as contaminated by the capitalist spirit of exchange—is quite unhistorical; as the Scots well understood, it applies more pervasively to the personalized politics of the Renaissance and absolutism than to commercial society.[54]

In Saint-Evremond's account, both prince and confidant yearn for personal intimacy but neither can escape the logic of their stations.[55] Rousseau reflects the same dilemma in contrasting the "two different sorts of commerce" in terms that oppose emotional intimacy, not to market relations, but to the clientelistic politics of the *ancien régime*:

> The only bond of my associations would be mutual attachment, agreement of tastes, suitableness of characters. . . . I would want to have a society around me, not a court; friends, and not *protégés*. I would not be the patron of my guests; I would be their host. This independence and equality would permit my relationships to have all the candor of benevolence; and where neither duty nor interest entered in any way, pleasure and friendship would alone make the law.[56]

intrigue and competitive struggle. This is analyzed by Simmel in *The Sociology of Georg Simmel*, pp. 40–57; Robert Mauzi, *L'Ideé du bonheur au XVIIIe siècle*, pp. 580–601; Daniel Gordon, *Citizens without Sovereignty: Equality and Sociability in French Thought, 1670–1789*, pp. 107–17, and, more intensively, Gordon's "Circular Discourse: The Cult of Conversational Sociability in Pre-Revolutionary France."

54. Tönnies evaluated capitalist society in terms of an antipodal contrast with an idealized image of "traditional" peasantry, but precisely this indictment was made abundantly by analysts of clientelistic and court politics preceding rational bureaucracy and capitalism. Many of La Rochefoucauld's *Maximes* are prototypic—for example, number 83: "What men have called friendship is merely association *[commerce]*, respect for each others' interests, and exchange of good offices—in fact, nothing more than a business arrangement from which self-love is always out to draw some profit" (La Rochefoucauld, *Maximes* [1665–78] in *Œuvres complètes*). See also chapter 5 of Norbert Elias, *Court Society,* from which a brief passage is quoted on p. 51 above.

55. It is anachronistic to endow the confidant, a political friend, with the emotional intimacy of modern friendship. Thus, Horatio is less Hamlet's friend than an exemplary confidant, sharing and aiding Hamlet's stratagems. Hamlet never shares with him the material of the great monologues, the secrets not of his strategy but of his soul. He rather confides to Horatio his suspicions and tactics, like that of the play-within-a-play, "after which we will both our judgments join" (III.ii.83–84). At the end he commands Horatio to remain alive to "report me and my cause aright" (V.ii.328). Both are resonant of late medieval companions' obligations to offer *consilium* and "maintain causes" as described in Maurice Keen, "Brotherhood in Arms."

56. Jean-Jacques Rousseau, *Emile* [1762], translated by Allan Bloom (New York: Basic Books, 1979), pp. 348–49.

Rousseau strikingly proclaims the coming of the modern friendship ideal. However, for almost the two preceding centuries, Montaigne's praise of friendship founded on elective affinity between two unique persons—"If you press me to tell why I loved him, I feel this cannot be expressed, except by answering: because it was he, because it was I"—found incomprehension even in those circles which appreciated La Rochefoucauld's remorseless unmasking of self-interested calculation behind every seemingly generous or selfless act. Appreciation of Montaigne's celebration of personal friendship divorced from station and practical services had to await the flowering of romanticism, in the first third of the nineteenth century.[57] Similarly, Montaigne's celebration of intention rather than result in judging the actions of friends made little sense when the practical utility of friendship was key to its purposes and ethic.[58] Clientelistic and absolutist politics did not, like capitalism, sustain a viable adversary culture, but at most, as in La Rochefoucauld's *Maximes,* one of disillusion.[59]

In contrast, the Scots construct a model of universal sociability in which anti-instrumental personal relations do not play a retreatist role, but pervade society as a source of moral order. According to Adam Ferguson:

> [I]n every instance of good will to men, the effects of a benevolent disposition may reach the object of it in beneficent and positive services; and be considered among the characteristics of a *social attachment,* upon whatever ground of connection it may be formed. Under this title we may consider the relations of consanguinity, of neighborhood or acquaintance, as well as attachments of predilection and choice, more properly termed the connection of friends.[60]

The new friendship does not express a "lowering of the moral standard," as in Nelson's account, but celebrates a moral corollary of commercial society: friendship no longer need benefit those directly involved by attacking or menacing others' interests, and is freed from the dilemmas and tensions of historic forms of friendship that combined Hume's "two different sorts of commerce."

57. Donald Frame, *The Reception of Montaigne in France,* chapter 1.

58. "It is not in the power of all the arguments in the world to dislodge me from the certainty I have of the intentions and judgments of my friend. Not one of his actions could be presented to me, whatever appearance it might have, that I could not immediately find the motive for it" (Montaigne, "Of Friendship" [1580], in *Essays,* p. 140).

59. In Molière's *Le Misanthrope,* Alceste, in his moral rage against false friendship, hypocrisy, and insincerity, has no choice but to retire from the world. In Madame de La Fayette's novel of 1678, *La Princesse de Clèves,* the protagonist's sensitive sincerity destroys her marriage and life. Marivaux's play of 1739, *Les sincères,* shows that sincerity itself is not immune to affectation and dissimulation.

60. Ferguson, *Principles of Moral and Political Science,* p. 361 (original emphasis).

For the Scots, the moral quality of exclusivistic bonds was corrupted by the ubiquity of interests stemming from *necessitudo;* "universal otherhood" is not a pale version of historically stronger forms of solidarity. The Scots understand commercial society not as causing an "attenuation of love," as Nelson has it, but as offering new possibilities of personal relations purged of pervasive instrumentalism, creating friendship in the modern sense.

CONCLUSIONS AND QUESTIONS

To SUMMARIZE BRISKLY the perspective on personal relations of these eighteenth-century social theorists: commercial society—in which "every man . . . lives by exchanging, or becomes in some measure a merchant" [61]—and impersonal and uniform political administration—"where the authority of law is always perfectly sufficient to protect the meanest man in the state" [62]— both facilitate a distinction, without extensive precedent, between sympathetic relationships that normatively exclude calculation and utility, and relationships oriented to instrumentalism and contract. This development enhances the moral quality of personal relationships and frees them from exclusivistic solidarities expressing pervasive competition. Friendship and other sympathetic bonds integrate individuals into the larger society, linking them to successively more inclusive but less intense groupings. Such personal relations are not survivals of earlier historical periods. Only in commercial and impersonally administered society can friendship connect, not some in struggle against others, but potentially all through forms of association that cumulatively contribute to a moralized civil society. Only with impersonal markets in products and services, and impersonal modes of administration, does a parallel system of personal relations emerge the ethic of which is constituted by sentiment and affect rather than calculation and utility.

This grand, if rough, working hypothesis has its weaknesses, but, compared with available alternatives, it emerges as persuasive and rugged. Indeed, much of the contemporary sociology of personal relations descends, if unknowingly, from the Scots' account; however, it shares neither their understanding that anti-instrumental ideals of personal relations are distinctively modern, nor the historical sociology underlying their analysis, nor, indeed, a sense that its task requires an informed sense of history.[63] It largely inherits the unexamined

61. Smith, *Wealth of Nations,* p. 37.

62. Smith, *Moral Sentiments,* p. 224.

63. For its indirect influence on Cooley and others of his seminal generation, see Allan Silver, "The Curious Importance of the Small Group in American Sociology," in Herbert Gans's edited collection, *Sociology in America.* For its expression in subsequent sociological research, see such examples as: Claude Fischer, *To Dwell among Friends: Personal Networks in Town and City;* Mark Granovetter, "The Strength of Weak Ties"; Edward O. Laumann,

assumption that anti-instrumental personal relations are antipodal in spirit, and historically prior, to modern society—an assumption that shapes its understanding of the present. Had sociology drawn self-consciously on a corpus of theory including the Scots, it might not have "rediscovered" primary groups earlier in this century or treated them as historical survivals. That "rediscovery," and the recurrent finding that such relations flourish in modern society, are ungrounded in a warranted sense of how our present stands in relation to those other presents, now past, that constitute history. A presentist misreading of the history of personal relations has dominated in sociology at least since Cooley's assumption of the historical as well as psychological priority of the "primary group."[64] This in turn affects understanding of personal relations today—whether, for example, we are to understand them as "communal" phenomena at odds with the Great Society, or tucked away in its interstices, or as distinctively modern phenomena causally dependent upon it.

Deep difficulties lie in the very concept most readily at hand to address these matters—that of "differentiation." In its ordinary use, the idea tempts us to imagine an "undifferentiated" past as one in which (say) "instrumentalism" and "sympathy" coexisted in the form and substance they have at present.[65] On this view, change consists of these entities, unchanged in essence, coming to inhabit different parts of a social structure. But are these "two different sorts of commerce," to evoke Hume's distinction again, the same in substance and meaning whether or not "differentiated"?

Consider, with a brevity necessarily desperate, a rich complex of ideas and practices that for centuries defined an important range of personal relations among privileged groups in Western history—namely, codes of honor. Men widely considered themselves honor-bound, if need arose, to sacrifice themselves nobly for others to whom they had promised loyalty—and also explicitly expected a variety of palpable rewards and resources from the same associations.[66] Are the intense loyalties, coexisting with the frank expectation of re-

Bonds of Pluralism: The Form and Substance of Urban Social Networks; S. M. Lipset, Martin Trow, and James Coleman, *Union Democracy;* Barry Wellman, "The Community Question: The Intimate Networks of East Yorkers."

64. Cooley, *Social Organization,* chapters 1 through 5.

65. This is not necessarily among the various senses intended by the idea's progenitor, Spencer, or its most influential advocates in this century, Talcott Parsons and Niklas Luhmann.

66. From a large literature, see, illustratively, Merwyn James, "English Politics and the Concept of Honour, 1485–1642"; Roland Mousnier, *The Institutions of France under the Absolute Monarchy, 1598–1789,* 1:99–111; Kristen Neuschel, *Word of Honor: Interpreting Noble Culture in Sixteenth Century France;* Jonathan Dewald, *Aristocratic Experience and the Origins of Modern Culture.*

ward, found in the richly elaborated cultures of honor the same "conceptual stuff" as the loyalties of modern friends and the instrumentalism of market society? Or are they part of a qualitatively different complex of meaning? Is not the sense, setting, and substance of honor so distinctive that the imagery of "differentiation" smuggles the present into the past, and flattens questions that might otherwise be asked, both about past and present?

Such misunderstandings arise, in part, because modern ideals of friendship and personal life create privileged standards by which the quality of experience is evaluated. Only modern society has created a democratized arena of private and elective affinities, in which persons might culturally value each other for their "true," that is, their unproductive, selves. But modern ideals of personal relations, "purified" of practical urgencies, often contribute to a troubled contrast between private and public domains, privileging a personal morality whose ideal attributes need no longer accommodate the imperatives of *necessitudo*. Such ideals seem elevated and pure, compared with the exigencies of the public domain at its best—compromise, calculation, rationing, efficiency, the clash of contending interests. The contrast is gratuitously invidious, to the unmerited disadvantage of the public domain.

The significance of this invidious contrast is certainly greater for the various strains of anticapitalist "adversary culture," including its romantic, conservative, and left variants, than for most people in the context of everyday life. Still, the Scots' characteristic neglect of tensions intrinsic to "commercial society" did not lead them to consider that the emergence of a distinct domain of sympathy and benevolence in civil society might engender a sense of unease with the very world of markets and dispassionate administration they also celebrated. However, that these "two different sorts of commerce" are often at odds in felt experience is properly understood, not in terms of lost ideals of personal bonds eroded by modernity, but as internal to the modern condition.

REFERENCES

Adkins, A. W. H. 1972. *Moral Values and Political Behavior in Ancient Greece*. New York: Norton.

Allan, Graham. 1979. *A Sociology of Friendship and Kinship*. London: Allen & Unwin.

———. 1989. *Friendship: Developing a Sociological Perspective*. London: Harvester.

Anderson, Michael. 1971. *Family Structure in Nineteenth Century Lancashire*. Cambridge: Cambridge University Press.

———. 1977. "The Impact on the Family Relationships of the Elderly of Changes Since Victorian Times in Governmental Income Maintenance Provision." In *Family, Bureaucracy and the Elderly*, edited by Ethel Shanas and Marvin Sussman. Durham, NC: Duke University Press.

Annis, David B. 1987. "The Meaning, Value, and Duties of Friendship." *American Philosophical Quarterly* 24: 349–56.

Badhwaar, Neera Kapur. 1987. "Friends as Ends in Themselves." *Philosophy and Phenomenological Research* 48: 1–23.

Bagehot, Walter. [1872] 1948. *Physics and Politics.* New York: Knopf.

Bidart, Claire. 1993. "Les semblables, les amis et les autres: Sociabilité et amitié." Thèse de doctorat, Ecole des Hautes Etudes en Science Sociales, Marseilles.

Blundell, Mary Whitelock. 1989. *Helping Friends and Harming Enemies: A Study in Sophocles and Greek Ethics.* New York and Cambridge: Cambridge University Press.

Boltanski, Luc. *L'Amour et la justice comme compétences.* Paris: Métailié, 1990.

Bonhoeffer, Dietrich. 1972. *Letters and Papers from Prison.* Edited by Eberhard Bethge. New York: Macmillan.

Campbell, T. D. 1971. *Adam Smith's Science of Morals.* London: Allen & Unwin.

Caudwell, Christopher. [1938] 1948. *Studies in a Dying Culture.* London: Bodley Head.

Cooley, Charles Horton. [1909] 1962. *Social Organization.* New York: Schocken.

Cropsey, Joseph. [1957] 1977. *Polity and Economy: An Interpretation of the Principles of Adam Smith.* Westport, CT: Greenwood.

Defoe, Daniel. [1726] 1970. *The Complete English Tradesman.* New York: Franklin.

Dewald, Jonathan. 1993. *Aristocratic Experience and the Origins of Modern Culture.* Berkeley: University of California Press.

Dewey, John. 1927. *The Public and Its Problems.* New York: Holt.

Dibble, Vernon. 1978. "Transcendentalism and Sociology: The Case of Charles Horton Cooley." Wesleyan University, Department of History Seminar.

Elias, Norbert. [1969] 1983. *The Court Society.* New York: Pantheon.

Evans-Pritchard, E. E. 1933. "Zande Blood-Brotherhood." *Africa* 6: 369–401.

Farnsworth, Allan E. 1969. "The Past of Promise: An Historical Introduction to Contract." *Columbia Law Review* 69: 576–607.

Ferguson, Adam. [1767] 1966. *An Essay on the History of Civil Society.* Edinburgh: University of Edinburgh Press.

———. 1792. *Principles of Moral and Political Science.* 2 vols. Edinburgh: Creech.

Fischer, Claude. 1982. *To Dwell among Friends: Personal Networks in Town and City.* Berkeley: University of California Press.

Forster, E. M. 1924. *A Passage to India.* New York: Harcourt Brace.

Frame, Donald. 1940. *The Reception of Montaigne in France.* New York: Columbia University Press.

Friedberg, Barbara Jane. 1980. "Sympathetic Imagination as an Intellectual Ideal in Victorian Literature and Controversy." Ph.D. dissertation, Columbia University, Department of English and Comparative Literature.

Gaus, Gerald F. 1983. *The Modern Liberal Theory of Man.* New York: St. Martin's.

Goitein, S. D. 1971. "Formal Friendship in the Medieval Near East." *Proceedings of the American Philosophical Society* 115: 484–89.

Gordon, Daniel. 1990. "Circular Discourse: The Cult of Conversational Sociability in Pre-Revolutionary France." Paper presented at the annual meeting of the American Historical Association.

———. 1994. *Citizens without Sovereignty: Equality and Sociability in French Thought, 1670–1789.* Princeton, NJ: Princeton University Press.

Granovetter, Mark. 1973. "The Strength of Weak Ties." *American Journal of Sociology* 78: 1360–80.

Haskell, Thomas L. 1985. "Capitalism and the Origins of Humanitarian Sensibility, Part 2." *American Historical Review* 90: 547–66.

Herman, Gabriel. 1987. *Ritual Friendship and the Greek City.* New York and Cambridge: Cambridge University Press.

Hirsch, Fred. 1977. *Social Limits to Growth.* Cambridge, MA: Harvard University Press.

Hirschman, Albert O. 1977. *The Passions and the Interests: Arguments for Capitalism before Its Triumph.* Princeton, NJ: Princeton University Press.

Hume, David. [1749] 1978. *A Treatise of Human Nature.* Edited by L. Selby-Bigge. Revised edition by P. H. Niddich. Oxford: Clarendon.

Hutcheson, Francis. [1725, 1738] 1969. *An Inquiry into the Original of Our Ideas of Beauty and Virtue. Treatise II: An Inquiry Concerning the Original of our Ideas of Virtue or Moral Good.* Vol. 1, *British Moralists, 1650–1800,* edited by D. D. Raphael. Oxford: Clarendon.

Hutter, Horst. 1978. *Politics as Friendship: The Origins of Classical Notions of Politics in the Theory and Practise of Friendship.* Waterloo: Wilfred Laurier University Press.

James, Merwyn. 1978. "English Politics and the Concept of Honour, 1485–1642." *Past and Present,* supp. 3.

Keen, Maurice. 1962. "Brotherhood in Arms." *History* 47: 1–17.

Konstan, David. 1994–95. "Friendship and the State: The Context of Cicero's *De Amicitia.*" *Hyperboraeous* 1, no. 2: 1–16.

———. 1995. "Patrons and Friends." *Classical Philology* 90: 328–42.

———. 1996. "Greek Friendship." *American Journal of Philology* 117: (in press).

Krattenmaker, Thomas. 1976. "Interpersonal Testimonial Privileges under the 'Federal Rules of Evidence.'" *Georgetown Law Journal* 64: 613–68.

Kurth, Suzanne B. 1970. "Friendship and Friendly Relations." In *Social Relationships,* edited by George McCall. Chicago: Aldine.

La Fayette, Mme de. [1678] 1963. *La Princesse de Clèves.* Baltimore, MD: Penguin.

La Rochefoucauld. [1665–78] 1964. *Maximes.* In *Œuvres Complètes.* Paris: Editions Gallimard.

Laumann, Edward O. 1973. *Bonds of Pluralism: The Form and Substance of Urban Social Networks.* New York: Wiley.

Levinson, Sanford. 1984. "Testimonial Privileges and the Preferences of Friendship." *Duke Law Journal* 32: 631–62.

Lipset, S. M., Martin Trow, and James Coleman. 1956. *Union Democracy.* New York: Free Press.

Maisonneuve, Jean, and Lubomir Lamy. 1993. *Psycho-sociologie de l'amitié.* Paris: Presses Universitaires de France.

Marivaux. [1739] 1968. "Les sincères." In *Théâtre complet,* edited by Frédéric Deloffre. Paris: Editions Garnier.

Marshall, Alfred E. [1890] 1927. *Principles of Economics.* London: MacMillan.

Marx, Karl. [1857–58] 1973. *Grundrisse.* New York: Vintage.

Mauss, Marcel. [1938] 1985. "A Category of the Human Mind: The Notion of Person; the Notion of Self." In *The Category of the Person: Anthropology, Philosophy, History,* edited by Michael Carrithers et al. Cambridge: Cambridge University Press.

Mauzi, Robert L. [1960] 1979. *L'Idée du bonheur au XVIIIe siècle.* Geneva and Paris: Slatkine.

Meilaender, Gilbert C. 1981. *Friendship: A Study in Theological Ethics.* Notre Dame, IN: University of Notre Dame Press.

Mills, Laurens J. 1937. *One Soul in Bodies Twain: Friendship in Tudor Literature and Stuart Drama.* Bloomington, IN: Principia Press.

Mizuta, Hiroshi. 1975. "Moral Philosophy and Civil Society." In *Essays on Adam Smith,* edited by Andrew S. Skinner and Thomas Wilson. Oxford: Clarendon.

Montaigne, Michel. [1580] 1958. "On Friendship." In *Essays,* translated by Donald Frame. Stanford, CA: Stanford University Press.

Mousnier, Roland. [1974] 1980. *The Institutions of France under the Absolute Monarchy, 1598–1789.* Vol. 1. Chicago: University of Chicago Press.

Morrow, Glenn R. 1923. *The Ethical and Economic Theories of Adam Smith.* Cornell Studies in Philosophy, no. 13. New York: Longmans.

Musgrave, R. A. 1976. "Adam Smith on Public Finance and Distribution." In *The Market and the State: Essays in Honour of Adam Smith,* edited by Thomas Wilson and A. S. Skinner. Oxford: Oxford University Press.

Naegele, Kaspar. 1958. "Friendships and Acquaintances: An Exploration of Some Social Distinctions." *Harvard Educational Review* 28: 232–52.

Nelson, Benjamin. [1949] 1969. *The Idea of Usury: From Tribal Brotherhood to Universal Otherhood.* Chicago: University of Chicago Press.

Neuschel, Kristen. 1989. *Word of Honor: Interpreting Noble Culture in Sixteenth Century France.* Ithaca, NY: Cornell University Press.

Norton, David L. 1976. *Personal Destinies: A Philosophy of Ethical Individualism.* Princeton, NJ: Princeton University Press.

Nygren, Anders. [1930, 1936] 1982. *Agape and Eros: The Christian Idea of Love and Its Transformations.* Translated by Philip S. Watson. Chicago: University of Chicago Press.

Oncken, Auguste. 1897. "The Consistency of Adam Smith." *Economic Journal* 7: 443–50.

Paine, Robert. 1969. "In Search of Friendship: An Exploratory Analysis in Middle Class Culture." *Man* 4: 505–24.

Perkin, Harold. 1972. *The Origins of Modern English Society, 1780–1880.* Toronto: University of Toronto Press.

Phillipson, Nicholas. 1983. "Adam Smith as Civic Moralist." In *Wealth and Virtue: The Shaping of Political Economy in the Scottish Enlightenment,* edited by Istvan Hont and Michael Ignatieff. Cambridge: Cambridge University Press.

Pitt-Rivers, Julian. 1968. "The Stranger, the Guest and the Hostile Host." In *Contributions to Mediterranean Sociology,* edited by J. G. Peristiany. The Hague: Mouton.

Reiman, Jeffrey. 1976. "Privacy, Intimacy and Personhood." *Philosophy and Public Affairs* 6: 26–44.

Rousseau, Jean-Jacques. [1762] 1979. *Emile.* Translated by Allan Bloom. New York: Basic Books.

Saint-Evremond, Charles de. [1689] 1966. "Sur l'amitié." In *Œuvres en prose,* edited by René Ternois. Tome 3. Paris: Libraire Marcel Didier.

Silver, Allan. 1989. "Friendship and Trust as Moral Ideals: An Historical Approach." *Archives européenes de sociologie* 30: 274–97.

———. 1990. "The Curious Importance of the Small Group in American Sociology." In *Sociology in America,* edited by Herbert J. Gans. Newbury Park, CA: Sage.

———. 1990. "Friendship in Commercial Society." *American Journal of Sociology* 95, no. 6: 1474–1504.

Simmel, Georg. [1900, 1907] 1978. *The Philosophy of Money.* Translated by Tom Bottomore and David Frisby. London: Routledge & Kegan Paul.

———. 1950. *The Sociology of Georg Simmel.* Translated by Kurt Wolff. Glencoe, IL: Free Press.

Smith, Adam. [1759, 1791] 1976. *The Theory of Moral Sentiments.* Edited by D. D. Raphael and A. L. Macfie. Oxford: Clarendon.

———. [1776] 1976. *An Inquiry into the Nature and Causes of the Wealth of Nations.* Edited by R. H. Campbell and A. S. Skinner. Oxford: Clarendon.

Smith, Lacy Baldwin. 1986. *Treason in Tudor England.* Princeton, NJ: Princeton University Press.

Stone, Lawrence. 1977. *The Family, Sex and Marriage in England, 1500–1800.* New York: Harper & Row.

Suttles, Gerald. 1970. "Friendship as a Social Institution." In *Social Relationships,* edited by George McCall. Chicago: Aldine.

Teichgraeber, Richard III. 1981. "Rethinking *Das Adam Smith Problem.*" *Journal of British Studies* 20: 106–23.

Telfer, Elizabeth. 1970. "Friendship." *Proceedings of the Aristotelian Society,* pp. 223–42.

Tenbruck, Friedrich H. 1964. "Freundschaft: Ein Beitrag zu einer Soziologie der persönlichen Beziehungen." *Kölner Zeitschrift für Soziologie und Sozial Psychologie* 16: 431–50.

Thomas, Lawrence. 1987. "Friendship." *Synthèse* 72: 217–36.

Tönnies, Ferdinand. [1887] 1957. *Community and Society (Gemeinschaft und Gesell-schaft).* Translated by Charles Loomis. New York: Harper & Row.

Turner, Ralph. 1976. "The Real Self: From Institution to Impulse." *American Journal of Sociology* 81: 989–1016.

Wadell, Paul J. 1989. *Friendship and the Moral Life.* South Bend, IN: University of Notre Dame Press.

Wallas, Graham. [1914] 1936. *The Great Society: A Psychological Analysis.* London: Macmillan.

Wellman, Barry. 1979. "The Community Question: The Intimate Networks of East Yorkers." *American Journal of Sociology* 84: 1201–31.

Wolf, Eric. 1966. "Kinship, Friendship and Patron-Client Relations in Complex Societies." In *The Social Anthropology of Complex Societies,* edited by Michael Banton. London: Tavistock.

Wood, Gordon S. 1992. *The Radicalism of the American Revolution.* New York: Knopf.

THREE

Nationalism and the Public Sphere

Craig Calhoun

POLITICAL DISCUSSION COMMONLY starts with the state. It is, indeed, the creation of states as quasi-autonomous organizations (or actors) that produces the differentiation of politics from other aspects of social life and of discourse.[1] As a result, it is not surprising that we are led to assume state-centered views of the constitution of political communities. Modern political communities are given their boundaries in the first instance by common subjection to a state. The outcomes of past struggles—conquests, inheritances, civil wars, revolutions, anti-imperial revolts—are ratified through administrative centralization and integration. States define political communities not only domestically but in relation to other states—for example, by issuing passports and visas, by sponsoring shared educational institutions that maintain linguistic homogeneity internally and heterogeneity externally, and by encouraging domestic and restricting foreign markets. Not all states are equally effective, but the effectiveness of some reinforces the assumption that states are the necessary objects of political communities, even where they are not their source.

There is, however, a paradox in the use of states to define political communities. States may distinguish political communities from each other in various ways, and states and their personnel may also occupy a great deal of the public

Earlier versions of parts of this essay have benefitted from discussion at the V Conversaciones Internacionales de Historia, University of Navarre; the Washington University Conference on Strategies of Explanation in Social Science; the Robert F. Harney Program in Ethnic, Immigration, and Pluralism Studies at the University of Toronto; and meetings of the Center for Transcultural Studies in Chicago. The Swedish Collegium for Advanced Study in the Social Sciences provided support for its completion. The author is also grateful for comments from Jean Cohen, Lloyd Kramer, Krishan Kumar, and Jeff Weintraub.

1. Different definitions of politics would make this statement problematic. If one followed Hannah Arendt, for example, in extolling politics as a vital part of the *vita activa,* and denigrating administrative authority as the mere management of the necessities of life, one would avoid linking politics too strongly to states, and one would see politics sharply differentiated from the social. By the same token, the social would then appear as a very inferior and unfree dimension of life—and this raises all the questions about the politicization of the social that have been at stake in the social movements of the modern era. See *The Human Condition.*

sphere within each. Yet in modern usage, states are not in themselves political communities.

A state is not merely a country, but also a specialized apparatus of rule. A state is thus distinct from the people subject to its rule. The Roman state was not equivalent to the Roman people even in the Republican era, and still less was the state of imperial Rome equivalent to the peoples of the Roman Empire. In empires and in many other historical forms of rule, the relationship between state and people has commonly been distant and/or arbitrary. Hereditary elites were sharply distinguished from those they ruled. "Peoples" came under one or another state as a result of the conquest of the territories on which they lived, but neither their character nor that of the state that claimed them was necessarily altered by this. Some ethnic or other relatively broad groupings might have special claims on office or special capacities to influence rulers, as for example Romans did retain a special political access even as imperial Rome became more far-flung and multicultural. The Mughal state in India thus favored Muslims and Urdu speakers and its British successor favored Englishmen and English speakers, but in neither case was being a member of the favored group a guarantee of jobs or power. These groupings were not conterminous with the state apparatus but had to relate to it through discourse or action; the state was not constituted by its relationship to any such broad category of people. In these and most other cases, the relevant political community was not "the people," nor even any very large segment of the people, but rather the networks of elites given voice and influence by heredity or administrative position.

This narrower political community gave social identity to the state. Even where the state was tyrannical, some such political community existed and carried on some level of discourse, offering advice to the ruler and working out how to interpret his directives. Such political communities were always at least somewhat differentiated: courtiers and noblemen spoke with different backgrounds, interests, perceptions, and strategies. But by itself, the existence of this sort of political community did not necessarily constitute a *public* distinct from the state. Take the scholar-administrators of imperial China. They acted neither to influence a state from which they were distinct (as did Roman citizens) nor in place of a differentiated state apparatus (as in certain periods the citizens of Athens governed directly). Rather, this sort of political community was contained within the state.

In none of the cases just mentioned was the relevant political community "the people" as a whole, not even the people of the most favored ethnic classification. It was always a narrower elite. But we can still distinguish between those settings in which the political community was basically contained within the state and those in which it included a public conceptually and practically outside the state apparatus (even if many of the members of this public were insiders to the state). The extent and kind of distinction between the political community and the state is thus a crucial variable.

Also important is the relationship between the political community and the broader population. Modern states distinguished themselves from empires and other earlier forms of state largely by claiming and building a more intimate relationship to the populations they ruled. This was partly a matter of changing patterns of taxation, military mobilization, trade and production, and communications and transportation infrastructure.[2] The state penetrated more deeply into the daily lives of ordinary people, and did so more evenly throughout its territory. At the same time, three different sorts of ideological shifts made the relationship of people to state seem more intimate.

The first, and most recognized in political theory, was the extremely widespread influence of republican thought.[3] In this tradition, modern Europe saw itself as the heir of ancient Rome. Republicanism turned crucially on the notion of the public, and granted public discourse a powerful role, though it often retained a limited notion of the range of people constituting the political community that might carry on this public discourse.

Second, the Protestant Reformation encouraged a rethinking of the polity that emphasized the people—conceived first and foremost as God's chosen people or the people who shared religious revelation or understanding—rather than the public. Here the proper ancestor of modern Europe was not so much

2. Tracing these transformations in the nature and underpinnings of states has been one of the central tasks of historical political sociology, in different generations preoccupying, among many others, Max Weber, *Economy and Society* [1922]; Karl Deutsch, *Nationalism and Social Communication: An Inquiry into the Foundations of Nationality* (1953); and Michael Mann, *The Sources of Social Power* (2 vols., 1986 and 1993). Of course, the extent to which the categories of "the people" or "the public" become locally meaningful depends on other factors: internal connections among people, occasions for collective action, ideologies that root citizenship in popular consent or in the capacity of rulers to serve the interests of the people, and so forth.

3. For a compelling account of the role of republican ideas in a crucial early moment of modern political transformation, see J. G. A. Pocock, *The Machiavellian Moment*. Even modern monarchical states have been shaped by republican ideas. Of course, republicanism is not altogether new, as the example of Rome reminds us; Rome reminds us as well that transitions from republic to empire are also possible, and these have indeed occurred in the modern era, as, for example, the Union of Soviet Socialist Republics without announcement constituted itself in significant ways as an empire, both internally (with relation to the non-Russian republics) and externally (with relation to Warsaw Pact dependencies).

ancient Rome as the theocratic communities of the patristic era.[4] It is thus no accident that the Puritan influence on the English Civil War should offer us some of the first really modern invocations of the people as the source of legitimacy for the state.

Third, ethnic, cultural, and localist solidarities began to be invoked as the basis of political communities. Versions of this tendency appeared alongside republicanism, as in the Florentine patriotism of Machiavelli, and alongside religious invocations of the chosen people, as in Cromwell's English nationalism. But it also marked a distinct mode of claiming loyalty or legitimacy, as was evident in the successes both English and French kings found in invoking the alien other to help in the increasingly broad military mobilizations of the absolutist era.[5]

In short, three different modes of claiming a broader political community, one outside the state apparatus, became influential. I am designating these by the names *public, people,* and *nation* (though it should be noted that in everyday political rhetoric each of these terms has been used to refer to each of the three concepts I am trying to distinguish).

These new notions of political community reflected an expansion in the scope of political participation and in the role of the state in various forms of social mobilization and regulation. They also figured centrally in a changed understanding of legitimacy. During most of previous European history, the notion that legitimate right to rule ascended from the people to the rulers had been subordinate to an understanding of power as descending from God and other authorities through the various ranks of the nobility to lower levels. Claims based on the "ascending theory" were generally directed against efforts to translate papal authority into state-building or against the efforts of monarchs to institutionalize central states.[6] In the early modern era, a conceptual revolution helped to reconcile ascending theories of legitimacy, rooted in recognition of the political rights of the public, the people, or the nation, with centralized state-building.

This transformed understanding of the nature of political community and legitimacy was linked to the growth of new ideas about nonpolitical social

4. And in this sense, we see more of the modern notion of the "people" in relation to the state in the early histories of both Judaism and Islam than in either the Greece or Rome of classical antiquity, however beloved these were by early modern political theorists.

5. Shakespeare's paradigmatically English King Henry IV devotes a good deal of effort to constituting the unity of his quarreling Scottish, Welsh, and regionally diverse English followers by reference to the undeniable foreignness of the French.

6. See Otto von Gierke's *Natural Law and the Theory of Society* and Walter Ullmann's *Principles of Government and Politics in the Middle Ages.*

organization. These were articulated prominently in the early discourse of civil society. This term, adapted in part from an image of free medieval cities, referred both to the capacity of a political community to organize itself independent of the specific direction of state power and to the socially organized pursuit of private ends.[7] Self-organization might be accomplished through discourse and decision making in the public sphere, or through the systemic organization of private interests in the economy. The thinkers of the Scottish Enlightenment emphasized the latter in their account of early capitalist markets as arenas in which the pursuit of private ends by individual actors produced in aggregate an effective social organization not dependent on the intervention of the state. The market was thus a model for claims to the capacity for self-organization, as well as the realm of specific interests to be protected from improper manipulation. But the claims of civil society could also be linked—especially after Locke—to rejections of the absolute authority of monarchs and assertions of the rights of popular sovereignty. These arguments placed a new emphasis on the social integration of society as such rather than merely on the aggregation of subjects. In such a view, the state no longer defined the political community directly, for its own legitimacy depended on the acquiescence or support of an already existing political community.

These changes powerfully shaped both political discourse and the most material sorts of politics for succeeding centuries, including our own. They were also crucial in the production of a discourse of "society," for they made politics increasingly a sociological problem rather than just a matter of statecraft, princely wisdom, or sheer power understood solely in terms of relations among members of the state apparatus or its competitors. The political community had escaped the bounds of the state apparatus, and a new tension between the broad idea of the nation and generally narrower ideas of who constituted the proper custodians of the public good came to constitute more and more of political struggle.

In the present essay, I want to explore the close but complex relationship between the ideas of public, people, and nation. Each influenced the other from the time they took on their characteristic modern inflections. My major emphasis, however, will not be on the history of these ideas as such, but on the ways in which recognizing their interlinkage helps to shed light on the

7. Hegel looms too large in the most prominent recent general account of the political theory of civil society, Jean Cohen and Andrew Arato's *Civil Society and Political Theory*. This obscures the importance both of Scottish/English and French analyses and of the extent to which the discourse from the beginning emphasized capacity for nonstate social organization. This discourse was, of course, a crucial forerunner to the constitution of sociology.

modern discourse of nationalism. Nationalism has appeared recurrently as one of the greatest challenges to the ideal of rational collective decision making through peaceful discourse that has joined the term "public" to the projects of republicanism and democracy. Yet in many ways nationalist ideas are presumed by the more "successful" democracies, and nation-building has been closely related historically to the very rise of public life that has helped make modern democracy possible.

Even in academic analysis, too easy acceptance of the view that nationalism is a problematic but fading inheritance from primordial history has obscured recognition of its centrality to our modern ideas of publics and more generally of politically salient identities. Most basic is the notion that there is some one people that constitutes the proper referent of public discourse and the ground of democratic claims to self-governance. On such a view, American public discourse is—or ought to be—about the public goods appropriate to the American people. This implies, among other things, that this people is sufficiently unified that it can be adequately represented by a single, authoritative public discourse. Such views work to privilege certain definitions of the public at the expense of others. Not only are certain speakers given wider attention, recognition, or influence; certain topics are defined as properly public and others as merely private. At stake throughout this discussion is the issue of difference—that is, of the extent to which discourse involving the notion of public or the identity of nation recognizes or represses the plurality of identities that shape the lives of individuals, communities, and societies. Nationalism thus becomes the most frequently troubling instance of identity politics writ large, but it is not the only one.[8] Similar issues are involved in many invocations of "legitimate" publics and nonnationalist representations of peoples.

PROBLEMATIZING PUBLIC AND PRIVATE

THE VERY DISTINCTION of public from private took on new meaning in the early modern era with the notion that outside the immediate apparatus of state rule there existed both a realm of public discourse and action that might address or act on the state, and the private affairs of citizens that were legitimately protected from undue state regulation or intervention. Persons existed in dual aspects, just as the private affairs of officeholders came increasingly to be distinguished from their public roles.[9] The notion of a public realm is accordingly almost always ambivalent, referring to the collective concerns of the political community and to the activities of the state that is central to

8. See Craig Calhoun's edited volume, *Social Theory and the Politics of Identity.*

9. Like the separation of family finances from business finances, this is of course part of the Weberian story of modernization as rationalization.

defining that political community. This two-edged notion of the public in-scribes its parallel notion of the private. The private is simultaneously that which is not subject to the purview of the state and that which concerns personal ends distinct from the public good, the *res publica* or matters of legitimate public concern.

The idea of "public" is central to theories of democracy. It appears both as the crucial subject of democracy—the people organized as a discursive and decision-making public—and as object—the public good. This complex of issues has recently become an object of intense critical theoretical attention, especially in the English-speaking world, partly because the English translation of Jürgen Habermas's major book on the subject coincided with the fall of Communism and attendant concern for transitions to democracy.[10] As Habermas develops the theoretical problematic of the public sphere, for example, the basic question is how social self-organization can be accomplished through widespread and more or less egalitarian participation in rational-critical discourse.

Yet, as analyses of the exclusion of women from public life have shown most sharply, conceptualizations of "the public" have also worked in antidemocratic ways. The issue of "democratic inclusiveness" is not just a quantitative matter of the scale of a public sphere or the proportion of the members of a political community who may speak within it. While it is clearly a matter of stratification and boundaries (for example, openness to the propertyless, the uneducated, women, or immigrants), it is also a matter of how the public sphere incorporates and recognizes the diversity of identities which people bring to it from their manifold involvements in civil society.

All attempts to render a single public discourse authoritative privilege certain topics, certain forms of speech, and certain speakers. This does not mean that the flowering of innumerable potential publics is in and of itself a solution to this basic problem of democracy. On the contrary, democracy requires discourse across lines of basic difference. But this discourse can be conceptualized—and nurtured—as a matter of multiple intersections among heterogenous publics, not only as the privileging of a single overarching public. Nationalist thought, however, commonly rejects such notions of multiple and multifarious publics as divisive. The presumption that the nation is a unitary being is a staple of nationalist thought. And as such it seeps into deliberations on democracy and public affairs that are not explicitly nationalist. Yet where nationalism or any other cultural formation represses difference, it intrinsically

10. Jürgen Habermas, *The Structural Transformation of the Public Sphere* (Cambridge, MA: MIT Press, 1989; originally published in 1962); see also Craig Calhoun's edited collection, *Habermas and the Public Sphere* (Cambridge, MA: MIT Press, 1992).

undermines the capacity of a public sphere to carry forward a rational-critical democratic discourse.

The problem arises largely from an inadequate appreciation of the extent to which difference—what Hannah Arendt called "plurality"—is basic not only to human life in general but specifically to the project of public life and therefore to democracy.[11] Plurality is not a condition of private life or a product of quotidian personal tastes, in Arendt's view, but rather a potential that flowers in creative public achievements. Arendt accepted the classical Greek restriction on public participation precisely because she thought few people could rise above the inherent conformity imposed by a life of material production to achieve real distinction in the realm of praxis. But we need not agree with this exclusionary premise in order to grasp that the reason for a public discourse lies partly in the potential that various members will bring different ideas into shared intellectual consideration.

Part of Arendt's point in linking the distinction of public from private to that of praxis from mere work or labor is to present the public sphere as something more than an arena for the advancement or negotiation of competing material interests. This image is carried forward in Habermas's account, with its emphasis on the possibility of disinterested rational-critical public discourse and his suggestion that the public sphere degenerates as it is penetrated by organized interest groups. But Habermas's analysis subverts some of his own purposes. To presume that there will be only different policies for achieving objectively ascertainable ends—let alone ends reducible to a common calculus in terms of a lowest common denominator of interest—is to reduce the public sphere to a forum of Benthamite policy experts rather than a vehicle of democratic self-government. This is clearly not something Habermas intends to praise. Yet it is not as sharply distant from his account of the public sphere as it might at first seem. One reason is that Habermas does not place the same stress as Arendt on creativity. He treats public activity overwhelmingly in terms of rational-critical discourse rather than identity-formation or expression, which somewhat narrows the meaning and significance of plurality and introduces the possibility of claims to expertise more appropriate to technical rationality than communicative action.[12] Part of the

11. Arendt's exploration of the idea of a public sphere both influenced Habermas and stands as an important (and importantly different) contribution to this line of theory in its own right. See the comparison in Seyla Benhabib, "Models of Public Space: Hannah Arendt, the Liberal Tradition, and Jürgen Habermas," in Calhoun, ed., *Habermas and the Public Sphere*.

12. The last phrase of course borrows terms from Habermas's later work that are not used in *The Structural Transformation of the Public Sphere*.

background to this problem lies in the very manner in which "public" is separated from "private" in the eighteenth- and early-nineteenth-century liberal public sphere which is the basis for Habermas's ideal-typical construction.

The liberal model of the public sphere pursues discursive equality by disqualifying discourse about the differences among actors. These differences are treated as matters of private, but not public, interest. On Habermas's account, the best version of the public sphere was based on "a kind of social intercourse that, far from presupposing the equality of status, disregarded status altogether." [13] It worked by a "mutual willingness to accept the given roles and simultaneously to suspend their reality." [14] This "bracketing" of difference as merely private and irrelevant to the public sphere is undertaken, Habermas argues, in order to defend the genuinely rational-critical notion that arguments must be decided on their merits rather than on the identities of the arguers. This was as important a reason as fear of censors for the prominence of anonymous and pseudonymous authorship in the eighteenth-century public sphere. Yet it also has the effect of excluding some of the most important concerns of many members of any polity—both those whose existing identities are suppressed or devalued and those whose exploration of possible identities is truncated. In addition, this bracketing of differences also undermines the self-reflexive capacity of public discourse. If it is impossible to communicate seriously about basic differences among members of a public sphere, then it will be impossible also to address the difficulties of communication across such lines of basic difference.

The public sphere, Habermas tells us, is created in and out of civil society. Thus, the public sphere is not absorbed into the state, but addresses the state and the sorts of public issues on which state policy might bear. It is based *(a)* on a notion of public good as distinct from private interest, *(b)* on social institutions (like private property) that empower individuals to participate independently in the public sphere because their livelihoods and access to it are not dependent on political power or patronage, and *(c)* on forms of private life (notably families) that prepare individuals to act as autonomous, rational-critical subjects in the public sphere. A central paradox and weakness (not just in Habermas's theory but in the liberal conception which it analyzes and partially incorporates) arises from the implication that the public sphere depends on an organization of private life that enables and encourages citizens to rise above private identities and concerns. It works on the hope of transcending

13. Habermas, *Structural Transformation*, p. 36.
14. Ibid., p. 131.

difference rather than the provision of occasions for recognition, expression, and interrelationship.

The resolution to this issue depends on two main factors. First, the idea of a single, uniquely authoritative public sphere needs to be questioned, and the manner of relations among multiple, intersecting, and heterogeneous publics needs to be considered. Second, identity-formation needs to be approached as part of the process of public life, not something that can be fully settled prior to it in a private sphere.

Recognizing a multiplicity of publics, none of which can claim a completely superordinate status to the others, is thus a first step.[15] Crucially, however, it depends on breaking with core assumptions that join liberal political thought to nationalism. It is one of the illusions of liberal discourse to believe that in a democratic society there is or can be a single, uniquely authoritative discourse about public affairs. This amounts to an attempt to settle in advance a question which is inextricably part of the democratic process itself. It reflects a nationalist presumption that membership in a common society is prior to democratic deliberations as well as an implicit belief that politics revolves around a single and unitary state. It is normal, however, not aberrant, for people to speak in a number of different public arenas and for these to address multiple centers of power (whether institutionally differentiated within a single state, combining multiple states or political agencies, or recognizing that putatively nonpolitical agencies like business corporations are loci of power and addressed by public discourse). How many and how separate these public spheres are must be empirical variables. But each is apt to make some themes easier to address and simultaneously to repress others, and each will empower different voices to different degrees. That women or ethnic minorities carry on their own public discourses, thus, reflects not only the exclusion of certain people from the "dominant" public sphere, but a positive act of women and ethnic minorities. This means that simply pursuing their equitable inclusion in the dominant public sphere cannot be either an adequate recognition of their partially separate discourses or a resolution to the underlying problem. It is important to organize public discourse so that it allows for discursive connections among multiple arenas.

Recognizing the existence of multiple public spheres is thus not an alternative to asking many of the questions Habermas asks about *the* public sphere, that is, about public discourse at the largest of social scales and its capacity

15. See Geoff Eley, "Nations, Publics, and Political Cultures: Placing Habermas in the Nineteenth Century," and Nancy Fraser, "Rethinking the Public Sphere: A Contribution to the Critique of Actually Existing Democracy," both in Calhoun's *Habermas and the Public Sphere*.

to influence politics. It simply suggests that these questions need to be answered in a world of multiple and different publics. It is a political exercise of power to authorize only one of these as properly "public," or some as more legitimately public than others which are held to be "private." In other words, determining whose speech is more properly public is itself a site of political contestation. Different public discourses commonly invoke different distinctions of what is properly "private" and therefore not appropriately addressed in the public discourse or used to settle public debates. There is no objective criterion that distinguishes private from public across the range of discourses. We cannot say, for example, that either bank accounts or sexual orientations are essentially private matters. Varying public/private distinctions are potential (and revisable) accomplishments of each sphere of discourse.

A great deal of the discourse which takes place in public, and which is accessible to the broadest public, is not about ostensibly public matters. I do not mean simply that people take very public occasions like television appearances to talk about what is customarily considered private, like their sex lives. I mean that many topics of widespread concern to the body politic—like childbearing and child-rearing, marriage and divorce, violence of various sorts—are brought into discussions that are public in their constitution but that do not represent themselves as public in the same way the newspaper editorial pages do, and are not taken equally seriously by most participants in the more authorized public sphere. These matters are discussed in churches and self-help groups, among filmgoers and on talk-radio, among parents waiting for their children after school dances and those waiting for visiting hours to commence at prisons. How much the discourse of these various groupings is organized on the rational-critical lines valorized by Habermas's classical Enlightenment public sphere is variable—as is the case, of course, for any other public discussion. But it would be a mistake to presume a priori that one can be rational-critical only about affairs of state or economy, and that these necessarily comprise the proper domain of the public sphere. Conversely, relegation to the realm of the private can be in varying degrees both a protection from public intervention or observation and a disempowering exclusion from public discourse.

Of course, the differences among public spheres are important. Neither Habermas's emphasis on state-oriented discourse nor his emphasis on discourse that attempts to work on a rational-critical basis is arbitrary. Including people different from each other while making arguments rather than the identities of arguers the basis of persuasion is crucial to the meaningful constitution of a public sphere (as distinct from, say, a community). Simply to treat all kinds of more or less public discourses as public spheres in Habermas's sense would be to miss the center of his theoretical project. Unfortunately, Habermas invites some of this problem by employing a problematic distinction of public from private. This appears especially in his relegation of identity-formation (and therefore interest-formation) to the realm of the private.

Habermas presumes that identities will be formed in private (and/or in other public contexts) prior to entry into the political public sphere. This sphere of rational-critical discourse can work only if people are adequately prepared for it through other aspects of their personal and cultural experience. Habermas briefly discusses how the rise of a literary public sphere rooted in the rise of novel-reading and theater-going publics contributed to the development of the political public sphere, but he does not follow through on this insight. He drops discussion of the literary public sphere with its nineteenth-century incarnation, that is, as soon as it has played its role in preparing the path for the rise of the Enlightenment political public sphere. He does not consider subsequent changes in literary discourse and how they may be related to changes in the identities people bring into the political public sphere.

More generally, Habermas does not adequately thematize the role of identity-forming, culture-forming public activity. He works mainly with a contrast between a realm of private life (with the intimate sphere as its inner sanctum) and the public sphere, and assumes that identity is produced out of the combination of private life and the economic positions occupied in civil society.[16] Once we abandon the notion that identity is formed once and for all in advance of participation in the public sphere, however, we can recognize that in varying degree all public discourses are occasions for identity-formation. This is central to the insight of Negt and Kluge in their appropriation of the phenomenological notion of "horizons of experience" as a way of broadening Habermas's approach to the public sphere.[17] Experience is not something exclusively prior to and only addressed by the rational-critical discourse of the public sphere; it is in part constituted through public discourse, and at the same time continually orients people differently in public life.[18]

16. This of course anticipates Habermas's later distinction of lifeworld from system, which has been faulted for its failure to recognize the way in which families and other lifeworld institutions are organized through asymmetrical power relations including gender inequalities. See Habermas, *The Theory of Communicative Action;* and Nancy Fraser, *Unruly Practices,* and "Rethinking the Public Sphere."

17. See Oscar Negt and Alexander Kluge, *The Public Sphere and Experience.*

18. This formulation should be read as equally distant from Habermas and from the approach to experience common to many "new social movements," in which experience is made the pure ground of knowledge, the basis of an essentialized standpoint of critical awareness. See the sympathetic critique in Alan Scott, *Ideology and the New Social Movements.*

We can distinguish public spheres in which identity-formation figures more prominently, and those in which rational-critical discourse is more prominent, but we should not assume the existence of any political public sphere where identity-formation (and re-formation) is not significant.[19] Identity-formation and topical debate are hard to keep entirely separate.

Excluding the identity-forming project from the public sphere makes no more sense than excluding those of "problematically different" identities. Few today would argue (at least in the broadly liberal public spheres of the West) against including women, racial and ethnic minorities, and virtually all other groups clearly subject to the same state and part of the same civil society. Yet many do argue against citizenship for those who refuse various projects of assimilation. It is not just Germans with their ethnic ideas about national citizenship who have a problem with immigrants. The language of the liberal public sphere is used to demand that only English be spoken in Florida, for example, or that Arabs and Africans conform to certain ideas of Frenchness if they wish to stay in France. And for that matter, many other arguments— for example, that only heterosexuals should serve in the military—have much the same form and status. They demand conformity as a condition of full citizenship. Yet movement of people about the globe continues, making it harder to suppress difference even while provoking the urge. In a basic and intrinsic sense, if the public sphere has the capacity to alter civil society and to shape the state, then its own democratic practice must confront the questions of membership and the identity of the political community it represents.

Once we acknowledge that the definition of a political community is not immutably given by nationality or any other putatively natural or historically ancient factor, then we may approach it as a matter of civil society—that is, of the actual construction of social relationships (the alternative is to see it as a matter of pure will). It is not enough that we criticize "bad nationalism." Participation in a democratic public sphere obligates us to develop a good account of the identity of our political communities that faces up to necessary problems of inclusion and exclusion. This is not just a matter of letting "them" mingle with "us." A public sphere, where it exists and works successfully as a democratic institution, represents the potential for the people organized in civil society to alter their own conditions of existence by means of rational-critical discourse.[20] As a result, participation always holds the possibility not

19. Habermas's sharp exclusion of identity-formation from the public sphere is one reason why he is left with no analytic tools save an account of "degeneration" and "refeudalization" when he turns his attention to the mass-mediated public sphere of the postwar era.

20. In an era when political economy is in relative eclipse and discourse analysis and cultural studies are ascendant, it is worth reminding ourselves that the public sphere repre-

just of settling arguments, or planning action, but of altering identities. The "identity politics" common to "new social movements" is thus a normal and perhaps even intrinsic part of a successful, democratic public sphere. Even the very identity of the political community is at least partially a product, not simply a precondition, of the activity of the public sphere of civil society.

SOVEREIGNTY AND POLITICAL COMMUNITY

THROUGHOUT MUCH OF European history, discussions of legitimate rule focused on arguments about divine or natural right, on questions of succession, and on debates about the limits which should be imposed on monarchs. When this was the case, the question of national identity either did not arise or was marginal. Reference might be made to a monarch's rule over a "people" or various "peoples," but only rarely before the modern era was any attempt made to treat sovereignty as "rising" from the people.[21] Calling such peoples "nations" initially carried no particular political significance. But when questions of sovereignty began to turn on appeals to the rights, acceptance, or will of "the people," this changed. Though the term "nation" (rather than "people") was not necessarily invoked, the modern notion of a popular will always assumed the existence of some recognizably bounded and internally integrated population. This led political theory to depend on social theory: it was necessary to conceive of the society which a monarch ruled, not just the territory or feudatories. Arguments turning on some notion of people or popular will were not introduced simply in response to the preexisting "nationhood" of various peoples—that is, as a result of their high extent of common ethnicity—but rather were linked to increasing state administrative capacity in the "absolutist" era, decline in the acceptance of spatially dispersed (as opposed to compact and contiguous) territories, and the growth of market relations.[22] They were also the products of political struggle and political thought.

sents only potential, because its agreements must be brought to fruition, or at least brought into struggle, in a world of practical affairs where power still matters.

21. It was perhaps in medieval Germany that the disputes between "ascending" and "descending" theories of sovereignty were strongest (Gierke, *Natural Law;* Ullmann, *Principles of Government and Politics*). Descending theories were epitomized by divine right legitimations of sovereignty. Ascending theories, on the other hand, foreshadowed the birth of the more modern idea of nation or people with their notion that sovereignty was a grant of the people to the ruler. Claiming that this notion was crucial to ancient Germany, and invoking Althusius, Gierke used it as a rationale for arguments against absolutist rule and the domination of state over society. In general, the emerging ideas of nation and public drew heavily on both Roman Republican ideas and the discourse of natural law.

22. Perry Anderson, *Lineages of the Absolutist State;* Anthony Giddens, *The Nation State and Violence;* volume 2 of Michael Mann's *The Sources of Social Power;* Karl Polanyi, *The Great Transformation.*

The new sorts of claims on behalf of peoples figured prominently in and around the English Civil War, a conflict distinctively productive of theory. Even Hobbes offered a sharply novel version of the argument that absolute monarchy was justified by the fact that it served the interests of the people rather than solely by inheritance or divine authorization.[23] *Leviathan* was a book about the commonwealth, by which Hobbes meant the *res publica* of Roman law. There was no public to enjoy public goods, Hobbes argued, without the pacifying rule of a monarch. This transformed the several and separate individuals who were originally doomed to incessant war among competing private interests into a socially organized body, a people. So while monarchy served the interests of the people, they had no status as a society without the monarch and hence no group claims against the monarch. Similarly, in the language of this essay, Hobbes had little interest in the discourse among the people that might qualify them as a public.

But this does not mean that Hobbes had no conception of the unity of the people, their existence as *a* people. Hobbes is commonly misrepresented as a completely asociological thinker appealing only to the interests of discrete individuals. But he did have a notion of the body politic that both anticipated functionalism and reflected the organization of the cosmos as a system of re-semblances in the manner that Foucault has described as typical of the period.[24] This is embodied not just in the text of *Leviathan* but in its remarkable frontispiece in which the Great Body of the State is depicted, down to the chain mail armor of hundreds of tiny people. Hobbes thus recognized social differentiation; he simply saw it as deriving its overall meaning and potential for peaceful continuity from the state. Similarly, Hobbes clearly recognized the existence of families, and of local relationships like the hierarchies linking small farmers to gentry, squires to knights. Social life at this level did not depend on the monarch in the same way as the social organization of large-scale collectivities: counties, regions, nations. Influenced like many others of the early modern era by the traditions of Roman law, he distinguished those sorts of relationships that might be established by private contract or connection from those entirely conditional on the institution of a public realm. The monarch or state might provide enforcement for the directly interpersonal relationships of the private realm, but it crucially brought into being the indirect relationships of the public realm; these existed only through its mediation. They were public, thus, not because of discourse among the different members of the political community, but because the state itself made them so.

23. Thomas Hobbes, *Leviathan* [1651].
24. Michel Foucault, *The Order of Things: An Archaeology of the Human Sciences.*

Hobbes's argument transformed from within a tradition of seeing political community defined entirely by subjection to a common ruler. Instead of locating that subjection in a hierarchy of intermediate authorities (as, for example, the inhabitants of a given region might fall into a different political community with the conquest or shifting allegiance of a superordinate nobleman), Hobbes treated each individual as directly a member of the state.[25] The political community thus became the whole people, though this people was deprived of the political capacities offered to the publics of most republican theory.

Hobbes's arguments were challenged almost immediately by others who, despite their predominant liberalism, appear in retrospect to anticipate nineteenth-century ethnic nationalism. They attempted to show the priority of political community to particular power structures. The theoretical device of social contract thinking, for example, was expanded with the idea of a "dual contract" in which a first contract bound prepolitical agents into a political community and a second bound that community (more contingently) to a ruler or a set of laws. The main initial development was to locate more and more of the political initiative and basis for evaluation in the socially organized people. In the long run, such arguments were often integrated with claims to ancient, even primordial peoplehood as parts of nationalist political programs of various stripes. But "the people" at this juncture meant mainly the politically active elites. After the Glorious Revolution, for example, Locke published a political theory (written earlier) that appealed not only to the interests of the people as a collection of discrete individuals with different roles to play in the body politic (Hobbes's image), but to the citizenry as a body laterally connected through communication, a public.[26] This prefigured aspects of democratic theory, but was also well suited to the context in which Locke published it: a monarchical restoration (which the English perversely call their Revolution) which in fact accorded a leading role to a revitalized, open, and internally communicative aristocracy. It was arguably among this aristocracy that English nationalism had its origins, encouraging a conception of a political community strongly distinct from and able to challenge the monarch.[27]

25. Paradoxically, Hobbes's account also anticipated the tradition of civic nationalism associated most commonly with the French Revolution. Though Hobbes's theory supported monarchy rather than revolution, it suggested that any individual conforming to the institutions of political rule could be a member of the body politic. It was assimilationist rather than ethnicist.

26. John Locke, *Two Treatises of Government* [1689].

27. Hans Kohn's *The Age of Nationalism* remains perhaps the best treatment of this dimension of the origins of English nationalism. See also Liah Greenfeld's *Nationalism: Five Roads to Modernity,* though note that she gives remarkably little attention to the extent to which the aristocratic proponents of nation against king were opponents of the more demo-

With the rise of claims to popular sovereignty and republican rule, the notions of "nation" and "people" were increasingly intertwined. In the first place, claims to nationhood offered a cultural basis for the demarcation of potentially sovereign political communities. The importance of this underpinning was pervasive in democratic theory, though not always explicit. Locke, for example, took the existence of discrete "peoples" more or less as a given. His treatments of conquest focused on the legitimacy of the subjection of conquered peoples, not the possibility of their absorption into an enlarged nation. In general, democratic theory was written as though its province was simply to formulate procedures and arrangements for the governance of such communities, not to address their constitution as particular peoples. Discussions of constitution in democratic theory still tend either to imagine a world without established communities or to imagine that the boundaries of a political community are not problematic.

In the real world, however, peoples were and are always constituted as such in relation to other peoples and out of the refractory stuff of preexisting communities and claims to loyalty and peoplehood. Democratic theory can ignore this only because it tacitly assumes what certain nationalist ideologues (like Fichte) explicitly asserted: that everyone is a member of a nation and that such nations are *the* relevant political communities. In practice, however, there is often no obvious or uncontested answer as to what the relevant political community is. Nationalism, then, is not the solution to the puzzle but the discourse within which struggles to settle the question are most commonly waged (too often with bullets and bombs as well as words). As such a discourse, it marks nearly every political public sphere in the contemporary world as an inescapable, if often unconscious, rhetoric of identity-formation, delimitation, and self-constitution. Nations are discursively constituted subjects, even if the rhetoric of their constitution is one that claims primordiality or creation in the distant, seemingly prediscursive, past.

It is only as nationalist discourse becomes institutionalized in a public sphere that "nation" or "people" are constituted as such. Thus nationalist rhetoric shapes the internal discourse of nearly every state, not just those marked by empire, alien rule, or ethnic conflict; it operates to constitute the nation (the public, the people) as a putative actor—the claimant to ultimate sovereignty—in relation to the state. "Nationalism," Gellner has thus averred, "is primarily a political principle, which holds that the political and the national unit should be congruent." [28] But as Durkheim noted long before, it

cratic assertions of the rights of Englishmen by Levelers, Diggers, and others. The notion of "nation" was not only elitist but repressive at its origins.

28. Ernest Gellner, *Nations and Nationalism*, p. 1.

is usually the apparent disjunction of people and state which brings the category of nation and the phenomenon of nationalism into play.[29] Grounding political legitimacy in notions of "the people" allows nationalists to assert a disjuncture between even a domestic government and its society if that government fails to serve the putative needs or interests of the nation. This rhetorical severing of state (or government) from society, in fact, joins the transitions of 1989 to the great modern revolutions more than any similarities in the social processes of transformation themselves.[30] But this rhetoric is paradoxically linked both to the sphere of public discourse within which intellectuals help to produce the national identity and engage in arguments about the public good, and to the nationalism that not only defines the society that is distinct from the state but often represses rational-critical public argument in favor of conformity to the national mission, destiny, or identity.

The issue arose sharply in the French Revolution of 1789. The development of an active public sphere, a strong exemplar of both rational-critical discourse and creative thought about matters of the public good, was a crucial precursor to revolution; and it flowered enormously in the early phases of the revolution itself, as public debate spread from salons and the National Assembly to innumerable neighborhood clubs and public gatherings.[31] Flourishing in print as well as oral debate, this public sphere presented "the people" as a capable political force to be counterposed to the king and to *ancien régime* elites more generally. But the very invocation of the people also threatened the institutions of the public sphere. It fueled both the illusory ideal of direct democracy and the rise of Jacobinism. The ideas of nation and sovereign people fused, encouraging the notion that the people ought to speak with a singular voice. Similarly, the people as assembled in public gatherings displaced both broader ideas of representation and occasions for reflective discussion.

Article 3 of the 1789 *Declaration of the Rights of Man and Citizen* declared: "The principle of all sovereignty resides essentially in the Nation. No body, no individual can exercise any authority that does not expressly stem from

29. Emile Durkheim, *Textes,* vol. 3, edited by V. Karady (Paris: Editions de Minuit, 1950), pp. 179–80.

30. Cohen and Arato, *Civil Society and Political Theory.*

31. Interesting uses of Habermas's public sphere concept to inform analyses of the French Revolution can be found in Keith Michael Baker, *Inventing the French Revolution,* and "Defining the Public Sphere in Eighteenth-Century France: Reflections on a Theme by Habermas," in Calhoun, ed., *Habermas and the Public Sphere;* and Joan Landes, *Women and the Public Sphere in the Age of the French Revolution.*

the nation." [32] Though the crucial term changed, the discourse of nationalism continued to dominate the construction of the comparable article in the Constitution of 1793: "Sovereignty resides in the people. It is one and indivisible, imprescriptible and inalienable." [33] Such ideas linked the revolution directly to the tradition of Rousseau and the idea of general will.[34] Rousseau (like Ferguson in another tradition) also developed ideas of the social cohesion of the members of a nation far beyond Locke. His *Considerations on the Government of Poland* emphasized patriotic education capable not only of binding citizens to each other and imbuing each with love of *la patrie*, but also of making each a distinctively national person, giving each mind a "national form." [35] Montesquieu's appeal to the "spirit" of laws had presaged a modern discourse of national cultures and characters.[36] In the French Revolution, especially as it was interpreted on the European continent and celebrated in successive French political struggles, the nation had actively constituted itself as a sovereign being. One catch was that appeals to this sovereign being could often be deployed as "trump cards" against other loyalties and against critiques rooted in various internal differences among the members of the nation. Only the properly national interests could be legitimate or authoritative in the public realm; more specific identities—for example, those of women, or workers, or members of minority religions—could at best be accepted as matters of private preference with no public standing. Too often the pressure for national unity became a pressure for conformity even in private life.[37]

The rhetoric of nationalism is sometimes described as inherently "collectivistic" rather than "individualistic," but this is a misleading opposition. The idea of the nation depends very much on individualism. It establishes the nation both as a category of similar individuals and as a sort of "superindividual." As a rhetoric of categorical identity, nationalism is precisely not focused on the various particularistic relationships among members of the nation. But here a crucial differentiation among nationalisms arises. To what extent do nationalist rhetorics depend on the recognition of differences among members

32. See Jacques Godechot's *La pensée révolutionnaire en France et en Europe, 1780–1799*, p. 116.

33. Godechot, *Pensée révolutionnaire*, p. 214.

34. Jean-Jacques Rousseau, "The Social Contract" [1762].

35. Jean-Jacques Rousseau, *Considérations sur le gouvernement de Pologne* [1782].

36. Montesquieu, *The Spirit of Laws* [1748].

37. See, for example, the insightful discussions of the ways in which nationalist ideologues have tried to impose certain standards of proper sexual behavior in the edited volume by Andrew Parker and others, *Nationalisms and Sexualities;* and George L. Mosse, *Nationalism and Sexuality: Middle-Class Morality and Sexual Norms in Modern Europe.*

of the nation (both as individuals and as members of smaller collectivities) and thereby gain constitution through the discourse of this differentiated public? Or, conversely, to what extent do nationalist rhetorics posit the nation as a unitary people in which the identity of each is merged into that of the whole?

THE UNITY OF NATIONS

NATIONALIST RHETORIC has generally stressed the essential similarity of the nation's individual members.[38] It is rare to find comparable emphasis on the constitution of the nation through the discourse of a public of highly differentiated members.[39] This is a crucial implication of the rhetorical appeal to presumed ancient ethnicity or peoplehood that was invoked in struggles over political sovereignty.

But of course this is not "mere rhetoric"; it reflects significant social changes in the modern era. The rise of the state and the capitalist transformation of trade and production relations had brought increasing integration to large collectivities of people. The raising of citizen armies had not only reinforced national identity against the nation's enemies, but brought together soldiers from different regions and occupations. Roads and later railroads provided an infrastructure that both joined the various parts of the nation and linked regions more strongly within state borders than across them. Proliferation of print (and later broadcast) media, schools, and administrative offices all encouraged linguistic standardization and both directly and through common language helped to produce national patterns of culture and behavior. This notion is rooted in positive historical developments; it is not ideologically arbitrary. Tocqueville, for example, wrote of how the eighteenth-century expansion of state administration had paved the way for the French Revolution by rendering France "the country in which men were most like each other."

> Behind such diversities as still existed the unity of the nation was making itself felt, sponsored by that new conception: "the same laws for all." . . . Not only did the provinces come to resemble each other more and more, but within each province members of the various

38. See Craig Calhoun, "Nationalism and Ethnicity," pp. 211–39, for further discussion of this issue of individualism and the categorical identity of nations. Of course, nationalist rhetoric has often employed organic metaphors like "body," but even when doing so it tends to emphasize both the direct bond between individual and nation and similarities among individuals.

39. Liberal variants were distinct from more extreme, repressive ones largely by the greater scope they granted to a private realm in which individuals might pursue different sorts of lives, and the lesser justification they saw for the nation to transgress this boundary between public and private.

classes (anyhow those above the lowest stratum) became ever more alike, differences of rank notwithstanding.[40]

As Watkins has shown, this extended even to childbearing. Fertility rates, which once varied from locality to locality, became strikingly uniform within nineteenth- and twentieth-century European nation-states.[41]

All these changes helped to create a new discourse of "public affairs," the affairs that represented the interests of the integrated nation. It was in this discourse, not in any material reality of exchange networks, that national economies, for example, were constituted. The description of the economy as a self-regulating system of exchanges, that is, did not in itself constitute the unity of domestic versus foreign trade. Such inner/outer distinctions were produced in a public discourse organized at the level of states, and then reproduced in state administrative policies and accounting procedures. In maintaining boundaries in this way, states were innovating, not simply protecting the interests of long-established national communities. So long as discourse (and identity) remained overwhelmingly local, most people invested relatively little concern in large-scale boundaries. Concepts like "the wealth of nations" or "trade surplus or deficit" could only be developed in a supralocal public sphere. It was precisely on the basis of the perspective afforded by the constitution of the British and French publics, and in works addressed to those publics, that Adam Smith and the physiocrats could constitute their competing accounts of how "national economies" work and relate. In these discourses, the national and the international were always intertwined. The eighteenth and nineteenth centuries indeed saw an increasing organization of exchange relations and capital accumulation at the national level. But as mercantilist arguments suggest, this came at the expense of some international organizations and processes as well as at the expense of local autonomy. The innovation was driven largely by the emergence of spheres of public discourse which addressed the relationship between aggregated private interests and state institutions.

In France, a growing national integration was spearheaded by a central state of long standing. In Germany, the central state was added fairly late, on top, as it were, of a variety of regions more or less widely understood as "German" in their language and culture. But despite their differences, both French and German stories thematize nationalism as an aspect of amalgamation of disparate regions into a superordinate state. In the territories of the declining

40. Alexis de Tocqueville, *The Old Regime and the French Revolution* [1856] (New York: Doubleday, 1955), pp. 103–4.
41. See Susan Cott Watkins, *From Provinces into Nations.*

Austro-Hungarian Empire, by contrast, nationalist discourse was generally invoked by separatists against the more central power. This is in part because the Hapsburgs self-consciously maintained an empire of the old style; they did not attempt to integrate their dominions into a modern nation-state. That is, they did not attempt to treat their subjects as more or less interchangeable members of the polity, to impose linguistic uniformity, to build an infrastructure rendering communication and commerce easy throughout the realm, to replace narratives of conquest with those of primordial ethnic commonality, or to base claims to legitimacy on the interests or will of "the people."

Imperial rule—in the Austro-Hungarian case or most other historical examples—is precisely *not* the attempt to forge a unity between nation and state. Empires are organized through the coexistence—albeit often hierarchically structured—of a number of distinct "peoples" or "communities." These need not enter into any public discourse with each other, nor indeed into many collective activities. Their economic relations are typically matters of market exchange, not cooperation in production, and while imperial armies may mobilize members of different ethnic groups, they are generally organized more on the model of mercenaries than citizen-soldiers.

Parts of empires can be transformed into nations by the creation of quasi-autonomous public spheres. This is as characteristic of metropoles as peripheral regions. As the Ottoman Empire declined, for example, it was just as novel a project to engender a national consciousness and project of state formation in Turkey as in Egypt, and early projects for pan-Islamic nationalism grew in the same soil. Among the most problematic settings are the frontiers between former or declining empires. The disastrous contemporary situation in the Balkans, for example, is not simply the result of ancient ethnic hatreds, nor entirely produced by the forced integration of Yugoslavia under Communism, nor conjured out of nothing by the ideological and military manipulators who have turned the discourse of nationalism into the project of ethnic cleansing. It is rooted in the long history of the region as a frontier in which neither of the relatively stable imperial regimes—Ottoman or Hapsburg—achieved clear hegemony. Local ethnic groups were not only divided by religion and military enlistment, they were in some cases resettled precisely to serve as buffers and prevent both sociopolitical and military consolidation. As empires receded from this frontier, they left behind not spatially compact and socially integrated nations but fragmented and interspersed ethnic communities. Pockets of Serbs, for example, were located in the middle of Croatian farm districts because their reputation as fighters made the Hapsburgs think they would stiffen defense against the Turks. Even tiny cities like Mostar were miniature metropolises, housing a range of religions and ethnicities.

Once they were no longer ruled from distant imperial centers, however, the members of these different ethnic groups were called upon to form their own public discourses to organize collective affairs. In such cases, elites who were previously subordinates in larger imperial hierarchies helped to promote national culture (including language and literature as well as nationalist ideology) partly as a project that would put them on top of the new or newly independent nation. Either the new public spheres would incorporate diverse cultures into regionally compact polities—as attempted most recently by Bosnia-Herzegovina—or the public spheres would be defined on ethnic lines and offer implicit bases for projects of ethnic nationalist reorganization of territory and population—as in the Serbian counterpart. But note that in either case the institutionalization of a public sphere was at the heart of the project of defining the nation, whether in terms of the civic institutions of a territorial polity or in terms of ethnic unity.

In many other cases, imperial rule involved the appropriation or development of subordinate state institutions that encouraged nationalism by making the contrast between alien, imperial rulers, and indigenes powerful. Such contexts frequently nurtured ideologies that represented the colonized as unitary peoples joined by common membership in a single national category (not least because colonizers so frequently justified their rule by claiming that the locals were internally disunified and needed outside help to keep the peace). This representation of "natives" as a single category combined with the stunting of careers in the imperial bureaucracies to make ideas of legitimation by consent or participation of the governed attractive to colonized elites, thus further reinforcing links between the project of instituting a single public sphere and gaining national autonomy.[42] Rendered subalterns in such a situation, nonimperial elites might find attractions in the political strategy of forging closer links with peasants and others whom they could claim to represent as a nation against the imperial power. Not only were Western-educated elites frustrated by limited possibilities for upward mobility. Displaced by new regimes, even traditional overlords who might otherwise have supported other, more elitist, doctrines of legitimacy often adopted and/or reinvented the notion that legitimacy should depend on the will of those governed. This happened in both

42. See Partha Chatterjee, *The Nation and Its Fragments: Studies in Colonial and Post-Colonial Histories;* and Benedict Anderson, *Imagined Communities: Reflections on the Origin and Spread of Nationalism.*

India and China, for example, and in varying degrees in much of Latin America and Africa.

The "modernizing" elites who were active in the development of both early public spheres and anticolonial nationalist movements pursued similar projects in a variety of settings—increased literacy and freedom of publication, for example. In a wide range of late-nineteenth and early-twentieth-century contexts, for instance, they pursued nationalism and internationalism simultaneously in a way reminiscent of Europe's "Springtime of Nations" and as part of a project of replicating Europe's Enlightenment. This was true of such otherwise diverse movements as Spain's "generation of 1898"; Turkey's "Young Turks" and secular nationalists under Atatürk; and China's student and intellectual protesters of May 4, 1919, and the "New Thought" movement. These examples suggest (*a*) how nationalism thrived as a modern discourse, not simply an ethnic inheritance; (*b*) how nationalism and the creation of cultural publics and political public spheres went hand in hand; and (*c*) how much global discourses and material factors affect these processes, helping to produce such similar movements nearly simultaneously in widely dispersed and culturally diverse settings. In anticolonial movements it is also especially easy to see the deep mutual interdependence of culture-forming, identity-forming, and political discourse.

Part of the story of the end of empire was the division of the world into formally equivalent national states, each of which was or should be sovereign. This discursive principle became normative well before the Hapsburgs and Romanovs were finally forced to abandon their very different sorts of states, and paved the way for the still problematic efforts to align states and nations within their former domains. But gradually, at least, older political organizations like empires, quasi-autonomous principalities, and free cities did give way to a more standardized system. This pattern was effected by international public discourse, not just by military power or diplomatic negotiation. By the second half of the twentieth century, it was clearly anomalous for any state to remain under the explicit political tutelage of another, and where such relations existed they were commonly subjected to campaigns to undo them.

But of course the equivalence of the national states recognized in this international public sphere is a formal property of the discourse not matched by material equivalence of power, internal organization, or loyalty of citizens. The discourse of nationalism demands that San Marino, two dozen square miles with 24,000 citizens, be seen as formally equivalent to China or the United States. It is, for example, a full member of the United Nations. The equivalence of states is emphasized especially in arenas like the United Nations, not only because the discourse of nationalism predominates, but because attention is paid to the whole system of states at once. Even in interstate relations where disparities of power and scale matter substantially, however, the rhetoric of equivalence is commonly observed.

This establishes, among other things, a new version of the old public/private division.[43] The international affairs of the presumptively equivalent states are public and addressable in the international public sphere while their internal, domestic affairs are treated as private. Attempts to challenge the formal equivalence of states by suggesting that international recognition should be linked to democratic institutions or by condemning domestic human rights abuses are as problematic within this division of public and private as attempts to intervene in families on behalf of the rights of children or spouses have been. Appearing as actions of the powerful against the weak, they have often backfired and rallied popular nationalist sentiments to the cause of elitist governments.[44] That the discourse of nationalism is available in an international public sphere for adoption in disparate settings is made clear by the history of anticolonial nationalisms.

In colonial (and postcolonial) settings, as in the West, the crucial question remains to what extent the constitution of a citizenry and the idea of nation reflect the notion of a differentiated public or that of a unitary people. What occasioned the issue was engagement with each other in common projects—those of self-rule or of resistance to colonialism. Colonial rule, like that of empires generally, allowed groups of people quite different and detached from each other to coexist and interact partly because it called on them to undertake no common projects not initiated by the state.[45] The creation of a political community called for new kinds of interrelationships, and something more than a "live and let live" cosmopolitanism. Faced with the challenge of building either anticolonial movements or postcolonial governments, diverse populations could follow, sometimes in combination, various paths: to separate

43. For many nationalists, moreover, it would appear that in a serious sense the sorts of politics that are domestically illegitimate because they prize interpersonal differences over national unity are legitimate in the international public sphere, since the differences among nations are as essential as the similarities of persons within nations.

44. For further discussion of the implications of the international discourse of nationalism—in effect an international public sphere constituting nations as members—see Craig Calhoun, "Nationalism and Civil Society," pp. 387–411.

45. This is a crucial contrast between the empire and the nation-state, or, as Jeff Weintraub has noted, between the cosmopolitan city and the polis. In the cosmopolis or empire, since "heterogeneous multitudes were not called upon to be citizens, they could remain in apolitical coexistence, and each could do as he wished without the occasion to deliberate with his neighbors" ("The Theory and Politics of the Public/Private Distinction," on p. 26 in this volume).

along the lines of their differences, to repress their differences, or to constitute their unity through discourse across the lines of their differences. One of the crucial questions of the modern era is how often and under what circumstances the third option—meaningful, politically efficacious public discourse without fragmentation or repression of difference—can be achieved.

CONCLUSION

THE HISTORY OF NATIONALISM, in short, is not a story of the inheritance and expression of primordial ethnic identities. Nor is it a narrative in which purely arbitrary boundaries are imposed by sheer force of will on indifferent populations. It is, rather, an aspect of the creation of socially integrated political communities in which a large-scale, identity-forming collective discourse was possible.

This was partly a matter of ideological transformation, as the meaning of categories like "the people" changed with transformed understandings of the sources of political legitimacy. It was partly a transformation of material infrastructure, as new transport and communications technologies enabled people in disparate parts of polities to come into closer touch with their compatriots. It was obviously a matter of economic integration, and perhaps above all it was a matter of growing state administrative capacity. But it is crucial not to see the rise of large-scale collective identities like "nation" as simply a reflection of the growth of specific states or of state power generally.

The discourse of nations and nationalism was from its beginning linked to the creation of political publics. Such political publics took on their important modern character when they ceased to be contained within the realm of state administration, yet retained the capacity to influence the state. These publics were multifarious, not singular and integral at the level of states; to modify Habermas's term, thus, we should understand the public sphere to be a sphere of publics. The identities of members were and are formed and revised partly through their participation in the public sphere, not settled in advance. It is this, above all, that has complicated the relationship of nationalism to democracy. For nationalist ideas fixed the most basic of collective political identities in advance of public life, and could and often have become sharply repressive of claims to various competing identities. Yet in so doing, nationalism was at least partly complicitous with democracy, not in simple opposition to it. For nationalism allowed the domestic public life of democracies to proceed with a tacit assumption of the boundaries of the political community, and democratic theory and discourse had—and has—little coherent answer to why such boundaries should exist.

REFERENCES

Anderson, Benedict. 1991. *Imagined Communities: Reflections on the Origin and Spread of Nationalism.* Rev. ed. London: Verso. Originally published in 1983.

Anderson, Perry. 1974. *Lineages of the Absolutist State.* London: New Left Books.

Arendt, Hannah. 1958. *The Human Condition.* Chicago: University of Chicago Press.

Baker, Keith Michael. 1990. *Inventing the French Revolution.* Cambridge: Cambridge University Press.

————. 1992. "Defining the Public Sphere in Eighteenth-Century France: Reflections on a Theme by Habermas." In *Habermas and the Public Sphere,* edited by Craig Calhoun. Cambridge, MA: MIT Press.

Benhabib, Seyla. 1992. "Models of Public Space: Hannah Arendt, the Liberal Tradition, and Jürgen Habermas." In *Habermas and the Public Sphere,* edited by Craig Calhoun. Cambridge, MA: MIT Press.

Calhoun, Craig. 1993. "Nationalism and Civil Society." *International Sociology* 8, no. 4: 387–411.

————. 1993. "Nationalism and Ethnicity." *Annual Review of Sociology* 19: 211–39.

Calhoun, Craig, ed. 1992. *Habermas and the Public Sphere.* Cambridge, MA: MIT Press.

————. 1994. *Social Theory and the Politics of Identity.* Oxford: Blackwell.

Chatterjee, Partha. 1993. *The Nation and Its Fragments: Studies in Colonial and Post-Colonial Histories.* Princeton, NJ: Princeton University Press.

Cohen, Jean, and Andrew Arato. 1992. *Civil Society and Political Theory.* Cambridge, MA: MIT Press.

Deutsch, Karl Wolfgang. 1953. *Nationalism and Social Communication: An Inquiry into the Foundations of Nationality.* Cambridge, MA: MIT Press; New York: Wiley.

Durkheim, Emile. 1950. *Textes.* Vol. 3. Edited by V. Karady. Paris: Editions de Minuit.

Eley, Geoff. 1992. "Nations, Publics and Political Cultures: Placing Habermas in the Nineteenth Century." In *Habermas and the Public Sphere,* edited by Craig Calhoun. Cambridge, MA: MIT Press.

Fichte, Johann Gottlieb. [1807] 1968. *Addresses to the German Nation.* New York: Harper & Row.

Foucault, Michel. 1966. *The Order of Things: An Archaeology of the Human Sciences.* New York: Random House.

Fraser, Nancy. 1990. *Unruly Practices.* Minneapolis: University of Minnesota Press.

————. 1992. "Rethinking the Public Sphere: A Contribution to the Critique of Actually Existing Democracy." In *Habermas and the Public Sphere,* edited by Craig Calhoun. Cambridge, MA: MIT Press.

Gellner, Ernest. 1983. *Nations and Nationalism.* Ithaca, NY: Cornell University Press.

Giddens, Anthony. 1984. *The Nation State and Violence.* Berkeley: University of California Press.

Gierke, Otto von. 1934. *Natural Law and the Theory of Society.* Cambridge: Cambridge University Press.

Godechot, J., ed. 1964. *La pensée révolutionnaire en France et en Europe, 1780–1799.* Paris: Armand Colin, 1964.

Greenfeld, Liah. 1992. *Nationalism: Five Roads to Modernity.* Cambridge, MA: Harvard University Press.

Habermas, Jürgen. [1962] 1989. *The Structural Transformation of the Public Sphere.* Cambridge, MA: MIT Press.

———. 1984, 1987. *The Theory of Communicative Action.* 2 vols. Boston: Beacon Press.

Hobbes, Thomas. *Leviathan.* [1651] 1968. Harmondsworth: Penguin.

Kohn, Hans. [1944] 1968. *The Age of Nationalism.* New York: Harper & Row.

Landes, Joan. 1988. *Women and the Public Sphere in the Age of the French Revolution.* Ithaca, NY: Cornell University Press.

Locke, John. [1689] 1950. *Two Treatises of Government.* London: Dent.

Mann, Michael. 1986, 1993. *The Sources of Social Power.* 2 vols. Cambridge: Cambridge University Press.

Montesquieu. [1748] 1980. *The Spirit of Laws.* Berkeley: University of California Press.

Mosse, George L. 1985. *Nationalism and Sexuality: Middle-Class Morality and Sexual Norms in Modern Europe.* Madison: University of Wisconsin Press.

Negt, Oscar, and Alexander Kluge. 1993. *The Public Sphere and Experience.* Minneapolis: University of Minnesota Press.

Parker, Andrew, Mary Russo, Doris Sommer, and Patricia S. Yaeger, eds. 1992. *Nationalisms and Sexualities.* New York: Routledge.

Pocock, J. G. A. 1975. *The Machiavellian Moment.* Princeton, NJ: Princeton University Press.

Polanyi, Karl. 1944. *The Great Transformation.* Boston: Beacon Press.

Rousseau, Jean-Jacques. [1762] 1962. "The Social Contract." In *Social Contract: Essays by Locke, Hume and Rousseau,* edited by Ernest Barker. New York: Oxford University Press.

———. [1782] 1963. *Considérations sur le gouvernement de Pologne.* New York: French and European Publications.

Scott, Alan. 1990. *Ideology and the New Social Movements.* London: Unwin Hyman.

Tocqueville, Alexis de. [1856] 1955. *The Old Regime and the French Revolution.* Garden City, NY: Doubleday.

Ullmann, Walter. 1977. *Principles of Government and Politics in the Middle Ages.* Harmondsworth: Penguin.

Watkins, Susan Cott. 1991. *From Provinces into Nations.* Princeton, NJ: Princeton University Press.

Weber, Max. [1922] 1968. *Economy and Society.* Berkeley: University of California Press.

Humankind as a System: Private and Public Agency at the Origins of Modern Liberalism

Daniela Gobetti

THIS ESSAY TELLS the story of the contribution of a few seventeenth- and eighteenth-century Natural Law theorists to the elaboration of the liberal distinction between private and public. This inquiry is of more than historical interest because, despite the profound social changes and theoretical revolutions of the last three centuries, the conceptual apparatus which continues to underlie our use of the pair private/public has its roots in the modern contract theorists.

I believe this can be asserted with confidence if the pair is considered in its juridical dimension. We are indebted to early modern Natural Law theorists, British ones in particular, for formulating a conception of the "citizen" as the holder of legal powers, and for giving us the notion of harm[1] as the criterion of distinction between private and public *jurisdictions*—that is, between the "private" jurisdiction of the citizen/subject and the "public" jurisdiction of the body that makes decisions for a politically unified group.[2] Private jurisdiction extends to all the activities in which an adult engages without

I wish to thank Jeff Weintraub for giving me the occasion to publish this essay and for helping me focus and shorten a piece that was originally far too long. His intelligent reading and patient editing made my work better. Mistakes and shortcomings are all mine.

1. For a key statement, see John Locke, *A Letter Concerning Toleration* [London, 1689], p. 42: "The part of the Magistrate is only to take care that the Commonwealth receive no prejudice, and that there be no Injury done to any man, either in Life or Estate." Natural Law theorists all employed the notion of injury, which derives from Roman law, to convey the idea that the violation of what belongs to a person according to the law of nature constitutes harm. (See Karl Olivecrona, "Locke's Theory of Appropriation.") Locke is the one who explicitly uses the concept of "injury" in order to distinguish between private and public jurisdictions.

2. The jurisdictional approach underlies classical liberal accounts of society. See, for one, Isaiah Berlin, *Four Essays on Liberty* (pp. 164–65): "If I wish to preserve my liberty, it is not enough to say that it must not be violated unless someone or other . . . authorizes its violation. I must establish a society in which there must be some frontiers of freedom which nobody should be permitted to cross." See also Jeremy Waldron, *The Right to Private Property,* pp. 295–96.

harming or endangering others, taken individually or collectively. Harm can be inflicted by commission—killing, injuring, or damaging people and their possessions—or by omission—not helping, defending, or supporting our fellows when it is possible to do so without detriment to ourselves. When harm is done, intrusion on the part of public authority into the person's private jurisdiction is legitimate. Otherwise, there is a wide array of activities, roughly defined by what these thinkers call natural rights, which is left to the discretion of each individual.

However, underlying these juridical implications is a more profound and less obvious innovation. According to the model that had been dominant in Western political philosophy since classical times, paradigmatically set forth in book 1 of Aristotle's *Politics,* the distinction between private and public corresponds to a division between two institutional domains—the private domain of the household and the public domain of the body politic—which is objectively given and grounded in nature. But in Natural Law theory and more generally in liberal theory, underneath the distinction between private and public jurisdictions there lies a distinction between modalities of agency within the individual.[3] These jurisdictions are not given by nature or history; rather, they are the outcome of the actions, and derived from the capacities, of the basic units of all human associations, individuals.

Natural Law theorists present all the powers and capacities that we attribute to either the individual citizen/subject or the state in political society as powers and capacities of each adult in the prepolitical (but it is more correct to say pregovernmental) "state of nature." When an individual engages in activities that are beneficial to himself and harmless to others he acts in his private capacity. But when his activities are harmful to others, or when he punishes the aggressor, he enters his public "mode." In the former case he makes himself liable to being treated as a public enemy, and in the latter he exercises the power of life and death, which is the hallmark of public authority. What allows the person to choose the right course of action is the capacity to assess the moral and legal consequences which his actions will have for himself and others. In other words, the agent can take distance from his immediate desires and urges, and look at his conduct from outside, as it were, thus evaluating

3. So that commentators move from one theme to the other, sometimes inadvertently: see, for example, Stephen R. Munzer, *A Theory of Property,* pp. 88–89; and Iris M. Young, "Impartiality and the Civic Public," in the edited volume by Seyla Benhabib and Drucilla Cornell, *Feminism as Critique: Essays in the Politics of Gender in Late-Capitalist Societies,* p. 74.

its legitimacy.[4] It is this capacity, together with the power of enforcement, which will be delegated to, or shared with, public institutions when exit from the state of nature becomes imperative.

An understanding of the jurisdictional distinction between private and public domains in Natural Law theorists thus requires an analysis of their conceptions of agency, in both their abstract determinations and their concrete underpinnings. Who is endowed with the capacities for private and public agency, and on what grounds? In this respect, we have been aware of the class bias in modern Natural Law theory for quite some time.[5] In more recent years feminist theorists have argued that there is a gender bias as well, and that it is closely tied to the Natural Law theorists' treatment of private and public. They have reminded us of the fact that seventeenth-century writers relegated women to the family-household, subjected them to the quasi-discretionary power of their husbands, and excluded them from public life.[6] The rigid distinction between the "private" world of the family and the "public" world outside it is the conceptual tool which Natural Law theorists adopt so as to translate the exclusion of women from the latter into a normative precept for the good society. The free and autonomous agents who populate the state of nature and rely on contract making in order to regulate their relations are all males; only males engage in the political act that gives life to civil society, and thus can claim full membership in the body politic. The family-household is left behind, structured by a hierarchy between the sexes which is dictated by God and nature.

While these readings have been illuminating, I would argue that they are also incomplete, and thus misleading if taken by themselves. Natural Law thinkers are indeed concerned with the problem of reconstructing a more or less hierarchical social order out of egalitarian and voluntaristic premises. But

4. Since it denotes capacities of the agent, the pair private/public has increasingly been used to denote an intrapersonal distinction. For example, Thomas Nagel, in *Equality and Partiality* (p. 4), argues that any social arrangement governing the relationship between individual and collective depends on a "corresponding balance . . . between the personal and the impersonal standpoints" within the self.

5. Crawford B. Macpherson has provided an influential Marxist interpretation of this kind of bias in *The Political Theory of Possessive Individualism, Hobbes to Locke.*

6. See Carole Pateman, "The Patriarchal Welfare State," in *The Disorder of Women* (pp. 183–84): "Men have been seen both as heads of families—and as husbands and fathers they have had socially and legally sanctioned power over their wives and children—and as participants in public life. Indeed, the 'natural' masculine capacities that enable them, but not their wives, to be heads of families are the same capacities that enable them, but not their wives, to take their place in civil life."

the dynamic between egalitarian premises and inegalitarian conclusions in their thought is more complex and unstable than such interpretations suggest. In particular, domestic society is neither theoretically "forgotten" [7] nor simply treated as unproblematically hierarchical. Rather, Natural Law theorists were led to revise the dominant models of both the household and the political domain in profound ways, and in the process to plant the philosophical seeds for a more universalist egalitarianism than they themselves were willing to accept.

Partially in response to these concerns, I wish to suggest in this essay that contract theorists worked with two conflicting and unreconciled views of the social universe of "citizens," and with two models of the requisites for citizenship. One model sees the citizen as fundamentally an appropriator of resources (of various kinds, as we shall see, not only material ones); on this view, citizenship is exclusive to adult male property-owners. On the other view, which is emergent though not explicitly upheld, citizenship may be inclusive of all adults, at least in principle. Here the citizen is an autonomous agent, capable of reading the unwritten law of nature and of responsible and reasonable conduct. In this latter model, appropriation of resources is relegated to being only one of the possible expressions of the person, and is no longer the prerequisite for exercising the rights of citizenship.

Two views of the boundary between the private and the public domains correspond to these two models of citizenship. One reproduces the classical distinction between household and body politic, though in modified form. The other view sees each sane adult as having legitimate jurisdiction over a private domain. The contours of this private domain do not coincide with any particular institution—the family, the economy, the church, and so forth—but are in constant flux, because they depend on the partially unpredictable activities in which the person chooses to engage, and on the impact which these activities have on the lives and rights of others. However, the latitude granted to the person in defining the features of her private domain implies that a heavy responsibility will fall on her shoulders as a public agent. Constant evaluation of her own and her fellow citizens' choices, willingness to negotiate the shifting boundaries between private and public domains, and a high degree of tolerance for the idiosyncratic expressions of the preferences of others become the basic ingredients of public agency in a liberal society.

Natural Law theorists embarked on the journey from an exclusive conception of citizenship to an inclusive one by revising the classical model which

---

7. As Pateman puts it in "Feminist Critiques of the Public/Private Distinction," *Disorder of Women,* p. 122.

saw the citizen as the head of household, that is, the *dominus* who controls both material resources and human chattel. They could no longer accept the continuum—expressed authoritatively in Roman law—between power over humans and ownership of things. It is this conceptual move that induced them to reject naturalistic grounds of personal and political authority, and to hypothesize an egalitarian state of nature. A recollection of this discussion will thus be the starting point of my narrative.

PROPERTY AND POWER IN NATURAL LAW THEORY

AS IS THE CASE with many other concepts of modern political theory, the juridical definition of the pair private/public has come to us from the *Corpus Iuris,* the summa of Roman laws and jurisprudential opinions commissioned in the sixth century A.D. by Justinian. The key statement in the *Corpus Iuris* reads, "*Publicum ius est, quod ad statum rei Romanae spectat, privatum, quod ad singulorum utilitatem pertinet*" ("Public law is that which regards the condition of the Roman commonwealth, private that which pertains to the interests of single individuals").[8]

Jurists and political thinkers who, throughout the Middle Ages, appropriated Roman law as the basis for their political thinking reproduced this definition automatically, without feeling the need for any clarification. For jurists, the distinction regarded, as in the original text, the two fundamental branches of the law.[9] For political thinkers, the pair increasingly came to be used to distinguish the domain of personal control of the citizen/subject, the "private," and the domain properly controlled by the state, the "public."

If we ask: who are the "individuals" of whom "private" is predicated? what are their "interests"? what is the entity of which "public" is predicated, and what are its "interests"? mainstream thinkers would not hesitate to answer: heads of households are the "individuals" in question; and the household, including all the animate beings and inanimate items in it, constitutes their "interest." As for the "public," it is those same heads of households who are citizens; they leave behind their private concerns and personal relations, and meet their peers in the public domain. It is what these citizens have in common—concern for internal security, external defense, and material welfare—that constitutes the "public interest." The social universe of the politically active in classical republicanism, and of the full members of the body politic in philomonarchic writers, is restricted to the adult independent males who

8. *Corpus Iuris Civilis,* edited by P. Krueger and T. Mommsen (Dublino and Turici: Apud Weidmannos, 1966), *Institutiones* I.I.3 (translation mine).

9. Norberto Bobbio, "Pubblico/privato," in *Enciclopedia XI: Prodotti-Ricchezza* (Turin: Einaudi, 1980), pp. 401–15.

control the means of production and reproduction: land, cattle, servants (or slaves), wives, and children.

This picture began to change with the early-seventeenth-century Protestant theorists such as Grotius, who, in the footsteps of the Spanish Jesuits, Suárez in particular, revived and profoundly modified medieval Natural Law theory, transforming it from a theory centered on natural laws into one centered on natural rights.[10] Natural Law writers began to look at the relations that heads of household establish independently of the political ruler, beginning in the fictional condition that would become known as the state of nature. Appropriation, production of goods, and exchange, which were part of the public domain for both republican and philomonarchic thinkers, are activities in which *free men* engage before government is instituted. And as is well known, it is conflict ensuing from the activity of *homo faber* types that leads to the state of war and necessity for the institution of government.

If we return to the questions: who are the individuals of whom "private" is predicated? what are their "interests"? this newly discovered domain of production and exchange ("economic" in the modern sense) and the activities occurring in it suddenly occupy center stage. Economic relations among heads of household, formerly a central concern of public jurisdiction, are "privatized." On the other hand, *only* relations *among heads of household* generate those conflicts—mainly (except for Hobbes) over the appropriation of material resources—that will require the institution of the state. The boundary line between private and public no longer separates the household from the politically significant interaction of adult free males in the public domain. Rather, that line now separates the privatized sphere of production and exchange from the public domain of the state and its legal order, where mediation and regulation of conflict take place.

This reading of the achievement of seventeenth-century Natural Law theorists has by now a long and distinguished history. Very recent scholarship has reinforced it.[11] But while this reading is correct in many ways, it does not tell us the whole story. Especially in recent years, feminist scholars have contended

10. See Richard Tuck, *Natural Rights Theories.*

11. On the Marxist side, see Macpherson, *Possessive Individualism.* On the liberal side, see Karen Iversen Vaughan, *John Locke, Economist and Social Scientist,* p. 94; John G. A. Pocock, "Virtues, Rights, and Manners: A Model for Historians of Political Thought," in *Virtue, Commerce, and History,* pp. 37–50; James Tully, *A Discourse on Property: John Locke and His Adversaries;* Istvan Hont and Michael Ignatieff, "Needs and Justice in the *Wealth of Nations,*" in their edited volume, *Wealth and Virtue: The Shaping of Political Economy in the Scottish Enlightenment,* pp. 1–44.

that the newly discovered freedom of, and capacity for, autonomous actions which structure the state of nature and the world of contractual relations does not break through the walls of the domestic association, over which the adult male continues to rule undisturbed.[12] Freedom and independence in the state of nature, control over the exclusive acquisition and use of the means of survival and enrichment, conflict over the allocation of relatively scarce resources, and "exit" from the state of war through a contract which institutes civil society are the basic concepts with which the modern school of Natural Law works.[13] It is precisely this set of concepts, critics contend, that contract theorists did not apply to the domestic association.

Therefore, the "privatization" of economic relations cannot and should not be taken as entirely redefining the boundary between the private and the public domains. The traditional boundary remains valid, and is actually reinforced, between the family on one side and both the market economy and the state on the other. In Carole Pateman's words:

> In the new social world created through contract, everything that lies beyond the domestic (private) sphere is public, or "civil," society. Feminists are concerned with *this* division. In contrast, most discussions of civil society and such formulations as "public" regulations versus "private" enterprise presuppose that the politically relevant separation between public and private is drawn *within* "civil society" as constructed in the social contract stories.[14]

Whether left aside because domestic relations are not centered on negotiation and conflict over relatively scarce resources, or because the supposedly natural asymmetry between the sexes is not called into question, the family in Natural Law theories is therefore taken to be a "residual" category. Thinkers are said to ignore it: for liberally minded commentators, because market relations are extradomestic by definition; and for feminist critics, because male writers aim at reinforcing the power of men over women, at the historic moment when the

12. In addition to Pateman, see Susan Moller Okin, "Women and the Making of the Sentimental Family." Seyla Benhabib (*Situating the Self,* pp. 154–55) thus summarizes the sexual politics of modern political philosophy in general: "The sphere of justice from Hobbes through Locke and Kant is regarded as the domain where independent, male heads of household transact with one another, while the domestic-intimate sphere is put beyond the pale of justice and restricted to the reproductive and affective needs of the bourgeois paterfamilias."

13. For an excellent account of the conceptual framework shared by all Natural Law theorists, see Norberto Bobbio, "The Conceptual Model of Natural Law Theory," chapter 1 of his *Thomas Hobbes and the Natural Law Tradition.*

14. Pateman, "The Fraternal Social Contract," in *Disorder of Women,* p. 34.

group of "brothers" replaces the "patriarchal father" as the source of legitimate political authority, and as the "ideal-type" of male sexuality.[15]

As I have indicated, I wish to offer an alternative view of the relationship between private and public that emerges from seventeenth- and eighteenth-century writers. With the rejection of a directly "natural" or God-given basis for authority, two concepts and their relations become central to modern Natural Law theories and to these recent criticisms: property and consent. It is the issue of the justification of private appropriation of resources, on the one hand, and the question of the consensual creation of institutions, on the other, that structures the Natural Law theorists' analyses of the state of nature and its transformation into civil society. It is as *private proprietors* that heads of households negotiate the institution of political authority through the social contract. I will therefore begin with a closer analysis of how Natural Law theorists understand private property and its relevance to the consensual institution and legitimation of power relations.

For Natural Law theorists, the concept of property is central to understanding the condition of human beings in the state of nature. As Richard Tuck has well illustrated, the debate over property pervaded late medieval and Renaissance political thinking.[16] Seventeenth-century writers might be said to conclude, rather than to begin, the debate on whether individuals are entitled to the exclusive appropriation of resources before government comes into existence.

It is significant that this debate is mostly carried on in Latin, including its latest expressions.[17] In Latin, property is *dominium. Dominium* is the power that an owner exercises over his legitimately acquired resources. Etymologically, the word derives from *dominum,* which is a modifier of *domus:* the *domus* is the household. *Dominium* is the power over resources which a *dominus,* that is, a head of household, exercises over his *domus.* As is well known, the resources that the *dominus* controlled included slaves, which were considered items of property as if they were material objects. The Roman conception of *dominium* thus linked tightly the ideas of owning property and exercising

---

15. Ibid., p. 41: "The motive for the brothers' collective act [parricide] is not merely to claim their natural liberty and right of self-government, but to gain access to women." There are exceptions to this line of argument. Melissa Butler, "Early Liberal Roots of Feminism: John Locke and the Attack on Patriarchy" (pp. 67–88), argues that Whig thinkers rejected the biblical basis for the political subordination of women, even though they accepted arguments made on empirical grounds.

16. Tuck, *Natural Rights,* chapters 1 and 2.

17. Including Hobbes's *De Cive,* Pufendorf's works, and Locke's *Letter Concerning Toleration,* first published as *Epistola de Tolerantia.*

power. It did this in two distinct but related ways. To own property means to exercise power of a kind over things: for the Roman jurists, ownership is *ius utendi, fruendi, et abutendi,* the right to use, enjoy, and abuse whatever is in our full legitimate possession.[18] And to own property means to exercise power in the more obvious sense that the property-item "slave" can be used and abused only if he is in the legitimate power of his master. Thus we can say: I own something or someone, therefore I have the right to exercise power over it/him. But can we say: I have the right to exercise power over something or someone, therefore I own it/him?

The debate among seventeenth-century Natural Law theorists on the nature of our relation to resources in the state of nature may be seen as an attempt to answer this question, through an analysis of the three concepts that were linked in Roman law: property, use/abuse, and power. But the question of whether the de facto exercise of power is a legitimate foundation of ownership split into three. The first is: Do I have exclusive property of material resources, such as food, drink, cattle, and land, over which I exercise power in the sense that I *use* them in the state of nature in order to survive? The second: Do I have exclusive property in other kinds of resources, such as my personal skills and capacities, which can be said to be *in my power*? And the third: Do I have exclusive property of other persons *over whom I exercise power*?

PUFENDORF

THE CONTINUUM BETWEEN ownership, use, and power which characterized the Roman approach was problematic for Natural Law theorists. In particular, while use could be accepted as a legitimate ground for the exclusive appropriation of things, questions were raised about the legitimacy of inferring ownership out of the exercise of power over human beings. Pufendorf confronted the problem explicitly. In his *Law of Nature and Nations,* he writes:

> But altho' *Dominion [imperium],* which is properly the Right of governing Another's Person, when establish'd with the free Consent of the Subject, cannot, regularly, be transferr'd without his good liking . . . Yet so long as the Subjects enjoy any Remains of Liberty, we cannot in seriousness say, that the Men themselves are thus alienated or made over, but only the Right of governing them, as being join'd with some Use or Advantage. Every Sovereign may indeed, as Mr Hobbes remarks, say of his Subject *hic, meus est, this Man is my property;* yet 'tis in a quite different sense that we call a *Thing* our *own.* For, by the former Expression, I mean no more, than that I and none

18. Barry Nicholas, *Introduction to Roman Law,* p. 154.

else have the Right of governing such a Person; yet so as to be myself under some kind of obligation to him, and not impower'd to exercise that Right upon him, in an unlimited absolute manner. But, on the other hand, the Property I claim over a Thing, implies a Right of using, spoiling, and consuming it, to procure my Advantage, or to satisfy my Pleasure; so that what way soever I dispose of it, to say it was *my own* shall be a sufficient Excuse.[19]

Pufendorf thus rejects the legitimacy of classifying as "ownership" the relationship between the ruler and the ruled. This means that we need a different vocabulary to speak about power relations. It also means, as Pufendorf's text shows, that we can no longer assume without further reflection that the exercise of power has the same characteristics as the ones implied in the relation of ownership. If we do not own a person who is in our power, can we use her, enjoy her, and abuse her to our pleasure as we can do with things? And more importantly, can use, interpreted broadly as a synonym of the de facto exercise of power, still be the ground upon which power relations can be legitimated?

In response to these concerns, Pufendorf contends that power can be legitimately acquired only when an individual gives his/her consent to being ruled by another person. This is true of *all* power relations: of the political power relation between sovereign and subject, as well as of the personal power relations between husband and wife, and master and servant.

> We suppose before-hand, that all Human Persons, whether of one Sex or the other, are naturally equal in Right; and that no one can claim the Sovereignty over another, unless it be obtain'd by the free Act of one of the Parties. . . . Therefore whatever *Right* a Man holds over a Woman, in as much as she is by nature his *Equal*, he must acquire, either by her Consent, or by the Sword, in a just War.[20]

19. Samuel Pufendorf, *Of the Law of Nature and Nations* (London, 1717), book VI, chapter III, vii, p. 385. In the Latin edition—Samuelis Pufendorfii, *De Jure Naturae et Gentium* (Londini, 1672), p. 483—one finds not *dominium,* but *imperium,* which in Latin denotes political (and military) power. Pufendorf thus emphasized his departure from the identification of power and ownership, which were conflated in the Latin word *dominium.* The English translator apparently chose, on the contrary, to emphasize the similarity between the two, by translating *imperium* as *dominion,* rather than *power.*

20. Pufendorf, *Nature and Nations,* VI, I, ix, p. 133. Hobbes's influence on Pufendorf is evident here; compare *Leviathan* [1651], edited by C. B. Macpherson (Harmondsworth: Penguin, 1980), chapter XX, p. 253.

Consent is thus constitutive of the power that the superior exercises over the inferior.[21] For Pufendorf this was the only solution to the problem of legitimating power relations, because morally valid claims are not things which we find in nature—*enthia physica*—but are rather the product of the human capacity to superimpose moral features—*enthia moralia*—on natural events. When we deal with power, which was for Pufendorf the generic term for our capacity to be active, not all expressions of power are morally acceptable, as was the case for Spinoza. Through the interpretation of the Law of Nature, we can discriminate between acceptable and unacceptable expressions of power. Pufendorf thus broke the connection between property and power; when we assign power to another human being, we grant him the right to govern us, but we do not assign him property rights over us.

Yet in fact the separation between property and power is less stark than these formulations seem to suggest. Pufendorf offered a very unconventional approach to what "claiming a right" means, an approach which sees a right as the product of an act of recognition by the parties involved in a transaction. But Pufendorf could not accept the full implications of his own intuition, in particular in the case of power. If legitimate authority comes into being when we recognize that another is entitled to exercise power over us, all we have to do is to express that recognition, and make our actions conform to the commands of our superior. On the contrary, Pufendorf contended that, in instituting a power relation, we transfer some of our natural capacities to the other person.

> A *perfect Promise* is, when a Man not only determines his Will to the Performance of such or such a thing for another hereafter, but likewise shews that he gives the other a full *Right* of challenging or requiring it from him. When we engage to give away a particular thing, or to perform a particular Service, the former is a Kind of *Alienation* of our Goods, or at least somewhat in order to it; the latter is an *Alienation* of some part of our Natural Liberty.[22]

---

21. Pufendorf makes this explicit while commenting on the work of a contemporary, J. Friedrich Hornius, who in *De Civitate* contends that the woman's consent is reduced to accepting the man who asks her in marriage, since the man's power is established by God. Pufendorf writes: "And that the Woman, for this reason, lies under no Obligation to obey, before she hath by her own Consent, submitted to the Rule and Authority of an Husband . . . Her own Covenant and her Subjection consequent upon it, are the *immediate* and nearest Cause productive of *the Husband's Power*" (*Nature and Nations*, VI, I, xii, p. 337).

22. Ibid., I, III, V, vii, p. 50.

If by instituting a power relation we *alienate* the resource that is the object of a transaction, the connection between power and property is reestablished. This holds true at least in the case of the relationship between ourselves and our personal resources, of which liberty is the most important. But the consequences of reintroducing a proprietary language are momentous, for the conceptual universe typical of this language is reintroduced with it. If individuals alienate their natural resources to others, others must acquire them, that is, become the proprietors of these resources. The beneficiary may use them, as he uses his material property. And since this procedure is central to the alienation of liberty, in instituting a power relation we impair our natural liberty, and we grant another person to right to use and enjoy it, if not abuse it. We can transfer all of our natural liberty to another, thus enslaving ourselves. But what are slaves if not items of property of the master? The case of full self-enslavement shows that there is a difference of degree, not of kind, between the exercise of power and the enjoyment of property rights.

We may decide, as would Locke, that self-enslavement is illegitimate. But even a limited alienation of personal liberty is consequential for social arrangements. We can measure the effects of this move on Pufendorf's own view of domestic relations. The original equality of the state of nature no longer holds, once the woman and the servant have accepted the power of the husband/master, thereby alienating their natural liberty and impairing their capacity for agency. And this loss of private agency entails the loss of public agency.

> *Fathers of Families,* who being the chief Rulers before the Institution of Publick Governments, brought into such Governments the Power which they before held over ther Wives, their Children, and their Servants. So that this Inequality being more Ancient than the Erection of Civil Society, can by no means owe its Original to them; nor do they [public governments] give this Power to the Fathers of Families, but leave it in their Hands as they found it.[23]

The fathers of families who institute civil society through a contract thus bring with them the resources that they acquired in the state of nature: land, goods, and power over their domestic dependents. According to the classical liberal reading, it is conflict among these male proprietors over the allocation of scarce resources that turns the state of nature into a state of war.

Having taken the step of arguing that power can be legitimated only by consent, Pufendorf would then appear to have effectively annulled the consequences of this innovation. But Pufendorf's insistence that, by alienating part of their natural liberty, household dependents do not thereby become items

23. Ibid., III, II, ix, p. 186.

of property of the head of household, means that all adults, even women and servants, are endowed with a degree of personal agency which cannot be eliminated. This leftover agency is not enough to enable dependents to be active in the public arena, even if they leave the household. However, when they legitimate the power of their husbands or masters, women and servants do not become things, but remain persons. They allow their superiors to govern them, to use their capacities—but not to use, enjoy, and abuse them as they may do with things.

Paradoxically, this kernel of agency is also what makes dependents vanish from the political arena. *They* have curtailed their liberty by instituting the head of household's power. *They* have subtracted themselves and their concerns from public scrutiny and protection, by impairing their capacity for agency and entrusting themselves to the husband/master. On the other hand, they may not become the *objects* of conflict among heads of households, for they partially remain *subjects*. Their consent is required for any change in their status: nobody may buy them and sell them; nobody may transfer them at his pleasure; nobody may steal them. Insofar as they belong to a household, they are managed together with the material resources that make up the private domain of their superior, for the state accepts as a fait accompli the fact that a private citizen exercises power over other members of society, even if they are not slaves. But domestic dependents are not his private possession. Thus the power of the head of household, which may have stretched to the exercise of the power of life and death in the state of nature, is immediately curtailed once civil society is instituted. The state, which is retreating from the economic domain, sets stricter limits to the power of the head of household over domestic dependents than to his power in economic matters.

Pufendorf's theory offers us as good an example as any of the consequences of operating with a basic assumption of Natural Law theory: individuals have jurisdiction over the skills and capacities that define them as agents—which they can potentially alienate to others. This means that my identity as an agent depends on what type of jurisdiction I control. The active citizen is necessarily an individual who has maintained independent control over his private jurisdiction. He is capable of political agency *because* he has employed personal agency correctly and successfully. But the relationship of reciprocal implication between agency and jurisdiction also means that we can infer what kind of agent a person is by looking at her jurisdiction. Thus women and servants have impaired their status as political agents *because* their private jurisdiction is to a large degree—and, in principle, by their own choice—under the control of their domestic superior.

Subsequent thinkers would begin the journey that has led to severing this connection between jurisdiction and agency. We do not have jurisdiction over our agency, but rather over the things which we can do thanks to being autonomous agents. This would finally result in the notion that the citizen is indeed the autonomous agent, that is, the person who can act in both her private and public capacity, but not necessarily a person who controls a specific jurisdiction. The first to move decisively in this direction was Locke, although he did so ambiguously enough as to create serious problems of interpretation for his readers.

LOCKE

THE SEPARATION OF *dominion* from *property,* which Pufendorf introduced, would be strengthened and refined by Locke, partially in response to Sir Robert Filmer's contention that Adam received from God proprietary rights in the earth and his fellow human beings.[24] While Locke agreed that God enjoyed power over, and property in, his creatures, his rejection of Filmer's grant of this kind of power to a human being was uncompromising. Nor can ownership of material things, in itself, legitimate power over other individuals. In the *First Treatise* Locke writes:

> But yet, if after all, any one will needs have it so, that by his Donation of God, *Adam* was made sole Proprietor of the whole Earth, what will this be to his Soveraignty? And how will it appear, that *Property* in Land gives a Man Power over the Life of another? Or how will the Possession even of the whole Earth, give any one a Soveraign Arbitrary Authority over the Persons of Men?[25]

In response to Filmer, Locke argues that God has given the earth to all human beings in common, which means that neither power nor property-ownership comes directly from God or from nature. However, if the natural condition is one of equality, how did it come about that some human beings have power over others, and that private property has replaced common property? Do we "acquire" power? Do we "acquire" property? How do we go about doing so?

24. Filmer, whose most influential work was *Patriarcha* [1680]—the chief target of Locke's *First Treatise*—presented his most explicit and radical version of the identification of property and dominion in another piece highly critical of Natural Law theory, *Observations Concerning the Originall of Government, upon Mr Hobs 'Leviathan', Mr Milton against Salmasius, H. Grotius 'De Jure Belli'* [1679] (in *Patriarcha and Other Writings,* edited by J. P. Sommerville; see especially p. 187). Locke commented on this work by Filmer in one of his notebooks; see Peter Laslett's introduction to John Locke's *Two Treatises of Government* [1689] (New York: Mentor, 1965), pp. 45–46.

25. Locke, *Two Treatises,* I, paragraph 41, p. 205.

Locke wished to argue that legitimate appropriation is independent of social relations, so as to avoid the problem—pointed to by Filmer—that consensus would have to be universal if the legitimacy of private property depended on agreement among the parties.[26] As is well known, Locke argues that ownership of our own labor legitimates our claim that the product with which we have mixed it is exclusively ours. In other words, it is because we all have equal and legitimate access to a personal resource, our labor, that we are entitled to claim property in resources external to us. The validity of our title does not depend on the recognition that others grant to it, as Pufendorf had contended.

However, Locke's ingenious though analytically problematic solution[27] to the question of the acquisition of private property could not work for the acquisition of power. Power is by definition something that we can have and exercise only over others, and therefore in the context of human relations. If power, like private property, is not instituted by God or nature, what other device do we have to introduce it except human contrivance, that is, contract, and what other means do we have to legitimate it except consent?[28] Locke thus had to adopt Pufendorf's (and Hobbes's) solution, according to which contract is the instrument for the institution of power, and consent is the only possible source of legitimation of its exercise.

However, unlike Grotius, Pufendorf, and Hobbes, Locke imposed severe limits on the range of acts to which we can freely consent. Aware that the capacity to alienate one's liberty had been used to legitimate both self-enslavement and the institution of an absolute ruler, in his chapter "On Slavery" Locke offered a restrictive interpretation of the latitude which God has left us with regard to our personal resources:

> This *Freedom* from Absolute, Arbitrary Power, is so necessary to, and closely joyned with a Man's Preservation, that he cannot part with it, but by what forfeits his Preservation and Life together. For a Man, not having the Power of his own Life, *cannot,* by Compact, or his own Consent, *enslave himself* to any one, nor put himself under the Absolute, Arbitrary Power of another, to take away his Life, when

26. R. Filmer, *The Anarchy of a Limited or Mixed Monarchy* (in *Patriarcha and Other Writings*), pp. 140–41.

27. Already mentioned by Grotius; but he listed it as one of many possibilities, especially first occupancy. Locke's solution has been criticized as analytically inconsistent: see John P. Day, "Locke on Property"; and Waldron, *Right to Private Property,* chapter 6, especially pp. 184–91.

28. I am not saying that there are no alternatives: history is one (as Hume would emphasize), functional homeostasis another. But Locke considered them only in marginal cases.

he pleases. No body can give more Power than he has himself; and he that cannot take away his own Life, cannot give another power over it.[29]

We cannot give away our own life because it is not ours, and unless we forfeit it by committing a heinous crime, only God, its legitimate owner, is entitled to decide when and how it can be taken from us. But as this very example indicates, Locke does not abandon the proprietary approach completely. Even if we do not have complete power over our lives, each one "has *Property* in his own *Person*. This no Body has any Right to but himself."[30] "Person" is a juridical category which summarizes the capacities of an actor at law. For Locke, this includes the capacity to make out and interpret the law of nature, and to apply it when engaging in transactions with others, contracts in particular. But why do we have to be *proprietors* in our own persons, that is, in the capacities that make us independent agents? The first obvious answer is that we have to be proprietors in our own persons because this makes us proprietors of our labor, which in turn entitles us to appropriate external resources.

However, there is much more than labor in one's personality. Can we do with other features of our personality what we do with labor, that is, transfer them into something or, more problematically, to someone else? Does granting another person the right to exercise power over us, even if it is not the power of life and death, mean that we have *alienated* some of our personal capacities to him? Does the beneficiary become the proprietor of the personal resources over which he now exercises control?

The two test cases for answering these questions are provided by the master/servant and the husband/wife relations. In each case, the two parties agree to a contract whereby the future servant and the future wife put their resources at the disposal of the master/husband. Women do it, because marriage requires the discharge of sexual services. And servants, because providing services for a master means to grant him the power of disposing of their persons, of their bodily movements, and of their mental skills. No one can control these capacities without the consent of the bearer. Being a proprietor does not grant the master power over the servant. Being a man does not grant the husband power over the woman. Only the parties engaged in the transaction can authorize the beneficiary to use their personal capacities. But do they alienate these capacities?

29. Locke, *Two Treatises*, II, paragraph 23, p. 325.
30. Ibid., II, paragraph 27, pp. 328–29.

Locke employs the language of buying and selling when discussing the transaction between master and servant.

> *Master* and *Servant* are Names as old as History, but given to those of far different condition; for a Freeman [unlike a slave] makes himself a Servant to another, by *selling him* [emphasis added] for a certain time, the Service he undertakes to do, in exchange for Wages he is to receive: And though this commonly puts him into the Family of the Master, and under the ordinary Discipline thereof; yet it gives the Master but a Temporary Power over him, and no greater, than what is contained in the *Contract* between 'em.[31]

Although modern readers are tempted to read this passage as introducing the modern notion of the alienation of labor, it is apparent from Locke's words that the servant, by selling his labor, also changes his civil status. He becomes a member of the master's household, or estate. This implies that the power of the master, although falling short of the power of life and death, is greater than the power of an employer who controls only the worker's labor time.[32] It also implies that the master *acquires* and *incorporates* the personal capacities that the servant has *sold* to him, so that they become part of his "estate." An indirect confirmation can be found in Locke's famous argument that mixing *labor* with nature is the ground for legitimate appropriation.

> Thus the Grass my Horse has bit; *the Turfs my Servant has cut* [emphasis added]; and the Ore I have digg'd in any place where I have a right to them in common with others, *become my Property* [emphasis added], without the assignation or consent of any body. *The labour that was mine* [emphasis added], removing them out of that common state they were in, hath *fixed* my *Property* in them.[33]

Thus the master does not merely appropriate the products of the servant's labor, but his labor, to the point that he no longer distinguishes between his own and the servant's laboring activity and capacity. It seems fair to conclude that in the case of master and servant there is a transference, we may well say alienation, of capacities from the dependent to his superior.

In sharp contrast, there is no reference to buying and selling in Locke's discussion of the marriage contract, through which man and woman give life to the family. The family is a society of mutual help and support between two adults who need to collaborate in the enterprise of rearing and educating

31. Ibid., II, paragraph 85, pp. 365–66.
32. Echoes of this language and its implications last until Marx.
33. Locke, *Two Treatises,* II, paragraph 28, p. 330.

children. Like all people forming a voluntary association, the parties have to curtail their individual freedom to a degree in order to act in concert. But this is not in itself a reason why there could not be a balance of power between man and woman, as there is among the members of a body politic who, taken one by one, do not acquire or lose any more power than the others do.

There are passages in Locke that reflect this approach. He grants women remarkable latitude in negotiating the marriage contract;[34] he concedes that a family may be under the control of a "mistress" as well as of a "master," that women can separate from their husbands, and that the children may remain in the mother's care, rather than the father's.[35] In other words, women are competent to perform the negotiation of the terms of the marriage contract, both in the state of nature and in civil society, and they are competent to manage their own lives outside marriage. Women maintain control of what belongs to them by contract, and of what they have acquired through their own labor.[36] If a woman signing a marriage contract does not alienate part of her agency, as servants do for Locke, then she should not be incorporated into her husband's "estate." At times Locke appears to confirm this.

> For all the ends of *Marriage* being to be obtained under Politick Government, as well as in the state of Nature, the Civil Magistrate doth not abridge the Right, or Power of either naturally necessary to those ends, *viz.* Procreation and mutual Support and Assistance whilst they are together; but only decides any Controversie that may arise between Man and Wife about them.[37]

However, Locke retreats from a fully egalitarian approach, and chooses an awkward compromise between granting full agency to the woman and denying it altogether.

> But the Husband and Wife, though they have but one common Concern, yet having different understandings, will unavoidably sometimes have different wills too; it therefore being necessary, that the last Determination, *i.e.* the Rule, should be placed somewhere, it naturally

34. In the *First Treatise* (paragraph 47, pp. 209–210), in part to reject Filmer's politicization of family relations, Locke writes: "But there is no more Law to oblige a Woman to such a Subjection [to her husband], if the Circumstances either of her Condition or Contract with her Husband should exempt her from it, than there is, that she should bring forth her Children in Sorrow and Pain, if there could be found a Remedy for it. . . . Neither will any one, I suppose, by these Words, think the weaker Sex, as by a Law so subjected to the Curse contained in them, that 'tis their duty not to endeavour to avoid it."

35. Locke, *Two Treatises,* II, paragraph 82, p. 364.

36. Ibid., II, paragraph 183, pp. 437–38.

37. Ibid., II, paragraph 83, p. 365.

falls to the Man's share, as the abler and the stronger. But this reaching but to the things of their common Interest and Property, leaves the Wife in the full and free possession of what by Contract is her peculiar Right, and gives the Husband no more power over her Life, than she has over his.[38]

There is no other way to make sense of this passage but by separating the different strands contained in it. At least to a modern reader, these strands belong to arguments which are mutually incompatible. But it is their incompatibility that allows us to infer two visions of the relationship between private and public in Locke's work.

One line of argument points to a reassertion of the Pufendorfian model, in which the head of household incorporates the personal and material resources of his dependents. But in the case of the conjugal relationship this occurs in a curiously roundabout way. The functioning of the family, as of any other society, requires a majority to rule it—in Locke's words, to "move" it.[39] Locke thus devises an artificial majority for the married couple, where no majority is possible, by assigning greater "weight" to the husband; the wife voluntarily accepts that the husband has his way in their small society.[40] But instead of contending that the woman has tilted the balance by alienating part of her power to the husband, Locke resorts to the more traditional view that natural inferiority justifies the woman's decision to give her consent to her husband's authority. The end result is that the wife does curtail or suspend her personal agency in legitimating the husband's power. He will take decisions for both of them and their small association, managing their common resources and making choices which will be binding for her even if she disagrees. Does he appropriate the capacities which she has impaired by accepting his authority? Locke does not use this language; but for all practical purposes, the husband can dispose of them as if he had incorporated them into his own person.

It is now time to look at the consequences of the transactions in which adults engage in the state of nature from the point of view of the distinction between private and public. Human beings do come into the world sharing the same condition of freedom and equality, for all sane adults are competent to understand, interpret, and enforce the law of nature. However, some individuals decrease their original allotment of resources by negotiating contracts that entitle the beneficiary to exercise power over them, provided that it is not the power of life and death. Locke thus presents the adult male as the

38. Ibid., II, paragraph 82, p. 364.
39. Ibid., II, paragraph 96, pp. 375–76.
40. See Mary Lyndon Shanley, "Marriage Contract and Social Contract in Seventeenth-Century English Political Thought," *Western Political Quarterly* 32 (1979): 89.

potential beneficiary of transactions through which he has acquired both material possessions and the personal resources of others, and has incorporated them into his "estate." The head of household is a proprietor, one whose property is made up not only of land and money, but also of the services and capacities of others. Being a proprietor and being capable of acquiring more property are undoubtedly central to his being a full agent.[41]

The proprietary conception of agency reproduces, in modified form, the classical distinction between private and public as the contrast between the household and the body politic. "Private" is all that is under the personal control of heads of households, all that they have acquired without harming others. "Public" is what regards the same heads of households, when harm has been done or threatened. But the classical picture has been modified because of the privatization of material exchange, and because it is only actual or potential harm to the welfare of others that justifies the intervention of public authority.[42] The "citizen" of classical and early modern theory would step into the public domain by leaving the household and encountering his peers. But the citizen of modern Natural Law theory steps into the public domain only when his relations with others threaten to be harmful for some or all the parties concerned.

The private domain thus includes all the activities in which the proprietor engages independently of the control of the state over harmful actions: they range from getting married to educating his children, from worshiping God to producing and trading goods.[43] Some of these activities occur "in private," that is, within the walls of the house; some occur "in public," as is the case with production and exchange. But their juridical status is the same: they are private concerns of the adult male who performs them.

In this model the citizen is undoubtedly the Pufendorfian head of household who has acquired personal and material resources in the state of nature. He must be an adult male and a property-owner: being only one of the two will not do. Male heads of households constitute the group of peers whose

41. Laslett emphasizes the link between property and personality in his Introduction to *Two Treatises*, p. 116 (though he contends that, for Locke, our natural equality is not impaired by differentials in property ownership).

42. That is, the aim of the state is no longer the pursuit of justice as complete virtue. But for Locke harm could be inflicted by commission and by omission—by not helping and defending others. Thus in civil society the government is granted broad "redistributive" powers, which appear to be in conflict with the aim of protecting property acquired by individuals before the institution of civil society.

43. Locke, *Letter Concerning Toleration*, p. 34.

relationships become antagonistic and require the institution of political rule. For Natural Law theorists it was still the case that dangerous conflict arises only among equals; domestic dependents do not represent enough of a threat for their superior. They do not threaten him because they depend on him, and because they have freely consented to being ruled by him. Dependents are reified sufficiently to be under the control of the head of household, though they are not reified sufficiently to make it possible to handle them as if they were things.[44]

This *partial* reification is the ultimate reason for the ambiguities that characterize Locke's treatment of the juridical and political condition of dependents. Contract thinkers who were willing to accept the legitimacy of self-enslavement could build a conceptually consistent theory of power relations. By rejecting the legitimacy of complete self-alienation, Locke leaves dependents equal to their private superiors in the crucial matter of the power of life and death. And since this power is the fundamental mark of *political* authority—"*Political Power* then I take to be *a Right* of making Laws with Penalties of Death"[45]—dependents and husbands/masters are indeed ultimately equal insofar as political power is concerned. But this equality means only that everyone has the right to defend oneself from a master or a husband who threatens his/her death. It does not mean that a servant and a wife can exercise the prerogatives of citizenship, for they have curtailed the capacities that enable people to act as citizens, by entrusting themselves to a private "caretaker."

Clearly, it is logically inconsistent to assert that inequality in matters of lesser importance—for whom you work, for how many hours, for whom you must reserve your sexual services and affection, whether you are paid for your labor or you work at home, and so forth—should overrule equality in matters of greater importance—that we are all equal when our lives are in question—thus turning a private dependent into a noncitizen. And it is likely that one of Locke's intentions in constructing this baroque and untenable theory was to keep women—and servants—in their place. But I wish to suggest that subjecting Locke to the pragmatist-ideological test—*cui prodest?*—and finding him wanting is not the most interesting way to close the argument. It is not interesting theoretically, for the ambiguities are there, and they are fascinating to explore. It is not interesting historically, for the subsequent history of the West, and then of the world, showed that interpreters and agents recognized

44. For a more extensive discussion, see Daniela Gobetti, "Goods of the Mind, Goods of the Body, and External Goods: Sources of Conflict and Political Regulation in Seventeenth-Century Natural Law Theory," *History of Political Thought* 13 (1992): 31–49.

45. Locke, *Two Treatises*, II, paragraph 3, p. 308.

these ambiguities and exploited them, pushing and pulling them in various directions—stressing, in particular, the egalitarian elements and finding in them a ground for legitimating an inclusive conception of citizenship.

I thus wish to take the pieces of Locke's theory that point in a universalist direction and see what conception of the requisites for citizenship, and of the distinction between private and public, can be built on them.

If every adult has the capacity for interpreting and enforcing the law of nature in order to preserve herself (and others whenever possible), then every adult has both personal and political agency. That is, every adult is capable of consulting the law of nature both in order to make choices regarding her personal life and in order to assess whether the safeguarding of these personal activities and their outcomes requires the use of "political" power.

But this means that if all sane adults are full agents, each person's private domain will coincide with all the activities in which she engages, provided that these activities do not harm others. The boundary line between private and public can no longer be drawn between the household and the body politic, for interaction within the household may lead to conflicts that require the use of the power of life and death in the state of nature, or the intervention of the magistrate in civil society—"the Civil Magistrate . . . decides any Controversie that may arise between Man and Woman about them." If one wishes to maintain the spatial metaphor, the private domain of each adult is like a bubble with flexible contours. It follows the agent who is at its center wherever the agent takes it: into the house, to church, to market, and even inside herself. It can be punctured when harm is threatened or done. It can be recreated, after the damage has been repaired, or the guilty party has compensated the victim. These bubbles interact, overlap, and grow when individuals form relations and associations in order to achieve their aims. How permeable the bubble is depends on how strict or broad the definition of harm is: for Locke harm was physical aggression and damage; for Mill it would be psychological distress as well.

On this account, the central feature of agency is the capacity for the autonomous interpretation of the law of nature, rather than the appropriation of personal and material resources. The relationship between appropriation and rights of citizenship has become contingent, because, in principle, how the individual fares in appropriating personal and material resources is inconsequential for her political status. Locke concedes as much in saying that differentials in property in material or personal resources do not alter the natural equality of human beings with respect to the power of life and death. And appropriation, rather than being the central expression of agency, is merely one activity among the many available to the person.

This shift in focus is even more consequential than it seems at first reading. The citizen is a person capable of making decisions about a broad range of activities which are all permissible to her, but she is not required to engage in any one activity rather than another. She can marry or not, have or not have children, choose among several religious faiths, spend her life cultivating her mind, give her goods to the poor, make a living by trading or by cultivating the land, and so forth. In other words, the person can choose the activities that she deems most conducive to her own welfare. This does not mean that she can do whatever she wants, because she must ascertain that what she wants to do is compatible with the dictates of the law of nature. First, she must assess whether her choices are potentially harmful to others, and if so refrain from implementing them. Second, she may be required to support or to help others, that is, to help take care of the common good. But when it comes to activities that fall into neither of these two categories, the person's private choices do not affect her rights as a citizen.

It is this third set of activities that constitute the private domain of each agent, and the "broadening" of such private activities has been considered by liberal thinkers, from Constant through contemporary epigones of classical liberalism, to be one of the defining traits of liberal society and one of its glories. But what does this "expansion" of the private domain mean, if we look at its implications for a theory of citizenship? In particular, what relationship is there between a "broadened" space for private agency and the semi-implicit universalistic theory of citizenship contained in the writings of protoliberal Natural Law theorists? I shall turn to Hutcheson to offer a brief answer to this question.

HUTCHESON

THE "EXPANSION" OF the private domain is often explained as a process of "liberation" of the private from the public, as Marx put it. But I wish to suggest that, normatively, this liberation/expansion is the consequence of an-other move, the above-mentioned severing of the link between private perfor-mance and rights of citizenship. To put it in other terms, it is the expansion of the realm of "things indifferent" that opens the way to freeing private activi-ties from public control. Activities are "liberated" from state regulation be-cause they become indifferent to keeping the peace and ensuring the common good. But this means, as said above, that they become indifferent to the requi-sites for citizenship. Thus, it becomes possible to conceive more abstractly of the characteristics typical of a citizen, and it is *this* move that leads to an authentically universalistic view of the body politic. Both these moves are pres-ent in Hutcheson, who maintains a more egalitarian view than Locke in matters political, and is also more direct than Locke in granting that political inequality is a historical construct, which might be justified on consequentialist grounds, but may not be on *a prioristic* ones.

Hutcheson's egalitarianism is ethical, before being juridical or political, for his main concern was to inquire into the moral foundations of legally enforceable principles and norms. It seems fair to say that his strong interest in ethics (and religion) may have made it easier for him to accept egalitarian assumptions. As his legal and political theory is almost wholly dependent on his moral theory, it becomes almost impossible for him to retreat to an unproblematic inegalitarian stance when he discusses natural rights, the social contract, and civil society.

Hutcheson starts from the assumption that all adults are capable of behavior according to moral principles, the fundamental one being the pursuit of the good, defined as "the greatest happiness of the greatest number." [46] Subsequent developments of utilitarianism would stress that what mattered was the pursuit of the aggregate happiness of the group of individuals under consideration, rather than the pursuit of the sum total of the happiness of each and every one. On the contrary, Hutcheson emphasized the need to maximize collective pleasure by guaranteeing that each individual attained the highest level of happiness available to her. He then harmonized individual and collective pleasure by contending that, upon reflection and the refinement of the moral sense, the individual would discover that what gave him the highest level of happiness was the pursuit of the general welfare. [47]

I emphasize this point not to enter into a detailed discussion of Hutcheson's moral theory—for which there is no room here—but to draw the reader's attention to the very deep roots of Hutcheson's individualism and egalitarianism. No one is excluded from the number of the "greatest number": not children, not women, not servants. (Not even animals, for Hutcheson is one of the first, at least to my knowledge, who discusses our moral duties toward "brutes.") In order to further the general welfare, every individual must be capable of evaluating the impact of her choices on the happiness and well-

---

46. *A Short History of Moral Philosophy* (London, 1755), volume II, book II, chapter IV, section iii, p. 218 (hereafter *SMP*). All quotations from Hutcheson are taken from the facsimile editions reprinted in *Collected Works of Francis Hutcheson*, 7 vols. (Hildesheim, NY: Georg Olms Verlag, 1969, 1971).

47. Hutcheson, preface to *Essays on the Nature and Conduct of the Passions and Affections* (London, 1728), p. viii: "It may perhaps seem strange, that when in this *Treatise* Virtue is suppos'd *disinterested;* yet so much Pains is taken, by a *Comparison of our several Pleasures,* to prove the *Pleasures* of *Virtue* to be the greatest we are capable of, and that consequently it is our true *Interest* to be *virtuous.*"

being of others. In fact, according to Hutcheson, every individual possesses a specific faculty, the moral sense, which gives her the capacity to understand and fulfill her obligations, as well as to evaluate the actions of others.

The capacity to evaluate the moral quality of our actions and intentions and of the actions of others is then translated into the capacity to recognize our rights and duties and those of our fellow human beings.

> Our notion of *right* as a moral quality competent to some person, as when we say one has a *right* to such things, is a much more complex conception. Whatever action we would deem either as virtuous or innocent were it done by the agent in certain circumstances, we say he has a *right* to it. Whatever one possesses and enjoys in certain circumstances, that we would deem it a wrong action in any other to disturb or interrupt his possession, we say 'tis *his right*, or he has a *right* to enjoy or possess it. Whatever demand one has upon another in such circumstances that we would deem it wrong conduct in that other not to comply with it, we say one has a *right* to what is thus demanded.[48]

Having endowed human beings with such remarkable capacity for assessing moral facts and their juridical implications, Hutcheson suggests that a long-standing, peaceful state of nature preceded the institution of political society and the centralization of the power of life and death. Domestic and economic relations arose over time among individuals who were perfectly competent to live a peaceful social life, in which self-restraint took the place of the enforcement of norms on the recalcitrant. But even after growing complexity and discord made the state necessary, signs of this egalitarian and self-balancing condition remain strong.[49]

So strong that the egalitarian and self-balancing state of nature is not superseded by political society, but is only subsumed under it, and remains a powerful and semi-independent realm of action within a "politicized" domain. "Civil/political society" is becoming civil society *tout court,* that part of the social structure that lives alongside and in partial opposition to the state, which has been founded to protect and preserve civil society itself.

We find in Hutcheson two accounts of the relationship between civil soci-

---

48. Hutcheson, *A System of Moral Philosophy* (London, 1755), I, II, III, i, p. 253.

49. One of them being a quite liberal and egalitarian view of marriage and domestic society. Man and woman are placed on a much more equal footing than ever before. Hutcheson supports both spouses' right to ask for a divorce, condemns adultery on both sides, rules out the idea that domestic power must be vested in the male, and assigns to the magistrate the duty to intervene when the two parties become unable to find a common ground (Hutcheson, *SMP,* II, III, I, v, p. 159).

ety and the state, or, if you prefer, two different accounts of the consequences that the foundation of the state has for the unregulated, self-balancing social relations of the state of nature.

The first account reproduces the Pufendorfian/Lockean account, with slight modifications. The state is founded by heads of households, who, albeit equal to their wives and, supposedly, to their servants, suddenly subsume their dependents under themselves and represent them vicariously when they institute political rulership.[50]

The second account is simply juxtaposed to the first. I should emphasize that it is not an explicit alternative to the Pufendorfian/Lockean model just summarized. It is the fruit of Hutcheson's looking at the complex social dynamics of his own society and seeing something that the account of Natural Law theory does not allow him to articulate. It is as if Hutcheson were looking at the world of society and politics through a prism, and by rotating it he could catch a glimpse of a different image, with different nuances and shapes, which could not be seen by holding the prism in its usual position. The two accounts are never brought together, compared, and reconciled. Hutcheson articulates the second account by reflecting upon the various types of rights and the natural and artificial persons of which we can predicate them.

In *A Short Introduction to Moral Philosophy,* Hutcheson proposes two classifications of rights. The first distinguishes between "private" rights, rights of "economics," and rights of "politics." Private rights regard individuals; rights of economics regard the domestic association; rights of politics refer to government.[51] Individuals can sacrifice part of their private rights for the good of an association they are forming with others (read: domestic society). Once they have performed that operation, they are no longer fully competent and will be represented by their superiors in the political domain.

The second classification distinguishes rights of persons (or private), of societies and corporations (or public), and of mankind (or common to all). Rights of persons concern each individual; rights of societies concern all associations, political or not; and rights of mankind concern all human beings conceived as a totality without any institutional embodiment.[52] This totality, which Hutcheson calls "the publick" or "mankind as a system," provides the abstract normative principle which a person must take into consideration when evaluating the consequences of her actions for her fellow human beings. This abstraction is formidable indeed, for Hutcheson assigns perfect rights to it—rights which must be enforced when someone violates them. "Mankind

50. Unlike Locke, Hutcheson is explicit on this point. See *SMP,* II, III, V, iii, p. 229.
51. Hutcheson, *A Short Introduction to Moral Philosophy* (Glasgow, 1747), p. i.
52. Hutcheson, *Short Introduction,* II, IV, ii, p. 141.

as a system" thus constitutes a new, noninstitutionalized public subject, domain, and set of concerns. And from this new public no one can be excluded, for all one needs to function properly in it is to exercise her moral sense and *interpret* the juridical implications of moral evaluations. The faculty of interpretation, which Hutcheson calls "judgment"—as Kant would later, in a different context[53]—is in fact brought to center stage.

> Our rights are either *alienable* or *inalienable*. . . . Thus our right to
> our goods and labours is naturally alienable. But where the translation
> cannot be made with any effect . . . the right is unalienable. . . .
> Thus no man can really change his sentiments, judgments, and inward
> affections, at the pleasure of another. . . . The right of private judgment
> is therefore unalienable.[54]

Private judgment is the central feature of autonomous agency, and its factual and normative inalienability ensures that every adult is an autonomous agent. In principle, the journey has been completed from the citizen as proprietor, whose visible standing in the world testified to his moral character and inner disposition, to the citizen as an interpreter of morally relevant phenomena, and of ethical and legal norms. The activity of interpretation is pervasive and inescapable. No social relation and no transaction are imaginable without assuming that the adults engaging in them exercise their capacity for assessing the personal and collective consequences of their choices.

CONCLUSION

HUTCHESON CAN THUS be said to conclude the journey which led Natural Law theorists to reject the figure of the citizen as the *dominus,* the propertyholder and the master, by making the link between private acquisition and public rights contingent rather than necessary. The citizen has become the autonomous agent, who can act following the laws of nature, by assessing the possible or actual consequences of his own and others' actions. As I have tried to show, the journey was bumpy and slow, full of dead ends and hesitations. Toward the (provisional) end of the journey, the features of the contemporary citizen, that is, our features as citizens, have all emerged.

The modern citizen is a moral, rather than a political animal. She is alone with her conscience, first, and her judgment later. She moves into the world not from within the massive walls of a premodern household, but from the fragile private world of her interiority. From this lonely, often solipsistic do-

---

53. Hannah Arendt has made us aware of the political dimensions of Kant's notion of judgment in her *Lectures on Kant's Political Philosophy.*

54. Hutcheson, *SMP*, I, II, III, iv, pp. 261–62.

main she judges her fellow human beings, their words and their deeds. She recognizes some of those words as advancing valid claims, that is, enforceable rights, and she recognizes her duty to respect those claims. Others are thus present in her mind as another "self," or, rather, as her own "self" seen from outside.[55] If she plays this game correctly, a long and peaceful state of nature will be her city, her informal public, her "humankind as a system." She will need no rulers, no prisons, no guards. But since frailty is part of human nature, this condition will not last. When others trespass, she is entitled to enforce the respect of her rights or of the rights of others on the trespasser. She is entitled to ask for redress, to punish, if necessary to kill. The modern citizen is, ultimately, an enforcer.

The solitude and isolation which are the mark of the modern citizen—her authentic, fragile private domain—almost force a universalistic conception of the universe of "citizens" on the writers who stand at the origins of modern political theory. If the peaceful working of social relations depends on the correct working of private judgment, which is actually unreachable for inspection and verification, and which we cannot wish to reach even if we could, we shall be forced to concede that all human beings possess it. Once we have taken this step, we can either recoil from it, fearing its consequences, as Hobbes did, and make all give up that capacity except for the sovereign, or we can start the journey toward democracy, where direct participation becomes logically inevitable.

Direct democracy is logically, but not historically, inevitable. Although the last two hundred years have seen a slow but seemingly irreversible progression toward more and more participation by citizens in public affairs, we may now be facing the same predicament that Hobbes faced. Can we implement fully the prescriptions implicit in a truly universalistic conception of citizenship? Can we find a solution to problems which range from the tyranny of the majority—already lurking under the surface in Hutcheson's account of "mankind as a system"—to the costs and inefficiency of direct ruling by the "people," from finding a counterbalance to the subjectivism and solipsism typical of modern individualism, to finding an acceptable compromise between defending particular cultures and mores without jeopardizing the universalistic import of the modern theory of rights?

Maybe we can. But what happens when the faculty of judgment itself seems to have been lost and when, on the basis of what is for us a completely erroneous, privatistic interpretation of the laws of nature—or of the American constitution—citizens take it on themselves to enforce their own sacred views? What

55. Thomas Nagel, *Equality and Partiality*, chapter 2, pp. 10–20.

can be done in Bosnia? What can be done at Waco, and after the bombing of the Federal Building in Oklahoma City? Can we brush off these extreme cases as aberrations, marginal absurdities, or should we not think of them as the tip of the iceberg, the radical but logical implementation of some of the premises of modern democratic theory? In very recent years, growing participation and trust in private judgment have been unleashing forces that we naively thought had been tamed once and for all. History sometimes seems to be actualizing the logical implications of abstract thought more rapidly than we are ready for them, thus bypassing us, interpreters, who are toying with moderate but obsolete recipes. I believe we are at such a juncture, debating problems and solutions that are inadequate to the reality they are called to address. But I do not believe that "the owl of Minerva spreads its wings only at dusk." The theories of the writers I considered in this essay are endowed with remarkable prophetic power, which, as is the case with real prophecy, was partially invisible even to them. What they meant to say did not exhaust the meaning of what they said. I believe this is an important lesson for us to learn.

References

Arendt, Hannah. 1989. *Lectures on Kant's Political Philosophy.* Chicago: University of Chicago Press.

Benhabib, Seyla. 1992. *Situating the Self.* New York: Routledge.

Benhabib, Seyla, and Drucilla Cornell, eds. 1987. *Feminism as Critique: Essays in the Politics of Gender in Late-Capitalist Societies.* Cambridge: Polity Press.

Berlin, Isaiah. 1969. *Four Essays on Liberty.* Oxford: Oxford University Press.

Bobbio, Norberto. 1980. "Pubblico/privato." In *Enciclopedia XI: Prodotti-Ricchezza,* pp. 401–15. Turin: Einaudi.

———. 1993. *Thomas Hobbes and the Natural Law Tradition.* Chicago: University of Chicago Press.

Butler, Melissa A. 1981. "Early Liberal Roots of Feminism: John Locke and the Attack on Patriarchy." *American Political Science Review* 11:67–88.

Corpus Iuris Civilis. 1966. Edited by P. Krueger and T. Mommsen. Dublino and Turici: Apud Weidmannos, 1966.

Day, John P. 1966. "Locke on Property." *Philosophical Quarterly* 16:207–20.

Filmer, Robert. 1991. *Patriarcha and Other Writings.* Edited by J. P. Sommerville. Cambridge: Cambridge University Press.

Gobetti, Daniela. 1992. "Goods of the Mind, Goods of the Body, and External Goods: Sources of Conflict and Political Regulation in Seventeenth-Century Natural Law Theory." *History of Political Thought* 13:31–49.

———. 1992. *Private and Public: Individuals, Households and Body Politic in Locke and Hutcheson.* London: Routledge.

Hobbes, Thomas. [1651] 1980. *Leviathan.* Edited by C. B. Macpherson. Harmondsworth: Penguin.

Hont, Istvan, and Michael Ignatieff, eds. 1985. *Wealth and Virtue: The Shaping of Political Economy in the Scottish Enlightenment.* Cambridge: Cambridge University Press.

Hutcheson, Francis. 1969, 1971. *Collected Works of Francis Hutcheson.* 7 vols. Hildesheim, NY: Georg Olms Verlag.

Locke, John. [1689] 1983. *A Letter Concerning Toleration.* Edited by J. Tully. Indianapolis, IN: Hackett.

———. [1689] 1965. *Two Treatises of Government.* Edited by P. Laslett. New York: Mentor.

Macpherson, C. B. 1962. *The Political Theory of Possessive Individualism: Hobbes to Locke.* Oxford: Oxford University Press.

Munzer, Stephen R. 1990. *A Theory of Property.* Cambridge: Cambridge University Press.

Nagel, Thomas. 1991. *Equality and Partiality.* New York: Oxford University Press.

Nicholas, Barry. *Introduction to Roman Law.* Oxford: Clarendon Press, 1962.

Okin, Susan Moller. 1981. "Women and the Making of the Sentimental Family." *Philosophy and Public Affairs* 11:65–88.

Olivecrona, Karl. 1974. "Locke's Theory of Appropriation." *Philosophical Quarterly* 24:220–34.

Pateman, Carole. 1989. *The Disorder of Women.* Cambridge: Polity Press.

Pocock, J. G. A. 1975. *Virtue, Commerce, and History.* Cambridge: Cambridge University Press.

Pufendorf, Samuel. 1717. *Of the Law of Nature and Nations.* London: R. Sare.

Pufendorfii, Samuelis. 1672. *De Jure Naturae et Gentium.* Londini: Scanorum.

Shanley, Mary Lyndon. 1979. "Marriage Contract and Social Contract in Seventeenth-Century English Political Thought." *Western Political Quarterly* 32:79–91.

Tuck, Richard. 1981. *Natural Rights Theories.* Cambridge: Cambridge University Press.

Tully, James. 1988. *A Discourse on Property: John Locke and His Adversaries.* Cambridge: Cambridge University Press.

Vaughan, Karen Iversen. 1980. *John Locke, Economist and Social Scientist.* Chicago: University of Chicago Press, 1980.

Waldron, Jeremy, ed. 1984. *Theories of Rights.* London: Oxford University Press.

———. 1988. *The Right to Private Property.* Oxford: Clarendon Press.

Young, Iris M. 1987. "Impartiality and the Civic Public." In *Feminism as Critique: Essays in the Politics of Gender in Late-Capitalist Societies,* edited by Seyla Benhabib and Drucilla Cornell. Cambridge: Polity Press.

Rethinking Privacy: Autonomy, Identity, and the Abortion Controversy

Jean L. Cohen

"A well-protected private autonomy helps secure the generation of public autonomy just as much as, conversely, the appropriate exercise of public autonomy helps secure the genesis of private autonomy."
—Jürgen Habermas, "Paradigms of Law"

"[The point is] . . . to affirm the moral judgement that women are entitled to be treated as individuals rather than restricted because of their sex, but also the moral judgment that the group to which they belong may no longer be relegated to an inferior position."
—Nadine Taub and Wendy Williams,
"Will Equality Require More Than Assimilation,
Accommodation, or Separation from
the Existing Social Structure?"

THE PUBLIC/PRIVATE DISTINCTION has once again become a central concern to political theorists, for a variety of reasons. On the one side, the debate over "privatization" centered on the relationship between the state and the market economy has been refueled by the developments in the former Soviet bloc. On the other side, debates over how to conceptualize and draw the boundaries between personal privacy and legal/political regulation have taken on a new urgency, due in part to certain technological developments, in part to the emergence of an increasingly aggressive "identity politics." While these two fields of debate are not entirely unrelated, they raise different issues; and my concern in this essay is with the second. I shall attempt to offer a defense and a "redescription" of personal privacy rights as a contribution to the task of theorizing an egalitarian, democratic, and liberal politics of "identity" that is adequate to modern civil societies.[1]

1. For a previous effort along these lines, on which I have drawn extensively in the present essay, see Jean L. Cohen, "Redescribing Privacy: Identity, Difference, and the Abortion Controversy." For the larger theoretical position that informs my argument, see Jean L. Cohen and Andrew Arato, *Civil Society and Political Theory.* I would like to thank Martha Fineman, Frank Michelman, Kendall Thomas, and Michel Rosenfeld for their helpful comments on earlier versions of the argument, and Jeff Weintraub for his perceptive reading and valuable suggestions.

Recent technological innovations, ranging from sophisticated surveillance techniques to biotechnologies that can penetrate into what were formerly construed as the most private and impenetrable of areas (the womb, the genes, and so forth), have brought home to many of us the importance of protecting personal privacy from unprecedented possibilities of intervention. But the rise of identity politics in a number of guises—ranging from "multiculturalism" to politically oriented religious fundamentalisms, from feminism and gay liberation movements to ethnic, racial, and nationalist politics—has served to highlight the ambiguities of privacy discourses and of privacy rights. Indeed, criticisms of the ways that the public/private distinction has figured historically in both the liberal and democratic traditions seem to proliferate endlessly these days. The critics have challenged both the possibility and the desirability of drawing boundaries between public and private, based on the suspicion that all such boundaries ultimately serve the purposes of exclusion, denigration, and domination over those designated as "different." Increasingly these criticisms have been cast in the framework of a more general challenge to "enlightenment thinking" as a whole—especially from the standpoint of the various forms of identity politics—that seeks to unmask the pseudo-neutrality, the homogenizing thrust, and the denial or exclusion of difference that are claimed to be inherent in enlightenment universalism and in all of the categories of enlightenment thought, including and especially the public and the private.

Despite the cogency of many of these analyses, however, the politics of identity has begun to show its dark side—as the emergence of virulent forms of nationalism, racism, ethnocentrism, and intolerant group particularism all over the world witness. One wonders whether the radical critiques of enlightenment universalism have not played into the hands of the antidemocrats by depriving us of the language and conceptual resources indispensable for confronting authoritarian, xenophobic, and regressive tendencies. These resources ought to be critically interrogated, reshaped, and reappropriated, not discarded out of hand. As I will try to show, these resources include the discourses of privacy and privacy rights.

Critiques of the public/private distinction are coeval with feminist theory. From its inception, feminist politics has targeted the legal disabilities and discriminatory laws that excluded women from the "public" spheres of work and politics (and which disadvantaged them once they got there), while feminist theory has challenged the cultural stereotypes about gender linked to conceptions of the public/private distinction that justified these exclusions. By now the main charges should be familiar: despite its obvious inadequacy to capture the institutional complexity of modern civil societies, a dichotomous conception of the social structure as divided into a "public" and a "private" sphere (identified with male and female genders, respectively) has played a key role in ideologies justifying both the exclusion of women from full membership in the political community and the denial of equality of opportunity in economic life. It has also helped to perpetuate the ascription of status on the basis of cultural stereotypes about gender, to screen out issues designated as "private" from public debate, and thus to shield the asymmetrical power relations governing the gendered division of labor and other aspects of "intimate relationships" within the home from the demands of justice. Indeed, apparently neutral discourses of privacy *and* of publicity have all too often been conducted on the basis of male norms, and have served male interests. As innumerable feminists have insisted, the public/private dichotomy has thereby served to reinforce and perpetuate social hierarchies and inequity between the sexes in all spheres of life.[2]

All this is true. However, it is not necessary to map the abstract concepts of public and private onto a dichotomous model of the social structure, nor to use the terms in stereotypically gendered ways. Like all contested concepts, "public" and "private" are open to reinterpretation and can be deployed in a variety of discourses. I will thus not seek in this essay to directly engage and refute the versions of feminism that reject the very distinction between the public and the private; other feminist scholarship has already done a good job here.[3] I will concentrate instead on developing a conception of privacy that is an adequate complement to feminist reconceptualizations of public space.

On the one hand, I remain convinced that the concept of the public sphere and the idea of deliberative democracy remain crucial to the theoretical and practical project of democratizing society. We therefore remain indebted to the problematic introduced in Habermas's 1962 *Strukturwandel der Öffentlichkeit*.[4] Of course, neither the original liberal model of public space reconstructed in this early book nor Habermas's own subsequent attempts to develop an alternative are entirely satisfactory. In this respect, recent work within feminist theory that has insisted on the indispensability of the concept of public space for a democratic feminism, while attempting to rethink the public realm in

2. For a now-classic statement of these problems, see Carole Pateman, "Feminist Critiques of the Public/Private Dichotomy."

3. For a recent summary, see Anne Phillips, *Engendering Democracy*, pp. 92–119.

4. Translated as *The Structural Transformation of the Public Sphere: An Inquiry into a Category of Bourgeois Society*. For some recent work in democratic theory that has also emphasized these concerns, see the essays in Craig Calhoun's edited volume, *Habermas and the Public Sphere*, along with John Druzek's *Discursive Democracy*, James Fishkin's *Deliberative Democracy*, Thomas Spraegens's *Reason and Democracy*, and Anne Phillips's *Engendering Democracy*.

ways that can render it more "woman- and difference-friendly," has been especially important.[5] While current approaches in this area are hardly free of difficulties,[6] the problem of restructuring the public sphere so as to reconcile inclusion and equality with diversity or "difference" has generated a substantial and valuable feminist discourse.

On the other hand, the project of reconciling universality and particularity, autonomy and identity, cannot be solved entirely at the level of the public sphere, even if the latter is understood to comprise multiple publics and to assume varied forms at different levels of the social structure. At the very least, some of the fundamental preconditions of genuine participation in public citizenship *and* of building and defending unique identities will depend on maintaining the necessary political and legal protections of privacy. In short, both the protection of "voice" (and of a multiplicity of "voices") in the public sphere *and* the protection of privacy are crucial to any project of democratization that tries to avoid exclusion, leveling, and homogenization. But the normative rethinking of the public in feminist theory has not been matched, so far, by an equivalent effort at rethinking the correlative category of the private.

To be sure, feminist theory has hardly ignored "the private"; rather, it has for some time been engaged in critical and genealogical investigations of the power strategies subtending privacy discourse. Feminist theorists have long argued that "the personal is political," meaning that the apparently "natural" private domain of intimacy (the family and sexuality) is legally constructed, culturally defined, and the site of power relations. For the most part, the emphasis has been on the critical deconstruction of privacy rhetoric as part of a discourse of domination which legitimizes women's oppression.

But "unmasking" (or, in more contemporary jargon, "deconstructing") the deployment of concepts that serve the ends of domination is only one-half of the task of critique. It is now up to us to move beyond a hermeneutics of suspicion and to redescribe the good that privacy protects in terms that are

5. I have in mind such recent work as Seyla Benhabib, *Situating the Self,* chapters 3, 5, and 6; Nancy Fraser, "Rethinking the Public Sphere: A Contribution to the Critique of Actually Existing Democracy," in Craig Calhoun, ed., *Habermas and the Public Sphere;* and Iris Young, *Justice and the Politics of Difference,* especially chapters 4 and 6.

6. For some discussion, see Jean L. Cohen, "The Public, the Private, and the Representation of Difference," pp. 3–9. Briefly, I would argue that most of these analyses—including those mentioned in the previous footnote—lack a sufficiently *differentiated* conception of the public sphere. Working out such a conception, adequate to the problems and opportunities of complex and differentiated modern societies, requires an effort of both normative and institutional analysis that has only begun.

woman-friendly.[7] In this essay I will therefore attempt to formulate a concept of the private that can serve as the correlative of a differentiated notion of the public and—in the form of a right to privacy—provide the protection for levels of autonomy and plurality which no combination of democratic publics can, by itself, achieve.

I will address these issues through the prism of the debate in American legal and political theory over the privacy justification for reproductive rights in the United States. This controversy provides an illuminating context for rethinking the significance of privacy for democratic concerns, including specifically feminist ones, because it reveals both the importance of privacy rights to women and the paradoxes that such rights entail. As is well known, a woman's right to decide upon an abortion in the United States was constitutionally protected, as part of her fundamental "right to privacy," in the 1973 Supreme Court decision *Roe v. Wade*.[8] Both abortion rights and the idea of a constitutional right to privacy have been challenged ever since. I will argue that a constitutionally protected right to personal privacy is indispensable to any modern conception of freedom and that without reproductive freedom, secured in part by such a right, women are deprived of the good that privacy rights are meant to, and should, protect for all of us.

As a starting point, I will consider two recent challenges to the privacy justification for abortion rights, both of which target what are taken to be its flawed conceptual and normative presuppositions, albeit from opposite points of view. The first of these critiques, articulated by feminist legal theorists who favor grounding abortion rights in equal protection arguments, charges that privacy analysis reinforces an ideological, liberal model of the public/private dichotomy that has long been used to justify gender inequality and private male power within the patriarchal family, along with exclusionary and discriminatory treatment of women outside the domestic sphere.

The second, articulated by "communitarian" critics of liberalism, argues that constitutionalized individual privacy rights undermine community values and solidarity. This, they claim, is due to the atomistic and adversarial conception of the individual that allegedly underlies these rights. While the first critique offers an alternative justification for abortion rights, the second challenges the very idea of individual rights in this domain.

We seem to be facing different forms of what I shall call the "paradox of

---

7. For the concept of "redescription," see Richard Rorty, *Contingency, Irony, and Solidarity*, pp. 79–80; however, I should add that I do not subscribe to Rorty's understanding of the public/private dichotomy.

8. *Roe v. Wade*, 410 U.S. 113 (1973).

privacy rights." According to the first argument, the attempt to correct the flaws of domestic privacy with more privacy seems quixotic: how can private power (over women) be undermined by privacy rights? From the communitarian perspective, on the other hand, to accord decisional autonomy to women in family matters through the vehicle of privacy rights is to purchase individual choice at the price of community solidarity.[9] And there is yet a third dimension to the "paradox of privacy" pointed out by critics in both camps: while privacy rights purport to be the means for protecting individuals from state power, they also reinforce the disintegrative, atomizing, and leveling tendencies in modern society, thereby exposing people to increased regulation by state agencies, and in the process destroying both the solidarity of the family community and the autonomy of the individual.

This essay will attempt to counter the objections from both quarters by contesting their interpretations of what is entailed by privacy justifications of the sort found in *Roe,* and by redescribing the good that privacy rights are meant to protect. The paradoxes of privacy are not unavoidable—they stem from the trap of ideology into which both critiques fall. In short, both approaches assume that what they take to be the liberal interpretation of privacy rights is definitive of such rights, and thus both propose to abandon the discourse of privacy altogether. Both critiques are consequently rather one-sided: the first, because it considers only the subordination of juridical practice to the preservation of a system of domination; the second, because it confuses the formal with the substantive meaning of individuality attached to privacy rights.[10] The first approach misses the normative and empowering dimensions of privacy rights because it is preoccupied with unmasking the functional role they can play in preserving inequality and hierarchy. The second is distracted by the old atomistic assumptions subtending many liberal justifications of privacy (and other individual rights). Thus, it fails to grasp the real importance of rights guaranteeing decisional autonomy, inviolability of personality, and a sense of control over one's identity needs to socialized, solidary individuals in the domain of "intimacy"—a complex of rights for which "privacy" has increasingly become the umbrella term.

9. There is a specifically feminist version of this communitarian argument: namely, that such a move from "status" to "contract" *apparently* frees women to shape their own lives, but at the price of buying into a possessive individualist model of the self that denies a reality women know especially well—the centrality of interdependence, of interconnectedness, and of relationships of care in constituting the self. For a useful discussion, see Linda C. McClain, "The Poverty of Privacy?" pp. 119–74.

10. For an excellent theoretical analysis and critique of both types of reductionism, see Claude Lefort, "Politics and Human Rights," in *The Political Forms of Modern Society,* pp. 239–72.

The task before us is to break with functionalist and other worn-out interpretations of privacy without jettisoning the valid principles protected by privacy rights. Precisely because the issues, relations, and arrangements once construed to be purely private, "natural," and thus beyond justice have become matters of public debate and political struggle, precisely when boundaries are being redrawn, and when meanings have become destabilized, it is time to enter the fray and rethink privacy rights in ways that enhance, rather than restrict, freedom *and* equality.

Indeed, I shall argue that one of the most important examples of normative learning in the twentieth century is the recognition that personal privacy is a good for every individual that deserves to be protected in its own right, on grounds that ought to be differentiated—legally and morally—from those pertaining to private property, freedom of contract, or "entity" privacy (that is, attached to the patriarchal family as a unit).[11] Many of us intuitively acknowledge the importance of this development, despite the confusion and controversy over the very meaning of privacy—a confusion that derives in part from the old associations of privacy with property and the patriarchal family. But neither of these associations is necessary or essential. It is true that the notion of private property used to serve as the symbolic center of the personal rights complex, but it neither can nor should do so any longer.[12] It is thus no accident that, over the course of the past thirty years, there have been increasing efforts to reorganize this complex around the principle of personal privacy, with the notions of inviolability of personality, intimacy, and bodily integrity at its core; in the process, privacy jurisprudence has become a key symbolic shield for individual identity needs against majoritarian intolerance. As we shall see, it is precisely this new thrust in privacy doctrine, articulated fairly recently by the Supreme Court in a number of rulings granting "decisional autonomy" to individuals over intimate personal matters, that communitarian critics challenge.

What does personal privacy entail? It is clear that among the dimensions of personal privacy recognized by the Supreme Court today, the "right to be let alone" (freedom from unwarranted intrusion or surveillance) and "decisional

11. For a discussion of the distinction between "entity" privacy and personal privacy, see Martha Albertson Fineman, "Intimacy Outside of the Natural Family: The Limits of Privacy," *Connecticut Law Review* 23 (1992): 955.

12. The reasons are too complex to go into here, but they have to do in part with the rise of the interventionist welfare state and the related demotion of property from a sacred principle to an economic concept. See Jean Cohen, "Redescribing Privacy," pp. 105–12; and Jennifer Nedelsky, "American Constitutionalism and the Paradox of Private Property," in Jon Elster and Rune Slagstad's edited volume, *Constitutionalism and Democracy.*

privacy" (freedom from undue regulation or control) in the domain of intimacy are central. Of the two, the first, especially as concerns the most intimate details of one's personal life, is far less contested than the second. The right to be let alone emphasizes informational privacy—control over the acquisition, possession, and spread of information about oneself, along with control over access or attention by others, be they private individuals, organizations, or public officials. This principle, if not its applications, is widely accepted today. The debates are over the extent, rather than the very idea, of our "right to be let alone."

The controversy on which I will focus here revolves primarily around the second prong of the privacy doctrine, namely, privacy construed as involving decisional autonomy vis-à-vis the "zone of intimacy"—marriage, divorce, sexual relations, procreation, child-rearing, abortion, and so forth.[13] This is the arena where the battle rages and where the very principle, rather than the reach, of an individual right to privacy is being contested.

THE FEMINIST EGALITARIAN CRITIQUE
OF PRIVACY ANALYSIS

As INDICATED ABOVE, feminist legal theorists who argue for abandoning the privacy justification for reproductive rights (preferring some version of equal protection doctrine) claim that privacy discourse reinforces a misleading liberal model of society/state relations that conceals gender hierarchies and obscures the social reality it helps to constitute, instead of opening it up to public scrutiny.[14] On this model, the state is construed as the public sphere—the locus of power—while all that is nonstate is construed as the private in an undifferentiated manner. Accordingly, the right to privacy "is based on the assumption that as long as the state does not interfere with private life,

13. Of course, control over access to oneself is not only a matter of informational privacy. It also involves control over the degrees of intimacy one wishes to have with others. Thus, "going public" over issues such as marital rape can be construed as an effort to secure privacy as decisional autonomy, and bodily integrity, for wives.

14. While many feminist theorists have invoked equal protection principles to protect reproductive rights, including abortion, most have presented arguments that would allow for a synthetic use of both sets of principles: privacy and equality. (For a list of references, see my "Redescribing Privacy," pp. 49–50.) The theorists I have in mind here are those who reject privacy analysis altogether, on both normative and strategic grounds, and wish to replace, not supplement, it with some version of equal protection doctrine. See, for example, Catharine A. MacKinnon, "Privacy v. Equality," in *Feminism Unmodified;* Frances E. Olsen, "A Finger to the Devil: Abortion, Privacy and Equality," pp. 377–82, and "Unraveling Compromise," p. 105; and (with special reference to pornography, abortion, and surrogacy) Cass R. Sunstein, "Neutrality in Constitutional Law," p. 1.

autonomous individuals will interact freely and equally." [15] The very concept of privacy, then, allegedly presupposes an ideological notion of a "natural," prepolitical sphere of life where relations are based on consent between free and equal adults.

But this dualistic model is superimposed in liberal privacy doctrine upon another—namely, the boundary between domestic life and the rest of society. When the private means the home, however, it is construed as the sphere of dependency, of "natural" hierarchical relationships and particularistic bonds, not as the locus of equal rights-bearing autonomous individuals. Here, of course women have been positioned, like children, as dependents. Yet their subordinate status within the family is considered to be as voluntarily assumed as is their entry into, and chance to exit from, the so-called marriage contract. [16] On this model, then, privacy attaches to an entity, the family, shielding its internal "natural" intimate relations from public intervention and scrutiny.

Although they are not always clear about the distinction between these two conceptions of privacy, feminist critics of privacy rights argue that both models inform and distort the reasoning in privacy doctrine even when privacy rights are being accorded to women. In her classic critique of *Roe v. Wade,* Catharine MacKinnon has argued that "the legal concept of privacy can and has shielded the place of battery, marital rape, and women's exploited labor." [17] Thus, even though the privacy right articulated in *Roe* was framed as an individual right, in MacKinnon's view, it nonetheless shores up the negative aspects of "entity" privacy. Accordingly, the state secures privacy by centering its self-restraint on the home and the bedroom, by staying out of marriage and the family, by not intervening. Thus, the privacy justification for abortion rights does nothing to undermine traditional gender stereotypes about the proper role of women in society, nor does it challenge inegalitarian patterns of male dominance and female subservience in the private sphere.

I believe this interpretation is wrong. I argue that MacKinnon and the others are mistaken in interpreting the legal concept of privacy simply as a vehicle that "has preserved the central institutions whereby women are deprived of identity, autonomy, control, and self-definition." [18] Rather, the recent developments in privacy law have begun to secure precisely these goods to women—that is why they are so hotly contested. The least convincing part of the analysis (adopted by Sunstein and Olsen) is the charge that the privacy justification in *Roe* and its progeny reinforces the old ideology of entity privacy

15. Olsen, "Finger to the Devil," p. 378.
16. See Carole Pateman, *The Sexual Contract,* pp. 154–88.
17. MacKinnon, "Privacy v. Equality," p. 101.
18. Ibid.

regarding the family, by resting on a conception of a sacrosanct private sphere identified with the marriage and the home. Indeed, this is an odd interpretation of *Roe,* the very decision that guaranteed a right of decisional privacy regarding abortion to women *as* individuals, not as wives, securing the privacy of a woman's communication with her doctor, not with her spouse, with respect to an activity that does not take place in the home, but in hospitals and clinics! Moreover, the Court has consistently overturned husband notification provisions in state law, thereby challenging the patriarchal model of the family along with gender stereotypes. The strong argument against husband notification rules made by the plurality in the 1992 decision on abortion rights in *Planned Parenthood v. Casey,* which cites family violence including battery and rape of wives by their husbands, supports my point.[19] The decision notes the role secrecy plays in shrouding abusive families and explicitly rejects the old common-law understanding of a woman's role in the family along with the view that entity privacy trumps individual privacy within the marital unit.

To be sure, what I have been calling "entity privacy" has had the negative effects on women described by many. The old entity approach to privacy, found in the common law, protected privacy for the family unit. We continue to be burdened with the ideology that justified this conception of privacy by associating interdependency and the need for protection with the lack of autonomy and rightlessness. It is also incontestable that deploying the term "private" to designate institutions and spheres of life as off limits to the principles of justice (be it the factory or the family) is indefensible. This ideology has most certainly played a role in preventing the democratization of the family and in keeping important issues out of the public sphere.

But to construe the personal privacy rights protected by *Roe* as continuous with the old assumptions of common-law entity privacy is silly.[20] By granting privacy rights to women *as individuals* (married or not) with respect to reproductive decisions and intimate relationships, the ideology of family privacy that had been used to justify rigid gender norms and patriarchal power relations, predicated on the denial of full legal personhood to women, is *exploded.* Indeed, by gaining individualized privacy rights, women can at last accede to the status of full legal personhood and begin to demand both protection and autonomy, both rights and legal benefits, within, as well as for, intimate relationships. They can also demand state action in the form of protection of their rights as persons within the family, while retaining control over the intimate decisions that individual privacy rights afford.

19. *Planned Parenthood v. Casey,* 112 S. Ct. 2827–32 (1992).

20. See my "Redescribing Privacy," pp. 48–65, for a more detailed analysis of these issues as well of the problems that abortion funding decisions pose for privacy analysis.

Going one step further, one can argue that *both* sorts of privacy rights involve important protections. While "entity privacy" has shielded the patriarchal family and all its disturbing practices from the demands of justice, this need not be the case. The ideological conception of the "normal" (patriarchal) family has been traditionally presupposed by entity privacy, but it is not logically entailed by it. Other family forms and other intimate relationships could all benefit from "entity" privacy—that is, from protection against undue state regulation and intervention. Once we acknowledge that "the family" is not a natural but a conventional civil association, that what counts as a family varies over cultures and over time, that law plays an important role in constituting families, we can ask what, if anything, about the nature of the protected relationship is *worth* protecting.

In other words, once we abandon the old ways of construing intimate associations and their relation to state power and law, we must still address the question of whether and how to draw a boundary within the terrain of the social. If we redescribe entity privacy as the privacy of intimate relationships, the answer will be evident. In short, I want to invoke the notion of relational privacy to cover what entity privacy covered without its patriarchal baggage. As such, relational privacy protects the intensely personal communicative interaction among intimates from unwarranted control or intervention by the state or third parties, with one key proviso: that the demands of justice are not violated within the relationship.

Intimate relationships are characterized by a particularly vulnerable, fragile sort of interpersonal communication which would fall apart or become seriously distorted if the principles of publicity (open access, inclusion, availability of information) were applied to them. In other words, information, access, and internal communication, crucial for the special trust involved in intimate relationships, must be under the control of the intimate associates themselves. Intimacy requires privacy—a special boundary vis-à-vis the outside, protective of the special bondedness inside. This is what relational or associational privacy rights secure.[21] Thus, even if we acknowledge all the criticisms of the ideological versions of the public/private dichotomy, we still need the concepts of privacy and privacy rights.

However, any type of intimate association can involve power and exploitation. Individuals need protection *within* and not only *for* intimacy. Thus while "entity" privacy ought to serve as the protective shield for the fragile communicative relationships that constitute intimacy, individual privacy rights ought

21. See Kenneth L. Karst, "The Freedom of Intimate Association," *Yale Law Journal* 89 (1980): 624.

to serve as protection for the personal and bodily integrity of "family" members, should these relationships become distorted or break down.

In this regard, it seems that the communitarian critics of "the new privacy" are closer to the truth when they argue that *Roe abandoned* the traditional conception of family privacy. But this is precisely what they object to. Let us turn to their analysis.

THE "PERNICIOUS DEVELOPMENT OF PRIVACY DOCTRINE"

TWO INFLUENTIAL COMMUNITARIAN critiques of the right to privacy, as it is applied to the zone of intimacy, are provided by Michael Sandel and Mary Ann Glendon.[22] Both argue against the new developments in privacy doctrine in this domain, because these allegedly rest on an unconvincing claim to neutrality vis-à-vis the question of the value of fetal life, and because they privilege individualistic over community values. Both reject the pivotal decision in *Roe v. Wade* on these grounds. Due to constraints of space, I can address only the second consideration here.[23]

Sandel and Glendon each note, with dismay, the development of privacy doctrine from a "traditional" concern to keep certain personal, intimate facts from public view, or informational privacy, to a contemporary right to engage in certain conduct without governmental restraint, in the name of individual choice.[24] But for both thinkers, the important change is not the application of the notion of privacy to the "zone of intimacy" but rather the shift *within* the intimate zone, from informational privacy to decisional autonomy, and from substantive justifications appealing to communal values and prized traditions or practices, to individualist justifications.

Since, like so many communitarians, Sandel and Glendon are enamored with "the family" and "family values," they do not object to the reasoning in the landmark case of *Griswold v. Connecticut* where the Court, for the first time, explicitly recognized a constitutional right to privacy and found it to apply to the right of married couples to use contraceptives.[25] For both agree

22. Michael J. Sandel, "Moral Argument and Liberal Toleration: Abortion and Homosexuality," pp. 521–38. See also Sandel, "Religious Liberty—Freedom of Conscience or Freedom of Choice?" pp. 597–615, and "The Procedural Republic and the Unencumbered Self," pp. 81–96. See Mary Ann Glendon's *Abortion and Divorce in Western Law,* and *Rights Talk.*

23. For a discussion of their first objection, see my "Redescribing Privacy," pp. 69–92.

24. Sandel, "Moral Argument," p. 324; Glendon, *Abortion and Divorce,* pp. 36–37.

25. *Griswold v. Connecticut,* 381 U.S. 479 (1965). Of course, serious constitutional critics of privacy doctrine have objected very strongly to the "right to privacy" discovered

that the Court justified the privacy right it proclaimed in *Griswold* on teleological rather than on voluntarist grounds: the right to privacy was defended not for the sake of letting people lead their sexual lives as they choose, but rather for the sake of affirming and protecting the social institution of marriage, and the human goods realized in it (intimacy, harmony in living, bilateral loyalty, a sacred association). *Griswold,* in short, affirmed a social practice and tradition valued by the community.[26]

The shift within the intimate sphere to voluntarist and individualist arguments began, according to Glendon and Sandel, with the case *Eisenstadt v. Baird* (1972), which involved a law restricting the distribution of contraceptives to unmarried persons.[27] Here the Court struck down the law through the explicit innovation which "redescribed the bearers of privacy rights from persons qua participants in the social institution of marriage to persons qua individuals, *independent of their roles or attachments."* [28] Moreover, privacy was no longer conceived as freedom from surveillance or disclosure of intimate affairs, but rather as protecting the freedom to engage in certain activities without governmental restriction. Sandel cites the now famous statement in *Eisenstadt* as proof of these "invidious" innovations: "If the right of privacy means anything, it is the right of the *individual,* married or single, to be free from unwarranted governmental intrusion into matters so fundamentally affecting a person as the decision whether to bear or beget a child." [29]

As is well known, one year later this reasoning was applied in *Roe* where the privacy right was extended to "encompass a woman's decision whether or not to terminate her pregnancy." Moreover, the language of decisional autonomy was made quite explicit in the 1977 majority opinion in *Carey v. Population Services International,* where Justice Brennan argued that the constitutional protection of individual autonomy in matters of childbearing is not

---

in *Griswold.* Their position is that since a right to privacy appears nowhere in the text of the Constitution, we have no such right. On these grounds, *Griswold* is as flawed as *Roe.* See Robert Bork, *The Tempting of America,* pp. 112, 115–16; and John Hart Ely, "The Wages of Crying Wolf: A Comment on *Roe v. Wade."*

26. Sandel, "Moral Argument," p. 527. According to Glendon (*Abortion and Divorce,* p. 36), what *Griswold* protected could thus be construed as some sort of family right. As such, privacy protected an entity—the family as a unit—against intrusion and seemed continuous with the traditional common-law concept of family or "entity" privacy (in the sense discussed by Fineman, "Intimacy Outside of the Natural Family").

27. Cited in Glendon, *Abortion and Divorce,* p. 36, and Sandel, "Moral Argument," p. 527.

28. Sandel, "Moral Argument," p. 527.

29. *Eisenstadt v. Baird,* 405 U.S. 453 (1972); cited in Sandel, "Moral Argument," p. 528.

dependent on the element in *Griswold* which forbade the restriction on the use of contraceptives because it would bring police into marital bedrooms. Rather, Justice Brennan maintained that the autonomy rights of individuals were really at the core of what even Griswold protected.[30] Indeed, Brennan maintained that the teaching of *Griswold, Eisenstadt,* and *Roe* is that the Constitution protects individual decisions in matters of childbearing from unjustified intrusion by the state. Later decisions upholding abortion rights also used the language of decisional autonomy to describe the privacy interest at stake. And in his important dissent in *Bowers v. Hardwick,* Justice Blackmun summarized what was at issue in the Court's previous privacy decisions:

> We protect those rights not because they contribute . . . to the general public welfare, but because they form so central a part of an individual's life. "The concept of privacy embodies the 'moral fact that a person belongs to himself and not others nor to society as a whole.'" . . . We protect the decision whether to have a child because parenthood alters so dramatically an individual's self-definition.[31]

The Court thus clearly construed the new privacy as securing decisional autonomy to individuals over certain intensely personal concerns.

Now it is time to discover just what is so objectionable about this development. Here I can only take up one set of criticisms, to wit, the objection to the conception of the self allegedly underlying the very idea that privacy rights secure decisional autonomy to the individual with respect to personal matters.

PRIVACY AS AUTONOMY: THE ISOLATED, DISEMBEDDED SELF?

THE COMMUNITARIAN ARGUMENT leveled against the principle of an individual right to personal privacy protecting decisional autonomy is that such a right presupposes an atomistic (Glendon) or voluntarist (Sandel) concept of the individual and a philosophical anthropology of the self that is both incoherent and incompatible with moral responsibility. Glendon and Sandel each make this charge, albeit with differing degrees of sophistication. Glendon argues that the Court's rulings protecting decisional autonomy embody a view of society as a collection of separate, autonomous, self-sufficient individuals.[32]

30. *Carey v. Population Services International,* 431 U.S. 678 (1977); cited in Gerald Gunther, *Constitutional Law,* 11th ed., pp. 515–16.

31. *Bowers v. Hardwick,* 478 U.S. 186 (1986). This case involved a challenge to the constitutionality of a Georgia statue criminalizing consensual sodomy. The Court's majority decision rejected the claim that the right to personal privacy applied to homosexual activity; but Justice Blackmun wrote a vigorous dissent to this decision.

32. Glendon, *Abortion and Divorce,* p. 35, and *Rights Talk,* pp. 47–75.

This "flaw" in privacy doctrine is, according to Glendon, distinctively and deplorably American.[33] In short, she construes the right to privacy in American constitutional law simply as the *right to be let alone,* which in turn presupposes a conception of the individual as autarkic, isolated, and sovereign. It is the atomism of the concept of the individual presupposed by the new privacy doctrine that she dislikes.

Sandel's critique of the principle of privacy as autonomy goes even deeper, to challenge the voluntarist conception of individual agency that it allegedly presupposes. Recall his famous argument against Rawls, contending that the liberal conception of justice, which privileges the idea of equal rights over substantive conceptions of the good, rests upon an anthropological concept of the self which is not only isolated, atomistic, and autonomous, but also radically unsituated.[34] The essentially unencumbered self is a "subject [. . .] of possession, individuated in advance and given prior to [its] ends."[35] This self adopts a distanced attitude toward all possible life goals and voluntaristically chooses its own conception of the good as if this were one among many dispensable preferences. Accordingly, the autonomous unencumbered self is construed as external to its own identity. It has no constitutive attachments, but merely a set of preferences from which it can pick and choose.

It is this self that is allegedly presupposed by the new privacy doctrine. Thus, in its privacy cases, it is the Court's individualism which Sandel abhors, for the Court seems to conceive intimate relationships as entirely the product of personal choice, instead of as constitutive of the persons who participate in them. In short, the new privacy rights undermine both community (in this case, family) and concrete identity because they rest on a voluntarist, disembedded conception of the self which is in turn subsumed under abstract universalist principles (rights) that deny and even undermine the particular identities of situated individuals.

Against this conception of the self, Sandel insists that everyone is radically situated—their identities, self-understandings, and values are shaped through community-mediated communicative processes of socialization. Thus, on theoretical grounds, the liberal conception of the self as a solipsistic presocietal being presupposed by the new privacy rights is impossible. Moreover, our moral experience belies voluntarism, for in order to have moral intuitions we must view ourselves as particular persons situated within this family, this community, this nation or people, as bearers of this history and this particular

33. *Rights Talk,* pp. 50–51.
34. Michael J. Sandel, *Liberalism and the Limits of Justice,* pp. 179–83.
35. Michael J. Sandel, "Justice and the Good," in his edited volume, *Liberalism and Its Critics,* p. 166.

identity. We are not separate from, but tied to and defined by, our aims and attachments, and these flow from our embeddedness in a specific context and community which is constitutive of who we are and to which we owe duties of loyalty. We also owe particular duties of responsibility to the concrete specific people with whom we have special relationships. If we assume that subjects are socialized through communication, we must see them as members of communities, sharing community values and traditions and having concrete identities and relationships. Individuals do not create their moral vocabulary ex nihilo; it is inherited from the traditional understandings into which they are socialized and which, in turn, nourish their capacity to be moral agents as well as their self-understandings, providing the content of their particular identities. Sandel thus sees us as particular, albeit self-interpreting beings, able to reflect on our history and to revise to some extent our identities, but situated nonetheless.

Now if he and Glendon were correct about the conception of the self which they impute to the new privacy doctrine, they would have a strong case. But they are not correct. There is no obvious connection between either the atomist or the voluntarist conception of the self articulated above and the general notion of the rights-bearing individual. Nor does the new privacy doctrine entail the particular version of liberalism targeted by this critique. In short, there is no necessary *conceptual* connection between privacy rights that secure personal decisional autonomy in certain domains and the ideological version of the self just described. If it has been so interpreted in the past, then it is time to change the interpretation, not to jettison the principle of individual privacy rights.[36]

The argument of both Glendon and Sandel is based on a category error: abstract concepts such as legal personality, fundamental individual rights, privacy, or decisional autonomy are not equivalent to an ontological description of the self or a particular concept of agency.[37] The principle that individual privacy rights protect decisional autonomy (choice) regarding certain personal

36. This point is powerfully brought out by Claude Lefort in "Politics and Human Rights." Lefort shows that what appears to be separation reinforced or created by individual rights, especially privacy rights, is actually a modality of one's relation to others, but one which escapes all corporate models of the social whole. As such, basic rights construct the conditions for interaction and communication (that is, certain structures of mutual recognition); they do not presuppose atomism—a mistake shared by the "bourgeois" understanding of rights and by many of its critics (see especially p. 257). Lefort thus provides a solution to the second "paradox of privacy rights" mentioned in the introduction of this essay.

37. See Jeremy Waldron's essay in his edited volume, *Nonsense upon Stilts,* pp. 166–90, for a cogent reply to the claims that personal rights entail an abstract or atomist conception of the individual.

or intimate concerns can go quite well with a recognition of the intersubjective character of processes of personal identity formation, and an awareness of the historical, contextual sources of our values. Indeed, decisional autonomy could be said to presuppose the communicatively mediated processes of moral and ethical development that make practical reflection and reasoning possible. None of these insights, however, obviates the need for privacy as decisional autonomy when it comes to certain choices for the socialized, embedded, interdependent, communicative individual who views her identity needs as constitutive of who she is. Only if decisional autonomy is respected in every person, however situated, only if the individual's capacity for moral deliberation and justification, on the one side, and for ethical-existential self-reflection and self-interpretation (involving the possibility of partial revision of identities and conceptions of the good on the basis of new insights), on the other, are protected against coercion by the state or the majority of the "community" can the individual function as a moral agent at all. These values may come from the "community," but our attitude toward them is not thereby predetermined.

To be sure, there have been rather controversial attempts to justify the personal rights complex recently secured by the new privacy doctrine that appeal to a comprehensive conception of the autonomous individual. But one could accept the critique of the Kantian or Millian concept of autonomy without assuming that privacy rights have to entail this sort of justification or, for that matter, any comprehensive conception of the person or any overarching substantive moral worldview.[38] One could, in other words, argue that the principle of privacy rights rests on the *abandonment* of "the cult of wholeness" presupposed by general philosophies of man. Indeed, it rests on and secures (along with other sets of rights) the differentiation between our status as *legal persons* and our functioning as concrete unique individuals involved in specific relationships and particular communities, where we may indeed be quite engaged with others and deeply involved in the pursuit of substantial ideals of the good.[39] Sandel's critique, in short, mistakenly conflates the legal with the natural person. Legal personhood of course attaches to individuals, but it presupposes no particular conception of the natural individual or of the self.

In sum, personal privacy rights are meant to ensure domains of decisional autonomy for every individual, not an atomist or voluntarist conception of the

---

38. See Charles Larmore, *Patterns of Moral Complexity,* pp. 40–91, and "Political Liberalism," *Political Theory* 18, no. 3 (August 1990): 339–60.

39. While I agree with Larmore on this point, I do not follow him in labeling all that is nonstate as the private realm. For a model of civil society that breaks with the public/private dichotomy as a paradigm for the social structure, see Jean L. Cohen and Andrew Arato, *Civil Society and Political Theory.*

individual. They protect one's decisional autonomy vis-à-vis certain crucially personal concerns,[40] they do not dictate the kinds of reasons one gives for moral or ethical decisions or the reflective processes informing the decision. Thus, on the privacy justification for reproductive choice, a woman may decide for or against abortion on the basis of her community's values, her religious worldview, or her discussions with "significant others"—her relation to tradition, community, or loved ones is not in question here. Her right to decide does not dictate the basis of her decision. Decisional privacy rights designate the individual as the locus of decision making when certain kinds of ethical or existential concerns are involved—they do not dictate to whom one must justify one's ethical choices nor the kinds of reasons one must give. As Hannah Arendt argued long ago, such rights ascribe a *legal persona* to the individual that serves as a protective shield for her concrete unique identity, particular motives, and personal choices, but do not prescribe these. Rather, they provide the formal enabling conditions for her to pursue her conception of the good without unjust interference by the state or by others.[41]

Thus when the language of autonomy or choice appears in Court decisions, there is no reason to impute to the Court a voluntarist ideal of the person.[42] Ascribing decisional autonomy to individuals over certain issues does not commit the concept of privacy rights to a conception of the disembedded individual—it simply militates against state paternalism, whether in the guise of "community norms" or "majority will."

PRIVACY AND IDENTITY:
THE RIGHT TO INVIOLATE PERSONALITY

EVEN THOUGH THIS interpretation of the privacy right to decisional autonomy can be defended against the above criticisms, it is not sufficient to account

40. Needless to say, what counts as a crucial personal concern—what is considered to be an ethical decision about the good life or a moral issue of justice—changes over time and can be among the stakes of intense debate and conflict. Surely this is the case for abortion.

41. See Hannah Arendt, *The Origins of Totalitarianism*, pp. 267–302, for an excellent discussion of the protective role of the legal persona, and the principle of equality that is attached to it.

42. To be sure, there is little agreement today over how to define a *philosophical* concept of autonomy. For recent efforts to develop a nonmetaphysical, intersubjective, and woman-friendly concept of autonomy, see Jennifer Nedelsky, "Reconceiving Autonomy: Sources, Thoughts and Possibilities," pp. 7–33; Maeve Cooke, "Habermas, Autonomy and the Identity of the Self," pp. 269–91; and Kenneth Baynes, "Autonomy, Reason and Intersubjectivity." For a critique of this enterprise, see Christine Di Stefano, "Rethinking Autonomy."

for the issue of identity raised by the communitarian intervention. According to Sandel, we must proceed in our moral and legal reasoning on the assumption that we are dealing with concrete selves, not abstract persons, with individuals defined in and through their ends, for whom attachments and beliefs are constitutive of who they are, and whose goals are essential to their good and indispensable to their identity. The self-realization of the individual so understood is indeed tied to a social precondition—shared values and membership in solidary communities in which norms and traditions are transmitted and mutual recognition of concrete identities is granted.

Thus, when Sandel and Glendon speak of the community's conception of the good, and of the "right" of the community to institutionalize its values (community self-realization), they have apparently shifted terrain from issues of autonomy/justice to concern with identity/the good.[43] But they are wrong to restrict the issue of the good to the integrity of community values or common identity, as if there were, in highly differentiated, pluralist, and multicultural civil societies, a single overarching conception of the good, or a single substantive collective identity upon which we all agree.[44] This sort of philosophical realism vis-à-vis common identity is misleading, to say the least.

It also seems as if these theorists assume that the individual and the common good, individual and group identities, completely overlap. Since they patently do not, the need to protect the integrity of those dimensions of individual identities and conceptions of the good that are *different* from majoritarian interpretations of collective identity, or of the common good on any level, is a crucial one.

If certain versions of liberal theory have operated with a controversial notion of autonomy, the communitarians suffer from the opposite difficulty. They have not only tended to abandon the principle of autonomy altogether, but also to suppress the problem posed by the *difference* and potential conflict between individual and group identity. Group identity is, of course, part of the identity of the members of the group. But in modern pluralist, differentiated, civil societies, individuals belong to many different groups, play a variety of social roles, and have "communal" identifications that are operative on different levels of the social structure. The sources and inputs into individual identity are multiple and heterogeneous. Indeed, the fact that one is situated within a plurality of communities, that one must act out a number of often

43. Needless to say, the abortion issue straddles this fault line.
44. For an amusing critique of what he calls "the phantom community," see Stephen Holmes, "The Permanent Structure of Anti-Liberal Thought," in Nancy Rosenblum, ed., *Liberalism and the Moral Life.*

conflicting roles, ought to lead back to the acknowledgment of the centrality of individual agency and choice in the shaping of a life.[45] The personal dynamics of shifting involvements among separate spheres, roles, and commitments required by life in a highly differentiated modern society create the need and the possibility for each individual to develop a strong sense of self, along with the ability to form, self-reflectively affirm, and express *her unique identity* in an open multiplicity of contexts.

While people do not invent the traditions, patterns, norms into which they are at first socialized, as they become individualized they do invent and reinvent the unity of their lives and their unique identities (of course in interactive, communicative processes). They also contribute to reinterpreting and reinventing meanings, norms, traditions, and narratives. Both constituted and constituting, the identity of the concrete individual is not just a set of preferences among which we can pick and choose like clothes. But neither is it simply the product of communal values, social embeddedness, shared traditions, or a set of social roles. Indeed, all of these are open to conflicting interpretations on the part of individuals and subgroups within a particular society. Precisely because it is the task of individuals to develop and express their self-conceptions out of (and within) the multiplicity of memberships and affiliations, roles and structures, they are involved in, precisely because they require recognition for their concrete personalities, their opportunity for self-development and experimental self-presentation require protection. Such protection affords to the individual a *sense of control* over her self-definitions, over the self-creative synthesis that only she can fashion out of her various locations and backgrounds, in part through communicative interaction with others.[46] It is my thesis that in highly differentiated societies, the new privacy rights—precisely because they include both informational and decisional aspects—play an important role in protecting the capacities of individuals to form, maintain, and present to others a coherent, authentic, and distinct self-conception. It is also my claim that *by narrowing down privacy rights to*

45. To point out that individual identities are developed through communicative interaction and require recognition by others to survive intact in no way undermines this claim.

46. I do hope that I shall not be accused of realism and essentialism vis-à-vis individual identity, or of reinscribing a naive modernist conception of the unitary self and the fully autonomous rational subject, because of these statements. I acknowledge the multiple and often conflicting sources of identity, as well as the frequent contestation over the cultural codes and social practices that go into identity formation. But I also believe that the ability to develop and maintain a coherent sense of self is the sine qua non of successful individuation—a fragile process that needs protection. The sign that one is relatively successful in this project is one's ability to present one's sense of self through narratives that construct and reconstruct one's identity for affirmation and acknowledgment by others.

the right to be let alone, by assuming that decisional autonomy has to entail an arbitrary relation between the individual and her ends, and by saddling the new privacy with an abstract conception of the individual that allegedly ignores the real individuality of members of concrete communities, the communitarian critics have deprived themselves of an important source of protection for the integrity and authenticity of individual as well as group identities, which may differ from those which the state at any time seeks to promote.

In short, I contend that we can take up the concern for the situated dimensions of identity and argue that the new privacy rights protect both agency *and* identity, self-determination *and* self-realization, autonomy *and* authenticity, without prescribing a particular concept of the self on either level. What, if not a right to personal privacy (securing control over access and decision making to the individual), protects the variety of identities of individuals and groups living in modern civil societies from leveling in the name of some vague idea of community values or the majority's conception of the common good? To be sure, provision for the participation of every group on equal terms in the public spaces of civil and political society, such that no perspective is excluded, is an important way to empower people (through "voice") to assert, protect, and further develop their different individual and collective identities in public. Voice and participation in democratic public spaces certainly can help protect difference. But individual personal privacy rights are nonetheless indispensable. Personal privacy rights protect the constitutive minimal preconditions for having an identity of one's own. Moreover, they ensure respect and protection for *individual difference*—for individual identities which seem to deviate from the "norm" embraced by society at large (in law) or by one's particular subgroup.[47]

Thus, more is involved here than the right to be let alone. What is at stake is the protection of concrete, fragile identities and self-formative processes which are, indeed, constitutive of who we are *and* who we wish to be. I want to argue that, when properly understood, privacy rights guaranteeing decisional autonomy in certain personal matters protect these as well as the chance for each individual to develop, revise and pursue her own conception of the good and her identity. Let me formulate the standard that underlies this aspect of privacy as *the right not to have one's constitutive identity needs violated or interfered with by the state or by third parties without very compelling reasons indeed.* This standard militates against the imposition of an identity onto one which

47. This is hardly a new idea for liberals. However, my point is that such protection need not entail atomistic, voluntarist, or possessive-individualist conceptions of the self. Personal privacy rights can be severed from the property paradigm as well as from patriarchal assumptions regarding "entity" privacy.

one does not freely affirm and embrace. In short, it protects the principle of authenticity. Indeed, even if one's personal identity needs conflict with the majority's interpretation of community values, personal privacy rights protect them—unless, and only unless, they violate universal moral principles. This is why personal privacy rights (together of course with communicative rights) secure the right to be different.

Personal privacy rights do not prescribe what identities should be like; rather, they secure to every individual the preconditions for developing intact identities which they can embrace as their own. On the one side, by securing everyone's juridical personhood and decisional autonomy *equally*, privacy rights protect the claim of every concrete individual, no matter how different or odd, to be treated as a peer by members of the community. On the other side, privacy rights shield the personal dimensions of one's life from undue scrutiny or interference. As such, they protect the processes of self-development and self-realization that go into identity formation. The principle that articulates this idea in American privacy doctrine is the principle of *inviolate personality*.[48]

Of course, the crucial question of which personal concerns should be covered by privacy rights remains to be answered. Here we cannot avoid the issue of where to draw the boundary line between public and private. As we have seen, feminists have criticized traditional modes of drawing the boundary. Our success in bringing a wide range of previously excluded "personal" issues into the public view and debate, including abortion itself, is certainly to be seen as a democratization of public space. Indeed, the discursive conception of public space embraced by democratic feminists presupposes that the agenda is open, and that there is no way to predefine the nature of issues that can be publicly discussed as being, in essence, either public or private. It is *within* a generalized public discourse that the determination of what should fall under the protective cover of privacy rights, and what should not, is ultimately to be made. Moreover, the boundary line is permanently open to contestation and, of course, it shifts over time. Nevertheless, the boundary line must be drawn somewhere. As I have argued elsewhere, while processes of discursive will-formation decide the boundary between the private and the public,

48. For the classic statement of this principle as the core of what privacy rights should protect, see Samuel D. Warren and Louis D. Brandeis, "The Right to Privacy" (1890), reprinted in Ferdinand David Schoeman's edited volume, *Philosophical Dimensions of Privacy*, p. 85. Most commentators have focused only on the famous "right to be let alone," also articulated by Brandeis and Warren in this article. But this has led to a one-sided interpretation of our current privacy doctrine, as evidenced by Glendon's approach.

they cannot entirely abolish the private.[49] At the time I was concerned with articulating what a normatively defensible model of discursive public space presupposed. Now I am concerned with a normative conception of privacy. Let me turn to this directly and then return, in the next section of this essay, to the issue of what should fall under the protective shield of privacy rights.

Here I want to indicate what it means to enjoy a privacy right to decisional autonomy regarding certain personal concerns before identifying these concerns. In short, it means that one cannot be obliged either to reveal one's personal motives for these ethical choices or to accept, as one's own, the group's reasons or evaluations. Neither the source nor the particular content of the individual's motives for action can be regulated by the state in this domain. In other words, a right to personal privacy involves precisely the liberation from the obligation to justify one's actions in a discursive process by giving reasons which everyone together could accept as their own. To put it another way, privacy as decisional autonomy frees one from the pressure to adopt, as one's own reasons, the reasons which "everyone" accepts. Such a telos toward consensus holds for moral discourse strictly speaking, and might be an ideal for political decisions backed up by state sanctions, but it is not required for existential or ethical decisions covered by personal privacy rights. To put this another way, a privacy right entitles one to choose with whom one will attempt to justify one's ethical decisions, with whom one will communicatively rethink conceptions of the good, and indeed, whether one will discuss certain matters with anyone at all. For with respect to personal decisions shielded by the protective cover of decisional and informational privacy, it does not matter whether the reasons decisive for me could also be accepted by everyone else.[50] The state may not require me to reveal my reasons for acting in the domain in which I have the right to act on my own reasons. Thus the decisional autonomy of the legal subject in the domain protected by personal privacy rights involves informational privacy as well. This means

---

49. Jean Cohen, "Discourse Ethics and Civil Society," in David Rasmussen's *Universalism vs. Communitarianism*.

50. I owe this formulation to Klaus Guenter's paper, "Communicative and Negative Liberty," delivered at the conference on Habermas's then-forthcoming book, *Faktizität und Geltung*, at Cardozo Law School, New York City, fall 1992. Thus, regarding the abortion decision, this means that if my right to an early, safe abortion is covered by a general right to privacy, then the reasons for my decision remain my own, and I do not have to submit these to boards of doctors, judges, or any other external authority for approval.

that one has the liberty to withdraw certain concerns, motives, and aspects of the self from public scrutiny and control.[51]

Thus, as Glendon has noted, privacy rights do indeed mark off a protected sphere surrounding the individual, constituting an invisible shield around the person.[52] But this is not an institutional sphere; individuals carry their protective shield, their legal persona, with them wherever they are—within and in withdrawal from interaction. They are not thereby burdened with an asocial conception of individuality, as Glendon seems to believe. Instead, privacy rights shielding personality protect the integrity and inviolability of *socialized* interacting individuals.

It is by now a commonplace that although the practices and rituals of privacy vary across cultures, *every* society acknowledges the normative importance of privacy in some form.[53] Every society establishes what Robert Post has recently called "rules of civility" that safeguard respect for individual personal privacy and which are, in a sense, constitutive of both individuals and community.[54] Echoing Erving Goffman, Post argues that the integrity of individual personality is dependent in part upon the observance of social rules of deference and demeanor that bind the actor and recipient together. In following these "rules of civility," individuals establish and affirm ritual and sacred aspects of their own and the other's identities while confirming the social order.[55] The violation of these rules indicates a lack of recognition for personal dignity and can damage a person by discrediting her identity and injuring her personality, thereby disconfirming her sense of self. Thus, the reciprocal recognition of privacy is the condition of possibility of successful social interaction based on mutual recognition of the integrity of the participants.

Indeed, the normative nature of privacy lies precisely in the protection of

51. It would however be false to interpret this as implying that the individual's need interpretations are fixed and pre-given, or that she solipsistically opts out of any and every dialogic community when she makes personal decisions. My point is that it is up to her to choose with whom, when, and what to discuss regarding personal concerns. While her own reasons can be clarified or altered in such a discussion, what counts is not that she take on the reasons of the community at large, but that she arrive at personal reasons acceptable to herself for her projects, which can hopefully be acknowledged by particular significant others as appropriate for her. For, of course, no one can stand alone or affirm an identity by herself.

52. Glendon, *Rights Talk,* pp. 40, 52.

53. See Barrington Moore, *Privacy: Studies in Social and Cultural History;* and Robert R. Murphy, "Social Distance and the Veil," in Ferdinand David Schoeman, ed., *Philosophical Dimensions of Privacy.*

54. Robert Post, "The Social Foundations of Privacy: Community and Self in the Common Law Tort," *California Law Review* 77, no. 3 (May 1989): 963.

55. Erving Goffman, "The Nature of Deference and Demeanor," in *Interaction Ritual: Essays on Face-to-Face Behavior.*

what Goffman has called "the territories of the self"—a preserve to which an individual can claim "entitlement to possess, control, use, dispose of."[56] Defined by normative and social factors, these territories are a vehicle for the exchange of meaning: they serve as a kind of language through which persons communicate with each other.[57] But they are also central to the subjective sense that the individual has concerning her selfhood. What counts is not whether a preserve is exclusively maintained or shared, or given up entirely,

> but rather the role that the individual is allowed in determining what happens to his claim. An apparently self-determined, active deciding as to how one's preserves will be used allows these preserves to provide the bases of a ritual idiom. Thus, on the issue of will and self-determination turns the whole possibility of using territories of the self in a dual way, with comings-into-touch avoided as a means of *maintaining respect* and engaged in as a *means of establishing regard.* . . . It is no wonder that felt self-determination is crucial to one's sense of what it means to be a full-fledged person.[58]

On this normative conception of privacy it is clearly the *sense of control* over one's identity needs, over access to oneself, over which aspects of oneself one will present at which time and to whom, along with the ability to press or to waive territorial claims, that is crucial and *empowering.* Indeed, it is the sine qua non for understanding oneself to be an independent person—an individual worthy of respect and capable of establishing regard. In our society, the new privacy doctrine thus secures more than the abstract principle of respect for persons as choosers, more than secrecy and solitude: privacy rights conferring decisional autonomy over certain personal matters secure to the individual the legal recognition of her "ethical competence" regarding her self-definitions and her decisions regarding which aspects of herself she will bring into play at which times and with whom. Privacy rights thus protect and even help constitute a structure of mutual recognition and the social ritual by means of which one's identity is acknowledged, one's selfhood guaranteed.

> Privacy is an essential part of the complex social practice by means of which the social group recognizes and communicates to the individual—that his existence is his own . . . this is a precondition of per-

56. Erving Goffman, "Territories of the Self," in *Relations in Public,* p. 28. Similarly, Georg Simmel speaks of "the feeling . . . that an ideal sphere lies around every human being . . . [that] cannot be penetrated, unless the personality value of the individual is thereby destroyed," in the volume edited by Kurt Wolff, *The Sociology of Georg Simmel,* p. 321.

57. Goffman, "Territories of the Self," pp. 29–41.

58. Ibid., p. 60.

sonhood. . . . And this in turn presupposes that he believes that the concrete reality which he is, . . . belongs to him in a moral sense.[59]

The language of possession here should not mislead us—what is meant is that by virtue of privacy, one is able to maintain a sense of selfhood, of agency, and of personal identity, not that these are a form of alienable property. While a right to privacy that protects *inviolate personality* thus is universalistic, in that it establishes every individual as a legal person meriting equal concern and respect, what it protects is our particularity—our concrete and fragile identities. The right to inviolate personality protected by privacy rights articulates intersubjectively recognized personal boundaries that are the sine qua non for the establishment and maintenance of *authentic* identities.[60] It also protects the communicative infrastructure (the rules and rituals of civility) crucial to successful social interaction.

PRIVACY REDESCRIBED: BRINGING THE BODY BACK IN

LET ME RETURN to the problem of what "personal concerns" should be covered by the new privacy. Here I can only offer my own intervention in what I see as a highly politicized debate on this matter. For of course, as indicated above, the answer would ultimately depend upon the cultural self-understanding of societies and on the outcome of political contestation over cultural norms, codes, and social relations that constitute the practices, domains, and understandings of privacy at any given time.

Here I shall briefly address this issue by drawing out the implications of the normative meaning of privacy rights securing decisional autonomy to women in the area of procreation—an interpretation that does not proceed on the possessive-individualist or voluntarist model of the person, but rather

59. See Jeffrey Reiman, "Privacy, Intimacy and Personhood," in Schoeman, ed., *Philosophical Dimensions of Privacy*, p. 310, for a discussion of the normative coherence of the concept of privacy and of a right to privacy which rejects the possessive-individualist model of the self and challenges objectivistic interpretations.

60. For an enlightening discussion of the importance of this dimension of rights for the maintenance of an intact sense of self and self-respect to African-Americans in particular, see Patricia Williams, *The Alchemy of Race and Rights*. Against the critique of rights fashionable in certain legal circles, Williams argues that rights help establish boundaries that eliminate the overly personalized and contemptuous character of relationships between dominant (white) and subordinate (black) groups. Thus, personal privacy rights serve to prohibit others from acting upon the presumed transparency and utter availability of the bodies and identities of others. "But where one's experience is rooted not just in a sense of illegitimacy but in *being* illegitimate . . . then the black adherence to a scheme of both positive and negative rights—to the self, to the sanctity of one's own personal boundaries—makes sense" (p. 154).

builds upon the notion of situated, embodied, interactive individuality. Indeed, in order to understand *why* abortion rights—among other procreative concerns—are central to the concrete as well as the abstract dimension of our selves, we must replace the possessive-individualist conception of the relation of self and body that has dominated our thinking for so long with something better.

Since I have no space to make the argument in the philosophical depth it requires, I will simply summarize the results of recent work on the topic with the phrase: we are all embodied selves.[61] We do not happen to have bodies or choose to take them with us where we go like our purses; we are our bodies. By this I mean that our bodies, our symbolic interpretation of our bodies, and our sense of control over our bodies are central to our most basic sense of self, to our identity and our personal dignity. My body is not extrinsic to who I am. Of course, this is not a simple physical fact, for we can lose some body parts without losing our identity, and the symbolic meaning we give to our bodies is communicatively mediated, varying across cultures and over time. Nevertheless, our selves, our identities, are intricately implicated in our bodies and in what we make of them—for our bodies are our mode of being in the world.

Indeed, Goffman views the body as one of the core territories of the self. He argues that a sense of control over one's own body is crucial for maintaining an intact sense of self and to the ability to interact with others.[62] Self-confidence is predicated upon the sense that one can dispose freely over one's own body: that one can coordinate its functions autonomously and regulate access to it.[63] Without recognition by others of one's autonomous control

61. There is a burgeoning literature on the body. See John O'Neill, *Five Bodies: The Human Shape of Modern Society,* and *The Communicative Body;* Brian Turner, *The Body and Society;* Maurice Merleau-Ponty, *The Phenomenology of Perception;* Kendall Thomas, "Beyond the Privacy Principle"; Zillah Eisenstein, *The Female Body and the Law;* Thomas Lacquer, *Making Sex: Body and Gender from the Greeks to Freud;* Elaine Scarry, *The Body in Pain: The Making and Unmaking of the World.*

62. "Territories of the Self," p. 38; see also Reiman, "Privacy, Intimacy and Personhood," pp. 310–14.

63. Goffman was one of the first to study the destructive impact on the sense of self experienced by individuals in total institutions, subjected to the total loss of privacy and bodily integrity. More recently, Elaine Scarry has focused on the destructive impact on the self when one's bodily integrity is purposefully attacked as in the experience of torture (Scarry, *Body in Pain,* p. 49). Building upon this analysis, Axel Honneth has analyzed the sense of humiliation, the loss of the sense of self and of a coherent sense of reality, when one's bodily integrity (one's control) is not recognized by others. See Axel Honneth, "Integrity and Disrespect: Principles of a Conception of Morality Based on a Theory of Recognition."

over one's body, of one's bodily integrity, without at least this most basic acknowledgment of one's dignity, the individual's self-image is crippled (loss of self-confidence), as is the security she needs in order to interact successfully with others and to express her own needs and feelings. Thus the slogan, "our bodies, our selves," employed by women to defend their abortion rights, rings quite true—for what is at stake in the abortion controversy is precisely a woman's selfhood and identity. This is why the liberty interest in this case is deemed to be so personal, so intimate, so fundamental, thus meriting protection.

Now it is or should be obvious that to force a woman to endure an unwanted pregnancy is to force an identity upon her—the identity of pregnant woman and mother. And clearly her bodily integrity in the physical and emotional sense are at stake in laws that criminalize abortion. But so is her inviolate personality. Indeed these are intimately interrelated. This is not because women are identical with or own their wombs, or because a woman is or owns her fetus, but because the experience of pregnancy constitutes a fundamental change in her embodiment on the physical, emotional, and symbolic levels, and thus in her identity and sense of self. An unwanted pregnancy imposes not only a very powerful form of embodiment on the woman, in which she very much fears losing control over her bodily functions and her sense of self; it also imposes a new and undesired identity and a new intimate relationship onto the woman,[64] requiring heavy investments of herself with implications that go well beyond the physical discomfort or mere lifestyle issues which antichoice thinkers believe sum up the problem of an unwanted pregnancy for women.

To assert the importance of bodily integrity to privacy analysis is not to revive the paradigm of property, or to claim an absolute right to do with one's body as one pleases.[65] Rather, it is to argue that bodily integrity is central to an individual's identity and should be protected by privacy rights as fundamental, to be overruled only if a truly compelling state interest is at stake. In this respect I agree with Kendall Thomas's argument that the emphasis of privacy analysis on protected places, intimate associations, and autonomous choice is insufficient, for it fails to recognize "that 'privacy' is always *body-*

---

64. See Karst, "The Freedom of Intimate Association."

65. No right is absolute in this sense. The state may, for example, insist upon inoculation of children attending public school against certain diseases and it may take measures to protect public health that involve inoculation of adults as well. I address the question of limits to the right to abortion in terms of the stages of pregnancy in "Redescribing Privacy," pp. 87–92.

mediated." [66] Thus when women claim the "right to control our own bodies" they are claiming the right to define themselves.[67]

Nevertheless, the idea of bodily integrity, I would argue, gets at one crucial dimension of our situated identity—but not all dimensions of it. We are also situated individuals in the sense highlighted by communitarians: we develop self-definitions on the basis of culturally available resources in our lifeworld; we draw on our location in a specific set of institutions, relationships, and contexts; we make use (often creatively) of discourses that prestructure in part what can be said and thought; and, out of all this, we fashion our own creative contribution to our self-formative processes—our identity. Our relation to our body, our embodiment, is the crucial substratum of our identity, but not the whole of it. Once we recognize that identity formation takes place throughout our lives we can see that the symbolic meaning we give to our bodies and our selves has many sources and presuppositions. Respect for an individual's bodily integrity involves, as do the other components of privacy, recognition *within* interaction of the individual's own judgment in regulating access and information, and in making decisions involving her basic identity needs. While privacy in the sense of concealment is also a component of bodily integrity, it is (again) not the whole of it. Like the other dimensions of privacy, we need bodily integrity within as well as apart from interaction with others.

Thus, procreative issues are fundamental not only because, as Ronald Dworkin has argued, the "moral" issues on which such decisions hinge are quasi-religious, touching on the ultimate point and value of human life. Reproductive freedom is fundamental also because it involves the core of a woman's identity—her embodiment, her self-formative processes, her life projects, and her self-understanding are all at stake. All individuals need to

66. "Beyond the Privacy Principle," *Columbia Law Journal* (1992), pp. 1515–16. However, I reject Thomas's suggestion that we drop privacy analysis altogether; his argument points to redescribing, not abandoning, privacy discourse.

67. The harm in denying a woman this right is that it denies to her the sense that her body and her self are *hers* to imagine and construct. If the woman is cast as the container for the fetus, her sexuality and her identity are reduced to the maternal function. Small wonder that the debate over abortion is very much a debate over discourses and how the issue should be framed—with the stakes including the definition of women and their place in society. See Kristin Luker, *Abortion and the Politics of Motherhood,* for what is now a classic analysis of the genesis of and stakes in competing discourses of the abortion debate in the United States. See also Barbara Katz Rothman, *Recreating Motherhood: Ideology and Technology in a Patriarchal Society.* In my view, this is also a debate over who gets to define women's "difference," that is, their ability to become pregnant and create a child—the individual woman herself or others.

have some sense of control over their bodies, over their self-definitions, over the self-creative synthesis that only the individual can make out of her various locations, background, and future projects. Inviolability of personality, and the sense of control over the territories of the self including the body, remain indispensable for any conception of freedom. In the abortion issue in particular and in reproductive issues in general, both the abstract and situated dimensions of a woman's personality are involved. Ethical autonomy and the integrity of individual processes of identity-formation—to which our bodies are central, thus, bodily integrity—are the core of what a right to personal privacy does or should protect.

One's decisional autonomy, bodily integrity, inviolate personality—the "territories of the self"—deserve protection no matter where one is. The notion of a general, fundamental, constitutionally protected right to privacy covers all of these. Understood in this way, privacy could and should replace property as the symbolic principle around which the key complex of personal civil rights are articulated. To cast the right to abortion as a privacy right is to acknowledge women's "difference" while leaving it up to each individual woman how to define this difference.[68] At the same time, legal recognition of women's ethical competence regarding reproduction, sexuality, and intimate association acknowledges their equality. While women as women acquire "special protection" for their unique capacities (abortion rights are women's rights), their "difference" is not thereby reified; rather it is simultaneously acknowledged and left to them to construct. And I take it that this, after all, is the point of asserting the right to be "different" *and equal.*

68. In "Redescribing Privacy" (pp. 48–65) I also make the equality argument for abortion rights, arguing for a synthetic use of equal protection analysis, privacy analysis, and bodily integrity arguments.

REFERENCES

Arendt, Hannah. 1951. *The Origins of Totalitarianism.* New York: Harcourt Brace Jovanovich.

Baynes, Kenneth. 1990. "Autonomy, Reason and Intersubjectivity." Unpublished manuscript.

Benhabib, Seyla. 1992. *Situating the Self.* New York: Routledge.

Bork, Robert. 1990. *The Tempting of America.* New York: Free Press.

Calhoun, Craig, ed. 1992. *Habermas and the Public Sphere* Cambridge, MA: MIT Press.

Cohen, Jean L. 1990. "Discourse Ethics and Civil Society." In *Universalism vs. Communitarianism,* edited by David Rasmussen. Cambridge, MA: MIT Press.

————. 1992. "Redescribing Privacy: Identity, Difference, and the Abortion Controversy." *Columbia Journal of Gender and Law* 3(1):43–117.

————. 1993. "The Public, the Private, and the Representation of Difference." Paper presented at the annual meeting of the Conference for the Study of Political Thought, Yale University.

Cohen, Jean L., and Andrew Arato. 1992. *Civil Society and Political Theory.* Cambridge, MA: MIT Press.

Cooke, Maeve. 1992. "Habermas, Autonomy and the Identity of the Self." *Philosophy and Social Criticism* 18:269–91.

Di Stefano, Christine. 1990. "Rethinking Autonomy." Paper presented at the annual meeting of the American Political Science Association, San Francisco.

Druzek, John. 1990. *Discursive Democracy.* New York: Cambridge University Press.

Eisenstein, Zillah. 1988. *The Female Body and the Law.* Berkeley: University of California Press.

Ely, John Hart. 1973. "The Wages of Crying Wolf: A Comment on *Roe v. Wade.*" *Yale Law Journal* 82:920.

Fineman, Martha Albertson. 1992. "Intimacy Outside of the Natural Family: The Limits of Privacy." *Connecticut Law Review* 23:955.

Fishkin, James. 1991. *Deliberative Democracy.* New Haven, CT: Yale University Press.

Fraser, Nancy. 1992. "Rethinking the Public Sphere: A Contribution to the Critique of Actually Existing Democracy." In *Habermas and the Public Sphere,* edited by Craig Calhoun. Cambridge, MA: MIT Press.

Glendon, Mary Ann. 1987. *Abortion and Divorce in Western Law.* Cambridge, MA: Harvard University Press.

————. 1991. *Rights Talk.* New York: Free Press.

Goffman, Erving. 1967. "The Nature of Deference and Demeanor." In *Interaction Ritual: Essays on Face-to-Face Behavior.* New York: Pantheon.

————. 1971. "Territories of the Self." In *Relations in Public.* New York: Harper.

Guenter, Klaus. 1992. "Communicative and Negative Liberty." Paper presented at the fall conference on Jürgen Habermas, *Faktizität und Geltung,* at Cardozo Law School, New York.

Gunther, Gerald. 1988. *Constitutional Law.* 11th ed. New York: Foundation Press.

Habermas, Jürgen. 1989. *The Structural Transformation of the Public Sphere: An Inquiry into a Category of Bourgeois Society.* Cambridge, MA: MIT Press, 1989. Originally published as *Strukturwandel der Öffentlichkeit* (Neuwied: Luchterhand, 1962).

Holmes, Stephen. 1989. "The Permanent Structure of Anti-Liberal Thought." In *Liberalism and the Moral Life,* edited by Nancy Rosenblum. Cambridge, MA: Harvard University Press.

Honneth, Axel. 1992. "Integrity and Disrespect: Principles of a Conception of Morality Based on a Theory of Recognition." *Political Theory* 20, no. 2 (May): 190–93.

Karst, Kenneth L. 1980. "The Freedom of Intimate Association." *Yale Law Journal* 89:624.

Lacquer, Thomas. 1990. *Making Sex: Body and Gender from the Greeks to Freud.* Cambridge, MA: Harvard University Press.

Larmore, Charles. 1987. *Patterns of Moral Complexity.* New York: Cambridge University Press.

———. 1990. "Political Liberalism." *Political Theory* 18, no. 3 (August): 339–60.

Lefort, Claude. 1986. "Politics and Human Rights." In *The Political Forms of Modern Society.* Cambridge, MA: MIT Press.

Luker, Kristin. 1984. *Abortion and the Politics of Motherhood.* Berkeley: University of California Press.

MacKinnon, Catharine A. 1987. "Privacy v. Equality." In *Feminism Unmodified.* Cambridge, MA: Harvard University Press.

McClain, Linda C. 1992. "The Poverty of Privacy?" *Columbia Journal of Gender and Law* 3(1):119–74.

Merleau-Ponty, Maurice. 1962. *The Phenomenology of Perception* London: Routledge.

Moore, Barrington. 1984. *Privacy: Studies in Social and Cultural History.* Armonk, NY: M. E. Sharpe, 1984.

Murphy, Robert R. 1984. "Social Distance and the Veil." In *Philosophical Dimensions of Privacy,* edited by Ferdinand David Schoeman. Cambridge: Cambridge University Press.

Nedelsky, Jennifer. 1988. "American Constitutionalism and the Paradox of Private Property." In *Constitutionalism and Democracy,* edited by Jon Elster and Rune Slagstad. New York: Cambridge University Press.

———. 1989. "Reconceiving Autonomy: Sources, Thoughts and Possibilities." *Yale Journal of Law and Feminism* 1:7–33.

Olsen, Frances E. 1989. "Unraveling Compromise." *Harvard Law Review* 103:105.

———. 1991. "A Finger to the Devil: Abortion, Privacy and Equality." *Dissent* (summer): 377–82.

O'Neill, John. 1985. *Five Bodies: The Human Shape of Modern Society.* Ithaca, NY: Cornell University Press.

———. 1989. *The Communicative Body.* Evanston, IL: Northwestern University Press.

Pateman, Carole. 1983. "Feminist Critiques of the Public/Private Dichotomy." In *Public and Private in Social Life,* edited by S. I. Benn and G. F. Gaus. London: Croom Helm.

———. 1988. *The Sexual Contract.* Stanford, CA: Stanford University Press, 1988.

Phillips, Anne. 1991. *Engendering Democracy.* University Park: Pennsylvania State University Press.

Post, Robert. 1989. "The Social Foundations of Privacy: Community and Self in the Common Law Tort." *California Law Review* 77, no. 3 (May): 963.

Reiman, Jeffrey H. 1984. "Privacy, Intimacy and Personhood." In *Philosophical Di-*

mensions of Privacy, edited by Ferdinand David Schoeman. Cambridge: Cambridge University Press.

Rorty, Richard. 1989. *Contingency, Irony, and Solidarity.* New York: Cambridge University Press.

Rothman, Barbara Katz. 1989. *Recreating Motherhood: Ideology and Technology in a Patriarchal Society.* New York: Norton.

Sandel, Michael J. 1982. *Liberalism and the Limits of Justice.* Cambridge: Cambridge University Press.

———. 1984. "Justice and the Good." In *Liberalism and Its Critics,* edited by Michael J. Sandel. New York: New York University Press.

———. 1984. "The Procedural Republic and the Unencumbered Self." *Political Theory* 12, no. 1 (February): 81–96.

———. 1989. "Moral Argument and Liberal Toleration: Abortion and Homosexuality." *California Law Review* 77, no. 3 (May): 521–38.

———. 1989. "Religious Liberty—Freedom of Conscience or Freedom of Choice?" *Utah Law Review,* no. 3: 597–615.

Scarry, Elaine. 1985. *The Body in Pain: The Making and Unmaking of the World.* New York: Oxford University Press.

Schoeman, Ferdinand David, ed. 1984. *Philosophical Dimensions of Privacy.* Cambridge: Cambridge University Press.

Simmel, Georg. 1964. *The Sociology of Georg Simmel.* Edited by Kurt Wolff. Glencoe: Free Press.

Spraegens, Thomas. 1991. *Reason and Democracy.* Durham, NC: Duke University Press.

Sunstein, Cass R. 1992. "Neutrality in Constitutional Law." *Columbia Law Review* 92:1.

Thomas, Kendall. 1992. "Beyond the Privacy Principle." *Columbia Law Review* 92: 1431–1516.

Turner, Bryan. *The Body and Society.* London: Blackwell, 1984.

Warren, Samuel D., and Louis D. Brandeis. [1890] 1984. "The Right to Privacy." In *Philosophical Dimensions of Privacy,* edited by Ferdinand David Schoeman. Cambridge: Cambridge University Press.

Waldron, Jeremy, ed. 1987. *Nonsense upon Stilts.* New York: Methuen.

Williams, Patricia. 1991. *The Alchemy of Race and Rights.* Cambridge, MA: Harvard University Press.

Young, Iris. 1990. *Justice and the Politics of Difference.* Princeton, NJ: Princeton University Press, 1990.

The Displacement of Politics

Jean Bethke Elshtain

I AM KEENLY AWARE of the ways in which language can be misused and put at the service of political ideologies out of touch with the habits, dispositions, and limits of that world in which we live and breathe and have our being. A cautionary note—a skeptical attitude—is always in order when people come along, whether theorists or activists, and promise a complete overturning and remaking of words or things. Here I recall Martin Luther's discourse on language and limits from his essay, "On the Bondage of the Will." Luther wrote (in his characteristically pungent and no doubt politically quite incorrect style):

> Most people would be amused, or, more likely, infuriated if at this late hour a linguistic revolutionary threw overboard established usage, and tried in its place to introduce the practice of calling a beggar *wealthy,* not because he had any wealth, but because it was possible that a king might give him his—and talked in this way, not as a figure of speech, like sarcasm or irony, but with all apparent seriousness. Thus, he would call one who was sick unto death *perfectly healthy,* on the ground that another might give him his health. Or he would call an unlettered idiot *a learned man,* on the ground that another man might give him his learning. It is no different to say, *man has "free-will"*—merely on the ground that God might grant him His! By thus misusing language, anyone can boast he has anything; for instance, that he is the lord of heaven and earth—if God would give him that . distinction! But such talk is more appropriate to actors and confidence tricksters than to theologians! Our words should be correct, pure and sober—in Paul's phrase, "sound speech, that cannot be condemned." [Titus 2:8][1]

Why bring up Luther and risk losing the reader's sympathy right at the outset? For this simple yet vital reason: political theorists are no more exempt from abstracted folly than Luther's hapless "linguistic revolutionaries," and are similarly well advised to try to be of sound speech. I do not mean to be

---

1. See the edited volume by John Dillenberger, *Martin Luther: Selections from His Writings,* p. 189.

dour here. Luther himself was one who had tremendous fun with language—a pithy and powerful style, examples that grab you by the scruff of the neck and shake you a time or two. But his warning has to do with redefinitions so radical they aim to shatter, to implode, dense layers of imbricated wisdom and folly—our human heritage—in the interest of a preformed and even elegant theoretical agenda. I am suspicious, and in this essay that suspicion is put on display and articulated theoretically.

❏

To THINK WITH EVEN modest coherence about human life as we enter the next millennium is to be concerned about the integrity of that which is public and that which is private; but we need to begin by recognizing that the line between them cannot be drawn easily or definitively. Public and private are categories that bleed into one another. Neither is wholly self-contained, neither stable. Public and private are terms of ordinary discourse, but there is widespread disagreement, among theorists and ordinary citizens alike, over their respective meanings and applications. The content and range of public and private vary with competing modes of social thought and ways of life.

Public and private are always defined and understood in relationship to one another. One version of "private" means "belonging to or concerning a particular person or group, not open to or controlled by the public"; and "public," by contrast, means "of or pertaining to the whole, done or made in behalf of the community as a whole." In part, this contrast derives from the Latin origins of "public" in *pubes,* the age of maturity when signs of puberty begin to appear: then and only then does the child enter, or become qualified for, public things. *Publicus* is that which belongs or pertains to "the public," the people, as a whole. But there is another set of meanings: public as open to scrutiny; private as hidden in principle, not subject to the persistent gaze of publicity. Privacy covers matters not wholly revealed, and this barrier to full revelation is necessary in order to preserve the possibility of certain sorts of relationships. These related understandings have shaped our historic political philosophies and continue to reverberate in contemporary theoretical and political debates.

As with other terms of ordinary discourse, most of the time we take public and private for granted. For we are all shaped to and for ways of life whose public and private forms, linked to or embodied within a grammar of basic notions and rules, either nourish or distort our capacities for purposive activity. It is the task of the political theorist to take a critical look at the resources of ordinary language and their intersection with self-consciously constructed theories of social life which themselves depend on some level of shared meaning. Reflect, for a moment, on just how inescapable is our involvement in one of a number of competing perspectives that depend upon what we take to be the appropriate relationship between public and private life, for this will also shape our understanding of what politics should or should not attempt to define, regulate, even control.

Although one finds widespread disagreement over the respective meanings of public and private within and between societies, no society is without some form of public/private division. Brian Fay sees the public and the private as two of a cluster of "basic notions" that serve to structure and give coherence to all known ways of life and to the individuals who inhabit them. The public and the private as twin force fields help to create a moral environment for individuals, singly and in groups; to dictate norms of appropriate or worthy action; and to establish barriers to action. They bear particularly on such areas as the taking of human life, the regulation of sexual relations, the promulgation of familial duties and obligations, and the arenas of political responsibility. Public and private are embedded within dense webs of associational meanings and intimations and linked to other basic notions and distinctions: nature and culture, male and female, and each society's "understanding of the meaning and role of work; its views of nature; . . . its concepts of agency; its ideas about authority, the community, the family; its notions of sex; its beliefs about God and death and so on."[2] Such basic notions, taken together, constitute a society's realm of intersubjectivity: those ideas, symbols, and concepts that not only are shared but whose sharing reverberates within and helps to constitute a way of life on both its manifest and latent levels. The social and political theorist, then, recognizes that no idea or concept is an island unto itself. When we use a concept, particularly one of the bedrock notions integral to a way of life, we do not do so as a discrete piece of linguistic behavior but with reference to other concepts, contrasts, and terms of comparison.

Just as public and private are essentially contested concepts, implicating us in competing normative frameworks, so is politics. There are no neatly defined and universally accepted boundaries of politics. Essentially contested concepts are internally complex or refer to several dimensions (which are, in turn, linked to other concepts); open-textured, in that the rules of their application are relatively flexible; and appraisive or normative. For example: one political theorist may claim that a given situation is *unjust*. Another, committed to an alternative logic of explanation, might argue that to label that same situation *unjust* is to inflame matters, for what one is really looking at is an inescapable feature of certain cherished social institutions and relations which cannot and

2. Brian Fay, *Social Theory and Political Practice,* p. 78.

should not be tampered with in order to yield the sort of outcome required by a strong theory of justice.

The problem—what is an injustice, as opposed to a misfortune?—has taxed political philosophy from its inception and bears directly on public/private construals and contrasts. The late Judith Shklar writes in *The Faces of Injustice:* "When can we blame others and when is our pain a matter of natural necessity or just bad luck?"[3] Shklar is clear that the distinction is a vital one. Curiously, however, she herself moves to breach it when she contrasts a rigid and absolute divide separating injustice from misfortune to her own more flexible and skeptical approach to thinking about "personal and political injustice" and the ways we respond to it, "especially as victims."[4] This latter move leads Shklar to her own rather disconcerting elision of misfortune *to* injustice; thus, she claims that going through the world in a woman's body may not be an injustice, but it is surely a misfortune located precisely *in* women's bodies "and the part they play in the propagation of the species."[5] The female body itself enters the world wrapped in a shroud of misfortune. This is surely an odd move. To call being born female a misfortune rather than, say, a natural fact, no more and no less unfortunate than being a man—we are all, after all, mortal and subject to illness and decay of the flesh—slides all too easily into bathos. If I, as a woman, begin with the premise that I am already the victim of misfortune by being born female rather than male, it does not take much of a leap of the imagination to turn that natural fact into a social injustice. But this may or may not be the case. Skepticism—and categorical flexibility—are impaired and ill-served if embodiment itself comes under the pall of injustice *in situ.*

We see, then, how tempting it is to try to grapple with two interwoven distinctions—misfortune and injustice, personal and public—only to wind up muddying the waters. Given the unstable and uncertain character of these demarcations, it should come as no surprise that boundary shifts in our understanding of "the political" and hence of what is public and what is private have taken place throughout the history of Western life and thought.[6] The relatively open-textured quality of politics means that innovative and revolutionary thinkers are often those who declare politics to exist where it was not thought to exist before. Should their reclassifications stick over time, the meaning of politics may be transformed. Altered social conditions may also

3. Judith Shklar, *The Faces of Injustice,* p. 54.
4. Ibid., p. 14.
5. Ibid., p. 65.
6. For a more complete version of this story, with women as an organizing theme, see Jean Bethke Elshtain, *Public Man, Private Woman: Women in Social and Political Thought.*

provoke a reassessment of old, and a recognition of new, "political" realities. In the history of Western political thought there is a range of ways that public and private realms and imperatives have been ordered, including the demand that the private world be integrated fully within, or subsumed by, an overarching public arena; the insistence that the public realm be "privatized," with politics controlled by the standards, ideals, and purposes emerging from a particular vision of private life; or, finally, a continued differentiation between the two spheres with lots of "wiggle room" on the boundaries.

Take, as a current opening example of a public/private dilemma, the technology of "bioengineering" and the arena of concern and inquiry it has spawned—"bioethics." Bioethics is deeply implicated in each of the broad theoretical areas noted above, touching on that which is apparently private, indeed, intimate—for example, a couple's decisions to turn to AID, artificial insemination by donor—but also suffused with public questions and implications. What happens to a society's view of the family and intergenerational ties if more couples resort to artificial insemination? What are the effects on the psycho-social development of donor children? What are the responsibilities of the donor father, if any, beyond the point of sperm donation for pay? Do contractual agreements suffice to "cover" not just the legal but the political and ethical implications of such agreements? Does the wider society have a legitimate interest in such "private" choices given the potential consequences of "private" agreements? My point is that we cannot "seal off" attitudes towards surrogacy contracts, in vitro fertilization, sex selection as a basis for abortion, and genetic engineering to eliminate forms of genetically inherited "imperfection" from other features of a culture. None of these bioethical dilemmas takes place in isolation, but emerges within a culture and thus makes contact with the wider contests over meaning that culture generates. This essay is not about genetic engineering, but this brief mention may help to convey just how complicated the relationship between public and private dilemmas can become.

But minimally, a *political* perspective requires that some activity called "politics" be differentiated from other activities, relationships, and patterns of action. By the political I here refer to a specific version of what is public: that which is, in principle, held and considered in common and which is, in principle, open to public scrutiny. If all conceptual boundaries are blurred and all distinctions between public and private are eliminated, then by definition no politics can exist. In practical terms, the richness and vitality of political life and of private life enhance rather than exclude each other; if they are drained, singly or together, of their normative significance, we are all impoverished.

❏

LET ME NOW MOVE directly to the central concern of this essay, a phenomenon I characterize as the *displacement of politics*. If I am correct and this displacement is a growing phenomenon, especially in North America, on the level of elite opinion and popular culture alike, it bears deep implications for how we "think" and "do" politics in the years ahead.

A politics of displacement is a dynamic that fuses public and private imperatives in a way that is both volatile and dangerous. It is most likely to occur when certain conditions prevail: (1) established institutions and rules—public and private, secular and religious—are in flux, and people have a sense that the center will not hold; (2) there are no vital and established public institutions to focus dissent and concern about important issues in an ordered way; and (3) private values, exigencies, and identities come to take complete precedence over public involvement in the secular realm as a citizen. To the extent that such conditions pertain, everything gets construed as "political" because the boundaries of politics and privacy are blurred. By extension, there is no such thing as an authentically "private" sphere. Intimate life is pervaded by politics; private life becomes a recommendation or authentication of one's political stance. It follows further that the ante gets upped in political contestation because to argue against a position is to challenge someone's "private" or personal identity. This is muddled, of course, but it seems to be where we are at—to our own peril and that of our civic descendants.

This road may be paved with good intentions. Take, for example, the feminist slogan: "The personal is political." On the one hand, this can reasonably be called a liberating move, compelling us to attend to the undeniable fact that certain political interests were hidden behind a gloss of professed concern for the sanctity of the "private" realm. Feminists argued that political and ethical values themselves were trivialized when a whole range of crucial questions having to do with women, children, and families were "privatized" and sealed off as inappropriate to political discussion and debate. To politicize the notion of "separate spheres" and the many issues embedded within this broader construction was a vital opening move. Feminists committed to ideals of civility and civic culture recognized that there were many ways to carve up the universe of debate in social and political life. Well and good.

But from the beginning there were problems latent in the assertion that "the personal is political." In its "give no quarter" form in radical feminist argumentation, any distinction between the personal and the political was utterly eroded. Note that the claim was not that the personal and political are interrelated in important and fascinating ways previously hidden by sexist ideology and practice; nor that the personal and political may be analogous to one another along certain axes of power and privilege; but that the personal *is* political. What got asserted was an identity, a collapse of the one into the other. Nothing "personal" was exempt from political definition, direction, and manipulation—neither sexual intimacy, nor love, nor parenting.

A total collapse of public and private as central categories of explanation and evaluation followed. The private sphere fell under a thoroughgoing politicized definition. Everything was grist for a voracious public mill, nothing was exempt, there was nowhere to hide. Things got nasty fast.

For if there are no distinctions between public and private, personal and political, it also follows that no differentiated activity or set of institutions that are genuinely political, that can serve as common bases of order and purpose in a political community, exist. What does exist within such a collapse of public and private is a vision of pervasive force, coercion, and manipulation: power of the crassest sort suffusing the entire social landscape, from its lowest to its loftiest points. There are few alternatives in such a world: one is either victim or victimizer, oppressor or oppressed, triumphant or abject. Politics itself, as a differentiated sphere of human activity, disappears in this yearning for a totalistic solution to all human woes, a thoroughgoing fusion of all principles.[7] The possibility that certain vital relationships are possible *only* because they are enacted against a backdrop that thrusts some activities into the full glare of public scrutiny and preserves others against such scrutiny is simply foresworn, goes unattended like an abandoned grave site.

We have, of course, long been warned that the invasion of private life and speech is one of the major tools of control in totalitarian societies. People learn to censor themselves or, growing careless, may find that conversation around a kitchen table, or in the bedroom with one's spouse, becomes the public property of the police or, worse, of the entire society. Milan Kundera, for example, tells a chilling tale. In a 1984 interview with Philip Roth, Kundera notes a "magic border" between "intimate life and public life . . . that can't be crossed with impunity." For any

> man who was the same in both public and intimate life would be a monster. He would be without spontaneity in his private life and without responsibility in his public life. For example, privately to you I can say of a friend who's done something stupid, that he's an idiot, that his ears ought to be cut off, that he should be hung upside down and a mouse stuffed in his mouth. But if the same statement were

---

7. I tell the long version of this story in chapter 5 of *Public Man, Private Woman:* "Feminism's Search for Politics."

broadcast over the radio spoken in a serious tone—and we all prefer to make such jokes in a serious tone—it would be indefensible.[8]

Kundera recalls the tragedy of a friend, the writer Jan Prochazka, whose intimate "kitchen table" talks were recorded by the state police (in pre-1989 Czechoslovakia) and assembled into a "program" broadcast on state radio. "He finds himself in a state of complete humiliation: the secret eye observes him even when he kisses his wife in the bedroom or stands in front of the toilet bowl. Such a man can only die." Prochazka did. According to Kundera, *intimate life,* a creation of European civilization "during the last 400 years," understood as "one's personal secret, as something valuable, inviolable, the basis of one's originality," is now in jeopardy—and not just from the secret police in statist societies.

Consider two examples drawn from contemporary American society, both flowing from a collapse of the personal into the political, both therefore exemplifying the pseudo-politics that flows from a politics of displacement. My first example comes from the fraught arena of "violence against women," specifically, the battered women's movement. I am not as much interested in the many explanations for why women are abused (some of them are unconvincingly universalist and ontological "men are violent" pronouncements) as in the proposed solutions. Such solutions often proffer a double agenda: a short-term soporific and a long-range total reconstruction of social life.[9] The first step is to draw attention to male battering, often neglecting the uncomfortable evidence that women are the primary abusers of children. The second, and it is a move all fair-minded persons surely endorse, is to insist that domestic violence is not just a private affair. But if you are working from a perspective that erodes any distinction between public and private, the solutions start to take on many features of political totalism.

The standard totalist case works like this: we must, as part of the interim strategy, expand the arresting powers of the police and promote the jurisprudential conviction that women are a special legal category requiring special protections and procedures. (There is something of a paradox here, of course,

---

8. Milan Kundera, "In Defense of Intimacy," an interview by Philip Roth, *Village Voice,* June 26, 1984, pp. 42-44, quotations on p. 42.

9. My reference point is one of the standard feminist works on this subject, Susan Schechter, *Women and Male Violence: The Visions and Struggles of the Battered Women's Movement,* passim. The subtitle alone—"visions and struggles"—locates the reader as one who is either with or against the project: either struggling, lagging behind, or blocking the way to the new world.

for egalitarian feminists who respect some public/private distinction challenge the whole concept of special "protection." Radical feminists, at least for certain purposes, endorse a sweeping reaffirmation of the notion.) Scant attention gets paid to the danger that enhancing police prerogatives to intervene may lead to abuse of the society's least powerful—poor blacks, Hispanics, and so on. When this is acknowledged, it is usually deemed a chance worth taking. Mandated counseling, even behavioral conditioning of violent men, coupled with compulsory punishment, are common as part of the panoply of interim proposals, along with a refusal to think about potential abuses inherent in extending therapeutic powers and responsibilities to the state as part of its policing function.

While interim programs rely heavily on the state's policing apparatus (denounced in other contexts as part of the patriarchal order), the *solution* to the problem of ending violence once and for all requires a "total restructuring of society that is feminist, antiracist, and socialist." But it is unclear whether the resulting society would be democratic or whether, indeed, there would be any politics in it at all. Presumably, some sort of state apparatus must be on hand to plan the economy, redistribute resources, and so on (given the commitment to socialism), but this is not spelled out. In the new society,

> family life would be open for community scrutiny because the family would be part of and accountable to the community. Community-based institutions could hear complaints and dispense justice, and community networks could hold individuals accountable for their behavior and offer protection to women. If a false separation did not exist between the family and the community, women might lose their sense of isolation and gain a sense of entitlement to a violence-free life.[10]

The author of this plan for eviscerating any public/private distinction goes no further in specifying how a robust communitarian world—a future perfect gemeinschaft—is to be generated out of what she portrays as our current Hobbesian battlefield. Because she assumes that "total restructuring" will produce a moral consensus, she skirts problems of coercion and control otherwise implicit in the plan for hearing complaints and "dispensing" justice with no provisions for "innocent until proven guilty" or providing the accused with a defender. With every aspect of life opened up for community inspection, she prescribes a world democrats must find singularly unattractive. Even in old-fashioned traditional communities there was room for backsliders, town

10. Ibid., p. 239.

drunks, loners, dreamers, and harmless eccentrics. In this utopia of total scrutiny, total accountability, and instant justice, the social space for difference, indifference, dissent, and refusal is squeezed out. This is the way matters stand unless or until feminists who share this theoretical orientation tell us how the ideal community of scrutiny would preserve any freedom worthy of the name.

I doubt, in fact, whether those making such proposals have really considered the implications of their arguments. For example, just thirty pages after her paean to the intrusive communities of a reconstructed future, the author of the proposal quoted above asserts unequivocally that "who women choose as emotional and sexual partners cannot be open for public scrutiny"—an embrace of the public/private distinction and the value of privacy at odds with her image of the reconstructed society.[11] There seem to be some loose theoretical threads dangling here.

My second example is taken from the intense and uncompromising arena of identity politics. Recall, again, a central characteristic of a politics of displacement: private identity takes precedence over public ends or purposes. Here, the citizen gives way before the aggrieved member of a self-defined group identity. And because the group is aggrieved, offended in a way that permits no compromise, civility—rule-governed activity that allows a pluralist society to exist and to persist over time because not everything is up for grabs and because I cannot always get everything I want—is often scornfully rejected. The assault on civility flows from the embrace of what might be called a politicized ontology of being. One dimension of this dangerous game of ontic politics is that persons are more and more judged not by what they do or say but by what they presumably *are*. And what you are is what your racial or sexual identity dictates. One's identity becomes the sole ground of politics and the sole determinant of political good and evil. Those who disagree with one's "politics," then, become enemies of one's identity.

For my example of identity politics I turn to gay liberation—by contrast to what might be called a gay agenda of equal rights that emphasizes an inclusive strategy to attain the dignity of political standing and citizenship. The starting point that gays are oppressed has led to rather different sorts of claims against the social order: either that society has no business concerning itself with the private sexual preferences of anybody, including gays; or that government *must* intrude in the area of private identity because gays require a unique sort of public protection. From the beginning of the movement for gay liberation there was tension in the claim that gays, as an oppressed class, were forced

11. Ibid., p. 271.

to call upon the very society which was oppressing them to protect their rights, if not to bring about their revolution by fully legitimating a homosexual ethos.[12]

A politics of democratic civility and equity holds that gays or any other group of citizens have a right to be protected from intrusion or harassment, as well as the right to be free from discrimination in employment, housing, and other areas. This I take as a given if a public/private distinction protecting both personal dignity and political inclusion is to be cherished and upheld. It is therefore an inescapable imperative in our constitutional system; ignoring or violating it is not merely an illegality, but an assault upon our constitutive political ethic.

But no one has a *civil right*, whether as a gay, a devotee of an exotic religion, or a political dissident, to public approval or sanction of one's activities, preferences, values, or habits. To be publicly legitimated—or "validated" in today's tedious therapeutic lexicon that makes human beings sound like parking tickets—in one's activities and values may be a political aim, but it is not a civil right. And in the quest to attain sanction for the *full* range of who one is— as a devotee of sadomasochism or a cross-dresser or whatever, the variations are nigh endless—one puts one's life on full display, one opens oneself up fully to *publicity* in ways others are bound to find quite uncivil, in part because a certain barrier—Hannah Arendt would call it the boundary of shame—is blatantly breached.

Shame or its felt experience as it surrounds our body—its functions, passions, and desires—requires appearances and symbolic forms, veils of civility that conceal some activities and aspects of ourselves even as we boldly or routinely display and reveal other sides of ourselves as we take part in public activities in the light of day for all to see. In an odd way, when one opens one's body up to publicity and when one's intimate life is put on display, one not only invites titillation and disapproval—these are not an overwhelming argument against such display, for one could, after all, slowly win approval for one's making a public "thing" out of oneself—but one invites the exploitation of one's own body to a variety of ends. Shame is central to safeguarding the freedom of the body; small wonder, then, that so many philosophers and theologians and political theorists find in shame a vital and powerful feature of our human condition that we would overturn, or invite others to overturn, at our peril. This is not to embrace any call for duplicity, disguise, or secretive withdrawal. Rather it means holding onto something that is vital for our public

12. Again, a longer version is available in Jean Bethke Elshtain, "The Paradox of Gay Liberation," *Salmagundi*, no. 58–59 (fall 1982–winter 1983): 250-80.

life as well: the privacy and possibility for solitude constitutively necessary for a rich personal life and human dignity—in order to *know* and thus to work to attain that which is self-revelatory, public, central to human solidarity and fellowship, to what is in common.[13]

Traditionally, in Western societies governed by notions of rights and the rule of law the politically and culturally "different" have embraced certain principles of civility as their best guarantee that government would not try to coerce them to concur with the majority. Militant gay liberationists, however, seek government protection and approval, not so much to prevent intrusion as to legitimate public assertion of private behavior in a manner that goes well beyond the norms of civility. The end point of these claims against society requires public remedies—and disclosures called "outing" that those committed to civility oppose—which might well have the practical result of strengthening the ethos of a society of scrutiny: nothing is exempt, if not from one's "enemies" then, ironically, from one's ostensible friends and allies. The demand for public "validation" of sexual preferences, by ignoring the distinction between the personal and political, threatens to erode authentic civil rights.

What follows from this version of "the personal is political" is the presumption that being gay *in itself* is a political act, condition, statement, or claim. Hence the early argument that gays "do not get validated by our participation in anti-war marches": only the eruption of the personal-political "is a total revolutionary movement."[14] Politics is an "eruption of radical feelings."[15] Such notions die hard in a therapeutic culture like our own, where personal authenticity becomes the test of political credibility. One can cure one's personal ills only through political rebellion based on sexual identity. The sorts of demands that issue from such politics go far beyond a quest for social and economic justice; nothing less than personal happiness, sexual gratification, and pleasure is claimed as a *political* right. The cause of justice and the pursuit of pleasure are conflated.

The demands of such a politics upon gays themselves are extreme, for every aspect of their lives must serve as a political statement and force. There is good reason to be skeptical, even queasy, about all this. For in addition to the erosion of any distinction between public and private spheres, this version of identity absolutism shares with other modes of twentieth-century expressivist politics a celebration of "feelings" or "private authenticity" as an alterna-

13. See the provocative discussion by Dietrich Bonhoeffer in his *Ethics*.

14. Karla Jay and Allen Young, eds., *Out of the Closets: Voices of Gay Liberation*, pp. 24–25.

15. The 26 to 6 Baking and Trucking Society, *Great Gay in the Morning*, p. 8. One unanswered question is why the eruption of "feelings" will necessarily cut one's own way.

tive to public reason and political judgment. The imperative that political acts must, in principle, be subject to a particular kind of public scrutiny and debate becomes a fuzzy nicety, readily discarded, if politics begins with eruptions of feelings and consists in direct reactions to such experiences.

Where is the check on overpersonalization? There is none. Each expression of personal feelings is accepted as valid (*if* it comes from the "liberated"), and politics, in turn, simply reflects and refracts those feelings. The writer or activist hopes to forge a connection between quivering psyches. It is perhaps useful at such a juncture to remind those embracing a world without a public/private distinction that the actual world is much wider, deeper, and more mysterious than a wholesale mapping of the subjective self onto the world allows. It is filled with intractable stuff, concrete entities and stubborn realities, veils as well as mirrors, all sorts of people with deeply ingrained predispositions, structures of power and authority that both constrain and enable—much more in heaven and earth, in other words, than is dreamt of in the illusion that expressing the authentic self, taken neat, constitutes a politics. To project one's urges and rages directly onto the world is to eradicate altogether a prime requisite of politics—the need for judgment based on criteria which are public in nature.

When utopians of any stripe assault the idea of a political standing, in and through an ideal of citizenship, which is not reducible to the terms of one's private existence, they promote the abolition of politics and its replacement either by administration or by a fantasy of a wholly transparent community in which all that divides us has been eliminated—or, alternatively, in which our divisions are made perfectly manifest, are "beyond compromise." At the height of the 1960s Civil Rights movement, Martin Luther King declared: "We're not asking you to love us. We're just asking you to get off our backs." That is a perfect summary of Isaiah Berlin's principle of "negative liberty" and of the difference between private and public demands, as well as an endorsement of what might be called *practical* by contrast to utopian or totalist politics.

In a world of practical politics, blacks and whites, men and women, gays and straights can come together around sets of concrete concerns. Temporary alliances are formed, depending on the issues; but the assumption is never that things will automatically divide by identity. There is no way to arrive at fully shared common understanding, or intimacy writ large. But there are, and there *must* be within a world of democratic politics, ways for people who differ in important, not trivial ways, to come together to "do" practical politics in a shared public arena. For this to be possible, we must recognize that public action and private intimacy have different requirements. As Harry Boyte writes:

The concept of public arena reintroduces a distinction between public life and private experience that modern therapeutic language ("shared feelings"; "self-esteem") and protest language (where every issue becomes the occasion for a Manichean division between good and evil) both obscure. Such a distinction is based not on the classic republican ideal of civic virtue detached from private interests. It grows instead from recognition that although people's self-interests lead them to public action, the best principles of action in public are different from those in private. Moreover, through productive, practical politics one's interests can broaden. In public we can learn to work with people with whom we disagree sharply and do not want to live "in community."[16]

When I was in graduate school in the late 1960s, it was in vogue to mock the warnings of Berlin about the dangers inherent in many visions of "positive liberty," turning as they did on naive views of human perfectibility and, it followed, sentimental views of politics. Berlin was accused of being a "liberal sell-out," a faint-hearted compromiser; and any distinction between private and public was accused of being timid and ideologically mystifying. But compromise, not as a mediocre way to do politics, but as the *only* way to do *democratic* politics, is itself an adventure. It lacks the panache of revolutionary violence. It might not stir the blood in the way a "nonnegotiable demand" does. But it presages a livable future. Berlin also reminds us that a "sharp division between public and private life, or politics and morality, never works well. Too many territories have been claimed by both." But to collapse public and private altogether in the search for total harmony or total justice is an even worse prospect, for

> the best that one can do is to try to promote some kind of equilibrium, necessarily unstable, between the different operations of different groups of human beings—at the very least to prevent them from attempting to exterminate one another, and, so far as possible, to prevent them from hurting each other—and to promote the maximum practicable degree of sympathy and understanding, never likely to be complete between them.[17]

This, then, is a plea for practical politics within a polity characterized by civility but not indifferent to the possibility of achieving provisional and ephemeral moments of civic virtue.[18]

16. Harry Boyte, "Redefining Politics, Part II," *Responsive Community* 3, no. 2 (spring 1993): 87.

17. Isaiah Berlin, *The Crooked Timber of Humanity,* pp. 32, 47.

18. For a more extended presentation of my own arguments for this kind of democratic politics, see Jean Bethke Elshtain, *Democracy on Trial.*

We live in an era when we are not well served by the old political categories as we witness, to our astonishment, the political realities of a half-century crumple and give way. The drama of democracy, of conflict and compromise, turns on our capacity for making distinctions and offering up judgments. It turns on our recognition that the rules of conduct which flow out of private relationships—intimacy, fidelity, self-disclosure—are not altogether transferrable to public relationships where different criteria, including the capacity for provisional alliances—no permanent enemies; no permanent friends—are required. We need to remind ourselves and teach our children what it means to be held accountable to the diverse and various rules of public life by contrast to private relationships if we are to avoid a disastrous overfamilializing of politics. To engage in politics is to be called out; to go beyond; to enter the unfamiliar.

Every social and political theory encompasses some ideal of a preferred way of life. Although there are a handful of contemporary theorists of the postmodern or deconstructive school who disdain any and all normative standards, the vast majority of social and political thinkers, past and present, insist that no way of life can persist without a deeply, widely, if somewhat roughly shared cluster of basic notions. Those of us who locate ethical concerns at the heart of our political theories should hope for a world in which both private and public lives bear their own intrinsic dignity and purpose and are allowed to flourish.

A richly complex private sphere requires some freedom from all-encompassing public imperatives to survive. But in order to flourish, the public world itself must nurture and sustain a set of ethical imperatives that include a commitment to preserve, protect, and defend human beings in their capacities as private persons, *as well as* to encourage and enable men and women alike to partake in the practical activity of politics. Such an ideal seeks to keep alive rather than to eliminate tensions between diverse spheres and competing values and purposes. There is always a danger that an overweening polity will swamp the individual, as well as a peril that life in a polity confronted with a continuing crisis of identity may decivilize both those who oppose it and those who would defend it. There is, then, no definitive answer. But here is a usable slogan: Public and private, *sic et non*. Only in the space opened up by the ongoing choreography of these categories can politics exist—or at least any politics that deserves to be called democratic.

R EFERENCES

Berlin, Isaiah. 1992. *The Crooked Timber of Humanity.* New York: Vintage.
Bonhoeffer, Dietrich. 1965. *Ethics.* New York: Macmillan.

Boyte, Harry. 1992. "Redefining Politics, Part II." *Responsive Community* 3, no. 2 (spring): 83–89.

Elshtain, Jean Bethke. 1982–83. "The Paradox of Gay Liberation." *Salmagundi,* no. 58–59 (fall–winter): 250-80.

———. 1993. *Public Man, Private Woman: Women in Social and Political Thought.* Princeton, NJ: Princeton University Press, 1981. Second edition with new epilogue published in 1993.

———. 1995. *Democracy on Trial.* New York: Basic Books.

Fay, Brian. 1975. *Social Theory and Political Practice.* London: Allen & Unwin.

Jay, Karla, and Allen Young, eds. 1972. *Out of the Closets: Voices of Gay Liberation.* New York: Douglas Books, 1972.

Kundera, Milan. 1984. "In Defense of Intimacy." Interview by Philip Roth. *Village Voice,* June 26, pp 42–44.

Luther, Martin. 1961. *Martin Luther: Selections from His Writings.* Edited by John Dillenberger. Garden City, NY: Doubleday Anchor.

Schechter, Susan. *Women and Male Violence: The Visions and Struggles of the Battered Women's Movement.* Boston: South End Press, 1982.

Shklar, Judith. *The Faces of Injustice.* New Haven, CT: Yale University Press, 1990.

The 26 to 6 Baking and Trucking Society. 1972. *Great Gay in the Morning.* Washington, NJ: Times Change Press.

Public and Private in Theory and Practice:
Some Implications of an Uncertain Boundary

Alan Wolfe

A Misleading but Necessary Division

THE THEMES OF THIS ESSAY can be summarized in three propositions. First, the distinction between the public and the private, as other contributors to this volume have emphasized, is a slippery one, incapable of being established in a way that accords either with an adequate empirical description of the major institutions of modern society or with satisfactory normative justifications.[1] Second, despite this inadequacy, some forms of the public/private distinction are nonetheless necessary both to understand and to improve society. Third, because we need to draw distinctions between public and private, but also cannot accept any sharp and consistent way of doing so, we are best off if we give up the effort to force all moral, political, and theoretical issues into a dichotomous public/private framework; rather, we should recognize the existence of a third realm of social life, intermediate between public and private, that can resemble either in particular instances, but that also can be equated with neither.

Public and Private in Contemporary Social Theory

SOCIOLOGISTS, WHO BOTH TRY to understand and (often) to make normative judgments about society, have long understood that some forms of social behavior ought to (and do) take place under the full gaze of others, while other forms of social behavior take place in relative isolation, properly screened from the observation and judgment of others. The two contemporary thinkers who best illustrate the significance of emphasizing one or the other are Erving Goffman and Jürgen Habermas. Both recognize that there is, and ought to be, a distinction between public and private. But each has a clear preference for which is real and which is inauthentic.

Goffman, who speaks for a tradition of sociological realism and inside-dopesterism, leaves the impression that the "real" reality is always offstage and behind closed doors. Indeed, the door may be the most important of all of

1. See, in particular, the introductory essay by Jeff Weintraub in this volume.

Goffman's images. Imagine, he asks us, the frustration of the gas station mechanic who is forced by the spatial design of his service station to work on cars directly in front of their owners, with no door behind which he can retreat.[2] For Goffman, the area behind the door allows people to let off steam:

> The backstage language consists of reciprocal first-naming, cooperative decision-making, profanity, open sexual remarks, elaborate griping, smoking, rough informal dress, "sloppy" sitting and standing posture, use of dialect or sub-standard speech, mumbling and shouting, playful aggression and "kidding," inconsiderateness for the other in minor but potentially symbolic acts, minor physical self-involvements such as humming, whistling, chewing, nibbling, belching, and flatulence.[3]

It is hard not to conclude from Goffman's occasionally cynical tone and language that he views human nature in non-Rousseauian terms. People have to be accepted as they are, warts and all. To the degree that back regions allow people to "regress," they are serving an important sociological function. And because they are, no account of modern society will ever be adequate unless it allows room for private spaces in which individuals can simply be themselves.

Goffman is not an explicitly normative thinker, but the implication runs through his work that if something is functionally necessary, it is also serving an important moral and ethical purpose. Just as he points out how many of our biological functions take place in private,[4] he seems to suggest that some of our most important social functions are and ought to be private as well. It is not that Goffman has little regard for public encounters; his writings demonstrate in fine detail how rituals of performance smooth out the potential awkwardness of interaction, making social life possible. But Goffman tends to worry more about the abuses of enforced publicity than about the irregularities of private conduct. This is most apparent in his reflections on total institutions—worlds without doors—for his concern is that too much public exposure can result in both unchecked public authority and private degradation. Asylums, by eliminating backstage regions, become for Goffman a metaphor of the totalitarian potentialities of inescapable visibility. However unflattering we may sometimes appear (even to ourselves) in private, it is precisely such behaviors which demand protection against institutionalist (and reformist) inclinations.

2. Erving Goffman, *The Presentation of Self in Everyday Life*, p. 115.
3. Ibid., p. 128.
4. Goffman's most "biological" account is in *Relations in Public: Microstudies of the Public Order.*

Even the far less threatening public encounters of everyday life are sometimes treated by Goffman as potentially full of traps. Individuals in frontstage regions are "on guard," monitoring their own performances so as not to give off wrong impressions. The constraints of being in public are enormous, because performances are rarely natural and spontaneous. The great terror of being in public is that, in spite of all one's efforts to control the presentation of self, one can still slip. We can never be fully in charge of all the impressions we give off, no matter how carefully we try to monitor them. The public realm, in Goffman's account, is treacherous turf. Unless we have frequent opportunity to retire backstage and collect ourselves, we are certain to stand exposed in public at some point, revealed as something other than what we have tried, with such determined work, to construct about who we are. The fact that action in public is dramaturgical does not mean that the public sphere is impoverished; Goffman appreciates a good performance as much as anyone. But Goffman's tone nonetheless manages to convey a sense that authenticity, if it is ever to be found in modern society, is more likely to be found in the shadows than in the sunlight.

This priority of private over public is reversed in the thought of Jürgen Habermas. Habermas's thought, like Goffman's, is subtle and has shifted in emphasis over the course of a long concern with these matters. Nonetheless, even at the risk of simplification, one can say that certain clear themes emerge in his work that reveal a preference for the public world over the private. There might once have been a kind of positive feedback between the two; but with the rise of "organized capitalism" and modern mass society, the private, or intimate, spheres of society lose their authentic character. The family, for example, is now private in appearance only: "The shrinking of the private sphere into the inner areas of a conjugal family largely relieved of function and weakened in authority—the quiet bliss of homeyness—provided only the illusion of a perfectly private sphere." [5] Indeed, the realm of the family "has started to dissolve into a sphere of pseudo-privacy." [6] At the same time that privacy has become illusory, so has publicity, at least as understood by eighteenth-century intellectuals. Cultural consumption creates a "pseudo-public or sham-private world," the audience has been "turned into a travesty," and "the world fashioned by the mass media is a public sphere in appearance

5. Jürgen Habermas, *The Structural Transformation of the Public Sphere: An Inquiry into a Category of Bourgeois Society,* translated by Thomas Burger (Cambridge, MA: MIT Press, 1989; originally published in German in 1962), p. 159.

6. Ibid., p. 157.

only."[7] The structural transformations brought about by modern capitalism turn both the private and the public into hollow shells of what they were at the height of bourgeois culture.

Even though both realms thus tend to be inauthentic, Habermas strives to breathe life back into only one of them. The most consistent theme in his oeuvre is the need to carve out and protect a public space in which rational communication and critical discourse can take place. Habermas devotes little attention to the modern private world, even as a precondition for a healthy public one. The private sphere, to be sure, is colonized by the invasive force of the market, just as the public sphere is taken over by the administrative logic of the state. We are meant to lament the passing of a world in which individuals could be more autonomous and self-directed by looking within themselves for their authenticity. But even this conception of privacy, with its Weberian overtones of this-worldly asceticism, has little to say to modern individuals who seek to turn away from the public to find themselves alone with family and friends.[8] Privacy, which was once a good, has under conditions of modernity been transformed into "privatism," which, all things considered, is a bad.

Habermas not only distinguishes normatively between the private and the public; he also redefines them, especially the public sphere, in ways that express a concern for the conditions of democratic citizenship and rational deliberation that is largely absent from Goffman. Habermas's treatment of publicity, unlike Goffman's, is not primarily concerned with visibility, but with openness of deliberation and judgment; life in Goffman's total institution is entirely visible (and in that sense public) but is not marked by rational discussion and accountability (which, by Habermas's definition, renders it not public). Thus, Goffman and Habermas differ over the normative value of public and private in part because they differ over how they understand public and private. Goffman's preference for backstage regions, and his analysis of interaction ritual in the frontstage, often simply disregard the questions of citizenship and its requirements so central to Habermas.

Yet Goffman also offers something which Habermas tends to miss. Precisely because rational deliberation is so central to our public role as citizens, too great an emphasis upon it works to the neglect of things we do with no

7. Ibid., pp. 160, 161, 171. Habermas uses the terms "manufactured" and "manipulated" with respect to the public sphere in many places: see pp. 219, 222, 232, 236, and 247.

8. Jürgen Habermas, *Lifeworld and System: A Critique of Functionalist Reason,* vol. 2 of *The Theory of Communicative Action* (Boston: Beacon Press, 1987), pp. 323–26.

particular collective purpose in mind. When he examines the kinds of "public" interaction to which Goffman pays so much attention, Habermas contrasts the requirements of rational communication with the requirements for performance or dramaturgical action, only to find the latter wanting. Communication in Habermas's sense involves cognition, justifiable beliefs, and explicit intentions, whereas performance involves emotions and subjective feelings. Even more important, the kind of action that assumes public stages behind which individuals are "really" themselves involves deception rather than truthtelling; far from seeking rational consensus, "dramaturgical action can take on latently strategic qualities to the degree that the actor treats his audience as opponents rather than as a public."[9] In Habermas's view, it is certainly the case that people act strategically, but they can do so constructively only if a larger public world against which their actions can be judged is assumed. It is, finally, claims to truth that establish the possibility of impression management, not the ability to manage impressions backstage that constitute the precondition for public performance.

Both Goffman and Habermas are valuable social thinkers. Each gives particular weight to one side or the other of the public/private distinction, reminding us, in the process, that both are central to the human condition. Yet each, in stressing one side or the other of the dichotomy, seems to miss something important as well. As a social scientist interested in describing how humans act, Goffman often glosses over the ways in which private and public selves reinforce each other. Some backstage regions are (quasi-) public as well as private; Goffman's backstage men, griping, joking, being vulgar, are doing so *with each other;* theirs is a social world, if not fully a public one, with its own forms of performance and ritual. Moreover, we often retreat to the back of the stage in part to be a more effective performer frontstage; we are "getting our act together," not because our internal self demands it, but because social life requires it. And there is, finally, no such thing as a "total" institution; even Goffman's asylums take control of people's bodies, not necessarily their minds. Rebellions within "total institutions" are not unknown; when they occur, we discover that such institutions were not quite so "total," after all, as their public faces implied.

Nor does Goffman's occasional attempt to establish moral supremacy for the private always convince. Leave alone, for the moment, the fact that sometimes we might need asylums, that individuals can be so self-destructive that they require supervision and care. Privacy in itself is morally ambiguous. Indi-

---

9. Jürgen Habermas, *Reason and the Rationalization of Society,* vol. 1 of *The Theory of Communicative Action* (London: Heinemann, 1984), p. 93.

viduals can use private spaces to develop their character, demean others, plan rebellions, collect stamps, masturbate, read Tolstoy, watch television, or do nothing. Any effort to address the moral benefits (and costs) of privacy involves the question of privacy for what—precisely the kind of question that Goffman, with his relative neglect of Habermasian questions of moral and civic discourse, is ill-prepared to address. Privacy, in short, is in many ways a *public* good. No society can effectively accord a moral value to privacy without encouraging and protecting collective action: either in the smaller-scale social groups which figure out what they really want, or in the larger institutions of law and democratic citizenship which, à la Habermas, enable a society to make legitimate distinctions between what it values and what it condemns.

Correspondingly, Habermas's concentration on rational discourse justified by publicly available standards fails certain empirical and normative tests. Very few actual speech situations are "ideal," and interaction in the public sphere rarely conforms to the requirements of purely "rational-critical discourse." Habermas knows this, of course: these models are explicitly offered as counterfactual normative standards. But while it is important for a moral philosopher to set a standard, it is also important for a sociologist to recognize why people frequently fail to meet it. Nor is it clear that we should always meet Habermas's standard even if we could. If we always need to provide rational grounds in defense of what we do, we lose the ability ever to escape from the tyranny of good intentions and consequences. Perfect Habermasian communicators may fear giving in to their rages, irrational urges, and prejudices, even when no one else is around. If they do, they lose a part of their humanity, for surely part of being human is accepting imperfections along with a desire to improve and better the moral community. Even democratically arrived at decisions, which epitomize the arena where we most value deliberation and rationally determined consensus, are not always the best decisions. Politics, including democratic politics, has often been well served by jerry-built compromises hammered out by hard-nosed politicians more interested in striking a deal—one, moreover, usually determined by the "private" interests they serve—than in reaching a justifiable conclusion. Habermas's model of public discourse guided by rational and universalizable standards lacks a certain realism, a feel for the nitty-gritty of actual social interactions—including the very features so emphasized by Goffman.

Boundaries are the stuff of sociology,[10] and in modern societies no boundary seems quite as important, yet quite as porous and ambiguous, as the one

10. On the importance of boundaries for social life, see Eviatar Zerubavel, *The Fine Line: Making Distinctions in Everyday Life;* and Michèle Lamont and Marcel Fournier, eds., *Cultivating Differences: Symbolic Boundaries and the Making of Inequality.*

between private and public. Modern individuals require both a realm of private self-expression and intimacy buffered from the larger world of politics and a sense of belonging to a larger community that expresses obligations to all its members, even if they are strangers. In an essay devoted to themes similar to the ones being developed here, Richard Rorty does not discuss Goffman, but contrasts Habermas's work with that of Foucault, emphasizing that "Foucault is an ironist who is unwilling to be a liberal, while Jürgen Habermas is a liberal who is unwilling to be an ironist." [11] One does not have to be a liberal ironist to recognize that the world will be a richer place if people can both live in Goffman's backstage territory and still come forward to Habermas's frontstage to work out their common lives by commonly agreed to, even rational, standards. We cannot take care of our public business without recognizing that we have private selves, and we cannot appreciate a private self unless we understand ourselves as public creatures. Neither Goffman nor Habermas makes a completely convincing case for either the private or the public, which suggests that, as difficult as it may be to justify one or the other, both are essential to the way we live now—and to each other as well.

PUBLIC AND PRIVATE IN CONTEMPORARY POLITICAL PRACTICE

IF THE TREATMENT of the public/private distinction in theory is not always satisfactory or free of confusion, neither is its use in practice. The level of confusion is increased by the fact that the lines along which left and right have historically divided on these issues seem to be in a complicated process of transition, if not disorientation. A pattern that was consolidated in response to the twin experiences of depression and global war, and that endured for most of the past half century, led the left to worry primarily about excessive privatism and to argue for a greater role for public policy, while the right has emphasized a defense of private decisions—both familial and economic. (The exceptions, cases where the left preferred privacy or protections against public authority, while the right took opposite positions, will be discussed shortly.) Recent events suggest that these affinities may be changing, with important implications for how we ought to think about the moral and political significance of the private and the public.

The most obvious reason for the left's preference for the public was its hostility to private property and the concentrations of private power it generates—even though, at an earlier historical conjuncture, the liberation of private property was understood as a progressive doctrine. A second source was

11. Richard Rorty, *Contingency, Irony, and Solidarity,* p. 61.

the left's preference for cosmopolitanism and universalism; to remain in private, from such a perspective, was to prefer the parochial, the local, and the premodern to the complex and the distant.[12] Third, left movements believed, in general, that matters carried out in secret were illegitimate; no better example could be found than the war in Vietnam, which, because of the way it was carried out, naturally encouraged a faith in publicity. A fourth source of the left's uneasiness with privacy was the feminist movement, which understood the "private" family as artificial and based on the exploitation of women; questioning the ideology of the public/private distinction became one of the core intellectual agendas of contemporary feminism.[13] Fifth, affairs in public were generally understood to be more democratic, more accountable, and more subject to equitable rules than affairs in private; to accept a large role for the private realm, in that sense, seemed to justify inequality and undemocratic practices.

These "natural" affinities between the left and the public sphere are, needless to say, the reverse of the right's preference for the private sphere. At least since the New Deal, when planning and centralized management became the hallmarks of economic policy, conservative movements, particularly in the United States, shared a Hayekian suspicion of centralized power. The trouble with the public sector, this point of view holds, is that society is so complex that no comprehensive public authority can guide all acts to their appropriate destination. Under such circumstances, we are far better off allowing private individuals to make private decisions, especially if we have faith that markets can guide those decisions toward an unplanned, but nonetheless harmonious, equilibrium.[14] As in economics, so in politics. State and local governments, which are less "public" than the national government, ought to be preferred when government is necessary. Parents, not bureaucrats, should determine which schools their children ought to attend.[15] The best society is the one that allows the freest scope for the maximum number of private choices.

Although left and right still usually find themselves lined up on different sides of the public/private distinction, the rise of cultural and identity politics

12. For one example, see Lawrence Kohlberg, "The Future of Liberalism as the Dominant Ideology of the West," in Richard W. Wilson and Gordon J. Schochet's edited volume, *Moral Development and Politics,* pp. 55–68.

13. See the essays in Michelle Zimbalist Rosaldo and Louise Lamphere, eds., *Woman, Culture, and Society,* and Rayna Reiter, ed., *Toward an Anthropology of Women.* The pitfalls and advantages of this way of thinking are treated with greatly subtlety in Jean Bethke Elshtain, *Public Man, Private Woman: Women in Social and Political Thought.*

14. A recent, cogently argued, defense of this way of thinking is Richard Epstein, *Forbidden Grounds: The Case against Employment Discrimination Laws.*

15. See John E. Chubb and Terry M. Moe, *Politics, Markets, and America's Schools.*

has changed the affinities just described. Conservatives favor private decisions, but not (at least most of them) a women's right to have an abortion. They are generally unsympathetic to the idea of treating religion as a matter of purely "private" belief, preferring more public manifestations of a common faith. No one, many conservatives believe, should be "free" to have children at the age of fourteen, especially if they expect government help. When it comes to moral and cultural issues, many conservatives drop Hayek; planning, intervention, and reliance on governmental incentives to encourage the "right" kinds of behavior are favored over laissez-faire.[16]

As conservatives swing one way, leftists swing the other—or, rather, they seem to be swinging several ways at once. Although the left has long stood for a preference for the public over the private in matters of economic and social policy, it also privileged the private in matters of conscience and free speech. The left's increasing focus on issues of the second kind, epitomized by its overwhelming support for a "pro-choice" position on abortion, might seem to indicate that it is now building on the exception rather than the rule. But this limited preference for the private is also changing under the impact of identity politics. The right to privacy, enshrined as a liberal goal since first articulated by Louis Brandeis,[17] does not, many on the left believe, include the right to buy a house in a particular neighborhood or to send one's children to a private school if the effect is to perpetuate racial segregation;[18] the right to vote on the basis of race;[19] the right to enjoy pornography (if one is a male);[20] or the right to harbor hateful thoughts about the powerless and oppressed.[21] It might be argued that these acts are not truly private, since they can affect others; but that criterion, pursued far enough, could eliminate the category of the private altogether. The inconsistency, if it was an inconsistency, between state intervention into the economy, which the left favored, and state

16. Not all conservatives do. One who expresses skepticism about governmental regulation of sexuality, for example, is Richard Posner, *Sex and Reason.*

17. For a recent indication of this commitment, see Ellen Alderman and Caroline Kennedy, *The Right to Privacy.*

18. Charles R. Lawrence III, "If He Hollers Let Him Go: Regulating Racist Speech on Campus," in Mari J. Matsuda, Charles R. Lawrence III, Richard Delgado, and Kimberlè Williams Crenshaw, *Words That Wound: Critical Race Theory, Assaultive Speech, and the First Amendment*, p. 63.

19. Lani Guinier, *The Tyranny of the Majority: Fundamental Fairness in Representative Democracy*, pp. 124–27.

20. See Andrea Dworkin, *Pornography: Men Possessing Women;* and Catharine A. MacKinnon, *Only Words.*

21. Mari Matsuda, "Public Response to Racist Speech: Considering the Victim's Story," in Matsuda et al., *Words That Wound*, p. 18.

intervention into matters of thought, which the left opposed, may be fading. As Cass Sunstein has argued, "The notion of laissez-faire is no less a myth— a conceptual error—for speech than it is for property." [22] We therefore ought to have a "New Deal" for free speech, one which views government as capable of protecting speech as much as it can threaten it.

The point of these comments is not to accuse either the right or the left of opportunism or sloppy thinking, although I do think that both sides often need to make a more compelling case why the line between private and public should be drawn in one place on some issues and somewhere else on others. Such changes, rather, can be taken as further indications of why it is so difficult to pinpoint exactly where the public ends and the private begins. It is not so much the case that the right and left have switched sides on the public/private distinction, although in some ways they have; what is more important is that the distinction itself shifts as political activists try to apply it to relatively new areas of public policy. When that happens, the results drive home the limitations of relying on the public/private distinction to provide clear answers to our moral and political dilemmas.

Consider the case of the family. However one defines the boundary between public and private, family life has generally been considered to have a special claim to be sheltered from public scrutiny and control. The first significant case to expound a constitutional right to privacy, *Griswold v. Connecticut,* pointed to the marital bedroom as a place into which the state should not peek.[23] *Griswold,* in turn, was built upon by the majority in *Roe v. Wade,* which found in the right to privacy reasons to protect women against government interference with their right to have an abortion.[24] Yet as feminism became a political force in the 1970s and 1980s, some women began to agree with the notion that "for women, the private is the distinct sphere of intimate violation and abuse, neither free nor particularly personal." [25] Awful things can take place within bedrooms—rape and child abuse, for example—and it would be an odd political position for those on the left to claim that the state had no claims to intervene when such abuses occurred because commitment to the defense of privacy prevented it. Many writers believe that privacy was the wrong basis for *Roe;* it would have been better to uphold a woman's right

22. Cass R. Sunstein, *Democracy and the Problem of Free Speech,* p. 41.

23. 381 U.S. 479 (1965). Those in favor of abolishing Connecticut's regulations on birth control tended to be upper-class Republican women, while those against tended to be working-class Catholic Democrats. See David J. Garrow, *Liberty and Sexuality: The Right to Privacy and the Making of Roe v. Wade.*

24. 410 U.S. 113 (1973).

25. Catharine A. MacKinnon, *Toward a Feminist Theory of the State,* p. 168.

to abortion on the basis of the equal protection clause of the Fourteenth Amendment, the general notion of personal autonomy, or even the antislavery amendments to the U.S. Constitution.[26]

Whatever position one takes on the priority to be assigned to privacy and autonomy, so long as issues of this sort are framed simply as a choice between privacy on the one hand and public scrutiny, symbolized by the state, on the other, we are unlikely to find satisfactory legal or normative principles. For what is really at stake in this debate are internal conflicts within one of these realms rather than a straightforward conflict between private and public: some people want to protect the privacy and autonomy of *individuals* who happen to live in families, while others uphold the privacy and autonomy of the *family* as a unit.[27] If the family stands in the private realm, in short, it contains its own internal version of the public/private distinction: either the family is a (usually temporary) association of private individuals, a position sympathetic to most versions of feminism, or it is a quasi-public society with its own rules and sanctions, a position generally favored by conservatives. In this sense, both the left and the right could plausibly claim to be protecting privacy and the private realm against unwarranted public intrusion; what differentiates them is the way they conceive the private realm, and especially their understanding of the moral status of the family as a "private" institution.

Similar issues arise over hate speech and pornography. Freedom of expression has long been a goal of the left, which, far more than the right, has elevated the right of an individual to read, see, and do what he or she likes to near-absolute status. It therefore seems like a contradiction in principle for individuals on the left to support university speech codes or to join with conservatives in seeking to regulate pornographic expression. (In a similar way, conservatives rarely known as strong supporters of academic freedom rely on this quintessentially liberal notion in their opposition to university speech codes.) But, as with the family, the question of whether support for regulation of speech constitutes a shift from one side to the other of the public/private

26. Ruth Bader Ginsberg, "Some Thoughts on Autonomy and Equality in Relation to *Roe v. Wade*," pp. 375–86; Kathryn H. Snedaker, "Reconsidering *Roe v. Wade:* Equal Protection Analysis as an Alternative Approach," pp. 115–37; and Andrew Koppelman, "Forced Labor: A Thirteenth Amendment Defense of Abortion," pp. 480–535. See also the essay by Jean Cohen in this volume, "Rethinking Privacy: Autonomy, Identity, and the Abortion Controversy."

27. As Cohen points out in her contribution to this volume, the key shift was marked by *Eisenstadt v. Baird*, 405 U.S. 453 (1972): "If the right to privacy means anything, it is the right of the *individual*, married or single, to be free from unwarranted governmental intrusion into matters so fundamentally affecting a person as the decision whether to bear or beget a child" (quoted by Cohen in "Rethinking Privacy," above, p. 145).

distinction has no clear answer, for, once again, the distinction itself moves just as much as do left and right.

The traditional conservative argument in favor of regulating pornography holds that offensive material should not violate community standards of appropriate conduct. The "community" in this sense becomes a stand-in for the "public": when private action violates public sensibility, the latter must trump the former. The feminist argument against pornography, by contrast, is not that it offends the standards of an entire community, but that it is harmful to a specific group, women, just as the case in favor of speech codes is based on the idea that they seek to protect not everyone, but only those against whom racism or discrimination has been practiced.[28] Neither women nor blacks constitute a "public" in the sense that the entire community is public. This is both a strength and a weakness for those arguing in favor of regulation of pornography and hate speech. The strength is that they are not necessarily calling for censorship in an abstract sense; the harm they identify, being limited and particular, ought to be remediable through less drastic remedies than complete suppression. But the weakness of their case turns on the same point: because the harm is less community-wide, there is less of a compelling reason for everyone to join together in calling for a ban on the offensive speech or images. The semipublic, semiprivate nature of identity groups colors both sides on the issue. Those generally opposed to regulations on pornography or hate speech conceive of people as individuals first and members of identity groups second. Those in favor of such regulations believe that the quasi-public character of such groups takes priority over the private interests of the individuals who compose them.

One final example of the way the boundary between public and private shifts in political debate involves appropriate responses to the AIDS epidemic. It now seems axiomatic that gays and others against whom discrimination has been common should support efforts to protect against invasions of privacy associated with testing, notification, record-keeping, and hospitalization, a position that reached as far as keeping results of AIDS testing of infants secret from their own mothers.[29] But this represents something of a historic transformation for American liberals, who, earlier in this century, understood compulsory vaccination, tuberculosis testing, and other such measures as essential to progress and equality. In the shift of language associated with the politics of this disease, officials who wanted to take strong measures to protect the "public" health were castigated as homophobic if such actions interfered with the

28. Matsuda, "Public Response," p. 36: "Hateful verbal attacks upon dominant-group members by victims is [*sic*] permissible."

29. Elinor Burkett, *The Gravest Show on Earth: America in the Age of AIDS*, p. 237.

rights of gays to keep their sexual preference private.[30] The conflict between public health and private action, many gay activists maintained, had to be resolved in favor of the latter, for homosexuals had won, and could not afford to lose, "our right to do with our own bodies as we choose."[31]

But once again this insistence on the priority of the private over the public left unclear exactly what kind of acts and institutions were in fact private. Sexual acts, after all, usually take place between two (or more) individuals and in that sense are anything but private—if by that term we mean "what is individual, or pertains only to an individual."[32] Furthermore, the results of these sexual encounters generally affected third parties—and fourth, fifth, ad infinitum—in the long run. But one special conundrum was brought out by the politics of AIDS when what was at stake was not sex per se but, for example, sex in bathhouses. Bathhouses are commercial institutions—but does that make them private or public? "If people want to continue dangerous sex in the privacy of their homes—so be it, that is their right," said one gay activist, Larry Littlejohn. "They are foolish to do so. However, bathhouses and public places. They are licensed by the city; they are the proper subject of public policy considerations."[33] But this was decidedly a minority position in the San Francisco gay community in the early years of the AIDS epidemic. Far more common was a position which held that since sex was by definition an intimate act, then it was sex itself which constituted the private realm, not the place in which sex took place. Bathhouses were in that sense no different from the marital bedrooms protected by *Griswold*. According to papers filed in a San Francisco controversy over whether the bathhouses should be closed,

> There is simply no legal basis to distinguish the right to engage in consensual sexual activity in defendants' premises from the right to engage in consensual sexual activity in hotels or private homes. [There is] no difference between someone who rents a cubicle in a bathhouse and someone who makes a mortgage payment on his house.[34]

30. See Stephen C. Joseph, *Dragon within the Gates: The Once and Future AIDS Epidemic.*

31. From an editorial in the *Bay Area Reporter,* as cited by Ronald Bayer, *Private Acts, Social Consequences: AIDS and the Politics of Public Health,* p. 36.

32. See Weintraub, "The Theory and Politics of the Public/Private Distinction," p. 5 of this volume.

33. Bayer, *Private Acts,* p. 34. Of course, the Supreme Court did not extend to homosexuals the right to practice "sodomy" in the privacy of their own bedrooms: *Bowers v. Hardwick,* 478 U.S. 186 (1986).

34. Bayer, *Private Acts,* p. 50.

The battle over the bathhouses once again reveals how the line between private and public—as well as the line between left and right—can shift in surprising ways. At the start of the twentieth century, it was the American right which insisted that private contracts ought not be regulated by public law; *Lochner v. New York* (1905) expressed the high point of that doctrine.[35] *Lochner* was effectively overruled by the New Deal Supreme Court, to general legal acceptance, but the notion that commercial bathhouses should be left unregulated would return us to a situation in which allegedly private actions would be given more weight than public regulation. Some writers identified with gay politics do believe that we ought to go back to *Lochner* for law on this point.[36] And the issue was also raised by abortion rights activists in Florida, who maintained that a state law designed to shut down unsafe "abortion mills" ought to be opposed because it was a short step to the regulation of abortion itself. "The fault with *Lochner*," Lawrence Tribe has written in this context, "lay not in judicial intervention to protect 'liberty'—including the 'liberty' of workers and of businesses—but in a misguided understanding of what 'liberty' required."[37] As the century comes to an end, in other words, disagreement still exists about whether businesses which provide a "public" clientele with "private" services exist in the public sector or the private.

Each of these examples illustrates how the shifting and uncertain boundary between public and private makes it close to impossible for anyone to believe in the sanctity of one over the other in all cases. Just as neither Goffman nor Habermas can make a completely convincing case for the priority of one or the other in theory, political practice does not allow for consistency in either direction. This is not necessarily a bad thing. For what may be taking place in American politics is that the right and the left have come to respect the other's preference for one side or the other of the public/private distinction— if only on issues favorable to the agenda of each. If gay activists and feminists worry about intrusive regulations of businesses which provide services for which they care deeply, perhaps they will come to understand that more private choice in schooling, medical care, or retirement is not necessarily a bad thing. If, on the other hand, conservatives come to appreciate the importance of public intervention into decisions involving sexuality or morality, they may also come to understand how such intervention can protect the natural environment or the airwaves as well. The shifting boundaries between public and

---

35. 198 U.S. 45 (1905).
36. H. N. Hirsch, *A Theory of Liberty: The Constitution and Minorities*, pp. 72–75.
37. Lawrence Tribe, *Abortion: The Clash of Absolutes*, p. 86.

private suggest that both private freedom and public order are important values. The question is rarely whether one should completely trump the other. It is much more often a question of how what we value most about both can be best protected.

TOWARD AN APPROPRIATE TRICHOTOMY

AS THE SHIFTING POLITICS of the public/private distinction indicates, when we try to address our moral dilemmas by assigning institutions and practices exclusively to one sphere or the other, we often rely on a false dichotomy, digging ourselves deeper into political conflicts from which the public/private distinction was supposed to rescue us. The notion that this distinction, valuable as it has been, is not as conceptually self-evident as both social theory and political practice sometimes would have it is strengthened by the number of thinkers who have viewed it as insufficient. Nearly all the leading sociological theorists, especially Emile Durkheim and George Herbert Mead, tried to define a realm of social life that was dominated neither by private calculation of self-interest nor by sovereign collective authority.[38] Along similar lines, Hannah Arendt's distinctions between the public, the private, and the social were meant to remind her readers that while some societies in the past could adhere to a dichotomous public/private division, the situation in modern society is complicated by the rise of the "social." [39] Finally, the revival of interest in "civil society" among contemporary writers indicates a desire to posit a realm of social life that contains elements of both the public and the private without fully being equated with either one.[40]

Efforts to revitalize notions such as civil society have come in for substantial theoretical and empirical criticism,[41] and it is not my intention to defend them here. But however one chooses to formulate a trichotomy, our society, and most of those like it, clearly contains institutions and practices that are neither fully public nor fully private. Terminology being contentious here, let me formulate the trichotomy this way: there is a *private* sector in which we appropriately judge behavior by whether it maximizes individual freedom or self-interest; a *public* sector in which we make decisions that are meant to apply equally to everyone in the society (even as we recognize the near impossibility of doing this); and a realm of distinct *publics*. These publics—by which I mean families and kinship networks, associations, ethnic and racial groups, linguistic communities, and other similar communities of interest, identity,

38. I go into much more detail in *Whose Keeper? Social Science and Moral Obligation.*
39. See Hannah Arendt, *The Human Condition.*
40. For one example, see Wolfe, *Whose Keeper?* passim.
41. See Adam Seligman, *The Idea of Civil Society.*

and belief—are on the one hand collective: they are guided by shared norms, can impose sanctions on members, and try to perpetuate themselves as groups at the cost of overriding individual preferences. But—hence the plural—such publics are not authoritative for the entire society; there are too many of them. It is for this reason that they are, on the other hand, partially private: they can protect individual members against intrusive state intervention from outside, express particularistic rather than universalistic needs, and allow the individual members within the group to develop their personal identities (and self-confidence) more fully.

Those who value private autonomy whenever it comes into conflict with collective authority (or vice versa) have no need for a middle-range realm of associations. An example of this tendency is John Stuart Mill's *On Liberty,* which makes a very strong defense of the private over the public (and, in so doing, contradicts some of the author's other writings).[42] Mill, in this essay, cares not a whit whether private expressions of liberty are curtailed by public authority or by the opinions of neighbors, friends, and associates. Indeed, in some ways the latter forms of suppression and censorship are worse than the former. "Society," he writes,

> can and does execute its own mandates; and if it issues wrong mandates
> instead of right, or any mandates at all in things with which it ought
> not to meddle, it practices a social tyranny more formidable than many
> kinds of political oppression, since, though not usually upheld by such
> extreme penalties, it leaves fewer means of escape, penetrating much
> more deeply into the details of life, and enslaving the soul itself.[43]

I believe that Mill is wrong here. There is good reason to prefer the "soft" forms of coercion associated with society to the "hard" ultimate monopoly of violence held by the state. Not only are the sanctions possessed by social groups in modern societies less punitive than those possessed by government, the possibility of "exit" from them is greater, the means of deploying them are usually more ambiguous and "coded," and they do not, by definition, extend to everyone in the society. If, moreover, we accept that group membership is to a significant degree socially constructed and voluntary—modern individuals can change their affiliations with amazing ease compared to any other people who ever lived on this planet—then intermediate groups seem like an ideal way to preserve both freedom on the one hand and normative constraints on the other; their status as neither fully public nor fully private

42. A point documented in Gertrude Himmelfarb, *On Liberty and Liberalism: The Case of John Stuart Mill.*

43. John Stuart Mill, *On Liberty,* p. 4.

might allow them to respond to needs both for autonomy and withdrawal from the gaze of others and for affecting the behavior of others and being affected by them in turn.

Some indication of how this might work is illustrated by the example most often at the center of controversies over the private and the public: abortion. *Roe v. Wade* gave a strong endorsement to privacy as the justification for removing just about all restrictions on a woman's right to choose, especially in the first trimester of pregnancy, and privacy remains the preferred ground for the defense of abortion in Jean Cohen's contribution to this volume. Opponents of a woman's right to control her own body, by contrast, generally cite the interest of the entire community in such decisions: the notion of an overriding "right to life" expresses a common commitment to a value which defines "our"—that is, the Judeo-Christian—way of life. In the backlash against *Roe,* new restrictions on an absolute right to an abortion have been imposed, such as a waiting period, the need for minors to obtain parental consent, mandatory counseling, and record-keeping and reporting.[44] Because such compromises nibble away at a right deemed to be, in Lawrence Tribe's phrase, "fundamental," Tribe and others like him see them as unacceptable.[45] But what may work in their favor is that they are efforts, on the one hand, to preserve the right to an abortion—the Court has been clear on that—while at the same time allowing for the input of publics, rather than the public, in the decision. Parental consent asks that the parents of a minor be included in the abortion decision; the requirement of a waiting period presupposes a time for reflection and discussion with significant others. Such compromises, however awkward or imperfect, are attempts to walk the line between 100 percent autonomy and 100 percent regulation. They represent a recognition that the family is composed of individuals but not only composed of individuals; it is, in that sense, neither private nor public.

Similar lessons can be applied to the controversies over hate speech and pornography discussed earlier in this essay. It is not always clear whether the groups most often cited on behalf of identity politics—such as women, African Americans, gays, the disabled, Latinos—are in fact groups which bind their members or only potential groups being called into being by making claims for their identity. But to the degree that claims are made and accepted on their behalf, they become groups that are in one sense large and inclusive but in another sense particular and specific, which means that they can find

44. *Webster v. Reproductive Health Services,* 492 U.S. 490 (1989); and *Planned Parenthood of Southeastern Pennsylvania v. Casey,* 112 S. Ct. 2791 (1992). However, the court struck down spousal consent requirements in *Casey.*

45. *Abortion: The Clash of Absolutes,* p. 11.

themselves on either side of the public/private distinction. With respect to the individuals who belong to them, such groups are public in the sense that they attempt to shape the attitudes, norms, and behavior of their members to meet collectively defined goals. But since they exist pluralistically in competition with other ethnic and identity groups, they are private in the way religion has usually been considered private in the United States. Long before the regulation of pornography or hate speech became an issue,[46] Americans settled religious disputes which bedeviled other countries by relying on both the public and private aspects of religious membership and belief.[47] With occasional exceptions,[48] America has no official public religion. But Americans also believe that a generalized "civil religion" ought to reinforce widely shared general beliefs for society as a whole and that specific religions should be responsible for the moral training and development of those who adhere to them.[49]

This suggests that a similar "separation of ethnicity and state" might help put into context some of the tensions around identity politics.[50] African-American organizations and leaders, for example, have a strong moral duty to call attention to racist attitudes and actions, which they accomplish both by raising consciousness among individual African Americans and by holding white Americans to a "civil" standard of commonly agreed-upon norms. But it does not follow that they are justified in seeking public laws regulating private speech. To do so would be to equate the group's interest in policing speech offensive to itself with the common interest, functionally similar to the idea that the specific beliefs of Protestants should become the common religious beliefs of all. By investing public authority behind the agenda of a group that is one (or more) among publics, I believe, speech codes upset the appropriate balance between public and private too much in one direc-

---

46. The Supreme Court at earlier periods did deal with offensive "fighting words" or with "group libel," but these decisions atrophied over time, never becoming important precedents for current battles. See *Chaplinsky v. New Hampshire*, 315 U.S. 568 (1942); and *Beauharnais v. Illinois*, 343 U.S. 250 (1952).

47. See Robert T. Handy, *Undermined Establishment: Church-State Relations in America, 1880–1920*.

48. Such as Justice Brewer's remark, in a unanimous Supreme Court case, that the United States "is a Christian nation." See *Church of the Holy Trinity v. United States*, 143 U.S. 457 (1892), p. 471.

49. See Robert N. Bellah, *The Broken Covenant: American Civil Religion in a Time of Trial*.

50. As proposed, for example, by Nathan Glazer, *Ethnic Dilemmas, 1964–1982*, pp. 126–44. For a critique of this notion, see Will Kymlicka, *Multicultural Citizenship: A Liberal Theory of Minority Rights*, p. 115.

tion. Relying on the ambiguous status of ethnic and racial groups is a better way to balance respect for private thoughts with a public interest in civil discourse.

As Jeff Weintraub notes in his essay for this volume, the public/private distinction has been one of the truly "grand dichotomies" of Western thought. Yet Weintraub and many other contributors (including myself) are somewhat uncomfortable with it, made uneasy by the realities it does not explain and the moral and legal conflicts it cannot resolve. But history may be in the process of easing some of our worries. It is by no means certain that the preoccupation with the public/private dichotomy that now shapes so many highly charged controversies will continue indefinitely. Some of the crucial historical developments that have fueled the intensity and absolutism of public/private debates in our century seem to have run their course. On the one hand, the movement representing the ultimate elevation of the public over the private—Communism—has been toppled in its primary home and generally discredited, and even such tame versions of public predominance as Keynesianism and the welfare state are in disarray. On the other hand, in Western societies the long battle to establish a private realm of free speech, thought, and religious practice protected from public scrutiny has essentially been won; defending it remains important, but no longer calls for the kind of all-or-nothing absolutism often necessary to carve it out in the first place. To be sure, there are, especially in the United States, strong forces behind reassertions of public morality, but attempts to legislate the moral superiority of heterosexuality over homosexuality or control over women's right to abortion commonly fail—so strong is the American leaning toward a version of libertarianism. And political correctness, whatever one thinks of it, is not McCarthyism.

In this country, at least, the immediate political future is likely to be one in which the private comes to be preferred over the public in both economic and moral matters. Yet there are also reasons to expect that, once the current flirtation with privatism runs its course, a counteremphasis on the importance of a public sector will emerge. If so, one hopes that new efforts to revitalize a sector emphasizing what Americans have in common will acknowledge the degree to which private and public are inevitably intertwined. In economic policy this means that a revitalized public sector will not substitute itself for private decisions but try to play a more indirect role in shaping them toward publicly decided ends. In matters of sexuality and morality, this means that efforts to stress the common interests we have in the behavior of others are not accompanied by attempts to restrict excessively the private behavior of those for whom we have little respect. The public/private dichotomy as we have known it, in reminding us of the importance of both individual autonomy and collective purpose, has done its work. What we need is what efforts to trichotomize the problem emphasize: a way of recognizing the importance of both the public and the private without absolutizing either.

REFERENCES

Alderman, Ellen, and Caroline Kennedy. 1995. *The Right to Privacy.* New York: Knopf.

Arendt, Hannah. 1958. *The Human Condition.* Chicago: University of Chicago Press.

Bayer, Ronald. 1991. *Private Acts, Social Consequences: AIDS and the Politics of Public Health.* New Brunswick, NJ: Rutgers University Press.

Bellah, Robert N. 1975. *The Broken Covenant: American Civil Religion in a Time of Trial.* New York: Seabury.

Burkett, Elinor. 1995. *The Gravest Show on Earth: America in the Age of AIDS.* Boston: Houghton Mifflin.

Chubb, John E., and Terry M. Moe. 1990. *Politics, Markets, and America's Schools.* Washington, DC: Brookings Institution.

Dworkin, Andrea. 1989. *Pornography: Men Possessing Women.* New York: Dutton.

Elshtain, Jean Bethke. 1981. *Public Man, Private Woman: Women in Social and Political Thought.* Princeton, NJ: Princeton University Press.

Epstein, Richard. 1992. *Forbidden Grounds: The Case against Employment Discrimination Laws.* Cambridge, MA: Harvard University Press.

Garrow, David J. 1994. *Liberty and Sexuality: The Right to Privacy and the Making of Roe v. Wade.* New York: Macmillan.

Ginsberg, Ruth Bader. 1985. "Some Thoughts on Autonomy and Equality in Relation to *Roe v. Wade*," *North Carolina Law Review* 83 (January): 375–86.

Glazer, Nathan. 1983. *Ethnic Dilemmas, 1964–1982.* Cambridge, MA: Harvard University Press.

Goffman, Erving. 1959. *The Presentation of Self in Everyday Life.* Garden City, NY: Doubleday Anchor.

———. 1971. *Relations in Public: Microstudies of the Public Order.* New York: Harper.

Guinier, Lani. 1994. *The Tyranny of the Majority: Fundamental Fairness in Representative Democracy.* New York: Free Press.

Habermas, Jürgen. [1962] 1989. *The Structural Transformation of the Public Sphere: An Inquiry into a Category of Bourgeois Society.* Translated by Thomas Burger. Cambridge, MA: MIT Press.

———. 1984. *The Theory of Communicative Action.* Vol. 1, *Reason and the Rationalization of Society.* London: Heinemann.

———. 1987. *The Theory of Communicative Action.* Vol. 2, *Lifeworld and System: A Critique of Functionalist Reason.* Boston: Beacon Press.

Handy, Robert T. 1991. *Undermined Establishment: Church-State Relations in America, 1880–1920.* Princeton, NJ: Princeton University Press.

Himmelfarb, Gertrude. 1974. *On Liberty and Liberalism: The Case of John Stuart Mill.* New York: Knopf.

Hirsch, H. N. 1992. *A Theory of Liberty: The Constitution and Minorities.* New York: Routledge.

Joseph, Stephen C. 1992. *Dragon within the Gates: The Once and Future AIDS Epidemic.* New York: Carroll & Graf.

Kohlberg, Lawrence. 1980. "The Future of Liberalism as the Dominant Ideology of the West." In *Moral Development and Politics,* edited by Richard W. Wilson and Gordon J. Schochet. New York: Praeger.

Koppelman, Andrew. 1990. "Forced Labor: A Thirteenth Amendment Defense of Abortion." *Northwestern University Law Review* 84 (winter): 480–535.

Kymlicka, Will. 1995. *Multicultural Citizenship: A Liberal Theory of Minority Rights.* Oxford: Clarendon.

Lamont, Michèle, and Fournier, Marcel, eds. 1992. *Cultivating Differences: Symbolic Boundaries and the Making of Inequality.* Chicago: University of Chicago Press.

Lawrence, Charles R., III. 1993. "If He Hollers Let Him Go: Regulating Racist Speech on Campus." In *Words That Wound: Critical Race Theory, Assaultive Speech, and the First Amendment,* by Mari J. Matsuda, Charles R. Lawrence III, Richard Delgado, and Kimberlè Williams Crenshaw, pp. 53–88. Boulder, CO: Westview.

MacKinnon, Catharine A. 1989. *Toward a Feminist Theory of the State.* Cambridge, MA: Harvard University Press.

———. 1993. *Only Words.* Cambridge, MA: Harvard University Press.

Matsuda, Mari. 1993. "Public Response to Racist Speech: Considering the Victim's Story." In *Words That Wound: Critical Race Theory, Assaultive Speech, and the First Amendment,* by Mari J. Matsuda, Charles R. Lawrence III, Richard Delgado, and Kimberlè Williams Crenshaw, pp. 17–51. Boulder, CO: Westview.

Mill, John Stuart. [1859] 1956. *On Liberty.* Indianapolis: Hackett.

Posner, Richard. 1992. *Sex and Reason.* Cambridge, MA: Harvard University Press.

Reiter, Rayna, ed. 1975. *Toward an Anthropology of Women.* New York: Monthly Review Press.

Rorty, Richard. 1989. *Contingency, Irony, and Solidarity.* New York: Cambridge University Press.

Rosaldo, Michelle Zimbalist, and Louise Lamphere, eds. 1974. *Woman, Culture, and Society.* Stanford, CA: Stanford University Press.

Seligman, Adam. 1995. *The Idea of Civil Society.* Princeton, NJ: Princeton University Press.

Snedaker, Kathryn H. 1987. "Reconsidering *Roe v. Wade:* Equal Protection Analysis as an Alternative Approach." *New Mexico Law Review* 17 (winter): 115–37.

Sunstein, Cass R. 1993. *Democracy and the Problem of Free Speech.* New York: Free Press.

Tribe, Lawrence. 1990. *Abortion: The Clash of Absolutes.* New York: Norton.

Wolfe, Alan. 1989. *Whose Keeper? Social Science and Moral Obligation.* Berkeley: University of California Press.

Zerubavel, Eviatar. 1991. *The Fine Line: Making Distinctions in Everyday Life.* New York: Free Press.

Home: The Promise and Predicament of Private Life at the End of the Twentieth Century

Krishan Kumar

"The home is an aspect of life and at the same time a special way of forming, reflecting, and interrelating the totality of life."
—Georg Simmel, "Female Culture" (1911)

❏

"Home is a barbarous idea; the method of a rude age; home is isolation; therefore anti-social. What we want is Community."
—Benjamin Disraeli, *Sybil* (1846)

❏

"It is part of morality not to be at home in one's home."
—Theodor Adorno, *Minima Moralia* (1951)

NO PLACE LIKE HOME

THE "RETURN TO HOME" is a popular and powerful slogan of our time. Central and East Europeans want to return to the "common European home." Ethnic and nationalist groups throughout the world make renewed claims to their "homelands." Feminists no longer denounce the very idea of home as enslaving but, some of them at least, draw attention to the potentially enabling and enhancing activities of the home. More diffusely, a number of cultural movements in Western societies have focused a new attention on the home, as perhaps the sole remaining site of satisfaction in late industrial society. Home, *Heimat,* in one form or another, is enjoying a somewhat unexpected renaissance.[1]

The discovery, or rediscovery, of the home is new or striking not so much for the fact of it as for its reevaluation of the home. Home is now positive. Home is good—precisely, "homely," like wholesome (and preferably home-

I should like to thank my co-editor, Jeff Weintraub, for help with this piece.

1. See, for some examples from Europe, David Morley and Kevin Robins, "No Place Like *Heimat:* Images of Home(land) in European Culture."

baked) bread. This is no news to the bulk of the population. Home has always been celebrated by them. There is indeed, it has generally been held, no place like home. But a shift seems to have occurred at the level of high culture, or ideology. There the home had been regarded with a certain lofty disfavor; now it has been endowed, by many intellectuals, with the warm glow of approbation.

When earlier sociologists and cultural critics proclaimed the "home-centered society," or discovered the "privatized worker" and the "privatized society," it was generally to express a sense of loss. Private life, understood as domestic or personal life, was seen to flourish at the expense of public life, understood as civic or cultural pursuits. The privatized worker no longer took much interest in union or plant activities, except insofar as these affected his take-home pay. The privatized "citizen" was hardly a citizen at all; his or her political life was largely reduced to the act of voting, usually for the person or party which promised most in the way of home-based consumption.[2]

Now the claim is that these were contrasts with an imaginary golden age of citizenship and public involvement. Or, even if people were formerly more socially conscious and politically active than now, this was out of necessity, not desire.[3] Now that most people in advanced industrial society have reached a certain level of comfort and security, they have expressed their clear preference for private over public life. Even in the former Communist countries of Central and Eastern Europe, intellectuals anxious to strengthen the democratic currents of the 1989 revolutions have been horrified by the rapid mass retreat from the public realm, and the rush to embrace private, purely personal concerns.[4]

One way in which the attachment to home most clearly seems to express itself is in the widespread passion for home ownership—widespread at least

2. For a general statement of the decline of the public sphere, see Jürgen Habermas, *The Structural Transformation of the Public Sphere*. For British examples, see John H. Goldthorpe et al., *The Affluent Worker in the Class Structure;* and Martin Pawley, *The Private Future: Causes and Consequences of Community Collapse in the West*. For an American example, see Philip Slater, *The Pursuit of Loneliness: American Culture at the Breaking Point*. There is a good discussion of the sociological literature of the 1960s and 1970s on "privatization" in Arthur Brittan, *The Privatised World,* pp. 45–76; see also Graham Crow, "The Post-War Development of the Modern Domestic Ideal," in Graham Allan and Graham Crow, eds., *Home and Family: Creating the Domestic Sphere,* pp. 14–32.

3. Albert Hirschman is probably nearer the truth when he says that there have been *cycles* of public involvement and disengagement in recent Western history. See his *Shifting Involvements: Private Interest and Public Action*.

4. See G. M. Tamas, "The Legacy of Dissent," and Eva Kolinsky, "Exodus to the Private Realm."

among English-speaking peoples. In Britain more than two-thirds of all homes are now privately owned—compared with one-third thirty years ago—and more than three-quarters of the population wish to be homeowners. More remarkably, even among the poorest sections of the population attachment to home ownership is so tenacious that in a recent study 80 percent of the sample were found to be homeowners. Explaining this finding, one of the researchers said that for this group, "home is a haven." [5]

Once this clinging to the home might have been pitied. It would have been regarded as the expression of a truly impoverished life, in moral and cultural terms. Now it is celebrated by intellectuals of both the New Left and the New Right. The Right, not surprisingly, sees it as the healthy sign of a "people's capitalism," and the moral as well as the material foundation of a "property-owning democracy." The Left, which might previously have regarded it as suspiciously "petit bourgeois," now embraces it almost as wholeheartedly. The Left's traditional indifference to the concerns of private life, its contempt for the aspirations of ordinary people are, many Left intellectuals now feel, a principal cause of the Left's declining fortunes—especially in these post-Fordist, postmodernist times.[6]

As the focus of private life, the home—especially one's privately owned home—emerges as a consecrated place. More than ever before it is regarded as the principal source of identity and personal fulfillment. Public life is alienating when it is not actually corrupting; private life, centered on the home, correspondingly expands in importance. A powerful statement to this effect comes from Peter Saunders, one of the foremost British advocates of the home-centered society.

> The home is a core institution in modern society. It shelters the smallest viable unit of social organization—the household—and basic patterns of social relations are forged, reproduced and changed within it.

5. Preliminary findings of the study, by Angela Dale and others, were reported at the annual meeting of the British Association for the Advancement of Science, Keele University, August 1993: see the *Independent,* August 31, 1993. For the figures for home ownership in Britain, and on the widespread desire to become home owners, see Peter Saunders, *A Nation of Home Owners,* pp. 14, 60–65. The increase is plotted from an estimate of 10 percent home ownership at the time of the First World War. Comparison with other industrial countries shows the strong Anglo-Saxon lead in home ownership. Saunders attributes this preference to the long-standing cultural value of "individualism" among English-speaking peoples (pp. 18, 40–41).

6. See, for the Left, Stuart Hall and Martin Jacques's edited volume, *New Times: The Changing Face of Politics in the 1990s.* A good example of the Right's celebration of family and private life is Ferdinand Mount (a former policy adviser to Margaret Thatcher), *The Subversive Family.*

It is the place with which individuals can most readily identify and it easily lends itself to the symbolic expression of personal identity. It offers both physical and psychological shelter and comfort. It is the place where the self can be expressed outside of social roles and where the individual can exert autonomy away from the coercive gaze of the employer and the state. It is the private realm in an increasingly public and intrusive world. For many of us, its integrity is of the utmost value in our lives.[7]

How does this assessment stand up? How far, even if it were thought desirable, is the home capable of discharging this solemn task in contemporary conditions? What implications does this widely expressed position carry for the relation between private and public life? Where precisely, in any case, does the home stand in that relationship? It may seem to belong unequivocally, as Saunders assumes, to "the private realm." But that is to begin, not to end, the inquiry. For what is the nature of that "private" to which it is said to belong? Is it no more than the home? Is everything else "public"? If so, has this always been the case? What may have been the changing definitions and boundaries of the private and the public, and how has this affected our thinking about the role and place of the home? To raise these questions is to become aware that, in dwelling on the home, we are forced to reflect in the most general way on the nature of public and private life in modern societies.

WHAT IS THE HOME? WHERE IS THE HOME?

"HOME," SAYS ERIC HOBSBAWM,

> in the literal sense, *Heim, chez soi,* is essentially private. Home in the wider sense, *Heimat,* is essentially public . . . *Heim* belongs to me and mine and nobody else. Anyone who has been burglarized knows the feeling of intrusion, of a private space violated. *Heimat* is by definition collective. It cannot belong to us as individuals.[8]

This is a necessary beginning. It is clear that many of the current calls for a "return to home" refer to home as *Heimat,* homeland, rather than to the home of private life. Such was the home of Gorbachev's "common European home"; such too is the home that the exiled South African poet Breyten

---

7. Saunders, *A Nation of Home Owners,* p. 311. A similar view, more restrained in tone, is expressed by R. E. Pahl, *Divisions of Labour,* pp. 321–24.

8. Eric Hobsbawm, introduction to the section on "Exile" in the special issue of *Social Research* on "Home: A Place in the World," edited by Arien Mack. For a "multilevel" concept of home, linking "home," "homeland," and beyond, see Aviezer Tucker, "In Search of Home."

Breytenbach has in mind when he says that "exile has brought it home to me that I'm African," that exile has made him more aware than previously that Africa is his real home.[9] *Heimat,* Hobsbawm has further remarked, is "almost always a social construction rather than a real memory. . . . At the limit, as when we look back across oceans or generations . . . it becomes an imagined community."[10] Edgar Reitz, the director of the well-known German television film *Heimat,* echoes this directly when he says that "the word is always linked to strong feelings, mostly remembrances and longing. Heimat always evokes in me the feeling of something lost or very far away . . . It seems to me that one has a more precise idea of Heimat the further one is away from it."[11]

There is an obvious overlap, not only etymologically but also in spirit, between *Heim* and *Heimat,* home and homeland. One can feel love and longing, nostalgia or homesickness—and their opposites?—for both. Both too are capable of physical displacement, since "home is where the heart is." But equally clearly the two senses of home belong to different discourses. The one is indeed primarily a matter of private life, the other of public life.

The reason why this is not immediately obvious is of course that "homeland" trades off the intimate, domestic, private connotations of "home." The public realm, when conceived as the homeland, is explicitly modeled on an idealized version of the private realm of the household or family. That is why the current enthusiasms for both home and homeland can draw upon the same emotional roots. They reflect a longing for the qualities of community, security, and sense of belonging that we traditionally associate with private family life, in an era when public life appears to have been drained of all vitality and significance. Thus there may well be a wish or a willingness to collapse the two domains into each other (with potentially disastrous consequences, as shown in several versions of nationalism and fascism). Nevertheless the two concepts, home and homeland, point to different realities and it is important to bear the distinction in mind—in analysis and, so far as possible, in social and political life as well.

I am concerned in this essay with the home of private life. But, as Jeff Weintraub makes clear in the introductory essay to this volume, the sense of "private" involved here is by no means unambiguous. It belongs largely to the third and fourth of the four paired oppositions of private and public that he distinguishes. That is, the home belongs to the private sphere primarily as the locus of the family and the household. It is thus "private" in a way quite different from the "privateness" of the market economy, for example. "*Hei-*

---

9. Breyten Breytenbach, "The Long March from Hearth to Heart," p. 79.
10. Hobsbawm, introduction to "Exile," p. 67.
11. Quoted in Morley and Robins, "No Place Like *Heimat,*" p. 4.

mat," as Hobsbawm emphasizes, "is by definition collective. . . . We belong to it because we don't want to be alone." [12] But this is equally true of *Heim,* though on a more intimate scale. What makes the home "private" is—following especially the work of Philippe Ariès—its association with the sphere of domesticity, intimacy, and privacy. This sets it against the public sphere of "sociability" as well as, more conventionally, the public spheres of the market and the state. [13]

These versions of the public/private distinction reflect, of course, the unprecedented "privatization" of the home and the family in modern times. Both Ariès and a number of feminist scholars—Weintraub's principal exemplars for his third and fourth sets of public/private distinctions—are concerned to trace the developments which have led to this situation, one which, for quite different reasons, they regard with disapproval.

For Ariès, the modern family (namely, home) emerges in splendid and embattled isolation out of a rather satisfyingly confused earlier condition where the boundaries between the private world of the family and the public life of the streets and society—of "sociability"—were faint and highly permeable. The family inhabited a world that was "neither private nor public, as these terms are understood today; rather it was both simultaneously." [14] This permeability applied to both the internal and the external relations of the family. The medieval household mixed up young and old, men and women, servants and masters, friends and family, intimates and strangers. It was open, almost like a café or pub, to the comings and goings of a multitude of diverse types of people, intent upon a bewildering variety of tasks concerned with business or pleasure.

Gradually, starting sometime in the early seventeenth century, this promiscuous world was ordered and tidied up. Houses—upper-class houses to start with—began to reflect a marked degree of segregation of the status and functions of husband and wife, parents and children, masters and servants, friends and family. Boundaries were more strictly drawn—in paths and hedges, bricks and mortar, as well as in social customs—between the private and intimate world of the home and family, and the public world of acquaintances, business associates, and strangers. Work and nonwork ("living") were rigidly separated and assigned to separate spheres. The area of sociability, of the forms of convivial urban social life, contracted. The "interstitial space" that had linked differ-

12. Hobsbawm, introduction to "Exile," p. 68.
13. See Jeff Weintraub, "The Theory and Politics of the Public/Private Distinction," in this volume.
14. Philippe Ariès, "The Family and the City in the Old World and the New," in Virginia Tufte and Barbara Meyerhoff's *Changing Images of the Family,* p. 30.

ent activities, private and public, vanished. "The whole of social life was absorbed by private, family living." The household, for its part, shrank to its nuclear core; home was reduced to the nonwork life of the nuclear or conjugal family of parents and a handful of dependent children. A "great void" opened up between the private sphere, identified more or less exclusively with the family, and the public sphere, seen as the threatening and to some extent uncontrollable outside world from which the family offered a refuge (the family became "*the* private domain, the only place where a person could legitimately escape the inquisitive stare of industrial society"). But for Ariès it is evident that the family is fighting a losing battle.

> In an attempt to fill the gap created by the decline of the city and the urban forms of social intercourse it had once provided, the omnipotent, omnipresent family took upon itself the task of trying to satisfy all the emotional and social needs of its members. Today, it is clear that the family has failed in its attempts to accomplish that feat, either because the increased emphasis on privacy has stifled the need for social intercourse or because the family has been too completely alienated by public powers. People are demanding that the family do everything that the outside world in its indifference or hostility refuses to do.[15]

15. Philippe Ariès, "The Family and the City in the Old World and the New," p. 29, and, for the previous quotations and the general account, pp. 29–41. In this piece Ariès's nostalgia for the earlier world (as well as a more Foucauldian cast of thought) comes out more strongly than in his longer and better-known account, *Centuries of Childhood: A Social History of Family Life,* especially pp. 327–99.

As Weintraub points out (p. 19), Ariès's account of the evolution of the family is not altered substantially by those of other historians more favorably disposed towards the modern family. See, for example, Edward Shorter, *The Making of the Modern Family;* and Lawrence Stone, *The Family, Sex and Marriage in England, 1500–1800.* For more recent work, emphasizing especially class differences in timing, see the lucid discussion by Tamara Hareven in "The Home and the Family in Historical Perspective." An important earlier contribution, which supports Ariès's account specifically in relation to the American family, is Barbara Laslett's "The Family as a Public and Private Institution: An Historical Perspective." For England, a useful general survey, again concluding essentially with Ariès, is Peter Williams, "Constituting Class and Gender: A Social History of the Home, 1700–1901," in Nigel Thrift and Peter Williams's edited volume, *Class and Space: The Making of Urban Society,* pp. 154–204.

For the changes specifically to the design of the home—with the increasing specialization of roles and functions within it, and the increasing insulation from the world outside— see Ariès, *Centuries of Childhood,* pp. 377–91; Witold Rybczynski, *Home: A Short History of an Idea,* pp. 51–121; Lawrence Stone, "The Public and the Private in the Stately Homes of England, 1500–1990"; Clifford Edward Clark, Jr., *The American Family Home.* All these writers recognize the importance of the Dutch bourgeois home of the seventeenth century as providing something of a model for later developments elsewhere; at the same time they

We shall need to consider this verdict later (and also Ariès's view that "the real roots of the present domestic crisis lie not in our families, but in our cities"—that is, in the character of public life). For their part, feminists arrive at a similar sense of crisis, but with a different emphasis and a different agenda. Feminist historians and sociologists largely accept the sketch of family history provided by Ariès, Stone, Shorter, and others. But no more than Ariès are they inclined to celebrate the rise of the "companionate marriage" or the family of "affective individualism." Unlike Ariès they feel little nostalgia for the past. But they share with him the view that, if one considers specifically the position of women, the household of the past gave them a greater degree of involvement in the general life of society than became possible in the modern nuclear family. Women were co-partners with men in the system of household production. They were frequently managers of large households. In both town and country they engaged in a large variety of tasks outside the home, in agricultural work and in the skilled trades. The coming of the nuclear family confined women almost entirely to the domain of the home. Their lives came to be centered on their children and their husbands. They were cut off from the productive life of society. In upper- and middle-class families even much of the housework was taken out of their hands. They lived their lives as a protected species within the walled-off domestic realm, its ornament and the guardian of the moral and expressive life of its members.[16]

---

acknowledge that in other countries the changes mostly began at the top of the society, in the great houses of the aristocracy and gentry, and later spread to other classes. That this began relatively early, even for the working class, see H. J. Daunton, "Public and Private Space: The Victorian City and the Working Class Household," in D. Frazer and A. Sutcliffe, eds., *The Pursuit of Urban History*.

16. Ariès, "The Family and the City in the Old World and the New," p. 41. Women's history is a thriving but controversial field. I do not mean to suggest anything more here than a general emphasis in its presentation of the past. For examples, see Ann Oakley, *Subject Women*, pp. 138–42; Stephanie Coontz, *The Way We Never Were: American Families and the Nostalgia Trap*. For the rise of the domestic ideology in Victorian England, and the idea of the family as not merely "*the* private domain" but also quintessentially "the woman's domain," see Walter E. Houghton, *The Victorian Frame of Mind*, pp. 341–93; also Leonore Davidoff and Catherine Hall, *Family Fortunes: Men and Women of the English Middle Class, 1780–1850*, especially part 3, pp. 317 ff. The dichotomy between the public world (of men) and the private world (of women) can be exaggerated, especially for the nineteenth century. See Karen V. Hansen, "Feminist Conceptions of Public and Private: A Critical Analysis," and her essay in this volume, "Rediscovering the Social: Visiting Practices in Antebellum New England and the Limits of the Public/Private Dichotomy."

For a defense of the home as properly the woman's realm, and indeed as "the supreme cultural achievement of women," see the characteristically subtle essay by Georg Simmel, "Female Culture," in *Georg Simmel: On Women, Sexuality and Love*, especially pp. 90–98.

The point to note is that both Ariès and the feminists share a concern with the exclusion of the family from the public life of society. In Ariès's case this exclusion is glossed as a decline of sociability, in the feminists' case as the decline of women's productive role and their confinement to domesticity within the small nuclear family. For both, the modern family is decisively privatized—to its loss, and to consequent suffering on the part of all its members, husbands and children as much as wives.[17]

The historical focus of both Ariès's and the feminists' accounts is the transition, broadly speaking, from medieval to modern society. It is this that allows them to see in the preindustrial family a degree of "publicity" wholly lacking in the modern family. For Hannah Arendt, employing a wider historical framework, neither in medieval nor in any other times have the family and household been anything other than private. Nor could it have been otherwise, since the very principle of the home is its privateness. Insofar as medieval society elevated the family to an important social and political role, making it almost the paradigm of society as a whole, to that extent medieval society denied itself any real engagement with the public realm.

For Arendt it is axiomatic that "the distinction between a private and a public sphere of life corresponds to the household and the political realms." She seems at times to share the "tremendous contempt" that she says the Greeks of the classical period displayed towards the domestic realm. But that is not her general position. Her general conviction is that there is a "profound connection between private and public," making both necessary for the full *vita activa* of the human condition. The public realm is reared on the foundation of the private; indeed, the private can effectively do without the public—that is largely what happened in the period of medieval Christianity, and it is happening now in our own time—but not the other way round. The private is the realm of necessity, concerned with "the maintenance of life," where human life is sustained and reproduced. Without this foundation there can be no realm of freedom, no public realm of politics. Arendt even argues that one particular aspect of the private, private property (though not wealth), is a condition of public participation. Private property provides a private home, a "particular location in a particular part of the world." This is a guarantee

17. See, for instance, Michèle Barrett and Mary McIntosh, *The Anti-Social Family.* Women have not been the only ones to point to the nuclear family as a source of illness and oppression. This has also been a strong theme within the "antipsychiatry" movement of R. D. Laing, David Cooper, and others. See, for instance, R. D. Laing, *The Politics of the Family, and Other Essays,* where he speaks of families as "the slaughterhouses of our children," and as the sphere of the "holocaust of one's experience on the altar of conformity" (pp. 101–2).

not simply of independence but of a necessary dark "hiding place" from the strong light of the public realm, which otherwise becomes intolerable. "A life spent entirely in public, in the presence of others, becomes, as we would say, shallow." The Greeks were negligent about this.

> The full development of the life of hearth and family into an inner and private space we owe to the extraordinary political sense of the Roman people who, unlike the Greeks, never sacrificed the private to the public, but on the contrary understood that these two realms could exist only in the form of coexistence.[18]

Arendt rescues the domestic sphere from contempt, however, only it seems to damn it more completely. The domestic sphere is the private sphere and, declares Arendt roundly, "to live an entirely private life means above all to be deprived of things essential to a truly human life." The private sphere is the realm of nature and necessity and, as such, while it may satisfy the human animal, it cannot satisfy the human being. Again and again Arendt points to the etymological connection between private and privation. The Latin *privatus* also seems to carry many of the connotations of the Greek *idiotes*, "a private person," from *idios*, private or personal. Private life is "idiotic," says Arendt, since it is "a life spent in the privacy of 'one's own,' . . . outside the world of the common." It is "a state of being deprived of something, and even of the highest and most human of man's capacities." Hence it was that "a man who lived only a private life, who like the slave was not permitted to enter the public realm, or like the barbarian had chosen not to establish such a realm, was not fully human." [19]

Arendt's diagnosis of the modern predicament is indeed that we have allowed the public to be swallowed up by the private. With the rise of the nation-state and the modern industrial economy, society has increasingly come to be thought of, and acted upon, as a sort of "super-human family." Society or "the social," in its modern guise, is the realm "where private interests assume public significance."

> We see the body of peoples and political communities in the image of a family whose everyday affairs have to be taken care of by a gigantic, nation-wide administration of housekeeping. The scientific thought

18. Hannah Arendt, *The Human Condition*, p. 54; for the previous quotations and the general argument, see pp. 23–69. She develops the idea that—"from the viewpoint of privacy"—the distinction between the public and private realms "equals the distinction between things that should be shown and things that should be hidden" on pp. 64–69.

19. Arendt, *The Human Condition*, p. 35. See also Barrington Moore, Jr., "Public and Private in Classical Athens," in *Privacy: Studies in Social and Cultural History*, pp. 82–83.

that corresponds to this development is no longer political science but "national economy" or "social economy" . . . ; the collective of families economically organized into the facsimile of one super-human family is what we call "society," and its political form of organization is called "nation." [20]

But there is a twist. The triumph of the social, of "society," does not un-equivocally mean the victory of the private—not, at least, of the private as privacy and intimacy. Intimacy, as developed by Rousseau and the Romantics, was set up precisely against the new concept of society. It was a rebellion against society's pressure towards conformity, against its soullessness. The family was the principal bulwark against this tendency, the protective shell within which intimacy and privacy could thrive. The development of modern society into "mass society," the culmination of its "collective housekeeping" in a nationwide system of bureaucracy, have overshadowed and undermined the family, the theater of intimacy. The social is a hypertrophied and distorted outgrowth of the private, classically conceived as the domestic sphere. Its victory has, however, meant not just the elimination of the classic realm of the public but also the virtual annihilation of the classic realm of the private. [21]

So, by a different route, Arendt nevertheless arrives at a conclusion strikingly similar to that of Ariès and the feminists: that the modern family and the modern home are incapable of discharging the heavy tasks so enthusiastically heaped upon them by the proponents of the home-centered society.

THE RETURN OF THE HOME

HOME ENTHUSIASTS ARE AWARE that the home has been under threat from mass, bureaucratized society. They accept that, as a result of "societal differentiation," many of the functions previously undertaken by the family have been taken over by the state and the wider society. But not only do they argue, as did Talcott Parsons and others at an earlier date, that this leaves the home and family freer to concentrate on their "expressive" tasks, which they are in any case better equipped to perform than any other agency in society. They also claim that in recent years the home has been regenerated and refortified by new technological developments. This in turn is allowing the home to regain much of the ground it lost during the first wave of modernization and industrialization.

The main developments here have to do with the microelectronic revolu-

20. Arendt, *The Human Condition*, pp. 28, 40.
21. For this development see *The Human Condition*, pp. 35–45.

tion and especially the spread of information technology in the home. This, it is argued, is putting production back into the home, as well as greatly extending the home's role as a provider of education, entertainment, and leisure services.

Already in the 1970s Scott Burns, using the United States as his example, had made the remarkable calculation that the modern household economy—which encompasses everything from the provision of food and shelter to child care and community services—amounted to nearly one-third of the gross national product. This productive effort, much of it the result of women's work, was needless to say invisible in the national accounts. Every new addition of household technology, from microwave ovens to videocassette recorders, increased the sum of goods and services produced in the home. Burns pointed to the absurdity of calling household goods, as was the usual custom, "consumer goods." "It is difficult to explain how an automobile owned by a cab company is capital equipment whereas it is a consumer bauble when owned by a household." [22]

Echoing this, Jonathan Gershuny argued that most household goods were in fact better described as "intermediate capital goods," used for the final delivery of goods and services in the home. Contrary to the widespread view that we were moving towards a service economy, we were actually moving towards a "do-it-yourself" or "self-service" economy. Analysis of investment and consumption trends over the past twenty-five years revealed a marked pattern of the substitution of household goods for marketed services. Instead of using public transport, we carry ourselves by car; instead of going out to concerts or to the cinema, we put on a record or watch TV; instead of sending or taking our clothes to the laundry or launderette, we wash them ourselves in our own washing machines; instead of going out to eat, or even buying in food from take-aways and fast-food restaurants, we buy ready-prepared meals to cook in the oven or microwave.

> Instead of capital investment taking place in industry, and industry providing services for individuals and households, increasingly, capital investment takes place in households, leaving industry engaged in what is essentially intermediate production, making the capital goods—the cookers, freezers, televisions, motor cars—used in home production of the final product.[23]

22. Scott Burns, *The Household Economy: Its Shape, Origins and Future*, pp. 14, 53.

23. Jonathan Gershuny, *After Industrial Society? The Emerging Self-Service Economy*, p. 81. Gershuny has continued to chart these trends—see, for example, *Social Innovation and the Division of Labour*, and (with Ian Miles) *The New Service Economy*.

Summarizing much of the newer research and thinking on the home, Hugh Stretton, one of its most ardent advocates, wrote this paean to it:

> In affluent societies . . . much more than half of all waking time is spent at home or near it. More than a third of capital is invested there. More than a third of work is done there. Depending on what you choose to count as goods, some high proportion of all goods are produced there, and even more are enjoyed there. More than three quarters of all subsistence, social life, leisure and recreation happen there. Above all, people are produced there, and endowed there with the values and capacities which will determine most of the quality of their social life and government away from home.[24]

This is the crucial question: the "values and capabilities" produced by the home, the culture of the home. It is not often addressed by these advocates of the home, intent on detailing such matters as the growth in home ownership and the vast expansion of household technology. But before we consider this question, we should note the continued claims made on behalf of the home as a result of its increasing penetration by the microelectronic revolution.

Gershuny had found that health and education were two of the main areas that had so far resisted the trend towards substitutability, the replacement of services by equivalent goods. But he noted that "it would only take some relatively minor technological developments . . . to convert the UK 'Open University' system into a complete university education which could be bought, once and for all, over the counter of some educational emporium." And he observed: "We cannot say for certain . . . that the same social forces that produced the home washing machine and the home music machine, will not in the future produce the home hospital machine or the home university." [25]

Great strides are being made in that direction, to the evident satisfaction of many home enthusiasts. The development of cheap video systems, home computers, CD-ROM, and a worldwide cable and satellite television network is making it possible for much of formal education, at all levels, to take place in the home. World-famous authors and lecturers have their thoughts permanently transferred to audiocassettes or videocassettes, which are then bought or loaned over the counter, or transmitted via cable or satellite. CD-ROM allows the works of whole libraries and picture galleries, in one's own country or abroad, to be read or seen at home on the home computer. Foreign languages are learned through home interactive systems. Suitably backed up by

24. Hugh Stretton, *Capitalism, Socialism and the Environment*, p. 183.
25. Gershuny, *After Industrial Society?* pp. 90–91.

textbooks and specially designed manuals, perhaps with local tutors in the background, a fully formed home educational system—a teaching machine—is at hand. It has the obvious appeal of cheapness and flexibility, enabling learning to be tailored directly towards individual needs. One can think of many reasons why it has so far not displaced conventional educational systems; but there is no doubting that the potentiality for such displacement exists, nor that many powerful forces would favor it.[26]

Things have not gone so far with health. But the increasing mechanization of the hospital, where the substitution of goods for services goes on apace, suggests what might be in store. Just as the giant computers of the past shrank to domestic scale, it is not too difficult to imagine much of the diagnostic and other machinery in hospitals being reduced to a size suitable for domestic use. Routine health matters might once more, as in earlier times, become largely a domestic affair.[27] Already it is possible for you to do a heart trace on yourself; to test your sight, hearing, and blood sugar levels; to test yourself for diabetes and bowel cancer. Women can test themselves for pregnancy. Soon they may be able to perform their own abortions, safely and cheaply. The most significant developments, however, may be in pharmaceutics. Many conditions that previously required institutional treatment, such as behavioral or mental disorders, are now increasingly dealt with at home, through self- or family-administered drugs. A whole battery of new drugs are being developed which aim to create an "invisible hospital," or invisible asylum or prison, around those thought to require treatment, surveillance, or control. The "medicalization of social problems" moves, to an extent, in the direction of the home-centered society. Cheapness is, again, a mighty motor of the change, though not the only one.[28]

The growth of home entertainment is so obvious a feature of recent times as scarcely to need documentation. The increasing miniaturization, portability, and cheapness of information goods are among the factors that have made the home the principal locus of entertainment for all members of the family. The video shop has become as routine a port of call as the supermarket (indeed, it is often now in the supermarket); the home computer supplies the facility

26. For some of the relevant technological developments in this area, see Ian Miles, *Home Informatics: Information Technology and the Transformation of Everyday Life*, pp. 17–26.

27. Mechanization could affect not just health care in the home. The film *Demon Seed* has a housebound Julie Christie impregnated by the family robot.

28. For a good discussion of some of the factors behind these developments, see Stanley Cohen, *Visions of Social Control*. For home-based health care, see Miles, *Home Informatics*, pp. 114–16; John Naisbitt, *Megatrends*, pp. 149–56.

for the endless array of computer and video games. Satellite and cable TV offer many households around thirty channels of varied viewing; after a slow start, most households have eagerly accepted the offer. The mega-multimedia corporation has for long regarded the home as the safest and softest sales target. For their part families do not need much telling that watching a video at home or subscribing to a movie channel, backed up by a TV dinner, will be a fraction of the cost of going to the cinema and having a meal afterwards—especially if travel and baby-sitting costs are thrown in.[29]

"Telebanking" and "teleshopping" are still in their infancy; but there are some strong forces behind them, and they too stress the cheapness and convenience of doing it all from home. In Britain "First Direct," a spin-off from one of the big banks, offers twenty-four-hour banking by telephone, with fewer and cheaper charges than conventional banks. Its success has not surprised those who find it increasingly dispiriting to cross the portals of a bank. As for TV teleshopping, all you need is a comfortable sofa, on which you sit television zapper in one hand, credit card in the other, and a telephone a few feet away. The television screen displays a panoply of goods, just a toll-free number away, twenty-four hours a day, seven days a week. The United States has predictably taken to this rather more than other nations so far. Annual turnover for the industry is already $2 billion and growing fast. The American QVC (Quality, Value, Convenience) channel has now also invaded the United Kingdom through a deal with Rupert Murdoch's BSkyB satellite network. Once more, the media moguls know when they are on to a good thing. People no longer make jokes about home shopping.[30]

Finally there is work. The return of work to the home has been one of the most publicized developments of recent times and, to the extent that it is occurring, represents perhaps the most far-reaching claim made by the champions of the home. The message has been carried across the globe by, among others, Alvin Toffler, both in his capacity as the best-selling author of *The Third Wave* and as an energetic publicist developing its themes via television, video, and the lecture platform.

Toffler sees the return of the "prosumer" of preindustrial times. Prosumers are neither producers nor consumers in the usual sense but people who con-

29. For Britain, the growth of home entertainment is most conveniently followed in the reports of the annual *Family Expenditure Survey* (London: HMSO). See also Miles, *Home Informatics,* pp. 96–101, 104–9.

30. On the growth of home shopping in the United States, see the report, "Shopping from the Sofa," in the *Independent,* June 20, 1993. On general developments in teleshopping and telebanking, together with the use of other home-based videotext services (Prestel, CompuServ, and so forth), see Miles, *Home Informatics,* pp. 73–75, 112–14.

sume what they themselves produce. This refers in part to the "self-service economy" mentioned earlier, and in general to the growth of the "informal" or "invisible" economy outside the market, mostly centered on the home and neighborhood. It also refers to the phenomenon of "the electronic cottage," which Toffler sees as "a return to cottage industry on a new, higher, electronic plane." In all industrial societies workers have moved from the making and handling of goods to the making and handling of information. This makes it increasingly possible for people to work at home, rather than travel to an office or factory. Most homes can be fitted with low-cost "work stations" involving a home computer, a telephone and fax, and a modem connection to national and international computer networks. Thus equipped, working at home is proving attractive to a variety of professionals, both self-employed and employees, such as architects, designers, academics, computer programmers, lawyers, accountants, and consultants in business and finance. It can also be made attractive to a host of less skilled workers, such as secretaries, salespeople, and bank and insurance employees. Here are the new "telecommuters," saving both themselves and the nation valuable time and energy.[31]

For Toffler these changes point the way to the return of "the home as the center of society." The family that works together sticks together. Home working strengthens and confirms the family. It counters the disintegrating tendencies so evident in high divorce rates. It may even lead to the revival of the "extended family," as other family members and coworkers join the nuclear family in the new home-based work environment. Toffler concludes with this ringing credo:

> I believe the home will assume a startling new importance in Third Wave civilization. The rise of the prosumer, the spread of the electronic cottage, the invention of new organizational structures in business, the automation and de-massification of production, all point to the home's re-emergence as a central unit in the society of tomorrow— a unit with enhanced rather than diminished economic, medical, educational, and social functions.[32]

It is beyond the scope of this essay to assess how far, and how fast, these various changes in a homeward direction may be occurring.[33] There are cer-

31. Alvin Toffler, *The Third Wave*, pp. 194–207, 265–88. Faith Popcorn estimates that currently nearly 25 percent of the American workforce can be classified as home workers (*The Popcorn Report*, p. 52). For Britain see Catherine Hakim, "Homeworking in Britain," in R. E. Pahl's *On Work*, pp. 609–32.

32. Toffler, *The Third Wave*, p. 354.

33. For a discussion, see Tom Forester, "The Myth of the Electronic Cottage," and the reply by Ian Miles, "The Electronic Cottage: Myth or Near-Myth?" See also the further

tainly some countervailing forces and trends. Adolescents and young people generally have shown, as always, a tendency to resist the embrace of home. The youth culture is to a good extent a street culture, although it can certainly be combined with a good deal of home activity, especially in middle-class homes. The movie industry has fought back against television by developing the "blockbuster" film, such as *Star Wars* or *Jurassic Park,* which is best seen on a big screen at a well-equipped cinema. Sport has tried, with some success, to win back the crowds by providing more comfortable venues and making sport more of a spectacle. Large, technologically sophisticated theme parks and cleverly designed entertainment complexes such as Disneyland have tried, again with considerable success, to woo people from their homes. So too have the new big shopping malls, which have tried to make shopping a day out for the family. Holidays and tourism have continued to grow, despite the recession of recent years.

But it is significant that most of these examples come from the field of entertainment and leisure. This is an area where the home has a strong record of resilience and recovery. It is constantly being replenished with fresh attractions, as now in "virtual reality" machines, which can simulate for you the experience of climbing Everest or going deep-sea diving. Certainly these countermovements have done relatively little to dent the home's commanding position in the field of entertainment. In other spheres the home has evidently come to occupy a strong, though not preponderant, position. Many powerful economic and political forces, sometimes glossed under the terms "post-Fordism" and "postmodernism," are contributing to its revived importance. The home has become a site rich in information and technical capacity. It is, at least potentially, a virtual powerhouse of production. It contains an alluring array of gadgets and instruments to occupy the time and attention of nearly all members of the family. It offers privacy and security, or seems to, in an urban environment that appears increasingly dirty and dangerous. It is constantly referred to as a haven, though a more accurate image might be an embattled fortress around which a protective moat has been thrown.

These images suggest a certain ambivalence, an uneasy mix of security and danger, fear and desire. What sort of life does the modern home offer? What *can* it offer? How realistic is it to think of it as a protected space of privacy and intimacy? Have we constructed a utopia of the home? The lofty claims

---

discussion in *Futures* 22 by Kevin Robins and James Cornford, "Bringing It All Back Home," (pp. 870–79) and the response by Ian Miles (pp. 880–85). For the conflicting trends—towards the home, and away from it—in the world of entertainment, see Anthony Smith, "The Electronic Circus." I have discussed the matter further in my *From Post-Industrial to Post-Modern Society,* especially pp. 154–63.

made on its behalf are one thing; the reality may be very different. To consider this is to consider not just the nature of the private but, as suggested by Ariès, Arendt, and others, the relation between private and public life.

INDIVIDUALISM AND THE FAMILY

MODERN SOCIETY IS generally seen as the theater of individualism. Especially in northwestern Europe and North America, where modernity first took hold and was most thoroughly promoted, individualism is associated with those twin engines of the modern world, Protestantism and capitalism. The cult of the individual, it has commonly been held, is the hallmark of modernity—at least Western modernity.[34]

This may hold up in the most general terms. But it ignores not just the persistence but the new creation of a variety of practices and institutions that in important respects countered and qualified the dominant individualism, seen at its strongest in the market economy. These included such forms as religious organizations, political associations, and trade unions. They also included the modern family.

We might say, with Durkheim, that many of these forms and practices were not, properly speaking, anti-individualistic, but were more the expressions of a "moral individualism" that was the antithesis of the egoism of the economy.[35] But in any case the qualification needs to be made. It is especially important with respect to the family. The rise of the private sphere of the family, as Ariès shows it, certainly meant the contraction of the public sphere of sociability— the wider social networks and the broad range of social activities in which the family had hitherto been implicated. "The family has advanced in proportion as sociability has retreated." But that contraction stopped at the boundaries of the nuclear family. Within the family, individual interests and desires had to be sacrificed to the needs of the whole family, especially those of its most dependent members, the children. It is in this sense that Ariès asserts that, in the modern age, "it is not individualism which has triumphed, but the family."[36]

34. This thesis is stated, and critically discussed, in Nicholas Abercrombie, Stephen Hill, and Bryan S. Turner, *Sovereign Individuals of Capitalism*. See also Peter L. Berger, Brigitte Berger, and Hansfried Kellner, *The Homeless Mind: Modernization and Consciousness*, pp. 174–76.

35. See Emile Durkheim, "Individualism and the Intellectuals" (1898), in Robert N. Bellah, ed., *Emile Durkheim on Morality and Society: Selected Writings*, pp. 43–57. This form of "moral individualism," as Durkheim goes on to show, is not merely not incompatible with, but almost seems to require, socialism.

36. Ariès, *Centuries of Childhood*, p. 393. For the importance of the family in modifying the "bare" individualism of the early capitalist economy, see Abercrombie, Hill, and Turner,

But, if so, the triumph has been short-lived. The family was probably at its most resilient in the nineteenth century, when for many it did play the part of a bulwark against the buffets of a rapidly changing world. The nineteenth-century novel is perhaps the best place to explore the interplay between family and society, as more or less equal partners. But the twentieth century has seen the decline and disintegration of the family as a community, as a collectivity expressing the common purposes of its members. Individualism's progress, interrupted and held in check in various ways, has continued apace. It has now invaded the family as well as other sectors of society. In the end it is individualism, not the family, that has triumphed. The family is no longer, nor can it be, a "haven in a heartless world."

Let us take a snapshot of the contemporary family and household. In Britain, 40 percent of all first marriages end in divorce (and the divorce rate for remarried people is even higher—you have to marry three times to be reasonably secure). Twenty-one percent—one in five—of families with dependent children are headed by a single parent. One in four households is a single-person household. The standard nuclear family of two parents and dependent children now accounts for only 15 percent of all families at any one time. The average number of children per family has dropped to 1.8. Thirty percent of all births are outside marriage. Thirty-five percent of single women aged between 25 and 34 are cohabiting. All these tendencies have been growing over the past quarter of a century, some of them—such as divorce and one-parent families—at an especially fast rate.[37]

These are familiar kinds of figures, much discussed in all Western societies. Two things in particular need to be said about them. First, they are, precisely, snapshots of family life caught at a particular moment; they do not reflect the full experience of individuals over time. We may move from membership of a two-parent family to a single-parent family and back again to a two-parent family; we may have gone from living in a three-person household to a one-

---

Sovereign Individuals of Capitalism, pp. 111–17; also the good study by Michael Anderson, *Family Structure in Nineteenth-Century Lancashire.*

37. For these figures, see the report of the Mintel research organization, *Family Lifestyles, 1993;* also *Family Spending: A Report on the 1992 Family Expenditure Survey* (London: HMSO, 1993); *Social Trends* (London: HMSO, 1993). There are some valuable essays on their meaning in David Clark's edited volume, *Marriage, Domestic Life and Social Change;* see also Diana Gittins, *The Family in Question: Changing Households and Familiar Ideologies.* For earlier figures, with good discussions of the trends, see R. N. Rapoport et al., eds., *Families in Britain;* Jonathan Gathorne-Hardy, *Love, Sex, Marriage and Divorce.* For the United States, which presents a largely comparable picture, see Andrew J. Cherlin, *Marriage, Divorce, Remarriage;* Sar A. Levitan and Richard S. Belous, *What's Happening to the American Family?;* Arlene S. Skolnick and Jerome K. Skolnick's *Family in Transition.*

person household; and so on. The life cycle puts us in different kinds of families at different times. Most of us will have experienced a variety of family styles over our total life span.

The second thing to say is that the figures, by themselves, tell us nothing, or next to nothing, about the satisfaction of individuals or the health of society. It is perfectly possible that individuals are much happier, and the condition of society much healthier, for the state of things suggested by these figures. They could reflect an increase in individual freedom and independence, or the growth of a welcome social diversity.

But what they cannot reasonably be held to do is indicate that the *family* is in a robust state of health—not, at least, as the family has been understood for the past two hundred years. They point to a family increasingly fragmented and disjointed, almost to the point of dissolution.[38] The snapshot of family

38. Figures such as these give rise to the familiar question of whether the glass is half full or half empty. For some people what is remarkable is not, for example, that more than a third of all marriages end in divorce but that, given the enormously increased life expectancy of the spouses, nearly two-thirds do not. I accept the force of that. My point is that these figures show the weakness and instability of the standard nuclear family, the family that clearly underlies the claims made on behalf of the home, and so throw into question the validity of those claims.

There is the much bigger question of the very definition of the family, and its complex history. It has been argued that there has never been merely one family form ("*the* family"), and that the nuclear family in particular has always been accompanied by a variety of other forms. What we may be seeing, therefore, in the current growth of one-parent families, one-person households, experiments with family communes, and the like, is simply the contemporary manifestation of the general plurality of family forms. Hence it is wrong to talk of "the decline of the family"; there is simply change. For such arguments, see Suzanne Keller, "Does the Family Have a Future?" in Skolnick and Skolnick, eds., *Family in Transition,* pp. 137–50; Jessie Bernard, *The Future of Marriage,* pp. 171–81; Gittins, *The Family in Question,* pp. 155–68; Barrett and McIntosh, *The Anti-Social Family,* pp. 29–40, 81–130. A related argument is that a concentration on the nuclear *family* neglects the possibility, revealed by recent research, that the *household* may be extended across a much wider range of kin, and involve many of them in its activities. See Patricia Wilson and Ray Pahl, "The Changing Sociological Construct of the Family."

Again, one has to accept the force of these arguments. But even those who make them admit that the nuclear family—and the nuclear family household—has established itself as the norm or ideal of all classes in Western society. That, indeed, is their complaint: that the modern bourgeois family, the nuclear family, has over the past hundred years or so come to dominate the aspirations, and to a good extent the practice, of all groups in society (see, for a good account of this process, Mark Poster, *Critical Theory of the Family*). It is largely because of this that the contemporary advocates of the home take it for granted that the nuclear family and the home are now more or less synonymous. They rest their claims for the desirability and vitality of the home on the desirability and vitality of the nuclear family. Any question mark over the nuclear family therefore poses a real challenge to their

life does not tell us much about the full range and quality of individual experience, but it tells us a great deal about family structure in contemporary society. The family may have held its own for a while as the sphere of private life counterposed to the public realm. But that depended on this private sphere's having a solidity and an autonomy that enabled it to fend off the pressures of society. This private sphere needed to hold on to a stable social space in which its actors could find fulfillment as members of a community, through a common solidarity. It needed also to maintain a certain distance from the public sphere, so that it could develop according to its own principles of morality and social existence. Now it has lost both that solidarity and its relative independence. The private sphere of the family, already precariously small, has shrunk further with the further inroads of individualism. It has been further privatized. It has narrowed right down its individual elements. In doing so, it has virtually annulled itself.

"Affective individualism," in too strong a dose, is inimical to the family. Like the "sentiment," the search for personal fulfillment, that Edward Shorter sees as the driving force behind the rise of the nuclear family in the eighteenth century, it is a corrosive force. Shorter finds the "postmodern family," an attenuated fragment, bidding farewell to the nuclear family: "The nuclear family is crumbling—to be replaced, I think, by the free-floating couple, a marital dyad subject to dramatic fissions and fusions, and without the orbiting satellites of pubertal children, close friends, or neighbours." [39]

It might seem as if to blame individualism for the decline of the family is to put the blame on the family itself, or at least its members. After all, is it not the self-assertion of women and children that has dissolved the largely patriarchal family? But Ariès and Arendt are at one with most feminists in arguing that this is not the case. Causality has flowed in the opposite direction.

---

claims. It is possible that other family forms might provide the basis for a different concept of home; but so far at any rate none other seems sufficiently desired, or sufficiently secure, to provide a sound basis for a new *general* concept of home. See, for the "interchangeability" of the home and the nuclear family today: Graham Allan, "Insiders and Outsiders: Boundaries around the Home," in Allan and Crow, eds., *Home and Family*, pp. 141–58.

39. Shorter, *The Making of the Modern Family*, p. 273. For an interesting account of how the forces of "romanticism," coupled to "self-assertion and self-concern," broke down the nineteenth-century American family, see David E. Stannard, "Changes in the American Family: Fiction and Reality," in Tufte and Meyerhoff, eds., *Changing Images of the Family*, pp. 83–96. The report of the Mintel research organization, *Family Lifestyles, 1993*, noting the declining size of families and the rise of the childless couple, attributed this to "a growing individualism among would-be parents," and the desire of individuals "to fulfil all sides" of their personalities (pp. 49–50).

Individualism is a social ideology carried by powerful social forces. The nuclear family was itself the result of individualizing currents that undermined older corporate ties. At the same time it acted partly to offset the individualism of the wider society. In its further development capitalist industrial society knocked away that prop. The family found itself unable to contain the individualism that increasingly motivated its members.

Ariès has already suggested one of the ways in which the nuclear family was undermined. It was "overloaded" or "overburdened" with tasks. The earlier family shared its burden—social, economic and emotional—with a variety of adults and children, kin and nonkin, who were part of the household. The household itself lived in a sea of sociability. The modern family, reduced to its nuclear core, was forced to rely almost entirely on the resources of its handful of members. At the same time, with the decline in sociability, it was cut off from civic and social life. It had to satisfy all the aspirations of its members—for love, care, companionship, consolation, nurture, protection—out of itself alone. This was an unrealistic aim. The nuclear family broke under the strain. It became the arena of a "destructive Gemeinschaft" whose ultimate effect was to turn all members of the family against each other. They faced the alternative of punishing each other within the family or of seeking their fulfillment outside it, each in his or her own way.[40]

Arendt has pointed to the other main cause of the nuclear family's downfall. The social space it occupied was increasingly colonized by other agencies and institutions from without. This is the process that Christopher Lasch has also described in his account of "the family besieged." For him, the family was not so much overloaded as invaded. Recognizing the inability of the nuclear family to fulfill its functions out of its own resources, social science and the "helping professions" sought to support the family in its role as provider and socializer. The result, however, was to undermine the autonomy of the family, and to strip its members of their competence and independence. The nuclear family became an appanage of the therapeutic state, which took upon itself

40. For Ariès's account, see note 15 above. See also Richard Sennett, "Destructive Gemeinschaft," in Norman Birnbaum's edited volume, *Beyond the Crisis*, pp. 171–97; and Sennett's *The Fall of Public Man*, especially part 4, "Intimate Society." For the harmful effects—on all its members—of the child-centered nuclear family, see Slater, *The Pursuit of Loneliness*, pp. 62–87. Christopher Lasch rightly points out that one source of "the theory of emotional overload"—that people expect more satisfaction from the family than it can provide—is, ironically, the work of Talcott Parsons. Parsons's functionalist defense of the nuclear family, as the home of expressive life, is reinterpreted as the condemnation of its members to privatism, psychic punishment, escapism, and neurotic withdrawal. See Lasch, *Haven in a Heartless World: The Family Besieged*, p. 145.

the right to intervene in family life and to discipline family members. The family was increasingly treated as a collection of individuals in need of protection from each other.[41]

There was one further kind of invasion, this time originating directly in the culture of individualism itself. As industrial societies moved from mass production to mass consumption, the home was targeted as a prime site of consumerism. Household "consumer goods" were the principal output of the new consumer industries. Some of these were initially promoted by evoking images of the traditional nuclear family. The family was pictured sitting together around the new television set as they had once sat around the hearth. But these cozy images of family togetherness were shattered by the more complete development of consumerism.

Consumer culture always had as its principal emblem the individual. It was individual freedom, spontaneity, and pleasure that it traded in. It came to appeal to family members as individuals—as individual men, women, adolescents, even infants, seeking their own fulfillment and the fullest extension of their personalities. And it supplied the goods, services, and images to match this. In doing so it pulled the family apart. Households were persuaded that they needed not one family car but two, three, or more cars so that every member of the family beyond a certain age could enjoy the freedom of the road, and have their own independence. Cable and satellite allowed television to move from broadcasting to "narrowcasting," giving virtually every family member the ability to choose their own programs in the privacy of their own room. Household consumer goods became smaller, cheaper, and more portable, suited to the different needs of different family members. If husband and wife still sat together in the downstairs parlor watching television, their teenage son was watching a video with his friends in his bedroom, while in another room his sister was curled up on her bed cocooned by her personal stereo system.

The "democracy of the microwave" adds further to the physical and social dispersal of the family. The *Wall Street Journal* wrote some years ago that the microwave was "the embodiment of Eighties-style individualism, turning each family member into a chef. Gone is the sanctity of the family meal."[42] Super-

41. For Arendt, see note 21 above; for Lasch, see note 40 above. Employing a more explicitly Foucauldian framework, Jacques Donzelot gives an account substantially like Lasch's: see *The Policing of Families.*

42. Quoted in Keith Botsford, "Ping, Unload, Zap and Refuel," *Independent*, October 7, 1989. The invasion of the family by consumerism and "the universal market" is well described by Harry Braverman, *Labor and Monopoly Capital: The Degradation of Work in the Twentieth Century*, pp. 272–83. And compare Ulrich Beck on "the dissolving post-

markets supply the microwavable convenience foods, which can be accumulated in the family freezer. Family members make their choice, each according to their own taste, and at whatever time is most convenient to them. A few minutes in the microwave and the dish can be hastily consumed at the table or hurried away to one's room, to be consumed alone or with friends. If the hearth is no longer the center of the home, no more is the kitchen or the dining room, with the family meal symbolizing unity and togetherness.

FROM HOME TO HOTEL?

WHAT IS A HOME? It cannot be defined by its functions since, as many people have pointed out, these can often be done better by a host of other institutions, from schools to health farms. Nor is it the same as a house, or even a household. Mary Douglas has used the contrast between home and hotel to show the essence of the idea of home. The idea of a hotel, she argues, is the complete antithesis of the home. Both feed and sleep their inhabitants; both provide many of the same amenities for relaxation and entertainment. But the commercial basis of the hotel puts it at the opposite pole to the communal idea of the home. The home is an "embryonic" or "virtual" community; the hotel is a "virtual market." "The idea of the hotel is the standard 'Other,' where every comfort has to be paid for, the mercenary, cold, luxurious counterpart against which the home is . . . measured." [43]

But Douglas makes another important distinction between home and hotel. "The idea of the hotel is a perfect opposite of the home, not only because it uses market principles for its transactions, but because it allows its clients to buy privacy as a right of exclusion." The home does allow, indeed exists, for privacy. But it must be a "limited privacy." [44] The overriding principle must be "enough solidarity to protect the collective good." In this sense, the private space of the home is a "public good" whose strength and survival depend on its members' willingness to subordinate their individual wishes to its collective needs. Members must attend regularly for common meals. They

---

familial pluralism of families," in Ulrich Beck, Anthony Giddens, and Scott Lash, *Reflexive Modernization*, p. 16. For an account of the individualized "cellular family" and "cellular household," as pictured and targeted by commercial organizations and market forecasters, see Alan Tomlinson, "Home Fixtures: Doing-It-Yourself in a Privatized World," in A. Tomlinson's *Consumption, Identity and Style*, p. 61.

43. Mary Douglas, "The Idea of a Home: A Kind of Space," p. 300. Others stress the essentially ambivalent character of the home, both a place of comfort and refuge and a place of fear and danger. See the contributions to "The Question of Home," a special issue of *New Formations* (summer 1992), vol. 17; and Robert M. Rakoff, "Ideology in Everyday Life: The Meaning of the House."

44. Douglas, "The Idea of a Home," pp. 304–5.

must take part in the sociable activities of the home, such as entertaining guests. ("Perhaps the most subversive attack on the home is to be present physically without joining in its multiple coordinations.") They must abide by the rules that govern permissible behavior and language.

Those committed to maintaining the idea of the home need to exercise "continual vigilance," even a certain degree of authoritarianism, in the upkeep of these collective activities. Too much opportunism and individualism leads to a breakdown of solidarity. The home becomes a household, or even something approaching a hotel. Members make regular financial contributions for their upkeep, or share the rent. They carefully monitor their contribution to household duties, adjudicating claims and conflicts according to the principles of equity and rationality. Beyond that they keep out of each other's way and pursue their private—that is, individual—lives.[45]

Douglas's distinctions seem to me persuasive. On that basis, we have clearly moved a long way from the home and are halfway towards the hotel. The family is increasingly a collection of individuals who, for the time, share the same household. The home, it is true, cannot in all cases be identified with the family—nonkin members have often played a vital part in making a home. But the modern home is the modern nuclear family. Its fate is linked to the fortunes of the nuclear family. The fragmentation of the nuclear family is the fragmentation of the home.

In the midst of his famous mid-Victorian paean to the home ("a sacred place, a vestal temple," and so forth), John Ruskin warned:

> So far as the anxieties of the outer life penetrate into it, and the inconsistently-minded, unknown, unloved, or hostile society of the outer world is allowed by either husband or wife to cross the threshold, it ceases to be home; it is then only a part of that outer world which you have roofed over, and lighted fire in.[46]

Not just the anxieties but the agencies of "outer life" have penetrated the home. If the home is a fortress, then the enemy is encamped within. The modern home was set an impossible task: to succor its members in isolation from, and to a good extent in opposition to, the life of the wider society. Small wonder that it should have succumbed in internal disorder and external regulation. Modern society is not all of a piece, but it is unthinkable that it

45. Ibid., pp. 297–303.

46. John Ruskin, *Sesame and Lilies* ("Of Queens' Gardens"), in E. T. Cook and Alexander Wedderburn's edited volume, *The Works of John Ruskin,* 18:122. On the rise of the family not merely as a private but as a sacred sphere, the sphere of subjectivity and meaning par excellence, see Eli Zaretsky, *Capitalism, the Family, and Personal Life,* pp. 36–77.

should allow so important an institution as the family to go its own way. It was impossible to stop the dynamic forces of modern society at the door of the nuclear family. Sociologists might speak of "functional differentiation" and a specialized role for the family as the guardian of private life; the reality has been more like a species of internal colonialism.[47]

The integrity and independence of the family is central to the rhetoric of politicians. So too the manufacturers and merchants have played up the home as the prime site of individual satisfaction, the place where we should be persuaded to spend most of our time and conduct most of our activities. They have supplied the home with a dazzling array of resources. In response, individuals have set about, with a conspicuous degree of success, in cocooning themselves in the home. The fear of violence in the streets, and the general deterioration of the urban environment, have reinforced this trend.[48] For better or worse, in the apparent absence of any alternative, individuals have settled for home. To that extent there is no denying, and no need to deny, the descriptive force of the "home-centered society."

But that is quite a different matter from the prescriptive endorsement of the home, in the manner of the home enthusiasts. That would be to accept the politicians' protestations and industrialists' propaganda at face value. The politicians have not protected the family, and the industrialists have not liberated the home. The home has been celebrated as never before, but it is also more vulnerable than ever before. The politicians declare its sanctity but at the same time systematically intervene in its affairs, taking upon themselves the mantle of the great protector of the home. Law and regulation have penetrated the family to the extent of making it a branch of the welfare state, a happy hunting ground for lawyers and social workers. That this gives some support and protection to individual family members cannot be doubted; what also cannot be doubted is that it immensely weakens the family as an institution. One does not have to be an apologist for the nuclear family to see that, in its current condition, it is simply incapable of carrying out the many special tasks assigned to it by the ideologues of the home. The private sphere of the family is a space that has been increasingly filled by outside forces.

So far as the building up of the material infrastructure of the home is

---

47. On the "underinstitutionalization" of the private sphere, and the weakness in particular of its key institution, the family, in relation to the public sphere, see Berger, Berger, and Kellner, *The Homeless Mind*, pp. 167–68.

48. For a lively account of the "cocooning" phenomenon in the United States, see Popcorn, *The Popcorn Report*, pp. 27–33, 78–84. There is a good account of cocooning, 1970s style, in Pawley, *The Private Future*, and in Slater, *The Pursuit of Loneliness* (see note 2 above).

concerned—the household technology revolution—this represents not so much a freeing as a comprehensive industrialization of the home. As with other forms of industrialization it is double-edged in its effects on creativity and autonomy. Not only does much domestic technology actually increase the work time spent on household chores,[49] it confirms and promotes a home-based life that is contrary in almost every respect to the idea of home, as usually understood. It is a life that isolates individuals from each other and encourages a degree of privacy that is hostile to the common purposes of the home. At the same time the content of that private life is to a good extent determined by outside agencies and outside purposes.

The new communications media, for instance, may be increasingly home-targeted. But far from confirming the sense of a specific place—a home, a locality with its own culture—they abolish the specificity of place and replace it with delocalized space. The home occupies a position in "homogeneous space"; it is simply the conduit for people, ideas, and images that are plucked from the global society and presented to individuals on the screens in their homes. "Face-to-face" family interaction, insofar as it still takes place, takes place in front of the television set, mediated by television images and influences.[50]

It may be that the degradation and displacement of the home was, as Ariès especially suggests, implicit in its very elevation as a proud isolated bastion standing against the rough currents of society. Joseph Rykwert observes that the word "home," in the Indo-European languages, comes from a root *(kei)* meaning "a settlement or a village," "so that 'home' becomes . . . a communal and neighborly manner of dwelling."

> I would argue . . . that a house . . . can be a true home only in such
> neighborly circumstances. While the lonely hearth will not quite make
> a home, therefore, yet the erection of the home-house into a castle

49. Most of which of course still fall on women. See Ruth Schwartz Cowan, *More Work for Mother: The Ironies of Household Technology from the Open Hearth to the Microwave.* On the industrialization and mechanization of the household, see also Siegfried Giedion, *Mechanization Takes Command,* pp. 512–627; Christine Hardyment, *From Mangle to Microwave: The Mechanization of Household Work.*

50. See Joshua Meyrowitz, *No Sense of Place: The Impact of Electronic Media on Social Behavior,* p. 147. Meyrowitz also suggests that the electronic media are encouraging the trend towards single-person households, since "living alone involves treating even family members like partial strangers," and this suits the pattern of association fostered by the electronic media. "In both electronic communication and single-living . . . the options of association are large and shared, but the choice is individual and idiosyncratic" (p. 148). On "delocalized space" and the loss of place, see also Gérard Raulet, "The New Utopia: Communications Technologies," pp. 40–41.

which defies its neighbors, and may be seen as quite separate from the public realm, makes it much less of a home.[51]

This seems to be the essential point: the cutting off of the home from the public realm. The relegation of the home to an isolated private sphere spelled its doom. It was too small, too vulnerable, to resist the incursions of the wider society, which in time developed powerful resources, and powerful reasons, for invading it. Connected to the wider society through the "interstitial space" of sociability, through the network of social activities and social institutions with which it overlapped in the seventeenth, eighteenth, and much of the nineteenth centuries, it could preserve some independence and give its members some space for privacy and intimacy. As the public realm of sociability contracted, the family became increasingly defenseless.[52] Private life, now identified exclusively with the family, suffered accordingly. Private life lives off the balance, or perhaps one should say, the interpenetration, of public and private. By itself it shrivels and dries up, turning in on itself in the form of narcissism and neurosis. The predicament of private life, of the home, at the end of the twentieth century, is the predicament of our public life, emptied of meaning for all but a handful of politicians and publicists.

51. Joseph Rykwert, "House and Home," pp. 56–57. On the extent to which homes in earlier times were seen as part of a communal (public) identity, rather than as expressing merely an individual (private) identity, see David M. Hummon, "House, Home, and Identity in Contemporary American Culture," in Setha Low and Erve Chambers, eds., *Housing, Culture, and Design,* pp. 211–12. On a similar idea of home as "a set of concentric circles," radiating out from the house of one's birth to the wider society and world beyond, see Vaclav Havel, "On Home," in *Summer Meditations,* translated by Paul Wilson, pp. 30–33.

52. On the decline of sociability, see Ariès, "The Family and the City," pp. 36–41. The decline of sociability is also at the center of Jane Jacobs's lament in *The Death and Life of Great American Cities.* More recently, though less incisively, it has also been chronicled as the decline in our time of the "third place"—the informal public life of cafés, coffee shops, and the like: see Ray Oldenburg, *The Great Good Place.*

REFERENCES

Abercrombie, Nicholas, Stephen Hill, and Bryan S. Turner. 1986. *Sovereign Individuals of Capitalism.* London: Allen & Unwin.

Adorno, Theodor. 1974. "Refuge for the Homeless." In *Minima Moralia,* translated by E. F. N. Jephcott. London: Verso.

Allan, Graham, and Graham Crow, eds. 1989. *Home and Family: Creating the Domestic Sphere.* London: Macmillan.

Anderson, Michael. 1971. *Family Structure in Nineteenth-Century Lancashire.* Cambridge: Cambridge University Press.

Arendt, Hannah. 1959. *The Human Condition.* New York: Doubleday Anchor.

Ariès, Philippe. 1973. *Centuries of Childhood: A Social History of Family Life.* Harmondsworth: Penguin.

———. 1979. "The Family and the City in the Old World and the New." In *Changing Images of the Family,* edited by Virginia Tufte and Barbara Meyerhoff. New Haven, CT, and London: Yale University Press.

Barrett, Michèle, and Mary McIntosh. 1991. *The Anti-Social Family.* Rev. ed. London: Verso.

Beck, Ulrich, Anthony Giddens, and Scott Lash. 1994. *Reflexive Modernization.* Cambridge: Polity Press.

Berger, Peter L., Brigitte Berger, and Hansfried Kellner. 1974. *The Homeless Mind: Modernization and Consciousness.* Harmondsworth: Penguin.

Bernard, Jessie. 1982. *The Future of Marriage.* 2d ed. New Haven, CT: Yale University Press.

Braverman, Harry. 1974. *Labor and Monopoly Capital: The Degradation of Work in the Twentieth Century.* New York: Monthly Review Press.

Breytenbach, Breyton. 1991. "The Long March from Hearth to Heart." *Social Research* 58, no. 1: 69–83.

Brittan, Arthur. 1977. *The Privatised World.* London: Routledge & Kegan Paul.

Burns, Scott. 1977. *The Household Economy: Its Shape, Origins and Future.* Boston: Beacon Press.

Cherlin, Andrew J. 1992. *Marriage, Divorce, Remarriage.* Revised and enlarged edition. Cambridge, MA: Harvard University Press.

Clark, Clifford Edward, Jr. 1986. *The American Family Home.* Chapel Hill, NC: University of North Carolina Press.

Clark, David, ed. 1991. *Marriage, Domestic Life and Social Change.* London: Routledge.

Cohen, Stanley. 1985. *Visions of Social Control.* Cambridge: Polity Press.

Coontz, Stephanie. 1994. *The Way We Never Were: American Families and the Nostalgia Trap.* New York: Basic Books.

Cowan, Ruth Schwartz. 1989. *More Work for Mother: The Ironies of Household Technology from the Open Hearth to the Microwave.* London: Free Association Books.

Crow, Graham. 1989. "The Post-War Development of the Modern Domestic Ideal." In *Home and Family: Creating the Domestic Sphere,* edited by Graham Allan and Graham Crow. London: Macmillan.

Daunton, H. J. 1983. "Public and Private Space: The Victorian City and the Working Class Household." In *The Pursuit of Urban History,* edited by D. Frazer and A. Sutcliffe. London: Edward Arnold.

Davidoff, Leonore, and Catherine Hall. 1987. *Family Fortunes: Men and Women of the English Middle Class, 1780–1850.* London: Hutchinson.

Donzelot, Jacques. 1979. *The Policing of Families.* Translated from the French by Robert Hurley. New York: Pantheon.

Douglas, Mary. 1991. "The Idea of a Home: A Kind of Space." *Social Research* 58, no. 1 (spring): 287–307.

Durkheim, Emile. 1973. "Individualism and the Intellectuals." In *Emile Durkheim on Morality and Society: Selected Writings,* edited by Robert N. Bellah. Chicago: University of Chicago Press.

Forester, Tom. 1988. "The Myth of the Electronic Cottage." *Futures* 20, no. 3: 227–40.

Gathorne-Hardy, Jonathan. 1983. *Love, Sex, Marriage and Divorce.* London: Triad/Granada.

Gershuny, Jonathan. 1978. *After Industrial Society? The Emerging Self-Service Economy.* London: Macmillan.

———. 1983. *Social Innovation and the Division of Labour.* Oxford: Oxford University Press.

Gershuny, Jonathan, and Ian Miles. 1983. *The New Service Economy.* London: Frances Pinter.

Giedion, Siegfried. 1969. *Mechanization Takes Command.* New York: Norton.

Gittins, Diana. 1993. *The Family in Question: Changing Households and Familiar Ideologies.* 2d ed. London: Macmillan.

Goldthorpe, John H., et al. 1969. *The Affluent Worker in the Class Structure.* Cambridge: Cambridge University Press.

Habermas, Jürgen. [1962] 1989. *The Structural Transformation of the Public Sphere.* Translated by Thomas Burger and Frederick Lawrence. Cambridge, MA: MIT Press.

Hakim, Catherine. 1988. "Homeworking in Britain." In *On Work,* edited by R. E. Pahl. Oxford: Basil Blackwell.

Hall, Stuart, and Martin Jacques, eds. 1989. *New Times: The Changing Face of Politics in the 1990s.* London: Lawrence & Wishart.

Hansen, Karen V. 1987. "Feminist Conceptions of Public and Private: A Critical Analysis." *Berkeley Journal of Sociology* 32: 105–28.

Hardyment, Christine. 1988. *From Mangle to Microwave: The Mechanization of Household Work.* Cambridge: Polity Press.

Hareven, Tamara. 1991. "The Home and the Family in Historical Perspective." *Social Research* 58, no. 1 (spring): 253–85.

Havel, Vaclav. 1992. "On Home." In *Summer Meditations,* translated by Paul Wilson. New York: Knopf.

Hayden, Dolores. 1984. *Redesigning the American Dream: The Future of Housing, Work, and Family Life.* New York and London: Norton.

Hirschman, Albert. 1982. *Shifting Involvements: Private Interest and Public Action.* Princeton, NJ: Princeton University Press.

Hobsbawm, Eric. 1991. Introduction to the section on "Exile." In "Special Issue: Home: A Place in the World," edited by Arien Mack. *Social Research* 58, no. 1 (spring): 67–68.

Houghton, Walter E. 1957. *The Victorian Frame of Mind.* New Haven, CT, and London: Yale University Press.

Hummon, David M. 1989. "House, Home, and Identity in Contemporary American Culture." In *Housing, Culture, and Design,* edited by Setha Low and Erve Chambers. Philadelphia: University of Pennsylvania Press.

Jacobs, Jane. 1961. *The Death and Life of Great American Cities.* New York: Vintage.

Keller, Suzanne. 1990. "Does the Family Have a Future?" In *Family in Transition,* edited by Arlene S. Skolnick and Jerome K. Skolnick. 5th ed. Boston: Little, Brown.

Kolinsky, Eva. 1993. "Exodus to the Private Realm." *Times Higher Education Supplement,* January 29: 15–18.

Kumar, Krishan. 1995. *From Post-Industrial to Post-Modern Society.* Oxford: Blackwell Publishers.

Laing, R. D. 1971. *The Politics of the Family, and Other Essays.* London: Tavistock Publications.

Lasch, Christopher. 1979. *Haven in a Heartless World: The Family Besieged.* New York: Basic Books.

Laslett, Barbara. 1973. "The Family as a Public and Private Institution: An Historical Perspective." *Journal of Marriage and the Family* 35(3): 480–92.

Levitan, Sar A., and Richard S. Belous. 1981. *What's Happening to the American Family?* Baltimore and London: Johns Hopkins University Press.

Meyrowitz, Joshua. 1986. *No Sense of Place: The Impact of Electronic Media on Social Behavior.* New York: Oxford University Press.

Miles, Ian. 1988a. *Home Informatics: Information Technology and the Transformation of Everyday Life.* London: Pinter Publishers.

———. 1988b. "The Electronic Cottage: Myth or Near-Myth?" *Futures* 20, no. 4: 355–66.

Moore, Barrington, Jr. 1984. "Public and Private in Classical Athens." In *Privacy: Studies in Social and Cultural History.* Armonk, NY: M. E. Sharpe.

Morley, David, and Kevin Robins. 1990. "No Place Like *Heimat:* Images of Home(land) in European Culture." *New Formations* 12 (winter): 1–23.

Mount, Ferdinand. 1982. *The Subversive Family.* London: Unwin.

Naisbitt, John. 1984. *Megatrends.* New York: Warner Books.

Oakley, Ann. 1982. *Subject Women.* London: Fontana, 1982.

Oldenburg, Ray. 1991. *The Great Good Place.* New York: Paragon House.

Pahl, R. E. 1984. *Divisions of Labour.* Oxford: Basil Blackwell.

Pawley, Martin. 1975. *The Private Future: Causes and Consequences of Community Collapse in the West.* London: Pan Books.

Popcorn, Faith. 1992. *The Popcorn Report.* New York: HarperCollins.

Poster, Mark. 1978. *Critical Theory of the Family.* London: Pluto Press.

Rakoff, Robert M. 1977. "Ideology in Everyday Life: The Meaning of the House." *Politics and Society* 7(1): 85–104.

Rapoport, R. N., et al., eds. 1982. *Families in Britain*. London: Routledge & Kegan Paul.

Raulet, Gérard. 1991. "The New Utopia: Communications Technologies." *Telos*, no. 87: 39–58.

Robins, Kevin, and James Cornford. 1990. "Bringing It All Back Home." *Futures* 22, no. 3: 870–79.

Ruskin, John. 1905. *Sesame and Lilies*. In *The Works of John Ruskin*, edited by E. T. Cook and Alexander Wedderburn. London: George Allen.

Rybczynski, Witold. 1987. *Home: A Short History of an Idea*. New York: Penguin.

Rykwert, Joseph. 1991. "House and Home." *Social Research* 58:1 (spring): 51–62.

Saunders, Peter. 1990. *A Nation of Home Owners*. London: Unwin Hyman.

Sennett, Richard. 1977a. "Destructive Gemeinschaft." In *Beyond the Crisis*, edited by Norman Birnbaum. New York: Oxford University Press.

———. 1977b. *The Fall of Public Man*. Cambridge: Cambridge University Press.

Shorter, Edward. 1977. *The Making of the Modern Family*. London: Fontana.

Simmel, Georg. 1984. "Female Culture." In *Georg Simmel: On Women, Sexuality and Love*, translated and edited by Guy Oakes. New Haven, CT, and London: Yale University Press.

Skolnick, Arlene S., and Jerome K. Skolnick, eds. 1990. *Family in Transition*. 5th ed. Boston: Little, Brown.

Slater, Philip. 1976. *The Pursuit of Loneliness: American Culture at the Breaking Point*. Rev. ed. Boston: Beacon Press.

Smith, Anthony. 1993. "The Electronic Circus." *The Economist*, September 11–17: 96–98.

Social Research. 1991. Special Issue: "Home: A Place in the World," edited by Arien Mack. 58, no. 1 (Spring).

Stannard, David E. 1979. "Changes in the American Family: Fiction and Reality." In *Changing Images of the Family*, edited by Virginia Tufte and Barbara Meyerhoff. New Haven, CT, and London: Yale University Press.

Stone, Lawrence. 1979. *The Family, Sex and Marriage in England, 1500–1800*. Harmondsworth: Penguin.

———. 1991. "The Public and the Private in the Stately Homes of England, 1500–1990." *Social Research* 58, no. 1: 227–51.

Stretton, Hugh. 1976. *Capitalism, Socialism and the Environment*. Cambridge: Cambridge University Press.

Tamas, G. M. 1993. "The Legacy of Dissent." *Times Literary Supplement*, May 14: 14–16.

Toffler, Alvin. 1981. *The Third Wave*. New York: Bantam.

Tomlinson, Alan. 1990. "Home Fixtures: Doing-It-Yourself in a Privatized World." In *Consumption, Identity, and Style*, edited by A. Tomlinson. London and New York: Routledge.

Tucker, Aviezer. 1994. "In Search of Home." *Journal of Applied Philosophy* 11, no. 2: 181–87.

Williams, Peter. 1987. "Constituting Class and Gender: A Social History of the Home, 1700–1901." In *Class and Space: The Making of Urban Society,* edited by Nigel Thrift and Peter Williams. London and New York: Routledge & Kegan Paul.

Wilson, Patricia, and Ray Pahl. 1988. "The Changing Sociological Construct of the Family." *Sociological Review* 36, no. 2: 233–66.

Zaretsky, Eli. 1976. *Capitalism, the Family, and Personal Life.* London: Pluto Press.

From Public Housing to Private Communities: The Discipline of Design and the Materialization of the Public/Private Distinction in the Built Environment

David Brain

IT IS DIFFICULT to imagine a critical discussion of architecture or the urban environment that did not, at some point, invoke the distinction between "public" and "private." Just as this dichotomy has been central to the institutional order of modern Western societies, it is ingrained in our practical experience of the spatial organization of social life and woven into the technical language and professional practices of architects and urban planners. An orienting framework for both common sense and expert knowledge, the public/private distinction has also figured prominently in the main tendencies of architectural and cultural criticism that have tried to address the social significance of the built environment. For at least three decades, these critical discussions have focused heavily on arguments about the quality and transformations of "public space"—expressing both the concerns of those who worry about the "end of public space" and the hopes of those who see signs of its reconstruction in what they optimistically call a "new urbanism."

The destruction of traditional public spaces has been linked to the "privatization" of the city, a process that involves the decay of older city centers, the creation of quasi-public spaces restrictively controlled by private interests, and the remaking of the city as a secure site for atomized consumption. Critics of shopping malls, atrium hotels, festival marketplaces, and "historical" urban centers have found in these new architectural forms both a reflection and a cause of the decline of civic culture and active political engagement. It has been argued that the creation of new spaces defined by their spectacular qualities rather than sedimented historical meanings, the packaging of space itself as an object of visual consumption, and the proliferation of signifiers in the urban landscape all tend to impoverish our experience of collective life. Beneath the superficial diversity of images, one finds symbolic emptiness and,

I would like to thank Jeff Weintraub for his heroic efforts quite beyond the usual duties of an editor. His careful reading, sensitive comments, and astute suggestions were responsible for much clarification of both ideas and writing.

in Mike Davis's words, a "post-liberal" city where "the defense of luxury has given birth to an arsenal of security systems and an obsession with the policing of social boundaries through architecture."[1]

Others are heartened by the revival of images of urbanity and public sociability in both rebuilt city centers and suburban "edge cities."[2] In defense of the much-maligned shopping mall, Witold Rybczynski has pointed out that "the atmosphere is enlivened by families eating lunch in the food court, excited teenagers swarming at the video arcade, young parents trailing children on the way to the movie theatre." He finds encouragement in the fact that people "are rubbing shoulders, they are in a shared space."[3] More theoretically sophisticated critics are a bit less sanguine, but still see glimmers of hope amid hyperreal transformations of public space. Self-consciously "postmodernist" responses to such postmodern tendencies have been touted by the popular press, by urbanists, and (not surprisingly) by architects as offering new spatial forms for a new urbanity.

As Weintraub notes in his essay for this volume, however, the public/private distinction is used to mean different things in different contexts—in ways that carry disparate and even conflicting implications. In critical discussions of the built environment, a great deal of confusion and question-begging has ensued from the fact that the various meanings of "public" and "private" are often invoked in ways that take advantage, intentionally or unintentionally, of the potential for slippage between them. One frequent result has been to mask or evade important ambiguities in the conception of "public space."

These ambiguities are often buried in relatively unexamined conceptions of what makes for "successful" public space and undertheorized normative images of urban sociability that blur the distinctions between the city as the center of cosmopolitan social life, as a political community, and as a constructed visual and spatial order. Such images are deeply rooted in the historical association of the physical forms of the city with particular forms of social and political life. From the Greek polis to the modern metropolis, the urban landscape has provided not only the context for distinctive patterns of sociability, but a vocabulary of images and metaphors fundamental to our conceptualizations of public life: the square, the market, the street. The city has been seen as both historical location and sociological basis for modern democratic

1. Mike Davis, "Fortress Los Angeles: The Militarization of Urban Space," in Michael Sorkin's edited volume, *Variations on a Theme Park: The New American City and the End of Public Space,* p. 155.

2. For a suggestive, if theoretically unsatisfying, account of the latter phenomenon, see Joel Garreau, *Edge City.*

3. Witold Rybczynski, "The New Downtowns," *Atlantic Monthly,* May 1993, p. 98.

politics. It was in the city that the "public" first took a visible and politically problematic form as a realm where "complex social groups were to be brought into ineluctable contact."[4] As Sorkin has pointed out: "The familiar spaces of traditional cities, the streets and squares, courtyards and parks, are our great scenes of the civic, visible and accessible, our binding agents."[5] Associated at once with the binding character of shared experience, democratic accessibility, and civic culture, visibility in public space is taken to imply both intelligibility and empowerment.

Because it has been tempting to assume that the city as *urbs,* as a dwelling place and an assemblage of material artifacts, reveals the fundamental character of the city as *civitas,* as a form of association, a moral order, or a political community,[6] the criticism of the visual qualities of built forms can dovetail seamlessly into criticism of social and political meanings without clear analysis of the connections. If it has seemed easy to slide over such questions, this is partly due to certain pervasive and typically implicit assumptions that go back to the complex elective affinities between early social-scientific analyses of "urbanism as a way of life"[7] and a variety of projects that shaped contemporary cities in the early part of this century. Chicago-school sociologists interpreted the spatial order of the city as an observable manifestation of the functioning of modern forms of social organization, with their accompanying moral order and distinctive pathologies.[8] As both a physical trace of social processes and itself a cultural component of those processes, the built environment of the city appeared as a privileged site where it is possible to see the tangible nature of social problems, trace their etiology, and render them susceptible to therapeutic intervention.[9]

4. Richard Sennett, *The Fall of Public Man: On the Social Psychology of Capitalism,* p. 17.

5. Michael Sorkin, introduction to *Variations on a Theme Park,* p. xv.

6. As Fustel de Coulanges explains in *The Ancient City, civitas* was the religious and political association of families and tribes, and *urbs* was its dwelling place and place of assembly (p. 134). See also Richard Sennett, *The Conscience of the Eye: The Design and Social Life of Cities,* p. 11.

7. Louis Wirth, "Urbanism as a Way of Life," *American Journal of Sociology* 44 (July 1938): 1–24.

8. Comte began a long tradition of organic metaphors in urban sociology, referring to cities as the "real organs" of the social body; cited in Mark Gottdiener, *The Social Production of Urban Space,* p. 25.

9. See Robert Park, "The City: Suggestions for the Investigation of Human Behavior in the Urban Environment," *American Journal of Sociology* (1916), vol. 20, reprinted in Richard Sennett's edited volume, *Classic Essays on the Culture of Cities.* The city, Park argues, should be treated as "a laboratory or a clinic in which human nature and social processes may be conveniently and profitably studied" (p. 130).

In the late nineteenth century, reformers thought that an urban environment that provided privacy for families, contact with natural elements, and public spaces characterized by an emphatic visual orderliness would be physically hygienic, morally uplifting, and socially integrating.[10] In the early twentieth century, such conceptions were incorporated into the professionalizing projects of city planners and architects. Where urban sociologists sought explanations for the social, political, and moral order in the spatial order of the modern city, the architectural profession approached the problem as a practical matter of constructing visible connections between built form and social order. Modernist architects, rather than approaching the city as an organism whose forms revealed the nature of its functioning, regarded it as a "machine for living" (to generalize Le Corbusier's memorable phrase) whose order needed to be engineered rather than merely discovered; but, in the process, they grounded renewed claims to professional authority in finding supposedly "objective" connections between architectural forms and underlying "functions."

Current critical discussions are generally far removed from both the organismic imagery of a century ago and the mechanistic imagery of modernist design. Still, they often reproduce the older tendency to treat the emergence of certain kinds of urban space as a more or less direct result of larger social forces—"late capitalism" and the "postmodern condition" have replaced such phenomena as "industrialization," "mechanization," and, more broadly, "modernization" in this role. However, an effective critical analysis of the dynamics of social space needs to be linked to a systematic examination of the processes by which it is produced. A crucial component of these processes is the active mediating role played by the professional practices of architecture. This is so not only because architects act as agents organizing economic, technological, social, and aesthetic considerations into specified building intentions, but because the discipline of design has also played a key role in constructing the symbolic vocabularies and representational practices which shape the experience and interpretation of meaning in the built environment. As a mode of cultural production, architecture thus operates at the seam between the city as material artifact and perception of the city as a form of association, and also, as I will try to show, at the practical intersection of the complex dimensions of the public/private distinction. Its characteristic modalities materialize conceptions of the relationship between visual, social, and political order—and thereby provide material and ideological underpinnings for assumptions about the social significance of the built environment.

This essay will explore some of the recent vicissitudes of the public/private

---

10. See Paul Boyer, *Urban Masses and Moral Order.*

distinction as both an organizing feature of the urban landscape and a constitutive element in the discipline of design by examining the "modernist" and "postmodernist" tendencies in American architecture, linking the institutional and cultural logic of their respective design practices to the kinds of social space they have typically helped to produce. In using the somewhat overworked labels of "modernism" and "postmodernism," I make no claims to diagnose a general cultural condition or identify the essence of the current period. "Modernism" refers here to design practices formed in the early twentieth century and dominant in American architecture by mid-century. The "postmodernism" with which I am concerned is limited to specific transformations in professional design since the 1960s, largely in self-conscious reaction against the modernist project. For the past decade, architectural examples have often been used as privileged illustrations of a more general "postmodern condition," both symptoms of broad cultural crisis and a creative response.[11] However, the explicit opposition of "modernism" and "postmodernism" within architecture predates these wider discussions.

This examination will approach the historical sociology of modernist and postmodernist architecture by focusing on paradigmatic exemplars produced by each of these modes of design: public housing during the 1930s, and planned suburban developments of the 1980s and 1990s that are sometimes labeled "private communities." The federal public housing programs of the New Deal provided a crucial site where American architects worked out their reception of European modernism as part of a reconstruction of the theoretical and practical foundations of their discipline. I would suggest that, in the past decade, planned suburban communities have taken on a similarly paradigmatic significance in relation to "postmodernist" architecture. These examples usefully mirror each other in a way that is marked, in each case, by a revealing oxymoron: while "public housing" involves a public provision of private residential space, the so-called private communities are characterized by the provision of certain kinds of public space within private developments (something also true, in somewhat different ways, of such exemplars of postmodern architecture as indoor shopping malls and atrium hotels).

This comparison illuminates both recent transformations in the character of "public space" and significant continuities rooted in the social organization of professional architecture. Each of these cases is paradigmatic at two (interrelated) levels: the level at which design practices give justification to built form

11. Fredric Jameson's seminal formulation of this position was in his article, "Postmodernism, or, the Cultural Logic of Late Capitalism," *New Left Review*, no. 146 (July–August 1984), pp. 59–92, and was later elaborated in chapter 1 of his *Postmodernism, or, The Cultural Logic of Late Capitalism* (Durham, NC: Duke University Press, 1991).

by embedding building intentions in a cultural as well as pragmatic context, and the level at which the practice of design itself is embedded in a broader social and historical context. In each case, the public/private distinction is a complex constitutive element in both the practices and outcomes of design. The ways that the public/private distinction is loaded with social significance and embodied in the built environment are thus shaped by the efforts of architects to respond to social and technological conditions affecting their professional role, while sustaining the coherence and cultural authority of their discipline and their collective capacity to give visual expression to what come to be seen as salient qualities of different kinds of social space.

THE PROBLEM OF PUBLIC SPACE

As WEINTRAUB HAS POINTED OUT, "public space" is commonly set in opposition to "private space" in order to highlight at least three very different senses of "public": the physical or social space in which one's activities are visible to diverse others rather than kept hidden from view; that region of relatively impersonal sociability characteristic of modern urban life, as opposed to the region of intensely personal concern; and that domain which pertains to common interests and collective decision making, as opposed to that which is left to individual choice and selfish interest. This last version of "public," which might be termed "political," contains within itself a further distinction: between the institutional domain associated with the application of sovereign authority to matters of common interest (above all by the state), and the metaphorical space of collective deliberation associated with the empowerment of a democratic community.[12]

As a normative and critical concept, "public space" is a good example of how several senses of "public" can be blurred by their tangible embodiment in the physical space of the city. Most simply, public spaces are spaces in which action is visible to unspecified others; but the condition of visibility implies social as well as spatial relations from the start. According to Roger Scruton, for example: "It is a space into which anyone may enter, and from which anyone may depart, without the consent of strangers, and without any declaration—however tacit—of a justifying purpose."[13] In public space, therefore, residents of the city can encounter diverse strangers in spontaneous

12. See Jeff Weintraub, "The Theory and Politics of the Public/Private Distinction," in this volume. For a discussion that addresses more explicitly the ambiguous meanings of "space" as well as "public," see also Jeff Weintraub, "Varieties and Vicissitudes of Public Space," in Philip Kasinitz's edited volume, *Metropolis: Center and Symbol of Our Times.*

13. Roger Scruton, "Public Space and the Classical Vernacular," in Nathan Glazer and Mark Lilla, eds., *The Public Face of Architecture: Civic Culture and Public Spaces,* p. 15.

meetings that are full of the dramaturgical possibilities of Goffmanesque interaction. In this stream of everyday encounters, social actors can engage in a variety of material and symbolic exchanges, display their status or identity, and constitute themselves as social actors in the abstract sense associated with the political practices and moral sensibilities of a modern democratic society.

Beneath many of the critical uses of the notion of public space one can discern an ideal of urban sociability that was given vivid and influential formulation by Jane Jacobs.[14] For Jacobs, to take one of her paradigmatic examples, the successful functioning of an urban street entails a fruitful tension between the relatively enclosed spaces of intimate personal relations and commonly accessible spaces in which individuals can find both necessary services and opportunities for establishing meaningful connections between private domains. A functioning urban street or neighborhood has to have density of activity and diversity of functions, but also an interconnectedness facilitated by physical arrangements and visual contact. A viable street has, as she puts it, eyes and ears: residences with windows and doors opening onto the street, and inhabitants in the habit of looking out.[15] On the same street, small retail establishments like stores, newsstands, and diners provide spaces that maintain the practical articulation of the public life of the street and the private regions that it serves. A diversity of uses creates a continuous stream of minor interactions between familiar strangers—a pattern of sociability characterized by a necessary degree of social distance and limited liability, but also by recognition, engagement, and a kind of trust that implies no private commitments.[16] Jacobs's complaint is that modern approaches to planning and design turn their back on the vitality of the street or neighborhood in favor of aesthetic formalism or the abstract functional conceptions associated with certain kinds of technocratic intervention.

Jacobs's analysis brings out a point often forgotten in discussions of public space, even when they claim inspiration from her work: the qualities of public space as "public" depend not only on the forms of the space itself or on what happens within it, but on the ways that the distinction between public and private is marked. What we think of as urban public life implies a modulation of interaction along a public/private continuum. As Jacobs points out, such patterns of interaction are rooted in the necessary and routine interactions among strangers that cumulate over time into a body of common experience and norms, in the micropractices of regulating presentations of self under conditions of visibility in particular kinds of places. But the quality of urban

14. Jane Jacobs, *The Death and Life of Great American Cities* (New York: Vintage, 1961).
15. Ibid., p. 35.
16. Ibid., p. 56.

public space also depends on its asymmetrical relation to the *private* spaces that look out on it, distinct but not disconnected. The articulation of public and private is expressed in the physical articulation of spaces where strangers can be encountered regularly, without their having to be let into one's private world, with spaces where private interactions can be carried on without being exposed to the eyes of strangers. The success of this articulation relies on a combination of social and spatial arrangements that enable a normatively regulated management of communication between public and private regions of social life as a practical matter of day-to-day social interaction.

For Jacobs and her many sympathizers, this normative conception of public space is tied to a critical contrast between the vitality of older neighborhoods and the relative lifelessness of the urban spaces created by modernist-inspired building and redevelopment schemes. These schemes certainly provide *open* spaces; but, to cite Scruton once more, "space does not become public merely by ceasing to be private." [17] Sennett makes the same point in arguing that the key problem is not the lack of commonly accessible space, but the systematic creation of "dead public space" by the elimination of significant social interaction.[18] This deadening of public space is in part the result of larger social tendencies such as suburbanization that have removed all but the poorer residents from many urban neighborhoods, as well as patterns of spatial separation that have segregated residential space from other functions. But it is also the predictable outcome of the conceptualizations of public space inherent in modernist design and planning paradigms, which entail a "rational" conception of built form as a direct and "objective" reflection of its function.

In Sennett's example of the open plaza in front of a modernist downtown office building, openness and visibility create isolation rather than sociability, by defining a space through which people pass rather than a space which people inhabit. The experience of place, however its distinctiveness might be marked by features added to the plaza, is subordinated to motion.[19] Although Sennett does not explicitly put the matter this way, this result is as much a matter of the conceived relation of form to function as it is a matter of the perceived openness of the space itself. If the environment prompts people "to think of the public domain as meaningless," as Sennett has suggested,[20] it is partly because the built environment is designed to represent its own functionality. Individuals are defined as "users," and addressed primarily as a crowd

17. Scruton, "Public Space and the Classical Vernacular," p. 17.
18. Sennett, *Fall of Public Man,* pp. 12–16.
19. Ibid., pp. 13–14.
20. Ibid., p. 12.

on their way elsewhere, perhaps facilitated in their passage but inhibited in their ability to recognize any commonality of their connection to the space, and induced to think of it purely in relation to their individual interests and goals. Instrumentally meaningful rather than valued in itself, such space is isolating and atomizing since others become merely competitors for space rather than sharing a meaningful occupancy.

To a large extent, critiques of the "postmodern" qualities of urban landscapes rely on similar images of urban sociability, but with increasing emphasis on visual experience and the placing of visual signifiers in the urban landscape, reflecting here a more general semiotic turn in cultural studies. Some recent work has also attempted to go beyond the earlier focus on sustaining the vitality of urban sociability to a concern with translating the urbane experience of difference into a distinctly political vision, of neighborliness into capacities for active citizenship.[21] In contrast with earlier critiques of the disruption of the spatial order of urban sociability, recent critiques of the city focus on the way a variety of conditions, ultimately linked to the workings of late capitalism, have disrupted any sort of coherent representation of social life in the forms and images of the city. These critiques identify the "postmodern" city with a proliferation of spectacular spaces and experiences; an effacement of history by constant reference to a fragmented and spurious past; and the coupling of this semiotic extravaganza with new forms of power and control.[22] Urban form is criticized not only as a more or less adequate technical support for desirable patterns of interaction, but also as a material representation in and through which urbane modes of sociability might be translated into the conditions for self-conscious political community.

These arguments reveal assumptions implicit in earlier criticism of urban space. A public space is both a site where certain kinds of social relations are enacted and a material representation of the normative dimensions of these interactions. Thus, one requirement of a "successful" public space is a certain type of intelligibility: it must be sufficiently abstract in its representational qualities to be inclusive, yet sufficiently defined to give it a tangibly intersubjective quality, enabling social actors to recognize its public character and to act meaningfully, appropriately, and efficaciously within it. The qualities that make urban space successfully "public" are in part a matter of spatial configuration and practices (patterns of movement and habits of interaction between

21. Again, Sennett provides a good example in *The Conscience of the Eye.*

22. For examples of this kind of criticism, see Sharon Zukin, *Landscapes of Power: From Detroit to Disney World;* Sorkin's edited volume, *Variations on a Theme Park;* Jameson, *Postmodernism, or, The Cultural Logic of Late Capitalism.*

diverse strangers), but also a matter of symbolic qualities of the built environment that convey significant and compelling representations of the modulations of public and private in social space.

Seen in this light, the problem of public space raises two kinds of issues that need to be sorted out. First, there is the question of the relationship between patterns of social activity encouraged, enabled, or inhibited by different configurations of built space and the meanings embodied in that space. While these issues have received increased attention, the connections involved are too often assumed rather than carefully investigated. At the same time, the dimension of meaning in the built environment raises a further set of questions, too rarely addressed explicitly, concerning the relationship between the meanings intentionally encoded in public spaces by the form-giving practices of architects and planners and the meanings experienced by those who use and inhabit these spaces. Analyses of the social significance of built space often rely implicitly on interpretive categories drawn from the discourse and practices of professional design—even when they are critical of those practices—without systematically examining either their underlying presuppositions or the social and historical formation of the representational practices within which they are embedded. As a first step toward delineating and examining these connections, we need to consider the ways that the symbolic connections between visual form and social order are constructed and mobilized within the practices of design.

ARCHITECTURE: SOCIAL SPACE BY DESIGN

THE PROFESSIONALIZATION OF architecture has not been a matter of monopolizing knowledge of building technology, which architects have never been able to do, but of organizing the process of giving intentional form to building tasks in terms of a distinctive and authoritative practice requiring specialized judgment. The key problem and, at the same time, the essential enabling condition of professional design is the historical emergence of a practical gap between form and function.[23] Historically, "architecture" first emerged from the background of "mere building" as that specialized category of building which gave monumental embodiment to divine and earthly power. The modern figure of the architect as the agent generally responsible for giving form to building intentions first appeared in the Renaissance, made possible by the zone of uncertainty that appeared with extension of the domain of architecture from the relatively exclusive realm of princely and ecclesiastical

23. See David Brain, "Practical Knowledge and Occupational Control: The Professionalization of Architecture in the United States," *Sociological Forum* 6, no. 2 (June 1991): 239–68.

power to the broader realm of "private" displays of wealth, power, and position.[24]

As a self-conscious practice of linking building tasks to formal ideals, architecture entails a rationalization of form with paradoxical consequences. Design practices must sustain a framework of interpretation in the context of which the motivation of architectural form can appear convincing or self-evident, and at the same time the significance of built form as architecture—as culture—rests on the persistence of the gap between form and function as a problem requiring an artful (rather than merely technical) solution.[25] The architect's role has always depended on the ability to call attention to the gap between form and function by the very effort to bridge it.

The distinction between public and private has been at the heart of the discipline, not only because architects must mark distinctions in the social functions of space in matching form to function, but also because the core features of the discipline of design emerged with the expansion in the domain of "architecture" to encompass the problem of giving adequate form to broader range of building tasks and to representations of more diverse forms of status and power. The discipline of design has been formed largely by the articulation of a domain of subjective judgment associated with architectural taste, in response to the problem of constructing a representational system that can operate in distinct registers as it shapes appropriate locations for a variety of private functions and personal experiences, and can give public form to the outward face of buildings that serve functions related to both public affairs and private interests. Taste, one might note, is simultaneously private and public: it is a characteristic of private judgment that is displayed indirectly by its embodiment in the world of things. In this way, artifacts serve as the public face of private feeling and experience, and architecture represents this articulation of public and private at the grandest scale.

These problems of articulating public and private in the context of mapping form onto function appear in a variety of guises. Most obviously, the discipline of design has had to confront not only the requirements of configuring space to meet expectations for privacy or visibility, but also the question of the appropriate visual representation of the relationships of interior spaces

24. See Magali Sarfatti Larson, "Emblem and Exception: The Historical Definition of the Architect's Professional Role," in Judith R. Blau, Mark E. La Gory, and John S. Pipkin, eds., *Professionals and Urban Form*, pp. 49–86.

25. Elsewhere I have examined the emergence of the uneasy mix of aesthetics and technical rationality that has characterized the architect's professional role: Brain, "Discipline and Style: The Ecole des Beaux Arts and the Social Production of an American Architecture," 807–68.

to exterior facades, of relatively hidden spaces to those open to movement or sight. Somewhat less obviously, the problems of relating historical styles to contemporary building intentions, or the visual order of architectural forms to the underlying demands of the building task, entail representational practices which refer to the public/private distinction in the ways they distinguish between what is to be represented and what is to be left implicit in giving appropriate expression to building intentions. Although distinct kinds of issues are involved in these and other choices, the practices of design transcribe them into interrelated problems of architectural representation. As a result, transformations in building practices reflect not only broad changes in the social patterning and cultural understanding of public and private, but also more immediate efforts within the discipline of design to transcribe changes in types of social space and in the circumstances of architectural production into "appropriate" practical articulations of this dichotomy.

Architectural practice assumes responsibility for the transcription of the normative dimensions of social space into built form when it constructs rules, norms, and practical strategies governing the intentional linking of form to function. Architects have shaped the representational qualities of the built environment by symbolically representing broad cultural meanings (for example, borrowing forms taken from Greek temples for banks, and so forth), but also by the ways they have inscribed their own intentionality and authority in the visible appropriateness of building form. As a result, the enacting of the public/private distinction in architectural artifacts has been regulated by the practical logic imposed on professional design by the historical formation of the discipline and the sociological conditions that sustain it.

Historically, the construction of a professional practice of design opened a gap between the representational order mobilized by professional form givers and more common understandings of architectural meaning. Modernism significantly widened this gap and redefined the relationship between the specialized discipline of design and the broader culture. In this way, the modernist reconstruction of the discipline of design added a new layer of ambiguity to the meaning inscribed in the built environment and contributed to persistent confusions in critical discussions of public space.

THE LOGIC OF MODERNIST DESIGN

ACCORDING TO STANDARD HISTORIES, modernism in architecture was an attack on an older architecture based on the connection of historical styles with elite taste. More immediately, it was a professional response to the perception that traditional styles could never be convincingly fitted to modern conditions, and would always appear as an imposture compared to the hard-edged rationality of other forms of modern technology. European modernism, particularly as represented by the experiments of the Bauhaus in the 1920s, was an effort to reconstruct the practice of giving form to buildings in order to maintain its distinctiveness while encompassing the demands of modern technical rationality. According to Mies van der Rohe, the goal of such an architecture was simple: "Create form out of the nature of the task with the means of our time." [26]

However, the modernist transformation of design involved not only a change in the vocabulary of architectural representation, but a reconstruction of the boundaries of the architectural, and a transformation of the way architectural forms were to be understood as fitted to building tasks. Modernist architects rejected the historicism of nineteenth-century architecture in favor of a transparently "rational" architecture based on the linkage of an abstract geometric order to a conception of building tasks in terms of organically structured and integrated systems of functions. The modernist set out to solve building problems as if they had never been solved before, conceiving functions in terms of generalized human needs, without reference to the forms they might have taken in the past or to particular cultural values. What was to be transparent was not just the walls, which might indeed be made of glass, but the way geometric forms were modulated as a (supposedly) direct and honest reflex of an inner functional logic. Modernist architects and planners went so far as to claim the ability to re-form social life to fit the demands of technology, the industrial system, and a modern democratic culture. This would require only removing the obstructions of tradition and outdated forms of privilege from "a new world which is forming itself regularly, logically, and clearly, which produces in a straightforward way things that are useful and usable." [27]

In the United States, public housing programs of the early 1930s provided a practical field in which architects were able to give technical motivation to this vocabulary of forms, to anchor aesthetic judgment in fundamental and "visible" facts of the building task, and to work out the fit between a new mode of design and the pragmatic concerns of the profession. In these projects, it was possible to locate architectural judgment at a level where the abstract geometries and "symbolic objectivity" of European modernism could be stripped of ideological association with left-wing politics and made to represent persuasive claims about the relationship of particular forms to particular

26. Mies van der Rohe, "Working Theses," reprinted in Ulrich Conrads's *Programs and Manifestoes on 20th Century Architecture*, p. 74.

27. Le Corbusier, *Towards a New Architecture*, p. 288.

functions.[28] In the process of responding to the demand for subsidized housing, architects simultaneously reconstructed the foundations of their own discipline.

In the late nineteenth century, architects had responded to criticism and jurisdictional challenges, particularly with regard to the problem of housing, by insisting on their claim to represent a distinctive sphere of cultural concerns.[29] During the Depression, however, the significance of the distinction between architecture and "mere building" shifted as a result of economic and political exigencies which restricted the opportunities for architecture in the traditional sense. The design of federally subsidized urban housing made it painfully clear that the distinctively "architectural" expertise of the traditional architect was largely irrelevant. Public housing programs left little or no room for decorative elaboration or rhetorical flourishes that could be recognized as architectural within existing frameworks of justification. Furthermore, the peculiarly "public" character of public housing could not be convincingly represented in the traditional mode for marking the articulation of public and private, which had relied on the cultural symbolism of the historical styles and on monumentality as the hallmark of the public domain.

Public housing raised the fundamental questions of the discipline with particular urgency, but also provided an ideal site for working out a new modality for relating form and function. First, the architect's authority to impose a formal ideal on the building task was given a new political space in which to operate. Whatever the constraints of budget or other guidelines, the bureaucratic context set clear parameters for the interaction between the client (an agency of the federal government) and the architect, defining a space within which the operation of a relatively autonomous expertise was not only possible but welcomed. The state, as the architect's client and acting on behalf of potential rather than actual residents, provided a useful buffer between the architect and a user whose needs were thereby defined in general, abstract, and quantifiable terms. Within the broad mandate of the New Deal programs, the architect was relatively free to invent the people for whom the projects were designed.[30]

28. See William Jordy, "The Symbolic Essence of Modern European Architecture of the Twenties and Its Continuing Influence," *Journal of the Society of Architectural Historians* 22 (1963): 177–87.

29. See Gwendolyn Wright, *Moralism and the Model Home: Domestic Architecture and Cultural Conflict in Chicago,* p. 200.

30. See Roger Montgomery, "Architecture Invents New People," in Russell Ellis and Dana Cuff's *Architects' People,* pp. 260–82.

One indication of the new relationship of functional form and visual order appears in the polemical reinterpretation of standardization that was a recurring theme in both modernist manifestos and more pragmatic proposals for reform. Catherine Bauer, a housing reformer, argued that "functional" standardization (in contrast with the ugly and wasteful standardization characteristic of existing market housing) would open up important new opportunities for design:

> For the first time, it is possible to build up groups and balanced masses and rhythms merely out of the varied forms required for specific functions. Standardized parts, instead of creating dull uniformity, become a positive force in creating a unified whole. Meaningless surface ornament, once applied to distract the eye from the unbearable bleakness and monotony underneath, becomes not only unnecessary but ridiculous. Good materials, simple lines, and geometric forms become, when combined with carefully designed and planted open spaces, all the elements necessary to an authentic modern architecture.[31]

Standardization, rather than representing the unfortunate lack of design, enabled architects to replace reliance on the application of "meaningless surface ornament" with an aesthetic that drew its force from the way modulations of form reflected the organization of functions and the way technical and economic constraints were made visible. A "modern" sensibility in aesthetic judgment would thus recognize the aesthetic qualities of architectural constructions as manifestations of their successful solution of pragmatic problems, in a way supposedly independent of the cultural associations of particular forms.

In the context of federal housing programs, architects found it possible to define the function of housing in terms of abstract features of the physical environment that could be referred to equally abstract conceptions of the needs of the residents for such things as light, air, open space, or privacy. In this way, "functional" standardization reflected principles of design associated with a rationally defined public good rather than the dictates of the market. At the same time, the scale of projects made it possible to relocate the aesthetic qualities of building from the no-longer-acceptable artifice of applied styles to the most fundamental modulation of forms in the massing of individual buildings and their relationship to one another on the site. This architecture gave pragmatic substantiation to the characteristically modernist claim: "Houses can

31. Catherine Bauer, *Modern Housing*, p. 164. Bauer echoes similar statements by Gropius, Le Corbusier, and Henry-Russell Hitchcock.

be designed, as they should be: from the inside out according to the physical and psychological needs of the tenants." [32] An "authentically modern" architecture extended the architect's authority beneath the visual appearance of the building to the organization of its functions.

The federally funded housing programs anchored these forms in the bureaucratic authority of the democratic state. Association of certain formal images with functional principles was effectively "naturalized" by incorporation into the practical guidelines of the Public Works Administration and the bureaucratic standardization later imposed by the Federal Housing Authority. The design guidelines published by the Public Works Administration in 1935 offered labor-saving hints for unit design and site planning that allowed the architect to submit preliminary plans without extensive research, and a routinized approach to meeting the expectations that would guarantee approval of a project. Emphasis was put on the site plan, and it was suggested that the architect might make use of wooden blocks, cut to scale to represent blocks of apartment units, in order to experiment with the visual effect of different arrangements and to present the resulting plan for approval. In this way, a formal aesthetic grounded in a planning paradigm was tied to a visual technique for demonstrating the rationality of design choices. This technical convenience reflects the radical decontextualization and analytical abstraction of function characteristic of the modernist architect's treatment of the public realm.

THE MODERNIST CITY

ALTHOUGH MODERNISM WOULD thus appear in key respects to be an especially "public" architecture—in terms of its orientation towards a technocratically defined public good authorized by sovereign authority, its anonymous and abstractly general conception of its ultimate clientele, and its aesthetic ideal of technical-rational "transparency"—a growing body of criticism has argued that its consequences for public life were in fact systematically catastrophic. The city of Brasilia provides an exemplary demonstration of these paradoxical implications of modernist design and planning, since here they were carried out on the most extensive scale, with none of the pragmatic adulterations that result from working with existing cityscapes and the conflicting interests vested in them.

Brasilia was planned and built from scratch on the central plateau of Brazil, intended to be a functional capital city and a symbol of Brazil's entry into a

32. Alfred Kastner, "The Architect's Place in Current Housing," *Housing Yearbook*, p. 234.

new political and economic age. Designed by Lúcio Costa and Oscar Niemeyer with the help of Le Corbusier, the city strikingly embodies principles
of design and planning developed between about 1928 and 1960 in the manifestos issued from organizational core of European modernism—the Congrès
Internationaux d'Architecture Moderne.[33] The city was laid out according to
an overall plan, organizing space for housing, work, and recreation around a
core devoted to civic and administrative functions, and woven together with
an elaborate system of arterial roads. Its architectural forms are innovative yet
standardized, and reflect the best modernist ideas with respect to the reconcep-
tualization of the functions of the city—including, in particular, the problem
of housing.

Holston's study of Brasilia as "the modernist city" par excellence, by combining a critical and historical account of its design with an ethnographic
investigation of the residents' actual experience of the city, sheds an unusually
clear light on the paradoxical relationship between modernist intentions and
the impact of modernist design on the character of social space. In the first
place, Holston points to Brasilia's peculiar transformation of the traditional
articulation of public and private in Brazilian cities. In the traditional city,
according to Holston, the street is a "figural void" defined by the ambiguous
opposition of open space and structures that frame and define it.[34] As a fundamental convention that structures the entire cityscape into a pattern of solids
and voids, this operates as a legible code that organizes understanding of the
geography of the city. The traditional street is an architectural organization
of the public and private domains of social life, both constituting and representing the articulation of the two in everyday sociability. The reversal of the
usual figure/ground relationship—where the building becomes figure and the
space around it the ground against which its form appears—was traditionally
a means to represent wealth and power as features of the public realm.

The modernist city does away with the street as a figural void, and inverts
the traditional order by designing every building as a monument to its function. As is evident in Brasilia, the result is paradoxical. On the one hand, the
city is intensely privatized. The absence of traditional streets and street corners
as places for social interaction leads to a sense of isolation and a feeling that
the city lacks human warmth. At the same time, the rational order of the city
is apparent only on the map, not at the level of experience as one moves
through the city. The visual regularity of both buildings and intervening spaces

---

33. For a discussion of Brasilia's high-modernist pedigree, see James Holston, *The Modernist City: An Anthropological Critique of Brasilia,* pp. 31–46.

34. Ibid., p. 120.

is experienced as unrelated to patterns of social life or interaction. Residents tend to meet friends and associates in their homes or private clubs, with the result that social life is interiorized and constricted, characterized by a pragmatic withdrawal into the household that runs counter to Brazilian cultural traditions.[35] This constriction is exacerbated by the design of the apartment units themselves. Semipublic spaces traditionally found in Brazilian homes had been eliminated, making them less useful as places where one might comfortably entertain relative strangers. Intended as an apotheosis of public life over class differences and prejudices, Brasilia achieved almost precisely the opposite effect, sharpening the spatial isolation of individuals and the experience of social distance between classes.

Although social life is privatized by its relocation within domestic space, in another sense the modernist city is entirely public. The organization of the city into functionally homogeneous zones according to predetermined categories of work, entertainment, shopping, and residence has the effect of limiting the use of public space to those with a specific reason for being there. At the same time, although typical urban functions are spatially separated, the distribution of housing according to work affiliation results in the experience of "a deep penetration of the roles and identities of work into residential life," opening up private space to organizational principles associated with the realm of work.[36] This experience is exacerbated by the undifferentiated monumentality of the buildings, and the fact that the apartments were designed to address the essential physical needs of the residents, irrespective of cultural traditions or the idiosyncracies of households in a specific social or historical context. Designing residential units for an abstract citizen results in the transparency of private space to normalizing frameworks derived from a purely technical conception of the household—seen, in Le Corbusier's terms, as a "machine for living." This symbolic transparency is emphasized by the actual transparency of the mostly glass facades of the apartment blocks in Brasilia.

As the apotheosis of the logic of modernist architecture, the example of Brasilia makes it clear how the pursuit of the modernist project yielded the curious achievement of simultaneously undermining the vitality of both private and public life. Through its characteristic combination of an emphasis on technical rationality with an aesthetic of abstract geometric form, modernism encourages a formalism and monumentality dramatically divorced from the level of concrete human interaction. Its way of conceiving the relationship between form and function implies a definition of the "public" domain in

35. Ibid., p. 107.
36. Ibid., p. 153.

terms of the abstractly generalizable characteristics of individual needs. As a mode of design, modernism shifted what could be called the "program of action" of architecture from design that addressed subjects at a discursive level of cultural meaning, as did the historically grounded design of the nineteenth century, to a mode of design intended to work its effects at the level of allegedly universal perceptual and psychological dispositions.[37] The constitution of the public realm is transformed from one occupied by moral agents with particular cultural orientations and competencies to one occupied by beings with physical bodies and uniform psychologies. Such beings are assumed to operate no differently in public than in private, and are not expected to acquire new virtues or recognize particular intersubjective truths. The functional organization of the built environment creates a uniformly abstract space that cuts across functions, across levels of scale from the household to the urban landscape, and across the traditional boundaries between public and private. Design based on the modulation of standardized forms in relation to rationally ordered functions dissolves visual representation of the seam between public and private.

AFTER MODERNISM

IN REACTION AGAINST what are now seen as the disasters of modernism, "postmodernist" tendencies in architecture have defined themselves polemically by their root-and-branch rejection of the modernist project. But it is not clear that they have entirely abandoned the impulse toward architectural self-aggrandizement inherent in modernism (and, indeed, in the logic of professional design), nor that they themselves have found genuinely workable solutions to the problems of public space in contemporary conditions.

Where modernist design sought to free itself from the arbitrariness of taste, with its questionable association with differences of class, postmodern architecture has involved an effort to ground design in the culture of everyday life, in the forms, images, and historical associations that constitute what Robert Venturi, in his polemically affirming way, calls "ugly and ordinary building." [38] Such a defense of the ugly and ordinary effects some basic inversions of modernist design practice. Just as modernist design enabled architects to locate the architectural in the most mundanely functional aspects of building, Venturi and other postmodern theorist/architects worked toward relocating the architectural amid the most mundanely symbolic aspects of building.

37. I draw the concept of "program of action" from Michel Callon and Bruno Latour, "Don't Throw the Baby Out with the Bath School!" in Andrew Pickering, ed., *Science as Practice and Culture*, pp. 343–68.

38. Robert Venturi, Denise Scott Brown, and Steven Izenour, *Learning from Las Vegas*, p. 93.

In pointed contrast with both the theorists of modernism and many of its critics, Venturi suggests that standardization is not a bad thing in itself, just standardization "without circumstantial accommodation and without a creative use of context." He suggests "an artful recognition of the circumstantial and contextual and of the inevitable limits of the order of standardization." [39] Furthermore, where modernism sought to reconcile inside and outside, to efface any indication of the seams between form and function, Venturi points to the contrast of inside and outside as a crucial source of the kind of contradiction which is the very stuff of "architecture" as an effort to give form to the visual experience of the built environment. Architecture should evoke a sense of containment and "the intricacy of things," an experience of the situation of spaces within spaces that is surprising and contradictory. In contrast with the formal purity of modernism, Venturi suggests a courting of complexity, contradiction, ambiguity, inconsistency, "expressive discontinuity," and allusions that promote a multiplicity of potential meanings.

What, one might ask, is the authoritative standpoint for this kind of design? Venturi takes issue with Peter Blake's comparison of the orderliness of the University of Virginia campus (as good design) with strip development on a typical Main Street: "Besides the irrelevancy of the comparison, is not Main Street almost all right? Indeed, is not the commercial strip of a Route 66 almost all right? As I have said, our question is: what slight twist of context will make them all right?" [40] The task of the architect is to derive significant building from the vernacular images that characterize Main Street, or other similarly "authentic" urban spaces. However, the original versions are, pointedly, only *almost* all right. The answer to Venturi's question (although not the one he offers directly) is that the necessary "twist of context" is the translation of these images into architecture by their association with the figure of the architect and by the incorporation of these vernacular images into a self-conscious practice. There is an element of populism in Venturi's position, but the underlying concern is the transfigurative power of the architect and the elaboration of the cultural space (metaphorically speaking) for professional design. [41]

In contrast with the ideologues of modernism, Venturi writes:

39. Robert Venturi, *Complexity and Contradiction in Architecture,* p. 44.
40. Ibid., p. 104.
41. In a recent book, Magali Sarfatti Larson has done an excellent job of situating the elaboration of "postmodern" architecture since Venturi in the social context of the profession, relating it to the division of labor within the profession and to the articulation of professional careers. See *Behind the Postmodern Facade: Architectural Change in Late Twentieth Century America.*

Designing from the outside in, as well as the inside out, creates necessary tensions, which help make architecture. Since the inside is different from the outside, the wall—the point of change—becomes an architectural event. Architecture occurs at the meeting of interior and exterior forces of use and space. These interior and environmental forces are both general and particular, generic and circumstantial.[42]

In this view, architecture properly involves a dramatization rather than a methodical effacement of the tensions between inside and outside, form and function, public and private. Like architecture derived from older historical styles, "postmodern" design conspicuously situates architecture at the seams or points of articulation between public and private. In doing so, however, it returns to the stylistic eclecticism of the nineteenth century without an established framework of taste to anchor it in bourgeois values and bourgeois order. Its reflexive irony constitutes a distinctively professional mode of architectural production. With what result?

THE POSTMODERN SUBURB

IF BRASILIA CAN BE SEEN as both a modernist utopia and an important cautionary example for critics of modernism, one utopian emblem of the "new urbanism" is the planned community of Seaside, developed in the Florida Panhandle by Robert Davis and designed by Andres Douany and Elizabeth Plater-Zyberk. Seaside has been praised for the design of its individual buildings (by a variety of architects) and for its embodiment of a new urbanistic image: a "neotraditional" community with human-scaled streets and public spaces organized around a symbolic center containing a mix of uses. This notion of a planned community based on an image of traditional small towns has attracted a great deal of attention among planners, architects, and the popular press.

Douany and Plater-Zyberk created a town plan intended to guide development along the lines of traditional towns by means of an elaborate architectural code that governs the design and construction of individual buildings. Rather than specifying a certain architectural style (as the planners of new towns did earlier in the century), they created an abstract language of spatial arrangements and architectural elements intended to insure that while each building may be a distinctive piece of architecture, it will be designed to sustain a consistently textured townscape.[43] Particular attention was paid to elements

42. Venturi, *Complexity and Contradiction*, p. 86.
43. Keller Easterling, "Public Enterprise," in David Mohney and Keller Easterling's edited volume, *Seaside: Making a Town in America*, pp. 53–55.

of design that give a definite character to the articulation of public and private: town squares, pedestrian paths, porches for sitting, fences that provide visual demarcation of private yards without completely isolating private space within.

Critics of Seaside have pointed out the obvious. It is not a complete and self-sufficient community, but a resort community with few full-time residents, made up mostly of second homes and relying on vacationing tourists to populate its streets. Douany's charismatic discussions of mixed-use town centers, where the store clerks live in cheap apartments above the stores, sharing the common spaces of the town with middle-class apartment dwellers and wealthy homeowners, can be criticized for naive treatment of the harsh realities of class and ethnic divisions. Although his town plans reflect many sound ideas, they are conceived abstractly in terms of functions and images of community, independent of broader social conditions and without engaging the real issues associated with existing urban landscapes.

What is not usually recognized is that Seaside is more than just a revival of traditional forms or an embodiment of new ideas about urban form. It is a paradigmatic realization of a mode of architectural production associated with a renewed focus on the problem of architecture's location at the cusp of public and private.[44] In this respect, it helps to transcribe recent trends in building and urban development into principles of design that operate under particular practical conditions, and implies a certain relationship between the production of visual order and the experience of community. In a setting like Seaside, the architects complain about restrictions on their freedom to design, but they operate as a "loyal opposition," working simultaneously within and against the code, looking for ways to push its limits but grounding their designs in the secure frame of reference that it provides. In this way, architects can work comfortably in the context of well-defined guidelines that set the parameters of form more definitely than any purely technical consideration. As a setting for professional design, such planning provides both a foundation for professional authority and a ground against which the figure of the architect as author of a unique vision can reappear with renewed vigor.

Seaside represents, in certain respects, a distillation of a planning paradigm out of the problems posed by more mundane suburban developments. These developments reflect a gradual shift in the form and meaning of the suburb, from the romantic suburban images of the nineteenth century to the so-called planned unit developments of the postwar period. Many of the more striking examples are in Florida, where large tracts of rural land on the fringes of

44. See Neil Levine's discussion of its significance as a break with modernism in "Questioning the View: Seaside's Critique of the Gaze of Modern Architecture," in Mohney and Easterling, eds., *Seaside,* pp. 240–55.

medium-to-small cities have been available to developers in a region where, because of climate, natural features, and a historical association with leisure, sudden residential communities with no geographic relation to an economic center could be marketed nationally to economically mobile buyers. Seaside has dozens of less theoretically sophisticated cousins, less explicit and self-conscious about their principles but nonetheless similarly revealing with respect to what is at stake in this kind of design.

What public housing was to modernism, such planned communities are to postmodern tendencies in design: both problem and opportunity. Developers have been pushed to increase the density of use of valuable land in order to maintain a sufficient level of profitability, reproducing urban density in a suburban setting. Political pressures brought to bear by environmentalists and regulatory agencies have created both incentives and legal frameworks necessary to support large-scale master planning by private developers. Finally, developers are faced with the constant risk of building too much, either because building outstrips demand, or because demand suddenly collapses. At the same time, there are limited possibilities for product differentiation, imposed by both cost and culture. Competitive pressures provide strong motivation for defining and differentiating marketable places. The solution is the suburban equivalent of brand names, but also the locating of the house in a setting that offers various amenities, access to services, confidence in property values, and a residential identity. Where the imagery of the romantic suburb of the late nineteenth century emphasized the relationship of the single house to nature, these new developments place central importance on the problem of giving practical definition to "community," although in a peculiar sense.

This peculiar process of constructing "community" is marked by three key characteristics. First, because of their scale of development and their location outside of the city proper, these postmodern suburbs involve a complicated intertwining of the interests of developers, architects, financial institutions, and the state. For approval of master-planned developments of sufficient scale to qualify as having "regional impact," there is a long process of negotiation carried on within the regulatory framework set up by the state. In this negotiation, the distinct agendas of these different players are dovetailed into one another. The planners develop a professional and political investment in the project, negotiating environmental and infrastructural exactions, including conservation of wetlands and wildlife habitats, wastewater management, development of public roads, provision for parks, fire stations, schools. The regulatory force of the state is, in turn, co-opted by the developer, helping to sustain and sanction long-term control over the course of development. These projects emerge as an alloy of private capital and public authority.

Second, these developments involve self-conscious efforts to create their own architectural vernacular. In these new planned communities, images derived from an actual or fictional history provide the basis for giving visual identity to suburban space in order to represent the coherence of a community and its distinctiveness as a marketable place. A fabricated vernacular represents "history in the making" (to use the unintentionally ironic words of an ad campaign for one of these communities), referring to a romanticized or fictitious past, or to an imaginary scenery derived from vague references to exotic places. In this way, newly produced residential space, often literally in the middle of nowhere, is located in history and given a legible identity. Both "history" and "community" are embodied in a pastiche of architectural styles, spatial arrangements, and a countryside of carefully designed scenes that become part of the real estate package. This visual quality is sustained by the mechanisms of detailed codes and design boards designated to approve all new construction.

One striking characteristic of these developments is that differences in class, status, and lifestyle are sorted out in spatial terms. Within a framework of master-planned development, different parcels are developed to suit distinct market segments: medium-to-large detached single-family houses, attached villas, condominiums, all in a range of flavors from the tastefully modest to the conspicuously upscale. The de facto boundary-defining character of suburban development is transformed into an intentionally manipulated and dramatized feature of community. In fact, it is *the* defining feature of these communities, the homogenizing function underlying the variations in styles. This categorical sorting of what the real estate people politely term "lifestyle choices" is linked to a shift in the architectural imagery from the isolated house in the garden to the rural village. Design criteria specified by the master plan sustain a visual homogeneity, and define the vocabulary in which difference is expressed, contained, or excluded. Each development has its own logo, its characteristic signage and street furniture, its palette of landscaping materials, and its carefully specified architectural look. The visual organization of segregated spaces becomes a crucial part of an image of community that relies on modulations of a consistently styled built environment to signal variations of wealth and status within an overall homogeneity. The effect is a landscape that is comforting and familiar, but which sharpens the experience of social distances. Much has been made recently of walled communities, but walls are typically more visual signifiers than effective barriers to uninvited entry.

Third, these communities define a particular mode of citizenship. The provision of recreational facilities, open space, and a variety of visual amenities constitutes a collective interest that is formalized in owners' associations. These associations act as the perfect night-watchman state, and buffer owners both from the usual dangers of urban development, with its cycles of decay and reinvestment, and from the need for involvement in local politics. The rights of citizenship, purchased with the property, revolve around visual consumption of the landscape. Responsibilities of citizenship are minimal but contractually specified and legally sanctioned: property owners are obliged to maintain a visual conformity to standards, and to take limited financial responsibility for the provision of certain collective goods. Contractual obligations and policing by homeowners' associations replace the need for any broader sense of trust or civic virtue among citizens.

Here we see a packaging of community, and a tangible construction of a specific kind of public realm which is operative in spatial practices and represented by visual images. In this version of community, the demands of sociability are reduced to a convenient minimum, since the rules of membership are formalized and a certain homogeneity of appearance is structurally as well as directly enforced. Since diversity is ordered and contained, and practical interdependence has been reduced to a minimum, there is little need for the continuous stream of minor interactions or the negotiation of an interaction order. There is no need for a modulated continuum of public and private space, since the private regions of household and personal lives are embedded in an abstractly defined but well-specified, well-illuminated, and legally circumscribed public realm. In short, the calculated imagery of community only underscores the effective absence of either a cosmopolitan or a civic public.

CONCLUSION

IT IS CLEAR THAT both public life and the spaces in which it takes place have undergone profound transformations. However, efforts to develop accounts of the "end of public space," or to elaborate critical alternatives to the perceived crisis, are persistently limited by the lack of a clear and concrete sense of what is meant by "public" and of how it is to be contrasted and articulated with "private." What is also missing in most of these discussions is an explicit analysis of the ways in which the relationship between visual and social order is mediated.

In this essay, I have tried to suggest some ways in which these theoretical problems need to be linked systematically to the technological modalities and social organization of the practices which give form and meaning to the built environment. In order to unravel the meaning and character of changes in the articulation of public and private, it is necessary to understand transformations in the way this articulation is mediated by the representation of the "public" character of built space in visual form, and to clarify the relationship between conceptions of public space and the practices of giving form to the built environment.

One source of confusion in recent critical discussions of the public/private distinction in the built environment has been the tendency for the representational practices of design, beginning with modernism, to effectively collapse this distinction or to reconstruct it in self-contradictory ways. Furthermore, while much criticism has been directed against the unintended consequences of modernist design, critical discussions of public space continue to struggle with a persistent ambiguity in the status of architecture as a cultural product that is a legacy of modernism. The modernist rhetoric of functionalism and objectivity, expressed in the abstract and self-referential character of modernist forms, reinforced the tendency to look for direct and "objective" links between visual form and social order, and to interpret built space with reference to an ideal type of technical rationality. The result is to obscure the mediating role of architecture and to mask its character as a specific system of representation.

In the case of planned suburban communities, we can see an intersection of the agendas of developers, home buyers, bankers, planners, and architects. The architects are not the most powerful of these interests, and are not always successful in shaping the outcomes as they might wish, but it is they who give tangible form to the convergence of these agendas and construct a discipline around it, translating what begins as a historically contingent constellation of interests into a durable technology and a transposable capacity to recognize certain virtues and value certain possibilities in the shaping of social space.

In the theoretical and practical passage from mundane suburban development to paradigmatic designs like Seaside, one can see a new reconfiguration of the historical identity of architecture as a cultural form. This reconfiguration reflects both a reaction to professional dilemmas created by modernist design and a creative response to contemporary conditions of professional practice. In this way, forms are enabled to make definite claims about their relationship to function, about their appropriateness and utility, and to address us as a certain kind of public.

Nineteenth-century architecture developed at the boundary between public and private, a boundary that was carefully aligned with the distinction between inside and outside, so that built form could be enacted as a public expression of private judgment. Modernist architecture, in attempting to dissolve the architect's historical reliance on the vagaries of taste, also dissolved the public/private distinction at the core of its representational order; in doing so, paradoxically, it only sharpened the distinction between those for whom architecture could be a public expression of private taste, and those for whom it was simply a technological form. "Public" space was thereby reduced to a matter of common access and visibility by the form-giving practices of modernism itself.

New modes of design have given up on the modernists' effort to rationalize form by yoking it to universalized functions, instead reemphasizing the particularity, contingency, and expressive possibilities of form freed from simple determinism and reasserting the importance of the articulation of public and private space as a central problem in architectural and urban design. However, where public space was once defined in opposition to the diverse private spaces it encompassed, and in terms of the responsibilities of the private citizen for things which transcend the individual and local, new forms of public space are circumscribed by private interests and crisscrossed with contractual relations; their "public" character is limited to the capacity to represent themselves as a response to an aggregated need for privacy. "Postmodernist" design has elaborated practical techniques for producing this distinctive kind of public space.

From an architecture of depth—a depth that depended on the transparency of the relationship between form and function—design since modernism has sought a return to an architecture of opaque surfaces. The cultural object of postmodernist architecture is located at the point where inside and outside, form and function, design intention and building problem, meet without any necessary reconciliation. But even as it appears to return to the historical fascinations of nineteenth-century eclecticism, this architecture involves a dramatic inversion. Where the stylization of private experience was once the condition of its representation in public and the constitution of a coherent bourgeois public realm, this new architectural modality stylizes public experience in a manner that valorizes the fact of choice rather than the substance of judgment. Where taste once allowed the individual to give visual representation to the capacities of a certain kind of subject, the multiplication of disconnected choices leaves the private sphere as an irreducible and unrepresentable core of experience. And where modernism dissolved the private into the public, postmodernist design moves in the opposite direction, but with the parallel effect of profoundly impoverishing both sides of the dichotomy. Public space is flattened into a manageable scenographic backdrop for a private realm without definitive content.

In the postmodern suburb, the public realm is narrowly and specifically defined, governed by rules of civility and propriety, a space inhabited by owners of property who share a symbolic and economic stake in its orderliness. These are functional spaces for living packaged as historical, a consciously planned and technically rational order of segregated spaces presented as a cultural order by drawing on a reconstituted (or even completely fabricated) history. These communities are defined by the imposition of an image of place on the abstraction of a market category, not by the practical engagement associated with a social space in which subjects are located in relation to one another as a result of deeply sedimented historical experience. Such public space, with its peculiar articulation between public and private, provides a framework for the coexistence of essentially disconnected individuals, whose interests are secured by delegated property management rather than shared responsibility or substantive political engagement.

In spite of postmodernist claims to have broken sharply with the heroic arrogance of modernist design, the public space of the "new urbanism" depends on the order-imposing authority of the planner and architect, an authority that rests on the coupling of the economic power of property owners/ investors with the authority of the state. Postmodernist design has reclaimed architectural problems which modernism attempted to reduce to technical issues within an overarching functionalism, reconstructing them as problems of form, meaning, and representation. Underlying these efforts, however, one can see the persistent struggle to sustain the cultural authority of the architect by organizing the shifting balance between private and public power within the discipline of design.

Whatever its aesthetic claims, architectural design is anchored in a practical setting that entails a complex institutional bargain with particular structures of power. For postmodernist design, private investment provides the framework within which the coherent articulation of a spatial order is achieved. This is not new in itself, since new towns and urban public spaces have been built with private money in the past, and architects have always welcomed opportunities to work on a large scale with the kind of unlimited and authoritative control that the rights of private property can offer.[45] One consequence of these new developments, however, is the translation of a reconfigured public/ private distinction into a new modality of architectural production.

It is ironic, but should be no surprise, that there is an intimate practical connection between the ordered visual diversity and expressive qualities of such designs, and a concern for security and social control that is both justified as a condition for the execution of grand designs and addressed in their implementation. Hence the ambivalence of the analogy drawn by critics between the contemporary city and the theme park as "a highly regulated, synthetic vision . . . that stands in for the more undisciplined complexities of the city." [46]

45. As Zukin points out, Jameson's discussion of the atrium hotel as a postmodern space ignores similar observations of hotel lobbies made by Henry James, and the arcades of Paris as public spaces constructed by private interests: Zukin, *Landscapes of Power*, p. 5.
46. Sorkin, "See You in Disneyland," in *Variations on a Theme Park*, p. 208.

It is by bringing public space *inside* that architects are empowered to reshape its representational qualities, and, in the process, ground the authority of their discipline and give coherence to our experience of built space.

One promising note in recent critical discussions is that they highlight both the political economy and the cultural politics of urban space, treating the built environment as an outcome of active production rather than a "naturally" evolving form. Most often, however, they leave out the crucial mediations in the production of urban space. Giving practical articulation to the public/private distinction in conjunction with the authoritative linking of form and function is both at the heart of the architectural profession's efforts at authorization of design, and at the core of recent efforts for recovering meaning and order in the city by rewriting its visual text. The result is a continuation of the fundamental link between structures of power and the effort to sustain a coherent landscape that characterized modernism as a consolidation of professional authority.

REFERENCES

Bauer, Catherine. 1934. *Modern Housing.* Cambridge, MA: Riverside Press.

Baxandall, Michael. 1985. *Patterns of Intention.* New Haven, CT: Yale University Press.

Brain, David. 1989. "Discipline and Style: The Ecole des Beaux Arts and the Social Production of an American Architecture." *Theory and Society* 18, no. 6 (November): 807–68.

———. 1991. "Practical Knowledge and Occupational Control: The Professionalization of Architecture in the United States." *Sociological Forum* 6, no. 2 (June): 239–68.

Boyer, Paul. 1978. *Urban Masses and Moral Order.* Cambridge, MA: Harvard University Press.

Callon, Michel, and Bruno Latour. 1992. "Don't Throw the Baby Out with the Bath School!" In *Science as Practice and Culture,* edited by Andrew Pickering. Chicago: University of Chicago Press.

Crawford, Margaret. 1992. "The World in a Shopping Mall." In *Variations on a Theme Park: The New American City and the End of Public Space,* edited by Michael Sorkin. New York: Hill & Wang.

Davis, Mike. 1992. "Fortress Los Angeles: The Militarization of Urban Space." In *Variations on a Theme Park: The New American City and the End of Public Space,* edited by Michael Sorkin. New York: Hill & Wang.

Easterling, Keller. 1991. "Public Enterprise." In *Seaside: Making a Town in America,* edited by David Mohney and Keller Easterling. Princeton, NJ: Princeton Architectural Press.

Fustel de Coulanges, Numa Denis. [1864] 1956. *The Ancient City.* Garden City, NY: Doubleday Anchor.

Garreau, Joel. 1992. *Edge City.* New York: Anchor Books.

Glazer, Nathan, and Mark Lilla, eds. 1987. *The Public Face of Architecture: Civic Culture and Public Spaces.* New York: Free Press.

Gottdiener, Mark. 1988. *The Social Production of Urban Space.* Austin: University of Texas Press.

Holston, James. 1989. *The Modernist City: An Anthropological Critique of Brasilia.* Chicago: University of Chicago Press.

Jacobs, Jane. 1961. *The Death and Life of Great American Cities.* New York: Vintage.

Jameson, Fredric. 1984. "Postmodernism, or, the Cultural Logic of Late Capitalism." *New Left Review,* no. 146 (July–August): 59–92.

———. 1991. *Postmodernism, or, The Cultural Logic of Late Capitalism.* Durham, NC: Duke University Press.

Jordy, William. 1963. "The Symbolic Essence of Modern European Architecture of the Twenties and Its Continuing Influence." *Journal of the Society of Architectural Historians* 22 (1963): 177–87.

Kastner, Alfred. 1938. "The Architect's Place in Current Housing." *Housing Yearbook.* Chicago: National Association of Housing Officials.

Larson, Magali Sarfatti. 1983. "Emblem and Exception: The Historical Definition of the Architect's Professional Role." In *Professionals and Urban Form,* edited by Judith R. Blau, Mark E. La Gory, and John S. Pipkin. Albany: SUNY Press.

———. 1993. *Behind the Postmodern Facade: Architectural Change in Late Twentieth Century America.* Berkeley: University of California Press.

Le Corbusier. [1931] 1986. *Towards a New Architecture.* New York: Dover.

Levine, Neil. 1991. "Questioning the View: Seaside's Critique of the Gaze of Modern Architecture." In *Seaside: Making a Town in America,* edited by David Mohney and Keller Easterling. Princeton, NJ: Princeton Architectural Press.

Mies van der Rohe, Ludwig. 1975. Working Theses. Reprinted in *Programs and Manifestoes on 20th Century Architecture,* edited by Ulrich Conrads. Cambridge, MA: MIT Press.

Mohney, David, and Keller Easterling, eds. 1991. *Seaside: Making a Town in America.* Princeton, NJ: Princeton Architectural Press.

Montgomery, Roger. 1989. "Architecture Invents New People." In *Architects' People,* edited by Russell Ellis and Dana Cuff. New York: Oxford University Press.

Park, Robert. 1916. "The City: Suggestions for the Investigation of Human Behavior in the Urban Environment." *American Journal of Sociology,* vol. 20. Reprinted in Richard Sennett, ed., *Classic Essays on the Culture of Cities* (New York: Appleton-Century-Crofts, 1969).

Rybczynski, Witold. 1993. "The New Downtowns." *Atlantic Monthly* (May).

Scruton, Roger. 1987. "Public Space and the Classical Vernacular." In *The Public*

Face of Architecture: Civic Culture and Public Spaces, edited by Nathan Glazer and Mark Lilla. New York: Free Press.

Sennett, Richard. 1978. *The Fall of Public Man: On the Social Psychology of Capitalism.* New York: Vintage.

———. 1990. *The Conscience of the Eye: The Design and Social Life of Cities.* New York: Knopf.

Sorkin, Michael. 1992. "See You in Disneyland." In *Variations on a Theme Park: The New American City and the End of Public Space.* New York: Hill & Wang.

———, ed. 1992. *Variations on a Theme Park: The New American City and the End of Public Space.* New York: Hill & Wang.

Venturi, Robert. 1966. *Complexity and Contradiction in Architecture.* New York: Museum of Modern Art.

Venturi, Robert, Denise Scott Brown, and Steven Izenour. 1972. *Learning from Las Vegas.* Cambridge, MA: MIT Press.

Weintraub, Jeff. 1995. "Varieties and Vicissitudes of Public Space." In *Metropolis: Center and Symbol of Our Times,* edited by Philip Kasinitz. New York: New York University Press; London: Macmillan.

Wirth, Louis. 1938. "Urbanism as a Way of Life." *American Journal of Sociology* 44 (July): 1–24. Reprinted in Richard Sennett, ed., *Classic Essays on the Culture of Cities* (New York: Appleton-Century-Crofts, 1969).

Wright, Gwendolyn. 1980. *Moralism and the Model Home: Domestic Architecture and Cultural Conflict in Chicago.* Chicago: University of Chicago Press.

Zukin, Sharon. 1991. *Landscapes of Power: From Detroit to Disney World.* Berkeley: University of California Press.

Rediscovering the Social: Visiting Practices in Antebellum New England and the Limits of the Public/Private Dichotomy

Karen V. Hansen

A NINETEENTH-CENTURY SEAMSTRESS, milliner, and one-time machine shop worker, Martha Barrett, has left a challenging legacy to social science and history. In the diaries she kept over thirty years, she documented the complexity of her everyday social life, which was filled with friendship networks, philosophical debates, struggles to find employment, political involvements, and considerations of the politics of women's fashions. Her account of a single day in 1853, on which she attended the Essex County Anti-Slavery Society convention, puts the challenge eloquently:

> Have had a beautiful time today. Went to the Convention. Mr. Burnham kindly called and took us over. Meeting had not commenced, found a goodly number collected together. But the audience increased steadily through the day. Stephen S. Foster spoke at some length on the position of the [spoilers]. . . . I like Stephen, but Parker is my favorite yet. He too made some remarks, also C. L. Remond and "Uncle Thomas." Dined at Mr. Harriman's with Parker, C. L. R. and his wife, Aunt Hetty. Two ladies from Manchester. Enjoyed myself very much. One of the ladies from M. wore the Bloomer dress. I envied her independense. I do like the dress, think it more convenient, healthy, and certainly prettier than the long skirts. I do hope I shall sometime have strength enough to put it on. Meeting not quite as interesting as in the morning. Took supper at Mr. Merrill's. Had quite a company. Parker, Stephen, James Buffum, James Babcock and wife, the Shermans, Geo. W. Putnam. W. J. Kenney, and Professor W. [P.] Allen from Central College, N.Y. The latter an exceedingly intelligent young man. Very interesting. He made a beautiful address in the evening. Beautifully eloquent. Several other speeches were made in the evening. Mr. Burnham brought us home. Huldah Shove and Mr. Pills-

Many thanks to Andrew Bundy for his astute reading of this essay and to Jeff Weintraub for his thoughtful and persistent probing of my theoretical argument.

bury accompanied us. Take it all together don't know when I've passed a pleasant day. It really seemed like an old time Essex Co. Meeting. But Essex Co. really is in a cold and lifeless state, as concerns anti-slavery. I wish it might be roused. I feel anxious about it. We used to be the banner county. It is sad to retrograde. I would I had the talent I would go the length and breadth thereof, and rouse the people from their apathy.[1]

According to the prevailing historical understanding, social life in nineteenth-century America was sharply dichotomized between public and private spheres, with women largely confined to the latter. But this model fails to capture the texture of Martha's life, as revealed in this characteristic passage from her diary. Her daily activities conjoined political, moral, social, and personal worlds in a way that makes them difficult to categorize as strictly public or private, however these terms are defined, and that undermines the assumption of a rigid separation between these two domains. Another formulation tied to the public/private dichotomy—the doctrine of "separate spheres" for men and women—would lead us to believe that Martha's everyday contacts consisted almost exclusively of other women. In fact, men appear frequently in Martha's diary as friends, visitors, and fellow activists.

The multidimensionality of Martha's life, and the lives of many ordinary working women like her, not only challenges us to rethink our picture of nineteenth-century American society. Its larger implications point to the problematic character of the public/private dichotomy itself as an analytic framework in history and the social sciences. When used as a binary model of social structure, the public/private dichotomy obscures the depth, breadth, and importance of informal interaction in everyday life as a field of practices that weaves these different realms together.

Through the prism of Martha Barrett's diary, for example, we see how political activity intertwines with daily life and informal interaction. As a woman, Martha could not vote. As an unmarried worker supporting herself largely through her needle skills, she had few monetary resources and limited ability to reshape the political system. But Martha hardly led an isolated, privatized existence, confined to domestic space. Through her complex interactions with others—as a friend, neighbor, and co-worker—she actively constructed and maintained a community of people upon whom she could rely for scarce resources, emotional support, a shared political perspective, and

1. Martha Osborne Barrett Diary, January 9, 1853 (James Duncan Phillips Library: hereafter JDPL). To facilitate the ease of interpreting the written words of my nineteenth-century subjects, I have modernized the capitalization and punctuation of excerpts from diaries and letters. However, I have left the spelling as it appears in the original documents.

goods and services. And these bonds shaped and supported a range of political commitments and activities.

On the other hand, Martha was acutely aware that the attractions of involvement in a social movement included the people she saw at meetings and her ties to them. In the passage just cited, an account of a single day, she mentions nineteen people. In 1858 she wrote about planning to attend another Essex County Anti-Slavery Society meeting: "Shall go if possible—am anticipating much pleasure, not only from listening to the speaking, but also in meeting some esteemed friends." [2] In a similar vein, years later Martha quoted from old minutes of the Ladies Unitarian Association to recall the political import of conversation at supposedly nonpolitical meetings: "One report read thus . . . 'Not much work was accomplished this afternoon, ladies being very much engaged in talking politics.' " [3]

This brief glimpse into Martha Barrett's life is enough to highlight some of the ways in which the public/private dichotomy fails to grasp the complexity of nineteenth-century life. This model assumes the separateness of political issues and private concerns. It does not account for the fluidity of activity where friendship and socializing meld into political discussion, which stimulates political action. In Martha's diary we find extensive evidence of personal attachments anchoring political behavior, and political beliefs shaping social behavior, such as which church to attend or what clothes to wear. More important, the public/private dichotomy fails to capture the large intermediate areas of communal interaction that filled the days of working people. This sociability—the means by which people constructed and maintained communities, mobilized social movements, and expressed moral sensibilities—is distinct from purely private interactions, often ruled by intimate emotion and particularistic obligations, and from strictly public affairs, which are ordered by legislation and formal organization.

Elizabeth Metcalf, a farm woman, inadvertently offered a preferable way to frame Martha's activities. She described her merriment at a quilting party at which a similarly broad variety of interactions took place: "We had a very social time." [4] Borrowing from Elizabeth's wisdom, I propose to frame the activities depicted in Martha's diary, and the similar activities of her contemporaries, as *social* rather than public or private. Along with thousands of other women whose economic, political, and associational lives have been docu-

2. Martha Osborne Barrett Diary, December 15, 1858.

3. Martha Osborne Barrett, "Paper Read before the Ladies' Unitarian Association," October 28, 1892 (Peabody Historical Society).

4. Elizabeth H. Metcalf to Chloe Metcalf, October 22, 1851 (Metcalf-Adams Family Letters, Museum of American Textile History).

mented by historians, Martha ignored the popularly disseminated dictates admonishing her to confine herself to domestic life and to avoid public involvements.[5] However, as the historical evidence from antebellum New England reveals, it was not only political activism, working for wages, and involvement in voluntary associations that pulled women out of the domestic realm, but sociality itself.[6]

Why should this seem surprising? The answer lies in the pervasive influence of the public/private dichotomy, which captured the imagination of feminist scholars during the 1970s and 1980s. Their search for a lost history and an explanation for the virtually universal subordination of women in otherwise very different cultures brought them to this organizing conceptualization by several intersecting routes. Feminists reasoned that the apparent contrasts between the cultures of men and women in a wide range of societies and historical periods had structural (as opposed to biological) origins. According to a very influential line of argument, one recurrent—possibly even universal—structural dimension of gender inequality has been the more or less total exclusion of women from the public realm and their disproportionate association with the private realm of domestic life; women's distinctively "private" activities are then systematically devalued as marginal or unimportant for society as a whole in comparison with the more "public" activities to which men have disproportionate or exclusive access—whether these involve hunting, politics, warfare, or business.[7] Feminists also called attention to the remarkable frequency with which women have been ideologically identified with the "private" pole of this domestic/public opposition, in contexts ranging from popular culture to the most abstract forms of jurisprudence and political theory.

5. See, for example, Ellen Carol DuBois, *Feminism and Suffrage* (1978); Mary P. Ryan, *Women in Public: Between Banners and Ballots, 1825–1850* (1990); Carroll Smith-Rosenberg, *Disorderly Conduct: Visions of Gender in Victorian America* (1986); Christine Stansell, *City of Women: Sex and Class in New York, 1789–1860* (1986); Dorothy Sterling, *Ahead of Her Time: Abby Kelley and the Politics of Antislavery* (1991); and Shirley Yee, *Black Women Abolitionists: A Study in Activism, 1828–1860* (1992).

6. This is, in fact, made strikingly clear by such prominent works as Nancy Cott, *Bonds of Womanhood: "Woman's Sphere" in New England, 1790–1835* (1977), and Smith-Rosenberg, *Disorderly Conduct;* however, neither the authors nor most readers of these books have usually drawn the conclusions from their evidence that I am drawing here. See also Karen V. Hansen, *A Very Social Time: Crafting Community in Antebellum New England* (1994).

7. For some landmark statements of this position, see Michelle Z. Rosaldo, "Woman, Culture, and Society: A Theoretical Overview," in Michelle Z. Rosaldo and Louise Lamphere's edited volume, *Woman, Culture, and Society* (1974), pp. 17–42; and Karen Sacks, "Engels Revisited: Women, the Organization of Production and Private Property," in Rayna R. Reiter, ed., *Toward an Anthropology of Women* (1975), pp. 211–34.

These themes have made a strong impact on some of the most vigorous approaches to the social history of the United States. In their search for roots of the oppression of women in American history, feminists found that the dominant ideology of the nineteenth century articulated a doctrine of "separate spheres" for men and women. For women's historians, the exploration of the public/private dichotomy in the United States has gone hand-in-hand with a discussion about the culture of separate spheres. This ideological formulation seemed to explain a great deal about the constraints on women's exercise of power and their limited access to political life.[8] Some have concluded that the industrial division of labor, combined with the formal exclusion of women from political power, effectively assigned women to the domestic realm and men to the public. Thus, this body of scholarship has usually treated the public/private dichotomy and the paradigm of separate spheres as largely interchangeable, and in so doing has tended to conflate two questions that, although related, are analytically distinct: Was everyday life in the nineteenth century sharply dichotomized between public and private domains; and, Were the lives of women and men as thoroughly gender-segregated as the ideology of separate spheres suggests? I intend to demonstrate that, in light of the historical evidence, both of these accepted pictures need to be fundamentally reassessed.

Feminists have also generated a vast literature that points to the inadequacies of the public/private framework for understanding the status of women in society.[9] These disparate criticisms emphasize its historical fluctuations and contest its meanings and uses in the academy. From the earliest phases of "second-wave" feminist scholarship after 1970, some feminist writers have emphasized that the dualism of the domestic/public model conceals the actual interconnectedness of the public and private spheres.[10] For example, the ability of some individuals to enter the labor market depends upon their freedom from the need to perform life-maintenance activities such as "providing food, washing and cleaning, and care of children," made possible "only because these tasks are performed unpaid" by women in the "private" sphere of the

8. For example, Cott, *Bonds of Womanhood;* Carl N. Degler, *At Odds: Women and the Family in America from the Revolution to the Present* (1980); Karen Halttunen, *Confidence Men and Painted Women: A Study of Middle-Class Culture in America, 1830–1870* (1982); Linda K. Kerber, "Separate Spheres, Female Worlds, Women's Place: The Rhetoric of Women's History," *Journal of American History* 75, no. 1 (1988): 9–39; and Smith-Rosenberg, *Disorderly Conduct.*

9. For an exemplary anthology of the recent historical literature, see Dorothy O. Helly and Susan M. Reverby's *Gendered Domains: Rethinking Public and Private in Women's History* (1992).

10. Elizabeth H. Pleck, "Two Worlds in One: Work and Family," *Journal of Social History* 10, no. 2 (winter 1976): 178–95.

household.[11] Exaggerating the differences between these domains also obscures the similarities, such as the fact that both are sites of labor, rendering women's everyday work within the home invisible.[12] In studying specific historical contexts such as the nineteenth-century United States, it has been suggested, the categories are often misleading because they were designed for middle-class application, and do not adequately address the broad experiences of white and free black working-class and farm women.[13] More generally, it has been argued that the attempt to transform gender-stereotyped prescriptive models of the public/private dichotomy into analytical frameworks tends in practice to reinforce the ideological stereotypes rather than undermine them. And, on the other hand, most efforts to use the public/private dichotomy in ways that are ostensibly gender-neutral (such as claiming that the internal workings of the family ought to be sacrosanct against legal or political intrusion because it is a "private" domain) actually operate to camouflage power inequalities between men and women and to prevent various types of "private" abuse from being recognized and combated.[14] More recently, from somewhat different perspectives, both feminist poststructuralists[15] and some black feminist theorists have attacked the artificial and distorting character of "either/or dichotomous thinking" in principle, arguing that it necessarily leads to both theoretical and practical dead ends.[16] However, despite these widespread (and unresolved) debates, criticisms, reassessments, and reformulations, a considerable range of scholarship in history and the social sciences—feminist and otherwise—continues to rely analytically on one or another form of the public/private dichotomy.[17]

11. Carole Pateman, "Feminist Critiques of the Public/Private Dichotomy," in S. I. Benn's and G. F. Gaus's edited volume, *Public and Private in Social Life* (1983), p. 296.

12. Nancy Fraser, "What's Critical about Critical Theory? The Case of Habermas and Gender," *New German Critique* 35 (spring–summer 1985): 97–131.

13. Hansen, *A Very Social Time;* and Nancy Grey Osterud, *Bonds of Community: The Lives of Farm Women in Nineteenth-Century New York* (1991).

14. Fraser, "What's Critical about Critical Theory?"; also see Pateman, "Feminist Critiques of the Public/Private Dichotomy"; and Linda J. Nicholson, *Gender and History: The Limits of Social Theory in the Age of the Family* (1986).

15. For example, Joan Wallach Scott, *Gender and the Politics of History* (1988); and Chris Weedon, *Feminist Practice and Poststructuralist Theory* (1987).

16. bell hooks, *Feminist Theory: From Margin to Center* (1984); and Patricia Hill Collins, *Black Feminist Thought: Knowledge, Consciousness, and the Politics of Empowerment* (1990).

17. Some feminists have proposed using the concepts in altered ways, without discarding them altogether: for example, Susan Ostrander, "Feminism, Voluntarism, and the Welfare State: Toward a Feminist Sociological Theory of Social Welfare," *The American Sociologist* 20, no. 1 (spring 1989): 29–41; and Michelle Z. Rosaldo's reconsiderations of

I have three goals in this essay: (1) to present evidence from antebellum New England that challenges our current image of nineteenth-century American society as sharply divided into public and private spheres; (2) to challenge, in addition, the identification of male and female with public and private, respectively; and (3) to suggest that the concept of the *social* mediates the falsely dichotomized categories of public and private and can help to reframe future debates.

As a number of the essays in this volume have emphasized, the terms "public" and "private" are used in shifting and even contradictory ways. But regardless of how they are defined, approaches that treat public and private as exclusive alternatives consistently ignore or underestimate one critical dimension—sociability.[18] As Kenneth Burke puts it, "a way of seeing is also a way of not seeing." [19] Thus, the dichotomous language of public and private directs attention either to the state and the market, or to family and intimate relations, eclipsing community life. Among neighbors and extended kin, people followed different rules of behavior than in familial settings, in the increasingly impersonal world of the market, or in public, formally structured, and legislated environments. The critical idea which emerges inductively from the historical evidence presented here is the concept of the social, which focuses squarely on the dynamics of communal interaction and more accurately captures the gender-integrated behavior of antebellum working women and men.

In particular, the visiting practices of working people provide a wealth of concrete historical evidence with which to explore the terrain of the social in antebellum New England. Visiting was a primary mode of interpersonal interaction, serving a wide range of overlapping functions. In effect, visits were a medium for exchange and reciprocity, as well as a practice through which people activated networks and created communities. Visiting provides a crucial example of a social practice that spans and mediates the public and private spheres. It obliterates any notion of their mutual exclusivity because visitors traversed households as well as outdoor common spaces, often cooperated in productive work while socializing, and discussed each other's moral behavior

---

her earlier position in "The Use and Abuse of Anthropology: Reflections on Feminism and Cross-Cultural Understanding," *Signs* 5, no. 3 (spring 1980): 389–417.

18. As Jeff Weintraub notes in the opening essay to this volume, "Attempts to use the public/private distinction as a dichotomous model to capture the overall pattern of social life in a society—as opposed to using one or another version for specific and carefully defined purposes—are always likely to be inherently misleading, because the procrustean dualism of their categories will tend to blank out important phenomena" ("The Theory and Politics of the Public/Private Distinction," p. 15).

19. Kenneth Burke, *Permanence and Change: An Anatomy of Purpose*, p. 49. Thanks to Jeff Weintraub for bringing this quotation to my attention.

in addition to national and local politics. In this way, visiting further reveals the inadequacy of a dichotomous model of social structure.

Visits were occasions for exchanging information, entertainment, comfort, and labor. Visiting expanded the contacts of those in the private sphere, broadening and deepening networks of social intercourse. It simultaneously provided fertile ground for discussing politics and creating political space that could ultimately affect local, state, and national governments. It also acted as a meeting ground for working men and women, who intermingled extensively while conducting their daily chores and constructing their communities. Through visiting, individuals propped open the doors of households in order to monitor familial interaction and individual behavior, establish neighborly and kin ties, create a forum for discourse, involve people in a communal network, and sustain a common life.

To begin with the evidence: most scholarship on women in the nineteenth-century United States has drawn predominantly on the ideology and experience of the middle class,[20] and this is especially true of historiography informed by the "separate spheres" perspective. But the relationship between public and private looks very different from the vantage point of working people's everyday lives. In order to explore the contours of life in antebellum New England, I turn to first-person narratives of working people—in the form of diaries, letters, and autobiographies. Textile workers, sailors, domestic servants, shoe binders, farmers, seamstresses, and day laborers articulate a rich and complex set of stories and images, full of detail that frequently challenges traditional analyses of their experience. Most of the approximately 170 people I have studied toiled at some kind of manual labor, skilled or unskilled, and none attended college. They lived in households that in 1850 owned an average of $978 worth of real estate and personal property.[21] By no stretch of the imagination can they be characterized as professional or socially elite. While these

20. Some important exceptions focusing on working-class women include Thomas Dublin, *Women at Work: The Transformation of Work and Community in Lowell, Massachusetts, 1826–1860* (1979); and Stansell, *City of Women.*

21. These figures regarding wealth come from the 1850 manuscript census. They are largely consistent with the figures computed by Thomas Dublin in his study of the social origins of female textile operatives. He found that the median property holdings of millhands' fathers in 1850 was $960, just slightly less than the average property holdings of other male heads of households of similar ages in the towns and villages where the fathers lived ($998): Dublin, *Women at Work,* p. 35. I have supplemented the main base of evidence for this essay—diaries of fifty-six men and women, twenty collections of letters, and nineteen autobiographies—by drawing on town histories, vital records, genealogies, manuscript censuses, and probate records. For a full analysis of these documents, and an explication of their use as sources of evidence, see Hansen, *A Very Social Time.*

subjects may not precisely represent the New England working population as a whole, at a minimum they clearly illustrate a broad range of what was *possible*. At best, given the preponderance of consistent evidence and the virtual absence of cases to the contrary, I have great confidence in the degree to which their testimony falls in line with the experiences of a broad spectrum of working people.

GENDERING PUBLIC AND PRIVATE

As STRUCTURAL FORCES transformed production in the nineteenth century, they also transformed how men and women supported themselves and how society viewed them and their work. Industrialization increasingly moved production out of the household, creating a separation between "home life" and "work life" and thus generating a new dimension of the private/public division. Men found many employment options outside of the home and farm environment, working as printers, weavers, machine shop workers—mechanics and artisans of all kinds. Single women similarly sought employment for wages, while married women confronted both a reorganization of their work within the household and an increasing devaluation of this work, as productive "work" came to be ideologically identified with the cash economy.[22] Since a majority of Americans lived in rural areas throughout the nineteenth century, agriculture continued to be the most common source of employment for men and women.[23] In rural areas, many women who had to contribute to the household economy also became "hired girls" on neighboring farms, contracted piecework in the "outwork" system—binding shoes, sewing buttons on cards, and making straw hats—or entered the developing network of textile factories in New England.[24] In addition, as many as one in four women taught school at some point in their lives.[25] But the seasonality of employment combined with the preindustrial character of agricultural and artisanal endeavors to sustain the household as a center of production and sociality in antebellum New England, even in the face of increasing industrialization.

22. For a penetrating analysis of these structural and ideological processes, see Jeanne Boydston, *Home and Work: Housework, Wages, and the Ideology of Labor in the Early Republic* (1990).

23. U.S. Bureau of the Census, *Historical Statistics of the U.S., Colonial Times to 1970.*

24. In the United States, women became the first industrial proletariat. Dublin finds that women constituted more than 85 percent of the workforce in the Hamilton Company mills in Lowell, Massachusetts, in 1836 (*Women at Work,* p. 26).

25. Richard M. Bernard and Maris A. Vinovskis, "The Female School Teacher in Ante-Bellum Massachusetts," *Journal of Social History* 10, no. 3 (March 1977): 333.

Not coincidentally, at the very moment that the industrial organization of work began paying cash wages, granting some women temporary economic independence and unprecedented freedom from family and community surveillance, a new ideology emerged that firmly located women's place in the home—the doctrine of "separate spheres." The new perspective corresponded neatly with the emerging separation of "work" from family life, of public from private space. More important, this separation—and the expectation that women conform to it—purportedly solved questions about the role of women in the new social order. The shift of production of household goods from home to factory meant that women's work at home was being usurped by industry. However, single women went into the factories in droves, leaving married women with children to cope with a changing economic context and a contradictory set of ideals.

The new domestic advice literature, oriented largely to white middle-class women, dovetailed with these structural changes. It advocated the construction of an ideological wall between public and private life and, in effect, between men and women. It relegated middle-class women to domestic life and men to the marketplace and world of politics. It promised men and women autonomy within their own separate spheres, free to reign with relatively little interference from the opposite sex. This ideology elevated the gendered division of labor to the height of religious principle.

A related ideological genre, the "cult of true womanhood," embellished the portrait of wives and mothers in the home.[26] Their place was by the hearth fires, tending the education of their children, guarding the morals of society, and alleviating the ill effects of calculating, harsh market relations. Women's reward for their confinement to the home was the promise of power, or at least influence, in the domestic sphere—"the empire of the mother."[27] The partner to the "true woman," the fashionable middle-class man, was to be an individual who exhibited ambition, courage, and strength, and "who was almost ascetically devoted to the work-related virtues."[28] Men, as breadwinners and political actors, were shaped by the instrumentalism of market exchange and formal political bargaining, and therefore needed domestication by the gentle hand of women. In fact, E. Anthony Rotundo finds middle-class men

26. Barbara Welter, "The Cult of True Womanhood: 1820–1860," *American Quarterly* 18, no. 2 (summer 1966): 151–74.

27. Mary P. Ryan, *The Empire of the Mother: American Writing about Domesticity, 1830–1860* (1985).

28. Ronald P. Byars, "The Making of the Self-Made Man: The Development of Masculine Roles and Images in Ante-Bellum America" (1979), p. 197.

wary of the "cage of domesticity," prompting some men to reject those aspects of life that held feminine associations—religion, culture, the home, and women themselves.[29]

In part, this prescriptive literature targeting middle-class women and men attempted to finesse the tension created by the separation of "work" from family life and the instrumental versus expressive modes of behavior associated with each realm. It posited gendered spheres of influence which would allow for greater specialization within each realm and counter the sphere of instrumental rationality with a realm of intimacy and emotion. How this literature affected actual behavior remains an open question. A further question is how this literature affected the working classes, if it did at all.

The widespread use of "separate spheres" as a theoretical construct has been bolstered by the revival of discussions about public and private in the last twenty years—from feminist quarters and elsewhere. One school of thought claims that the division of labor into paid production and unpaid reproduction did indeed create physically, emotionally, and culturally separate spheres for men and women. While subjecting the ideology of separate spheres to critical scrutiny, much influential feminist research has accepted the assumption that women's separation from men encouraged a distinct women's culture to flourish.[30] Some have suggested that this separate women's culture provided a crucial foundation for the emergence of the women's rights movement beginning in 1848.[31]

More recently, other feminist work has challenged the accuracy of the model of separate spheres for the nineteenth-century United States (and elsewhere), except insofar as it operated as ideology.[32] Nancy Grey Osterud has

29. E. Anthony Rotundo, *American Manhood: Transformations in Masculinity from the Revolution to the Modern Era* (1993), p. 105.

30. Cott, *Bonds of Womanhood;* Halttunen, *Confidence Men and Painted Women;* and Smith-Rosenberg, *Disorderly Conduct.* Lise Vogel argues that this vein of feminist scholarship achieved hegemony in the late 1970s through the 1980s, to the exclusion and retrospective erasure of competing perspectives that were informed by analytic categories such as class, racial difference, and exploitation: "Telling Tales: Historians of Our Own Lives," *Journal of Women's History* 2, no. 3 (winter 1991): 89–101.

31. Cott claims the separation of men from women cultivated a "unique sexual solidarity" upon which feminism built in organizing for social change: *Bonds of Womanhood,* p. 201.

32. The argument that the "separate spheres" model has outlived its analytic usefulness is made especially sharply by Linda Kerber in a panel discussion on women's history: Linda K. Kerber, Nancy F. Cott, Robert Gross, Lynn Hunt, Carroll Smith-Rosenberg, and Christine M. Stansell, "Beyond Roles, Beyond Spheres: Thinking about Gender in the Early Republic," *William and Mary Quarterly* 46 (July 1989): 565–85.

documented the extensive commingling of men and women in rural upstate New York: men and women mixed frequently, men routinely did household chores, and women labored in the fields.[33] Even in the middle class, Mary Ryan and Karen Lystra have found widespread evidence of the gainful employment of women outside the home and of women disregarding cultural dictates to observe more conservative romantic and sexual standards than men.[34]

Examining the lives of working people, as reconstructed from their own accounts, provides a means of reassessing both the models of the public/private dichotomy and of gender-segregated "separate spheres." As I indicated earlier, these two models need to be distinguished more carefully than is usually done, but it is useful to address them in tandem because the historical evidence calls both of them seriously into question. An important part of the solution to the limitations of both approaches can be found in the category of the social, which mediated between private and public and served as a meeting ground for men and women.

VISITING IN ANTEBELLUM NEW ENGLAND

IN NINETEENTH-CENTURY AMERICA, the practice of visiting was one of the many ways that people sustained their community life. I define a visit as an informal interaction between two people who know each other but who are not part of the same household. In effect, the involvement of a non–household member distinguishes a community interaction from a private, familial one.[35] In the antebellum context of economic transformation and cultural metamorphosis, the first-person accounts tell us a great deal about what was important in the lives of working men and women. In the diaries, visiting ranks second in frequency only to reports of the harsh New England weather. Piecing together these visits reveals a complex, gender-integrated practice that defies simple notions of public and private and challenges assumptions about the separateness of men's and women's lives.

As a catalog of community activity, these accounts document the elaborate networks of mutuality constructed by people in their daily rounds. In villages, small towns, and urban neighborhoods, people largely knew one another and

33. Osterud, *Bonds of Community*.

34. Mary P. Ryan, *Cradle of the Middle Class: The Family in Oneida County, New York, 1790–1865* (1981); and Karen Lystra, *Searching the Heart: Women, Men, and Romantic Love in Nineteenth-Century America* (1989).

35. Karen V. Hansen and Cameron Macdonald, "Surveying the Dead Informant: Quantitative Analysis and Historical Interpretation," *Qualitative Sociology* 18, no. 2 (summer 1995): 227–36.

business transactions intermingled with social ones. In the antebellum period, furthermore, sociability and work were often intertwined, as yet not entirely shaped by the forces of the market. While on social visits, women and men often shared and exchanged labor; that is, they created extensive, durable networks founded on reciprocity. Visiting served as a vehicle for the distribution of essential services in the community, such as caring for sick neighbors, which do not fall easily into public or private realms.

Visits recorded in diaries by both women and men involved the exchange of numerous goods and services. Purposeful and systematic but informal and unplanned, visits provided an occasion to cement ties and to exchange comfort, companionship, information, moral evaluations, entertainment, and labor. Visiting was part of an ordered system of exchange, built on the principle of mutual obligations binding neighbors and kin. It assumed general equality of station, mutual respect, and reciprocity. Participation in the system offered group membership and the status and honor it bestowed, aid in times of need, companionship, and access to the news circuit.

Formal institutions and structures of collective action—such as churches, schools, labor unions, and voluntary associations—also brought individuals together and connected them to a larger society. However, a focus on the more microsocial level of everyday face-to-face interaction is indispensable for understanding how the fabric of community life, which formed the crucial foundation for these institutions, was created and maintained by human action. It can also help to remind us that it was individual action and engagement with other people that set these larger institutions in motion. For example, Martha Barrett, mentioned earlier, became a member of the abolitionist movement by observing moral principles, acting on her beliefs, going to meetings, and socializing with other abolitionists. A rank-and-file activist in the abolitionist crusades of the 1850s and 1860s, Martha refused to attend services of ministers not staunchly opposed to slavery:

> Indeed I could not consistently attend church where a pro-slavery clergyman performs. I cannot call it worships for can the worship of an oppression, or an apologist for oppression, outrage and wrong be acceptable to a liberty-loving God of purity and truth?[36]

She also acted on her conscience (as abolitionist organizers advocated) by, for example, refusing to participate in Independence Day celebrations because she found them hypocritical:

36. Martha Osborne Barrett Diary, June 30, 1850 (JDPL).

Have had no school to day. It being Independent Day. I have staid quietly at home. I do not like to join in the usual rejoicings, for they seem a mocery while three millions of slaves are groaning in bondage in this own country.[37]

In another example, the Reverend Noah Davis, a former slave who purchased his own freedom, wrote about a similar phenomenon in the border South. He went visiting as part of his strategy to build the congregation of the Saratoga Street African Baptist Church he founded in Baltimore: "During this time we succeeded in getting a better place for the Sabbath school, and there was a larger attendance upon my preaching, which demanded reading and study, and also *visiting*, and increased my daily labors." [38] As sociologists have long observed, what appears to be happenstance on the surface may in fact be purposeful, systematic behavior of great importance. Ongoing human action made an organization an entity, a church a congregation, or abstinence from alcohol a social movement.

Visiting as Sociability

THE DIARY OF MARY MUDGE, a schoolteacher and seamstress living in Lynn, Massachusetts, provides an illuminating picture of the everyday life of an active visitor. On a typical day in March 1854, Mary wrote at length about what had happened at school. Then her visiting began in earnest:

> After dinner called into Harriett's . . . and expected to go up to Sarah's to spend the P.M., but while I was over to Aunt Sally's sister came over and said that some one wanted to see me. So I came home & found Jessee Attwill here. He wanted to know how Anna felt towards him. I got really vexed with him before he left for he got my last year's diary and read some of it after I told him I did not want him to. When he left I did not ask him to call again. B. to [corset] meeting. Marth & Anna spent the eve with me. I was determined to finish my sleeves so I sat up till 12 o'clk and finished them. B. came in a moment about 9 but left with so much as saying he was going home. Orrin says he is kind of sick. Saw the "Organ," a new newspaper today published at West Lynn. Mr. Lewis . . . called and made himself quite sociable. Says he gave $15 for the organ at Boston . . . church, a self

---

37. Martha Osborne Barrett Diary, July 4, 1849 (JDPL).
38. Reverend Noah Davis, *A Narrative of the Life of Rev. Noah Davis, a Colored Man* (Baltimore: John F. Weishampel, Jr., 1859), p. 37 (emphasis added).

conceited fellow I guess. Abba West made me a present of a pretty book- "Gems from [T. S]upper." [39]

In this partial entry for her day, Mary mentions eleven people. Two of those people were nuclear family members—her sister and Orrin—while the rest were neighbors and friends. We can assume that Mary saw more people (certainly her scholars at school, if not others), but did not write them down. While this day was more hectic than some, it was by no means unusual in Mary's life.

Mary was not a middle-class woman of leisure. She was a working woman, pressed to help her mother and save for her own future. Mary's widowed mother headed the household and took in two boarders in addition to caring for eight of her children. Two of Mary's brothers and one of the boarders in the house were "cordwainers," or shoemakers, as her father had been before them. While Mary was unmarried at twenty-four, she was by no means free of responsibility. Not only did she teach elementary school in Lynn, with a class ranging from thirty to forty-four students, she sewed for people, visited the sick, and kept numerous commitments to her friends and extended kin. The mysterious "B." of her diary, otherwise known as Philip C. Bryant, was her steady beau who two years later became her husband. A cordwainer eight years her senior, "B." brought some resources to their marriage, but at least through 1860 Mary continued to teach school.

Her diary is bursting with names, people, and relationships. Typically, her day included work and socializing, although it is often impossible for a twentieth-century reader to distinguish one kind of activity from another. By seeing people, naming them, engaging them, incurring their favor, repaying obligations, sewing for them, talking to them, Mary constructed her community and insured their reciprocal obligations to her. Through visiting, she activated her networks of friends and kin for mutual support, entertainment, and different kinds of exchange. Through her everyday practice of socializing, Mary navigated the economic hardships of life in an industrial city and buoyantly created a durable system of mutual dependency among her neighbors and kin.

Mary Mudge is one example of many. The chronicle of people in first-person narratives provides a measure of what working people in antebellum New England considered important in their lives. It also details for us the intricacies of daily life, the process of creating a web of interconnections, and the rhythms of cooperation and exchange. The historical documents reveal that people sustained their community through the practice of visiting.

39. Mary Mudge Diary, March 1, 1854 (Schlesinger Library: hereafter SL).

Working men and women did not always record the content of their inter-actions while visiting, but religiously documented their visits and visitors, indi-cating their importance as events. These diary entries map the human as well as geographic terrain of community life. John Plummer Foster, a farmer living in North Andover, Massachusetts, recorded his calls on Monday, December 21, 1857: "I went down to Boxford, and called at Edward Foster's, Caroline Batchelder's, Charles Spofford's, and Aaron Spofford's." [40] Again, the chroni-cle of names clues us to the centrality of these people in the life of John Plummer Foster. These visits provided some casual enjoyment, occasional con-flict, and a range of other forms of social intercourse; most important, they mapped a portion of the circle that John identified as his community.

In antebellum New England, women visited more than men, but men participated in this practice as well. Both men and women called upon family members, neighbors, and friends, often in gender-integrated environments. One hundred percent of the female diarists and 86 percent of the male diarists recorded visiting in their diaries. The sheer volume of visitors filtering in and out of everyday routines can seem astounding to us today. Both men and women interrupted their day's labors to visit someone or to provide refresh-ment for an unexpected caller. Both traveled great distances to help raise a barn, to quilt a bedcover, or to provide company for a lonely friend.

Within circles of friendship and family, a powerful sense of obligation mo-tivated people to visit. Sarah Holmes Clark, a married schoolteacher who had moved from Foxcroft, Maine, to Madison, Georgia, discussed the impact of *obligation* on how she spent her day.

> I was interrupted by company yesterday. I had visitors all day or nearly and this morning I devoted to visiting. I felt obliged to go as I am much indebted owing to my long illness, and I fear that people will think me very unsociable if I do not improve the first opportunity. The ladies of Madison visit a great deal. I sometimes wish that they would not come to see me quite as often as they do for if I pretend to pay all my visits in due season, I can find time to do nothing else. Besides, I consider it a task to make ceremonious calls. [41]

Company interrupted her labors but she owed it to her community to repay the attention she received while ill. Her neighbors successfully communicated a message to her: to be unsociable denied community commitments. It was unacceptable.

40. John Plummer Foster Diary, December 21, 1857 (JDPL).
41. Sarah Holmes Clark to Sarah Carter, October 29, 1854 (Holmes Family Papers, Massachusetts Historical Society: hereafter MHS).

It was not simply a matter of whether one did or did not make a visit, but also how one behaved once there. The host could insult the visitor if he or she did not observe the local rules regarding hospitality. William J. Brown, a free-born black man who lived his entire life in Rhode Island, wrote about visiting expectations and the use of alcohol in a waterfront neighborhood of Providence:

> If a person went out to make a call or spend the evening and was not treated to something to drink, they would feel insulted. You might as well tell a man in plain words not to come again, for he surely would go off and spread it, how mean they were treated—not even so much as to ask them to have something to drink; and you would not again be troubled with their company.[42]

While subjects visited as a form of entertainment, they also combined visiting with work. Many female diarists visited each other while doing piecework in order to enjoy another's company and to mitigate the loneliness of their task. In the example above, Sarah Holmes Clark experienced visits that affirmed friendship or that incorporated work differently from those which she characterized as "ceremonious." When visitors brought their work, she could work too. "There are so many ladies who take their work, and Southern ladies are very industrious, and spend a whole morning or evening with me. These are visits that I prize."[43] This kind of visiting did not interrupt the work in her life, and work did not distract from visiting. She happily combined the activities. For some employments, such as shoe binding, farming, sewing, or domestic work, arranging to work with someone else alleviated the isolation. Mary Mudge sewed in the company of her friends on at least a weekly basis. Sarah Trask regularly sewed the tops of shoes to their leather soles in a group of sister shoe binders: "At home today. Mrs. Claxton came in this afternoon with her work. Lizzy and LAB pass the afternoon with us."[44] And on another day, "A. A. B. came in with her work and we had a grand time."[45] The social dimension transformed the work into a more acceptable, if not always enjoyable, activity.

---

42. William J. Brown, *The Life of William J. Brown, of Providence, R.I. with Personal Recollections of Incidents in Rhode Island* (1883; reprint, Freeport, NY: Books for Libraries Press, 1971), p. 93.

43. Sarah Holmes Clark to Sarah Carter, October 29, 1854 (Holmes Family Papers, MHS).

44. Sarah Trask Diary, May 22, 1849 (Beverly Historical Society and Museum: hereafter BHSM).

45. Sarah Trask Diary, June 22, 1849 (BHSM).

Visiting and Economic Activity

THE LINE BETWEEN socializing while doing similar work and sharing work while socializing was virtually indistinguishable in most diary accounts. Many activities detailed by antebellum working people confound the distinctions between economic activity and socializing. Indeed, they reaffirm the interrelationships between neighborliness, friendship, communal cooperation, and economic survival. Farm labor illustrates this point. Much work on a farm could be done by one person only with great difficulty, so farmers arranged for coworkers, sometimes for pay, oftentimes not. For example, Samuel Shepard James, a New Hampshire farmer and surveyor, wrote about one Saturday in May 1860:

> Wind E. signs of rain. A.M. Piled up hemlock bark, about one cord. Mr. Small helped. J. Griffin. (Killed rooster—carried some to Father to eat—very sick yet). P.M. Small at home—with wife & girls down to store—down to Hodgdon's to get shoes made. Mrs. Bodge & children took dinner with us.[46]

In this example, Mr. Small is a hired man who helps regularly around the farm. J. Griffin is unidentified and could be paid help or a friendly neighbor.

Although working people engaged in many types of labor exchanges, here I will focus on caring for the sick, one specific type of service exchange prominent in working people's narratives. Illnesses routinely shortened lives and heightened infant mortality in the nineteenth century. For example, cholera and scarlet fever periodically infested communities, took many lives, and spread rapidly, their causes unknown and their contagion misunderstood.[47] Becoming ill always foretold economic hardship in the form of lost wages or unattended farm chores.

Regardless of their illness, the sick needed to be tended and "watched." Diarists used the means available—home remedies, herbs, bleeding, water treatments, prayers, even doctors—to try to cure the patient. In this historical context, the care of the sick person involved visiting to monitor the status of the patient and to bolster his or her morale. Watchers were not consistently distinguished from other visitors in diaries, but in practice their duties were all-encompassing: they were to perform any task that provided comfort for the patient. They would wait on the person, make him or her comfortable,

46. Samuel Shepard James Diary, May 26, 1860 (New Hampshire Historical Society: hereafter NHHS).

47. See, for example, Barbara Ehrenreich and Deirdre English, *For Her Own Good: 150 Years of the Experts' Advice to Women* (1979); and Charles E. Rosenberg, *The Cholera Years: The United States in 1832, 1849, and 1866* (1962).

administer medicine, and "watch" the patient. They watched for a change in the patient's condition. They watched to make sure the person was still alive. Mary Mudge scatters numerous accounts of sick visits in her diary. For example, on March 29, 1854, she chronicled her rounds:

> Called with Anna down to Mr Ambler's to inquire after Benjamin (he has a brain fever). His mother came to the door. She could hardly speak. Says she has no hopes of him. On our way home called at Sarah's. She is quite sick again. Her nurse let her go down stairs Sunday and she took a violent cold. Says she has been sicker this wk. than she has been at all.[48]

Two weeks later Mary notes that she "called into Mrs. Warren's tonight. She is very sick with 'Rheumatism' so that she cannot move." [49] Numerous other women also visited and cared for neighbors and kin. In accounts of daily calls, the diaries in particular document purposeful visits to check on and care for the sick.

The issue of obligation surfaced with special immediacy in the exchanges of caretaking labor. In light of her parents' recent death, Mary Giddings Coult felt supreme sensitivity to the issues of family obligation as well as her need to support herself. Her Uncle L. Colby came to get her to stay with her aunt and Hatty. "I must try to do all I can for them. If I do perhaps when I am sick some one will take pitty on a *poor lone orphan* and be as a Mother to me." [52] Her fear of her potential ill health and eventual death overrode her concerns about supporting herself. She determined that incurring family obligations better suited her needs in the long run. However, it was not unusual to pay a woman for her caretaking services, be she a neighbor, a sister, or a

Extended families examined in this study routinely called single women away from their paid employment to care for the sick. Schoolteacher Louisa Chapman wrote in 1849, "owing to the sickness of my mother, my school closes to-day." [50] As was a common practice for multitudes of mill girls, Mary Hall left her job as a weaver in a textile mill and returned to New Hampshire in response to one of her many calls to familial duty: "Heard from home to-day. Brother I. and sister J. sick and grandfather not able to walk or step. And father and mother wish me to come home." [51]

---

48. Mary Mudge Diary, March 29, 1854 (SL).
49. Mary Mudge Diary, April 14, 1854 (SL).
50. Louisa Chapman Diary, March 5, 1849 (JDPL).
51. Mary Hall Diary, May 27, 1831 (NHHS). It was rare for women to quit work to care for a friend as opposed to kin.
52. Mary Giddings Coult Diary, August 6, 1851 (NHHS).

niece. This system of mutual aid in caretaking was not fully separated from an individual's need for hard cash.

The Gendered Division of "Social Work"

NOR WAS IT ONLY women who considered nursing and "watching" a social obligation. While the historical literature identifies nursing as a woman's duty, evidence from my research shows that men often cared for the sick as well. With their higher wages and greater power, men who were teachers or factory workers typically did not leave their jobs for this purpose. However, male farmers and artisans, who had greater flexibility in work routines, did take time off to care for sick relatives and friends. In this and other ways, men also participated in the ongoing enterprise of "social work," the web of activities undertaken to activate and sustain social ties.[53]

Perhaps unsurprisingly, men's nursing focused almost exclusively on other men and boys—their fathers, male friends, and sons. J. Foster Beal, a box factory worker in Boston in the 1830s, chided Brigham Nims, a fellow factory worker and teacher, for not writing: "I guess you have forgot all about you being at Boston last Sept. when you was so sick, and I took care of you, doctored you up, even took you in the bed with myself." [54] Farmer John Plummer Foster was extensively involved in nursing his father who lived and worked with him. In 1834, he wrote in his diary:

> Friday. Fair and cold. I was half sick with a cold, did nothing but the chores, Father was taken in the evening with a slight shock of the palsy.
> Saturday. Fair and cold. I helped take care of Father.

Each day thereafter John gave an account of the weather and the condition of his father's health. The prominence of his father's illness in the diary provides a striking sense of its centrality to John's life. Occasionally John's distress erupted through his rote entries. "It is enough to make one's heart ache to

53. What I am calling "social work" parallels and extends the concept of "kin work" used by Micaela di Leonardo to denote those numerous activities (disproportionately attended to by women) that keep networks of kin in touch with one another—phone calls, cards, letters, holiday celebrations, and the like: "The Female World of Cards and Holidays: Women, Families, and the Work of Kinship," *Signs* 12, no. 3 (spring 1987): 440–53.

54. Letter from J. Foster Beal to Brigham Nims, December 17, 1834 (Roxbury Town Records, New Hampshire State Archives). For a more detailed discussion of their relationship, see Karen V. Hansen, " 'Helped Put in a Quilt': Men's Work and Male Intimacy in Nineteenth-Century New England," *Gender & Society* 3, no. 3 (September 1989): 334–54.

be with him, and see him, when he has his spasms."[55] Gradually, John began working again, but remained deeply concerned about his father's care. His father died five months later. It is interesting to note that he characterized his attendance to his father's needs as "helping." He saw himself as an assistant rather than a primary care provider. Even so, the number of men caring for other men makes clear that nursing was not exclusively a female vocation.

The widespread conformity to same-sex caregiving for men reflects a deep-rooted taboo against cross-gender touching and a concern for bodily modesty. The healing arts had long been a primarily female enterprise, and new nineteenth-century concerns about female chastity placed male-female physical intimacy in a particularly delicate situation.

In the primary exception to same-sex nursing, married men cared for their ill wives.[56] Sarah Holmes Clark wrote to her friend about the fine nursing skills of her husband. Given her current state of health, she insisted she could not possibly go North and leave his healing hands:

> Gilman has spoiled me since I have been sick so much. I cannot do without him for a nurse when my health is so poor. I depend on him as a child relies on its mother. I believe that no one could nurse me so well as he does, because no one loves me as well as he does. Gilman is the best husband in the world. If you do not believe it come and live with us and judge for yourself.[57]

In a second notable exception, two former slaves, James Mars and William Grimes, wrote in their respective autobiographies of their employment and skill in taking care of the sick. James Mars was called to the bedside of his former owner's unmarried adult daughter:

> As I had been accustomed to take care of the sick, she asked me to stop with her that night. I did so, and went to my work in the morning. . . . She asked what I thought of her; I told her I feared she would never be any better. She then asked me to stay with her if she did not get any better, while she lived. I told her I would. A cousin of hers, a young lady, was there, and we took care of her for four weeks.[58]

55. John Plummer Foster Diary, February 7–13, 1851 (JDPL).

56. And of course wives cared for their ill husbands. But here I am pointing to the ways that men as caretakers crossed gender boundaries.

57. Sarah Holmes Clark to Sarah Carter, August 1854 (Holmes Family Papers, MHS).

58. James Mars, *Life of James Mars, a Slave, Born and Sold in Connecticut* (1864), reprinted in Arna Bontemps's edited volume, *Five Black Lives: The Autobiographies of Venture Smith, James Mars, William Grimes, The Rev. G. W. Offley, and James L. Smith*, p. 53. See also William Grimes, *Life of William Grimes, the Runaway Slave, Brought Down to the Present Time* (1855), in the same collection, pp. 59–128.

James had a long-term acquaintance with this young woman, and she valued the skills and comfort he brought to her bedside. His skin color mitigated the taboo of male nurse to a female patient. Race overrode gender concerns. Had James not been black, it is highly unlikely that he would have been asked or allowed to care for this sick woman. However, because of his subordinate status as a black man—once slave, now free, but still not a full citizen—James did not pose a sexual threat.[59]

Same-sex nursing was not the only gendered dimension of the caretaking division of labor; but even where the customary roles of men and women differed, they did not divide neatly along public/private lines. As a rule, men stayed in their own households most of the time, while women acted as a mobile caretaking force, at times traveling long distances to care for sick relatives and friends, often staying with them. On the other hand, men typically shouldered the responsibility of going to get the doctor, nurse, neighbor woman, or midwife.

Men also engaged in other forms of shared and exchanged labor, such as quilting parties, typically assumed to be quintessentially female activities. Quilting parties joined the list of other communal occasions to pare apples, haul wood, shuck corn, and perform other chores that required many hands—both male and female. In character with other types of antebellum visiting, both work and leisure shaped these "bees," as they were called. The fact that men even attended these events challenges the notion that women's culture grew out of a separate female sphere where women did "women's work" to the exclusion of men. Although this was indeed a world that organized a division of labor by gender, working men were regularly involved in communal activities that brought men and women together. They did not religiously observe boundaries segregating men and women.

The working men of this study also did not follow the rigid division of labor within the household prescribed by the ideology of separate spheres. Fully 30 percent of the male diarists commonly recorded doing household chores, shopping for food, washing the laundry, or caring for children. Washing clothes, unquestionably a labor-intensive chore, required heating water; scrubbing layers of dirt; moving wet, heavy clothes from one tub to another; and wringing many yards of fabric free of excess water. Two or more people often did the wash, a task that would be difficult for one individual. Several women record washing clothes with their husbands. John Plummer Foster

59. The other major exception was of course doctors. By professional license they were granted access to women's bedsides, but not without complications (see, for example, Ehrenreich and English, *For Her Own Good*). Ministers were also acceptable watchers, visitors, or nurses; indeed, they were expected to call on the sick, regardless of gender.

took over responsibility for laundry during the periods when his wife was pregnant. Brigham Nims ironed clothes in addition to helping with the wash. While most indicators point to the fact that men who did laundry regarded their work as *assistance* rather than a responsibility, the fact remains that a significant minority consistently engaged in household labor.

The evidence outlined in this essay reveals a practice of gender mixing in daily life, not a radical separation of spheres for men and women. However, whether or not most subjects in my study were willing to cross their culturally prescribed boundaries, it remains true that a deeply gendered division of labor underlay their practices in the social sphere. I do not want to suggest that working people did not define some activities as appropriate only to men or to women. However, I do want to argue that they did not do so as rigidly or as universally as assumed. Rules for gender-appropriate behavior among working people did not strictly conform to the dictates of the culture of separate spheres. And the opportunities for negotiation and reinterpretation emerged most clearly in the social sphere.[60]

Transformations and Continuities

THE CONTINUING MASSIVE SHIFTS in the market economy over the course of the nineteenth century transformed activity in the social realm. Industrial capitalism reordered social life by fundamentally reorganizing large-scale production, indirectly generating a reorganization of work within the household, and—not least significant from the standpoint of this study—placing increasing constraints on opportunities to visit. Tasks such as producing textiles and caring for the sick became industrialized and professionalized over the nineteenth and twentieth centuries. This meant that families and neighbors performed fewer tasks for reciprocal exchange such as weaving, sewing each other's clothes, and caring for the sick. This process gradually diminished the place of labor in visiting practices, making them more purely sociable in nature. In addition, the progressive specialization of production separated it from leisure, rendering the sociability of exchanged and cooperative labor increasingly a relic of the nineteenth century. However, it would be premature to conclude that reciprocity, mutuality, and the informal exchange of services and support have ceased altogether to play an important role in the processes that knit communities together in the twentieth century.

---

60. I have focused in this essay on working people, but roughly similar principles of sociability may also have played a critical role for the middle class; however, their specific form and content need to be the subject of a separate investigation.

REFRAMING SOCIAL ACTIVITY

VISITING IN ANTEBELLUM New England is a subject of great interest in itself, but I have also tried to use this examination to demonstrate a larger point: the inadequacy of the public/private dichotomy as an analytic frame for orienting our historical understanding of nineteenth-century American society. Despite the continuing influence of this model in shaping both academic and popular thinking about gender, social structure, and politics in the nineteenth century, it conveys a distorted picture of culture and social organization, conceals or marginalizes important phenomena, and flattens out the complexity of the lived reality under the ideological veil of "separate spheres." In particular, it obscures both the importance and the dynamics of communal sociability in the everyday lives of ordinary women and men. Furthermore, the drawbacks of the public/private dichotomy for addressing this historical period raise more general questions about its limitations as an orienting paradigm in history, sociology, and political theory.

This flawed but tenacious theoretical framework profoundly shaped my own initial approach to studying antebellum society; and my recognition of its limitations emerged from my efforts to bring it to bear on the historical evidence. I gradually realized that the realities of nineteenth-century life, as conveyed by the first-person narratives I was examining, could not be squeezed into these rigidly dichotomous categories without great distortion and oversimplification.

As we have seen, the practice of visiting illustrates this point very clearly. According to both the nineteenth-century ideology of separate spheres and the categories of much current historiography, because women were barred from formal political life and, in some accounts, from the world of commerce, their lives were confined to the "private" sphere of domesticity. However, it seems absurd to describe the lives of the women I have studied, with their bustling rounds of varied activities and wide-ranging interactions, as private in any meaningful sense of the term; indeed, genuinely private activities occupied only a small corner of their lives. Their activities could appear "private" only if the term is used as a residual category to describe everything outside formal politics; but this is clearly inappropriate. On the other hand, it can also be misleading to categorize visiting as "public"—at least, if that is used as a blanket term to cover all activities outside the household. Visiting could easily slide over into political debate and sustain networks that energized social movements, such as abolitionism, which eventually targeted the state; but this was only one dimension of a rich and multifaceted practice. And, while the possibilities of political action and an active concern with public issues were part of these women's lives, their exclusion from full rights in the public realm of citizenship was a matter of real importance that our interpretive categories should not minimize or conceal.

In short, the historical documents yield a portrait of visiting as a densely textured practice that routinely blurred the supposedly rigid boundaries of public and private. At the same time, the evidence also makes it clear that visiting was an ordered *system* of social activity, one element in a complex field of communal sociability whose logic was not equivalent to that of either the public or the private realms, strictly speaking.

Once the realm of the social is examined carefully in its own right, it brings out another problematic aspect of the use of the public/private dichotomy in social history and historical sociology: current scholars, in utilizing the prescriptive model of the nineteenth-century ideology of separate spheres, often unintentionally reproduce the reductive gender stereotyping of that model rather than gaining a critical distance from it. "Private" and "public" can thus continue to be seen as what women and men *should* be because this division is "natural," "normal," and "inevitable." However, the historical evidence presented in this essay demonstrates how misleading these gendered preconceptions are—we find men involved in allegedly "private" and feminine activities, such as caring for the sick, and women out and about in the social sphere, hardly confined to their domiciles.

Reintroducing the Social

DESPITE THE NUMEROUS CRITICISMS of the public/private framework, calls to abandon these categories have largely fallen on unresponsive ears (except among poststructuralists). And, indeed, these concepts can be used to establish fruitful analytical distinctions, as many of the essays in this volume demonstrate; in particular, they can highlight important structural elements in modern societies that arguably have emerged with industrial capitalism and the modern state. The dangers come from treating public and private as exclusive alternatives within a dichotomous model of social structure. As Weintraub and others in this volume have also argued, the attempt to force social reality into such rigidly dichotomous frameworks impels scholars to use these categories in misleading or inconsistent ways. Either the dualism of the categories leaves out important areas of social life, or else one side of the dichotomy is expanded into a vague and overly broad residual category (as when everything not domestic is referred to as public), in which case significant distinctions are lost.

Therefore, rather than abandoning the concepts of public and private, I propose that they be included within a more differentiated and encompassing framework. I have already explained why I believe the concept of the social can usefully mediate the dualism of public and private. Here I would add that the common practice of conflating the market economy and the realm of formal politics under the term "public," in contrast to the domestic sphere, is also misleading, and the two need to be analytically distinguished. I would therefore propose a four-part orienting model: the public, the private, the market economy, and the *social.*

This is not offered as a universal model, uniformly applicable to all societies and historical periods. Given the continuous reality of historical change, frameworks of this sort are necessarily contextually drawn. This one is rooted most directly in the nineteenth-century United States, though I think that its categories, flexibly employed, may be useful in understanding aspects of other modern societies. But in any specific sociohistorical context—antebellum New England, for example—each of these categories will have a distinctive meaning and configuration, shaped by the historical contingencies of race, class, gender, and politics. It is also worth emphasizing that analytical distinctions, while useful and necessary, should not be reified: the boundaries between these realms are neither static nor, in most cases, rigid and impenetrable. In practice, they often overlap and blend fluidly into each other.

In the context of this inquiry, the *social* encompasses that field of activities mediating public, private, and market domains, linking households to neighbors and individuals to institutions. In antebellum New England, the distinctive principles of activity in the social realm included mutuality, reciprocity, voluntarism, and localism. The social was thus characterized by informal rules and fluid negotiation, as compared with the more formal legal and political structures of the public; the impersonal, competitive, self-interested calculation of the market economy; and the motivating forces of intimacy and particularistic obligation in the private.

In short, the notion of the social captures a field of activities and relationships that transcend the boundaries of households but are not predominantly shaped by the logic of the state or market. In New England, the social was manifested institutionally—in churches, schools, lyceums—as well as informally in a range of activities from visiting, gossiping, and churchgoing to attending lectures, joining social movements, caring for a neighbor's child, quilting, and the like. These are the everyday activities of communal sociability detailed in the diaries, letters, and memoirs of my subjects. Because the realm of the social constituted a meeting ground where interactions were rooted in everyday contacts and broadly shared assumptions, it also proved a fertile ground for politicization.

As an analytical prism, the category of the social helps us to recognize these everyday activities—often trivialized or ignored—as central to the creation and sustenance of communities. Furthermore, it highlights the critical role often played by women in these activities, and thus counteracts the exaggerated picture of their isolation and marginality often conveyed by approaches based on one or another version of the public/private dichotomy.

What I am calling the social is not really a new concept—it constitutes the essence of sociology and anthropology. Since the nineteenth century, the social realm, its definition, its dynamics, and its boundaries have been as embattled as those of the public and the private.[61] In recent years, as Alan Wolfe points out, academics have increasingly seen the tension between individual needs and collective restraint as regulated either by the state or the market. As economics and political science have gained ascendancy over sociology during the past two decades, the roles of culture and what Wolfe calls "civil society" have been eclipsed.[62] "One of the formative insights of 'classic' sociological thought," Jeff Weintraub notes in a discussion of Wolfe's argument, was precisely that there was more to society (and certainly to a *good* society) than the market and the state—and, accordingly, "that understanding social life required going beyond an exclusive focus on self-interest and coercion to explore the ties of attachment, solidarity, and obligation that bind together the social order."[63] Wolfe urges us to reassert the importance of this sociological endeavor. The investigation outlined in this essay is a prime example of what can be learned when communal interaction is placed at center stage.

If the social embraces the realm of communal sociability and informal interaction, network ties and mutuality between neighbors and extended kin, then the *private* centers on the household and activities that link the nuclear family and other household members. While the private was not rigidly segregated from the social—and, as I have argued, played a far less exclusive role in women's lives than is commonly suggested—I think it is analytically useful to recognize it as a distinct sphere of activity rooted in the family/household, with its privileging of intimate emotion, blood ties, particularism, and bodily needs. The private in antebellum New England, it should be noted, did not coincide with the individual. As Ryan attests, "The doctrine of privacy venerated not the isolated individual but rather a set of intense and intimate social

---

61. For an overview of many of these debates, which also emphasizes (in a somewhat different way) the need to break with a dichotomous model of social structure, see Jean L. Cohen and Andrew Arato, *Civil Society and Political Theory* (1992).

62. Alan Wolfe, *Whose Keeper? Social Science and Moral Obligation* (1989).

63. Jeff Weintraub, "Back to Basics," *Contemporary Sociology* 20, no. 5 (September 1991): 697.

relations, essentially those of the conjugal family. Privacy was a social construction, in other words, and as a consequence, a product of concrete historical actions."[64] Working people did not privilege privacy in the same way the middle class did; nonetheless, the realm of the private was a significant part of the landscape of everyday life for them as well.[65]

I define the *public* to encompass the state and all state-related activities, such as the law, the party system, and local, state, and national governments. The antebellum manifestations of the public included activities such as jury service, muster training, participation in town meetings, and voting—all accessible only to men. The laws allowed women to petition the government and to use the courts in a restricted manner, but otherwise they had access to the state only through unofficial political mobilization or influence on male citizens. In many states, these minimal formal rights were denied African Americans of both genders.

Here it is essential to emphasize the distinction between the *political* and the *public* because, as feminists have long argued, the two are not equivalent.[66] In this conception, politics are confined neither to the state nor to public space, but can take place in the social or in the private as well as in the public. All talk and action—from convening a family gathering to recruiting someone to attend an abolitionist church—have the *potential* to be politicized which may or may not be realized by the participants.[67] And conversely, the state performs many functions that are not purely political.

64. Ryan, *Cradle of the Middle Class,* p. 154.

65. On the middle-class privileging of privacy, see, for example, Lystra, *Searching the Heart.*

66. For example, the battle cry of the women's liberation movement was "the personal is political." This is not to say that there is a clear consensus among feminists regarding the precise contours and boundaries of the political. Almost all would reject as too narrow what Doug McAdam characterizes as the traditional academic conception of politics: "something that takes place in public domains between officially recognized political actors" ("Gender Implications of the Traditional Academic Conception of the Political," in Susan Hardy Aiken, Karen Anderson, Myra Dinnerstein, Judy Nolte Lensink, and Patricia Mac-Corquodale's edited volume, *Changing Our Minds: Feminist Transformations of Knowledge,* p. 61). On the other hand, not all would embrace as broad a conception as Joan Scott: "the process by which plays of power and knowledge constitute identity and experience" (*Gender and the Politics of History,* p. 5). One noteworthy effort to stake out a middle ground is Paula Baker, "The Domestication of Politics: Women and American Political Society, 1780–1920," p. 622.

67. Activities can also be spiritualized (converting someone to Christianity) or, as Nancy Fraser points out, personalized, familialized, or economized, or none of the above. See Fraser, "Rethinking the Public Sphere: A Contribution to the Critique of Actually Existing Democracy," *Social Text,* no. 25/26 (1990): 56–80.

While much feminist scholarship—and especially women's history—has tended to merge the formal political world and the market economy in the category of the "public," it seems to me important to recognize the *market economy* as a system analytically separate from both the public and the social. As with the other spheres, of course, its boundaries are not impermeable. In antebellum New England, as I have noted, market relations based on impersonality and cash payment could still be intertwined in complex ways with the more informal economy of reciprocity and mutual obligation. Fundamentally, however, the market economy operates with its own distinctive principles, cultural assumptions, values, and criteria for inclusion and exclusion; and, with the progress of industrial capitalism over the course of the nineteenth century, the distinctiveness of this sphere became increasingly salient.

Negotiating Boundaries

THE BOUNDARIES OF THE public, private, market, and social realms are not absolute; they shift depending on historical period and the situational context. Citing the work of other feminist authors, Susan Ostrander points out that "what have been defined as 'natural' public and private spheres of social life are in fact socially and historically constructed, and are representations of socially enforced patterns of gender." [68] So, for example, the socialization of production by industrial capitalism altered the boundaries and purposes of the private sphere. The factory system absorbed production, expanded the cash economy, and correspondingly shrank both the private sphere and the range of reciprocal exchange in the social sphere. The private sphere defensively erected less permeable ideological boundaries to ward off encroachment of the market and the state.

Historical actors sometimes purposely mobilized to shift the frame within which a particular activity was perceived and executed. One pertinent example, described by Mary Mudge, concerned limits to the acceptable boundaries of talk about her minister, Mr. Stetson. People gossiped about his liaison with Mrs. Trussant. Mary objected to such talk because it was about her minister, a person she regarded as above reproach. Much to her satisfaction, Mr. Stetson orchestrated a social repudiation of the rumors and a rebuke of the person(s) who dared to breach the boundary he preferred to maintain around his private life. Mary recorded his day of vindication in April of 1854:

> He was beautiful; so affecting that many of the congregation were in tears. Said they had tried to rob him of his good name, blast his reputation, &c. They say Mr. Short has said a good deal. I was glad

68. Ostrander, "Feminism, Voluntarism, and the Welfare State," p. 14.

he was there to hear him. The choir sang "Mark the perfect man, and behold the upright for the end of that man is *peace*" . . . [Aunt Sally] thinks it is too bad for them to talk so about the minister, so does B.[69]

This dispute about what constituted acceptable talk was in constant negotiation. Reverend Stetson marshaled his considerable resources—complete with evocative sermon, thematic hymns, confrontation with the suspected rumor-monger, and repentance of a guilty congregation—to draw firmly the boundary around his personal life. This episode was part of an elaborate process of determining what rightfully pertained to the social domain and what belonged more properly to the private sphere.

On the other hand, the social movements of the antebellum period constituted attempts to transform social and private concerns into public and political issues. For example, in the 1830s drinking alcohol was a widely practiced private and social activity. Temperance activists challenged this practice by lobbying individuals, churches, and governmental bodies to reassess the moral and political legitimacy of drinking. In addition to urging people to sign pledges of abstinence, activists successfully launched campaigns against the sale as well as consumption of alcohol that succeeded in establishing many "dry" towns throughout New England. In another example, abolitionists sponsored lectures that detailed the perilous conditions of slaves and petitioned the state to criminalize slavery. They struggled to muster public support for government intervention into the South's legal and economic system. In effect, both temperance activists and abolitionists tried to politicize and publicize what had previously been seen as acts of personal choice. They successfully shifted debate and action to reflect a new interpretation about appropriate boundaries between spheres of activity.

Shifting the Debate

DESPITE THE MANY CHALLENGES to the public/private dichotomy, different versions of it remain ubiquitous as orienting frameworks in history and the social sciences. In this essay, I have used an investigation of visiting in antebellum New England to demonstrate the inadequacy of the public/private dichotomy for framing our understanding of gender, society, and politics in the nineteenth-century United States. Though it may well have played an intellectually useful and stimulating role in past, it is clear that it has outlived its analytical usefulness. Building on this analysis, I have suggested the need to move to a more differentiated and encompassing interpretive framework that

69. Mary Mudge Diary, April 16, 1854 (SL).

can more effectively capture the complexity of social structure and culture in modern societies. One crucial element of such a framework must be an informed recognition of the *social* as a distinctive and significant realm that can mediate the falsely dichotomized alternatives of public and private, and that can offer both theoretical and practical alternatives to the exclusive logics of the market and the state.

Historical accounts of everyday life, such as those on which my analysis of visiting has been based, demand a conceptual approach that honors their complexity and weaves their multilayered implications into a theory of social structure adequate to this task. However, rediscovering the social is a matter of more than just historical interest. It can be argued that social isolation, more than simply injuring individual well-being, fundamentally threatens a democratic society. Democracy depends upon the engagement of individuals, not only with the state, but with each other.

REFERENCES

Primary Sources

Barrett, Martha Osborne. Peabody, Massachusetts. Diary, 1848–79. James Duncan Phillips Library, Peabody and Essex Museum, Salem, Massachusetts.

Brown, William J. [1883] 1971. *The Life of William J. Brown, of Providence, R.I. with Personal Recollections of Incidents in Rhode Island.* Freeport, NY: Books For Libraries Press.

Chapman, Louisa Ann. Ipswich, Massachusetts. Diary, 1848–49. James Duncan Phillips Library, Peabody and Essex Museum, Salem, Massachusetts.

Coult, Mary Giddings. Auburn, New Hampshire. Diary, 1851–54. New Hampshire Historical Society, Concord, New Hampshire.

Davis, Reverend Noah. 1859. *A Narrative of the Life of Rev. Noah Davis, a Colored Man.* Baltimore: John F. Weishampel, Jr.

Foster, John Plummer. North Andover, Massachusetts. Diary, 1848–88. James Duncan Phillips Library, Peabody and Essex Museum, Salem, Massachusetts.

Grimes, William. [1855]. *Life of William Grimes, the Runaway Slave, Brought Down to the Present Time.* Reprinted in Arna Bontemps, ed., *Five Black Lives: The Autobiographies of Venture Smith, James Mars, William Grimes, The Rev. G. W. Offley, and James L. Smith* (Middletown, CT: Wesleyan University Press, 1971), pp. 59–128.

Hall, Mary. Lowell, Massachusetts and Concord, New Hampshire. Diary, 1821–36. New Hampshire Historical Society, Concord, New Hampshire.

Holmes Family Papers. Shirley and Foxcroft, Maine. Correspondence, 1840–60. Massachusetts Historical Society, Boston.

James, Samuel Shepard Northwood, New Hampshire. Diary, 1839–1907. New Hampshire Historical Society, Concord, New Hampshire.

Mars, James. [1864]. *Life of James Mars, a Slave Born and Sold in Connecticut.* Reprinted in Arna Bontemps, ed., *Five Black Lives: The Autobiographies of Venture Smith, James Mars, William Grimes, The Rev. G. W. Offley, and James L. Smith* (Middletown, CT: Wesleyan University Press, 1971), pp. 35–58.

Metcalf-Adams Family Letters. Maine and Massachusetts. Correspondence, 1796–1866. Museum of American Textile History, North Andover, Massachusetts.

Mudge, Mary. Lynn, Massachusetts. Diary, 1854. Schlesinger Library, Radcliffe College, Cambridge, Massachusetts.

Nims, Brigham. Roxbury, New Hampshire. Correspondence. Roxbury Town Records, New Hampshire State Archives, Concord, New Hampshire.

Trask, Sarah E. Beverly, Massachusetts. Diary, 1849–51. Beverly Historical Society and Museum.

Secondary Sources

Baker, Paula. 1984. "The Domestication of Politics: Women and American Political Society, 1780–1920." *American Historical Review* 89(3): 620–47.

Benn, Stanley I., and Gerald F. Gaus. 1983. "The Liberal Conception of the Public and the Private." In *Public and Private in Social Life,* edited by S. I. Benn and G. F. Gaus. New York: St. Martin's Press.

Bernard, Richard M., and Maris A. Vinovskis. 1977. "The Female School Teacher in Ante–Bellum Massachusetts." *Journal of Social History* 10, no. 3 (March): 332–45.

Boydston, Jeanne. 1990. *Home and Work: Housework, Wages, and the Ideology of Labor in the Early Republic.* New York: Oxford University Press.

Burke, Kenneth. 1965. *Permanence and Change: An Anatomy of Purpose.* Indianapolis: Bobbs–Merrill.

Byars, Ronald P. 1979. *The Making of the Self-Made Man: The Development of Masculine Roles and Images in Ante-Bellum America.* Ph.D. dissertation, Michigan State University.

Cohen, Jean L., and Andrew Arato. 1992. *Civil Society and Political Theory.* Cambridge, MA: MIT Press.

Collins, Patricia Hill. 1990. *Black Feminist Thought: Knowledge, Consciousness, and the Politics of Empowerment.* Boston: Unwin Hyman.

Cott, Nancy. 1977. *Bonds of Womanhood: "Woman's Sphere" in New England, 1790–1835.* New Haven, CT: Yale University Press.

Degler, Carl N. 1980. *At Odds: Women and the Family in America from the Revolution to the Present.* Oxford: Oxford University Press.

di Leonardo, Micaela. 1987. "The Female World of Cards and Holidays: Women, Families, and the Work of Kinship." *Signs* 12, no. 3 (spring): 440–53.

Dublin, Thomas. 1979. *Women at Work: The Transformation of Work and Community in Lowell, Massachusetts, 1826–1860.* New York: Columbia University Press.

DuBois, Ellen Carol. 1978. *Feminism and Suffrage.* Ithaca, NY: Cornell University Press.

Ehrenreich, Barbara, and Deirdre English. 1979. *For Her Own Good: 150 Years of the Experts' Advice to Women.* Garden City, NY: Anchor.

Fraser, Nancy. 1985. "What's Critical about Critical Theory? The Case of Habermas and Gender." *New German Critique* 35 (spring–summer): 97–131.

———. 1990. "Rethinking the Public Sphere: A Contribution to the Critique of Actually Existing Democracy." *Social Text,* no. 25–26: 56–80.

Gamarnikow, Eva, and June Purvis. 1983. "Introduction." In *The Public and the Private,* edited by Eva Gamarnikow, David H. J. Morgan, June Purvis, and Daphne Taylorson, pp. 1–6. London: Heinemann.

Halttunen, Karen. 1982. *Confidence Men and Painted Women: A Study of Middle-Class Culture in America, 1830-1870.* New Haven, CT: Yale University Press.

Hansen, Karen V. 1989. " 'Helped Put in a Quilt': Men's Work and Male Intimacy in Nineteenth-Century New England." *Gender and Society* 3, no. 3 (September): 334–54.

———. 1994. *A Very Social Time: Crafting Community in Antebellum New England.* Berkeley and Los Angeles: University of California Press.

Hansen, Karen V., and Cameron Macdonald. 1995. "Surveying the Dead Informant: Quantitative Analysis and Historical Interpretation." *Qualitative Sociology* 18, no. 2 (summer): 227–36.

Helly, Dorothy O., and Susan M. Reverby, eds. 1992. *Gendered Domains: Rethinking Public and Private in Women's History.* Ithaca: Cornell University Press.

hooks, bell. 1984. *Feminist Theory: From Margin to Center.* Boston: South End Press.

Kerber, Linda K. 1988. "Separate Spheres, Female Worlds, Women's Place: The Rhetoric of Women's History." *Journal of American History* 75, no. 1: 9–39.

Kerber, Linda K., Nancy F. Cott, Robert Gross, Lynn Hunt, Carroll Smith-Rosenberg, and Christine M. Stansell. 1989. "Beyond Roles, Beyond Spheres: Thinking about Gender in the Early Republic." *William and Mary Quarterly* 46 (July): 565–85.

Lystra, Karen. 1989. *Searching the Heart: Women, Men and Romantic Love in Nineteenth-Century America.* New York: Oxford University Press.

McAdam, Doug. 1988. "Gender Implications of the Traditional Academic Conception of the Political." In *Changing Our Minds: Feminist Transformations of Knowledge,* edited by Susan Hardy Aiken, Karen Anderson, Myra Dinnerstein, Judy Nolte Lensink, and Patricia MacCorquodale, pp. 59–76. Albany: State University of New York Press.

Nicholson, Linda J. 1986. *Gender and History: The Limits of Social Theory in the Age of the Family.* New York: Columbia University Press.

Osterud, Nancy Grey. 1991. *Bonds of Community: The Lives of Farm Women in Nineteenth-Century New York.* Ithaca, NY: Cornell University Press.

Ostrander, Susan. 1989. "Feminism, Voluntarism, and the Welfare State: Toward a Feminist Sociological Theory of Social Welfare." *American Sociologist* 20, no. 1 (spring): 29–41.

Pateman, Carole. 1983. "Feminist Critiques of the Public/Private Dichotomy." In *Public and Private in Social Life,* edited by S. I. Benn and G. F. Gaus. New York: St. Martin's Press.

Pleck, Elizabeth H. 1976. "Two Worlds in One: Work and Family." *Journal of Social History* 10, no. 2 (winter): 178–95.

Rosaldo, Michelle Z. 1974. "Woman, Culture, and Society: A Theoretical Overview." In *Woman, Culture, and Society,* edited by Michelle Z. Rosaldo and Louise Lamphere, pp. 17–42. Stanford, CA: Stanford University Press.

———. 1980. "The Use and Abuse of Anthropology: Reflections on Feminism and Cross-Cultural Understanding." *Signs* 5, no. 3 (spring): 389–417.

Rosenberg, Charles E. 1962. *The Cholera Years: The United States in 1832, 1849, and 1866.* Chicago: University of Chicago Press.

Rotundo, E. Anthony. 1993. *American Manhood: Transformations in Masculinity from the Revolution to the Modern Era.* New York: Basic Books.

Ryan, Mary P. 1981. *Cradle of the Middle Class: The Family in Oneida County, New York, 1790–1865.* New York: Cambridge University Press.

———. 1985. *The Empire of the Mother: American Writing about Domesticity, 1830–1860.* New York: Harrington Park Press.

———. 1990. *Women in Public: Between Banners and Ballots, 1825–1880.* Baltimore: Johns Hopkins University Press.

Sacks, Karen. 1975. "Engels Revisited: Women, the Organization of Production, and Private Property." In *Toward an Anthropology of Women,* edited by Rayna R. Reiter, pp. 211–34. New York: Monthly Review Press.

Scott, Joan Wallach. 1988. *Gender and the Politics of History.* New York: Columbia University Press.

Smith-Rosenberg, Carroll. 1986. *Disorderly Conduct: Visions of Gender in Victorian America.* New York: Oxford University Press.

Stansell, Christine. 1986. *City of Women: Sex and Class in New York, 1789–1860.* New York: Knopf.

Sterling, Dorothy. 1991. *Ahead of Her Time: Abby Kelley and the Politics of Antislavery.* New York: Norton.

U.S. Bureau of the Census. 1975. *Historical Statistics of the U.S., Colonial Times to 1970.* Washington DC: Bureau of the Census.

Vogel, Lise. 1991. "Telling Tales: Historians of Our Own Lives." *Journal of Women's History* 2, no. 3 (winter): 89–101.

Weedon, Chris. 1987. *Feminist Practice and Poststructuralist Theory.* New York: Basil Blackwell.

Weintraub, Jeff. 1991. "Back to Basics." *Contemporary Sociology* 20, no. 5 (September): 696–98.

Welter, Barbara. 1966. "The Cult of True Womanhood: 1820–1860." *American Quarterly* 18, no. 2 (summer): 151–74.

Wolfe, Alan. 1989. *Whose Keeper? Social Science and Moral Obligation.* Berkeley: University of California Press.

Yee, Shirley. 1992. *Black Women Abolitionists: A Study in Activism, 1828–1860.* Knoxville: University of Tennessee Press.

The Shadow of the Leviathan: Public and Private in Communist and Post-Communist Society

Marc Garcelon

THE RISE OF POLAND'S Solidarity movement in August 1980 triggered a sea change in Western approaches to state and society under communism, putting to rest forever the image of an immutable, all-powerful communist monolith presiding over a stable—if politically and aesthetically repellent—alternative to Western society. By the end of the 1980s, the dissection of who was standing where on Lenin's tomb had been superseded by talk of a "reemergent society" and its increasing emancipation from the paralyzing grip of the Leviathan-state. However, from the start a curious ambiguity marked this discussion. Scholars transfixed by the Polish August, for instance, tended to interpret Solidarity in terms of the emergence of a "public sphere" and a "democratic revolution of citizenship." Others—especially students of things Soviet—saw in the pervasive corruption of the Brezhnevite "Party-state," the ubiquity of black market transactions, and the withdrawal of the populace from ideological engagement into particularistic circles of friends and families the "privatization" of the communist order. From this perspective—also expressed in Hungarian notions of an emerging "second society"—the reassertion of a resilient private life in the face of the public rituals of a decrepit officialdom stood out as the key development of the post-Stalin era.

Unfortunately, the tendency to place instances of both "public" political rebellion and "private" economic pursuits under the rubric of "the rebirth of civil society" only added to the confusion. A striking lack of consensus as to the meaning and analytical applicability of the concept of civil society accompanied the explosion of discourse centered on the term. The ambiguity of the use of "civil society" in relation to "late communism" is hardly surprising, as the history of "civil society" in Western discourse has been closely intertwined with diverse, at times tortuous, attempts to draw distinctions between the political and public, on the one hand, and the social and private, on the other.[1]

I would like to thank Steven Stoltenberg and Jeff Weintraub for their comments on earlier versions of this essay.

1. Contemporary Western treatments of civil and political society differ widely in terms of the concrete elements that different analysts subsume under each of these categories and

For example, ambiguities about whether civil society belongs to the "public" or the "private" realm, to "politics" or "antipolitics," pervade Western thought.

Many commentators on "reemergent society" in the Soviet bloc not only inherited such inconsistencies; they also tended to assume, explicitly or implicitly, that the meanings of "public," "private," and "civil society" remained broadly similar in communist and Western societies. The highly misleading character of these assumptions, already noted by some analysts before 1989, has been underlined by subsequent developments in "postcommunist" societies, marked by fragile "public spheres," resurgent ethnic politics, and the less than resounding success of "privatization" in the sense of marketization. Americans and Western Europeans who have turned to the discourse of civil society as a means of sorting out the tangled web of late- and postcommunist politics have thus inadvertently opened a can of nasty conceptual worms. Rather than helping to clarify our understanding of "the Leninist extinction," the incautious use of this discourse has often merely compounded the problems of understanding the historical character of Soviet-type society, its breakdown, and its continuing legacies in the postcommunist era. To avoid such pitfalls, concepts derived from the Western experience require careful interrogation and refinement in light of the historically distinctive features of Soviet-type societies.

Such problems are complicated by the diverse nuances of the language of public and private in Western social and political discourse itself. The roots of these conceptual ambiguities lie deep, extending from the heritage of ancient politics and Roman law, through eighteenth- and nineteenth-century debates about the nature of civil and political society, down to present-day, equivocal shadings of public and private common in everyday language. Finally, this knot of conceptual and comparative difficulties is further complicated by cultural-linguistic translation problems: Russian, for instance, has no unambiguous equivalents for either of the English words "public" or "pri-

---

the ways that they use these concepts to articulate an institutional portrait of a social order (see John Keane, "Despotism and Democracy: The Origins and Development of the Distinction between Civil Society and the State, 1750–1850," in Keane, ed., *Civil Society and the State: New European Perspectives,* pp. 35–71; and Jeff Weintraub, "The Theory and Politics of the Public/Private Distinction," in this volume). The concepts of civil and political society used in this essay have been modeled on Tocqueville's analysis of the structuring of "private interests" and "public liberty" in nineteenth-century America, with civil society understood to include both market relations and most voluntary associations (including religious congregations), and political society—or the public sphere—understood as an intermediate realm of interest representation and societal will-formation between state and civil society proper.

vate," nor has the centrality of the public/private distinction to Western political theory been reproduced in Russian (or Soviet) political thought.[2]

WESTERN ABSOLUTISM
AND COMMUNIST TOTALITARIANISM

HOW THEN TO PROCEED? Paradoxically enough, another troublesome concept—totalitarianism—represents a fruitful starting point. The liberal opposition to Italy's fascist movement originally coined the term "totalitarian," only to see it immediately co-opted as a positive self-description by Mussolini's "movement regime."[3] The concept of totalitarianism then found favor among critics of the Nazis. In the 1950s, Western scholars reconstructed it as the model for a new, historically distinctive form of autocracy established by Leninist and fascist dictatorships.[4] The concept seemed to parsimoniously capture striking features of communist regimes that distinguished them from both liberal democracies and traditional authoritarian regimes, such as the suppression of autonomous social as well as political life; the concentration of "absolute" political power in the hands of a one-party regime (the "Party-state"); and the elimination of independent economic producers in favor of a centrally planned and managed economy. Following a brief period of preeminence, the totalitarian model went into decline in the 1960s, in part due to its association with Cold War rhetoric.[5] Nevertheless, the model's metaphorical invocation of early modern absolutism provides a useful referent in conceptualizing basic features of Leninist domination. In particular, the understanding of "the public" as it developed under Western absolutism can help to untangle the problem of the public/private distinction viewed in the context of Soviet-type societies.

As other essays in this volume have emphasized, one major use of the public/private distinction in Western thought—though not the only one—has been to demarcate the boundary between the political and the nonpolitical.

2. I rely on Russian examples of conceptual and linguistic translation problems throughout this essay. While a number of the linguistic difficulties cited are therefore not necessarily relevant to other former Soviet bloc countries, I argue that the underlying problems of *conceptual* translation are relevant to all modern communist societies.

3. Simonetta Falasca-Zamponi, "The Aestheticization of Politics: A Study of Power in Mussolini's Fascist Italy" (Ph.D. dissertation, University of California, Berkeley, 1992), pp. 34–37.

4. Carl J. Friedrich and Zbigniew K. Brzezinski, *Totalitarian Dictatorship and Autocracy* (Cambridge, MA: Harvard, 1956).

5. For the best summary discussion of totalitarian theory and its variants, see Juan Linz, "Totalitarian and Authoritarian Regimes," in Fred I. Greenstein and Nelson W. Polsby's *Macropolitical Theory*, pp. 175–411.

Along these lines, sociological analyses influenced by the work of Alexis de Tocqueville and Max Weber have identified two rival conceptions of "the public" that emerged in tension with one another during the absolutist period in western Europe: the public as the visible expression of the unchallenged sovereignty of the territorial ruler, and the public as the political expression of a coming-together of particular interests from civil society.[6] The origins of the public as the visible sphere of action and prerogative of the sovereign ruler can be traced to Roman law and its revival during the drive of territorial monarchs to consolidate centralized rulership in the absolutist era. Absolutist regimes fixed in particular on the Roman idea that sovereign power *created* the "public" insofar as it represented all that was common to a society and thus forged a coherent collectivity out of an otherwise disparate array of particular individuals, groups, and interests. Indeed, both Roman and absolutist usage restricted the "private" to the merely particular.[7] The idea that the sovereign power creates the community as a whole "from above" through political rule, as theorized most dramatically by Hobbes, is emphasized by Marc Raeff in his account of the ethos of the Prussian *polizeistaat* under Frederick the Great.[8]

Modern republicanism, with its understanding of the public sphere as coalescing out of the sphere of private interests by means of debate and deliberation among a fraternity of formally equal citizens, stands in sharp contrast to the absolutist conception of politics. But let us first note that this republican understanding of the public developed in tandem with new conceptions of the private, since it arose alongside the formation of a "bourgeois" civil society of entrepreneurs, professionals, skilled urban artisans, and literati during the social transformations of the mercantilist phase of absolutism.[9] This period witnessed the spread of prosperous commercial towns, the regional standardization of commercial codes and financial instruments, the appearance of protomodern forms of capitalist enterprise, and the decline of feudal social and

6. See Gianfranco Poggi, *The Development of the Modern State: A Sociological Introduction*, pp. 67–85. Essentially, these two conceptions of the "public" correspond, respectively, to the first and second of the two categories outlined by Jeff Weintraub in his essay for this volume.

7. These conceptions of public and private are crystallized in an influential formulation from the *Corpus Juris Civilis*, the authoritative sixth-century compilation of Roman law: "Public law is that which regards the condition of the Roman commonwealth, private, that which pertains to the interests of single individuals" (translation borrowed from Weintraub's essay in this volume, p. 12).

8. Marc Raeff, *The Well-Ordered Police State: Social and Institutional Change through Law in the Germanies and Russia, 1600–1800.*

9. See Jürgen Habermas, "The Public Sphere: An Encyclopedia Article," *New German Critique* 1, no. 3 (fall 1974): 49–55.

political relations. Above all, these developments helped bring about the new market-oriented civil society of the early modern West.

With the spread of market relations, a distinctive pattern of societal integration coordinated "spontaneously" and horizontally within the regulative framework of civil law began to displace traditional forms of authority. As "legal-modern" capitalism matured, the newly legitimate pursuit of profits by particular interests bound by contractual obligations and legal norms more and more supplanted both the consumption-oriented economic activity of landed gentry and the pursuit of socially illicit gain by speculators and profiteers. The private no longer implied simply the particular, but now also the "rational" (in Weber's terms, the instrumentally calculating) pursuit of one's interests within a (nonpolitical) system of interdependence. The Roman-inspired identification of the private with the particular per se had given way to what will be called here the *civil particularism* of modern, "rational" capitalism. The struggle between absolutist prerogatives and the recognition of private (economic) rights associated with the rise of the market not only spurred attempts to conceptualize the new form of spontaneous social integration (Adam Smith's celebrated "invisible hand"); it also helped engender a *third* Western sense of the private, rooted in "personal life" and the pursuit of leisure activities conducted in a now rights-protected sphere of elective affinities and domesticity. For, unlike many earlier forms of domestic life, the domestic sphere of the modern middle class was now legally shielded from social ("public") scrutiny.[10]

When combined with the development of representative institutions and of informal arenas for discussion and debate, the new "private" sphere of civil society facilitated the emergence of a new "public" sphere of political society also autonomous from direct state control. This process in turn created fertile conditions for the revival of republican ideals associated with the Greek polis and with late-medieval and early-Renaissance Italian city-states. The formation of the modern republican tradition thus rehabilitated and developed an understanding of the public as creating itself "from below," and of the state as the representative of a politically self-organized society, in opposition to the absolutist conception of the public as the emanation of sovereign will and power.

10. The sense of the private as "a realm of personal life" apart from the "publicly visible" parallels Georges Duby's characterization of the private as "a zone of immunity to which we may fall back or retreat" (Georges Duby, "Foreword to *A History of Private Life,*" in Paul Veyne, ed., *A History of Private Life,* vol. 1, *From Pagan Rome to Byzantium,* p. viii). On this subject, see also Allan Silver, " 'Two Different Sorts of Commerce'—Friendship and Strangership in Civil Society," in this volume.

The decline of absolutism and the ascendance of constitutional democracy, however, by no means resolved the conflict between the public as the province of the sovereign state and the public as the realm of autonomous societal will-formation in favor of the latter, as Tocqueville took care to emphasize.[11] Contemporary language mirrors the historical complexity of Western institutional differentiation, as varying notions of "the public" have survived and acquired context-specific connotations, depending on particular theoretical, legal, and everyday usages of the term. For instance, Western economic discourse tends to refer to public property as the province of the state (that is, the sovereign power), and the private as the realm of civil (that is, nonstate) proprietorship. Western legal codes demarcate spheres of both public and civil law, with the former rooted in the legislation, generalization, interpretation, and application of constitutional doctrines and universal codes of conduct, while the latter deals with the regulation of contractual relations and the adjudication of civil ("private") disputes over individual rights and between particular parties.[12] Western political discourse speaks of the public interest in international affairs in terms of national sovereignty and realpolitik; but in domestic politics, notions of representation, societal will-formation, and "public opinion" predominate. These ambiguities permeate the language of everyday life: in speaking of the public, whether one has in mind mere social visibility, the general interest of a national community, prevalent social opinions, or state interests and prerogative becomes clear only in the context of a given discussion.[13]

Despite these complications and ambiguities, the main pattern of the institutionalization of public and private that has come to characterize Western modernity can roughly be captured by a fourfold typology of (constitutional) state, political society (or public sphere), civil society, and the private sphere of "personal life." The first two are, in different senses, "public," while the last two are, in different senses, "private." While noting the differentiation of these institutional spheres and the manifold tensions between them, it is important to emphasize that they are also in many ways complementary, and

11. "Appearances notwithstanding, . . . [the French Revolution] sought to increase the power and jurisdiction of the central authority. . . . Radical though it may have been, the Revolution made far fewer changes [in this respect] than is generally supposed" (Alexis de Tocqueville, *The Old Regime and the French Revolution*, pp. 19–20).

12. Max Weber, *Economy and Society: An Outline of Interpretive Sociology*, 2 vols., pp. 641–43.

13. The understanding of the public as a realm of mere social "visibility" closely follows the reconstruction of Philippe Ariès's notion of "sociability" put forward in Jeff Weintraub's essay in this volume.

that this overall configuration emerged from an interconnected set of historical processes. For example, the emergence and vitality of a market-centered civil society depends on more than the mere absence of state interference. More positively, it also requires—among other things—the regulative framework of a legal order based to a significant degree on impersonal, predictable, and enforceable norms, provided by a state that is both effective and, at the same time, subject to constitutional restraints. Similarly, while it is important to distinguish the "public" authority of the legislative and administrative state from the "public sphere" of autonomous participation and association, successful representative government also involves a complex interdependence between them.

The former Soviet bloc presented a very different picture, since official discourse and practice were monopolized by an extreme version of the absolutist model of state/society relations. Under communism, the Party-state subjected all forms of autonomous, socially visible expression to strict control, and politics remained in principle the exclusive domain of the Leninist "vanguard."[14] Furthermore, as Chairman Mao liked to say, "politics" was "in command," and thus Party-state priorities dominated the rest of social life. Given the centralized and hierarchical organization of such Party-states, and the monopolization of all political initiatives by the Party elite (only a few thousand people), social perceptions of politics crystallized around the highly visible, but carefully orchestrated and manipulated, presentation of state officialdom to the captive audience of society. This in turn drew a sharp boundary between the official actions of the "omni-visible" Party-state and the passive reception of rule by the great majority of the populace. The ubiquitous, ritualized language of "the leading role of the Party," trumpeted ad nauseam in the mass media and imposed in formally organized settings (from schools to union offices to artistic associations), continually reinforced the dividing line between Party-state leaders and everyone else. Habitual references to the Party elite as "the leaders," "the partocrats" *(partokraty),* or simply "them" reflected the sharpness of this distinction in everyday life.[15]

Stylized presentation of the persona of an exalted, "larger-than-life" ruler became a characteristic form of symbolically projecting the sovereign power of absolutist regimes,[16] and in this sense Leninist states revived and relentlessly

---

14. For a comprehensive account of the risks Soviet citizens faced if they engaged in any sort of autonomous political activity in the post-Stalin, pre-Gorbachev USSR, see Ludmilla Alexeyeva, *Soviet Dissent: Contemporary Movements for National, Religious, and Human Rights.*

15. See Teresa Toranska, *Them.*

16. See Poggi, *Modern State,* pp. 68–69.

developed a political style reminiscent of absolutism. But the structure of Party-state domination also radicalized the despotic tendencies of its absolutist predecessors in both form and substance. Thus, in contrast to the experience of Western absolutism, no officially recognized space remained in which an autonomous civil or political society could emerge, *especially* before the deepening of the general crisis of late communism that overwhelmed and consumed the Soviet empire in the late 1980s.

The absence of any ideologically recognized place for particular interests or individual rights in the communist order helps explain this difference. Where the absolutist monarchs of the early modern West had presided over the standardization of commercial activities on the part of propertied individuals within the confines of state regulation, Leninist rulers saw the market as the root of all evil, and viewed autonomous producers, owners, and traders as potential "class enemies." On the surface, "politics in command" had the advantage of solving a thorny problem that had haunted Western political thought since before the French Revolution: the general ("public") interest was to be reconciled with particular ("private") interests simply by denying any recognition whatsoever to the particular as a legitimate element of social life.[17] Indeed, a steady stream of state-organized scorn and vilification rained down on notions of particular interests and the individualistic pursuit of "the personal life." The absence of key institutional elements of early Western civil society such as contractual law, with its inherent conferral of social recognition on particularistic pursuits, became a defining aspect of Soviet-type communism.

Furthermore, the recognition by early modern absolutist regimes of the legitimacy of corporate *(standische)* bodies representing social estates and communities (such as parliaments and regional councils, artisanal and trade associations, chartered towns, and so forth) created fertile conditions for the later development of an autonomous civil and political society. These elements were historically much weaker in Russia than in the West—and the continuities between communist practice and the autocratic heritage of tsarism have often been noted.[18] But in the second half of the nineteenth century even the tsarist

17. Over forty years ago, J. L. Talmon, following Tocqueville, pointed to the Jacobin radicalization of the Rousseauian notion of "the general will" as a primary inspiration of what he called modern "totalitarian democracy" (J. L. Talmon, *The Origins of Totalitarian Democracy*). Lenin was an innovative heir of the Jacobin tradition, having internalized it in part via the writings of Marx and Plekhanov and in part via his exposure to the Russian populist tradition of the second half of the nineteenth century; see James H. Billington, *The Icon and the Axe: An Interpretive History of Russian Culture*, pp. 456–64, 524–32.

18. Raeff stresses (in *The Well-Ordered Police State*) how the acceptance by Western sovereigns of intermediate corporate bodies between the state and the mass of commoners facilitated both the restructuring of everyday life in line with the procedural rationality

regime—by tolerating the rise of an urban bourgeoisie and seeking to incorporate refurbished intermediate structures in its system of rule—witnessed the emergence of a fragile civil society in parts of Russia.[19] By contrast, the Party-state treated autonomous association per se as illegitimate, particularly during the periods of "socialist construction" in Russia and later in Eastern Europe. The Bolsheviks assaulted, paralyzed, and destroyed all forms of visible social autonomy as part of their project of engineering a "new socialist man" and eliminating all class distinctions. And, up to the end of the Stalinist era, the Party-state subjected society in toto to repeated mobilization campaigns, comprehensive paternalistic supervision, and mass repressions organized from above.[20] In the Stalinist years of "high" totalitarianism, one can speak at most of *vestigial remnants* of civil society that persisted in surreptitious "second-economy" activities and the domestic realm of friends and family.[21]

Thus, the systematic suppression of any independent public life followed from and complemented the Party-state's effort to suppress or destroy the "private sector." Communism in this way spawned a hypertrophied public realm in the sense of state sovereignty and officialdom, but an atrophied public realm in the sense of republican citizenship and political society. This contrast underscores the continued relevance of the totalitarian model as an ideal-type concept of a Leninist "movement regime," insofar as it identifies the radicalization of the absolutist principle of an all-powerful sovereign center as the key organizing principle of the Party-state. And it is only in this narrow sense of

---

necessary for the expansion of early capitalist economies, as well as the development of civil and political society; while the relative scarcity of such bodies and the failure of the tsarist state to enlist them in its early modernization projects under Peter the Great and Catherine II greatly impeded the formation of civil society in Russia.

19. See Edith W. Clowes, Samuel D. Kassow, and James L. West's edited volume, *Between Tsar and People: Educated Society and the Quest for Public Identity in Late Imperial Russia.*

20. Elemér Hankiss has documented the ubiquity of mobilization campaigns in the everyday life of the Hungarian town of Dunapataj between June 1947 and December 1950. Relentless ideological campaigns mobilized from above both created a tight web with which to draw "the masses" into the Party-state's utopian project, and paralyzed remnants of previous civil society and social autonomy. See Elemér Hankiss, *East European Alternatives,* pp. 11–49.

For the classic statement of the communist state as a "mobilization regime," see Richard Lowenthal, "Development vs. Utopia in Communist Policy," in Chalmers Johnson's edited volume, *Change in Communist Systems,* pp. 33–116, which lays out the nexus of state-building goals, repression, and societal reconstruction that Stalinist "modernization" entailed.

21. See T. H. Rigby, "The USSR: End of a Long, Dark Night?" in Robert F. Miller, ed., *The Developments of Civil Society in Communist Systems,* pp. 11–23.

an autocratic center carefully orchestrating displays of its own power and majesty that one can still apply a political concept of the "public sphere" to Soviet-type society, as the lack of an intermediate realm of social autonomy between Leviathan-state and populace entailed the absence of a public coalescing from below.[22] Thus the informal groups, voluntary associations, and even mass protests that did begin to emerge in parts of the Soviet empire toward the end of the communist period developed under conditions radically distinct from those that had fostered civil and political society under Western absolutism.

The lack of an independent civil and political society does not imply, however, that society under communism represented a totally atomized, machine-like replication of the totalitarian organizational principle. As many critics of this model have rightly pointed out, the totalitarian image, taken literally, oversimplifies the complexity of social activity and development during the Soviet period in Eastern and Central Europe and the USSR. Even under "high" totalitarianism, the monolithic "public face" of communist power masked a dense tangle of subterranean conflicts among leaders and functionaries; informal "bureaucratic lobbies" formed and splintered around various branches of industrial and military production; and quasi-autonomous forms of social and familial life persisted in the interstices of the Leviathan-state.[23]

22. The hypertrophy of state sovereignty under communism can be traced to the organizational and ideological history of the Bolshevik movement, and in particular to Lenin's single-minded and purely instrumental concept of politics as the struggle for class power and the practice of class dictatorship. Bolshevism subordinated all social priorities to the strategic and tactical needs of "the proletarian vanguard" in its Herculean struggle for communism. The fruit of this political conception was, in the end, the instrumentalization of entire societies as a means to the ultimate aim of the Party-state's "heroic combat tasks." Lenin's thinking was paralleled in many ways by that of the authoritarian and fascist right of the 1920s and 1930s, which subordinated all social priorities to the "heroic" political struggle of the "fatherland" against all "enemies." For Lenin's politics and Bolshevism as an "organizational weapon," see Ken Jowitt, *New World Disorder: The Leninist Extinction,* pp. 1–32; A. J. Polan, *Lenin and the End of Politics;* and Philip Selznick, *The Organizational Weapon: A Study of Bolshevik Strategy and Tactics.* For the interwar European right, see Hans Rogger and Eugen Weber, eds., *The European Right: A Historical Profile;* and Carl Schmitt, *The Concept of the Political.*

23. These realities were recognized by many advocates of the totalitarian model. Merle Fainsod, for instance, noted that behind "the monolithic facade of Stalinist totalitarianism . . . the plural pressures of professional bureaucratic interests found expression" and that the Party faced "hooliganism," "lawlessness" and a "substratum of ideological indifference" (Merle Fainsod, *How Russia Is Ruled,* pp. 579, 594–95).

In the 1960s, a number of Western political scientists put forward an "interest group" model of communist politics as an alternative to totalitarian imagery: see, for instance, Jerry F. Hough, *The Soviet Prefects: The Local Party Organs in Industrial Decision-Making;* and H. Gordon Skilling, "Interest Groups and Communist Politics: An Introduction," in Skil-

Though the post-Stalin period brought an end of mass terror, Stalin's heirs failed to reform the basic institutions of Leninist domination, presiding instead over the *routinization* of partocratic oligarchy.[24] Routinization entailed a shift away from incessant ideological campaigns, purges, and the like in favor of greater security and a collegial-bureaucratic esprit de corps among leaders and apparatchiki. The Khrushchev-era curtailment of terroristic shake-ups of officialdom had been intended as a means of rationalizing Party-state rule through the establishment of stable norms of administration and more meritocratic criteria of office holding; but when these measures were followed, not by meaningful democratization, but by Brezhnev's "period of stagnation" *(zastoi)*, they greatly strengthened the "rent-seeking" proclivities of dominant bureaucratic strata, who no longer feared sudden demotion, exile, or execution at the hands of capricious "revolutionary leaders."[25] Applying the stick of coercion more selectively, officialdom increasingly relied on the manipulative use of the carrot of rewards—in the form of promotions, bonuses, access to scarce goods, granting of lifetime tenure to officeholders, and so on—as the principal means of "getting things done" in workplaces and offices. The conservative drift of the post-Stalin Party-state marked the passage of the revolutionary ethos of Bolshevism: the Party appeared less and less as the "vanguard" of a monolithic "workers' state" and more and more as a hegemonic, privilege-seeking social estate presiding over a society integrated by a mixture of formally meritocratic hierarchies, extensive clientelistic networks, and straightforwardly traditional values of authoritarianism.[26]

---

ling and Franklyn Griffiths's edited volume, *Interest Groups in Soviet Politics,* pp. 3–18. While it was certainly important to take account of paticularistic interests at work behind the mask of Party unity, this model unfortunately tended to project the "playing field" of a pluralist society onto the radically distinct world of Soviet-type society. Interpreting communist politics as simply the "rational pursuit" of individual and group interests obscured some key features of these regimes. In the Soviet bloc, on the other hand, official ideology considered the discussion of interest groups a "bourgeois deviation," so that raising the problem of particular interests was crucial in breaking out of the distorted language of the regime and preparing the way for a more critical and sociologically realistic assessment of actual social realities; see Tatyana Zaslavskaya, "The Novosibirsk Report," pp. 88–108.

24. For the concept of Leninist routinization, see Jowitt, *New World Disorder,* pp. 1–49.

25. Jan Winiecki has argued that the best way to conceptualize the difference between "modes of wealth distribution" under modern capitalism and communism is a property rights approach that stresses the profit-seeking activity of capitalists, on the one hand, and the rent-seeking activity of officeholders in a redistributive state, on the other (Jan Winiecki, "Obstacles to Economic Reform of Socialism: A Property-Rights Approach," pp. 65–71.)

26. Stalin's revival of many of the trappings of tsarist autocracy after 1932 is well documented, from the reestablishment of traditional epaulets in the army to the promulgation

The extent and complexity of social development that had occurred in the shadow of Party dictatorship became much clearer following de-Stalinization. Especially striking were the paradoxical consequences of Soviet-style industrialization, which facilitated continued modernization in the narrow sense of urbanization, increasing levels of education, and the stabilization of birthrates,[27] while at the same time augmenting quasi-traditional forms of authority. Rather than creating avenues for new forms of societal expression that could serve as "feedback mechanisms" for the restructuring of the sociopolitical order, post-Stalin communist rulers turned to "goulash communism," a new modus vivendi between Party-state and society (widely dubbed by Western observers as "a new social contract") in which top officials would retain their autocratic status and exclusive control of the economy in return for open-ended growth and the provision of ever-higher living standards and more and better-quality consumer goods to the populace.[28] Thus, despite continuing urbanization and modestly rising standards of living through the mid-1970s, fundamental changes in the autocratic character of state-society relations did not come until the onset of comprehensive reforms in the Gorbachev era.[29]

While their institutional form endured, however, Soviet bloc regimes grad-

---

of his own persona as "father of the Soviet peoples," a direct adaptation of a traditional epithet for the tsar, "the little father of the people." See Nicholas Timasheff, *The Great Retreat*. The Brezhnev regime redoubled Stalin's earlier reinvocation of traditional authoritarian values, stressing the value of loyalty to "the socialist State" above all else. The Russian word for "State" *(gosudarstvo)* itself echoes the autocratic past, as the root of the word is the royal "Your Majesty," "Sire" *(gosudar')*. The Stalin-Brezhnev restoration of autocratic values was paralleled in the eastern European satellites after 1956 in the form of emergent varieties of "national communism," in which bloc leaders such as Ceauşescu in Romania and Jaruzelski in Poland tried to legitimate their status by linking themselves to past nationalist traditions.

27. For an overview of the achievements of Soviet urbanization, see Moshe Lewin, *The Gorbachev Phenomenon: A Historical Interpretation*, pp. 13–82.

28. For a concise statement of the idea that the "legitimation strategy" of the post-Stalin leadership in the Soviet bloc consisted of a de facto social contract based on diffuse expectations of an ever-rising standard of living, see Victoria E. Bonnell, "Workers and the State in the Soviet Bloc," *Workers under Communism*, no. 5 (Spring 1984): 24–30. Ken Jowitt emphasizes that this metaphor should be taken with a grain of salt, since in its actual operation the arrangement was "more protection racket than social contract" *(New World Disorder*, p. 252).

29. Exceptions to this institutional continuity were the Hungarian economic reforms of 1968, which nevertheless did not alter the political monopoly of the Party; Czechoslovakia's "Prague Spring" of 1968, aborted by Soviet invasion; and Poland during the period of "legal Solidarity" from August 1980 through the imposition of martial law in December 1981.

ually began to rot away from within. Though second-economy activities,[30] corrupt functionaries, and extensive clientelism were ubiquitous in Soviet society from the very beginnings of "socialist industrialization," [31] in the Stalinist period the Party-state attempted to stave off the potentially delegitimating consequences of such phenomena by means of relentless ideological drives, regular condemnations of "deviations" and "sabotage by enemy agents," and the projection of a mythic image of Stalin as the incorruptible leader battling a sea of recalcitrant petty officials. When the Party leadership abandoned "high" totalitarianism and its ethos of "heroic combat tasks," it thus also unwittingly cast aside the rationale behind its propagandistic dismissal of unsavory aspects of communist rule as ephemeral distortions of the transition period. With the fall of Khrushchev, moreover, goulash communism soon degenerated into a "normalization" of blatant forms of particularism manifest in flourishing clientelist and second-economy relationships, a situation that gave the lie to the Party-state's claim to be "the state of the whole people." As communist ideology withered into empty formalism and "the masses"—and the elites themselves—"lost faith" in the Party-state's earlier utopian project, the state's claim to be a "universal proprietor" and guardian of the general interest appeared more and more as a ruse designed to deflect attention away from the appropriation of privileges by members of the partocracy.

In a certain sense, then, Soviet-type societies did indeed undergo a massive process of "privatization." However, the particularistic activities of apparatchiki, black-marketeers, and patron-client chains in formally organized settings had little to do with the *civil particularism* of Western civil society. Instead, the particularism of Soviet-type societies predominantly took the form of pervasive networks of patron-client relationships and "instrumental-personal" ties. Furthermore, this particularism was distinguished—ironically enough—by its relatively unregulated and chaotic character. Thus, the gradual corruption of the Leninist order—and not "the rebirth of civil society"— emerged as the principal outcome of post-Stalin developments, generating a tendency which has insightfully been characterized as "communist neotradi-

30. "Second economy" is a widely used blanket term for a diverse range of semilegal and illegal transactions that permeated the "planned economies" of Soviet-type societies and involved everyone from managers of state enterprises to black marketeers. For nuanced schemata of the scope and variety of such transactions, see Aron Katsenelinboigen and Herbert Levine, "Market and Plan, Plan and Market: The Soviet Case," in *The Soviet Economy: Continuity and Change*, pp. 61–70.

31. See Hiroaki Kuromiya, *Stalin's Industrial Revolution: Politics and Workers, 1928–1932*, pp. 287–318.

tionalism."[32] The "neotraditional" model stresses the dynamics whereby the unintended results of a rigid and avowedly monolithic system of domination, bent on monopolizing and "rationally" coordinating the entire process of production and distribution, spawned a vast web of clientelistic authority relations and instrumental-personal ties that could be shaken up only by terroristic means.[33] With the relaxation of blatant terror in the post-Stalin period, the dynamics of party clientelism crystallized into an increasingly immovable system of "neotraditional" oligarchy: the de facto lifetime appropriation of formally public offices for the particularistic ends of entrenched functionaries striving for "booty."[34]

In the Brezhnev period, the personalistic and often arbitrary exercise of "neotraditional" authority remained unchecked by impersonal norms and rights enforced by an effective legal order. Despite the fetish of "planning" and rational social coordination in communist ideology, the administration of social and economic relationships in Soviet-type society took surprisingly ad hoc and incoherent forms. Under communism, legal codes had little empirical relevance as regulative mechanisms beyond the most mundane affairs of "family, housing, labor, inter-enterprise, and personal property disputes, along with a much smaller number of garden variety criminal cases."[35] As soon as a mundane matter acquired "political" significance, law lost its relevance, a phenomenon manifest in the routine violation of legal norms and administrative regulations by top officials and apparatchiki in "special circumstances." This in turn reduced the presence of formal rights in constitutional documents to a matter of public show that in no way established effective mechanisms of protection or recourse for ordinary citizens against official actions. The fictitious character of legal rights under communism demonstrates how legality always remained ideologically subordinate to *partiinost'*, "party-spiritedness," whose ethos placed the concrete priorities of "the vanguard" above any theoretical rights of "the masses."[36] Such institutional conditions rendered the emergence of either a civic "public sphere" or a civil "private sphere" exceedingly improbable.

32. My summary is adapted from two variants of "neotraditional" theory put forward in Jowitt, *New World Disorder;* and Andrew Walder, *Communist Neo-Traditionalism: Work and Authority in Chinese Industry.*

33. Walder, *Communist Neo-Traditionalism,* p. 24.

34. Jowitt, *New World Disorder,* p. 128.

35. Robert Sharlet, "Stalinism and Legal Culture," in Robert C. Tucker's *Stalinism: Essays in Historical Interpretation,* pp. 155–79 (quotation on p. 156).

36. Sharlet, "Legal Culture."

Consequently, the typology of state, political society, civil society, and the private sphere of "personal life," which is most useful for capturing the institutional differentiation of *Western* modernity, is less helpful and indeed misleading if applied directly to Soviet-type societies. Instead, I propose that the basic institutional configuration of Soviet-type society can most elegantly be captured by distinguishing between the realm of *officialdom;* the *"social"* realm of work, routine administration, and officially sanctioned and supervised associational life; and the *domestic* realm of family and friendship.

Officialdom included the ruling elite, its immediate administrative *apparat,* and the *nomenklatura,* the closed social stratum that formed around the Party's monopoly over appointments to all significant economic and administrative offices.[37] The *"social"* realm encompassed the enormous and complex social world that developed in the intermediate institutional spaces between the apex of the Party-state pyramid and the informal networks of friends and families— cutting across many of the lines that separate "public" from "private" in Western societies. Interaction in the "social" realm was organized not only according to ideological, meritocratic, and authoritarian-hierarchical principles, but also along lines of bargaining, reciprocal favors, mutual dependencies, networks of connections, dissimulation, circumvention of regulations and procedures, and the like. As the preceding discussion emphasizes, pervasive clientelism and unregulated particularism marked the "social" realm in the post-Stalin period. Finally, the *domestic* realm crystallized around ascriptive relationships, as well as networks based on intimacy, shared value commitments, and so on. As will be discussed shortly, this realm differed in significant respects from the sphere of "personal life" in Western societies and served as a subterranean "reservoir" of unorthodox and dissident practices and opinions.

Beyond the greater analytical appropriateness of this tripartite model for Soviet-type societies, drawing the distinction between "official" and "social" rather than "public" and "private" is closer to everyday linguistic usage as it developed in Russia and Eastern Europe under communism. Furthermore, it preempts a range of cross-cultural "translation" problems by separating out some of the various shadings of meaning clustered in Western notions of the "public." On the one hand, use of the adjective "official" to refer to highly visible, orchestrated Party-state activities and to the special status associated with *apparat* and *nomenklatura* positions, which closely follows linguistic custom in the former Soviet bloc, represents the best choice for translating "pub-

---

37. For the *nomenklatura* system of appointments and its far-reaching consequences, see Michael Voslensky, *Nomenklatura: The Soviet Ruling Class, An Insider's Report.*

lic" in the sense of state sovereignty and prerogative.[38] On the other hand, despite linguistic variations between different Soviet-type societies, for most of the communist period the "social" characteristically encompassed those realms of everyday life under the ultimate control of officialdom. In Russia, for instance, in everyday speech the adjective "social" *(obshchestvennyi* or its synonym *sotsial'nyi)* signified life at the workplace, in offices, in officially sanctioned associations, and at cultural or sporting events; and where a westerner would use "public" in the sense of social visibility or prevalent social opinion, a Russian would again use "social." [39]

As noted above, the increasingly cynical instrumentalism that prevailed in the activities and relationships of the "social realm" emerged as a particularly striking feature of everyday life in Soviet-type societies. While value commitments and a sense of obligation or responsibility did not entirely die out in the workplace and professional life, they tended to be restricted to very narrow strata, and were almost never connected to any sort of socialist idealism. Such value orientations tended to take four main forms: commitment to work as an end in itself (the professional ethos of a scientist, doctor, skilled worker, or artist); commitment to the state as an end in itself (the ethos of traditional authoritarianism); commitment to superiors or subordinates on a personal basis (the quasi-traditional ethos of obligation to a patron or client, at times blended with personal attachment); and finally, ideological commitment and what Susan Shirk has called "virtuocracy," the obedience of a subordinate to a superior out of loyalty to shared ideological convictions.[40] While virtuocracy had become vestigial by the Brezhnev era, it continued to function to a limited extent among pockets of high Party, military, and intelligence personnel long after the communist virtuocracy of "heroic" Bolshevism had faded away. No place, however, existed in the "social" realm for civic values of citizenship, publicity, and democratic representation. Until the very last phases of the communist period, the frustration of autonomous expression by the Party-

38. Russian has two words for "official" in the context of state (that is, public) affairs: *ofitsial'nyi* and *gosudarstvenny,* of which the latter is derived directly from the word "the state."

39. A cognate of the Western word public *(publichnyi)* exists in Russian, but on the whole it is used to refer only to a few things along the lines of brothels *(publichnye doma)* and public toilets *(publichnye tyalety),* and thus has a pejorative connotation. Of course, for many other former Soviet bloc countries, such linguistic noncorrespondence is not as extreme; but the social-structural differences between Western and Soviet-type societies remain, complicating translation of precise *concepts* of the "public" in any case.

40. Susan L. Shirk, *Competitive Comrades: Career Incentives and Student Strategies in China.*

state drove those committed to such values either toward risky conflicts with state security or toward withdrawal into the domestic realm.

STATE-ENGINEERED STRATIFICATION AND GENERALIZED STATE-DEPENDENCE IN SOVIET-TYPE SOCIETY

THE HISTORICAL PATTERN of industrialization under communism, and the resulting forms of division of labor and societal integration, developed in ways highly dissimilar to the patterns of social differentiation that marked Western history. Indeed, Soviet-type societies represented a curious hybrid of large-scale industrial organization, quasi-feudal social relations, and patrimonial rulership. One's status in the state-organized hierarchy of "workers, peasants and intellectuals"—what T. H. Rigby has termed "the mono-organizational society"—dramatically shaped one's life chances and material standard of living.

First and foremost, the state's direct administration of production and its system of "total redistribution" of producer and consumer goods engendered Soviet-style "industrial patrimonialism" with its concomitant pattern of "state-engineered stratification." [41] When combined with the Leninist variant of autocratic domination, this pattern "lumpenized" the vast majority of the population, in the sense that it terminated all independent property ownership beyond articles of personal consumption and subordinated all forms of professional and associational autonomy to Party supervision.[42] Above all, "the extra-economic compulsion and personal dependence of the producer" marked the political economy of Soviet-type communism.[43] The Leninist-engineered social order was thus "free" of both independent producers and the social support networks and traditions associated with the semiautonomous communi-

41. For the concept of "state-engineered stratification" (*gosudarstvenno-sproektirovannaia stratifikatsiia*), see Victor Zaslavsky, "Rossiia na puti k rynku." For an overview of the concept of the command economy and the formation of communist economic doctrines on the basis of Lenin's and Stalin's interpretation of Marx, see Gregory Grossman, "The Solidary Society: A Philosophical Issue in Communist Economic Reforms," in Grossman's *Essays in Socialism and Planning in Honor of Carl Landauer*, pp. 184–211.

42. The concept of "lumpenization" occurs widely in Gorbachev-era newspapers and scholarly journals. Indeed, for many Russian observers, the "basic characteristic [of Soviet society] is the total lumpenization *[lumpenizatsiia]* of the population" (quoted in Nina Beliaeva, Igor Malov, and Maxim Khrustalov, "Mnogopartiinost' v Rossii, 1917–1990 gg.," *Problemy Vestochnoi Evropy*, no. 31/32 [1991]: 79–163 [quotation on p. 79]). Ironically enough, "lumpenization" as used by Russians is very close to Marx's conception of "proletarianization": the progressive reduction of the majority of the populace to the dependent status of propertyless wage laborers.

43. Yevgeny Starikov, "Novye elementy sotsial'noi struktury," *Kommunist*, no. 5 (1990): 30–41 (quotation on p. 30).

ties of artisans, religious congregations, literati, and so on that served as bearers of early civil and political society in the West. Such conditions produced legacies that continue to shape the postcommunist experience of these societies. In particular, the absence of market relations, small property owners, and forms of autonomous association by strata sharing similar material or ideal interests meant that when voluntary associations did begin to emerge in late communism, they often found themselves wholly dependent on connections and patrons embedded in broader "supplying-redistributive networks" for the mobilization of material means for organization and action.[44]

Of course, the specific histories of the various Soviet bloc countries affected the degree of dependence of informal groups and opposition activists on bureaucratic and second-economy connections. In the exceptional case of Poland, where the Catholic Church had—quite anomalously—survived Stalinism as a relatively independent corporate body, the Church and social networks sustained by it were able to provide meeting rooms and other material means, as well as moral and social support, to many oppositionists. Then the emergence of Solidarity and the continued underground activities of its members and networks under martial law created a nascent, functioning political class as an alternative national leadership to the communist elite.[45] Reemergent society in Poland was thus much stronger and less dependent on the surviving structures of the Leviathan-state than in Russia or Romania, for instance, where state-dependence was more radical.

Kádárist Hungary, with its "hybrid" of command economy and bureaucratically embedded "market" phenomena, represented a second important exception to the Brezhnevite norm.[46] However, though Kádárism did indeed generate strata of "socialist entrepreneurs" among moonlighting workers and peasants,[47] Janos Kornai has convincingly argued that the "hybrid economy," while modifying elements of the command system, in no way transcended the fundamental structural pattern of a Soviet-type economy.[48] While the "quasi-market" differentiation of some social strata in Hungary seems to have facilitated its initially "quiet and seamless" political revolution, it has not spared

44. For an extended discussion of "the supplying-redistributive status groups and social estates" *(snabzhenchesko-raspredelitel'nye statusy-sosloviia)* that dominated Soviet-type societies, see Yevgeny Starikov, " 'Ugrazhaiut' li nam poiavlenie 'srednego klassa'?" pp. 192–96.

45. See Steven Stoltenberg, "An Underground Society: The Evolution of Poland's Solidarity, 1982–1989" (Ph.D. dissertation, University of California, Berkeley, 1992).

46. Hankiss, *Alternatives,* pp. 188–96.

47. See Ivan Szelenyi, *Socialist Entrepreneurs: Embourgeoisement in Rural Hungary.*

48. Janos Kornai, "The Hungarian Reform Process: Visions, Hopes, and Reality," *Journal of Economic Literature* 24 (December 1986): 1687–1737.

Hungary from the intractable problems of the immediate postcommunist period that plague all the countries of the former Soviet bloc to one degree or another, from ethnic politics to persistent forms of authoritarianism to so-called "*nomenklatura* privatization."[49]

In sum, conditions of generalized state-dependence intensified the difficulties and dangers that faced an average person contemplating open defiance of the command structure of the official order. The question then arises: Why, after successfully paralyzing and repressing visible forms of public social autonomy for so long, did certain Soviet bloc regimes begin to allow and even at times encourage the reemergence of autonomous social activity after Gorbachev came to power? The full answer to this question lies in the developmental history of the crisis of the European Soviet-type societies, especially in the protracted stagnation of their command economies and the inability of ideologically bankrupt and complacent Party-states to energetically confront economic failure. Without attempting to reconstruct these processes here, we may note that the conjuncture between the gradual fragmentation and demoralization of the communist ruling elites (presaged by earlier crises in East Germany, Hungary, Poland, and Czechoslovakia), and the opening up of opportunities for publicly visible activity from below triggered by the reforms of the Gorbachev government—especially the glasnost initiative—and its close allies in Poland and Hungary, played a decisive role in the reemergence of sustained and autonomous public action. From the standpoint of understanding the relations between public and private in the context of communist societies, it is especially interesting to trace the ways in which the process of autonomous mobilization from below in the late 1980s brought together informal networks of family and friends and the subculture of instrumental-personal ties in the "social" realm to help shape reemergent society.

BETWEEN OFFICIAL AND DOMESTIC REALMS: THE GENEALOGY OF SOCIAL ROLES UNDER COMMUNISM

BRINGING OUT THESE processes requires deepening our analysis of the world of everyday practice in Soviet-type society. So far, the discussion has focused primarily on the external perspective of the modeler of institutional patterns. But what happens when we switch to the perspective of the participant in everyday life? In daily life, the anonymous "everyman" of the post-Stalin period experienced the "official" public realm as something spectacular and "omni-visible," yet distant and remote from everyday routines. Our "ev-

---

49. David Stark, "Privatization in Hungary: From Plan to Market or From Plan to Clan?" *East European Politics and Societies* 4, no. 3 (fall 1990): 351–92.

eryman" was preoccupied not by Party-state activities, but by the "dual partic-
ularisms" of instrumental-personal ties in the workplace and the second economy, and of affective ties in the domestic realm of family and friendship.

Indeed, this central fact of daily life underscores the great ironic paradox
of sustained Party-state rule: the subordination of particular interests and the
individual's life course to the diktat of "total administration" resulted, not in
a harmonized society striving in unison to realize the "vanguard's" blueprint
of the general interest, but rather in the pervasiveness of particularistic orientations and the near obliteration of civic orientations. The tangled web of particularism that marked the social world of Soviet-type society was the unintended
consequence of the communist ideological project of "community without
participation," of the total subordination of society to "the vanguard" without
intermediate, autonomous forms of association or mechanisms of social integration beyond formulaic exhortation, coercion, and material incentives. Our
"everyman" thus found himself or herself ensnared in a net of social dependencies that, outside circles of friend and family, demanded the strategic manipulation of personalistic ties without the benefit of a system of individual rights,
a supportive environment of autonomous local communities and associations,
or institutional forms of remonstrance vis-à-vis powerful patrons or corrupt
or indifferent administrative organs. The Party-state's sweeping "colonization"
of the publicly visible thus unintentionally but radically "privatized" much
of social life, in the sense that the great majority of people withdrew entirely
from politics and associational activity and concentrated on "getting by and
getting along."

Though the idea of a profound and systematic tendency toward "privatization" in Soviet-type societies points to a crucial outcome of Leninist rule, it
can also be misleading if the *forms* of "privatization" involved are not carefully
specified and delineated. But this kind of explicit examination is surprisingly
rare, even in otherwise perceptive analyses. When Elemér Hankiss comments
on the emergence of "an alienated, individualistic, privatizing society" in Ká-
dár's Hungary,[50] or Vladimir Shlapentokh emphasizes the wide-ranging privatization of social attitudes as the single most significant development of the
Brezhnev era in Russia,[51] it is clear that "private" functions in their arguments
as a negative or residual concept, in the sense that everything that cannot be
understood in terms of the "official-public" logic of the Party-state appears
as ipso facto "private." But without further qualification, such an approach
can easily lead to collapsing the important distinction between three analyti-

50. See Hankiss, *Alternatives,* p. 85.
51. See Vladimir Shlapentokh, *Public and Private Life of the Soviet People: Changing
Values in Post-Stalin Russia,* pp. 13–14.

cally distinct phenomena: the private as *particularistic orientations per se;* the private as an expression of *legitimate civil interests* in a context bounded by formal rights, legal norms, and contractual relations (the *civil particularism* of Western society); and *privacy,* understood as the legitimate withdrawal from social groups or observation. Just as in the case of the "public," a failure to think through these multiple meanings of "private" and their sociohistorical specificity obscures the distinctive nature and significance of the private in Soviet-type societies.

Just as Western concepts of the public as an expression of sovereign power and of the public as an expression of political society are variations on the theme of the formulation and expression of general interests, so Western notions of the private variously conceptualize the expression of particular interests and experiences, as well as the contexts in which such interests and experiences are expressed. In Western economic and political discourse, the private often indicates the pursuit of *legitimate* civil interests, though a more residual and pejorative notion of the private as the *merely* particular is used at times in discussions of the "private interests" of powerful figures or other "special interests" perceived to have manipulated public policy or circumvented the formal "rules of the game." In many legal discussions and in everyday life, however, the private also indicates *privacy,* a rights-shielded realm of personal life experienced in the household or other settings legitimately "hidden" from general view. The private in the West thus connotes much more that the merely particular: in the majority of cases, what is referred to as "the private" assumes, in fact, a diffuse web of "laws and mores" [52] that regulate and direct the expression of particular interests and the pursuit of the personal life. This web of regulative norms and its formal exclusion of coercion as a legitimate means of pursuing one's interests is what secures both the relatively impersonal *and* the pacific character of Western civil society.[53]

In contrast, the centrality of personalistic ties and the potential for violent resolutions of conflicts of interests (whether by means of the denunciation of opponents to security organs, the participation of such organs in second-economy dealings, or the political—and sometimes physical—annihilation of opponents among rivals for Party-state leadership) distinguished the rampant particularism of Soviet-type societies. Under communism, one simply cannot

52. Alexis de Tocqueville, *Democracy in America,* p. 62.
53. See Norbert Elias, "Violence and Civilization: The State Monopoly of Physical Violence and Its Infringement," in John Keane, ed., *Civil Society and the State,* pp. 177–98. Of course, the extent of Western civil society has always been largely coterminous with that of the middle and—later—working classes, and has only intermittently and partially penetrated into certain (decidedly unpacific) enclaves such as urban ghettos.

speak of the private either in terms of the normatively recognized pursuit of legitimate civil interests (what I have been calling civil particularism) or in terms of an institutionally secured realm of personal life (the quintessential private sphere in the West). Rather, at the workplace, in offices, and in the second economy of barter exchange, patron-client relations, and informal connections, one is dealing with a generalized *unregulated* particularism (the subculture of instrumental-personal ties) experienced as an oppressive, at times dangerous, but nevertheless defining and compulsory aspect of the social world. The absence of an institutional framework for the adjudication of disputes, the designation of legitimate rights, or the pursuit of recourse against abuse led to the enforced passivity and depoliticization of much of the populace, but in no way engendered a *private market* economic realm of civil particularism comparable to Western civil society.

Privacy on the personal level was, further, highly constricted and largely ephemeral under communism. The domestic realm may at times have served as a "refuge" from official authoritarianism and unregulated particularism, but it was often characterized by the *lack* of personal privacy in the sense that crowded living conditions and the radical shortage of housing alternatives imparted to domestic life many features of a *traditionalistic* social world. Mutual dependency on family members and friends for aid and comfort, a web of customary obligations, and the close proximity and "mutual surveillance" of "neighbors for life" defined the parameters of the domestic realm. Indeed, a more traditional, *familial* privatism—as opposed to the *individualizing* privatism of liberal Western modernity—predominated in this realm.[54]

Moreover, the official order marginalized the familial privatism of the domestic realm insofar as it neither respected individual rights nor limited apparat penetration of families and informal social circles. Whereas in the West privacy is now secured for many citizens to an empirically significant degree by "the rule of law" and middle-class status, generalized social dependency under communism effectively prevented the institutionalization of secure spaces for an autonomous personal life. One's degree of personal privacy in Soviet-type society indeed depended on having one's own apartment in a decent-size city, a matter largely dependent on fortuitous circumstances of birth, connections, and educational and career opportunities. Barrington Moore has pointed out that historically the combination of authoritarian rulership, widespread social dependence on state patrons, and a lack of recognized rights dramatically reduces the extent of privacy in the sense of personal life.[55]

54. Jowitt, *New World Disorder*, pp. 39–43.
55. Barrington Moore, *Privacy: Studies in Social and Cultural History*, pp. 267–88.

And under communism, the reliable securing of "private spaces" for personal life was by and large limited to apparatchiki,[56] and then only after de facto lifetime tenure for most officials superseded Stalin's "revolutionary" policies of arbitrary and widespread turnover of personnel. Thus Soviet-type societies gave rise to a social world where unregulated particularism was rampant and yet very little privacy existed.[57] The marginalization of private space is echoed at the linguistic level in Russia, where no equivalent of the Western words for privacy is readily found.[58]

The various adaptive behaviors people improvised for coping in this social world manifested themselves in three basic modalities of "presenting the self." The first entailed the minimum required displays of loyalty, or at least acquiescence, to the official norms of life as defined and organized by the Party-state. A second was characterized by a bargaining persona oriented to particularistic patronage relationships, second-economy activities, and barter exchange, and was essential for the manipulation of *blat* ("pull" or "connections"). Finally, a third, more affective and personal "self" was reserved for face-to-face relations in the family, in limited informal social situations, and among close friends and trusted colleagues and co-workers.[59]

In the "social" realm of everyday interactions, a less differentiated array of

56. Jowitt, *New World Disorder,* p. 40.

57. This paradox underlines the inadequacy of an undifferentiated and purely residual concept of the private, in which "private" is simply equivalent to "nonstate," for understanding Soviet-type society. What such a purely negative conception *cannot* tell us is: what were the social forms and substantive contents of particular interests and personal life under communism?

58. When translating "private" from English into Russian, it is necessary to select one of a number of words, depending on the context. For instance, private property is rendered *chastnaia sobstvennost',* literally "individual property," whereas private life is rendered as *lichnaia zhizn',* "personal life." One can be on own's own or alone *(naedine),* be in seclusion or solitude *(uedinenie),* or perform a service or obtain a good on own's own time or on the side, that is, not during regular working hours or on the job *(chastnym obrazom);* but anyone who has tried to render the English word "privacy" literally and directly into Russian has experienced an obstinate translation problem.

59. Three other dispositions that were important in Soviet-type society were a "meritocratic collegiality" among some skilled workers and professionals (as mentioned above); the quasi-aristocratic, moralizing stance of certain intellectuals who consciously tried to reproduce the ethos of the precommunist Eastern European and Russian intelligentsia; and the "countercultural" affectations of youth and self-styled "artists and bohemians." While these three social personae played an important role in social change in late communism, they were concentrated among numerically small and segregated strata of the populace (see below). For the historic distinctiveness of the Eastern European and Russian intelligentsia, see Martin Malia, "What Is the Intelligentsia?" in Richard Pipes's edited collection, *The Russian Intelligentsia,* pp. 1–18.

"visible" social roles thus developed than the spectrum found in Western societies, with their extensive complex of public, civil, and private roles and their peculiar forms of individualism.[60] Communism can be said to have led to a more "classless" society than in the West, but only in this ironic sense of a narrower range of differentiated roles.[61] The use of language clearly signaled the role assumed at a given time: if one adopted the regime's official "newspeak" *(novoiaz)* with a straight face in a social encounter, it functioned at the least as an indicator of one's withdrawal—whether due to caution, fear, or expedience—from any "sincere" face-to-face encounter; while at other times the use of newspeak acted as a warning to stay in an "official" role-playing mode and thus served as a disciplining and enforcement mechanism. In the domestic realm, on the other hand, the playful parody of newspeak went hand-in-glove with Aesopian language as a principal means of passively resisting official norms. The general appropriation and strategic and ironic uses of newspeak thus functioned as a line strictly demarcating the "official-public" from both the "social" world of instrumental-personal ties and the domestic realm of friendship and family.

Of the various social spaces where "unofficial" personalistic relationships thrived in Soviet-type society, communist leaders at the height of the Stalinist period viewed the domestic realm with particular suspicion, seeing it as a subversive source of social autonomy. The Party-state tried to minimize this subversive potential via extensive networks of informers and social campaigns against familial loyalty, such as the state-sponsored cult of Pavlik Morozov.[62] Thus under "high" totalitarianism, families at times found themselves subject to direct mobilization under the imperatives of the Party-state's "combat tasks," and at all times faced a pervasive culture of fear and indifference which gripped the society around them. The impossibility of a truly "total" control

60. The greater differentiation of available roles in the West does not necessarily imply either greater social integration or that access to this highly differentiated role set has been generalized throughout all strata of society. As most sociologists since Durkheim have pointed out, a great variety of available social roles can generate anomie; and the exclusion of many from possible assumption of certain roles (via segregated socialization of the working class or "underclass," the gendering of roles, and so forth) has been widely noted.

61. Social atomization under communism inspires a further Durkheimian observation: if Western civil society is noteworthy for a pronounced anomie resulting from overly individualized and egoistic patterns of life, the communist social world could be said to have been strikingly distinguished by a prevalence of fatalistic resignation in the face of the "mechanical solidarity" imposed on "the masses" by the Party-state.

62. Pavlik Morozov was a boy lionized by Stalin's propaganda apparat for informing on his father to state security. Statues of Morozov were erected across the Soviet Union, and he was turned into an ideal figure in the iconography of the Young Communist League.

of a populace by the state meant, however, that private life continued and developed in amorphous, restricted, and hidden ways under the obscuring cover of totalitarian mobilization. Even under "high" totalitarianism, the domestic realm thus formed a "reservoir" of unofficial values, traditions, iconoclastic beliefs, and styles of passive resistance that persisted across generations. Together with subterranean oppositional sentiments, these values, traditions, beliefs, and styles persisted as latent "symbolic resources" that nascent informal associations and grassroots activists could activate and invoke in the late-communist period.

Just as importantly, the domestic realm's rich tapestry of informal networks and unofficial values, beliefs, and styles complemented the adaptive behaviors and particularistic ties emphasized in neotraditional theory. Instrumental-personal ties in the office and workplace had in fact long been linked to the maintenance of the domestic realm, insofar as the use of connections remained central to securing everything from decent food to living quarters to tolerance for small gatherings in apartments or other discreet places. But it was only with the sustained reemergence of autonomous society (in Poland, with the rise of Solidarity; in the rest of the eastern bloc, with the coming of the Gorbachev reforms) that such informal "instrumental-personal" networks could become intertwined with "affective solidary" networks in the domestic realm in ways that brought symbolic resources latent in the margins of the social world out into the open of a fragile new realm of public discussion and association.

THE PUBLIC SPHERE AND ITS PROSPECTS IN LATE- AND POST-COMMUNIST SOCIETY

THE APPEARANCE IN THE 1970s of oppositionists striving to create a persona of *public citizenship* signaled an attempt to break out of the passive web of roles that choked autonomous sociation under "actually existing socialism." The rejection of consigned resignation and enforced, stereotyped role-playing as a form of resistance was championed by a small number of dissidents as a possible strategy for creating what was increasingly termed a "civil society" from below.[63] Adopting the stance of an active citizen instead of a passive

63. Adam Michnik's samizdat essay "A New Evolutionism," perhaps the best-known document of the Polish intellectual opposition of the mid-1970s, contains in embryo the strategy of peaceful resistance and "evolution from below" that in various forms would become the principal orientation of the democratic opposition in much of the Soviet bloc: Adam Michnik, "A New Evolutionism," in *Letters from Prison and Other Essays*, pp. 135–48. For an overview of the developmental history of the "civil society" strategy in Poland, see Andrew Arato, "Civil Society against the State: Poland, 1980–81," *Telos*, no. 47 (Spring 1981): 23–47; and, with a cautionary note about the need to distinguish between "civil society" and "political society" in this context, Z. A. Pelczynski, "Solidarity and 'The Re-

subject, while claiming that formally recognized constitutional rights ought to be respected in practice, the democratic dissidents of the period immediately preceding Solidarity and perestroika foreshadowed the rise of voluntary associations and independent social movements on a larger scale.

State-engineered strata of professionals and intellectuals came to play a decisive part in this reemergence of autonomous social action in the Soviet bloc of the late 1980s. The dependence of the regimes on such "middle strata" for the reproduction of the social order—due to the crucial roles of professionals and intellectuals in state administration, technical enterprises, the mass media, and so on—combined with the high social standing and organizational competencies of these strata to put them in a position of wielding disproportionate influence in the rapid-fire events of the late 1980s. Additionally, professionals and intellectuals could not only appeal to symbolic resources latent in the domestic realm, but could also bring to bear symbolic resources *from outside*, from the West.[64] Thus prominent intellectuals, professionals, and (in some cases, such as Russia) former Party reformers came together to create an alternative locus of public authority to that of a splintering officialdom.

In the end, the fact that the web of neotraditional dependencies could be selectively yet creatively appropriated by voluntary associations and counterelites to secure the *material means* necessary for sustaining social movements (such as typewriters and xerox machines for printing and distributing samizdat) indicates the vitality of solidary networks of friendship and shared value commitment that had developed in the interstices of the Leviathan-state. Once limited opportunities for autonomous sociation opened up from above, both material means and alternative identities to those controlled and propagated by the state thus became available to many as "mobilizational instrumentalities" in the social world, despite the absence of a civil society under communism. Nascent, alternative public authorities soon began to proliferate, embodied in forms ranging from xenophobic ultranationalists to vaguely democratic advocates of "westernization." The former Soviet bloc's new counterelites, however, and especially the "democrats" outside of Poland, stumbled almost immediately after the collapse of the Party-state on the narrowness of their constituencies, their continued embeddedness in active and still powerful fragments of the redistributive social estates of the command economy, and their

---

birth of Civil Society' in Poland, 1976–81," in Keane, ed., *Civil Society and the State,* pp. 361–80.

64. For the crucial role of Western economic achievements and democracy as "international demonstration effects," alternative models to which many turned as communism faded, see Andrew C. Janos, "Social Science, Communism, and the Dynamics of Political Change," *World Politics* 44, no. 1 (October 1991): 81–112.

inability to harness the unregulated particularism of social and domestic life in the face of deepening economic chaos.

The outline of reemergent society drawn here raises troubling questions regarding the long-term problems of institutionalizing civil society and the public sphere in postcommunist societies. The diffuse web of laws and norms that undergird Western civil society cannot be brought about simply by "liberating" individual interests from the straitjacket of Party-state domination, as narrow economic liberalism at times seems to imply. And although many of the voluntary associations of reemergent society are implicit bearers of organizational principles of civil and political society (legality, publicity, representation),[65] such implicit principles have yet to be consolidated into stable democratic institutions and a democratic political culture. Most important, there is no direct correspondence between the newly achieved autonomy of sociation and such a democratic political culture, for authoritarian movements of nationalism and neofascism have mobilized alongside democratic political associations.

Indeed, authoritarianism is greatly augmented by the robust familial privatism of the domestic realm and the ethnic character of much social integration in many nations of the former Soviet bloc. Whether or not what Veljko Vujacic has called "the dual revolution of citizenship and nationhood"[66] will continue to develop along parallel tracks in a majority of these countries remains to be seen, as the Yugoslav catastrophe somberly reminds us. The social legacy of communism, with its landscape of state-dependent social strata and collapsing industrial enterprises, rampant unregulated particularism and neotraditional authority relations, may yet undermine the fragile solidarities of emergent citizenship and prevent the full institutionalization of civil and political society for many years to come. The shadow of the Leviathan still looms large over the postcommunist world.

65. Arato, "Civil Society against the State."
66. Veljko Vujacic, "The Dual Revolution of Citizenship and Nationhood in Eastern Europe" (University of California, Berkeley, 1990).

REFERENCES

Alexeyeva, Ludmilla. 1985. *Soviet Dissent: Contemporary Movements for National, Religious, and Human Rights.* Middletown, CT: Wesleyan University Press.

Arato, Andrew. 1981. "Civil Society against the State: Poland, 1980–81." *Telos,* no. 47 (spring): 23–47.

Beliaeva, Nina, Igor Malov, and Maxim Khrustalov. 1991. "Mnogopartiinost' v Rossii, 1917–1990 gg." *Problemy Vestochnoi Evropy,* no. 31/32:79–163.

Billington, James H. 1970. *The Icon and the Axe: An Interpretive History of Russian Culture.* New York: Vintage.

Bonnell, Victoria E. 1984. "Workers and the State in the Soviet Bloc." *Workers under Communism,* no. 5 (spring): 24–30.

Clowes, Edith W., Samuel D. Kassow, and James L. West, eds. 1991. *Between Tsar and People: Educated Society and the Quest for Public Identity in Late Imperial Russia.* Princeton, NJ: Princeton University Press.

Duby, Georges. 1987. "Foreword to *A History of Private Life.*" In *A History of Private Life.* Vol. 1, *From Pagan Rome to Byzantium,* edited by Paul Veyne, pp. vii–ix. Cambridge, MA: Harvard University Press.

Elias, Norbert. 1988. "Violence and Civilization: The State Monopoly of Physical Violence and Its Infringement." In *Civil Society and the State,* edited by John Keane, pp. 177–98. London: Verso, 1988.

Fainsod, Merle. 1964. *How Russia Is Ruled.* Cambridge, MA: Harvard University Press.

Falasca-Zamponi, Simonetta. 1992. "The Aestheticization of Politics: A Study of Power in Mussolini's Fascist Italy." Ph.D. dissertation, University of California, Berkeley.

Friedrich, Carl J., and Zbigniew K. Brzezinski. 1956. *Totalitarian Dictatorship and Autocracy.* Cambridge, MA: Harvard University Press.

Grossman, Gregory. 1970. "The Solidary Society: A Philosophical Issue in Communist Economic Reforms." In *Essays in Socialism and Planning in Honor of Carl Landauer,* edited by Gregory Grossman, pp. 184–211. Englewood Cliffs, NJ: Prentice-Hall.

Habermas, Jürgen. 1974. "The Public Sphere: An Encyclopedia Article." *New German Critique* 1, no. 3 (fall): 49–55.

Hankiss, Elemér. 1990. *East European Alternatives.* Oxford: Clarendon Press.

Hough, Jerry F. 1969. *The Soviet Prefects: The Local Party Organs in Industrial Decision-Making.* Cambridge, MA: Harvard University Press.

Janos, Andrew C. 1991. "Social Science, Communism, and the Dynamics of Political Change." *World Politics* 44, no. 1 (October): 81–112.

Jowitt, Ken. 1992. *New World Disorder: The Leninist Extinction.* Berkeley: University of California Press.

Katsenelinboigen, Aron, and Herbert Levine. 1981. "Market and Plan, Plan and Market: The Soviet Case." In *The Soviet Economy: Continuity and Change,* pp. 61–70. Boulder, CO: Westview Press.

Keane, John, ed. 1988. *Civil Society and the State: New European Perspectives.* London: Verso.

———. 1988. "Despotism and Democracy: The Origins and Development of the Distinction between Civil Society and the State, 1750–1850." In *Civil Society and the State: New European Perspectives,* edited by John Keane, pp. 35–71. London: Verso.

Kornai, Janos. 1986. "The Hungarian Reform Process: Visions, Hopes, and Reality." *Journal of Economic Literature* 24 (December}: 1687–1737.

Kuromiya, Hiroaki. 1988. *Stalin's Industrial Revolution: Politics and Workers, 1928–1932.* Cambridge: Cambridge University Press.

Lewin, Moshe. 1988. *The Gorbachev Phenomenon: A Historical Interpretation.* Berkeley: University of California Press.

Linz, Juan. 1975. "Totalitarian and Authoritarian Regimes." In *Macropolitical Theory,* edited by Fred I. Greenstein and Nelson W. Polsby, pp. 175–411. Reading, MA: Addison-Wesley.

Lowenthal, Richard. 1979. "Development vs. Utopia in Communist Policy." In *Change in Communist Systems,* edited by Chalmers Johnson, pp. 33–116. Stanford, CA: Stanford University Press.

Malia, Martin. 1961. "What Is the Intelligentsia?" In *The Russian Intelligentsia,* edited by Richard Pipes, pp. 1–18. New York: Columbia University Press.

Michnik, Adam. 1985. "A New Evolutionism." In *Letters from Prison and Other Essays,* pp. 135–48. Berkeley: University of California Press.

Moore, Barrington. 1984. *Privacy: Studies in Social and Cultural History.* Armonk, NY: M. E. Sharpe.

Pelczynski, Z. A. 1988. "Solidarity and 'The Rebirth of Civil Society' in Poland, 1976–81." In *Civil Society and the State: New European Perspectives,* edited by John Keane, pp. 361–80. London: Verso.

Poggi, Gianfranco. 1978. *The Development of the Modern State: A Sociological Introduction.* Stanford, CA: Stanford University Press.

Polan, A. J. 1984. *Lenin and the End of Politics.* Berkeley: University of California Press.

Raeff, Marc. 1983. *The Well-Ordered Police State: Social and Institutional Change through Law in the Germanies and Russia, 1600–1800.* New Haven, CT: Yale University Press.

Rigby, T. H. 1977. "Stalinism and the Mono-Organizational Society." In *Stalinism: Essays in Historical Interpretation,* edited by Robert Tucker, pp. 53–76. New York: Norton.

———. 1992. "The USSR: End of a Long, Dark Night?" In *The Developments of Civil Society in Communist Systems,* edited by Robert F. Miller, pp. 11–23. North Sydney: Allen & Unwin.

Rogger, Hans, and Eugen Weber, eds. 1966. *The European Right: A Historical Profile.* Berkeley: University of California Press.

Schmitt, Carl. 1976. *The Concept of the Political.* New Brunswick, NJ: Rutgers University Press.

Selznick, Philip. 1960. *The Organizational Weapon: A Study of Bolshevik Strategy and Tactics.* New York: Free Press.

Sharlet, Robert. 1977. "Stalinism and Legal Culture." In *Stalinism: Essays in Historical Interpretation,* edited by Robert C. Tucker, pp. 155–79. New York: Norton.

Shirk, Susan L. 1982. *Competitive Comrades: Career Incentives and Student Strategies in China.* Berkeley: University of California Press.

Shlapentokh, Vladimir. 1989. *Public and Private Life of the Soviet People: Changing Values in Post-Stalin Russia.* New York: Oxford University Press.

Skilling, H. Gordon. 1971. "Interest Groups and Communist Politics: An Introduction." In *Interest Groups in Soviet Politics,* edited by H. G. Skilling and Franklyn Griffiths, pp. 3–18. Princeton, NJ: Princeton University Press.

Starikov, Yevgeny. 1990. "Novye elementy sotsial'noi struktury." *Kommunist,* no. 5: 30–41.

———. 1990. " 'Ugrazhaiut' li nam poiavlenie 'srednego klassa'?" *Znamia,* no. 10: 192–96.

Stark, David. 1990. "Privatization in Hungary: From Plan to Market or From Plan to Clan?" *East European Politics and Societies* 4, no. 3 (fall): 351–92.

Stoltenberg, Steven. 1992. "An Underground Society: The Evolution of Poland's Solidarity, 1982–1989." Ph.D. dissertation, University of California, Berkeley.

Szelenyi, Ivan. 1988. *Socialist Entrepreneurs: Embourgeoisement in Rural Hungary.* Madison: University of Wisconsin Press.

Talmon, J. L. 1952. *The Origins of Totalitarian Democracy.* Boston: Beacon Press.

Timasheff, Nicholas. 1946. *The Great Retreat.* New York: Dutton.

Tocqueville, Alexis de. [1835, 1840] 1969. *Democracy in America.* Garden City, NY: Doubleday Anchor.

———. [1856] 1955. *The Old Regime and the French Revolution.* New York: Doubleday Anchor.

Toranska, Teresa. 1987. *Them.* New York: Harper & Row.

Voslensky, Michael. 1984. *Nomenklatura: The Soviet Ruling Class, An Insider's Report.* New York: Doubleday.

Vujacic, Veljko. 1990. "The Dual Revolution of Citizenship and Nationhood in Eastern Europe." University of California, Berkeley.

Walder, Andrew. 1986. *Communist Neo-Traditionalism: Work and Authority in Chinese Industry.* Berkeley: University of California Press.

Weber, Max. [1922] 1978. *Economy and Society: An Outline of Interpretive Sociology.* 2 vols. Berkeley: University of California Press.

Winiecki, Jan. 1990. "Obstacles to Economic Reform of Socialism: A Property-Rights Approach." *Annals of the American Academy of Political and Social Science,* no. 507 (January): 65–71.

Zaslavskaya, Tatyana. 1984. "The Novosibirsk Report." *Survey* 28(1): 88–108.

Zaslavsky, Victor. 1991. "Rossiia na puti k rynku." *Politicheskie Issledovanie,* no. 5: 65–79.

Reveal and Dissimulate: A Genealogy of Private Life in Soviet Russia

Oleg Kharkhordin

INTRODUCTION

IN THE SUMMER OF 1926 a student of the Leningrad Mining Academy named Davidson committed suicide. There was enough evidence to suppose that her partner in "civil marriage," Konstantin Korenkov, also a student of the same academy, was the reason for her suicide. Over the preceding year he had continuously humiliated her, calling her names like "rabble" and "Jewish creep," discussed with his friends his sexual relations with other women in her presence, and locked her up in their dorm room when she was a nuisance (such as when she was bleeding after one of three consecutive abortions). The day she committed suicide, Korenkov told Davidson that he was leaving for the Crimea to spend a summer vacation alone: why did he need her there when he had other women to meet? He left a loaded revolver in the top drawer of the desk and went down into the dorm's backyard to play soccer.

Said a witness:

> I have known Korenkov and Davidson since 1925. . . . I am not aware of the details of their family life, but I heard from others that they did not do very well together. On the day Davidson died, before the shot sounded, we were playing ball, and Korenkov was among the players. When we finished, we parted, and in half an hour I was told that Davidson had shot herself. Initially I did not believe it, and as they live upstairs and I live downstairs, I did not even go to check it out.[1]

Research and writing of this essay were supported by an SSRC/MacArthur Foundation Fellowship on Peace and Security in a Changing World. The author would also like to thank David Woodruff and Jeff Weintraub for their help in the editing of this manuscript.

1. Sofia Smidovich, "O Korenkovshchine" (On Korenkovism) [1926], in the edited volume by A. A. Guseinov, M. V. Iskrov, and R. V. Petropavlovskii, *Partiinaia etika: Dokumenty i materialy diskussii dvadtsatykh godov* (Party Ethics: Documents and Materials of the Party Discussion of the 1920s) (Moscow: Politizdat, 1989), p. 382. All translations from Russian not otherwise attributed, including this one, are mine.

Korenkov could not be put on trial for murder. However, the local Komsomol (Young Communist League) cell, of which he was a member, excluded him from both Komsomol and the Party on the grounds "of moral responsibility for the suicide of a comrade." The district Party Control Commission overruled this decision as too harsh a punishment, and substituted a "severe reprimand and warning" for it.

Shortly thereafter, in June 1926, Korenkov and his younger brother staged a holdup of the cashier's office of the Mining Academy. They heavily wounded the cashier and stabbed his wife to death. The brothers needed money for a vacation in the Crimea.

These two related episodes did not surprise many readers of newspapers at the time: 1926 was a year filled with press reports of such crimes as dismemberment and group rape. However, Sofia Smidovich, a former chairwoman of Zhenotdel, the section of the Party's Central Committee that was specifically set up to deal with problems of women's liberation, chose this story as representative of the most serious illness that was corrupting the body social in 1926.

Of course, she was appalled by the way Korenkov had treated his wife; of course, she linked his gangster behavior to this treatment. But the peculiar thing about her article was that these aspects were not its central concern: Smidovich wanted to expose a specific type of social illness she called "Korenkovism." The most dangerous feature of Korenkovism, she wrote, was that

> young people who encounter him [Korenkov] every day and watch his relations with poor Davidson, who perceive his unbelievable rudeness, cynicism and humiliation of her, do not react to this fact at all and ostracize him only after the commission twice rules him guilty of Davidson's death.

Smidovich finds the essence of Korenkovism in this nonchalant reaction of the dormitory inhabitants to their neighbors' private lives, the sphere where dark and ominous forces lurk:

> The private life *[lichnaia zhizn']* of my comrade is not of my concern. The students' collective watches how Korenkov locks up his sick, literally bleeding wife—well, this is his private life. He addresses her only with curse words and humiliating remarks—nobody interferes. What's more: in Korenkov's room a shot resounds, and a student whose room is one floor beneath does not even think it necessary to check out what's going on. He considers it a private affair *[lichnoe delo]* of Korenkov and Davidson.[2]

2. Smidovich, "On Korenkovism," p. 383.

What is interesting here is that Smidovich, the Bolshevik Feminist par excellence, chooses to focus not so much on the case's manifest misogyny as on the parlous condition of the collective that does not interfere in private lives. What is most serious is that the collective is tainted: it watches everything, as all the drama takes place in public sight, but it does not react. Consequently, what Smidovich is trying to cure is not the way men treat women, but the way individual lives are to be handled by the collective.

One should not simply denounce Smidovich, bringing in the judgment of a different epoch and a different society. Our task is to understand the intertwining of public and private life in Soviet Russia as it is represented, for instance, in Smidovich's fears and Korenkov's actions. And, as the later exposition will show, the Korenkov case is important because it not only exemplified, but was also instrumental in, the formation of the specifically Soviet configuration of public and private life.

To understand the long-term process by which this configuration emerged, however, we need to reconstruct the cultural practices that constituted the background for the episode just described. Bolshevism aimed, not merely to change institutions, but to radically transform everyday life and to create a new, morally redeemed individual—the much-celebrated "New Soviet Man." In fact, Soviet society did succeed in creating a new individual, though not precisely the one intended. The goal was to construct a new society that would make saintly zeal its central organizing principle; the result, the unfolding of which this essay will trace, was a society whose key constitutive practice was a pervasive and, in the long run, increasingly cynical dissimulation. In order to grasp the logic of both this curious project and its denouement, we must begin at the root—which means, ultimately, with the religious roots of the Russian Revolution of 1917.

THE BOLSHEVIK REFORMATION

CONCEIVING BOLSHEVISM AS A religion is hardly novel for Russian studies. Nikolai Berdiaev, an émigré Russian philosopher, gave a classic rendition of the thesis. According to him, Bolsheviks channeled the religious energy of the Russian people to suit Bolshevik aims, and in so doing became the malignant outcome of the benign millennial development of the Russian Orthodox Church. The Bolsheviks' facade of atheism should not deceive an astute observer, for it covers up the essentially religious mechanisms that explain the advent and dynamics of Communism in Russia.[3]

---

3. Nikolai Berdiaev, *Istoki i smysl russkogo kommunizma* (The Origins and Meaning of Russian Communism) (Paris: YMCA, 1955).

Berdiaev was pointing at the bedrock of Soviet civilization, but he did not concentrate on the change in Orthodox religious practices that the Bolsheviks inaugurated. This change, however, lies at the heart of Bolshevik successes and is similar to what another renowned Russian thinker, Pavel Miliukov, described as a transition from "ritualized piety towards the religion of the soul."[4] In his study of religious sectarianism in Russia during the eighteenth and nineteenth centuries, Miliukov outlined what he saw as a central feature of "spiritual progress" at this time: the change from mass ritual worship (the essence of traditional Orthodoxy) towards a deep individual belief, which was characteristic of the sectarians. I will hold that the same transformation occurred in Bolshevik conversions: a fervent individual belief replaced the stale sacramental piety of Orthodoxy.

Therefore, it would seem quite plausible to compare the Bolshevik revolution in Russia with the Puritan Reformation in England. Michael Walzer was first to outline the similarities in the radical politics presented by the two cases, and my argument will be greatly indebted to his study.[5] However, I will specifically concentrate on one aspect in which they seem analogous that is marginal to Walzer's brilliant analysis.

Both "revolutions of the saints" involved the transformation of collective belief in sacramental rituals into deep individual faith in a professed discursive doctrine. Although the discursive articulations employed in the Puritan and Bolshevik Reformations seem to be radically opposite, the former being formulated in religious and the latter in starkly atheistic terms, the changes in practice that the majority of the "reformed" experienced were similar. First, a believer was expected to renounce any mediation between himself or herself and higher truth. This truth was contained in a special body of texts, available to everybody for interpretation. Second, the acute individualization of belief was based on individual revelation and conversion. Third, neither Puritan nor Bolshevik "individualism" of belief led to respect for privacy.

The last similarity is most important for the present argument. The "sacred" character of the private space, which originated in what Steven Lukes calls the "mystical individualism" of Saint Augustine and Luther, was alien to both Puritans and Bolsheviks. For Lutherans, privacy was sacred because

---

4. Pavel Miliukov, *Ocherki po istorii russkoi kultury,* vol. 2, *Tserkov i Shkola* (St. Petersburg, 1897), p. 93; published in English-language translation as Paul Miliukov, *Outlines of Russian Culture* (Philadelphia: University of Pennsylvania Press, 1942).

5. See Michael Walzer, *The Revolution of the Saints: A Study in the Origins of Radical Politics.*

this was the realm where communion with God took place.[6] On the contrary, writes Michael Walzer,

> Puritan individualism never led to a respect for privacy. . . . Puritan zeal was not a private passion; it was instead a highly collective emotion and it imposed upon the saints a new and impersonal discipline. . . . Tender conscience had its rights, but it was protected only against the interference of worldlings, and not against "brotherly admonition."[7]

Almost the same obtains for Bolshevism. To understand how individualism—of a certain kind—and total disrespect for privacy coexisted in Bolshevism, one should take a closer look at the origins of the Bolshevik individual. The paradigmatic process in the formation of a Bolshevik individual is conversion to fanatical faith in the revealed Doctrine. The central practice of this conversion is captured by the Russian word *oblichenie*.

BOLSHEVIKS REVEALING AND REVEALED

OBLICHENIE IS THE CENTRAL term of *What Is to Be Done?* Usually translated as "exposure" by interpreters who assume that the secular meaning of the word was primary for Lenin, this word can also be translated as "revelation."[8] The word is crucial for the third chapter of this Bolshevik manifesto, which discusses the differences between Bolshevik and traditional trade-unionist politics. The word *oblichenie* is repeated so often that it provides the chapter with a certain rhythm. The refrain is the same: the objective of the Bolshevik party of the new type is "to organize political revelation."

First of all, Lenin opposes *oblichenie* to mere discussion and explanation. Explanations do not suit Bolshevik aims, according to Lenin; rather "agitation," which will arouse workers' passions on the basis of the revealed truth of exploitation, is needed.[9] A little later, in a characteristic excerpt, imaginary workers demand from revolutionary intellectuals that the truth of the crimes of government be *revealed* to them in a "vivid" way, not simply communicated:

> You intellectuals can acquire this [political] knowledge and it is your *duty* to bring it to us in a hundred- and thousand-fold greater measure than you have done up to now; and you must bring it to us not only

6. Steven Lukes, *Individualism*, p. 61.
7. Walzer, *Revolution of the Saints*, pp. 12, 301.
8. Vladimir Lenin, "What Is to Be Done?" [1902], in *Collected Works* (Moscow: Progress Publishers, 1964), vol. 4. (All quotations from Lenin will follow this translation, except that *oblichenie* will be translated as "revelation.")
9. Lenin, "What Is to Be Done?" pp. 400–401.

in the form of discussions, pamphlets and articles (which very often—pardon our frankness—are rather dull), but precisely in the form of vivid *revelations* of what our government and our governing classes are doing at this very moment in all spheres of life. *Devote more zeal* to carrying out this duty and talk less about "raising the activity of the working masses." [10]

Second, the mechanism of *oblichenie* is very simple. A Bolshevik propagandist reveals the crimes of the governing classes to the workers by positing a certain Truth beyond appearances; she or he reveals the vile intentions of the powers that be and the reality of class domination, which are presented according to Marxist doctrine. The reality revealed is not the apparent, everyday, proximate reality of the given factory that the worker experiences; rather, this is Reality as it functions in the world religions, the *ens realissimum*.[11] This Reality, which is not and cannot be directly perceived by the senses, becomes the Higher and Indisputable Reality which is available to the mind's eye in the inner light of Revelation. The Reality revealed in accordance with the Word—this is what a worker should receive from a Bolshevik. But, laments Lenin, an average worker still does not get it in 1902:

> Why do the Russian workers still manifest little revolutionary activity?
> . . . We must blame ourselves, our lagging behind the mass movement, for still being unable to organize sufficiently wide, striking, and rapid revelations of all the shameful outrages. When we do that (and we must and can do it), the most backward worker will understand, or *will feel,* that the students and religious sects, the peasants and the authors are being abused and outraged by those same dark forces that are oppressing and crushing him at every step of his life. Feeling that, he himself will be filled with an irresistible desire to react, and he will know how to hoot the censors one day, on another day to demonstrate outside the house of the governor who brutally suppressed a peasant uprising, on still another day to teach a lesson to the gendarmes in surplices who are doing the work of the Holy Inquisition, etc. As yet we have done very little, almost nothing, to *bring* before the working masses prompt revelations on all possible issues.[12]

Third, workers are capable of local "revelations" that will uncover the injustices of a given factory manager or a shopfloor supervisor, but they are unable to link these local injustices to the Doctrine, which would recast them as local

10. Lenin, "What Is to Be Done?" p. 417 (in the last sentence, emphasis is added to the first three words and Lenin's emphases are omitted).

11. See Mircea Eliade, *The Sacred and the Profane.*

12. Lenin, "What Is to Be Done?" p. 414 (Lenin's emphases are retained).

appearances of a single profound injustice. This link is to be revealed by a Marxist propagandist. His or her role, then, is akin to the role of the "seditious ministers" whom Hobbes held to be among the causes of the Civil War in England. William Perkins, the father of Calvinist "covenant theology" in England, wrote in the 1580s, in his book *The Whole Treatise of the Cases of Conscience,* that the duty of the preacher was "to apply . . . the doctrines rightly collected [out of the text] to the life and manners of men in simple and plain speech." [13]

According to Robert C. Tucker, Stalin was drawn to Lenin precisely by this project of linking the everyday experiences of workers to the Marxist Word. The chief stock-in-trade of Stalin as revolutionary, writes Tucker, was an impressive knowledge of the fundamentals of Marxism and an ability to explain them very simply to ordinary workers. "[His] seminary experience gave him a catechistic approach to teaching and a facility for finding homely examples which must have been effective in his worker classes." [14] This "catechistic" style was frequently found in Stalin's later writings, too, which often consisted of short lists of concise dogmatic answers to explicitly posed basic questions.

Other parallels between Puritan ministers and Bolshevik propagandists immediately come to mind here. Both acquired the knowledge of the Doctrine by the "self-taught Word," which was then to be disseminated among the laity. Sermons were the most popular type of literature in sixteenth-century England;[15] the newspaper *Iskra* became the tribune for the clear and simple sermons emanating from Bolshevik ministers. Lenin explicitly uses the word *propoved'*, meaning "sermon" in Russian; translators secularize it into "speech" and "propaganda" in the English-language edition.[16] The activities of the Puritan laity—taking copious notes on the sermons and participating in Bible study groups—were replicated in the workers' Marxist study circles in Russia. But the primary importance of individual reading for conversion was indisputable for both: hence, the program to teach everybody to read (no matter what it cost) was essential to the so-called Cultural Revolution in Russia. Russian "seditious ministers" were to stop at nothing in the project of giving everybody the opportunity to become a "saint."

The title of Perkins's book suggests another overlooked parallel. The objective of Puritan and Bolshevik revelations was the acquisition of godly Con-

13. Quoted in Walzer, *Revolution of the Saints,* p. 145.
14. Robert C. Tucker, *Stalin as Revolutionary, 1879–1929: A Study in History and Personality,* p. 116.
15. Walzer, *Revolution of the Saints,* p. 146.
16. Lenin, "What Is to Be Done?" p. 430.

science, a direct knowledge *(conscientia)* of Higher Truth. Bearing this in mind, one can see that the familiar "spontaneity/consciousness" dialectic constituting the basic argument of *What Is to Be Done?* may be reinterpreted as progress from the state of the unenlightened chaotic soul to Higher Conscience, that is, as a process of conversion. By responding to revelations, a worker-Bolshevik overcomes the spontaneous, profane movements of his soul.

Later the narrative of the ascent to Bolshevik Conscience became what Katerina Clark calls the "masterplot of Socialist Realism." [17] This masterplot was repeated in *every* Socialist Realist novel: a disciple, under the guidance of the wise teacher, overcomes enormous difficulties, learns to control passions by doctrinal insight, and thus rises to Conscience. Clark notes that literary techniques employed in these novels were virtually identical to the techniques of nineteenth-century Russian hagiography. What she does not say is that the plot itself was a narrative of conversion, the endlessly reiterated narrative of Protestant literature.

The model of conversion and acquisition of Higher Conscience, as formulated by Lenin and later epitomized in Socialist Realism, had to be linked to mundane life; sacred Reality had to be grounded in profane reality. How was an individual to prove to him or herself that he or she had achieved Higher Conscience (and was not still responding to spontaneous instincts)? In other words, how was a Bolshevik individual to be sure of acquired grace?

Here another meaning of the word *oblichenie* comes to the fore, different from the one discussed so far—that is from *oblichenie* as an activity of Bolshevik propagandists. The classic dictionary of the nineteenth-century Russian language captures this meaning with the following example: "Deeds, and not words, reveal *[ob-lichaiut]* the man, demonstrate his real face *[litso]* and his self *[lichnost']*." [18] In a sense, human beings are endowed with a personality, or a self, by this self-revealing *oblichenie.* Of course, having established his or her own *lichnost'* (literally meaning "personality," but also a word for "self" in Russian), the individual may become capable of revealing the crimes of others according to the true doctrine—the currently predominant meaning of *oblichenie,* illustrated in the dictionary by examples such as the following: "Good Conscience likes revelations."

Thus, fundamentally, the self of a Bolshevik is revealed by his deeds. The way to arrive at the knowledge of one's true self, then, is not through inner light or meditation. One acquires one's self through public deeds which might be said to literally en-person *(ob-lichaiut),* to endow a body with a true self

17. See Katerina Clark, *The Soviet Novel: History as Ritual.*

18. Vladimir Dal', *Tolkovyi slovar zhivago velikorusskago iazyka* (Dictionary of the Living Russian Language), 5th edition (Moscow: Russkii Iazyk, 1980), vol. 3, p. 596.

or personality *(lichnost')*. This insistence on the knowledge of oneself through public deeds, on the reception of one's self in these deeds (actually, on being endowed with one's self through one's deeds, because you cannot actively obtain it), is not uniquely Bolshevist. It seems likely that the Bolsheviks took it over from the Orthodox practice of *oblichenie* through penance.

Michel Foucault opposed penance and confession as two possible ways of knowing oneself in Christianity. In his sketch of the origins of the Western individual (which was to be developed in the unpublished volume 4 of the *History of Sexuality*), Foucault claimed that in the West confession eclipsed penance as the practical way to know oneself. Confession, introduced by Cassian, came to predominate in the West after a lengthy period of historical development. Once confessional practices merged with the fictional object called "sex" in the eighteenth century, Western individuals were produced as "deep subjects" who posit their secrets by confessions on matters of sex.[19]

However, the practice of penance, outlined by Tertullian and described by Foucault as one of the abandoned ways of knowing oneself in the West, seems to have survived as central in Orthodox Russia. Tertullian uses the phrase *publicatio sui* to designate the way a penitent knows him or herself. Only in going public, in publicizing one's self in public penance, can one know it: the self is constituted by this special kind of deed. Thus, Foucault writes:

> The acts by which [a penitent] knows himself must be indissociable from the acts by which he reveals himself. . . . Penance in the first Christian century is a way of life acted out at all times by an obligation to show oneself. . . . The Tertullian expression, *publicatio sui,* is not a way to say the sinner has to expose his sins. The expression means that he has to present himself as a sinner in his reality of being a sinner. [Why?] The showing forth of the sinner should be efficient to efface the sins.[20]

A penitent in a public ritual revealed his or her true self to the community, and in so doing liberated himself or herself from the sins and, in a sense, acquired a new true self, imbued with Conscience. Later, says Foucault, this practice of showing one's self by public penance contributed to the model of knowing oneself through public martyrdom.

I would suggest that this model constituted the bedrock of Russian civilization for ages. The examples are numerous and range from "holy fools in the

19. See Michel Foucault, *The History of Sexuality,* vol. 1, *Introduction.*

20. Michel Foucault, "Truth and Subjectivity" (transcript of the Howison Lectures delivered October 20–21, 1980, in the Howison Library of the University of California, Berkeley).

glory of God" to revolutionary martyrs. All make a specific claim to know truth *(pravda)* about themselves and the world. Originally the holy fools, who underwent castigation and self-humiliation in public, were the sole possessors of the truth. Afterwards, the Christian hero of Russian Orthodoxy, a saint who knows himself not through private confession but through public penance, was taken over by the Bolsheviks, who remolded the religious practices of *publicatio sui* to suit the new aim, that is, to reveal a Bolshevik atheist individual.

This individual may now know himself or herself through revolutionary martyrdom, or—in less heroic situations—through public display of deeds that reveal Higher Conscience. The emphasis on deeds and not words to judge a person is common to both Lenin and Stalin. Lenin stated it clearly in his first major work, *Who Are the "Friends of the People," and How Do They Fight against Social Democrats?* Stalin reinforced it, by casting it as the only "correct" way to know one's self, in his letter to the editors of the journal *Proletarskaia Revolutsiia* at the beginning of the 1930s. In discussing the disputed Bolshevism of Lenin, Stalin retorted to critics that no matter what personal documents might be found indicating that Lenin was a vacillating Bolshevik, he proved by his revolutionary deeds that he was not. And this proof by deeds was the ultimate truth, ruled Stalin.[21]

Two features of the Bolshevik constitution of *lichnost'* through *oblichenie*— that is, of constitution of the self through revealing deeds—are extremely important for us.

First, a Bolshevik may know himself or herself only through the eyes of the relevant public, which is primarily the Party. Thus, she or he may get an assurance of righteous behavior, which is indicative of the Higher Conscience, only from the Party. Therefore, disciplined obedience to the Party's will becomes essential to a given Bolshevik's assurance of grace. This obedience may or may not reveal the Conscience to the public, but discipline is an essential condition of entry into the realm of virtuous and saintly living.

One of the most saintly of Bolsheviks, Soltz, asserted that voluntary submission to Party discipline was the primary virtue of a Bolshevik:

> What is the difference between our discipline and the discipline of a military barracks . . . which kills every initiative and lively creative thought? Our discipline is voluntary, as the Party is also a voluntary union of persons, who may leave it at any time. We are a voluntary army which pursues a certain objective and wages war by common

---

21. Joseph Stalin, "O nekotorykh voprosakh istorii Bolshevisma" (Concerning Some Questions of the History of Bolshevism) [1931], in *Voprosy Leninizma* (Problems of Leninism) (Moscow: Gospolitizdat, 1952).

effort. The consciousness of this gives us moral satisfaction when we obey the Party, even while disagreeing with this or that decision.[22]

Second, if a Bolshevik self is constituted in and by the public gaze, then by definition it cannot be secret. It is all and always on display, because only by means of this display, in *publicatio sui,* can a Bolshevik self exist at all. This condition has far-reaching consequences. The Bolshevik self, contrary to the liberal self, cannot be meaningfully defended "against the encroachments of the public," because it exists only in the eyes of this public. *Lichnost'* is formed by *oblichenie,* and this *lichnost'* is what is always seen to be revealed to the public.

Consequently, *lichnaia zhizn'* (which is usually translated as "private life") is subject to constant public gaze also: only in the whole totality of one's deeds is the true *lichnost'* manifested. Hence one cannot close *lichnaia zhizn'* off; for a Bolshevik self closing off is absurd, because obstacles to a public (that is, Party) gaze would lead exactly to the inability of a Bolshevik self to emerge. A translation of *lichnaia zhizn'* as "private life" is thus misleading in important respects, and can give rise to serious confusions. The underlying meaning of *lichnaia zhizn'* helps explain the Bolshevik insistence—which seems both absurd and unacceptable from the liberal perspective—on the need for the "public" to keep "private" life under constant surveillance (and for the "private" to be exposed to the public gaze).

After the revolutionary public became institutionalized in the revolutionary state, this state had the complete right to interfere in the "private" lives of Bolsheviks; indeed, it was obliged to interfere in order to correct or prevent those deeds that were not representative of the Higher Conscience. Therefore, interference was the duty of a revolutionary public, embodied in the state; noninterference was appropriate only when everything was fine, and there was no need to interfere in the private life of a Bolshevik.

LICHNAIA ZHIZN' AND *CHASTNAIA ZHIZN'*

HOWEVER, THE RUSSIAN LANGUAGE has a second term, *chastnaia zhizn',* which is also usually translated as "private life." This phrase bears the connotation of partiality, as *chast'* means "a part of something" and *chastnyi interes* means "partial interest." If *lichnaia zhizn'* is subject to an ever-present public gaze, then *chastnaia zhizn'* is not necessarily so and may possibly be closed off from the public or even counterpoised to it. These two types of "private life" experienced different fates in Soviet Russia. If *lichnaia zhizn'* was continu-

22. A. A. Soltz, "O partiinoi etike" (On Party Ethics) [1924], in Guseinov, Iskrov, and Petropavlovskii, eds., *Partiinaia etika,* p. 265.

ously fostered by the regime and was subject to its unending care—and intrusive attention—then *chastnaia zhizn'* was fought and almost discursively assassinated. The largest Russian dictionary, published in the 1950s and 1960s, registered this near death.

All the examples of usage of *chastnyi* are connected with the prerevolutionary life that was swept away after 1917. "Private household," "private stipend," "private service," and "private philanthropy" all fell out of usage once the core of this sphere, private property *(chastnaia sobstvennost')*, was abolished by the Bolsheviks. In the section on *chastnyi* one finds only one example of a post-1917 usage, which, not surprisingly, pertains primarily to life abroad: "He had a salary of a head physician in the cantonal sanatorium. He had a private practice." [23]

The dictionary's examples of *lichnyi* cover a broader range. For example, it quotes the head of the Soviet government, Kalinin, who tells us that the Constitution "obliges us to care for public property, to put common interests ahead of private, individual ones *[stavit' obshchie interesy vyshe lichnykh]."* Then an example from the years of the Second World War states that "the private became public *[lichnoe stalo gosudarstvennym]*, anxiety for the fate of the motherland entered the hearts of Soviet people, and fused their ranks." The final example of usage belongs to the postwar years: "Perhaps, because Rudakov always hid his private life *[svoyo lichnoe]* so thoroughly, it was strange to see him in the role of a caring husband and a loving father." [24]

The very complicated entanglement of *obshchii/obshchestvennyi/gosudarstvennyi/lichnyi/chastnyi/individualnyi* (these are often translated into English as either "public" or "private," though they originally mean, respectively: common/social/state/personal/partial/ individual) still awaits an avid and careful student. For the time being I will concentrate only on the distinction between *lichnyi* and *chastnyi*.

For the sake of conceptual clarity, I will translate *lichnyi* as "personal" and *chastnyi* as "private" in the following exposition. *Lichnaia zhizn'* will be translated as "personal life" to signify the specifically Bolshevik sense attributed to it after the revolution: that is, life which does not involve official organizations, but is (ideally) as demonstrative of the Bolshevik personality as official life. *Chastnaia zhizn'* will be translated as "private life" to signify the way of life, related to private property, which the Bolsheviks fought and almost vanquished.

One should not forget, nevertheless, that the two together constitute what

23. *Slovar' sovremennogo russkogo literaturnogo iazyka* (Dictionary of Contemporary Russian Literary Language) (Moscow: Institut Russkogo Iazyka, 1955–68), 17:779.

24. *Dictionary of Contemporary Russian Literary Language,* 6:298.

is commonly referred to as "private life" in everyday English usage—that is, life within a family or with friends, and more generally life outside the realm of public duties and public organizations. I will try to trace the development of "private life" in Soviet Russia, keeping in mind both the public/private distinction in English and the *lichnyi/chastnyi* distinction in Russian.

A DRIVE FOR COMRADELY ADMONITION

IN THE COUNTRY WHERE the Bolshevik saintly individuals had finally gained power, the majority of the population was not saintly at all. More than that, this majority threatened to contaminate the saintly purity of the party ranks. A special body, the Party Control Commission, took over the function of estimating what appertained to the saintly conscience of a party member. The question of saintly behavior in mundane situations was the most difficult to resolve: what were the standards representative of higher conscience in such matters as sex, clothes, everyday contacts with neighbors, and the like?

While a "debate on party ethics," aimed at establishing these standards, proceeded in 1923–26, the humble Party members reported their "corrupt" comrades to the Central Control Commission (CCC). Comradely investigations were staged, which resulted in suspensions and exclusions from the Party. However, the leaders of the CCC were completely unsatisfied by the results of the campaign. The very establishment of an internal Party vice squad, according to them, was something abnormal. How could it be normal for a comrade, asked Soltz, one of the chairmen of the CCC, to bring another comrade before a Party prosecution, instead of influencing the faltering comrade into righteous conduct by comradely advice and admonition *(tovarishcheskoie uveshchevanie)?* He asserted:

> If, for example, your brother or your wife, your close friend makes a mistake, I am sure that you don't summon him immediately to the C[ontrol] C[ommission], but you try to resolve the problem among yourselves, because it would be strange if a son brought his father to the CC or to judicial prosecution.[25]

Soltz, a professional revolutionary since 1898, had in mind a romantic model to be reestablished: the tight comradely unity of the underground Bolshevik sect, which allegedly existed before the Revolution. Now this unity was diluted by the arrival of many new Party members, who represented "raw material" not tempered by the harsh conditions of underground discipline. But perhaps the reestablishment of this discipline could recreate the lost unity.

25. A. A. Soltz, "O partetike" (On Party Ethics) [1925], in Guseinov, Iskrov, and Petropavlovskii, eds., *Partiinaia etika*, p. 278.

Now, with the underground conditions gone, this discipline had to be imposed by what Soltz called "public opinion."

This opinion, Soltz clarified further, would be akin to the "aristocratic opinion" which had earlier made impossible the marriage of an aristocrat and a peasant; this opinion would ensure discipline and the conscientious behavior of Party members without any quasi-judicial bodies. Soltz not only advocated it, he tried to create it in fact. Many of his speeches simply recounted the points made in the official resolutions of the CCC. Soltz added nothing new to the content of the resolutions, but he specifically stressed that he was trying to establish "public opinion" on the righteous conduct.

In some sense, Soltz was a good self-conscious Austinian. He consistently repeated that his objective was communicating not simply locutionary meaning, but also illocutionary and perlocutionary effects. The refrain of his speeches is always the same:

> Comrades! Before everything else, I would like to tell you that on the question of party ethics we should have discussions instead of listening to reports with corresponding resolutions. . . . This is, comrades, what I wanted to tell you. It is extremely important that we exchange opinions here today, because we should create public opinion and not listen to reports.[26]

One has reasons to think of Soltz's "public opinion" as closer to Locke's "Law Of Opinion" than to Habermas's "critical publicity."[27] The mechanism of Soltz's "public opinion" is the mechanism of traditional family mores or of "aristocratic opinion," given and not reflected upon. Emelian Iaroslavskii, another co-chairman of the CCC, summed it up in the following manner: "We must constantly watch such vacillating comrades, and when we see the tiniest signs of danger threatening this comrade, we should warn him, help him get out of this situation."[28]

Mutual surveillance, construed as brotherly help, was not a novel Bolshevik invention. The congregation of Puritan saints, according to Walzer, also preserved the purity of individual conscience by means of the mutual control of its members. Thus, two Puritan theologians, Field and Wilcox, wrote in *The First Admonition to the Parliament* that a congregation was held together by

> "an order left by God onto his Church, whereby men learn to frame their wills and doings according to the law of God by *instructing* and

26. Soltz, "O partetike," pp. 273, 292.
27. See Jürgen Habermas, *The Structural Transformation of the Public Sphere.*
28. Emelian Iaroslavskii, "O partetike" (On Party Ethics), in Guseinov, Iskrov, and Petropavlovskii, eds., *Partiinaia etika,* p. 175.

admonishing one another, yea, and by correcting and punishing all willful persons and contemners of the same." . . . In his Kidderminster parish, Baxter reported, the enforcement of the moral discipline was made possible "by the zeal and diligence of the godly people of the place, who thirsted after the salvation of their neighbors, and were in private my assistants."[29]

This combination of mutual surveillance and private conscience, which Baxter reports, was not such an easy and "natural" achievement in the 1920s in Russia. However, as more and more workers and peasants joined the Party and moved upward, they contributed to the installation of mutual surveillance within the Party, first by bringing into the new milieu their traditional mutual control techniques, and second by providing a solid pretext for its installation. When a worker or a peasant became a Soviet or Party official, certain behaviors and comportments, which were heretofore fully accessible to the gaze of, and tolerated by, his or her peers, suddenly became intolerable for a Party member, and even more so for an official. These behaviors and comportments became a "personal" issue, which was indicative not only of individual corruption, but in some cases of a social illness as well.

The Korenkov case, described in the beginning of this essay, is representative of this transition. It combines all the essential elements involved in transition to the system of comradely admonition to prevent the corruption of conscience. First, certain comportments are becoming suspect. Mistreating one's wife became highly dubious for a Party member, though such beating up and physical humiliation were accepted in both workers' and peasants' families. As any misdemeanor was revealing of the corruption of the whole Bolshevik *lichnost'*, Korenkov's relation to his wife was an early sign of his corruption. This corruption was amply proved later, by his gangster assault; but the initial signs were demonstrative enough. Second, the means to be employed are implied. Smidovich clearly advocated the introduction of comradely admonition; she pronounced the students' community ill because it failed to provide such admonition. In fact, mutual surveillance already existed as everything happened in the public gaze, but there were no conscientious individuals to warn and admonish Korenkov before it was too late.

In characterizing Korenkovism as a typical social illness, Smidovich provides a second example of it. A certain Morgunov used his official position (as an employment instructor in a trade union) for sexual pleasures. He granted employment assignments to young women only after they agreed to have sex with him. One of the victims refused to have sex when she was brought into

29. Walzer, *Revolution of the Saints,* pp. 220, 221 (Walzer's emphasis).

a dirty basement in Moscow, so he raped her. Having been summoned to the preliminary investigation bodies, Morgunov denied the rape, but did not deny that

> having met her in the district office of the trade union as a teenager for whom he, according to his professional obligations, was supposed to find employment, he engaged in sexual intercourse with her and did not attach "much significance to this fact as one which could produce excessive talk and suspicion; he considered it his personal affair." [30]

The worker Morgunov did not see an issue here. He had presumably tried sexual relations with women before, in workers' dorms in the full sight of his comrades, and it did not produce suspicion. He had behaved according to traditional patriarchal mores which prescribe subjugating a resisting female to an aggressive male, and these mores did not give rise to excessive talk. He did the same in this case, and now honestly could not understand how a workers' state could punish him for such a trifle. Once again, if there had been a comrade to admonish and instruct Morgunov before he slipped from sexual license into criminal rape, corruption would never have occurred.

Until 1926, however, appeals to introduce comradely admonition in the Party and Soviet organizations were largely wishful thinking. Smidovich's articles signified the beginning of the new effort to introduce it seriously. The Chubarov Affair of 1926 marked a watershed. In discussing it I will follow the argument of the recent dissertation of Eric Naiman on the Soviet sexual debates of the 1920s.

To cut a long story short: twenty-four workers raped one peasant woman in Leningrad. Eight of the rapists were Young Communist League members, two were Party candidates. Vivid details of the story filled the pages of newspapers, creating a popular demand that the criminals, who were characterized in biological terms, as a lower species—"loathsome reptiles," and so on—be killed. As there was no adequate punishment for the crime of group rape to satisfy the popular sentiment (eight years of imprisonment was the maximum), prosecutors charged them with banditry, so that their subsequent conviction resulted in a death sentence for eight of the rapists. [31]

The campaign immensely heightened attention to the personal lives of Bolshevik believers. Although "the rural world saw and tolerated for some time

30. Smidovich, "On Korenkovism," p. 385.
31. Eric Naiman, "Sexuality and Utopia: The Debate in the Soviet 1920s" (Ph.D. dissertation, University of California, Berkeley, 1991).

violent group rape" in Russia before the 1920s, according to Moshe Lewin,[32] once peasants had moved into the city and become Party members, the Bolshevik congregation could not tolerate it at all. The dangerous transgression of rape testified to a degree of inner corruption in the Party of the saints, in comparison to which the corruption of the students' dorm (of which Smidovich complained) seemed innocent.

The most remarkable consequence of the incident was an article by Iaroslavskii, which appeared in *Smena* in October 1926. The article demanded that every communist cell must know what happened in the home lives of the Party and Komsomol members to eliminate dangerous potentialities before they became crimes. Every conscientious Communist should watchfully control the details of the sexual lives of his or her comrades, unless the party wanted such an affair to happen again. By 1927, according to Naiman, sex had become "a constant topic of non-debate." It was talked about but it was not debated, the party line being clear on these matters. Sex became a dangerous area where the impulses most corrupting to the higher conscience resided.

How did the majority of the Party members react to this dangerous linking of sex with political corruption? This majority, who were not part of the initial sect of the Bolshevik saints, but only recently recruited, had to respond somehow. Heretofore they could be moderately licentious, and change or combine partners. Irresponsible males could abandon their pregnant females or push them in the direction of suicide. But after 1927 the environment was no longer the same.

Here lies the origin of a second crucial practice constitutive of the Soviet individual. If the initial Bolshevik saint was constituted by conversion based on revelation *(oblichenie)*, then the Party members who joined the Bolshevik congregation later were predominantly formed by dissimulation *(litsemerie)*. Faced with the installation of an all-pervasive mutual surveillance within the congregation, they had to hide certain comportments from fellow comrades. And since these latecomers were the vast majority, dissimulation became the dominant practice of individualization in Soviet Russia.

Ken Jowitt has grasped this peculiarity of what he calls Leninist regimes, in which, he says, dissimulation ties public and private together.[33] However, for entities to be integrated in a dissimulative structure, they must exist in the first place. Jowitt appears to assume that dissimulation is used to shield a pregiven "private" life from official surveillance and interference. In contrast,

32. Moshe Lewin, *The Making of the Soviet System,* p. 55.
33. Ken Jowitt, *New World Disorder: The Leninist Extinction,* p. 72.

my contention would be that this "private" sphere was itself created by Leninist regimes, and dissimulation was the practice that established it. Dissimulation, therefore, would appear not as a derivative of a split between public and private (between *obschchestvennoe* and *chastnoe*) in Leninist regimes, but as a central practice constitutive of this split.

The workers and peasants moving into Party and Soviet offices, which were now filled with comradely vigilance, immediately learned the dubiousness of certain conducts, which they had to conceal both at work and at home. The practice of dissimulation not entirely new, but its form was now radically recast. As Michel Confino has shown,[34] collective dissimulation was practiced by Russian peasants against their feudal masters and the tsar's officials for ages. This dissimulation did not substantially differ from similar "weapons of the weak" as found, for example, in a contemporary Malaysian village:[35] the weak of the peasant world collectively practice dissimulation against the strong. The novel aspect of Bolshevik dissimulation was that it was primarily practiced individually against the members of the peer group, not collectively against superiors. This dissimulation was also different from the "theatrical presentation of the self" in everyday Western life[36] in that it was not secondary to the already existing individual self; on the contrary, Soviet dissimulation was instrumental in constructing the Soviet individual.

The new Bolsheviks now individualized themselves primarily by dissimulation, and this aspect is better captured in the etymology of the word *pritvorstvo* than of the word *litsemerie* (both mean "dissimulation" in English, though *litsemerie* is sometimes translated as "hypocrisy"). The latter literally means "the changing of faces" (a later stage in the genealogy of a dissimulating individual), while the former comes from the Church-Slavonic verb *pritvoriati*, meaning both to dissimulate and to close oneself, as in "to close the door" or in "to close oneself off." Peasants who became workers who became Bolshevik officials had to close themselves off from the comradely congregation; they started to individualize themselves by this practice of closure. They retracted certain parts of their conduct from the public gaze, and these parts constituted the almost completely invisible, most private spheres of their lives. This retraction of dubious conduct into the ultimate and safest privacy became registered in the 1930s and 1940s as the phenomenon of the Great Retreat.

34. See Michael Confino, *Société et mentalités collectives en Russie sous l'ancien régime*.
35. See James C. Scott, *Weapons of the Weak: Everyday Forms of Peasant Resistance*.
36. See, for example, Erving Goffman, *The Presentation of Self in Everyday Life*.

Universalizing Sainthood

IN DISCUSSING THE POLITICAL entrepreneurship of the Puritan saints, Michael Walzer suggested that godly magistracy was a far better description of the saints' true vocation than either capitalist acquisition or bourgeois freedom. This magistracy centered on secular repression to reform manners, with the rationale that "the men who refused to govern themselves would have to be governed nevertheless—until, in effect, they could be forced to be free."[37] The legislative initiatives of Puritans in the English Parliament included the repression of beggary and usury, and prohibitions on bearbaiting, dancing, swearing, Sunday sports, church ales, and alcoholism. Having given an overview of all proposed measures to reform manners, Walzer concludes:

> The "reformation of manners" was, or rather would have been, had
> it ever taken place on the scale which the ministers intended, the Puri-
> tan terror. . . . The revolutionary effort to establish a holy common-
> wealth in England failed. The rule of the saints was brief; the new
> forms of repression were never enforced through the decisive activity
> of a state police. . . . The fearful Puritan demand for total, state-
> enforced repression was slowly forgotten . . . . [However,] who can
> doubt that, had the holy commonwealth ever been firmly established,
> godly self-discipline and mutual surveillance would have been far more
> repressive than the corporate system?[38]

Where saintly Puritans failed in England, saintly Bolsheviks succeeded in Russia. The Holy Commonwealth was established in the USSR after 1929 with all the related consequences. Moshe Lewin describes this development according to a classical scheme of Ernst Troeltsch: the Bolshevik sect was becoming a Church in order to universalize sainthood. The new dogma was represented in *The Short Course of the History of the Communist Party,* edited by Stalin; a laicized version of sins was adopted, and Inquisition (secret police) raged to stamp out the heresies and bring the guilty to confess their sins publicly. After the terror subsided, the quasi-religious civilization was formed: "the sacred borders" separated it from the rest of the profane world; Lenin's Commandments were its guiding light; the outwardly secular demonstrations and public ceremonies took on the role of religious rites.[39]

I would like to add to this account two other elements, often overlooked,

37. Walzer, *Revolution of the Saints,* p. 224.
38. Walzer, *Revolution of the Saints,* pp. 226, 230–31, 305.
39. Lewin, *The Making of the Soviet System,* p. 305.

which involved a major restructuring of everyday practices. A thrust to universalize sainthood meant that everybody was to become a Bolshevik saint. Thus, everybody had to be able to interpret sacred texts; and everybody was to behave in such a way that their deeds would be revealing of the Bolshevik *lichnost'*, imbued with higher conscience. Consequently, the changes in everyday practices included the reinvigorated emphasis on individual reading and the reformation of manners.

Individual reading became the universal way to participate in the affairs of the Bolshevik church-state. Vera Dunham, in her account of the Soviet "middlebrow fiction" of the 1930s and 1940s, notes that it provided a Soviet citizen with "ersatz participation":

> The topical novel of the moment proved one of the few ways of meeting the people's need to understand their society's major workaday problems. . . . Read by party leaders, by cultural luminaries, and their wives, as well as by high school students and housewives in small towns, and by factory and farm workers throughout the land, fiction, taken as if it were life, turned into a sort of town hall, a platform from which the system justified itself. . . . The novel substituted for the reader's sense of participation in the social processes.[40]

Participation in reading and interpreting sermons was the only initial participation allowed to the layman on the road to becoming a lay saint in Puritanism, and the Bolsheviks did not substantially differ from their counterparts. However, this participation was essential to the quasi-religious civilization. In a special resolution of the Central Committee on November 15, 1938, Stalin rebuked everybody who tried to substitute the ritualized public reading of *The Short Course* for intensive individual study. The "educative" Socialist Realist fiction was to play the role of sermon and additional commentary on the Word.

Another overlooked achievement of Stalinist terror was the imposition of a new moral order, which bound everybody by a uniform system of norms of everyday behavior—and which, once imposed, effectively controlled deviance without the need for all-pervasive terror. To impose it, however, a profound terror was required; the saints, with their zeal and lack of scruples about the use of violence, were very useful in the creation of this new moral order (even as they were consumed by the terror themselves).

The Reformation of Manners started once the victory of "socialism in one country" was proclaimed in 1934. If the Holy Commonwealth had already arrived, how could the Bolsheviks tolerate the unreformed around them? Dun-

40. Vera Dunham, *In Stalin's Time: Middleclass Values in Soviet Fiction*, p. 25.

ham describes the shift of emphasis from *kultura* to *kulturnost'*, from the deep spirituality of the intelligentsia to an outward appearance of civilized conduct, which started in the 1930s and culminated in the 1940s. *Kulturnost'*, according to Dunham, meant a "mere program for proper conduct in public"; it was based on a mechanism of "conforming with prescribed preferences." [41]

The Stalinist regime all of a sudden devoted intensive attention to everyday manners; "impeccable conduct," which meant manageable, predictable, proper manners, became the center of the propaganda campaign. Obsession with *kulturnost'*, a "fetish notion of how to be individually civilized," started with elite attention to personal hygiene, and then spread in "admonitory and educative" fashion to the whole society; clean nails, abstinence from cursing and spitting, and a minimum of good manners now defined the model citizen.

Nicholas Timasheff documents this change in his book *The Great Retreat*. He argues that after Stalin proclaimed in 1935 that life under socialism should be "beautiful and joyous," the original Bolshevik ascetic self-abnegation became suspect. *Komsomolskaia Pravda* now wrote:

> We endorse beauty, smart clothes, chic coiffures, manicures. . . . Girls should be attractive. Perfume and makeup belong to the "must" of a good Comsomol girl. . . . Clean shaving is mandatory for a Comsomol boy. [42]

Manners were constantly discussed and taught. Dancing schools were opened in 1935. Public carnivals started in 1936, where people could demonstrate the dancing skills they had learned; these carnivals contributed to a sense of fun which now seems macabre. A journal *Moda* (Fashion) appeared in 1935 also, to give guidance about good taste in dress. *The Book of Tasty and Healthy Food* was quick to follow, with quotations from Politburo member Anastas Mikoyan, who among many things advocated "moderate civilized drinking." This book became the bible of *kulturnost'*; possessed by every family, it gave unobtrusive advice not only on cooking, but on civilized manners in consuming food and on the appropriate social setting for this activity.

The inculcation of basic manners was not the sole objective of the "new moral order"; rather, it was concomitant to all the other changes that Timasheff has called the Great Retreat. With Communist experimentation in every realm of life abruptly curtailed, many "traditional" values of prerevolutionary Russia were restored. Thus, the alleged sexual license of the 1920s was replaced by an emphasis on marriage as the most serious affair in life; disrespect towards elders and superiors had to be punished immediately; "cultural revolution"

41. Dunham, *In Stalin's Time*, p. 22.
42. Quoted in Nicholas Timasheff, *The Great Retreat*, p. 317.

in the schools was reversed to restore the tsarist educational system, with its ranks and honors; in literature, art, and theater experimentation had to yield in favor of the popular taste for the understandable and recognizable.

Timasheff explained this radical and sudden "retreat" by the need to strengthen the social basis of dictatorship in the face of the coming war. Stalin was held to have set aside the initial projects of communist transformation in favor of consolidating the dictatorial system, appeasing substantial groups of the population, and securing the efficiency of national labor.[43] This may be true, but the complementary explanation holds also: all the measures that contributed to the Great Retreat follow the simple logic of a saintly dictatorship becoming a Holy Commonwealth. Thus, we should not take the imagery of "retreat" entirely at face value in quite as simple or straightforward a sense as Timasheff seems to understand it; for most of the population, the Great Retreat meant adopting profoundly new modes of activity, which marked a new stage in the Bolshevik Reformation.

For example, the reassertion of the "old-fashioned" type of family was completely logical from the standpoint of the saint. Even Calvin, who admonished his followers to break loose from the unclean bondage of Catholic marriage ties and get away from France into Geneva, advised them to marry upon arrival, so each man could become master of a reformed household which was to be structured like a little parish, on godly principles.[44] The same happened with Bolsheviks. They always had the aim of "shaking and restructuring the family," [45] that is, of breaking down the old bondage and building new families that were to become what Lenin's wife Nadezhda Krupskaia called "the union of equal comrades building Communism together." Before 1934 this was an option for conscientious Bolshevik saints; afterwards, when everybody was to become a lay saint or die, this became a must.

Hence, the novel emphasis on the conscientious *lichnaia zhizn'* of every Soviet person (who was soon to become a lay Bolshevik with the advent of the Holy Commonwealth) emerged. Yet, as sexual transgressions were now held to be indicative of the corruption of saintly conscience, the Great Retreat signified not a radical break with, but a continuation of, the developments of the 1920s: the saintly standards were now imposed on a greater society. And if only Communists initially had to withdraw their sexual behavior from the

43. Timasheff, *The Great Retreat*, p. 358.

44. Walzer, *Revolution of the Saints*, pp. 48–49.

45. Leon Trotsky, "S chego nachat" (How to Begin), *Pravda*, August 17, 1923; an English-language translation is provided in Leon Trotsky, *Problems of Everyday Life* (New York: Monad Press, 1973).

public gaze, now this was required from every Soviet citizen. All Soviet people had to appear outwardly to be imbued with Stalinist virtue in sexual conduct.

A more radical novelty was contained in the fact that everybody was now supposed to have *lichnaia zhizn'* (which many Russians did not have before, in the sense that home and family life had not been considered a problematic matter either for them or for the authorities), and simultaneously to abandon *chastnaia zhizn'* (if they ever had one). The two terms, almost synonymous until the 1930s, and virtually indistinguishable for the mass of the population because both were largely a nonissue, parted ways. *Lichnaia zhizn'* (that is, personal life) became one of those lawful terrains where Bolshevik *lichnost'* was to reveal itself; *chastnaia zhizn'* (that is, private life) was increasingly associated with corrupt behavior per se.

Two narratives from 1935 will clarify this pattern. The first one is from the Komsomol journal *Young Guard*. A model collective of young metro construction workers gathers in a dorm to discuss questions of love. In the "cozy room of 14 Komsomol girls" a phonograph is playing and cakes are served on the white tablecloth—signs of *kulturnost'*. (Note, however, that fourteen [!] women living in one room is still considered to be "good living conditions.") At first defenders of the now obsolete Bolshevik "free love" stance and of bourgeois privacy are rebuked; then the central disputation is waged between two model women.

Vera loves a man who consistently overfulfills the plan, but who turns out to be uncultured *(nekulturny):* she cannot talk with him about anything but production plans. Nadezhda makes a rejoinder: this is not the worst case. A *nekulturny* by birth may join a kolkhoz or a factory, get promoted, acquire higher education, and end up as a *kulturny* engineer or manager. The truly "uncultured" person is the one who dissimulates. Nadezhda had been the victim of one of these; he "deceived her, saying that he loved her when in fact he was married." In the end a secretary of the Komsomol organization, pressed to draw a general conclusion, reluctantly sets the "correct line" in family matters: "Our family has serious tasks, because one works well when personal life is organized and rightly adjusted *[nalazhena]*." [46]

This narrative yields some interesting conclusions. The first crucial feature of the debate is that everyone has a specific story from their *lichnaia zhizn'* to tell, which is a novel feature for the genre of the didactic story. Previously,

46. Galina Ancharova, "Diskussiia u Komsomoltsev Metro" (Discussion in the Metro Workers' Komsomol Organization), *Molodaia Gvardiia* (Young Guard) 14, no. 7 (July 1935): 162–66.

everybody would denounce a single transgressor, who had made his or her *lichnaia zhizn'* an object of specific public attention or an issue of public debate, as Morgunov or Korenkov did, for instance. Now everybody has his or her own *lichnaia zhizn'*, worthy of relating in public. The novelty of this condition is felt by almost everybody present: potential speakers are very nervous, and they keep their life stories, written on little sheets of paper, handy; this may help them overcome the confusion of telling the narrative of their *lichnaia zhizn'* for the first time in their lives. Second, the standards in personal life are no longer set by mutual surveillance, and the Soltz-Iaroslavskii model of comradely admonition is temporarily abandoned. While these standards may be enforced by the collective, they are now set by leaders. Third, this personal life is righteous only when it is *kulturny* and well organized. The primary corruption of personal life is represented by the figure of the dissimulator, who certainly should not be part of one's personal life.

Another narrative clearly links *chastnaia zhizn'* to corruption. A corrupting dissimulator has a *chastnaia zhizn'* as opposed to a righteous *lichnaia zhizn'*. In a characteristic article entitled "The Private Life of the Engineer Mirzoev," *Pravda* engages in a campaign against "fluttering scoundrels" of whom Mirzoev is a genuine representative. The narrative is simple. They met at 7 P.M. in the city park, at 9 they danced, at 11 they decided to marry, and the next day they consummated their marriage. On the morning after—surprise, surprise—the poor girl did not find Mirzoev next to her. He had fled. When she tried to locate him through state agencies, she found out that he was being sought by criminal prosecutors for having married six times already. *Pravda* did not weep over the girl's misfortune, but called for a demonstration trial of such Mirzoevs, who committed such sins in their private lives.[47]

After a gradually mounting campaign, *chastnaia zhizn'* was discursively assassinated in 1938 by no less figure than Zhdanov. The pretext was formidable: top members of the Komsomol Central Committee were dismissed and executed for "lordly neglect" of the everyday life of the rank and file Komsomol members, which allegedly resulted in the infiltration of student dorms by Trotskyites and Bukharinites. Zhdanov specifically underlined that enemies of the people

> found one of the weakest spots of Komsomol, that is, everyday life, and declared everyday life a "private affair." They tried to corrupt the Komsomol cadres by means of moral degradation: through alcoholism and false drunken camaraderie. . . . The Komsomol leaders [*aktiv*] should not live their lives apart from the masses, as they used to hereto-

47. *Pravda,* July 19, 1935.

fore. . . . They should interfere everywhere where young people spend their time, untiringly enlighten and organize them.[48]

The point was made clear: treating life away from the work site as "private life" was an enemy strategy; "private life" had no right to exist anymore. At the same time the "personal life" of every Soviet youth was to be subject to constant surveillance and organization. Commenting on the results of the recent purge of Komsomol leaders, *Komsomolskaia Pravda* reasserted in the editorial: "Everyday life is not a private affair, it is the most crucial zone of class struggle; everyday life is inseparable from politics; and people who are not honest in everyday life, who are morally depraved, are depraved politically." [49]

Vigilant leaders were to exterminate "private life" and to foster the "personal life" of the people. The Stalinist years pushed the role of the leader to the fore: he (almost always he and not she) was the vigilant shepherd, taking care of his flock. He had to have both a stick and a carrot; the absence of either smacked of "lordly neglect."

THE COMRADELY SOCIETY

BY LATE 1940S AND EARLY 1950s, however, the new Bolshevik standards had been instilled in the masses, and the leaders could now rest. Not only the new standards but the mechanism of mutual surveillance was finally in place, and the masses had become capable of policing themselves without the vigilant shepherd. With Khrushchev's coming to power, this mass vigilance comes to be seen as the primary mechanism of social cohesion. Every collectivity—and not only the party cell—is to be a congregation, based on constant mutual surveillance and the reform or punishment of transgressors. Thus, in 1958, an article in *Komsomolskaia Pravda* entitled "Is It Necessary to Interfere in Personal Life?" restated the now well-established ideological dictum that

> We live . . . in a socialist society where comradely and friendly relations have been substituted for the lupine laws of capitalism. And we cannot be indifferent to what is called personal life, personal relations, because in the final account these personal relations inevitably become public [obshchestvennymi].

But the best means of regulating personal life, as described in the article, consist of "comradely sensitivity" and the "heart-to-heart talk." In the "real story" that constitutes the main body of the article, these means are applied to stop

48. Andrei Zhdanov, "Rech' na Yubileinom Plenume TsK VLKSM" (Speech at the Jubilee Plenum of the Central Committee of Komsomol), *Komsomolskaia Pravda*, November 4, 1938.

49. *Komsomolskaia Pravda*, December 15, 1938.

the crumbling of a workers' family. A veteran rank-and-file Communist, a worker from the same factory named Vera Pavlovna (an allusion to Chernyshevsky?), goes to "talk" with the members of the family, and the problem is fixed in a day. What would have happened, asks *Komsomolskaia Pravda*, "if . . . comrades were to come to a sudden stop in front of the invisible gate bearing the strict inscription 'Personal Life'?"[50]

An important clue to the attitude behind this didactic tale lies in the fact that the Russian word translated as "public" in the quotation *(obschchestvennymi)* is more literally, and more properly, translated as "social." In fact, contemporary Russian usage barely employs the word *publika* (the most common reference is to the audience in the theater), which has a strong archaic connotation when it is used at all. The English word "public" is usually translated as *obshchestvo,* the same word that is most often used for "society" in Russian. While this might appear to be merely a linguistic accident, it actually points to some deeper conceptual issues, which can be illuminated by drawing on Hannah Arendt's distinction between "the public" and "the social."[51] Arendt's conception of the historical advent of "the social" seems to capture nicely many of the emerging features of Soviet life in the transition to the "benign" society of the period from the 1950s to the 1970s. Thus, one is led to suspect that *Sovetskoe obschestvo* was indeed regulated by mechanisms of a "social" rather than a genuinely "public" character—and that using the word "public" at all in the Soviet context is profoundly misleading, if not outrageously erroneous.

According to Arendt, the classical form of the public/private divide in the Western tradition marks the separation between a "public realm" of political action and critical discussion about common concerns and a "private realm" of legitimate privacy and particularism centered on the household.[52] These two spheres, while distinct, are also complementary and mutually supportive. A key feature of the modern age, however, is that this borderline has increasingly been effaced by "the rise of the social," a new realm marked by a blend of impersonal administration and mass conformism, whose tendency is to undermine and supersede both "the public" and "the private." The majority of everyday modes of behavior, such as working for large organizations, are nei-

50. S. Garbuzov, "Nuzhno li vmeshivatsia v lichnuiu zhizn'?" (Is It Necessary to Interfere In Personal Life?), *Komsomolskaia Pravda,* January 4, 1958.

51. Here and in the following discussion I rely on the interpretation advanced in Hanna Pitkin, "Conformism, Housekeeping, and the Attack of the Blob: Hannah Arendt's Concept of the Social."

52. See Hannah Arendt, *The Human Condition.*

358

ther "public" nor "private," strictly speaking, but are "social" in this sense. On the one hand, "politics" in the sense of "public" action is displaced by command and administration. On the other hand, such formerly "private" tasks as education, welfare, and reproduction become the object of "social concern," while the "private sphere" shrinks to the smallest possible "intimate" sphere, in which obedient individuals engage in leisure activities and culture consumption.

Two features of "the social," both stressed by Pitkin, are especially significant for our purposes. First, "the social" is a "curiously hybrid" realm, neither "private" nor "public," that seems almost like an enormously overgrown family; members of the "social" realm are supposed to behave, and be treated, like members of a family. Second, "modern privacy in its most relevant function, to shelter the intimate, was discovered as the opposite of . . . the social." [53]

Whatever the value of this account for grasping Western developments, it sheds a great deal of light on the Soviet case. *Sovetskoe obshchestvo*, that is, Soviet society, was to be run like a family almost from its inception. Soltz called for the Party congregation to be run like a family; later the familylike mechanism of comradely admonition was imposed on the whole society, not only on the Party. And one crucial effect of the imposition of "the social," of *Sovetskoe obshchestvo*—that is, "Soviet society" as opposed to the "revolutionary public"—is the retreat of the private into the intimate. However, this retreat occurred differently from the one in the West. Private life did not shrink to intimacy in the sense of a legitimate and protected sphere of privacy. Both privacy and particularism were completely rejected and stamped out by the social: *chastnaia zhizn'* was discursively assassinated. The social, *Sovetskoe obshchestvo*, was to allocate and regulate both the quasi-public (the world of work) and the quasi-private (the world of personal life, of *lichnaia zhizn'*). There was no recognized sphere left which was not, in principle, part of the social.

The private, however, was reestablished as the "secret" but pervasive underside of the social, as the invisible sphere of the most intimate comportment, carefully hidden by individual dissimulation. This dissimulation was so thorough that it did not offer even a glimpse of the secret obverse of the social. This was the real Great Retreat. The Soviet people might actually appear to be a monolithic bloc of fighters for Communism, conforming to the official image and providing a referent for the horrifying concepts of some Western theoreticians of totalitarianism. *Chastnaia zhizn'* became invisible; it was hid-

53. Arendt, *Human Condition*, p. 38.

den not only from the leaders or from foreign observers, but—primarily, and for that reason, more thoroughly—from the pervasive surveillance of surrounding comrades.

EPILOGUE

MICHELLE PERROT, introducing a volume that deals with the influence of the French Revolution on private life, states that even if the revolution exploded the distinction of public from private in the short run, and denigrated the private in favor of the public, it reasserted this dichotomy in the long run.[54] The exposition of this essay points to the conclusion that something similar happened with the Russian Revolution. Bearing in mind Walzer's convincing argument that Puritan, Jacobin, and Bolshevik politics are simply three different examples of revolutions of the saints, this outcome may seem to have been a foregone conclusion.

However, this essay has also tried to articulate the differences between the "shaking and restructuring" of public and private in these Western revolutions and the changes that occurred in Russia. The Bolshevik revolution did not explode the distinction between public and private and then reestablish it in a different form. Rather, it swept it away and replaced it, in the long run, with a division between the "social," which consists of transparent "public" *and* "personal" lives, and an unseen, unrecognized private which does not exceed the most intimate. The dissimulation covering this intimate sphere became the most profound practice of Soviet society.

In this comparison another difference comes to the fore. It has been argued that the Marquis de Sade may be considered a logical corollary of the French Revolution. He is said to have put nature and reason in the hands of unrestrained egotism, and he did so in private, thus turning the private into a space of the cruelest enjoyment. He used revolutionary methods to achieve the most private of aims. De Sade is the *reductio ad absurdum* of the French Revolution, Lynn Hunt suggests in her contribution to the Perrot volume.[55]

But de Sade is a singular and visible absurdity, the kind of horrible exception that proves the benign rule, and which the revolution is capable of containing. The Russian Revolution, however, had its own horrible absurdities which it was unable to contain, because it could not see them. Dissimulation just covered them up. Contemporary Russian society may have inherited these

54. Michelle Perrot, ed., *A History of Private Life*, vol. 4, *From the Fires of Revolution to the Great War*, p. 9.

55. Lynn Hunt, "The Unstable Boundaries of French Revolution," in Perrot, ed., *From the Fires of Revolution*, p. 36.

along with the dissimulative structure of the Soviet self, which is perhaps the only stable legacy from the Soviet past.

Andrei Chikatilo, a humble schoolteacher and office worker, raped, killed, and cannibalized fifty-two people between 1978 and 1990.

> Judge Akubzhanov said Mr. Chikatilo succeeded in evading the arrest so long primarily because he was so unremarkable. In everyday life he was a father whose two children paid him little heed, a Communist Party member who always posted pictures of [the] Politburo in his workplace. Yet in his secret life he was an insatiable sadist, always on the prowl for a victim, never leaving home without a knife and rope in the event that he might find one, the judge said.[56]

56. Serge Schmemann, "As Shrieks Fill Court, Killer in Russia Is Sentenced to Die," *New York Times,* October 16, 1992.

REFERENCES

Ancharova, Galina. 1935. "Diskussiia u Komsomoltsev Metro" (Discussion in the Metro Workers' Komsomol Organization). *Molodaia Gvardiia* (Young Guard) 14, no. 7 (July): 162–66.

Arendt, Hannah. 1958. *The Human Condition.* Chicago: University of Chicago Press.

Berdiaev, Nikolai. 1955. *Istoki i smysl russkogo kommunizma* (The Origins and Meaning of Russian Communism). Paris: YMCA.

Bourdieu, Pierre. 1990. *The Logic of Practice.* Stanford, CA: Stanford University Press.

Clark, Katerina. 1981. *The Soviet Novel: History as Ritual.* Chicago: University of Chicago Press.

Confino, Michael. 1991. *Société et mentalités collectives en Russie sous l'ancien régime.* Paris: Institut d'Etudes Slaves.

Dal', Vladimir. [1859] 1980. *Tolkovyi slovar' zhivago velikorusskago iazyka* (Dictionary of the Living Russian Language). 5th ed. Vol. 4. Moscow: Russkii Iazyk.

Dunham, Vera. 1976. *In Stalin's Time: Middleclass Values in Soviet Fiction.* Cambridge: Cambridge University Press.

Eliade, Mircea. 1958. *The Sacred and the Profane.* New York: Viking.

Foucault, Michel. 1978. *The History of Sexuality.* Vol. 1, *Introduction.* New York: Pantheon.

———. 1980. "Truth and Subjectivity." Transcript of the Howison Lectures, delivered October 20–21 in the Howison Library of the University of California, Berkeley.

Garbuzov, S. 1958. "Nuzhno li vmeshivatsia v lichnuiu zhizn'?" (Is It Necessary to Interfere in Personal Life?). *Komsomolskaia Pravda,* January 4.

Goffman, Erving. 1959. *The Presentation of Self in Everyday Life.* Garden City, NY: Doubleday.

Guseinov, A. A., M. V. Iskrov, and R. V. Petropavlovskii, eds. 1989. *Partiinaia etika: Dokumenty i materialy diskussii dvadtsatykh godov* (Party Ethics: Documents and Materials of the Party Discussion of the 1920s). Moscow: Politizdat.

Habermas, Jürgen. 1989. *The Structural Transformation of the Public Sphere.* Cambridge, MA: MIT Press. Originally published as *Strukturwandel der Öffentlichkeit: Untersuchungen zu einer Kategorie der bürgerlichen Gesellschaft* (Neuwied: Luchterhand, 1962).

Hunt, Lynn. 1990. "The Unstable Boundaries of French Revolution." In *A History of Private Life.* Vol. 4, *From the Fires of Revolution to the Great War,* edited by Michelle Perrot. Cambridge, MA: Harvard University Press.

Iaroslavskii, Emelian. 1989. "O partetike" (On Party Ethics). In *Partiinaia etika: Dokumenty i materialy diskussii dvadtsatykh godov* (Party Ethics: Documents and Materials of the Party Discussion of the 1920s), edited by A. A. Guseinov, M. V. Iskrov, and R. V. Petropavlovskii, pp. 170–96. Moscow: Politizdat.

Jowitt, Ken. 1992. *New World Disorder: The Leninist Extinction.* Berkeley: University of California Press.

Lenin, Vladimir. [1902] 1964. "What Is to Be Done?" In *Collected Works,* vol. 4. Moscow: Progress Publishers.

Lewin, Moshe. 1985. *The Making of the Soviet System.* New York: Pantheon.

Lukes, Steven. 1973. *Individualism.* London: Blackwell.

Miliukov, Pavel. 1897. *Ocherki po istorii russkoi kultury.* Vol. 2, *Tserkov i shkola.* St. Petersburg: Mir Bozhii. Published in English-language translation as *Outlines of Russian Culture* (Philadelphia: University of Pennsylvania Press, 1942).

Naiman, Eric. 1991. "Sexuality and Utopia: The Debate in the Soviet 1920s." Ph.D. dissertation, University of California, Berkeley.

Perrot, Michelle, ed. 1990. *A History of Private Life.* Vol. 4, *From the Fires of Revolution to the Great War.* Cambridge, MA: Harvard University Press.

Pitkin, Hanna. 1990. "Conformism, Housekeeping, and the Attack of the Blob: Hannah Arendt's Concept of the Social." Paper presented at the annual meeting of the American Political Science Association.

Schmemann, Serge. 1992. "As Shrieks Fill Court, Killer in Russia Is Sentenced to Die." *New York Times,* October 16.

Scott, James C. 1985. *Weapons of the Weak: Everyday Forms of Peasant Resistance.* New Haven, CT: Yale University Press.

Slovar' sovremennogo russkogo literaturnogo iazyka (Dictionary of Contemporary Russian Literary Language). 1955–68. 17 vols. Moscow: Institut Russkogo Iazyka.

Smidovich, Sofia. [1926] 1989. "O Korenkovshchine" (On Korenkovism). In *Partiinaia etika: Dokumenty i materialy diskussii dvadtsatykh godov* (Party Ethics: Documents and Materials of the Party Discussion of the 1920s), edited by A. A. Guseinov, M. V. Iskrov, and R. V. Petropavlovskii, pp. 377–88. Moscow: Politizdat.

Soltz, A. A. [1924] 1989. "O partiinoi etike" (On Party Ethics). In *Partiinaia etika: Dokumenty i materialy diskussii dvadtsatykh godov* (Party Ethics: Documents and

Materials of the Party Discussion of the 1920s), edited by A. A. Guseinov, M. V. Iskrov, and R. V. Petropavlovskii, pp. 258–72. Moscow: Politizdat.

———. [1925] 1989. "O partetike" (On Party Ethics). In *Partiinaia etika: Dokumenty i materialy diskussii dvadtsatykh godov* (Party Ethics: Documents and Materials of the Party Discussion of the 1920s), edited by A. A. Guseinov, M. V. Iskrov, and R. V. Petropavlovskii, pp. 273–90. Moscow: Politizdat.

Stalin, Joseph. [1931] 1952. "O nekotorykh voprosakh istorii bolshevisma" (Concerning Some Questions of the History of Bolshevism). In *Voprosy Leninisma* (Problems of Leninism [editions published after 1934]). Moscow: Gospolitizdat.

Timasheff, Nicholas. 1946. *The Great Retreat.* New York: Dutton.

Trotsky, Leon. 1923. "S chego nachat' " (How to Begin). *Pravda,* August 17. Published in English-language translation in *Problems of Everyday Life* (New York: Monad Press, 1973).

Tucker, Robert C. 1973. *Stalin as Revolutionary, 1879–1929: A Study in History and Personality.* New York: Norton.

Walzer, Michael. 1968. *The Revolution of the Saints: A Study in the Origins of Radical Politics.* New York: Atheneum.

Zhdanov, Andrei. 1938. "Rech' na Yubileinom Plenume TsK VLKSM" (Speech at the Jubilee Plenum of the Central Committee of Komsomol). *Komsomolskaia Pravda,* November 4.

abolitionist movement, 281, 291, 297

abortion, 133–65; abortion mills, 195; conservative opposition to, 190; equal protection justification for, 137, 140, 140 n.14, 192; husband notification provisions, 142; the left's support for, 190; "our bodies, our selves" slogan for defending, 160; parental consent provisions, 198; privacy justification for, xiv, 137–38, 150, 191–92, 198; reasons for as private, 155 n.50; restrictions on, 198; right to as central to the self, 159; and right to life, 198; self-administered, 217; waiting periods, 198. See also *Roe v. Wade*

absolutism: Communism compared with, 310–11; nationalism and, 78, 88; personalized politics of, 65, 66; the public conceived by, 306; Roman law and, 14; and sovereignty's rediscovery, 13

Adam Smith problem, 62–63, 63 n.50

affective individualism, 211, 224

agape, 60, 61

agency, 103–32; of all sane adults, 124; central feature of, 124; the citizen as agent, 115–16; Locke on women's, 120–21; Natural Law theory on, 104–5; private judgment as feature of, 129; proprietary conception of, 122; women and servants alienating their, 114–15

AIDS, 193–95

alcohol consumption, 297

analytical Marxism, 9

antipsychiatry movement, 212 n

Arato, Andrew, 15 n.29, 79 n

architecture: design in, 246–48; mediating role of, 262; modern figure of the architect, 246–47; organismic approach of late nineteenth century, 240; practical setting of, 264; professionalization of, 246; public/private distinction in, 237, 247; reconfiguration of, 262; standardization in, 251–52,

256. *See also* modernist architecture; postmodernist architecture

Arendt, Hannah: on boundary of shame, 176; the city as envisioned by, 26; on the family, 212–14, 225; on plurality, 82; on politics, 75 n.1; on privacy rights, 150; on private life, 213; on property, 212; on public/private distinction, 212, 358–59; on public space, 2, 11, 14, 82, 82 n.11; tripartite model of society, 35, 35 n, 196, 213–14, 358–59

Ariès, Philippe: the city as envisioned by, 26; on decay of sociability, 24–25; on the modern family's emergence, 18–19, 21, 209, 210–12, 225; on the home as private, 209; "public" defined by, 17 n.35; on public life of sociability, 2, 7, 24; on public life of the old regime, 18; on public/private distinction, 19 n.40, 35

Aristotle: on citizenship, 12; on the household distinguished from the polis, 29–30, 35, 104; on natural inequality, 12, 29

artificial insemination by donor, 170

ascending theory of sovereignty, 78, 88 n.21

asylums, 183, 186

Austro-Hungarian Empire, 96

authority: authoritarianism in post-Communist societies, 329; authoritarian trappings revived in Soviet Union, 313 n.26, 314; civil society rejecting absolute, 79; in Communist neotraditionalism, 315–16; in feudal system, 13; market reforms displacing traditional forms of, 307; the nation as source of, 92–93; power as mark of political, 123; public authority of the state, 8, 11; Pufendorf on, 113; rejection of natural, 110. *See also* sovereignty

autonomy: privacy as, 146–50; Tocqueville on autonomous social organization versus the state, 308, 308 n.11

Azande, 58 n.38

Babylon, 26
Bagehot, Walter, 45
Balkans, 96–97
Barrett, Martha, 268–71, 280–81
bathhouses, 194–95
battered women, 173–75
Bauer, Catherine, 251
Beal, J. Foster, 287
Becker, Gary, 9
Bellah, Robert, 199 n.49
Benhabib, Seyla, 34 n, 109 n.12
Benjamin, Walter, 26 n
Benn, S. I., 4 n
Bentham, Jeremy, 9
Berdiaev, Nikolai, 335, 336
Berger, Peter, 21
Berlin, Isaiah, 178, 179
bioengineering, 170
bioethics, 170
biotechnology, 134
Blackmun, Harry, 146
Blake, Peter, 256
Blau, Peter, 9
blood-brotherhood, 58 n.38
Bobbio, Norberto, 1, 109 n.13
bodily integrity, 158–62
Bolshevism: Central Control Commission,
    345–46; comradely admonition in, 345–50;
    dissimulation in, 350; a Holy Common-
    wealth established by, 351–57; mutual sur-
    veillance in, 346–47, 357; a new society as
    aim of, 335; and *oblichenie,* 337–43; Party
    Control Commission, 345; Puritan Reforma-
    tion compared with, 335–37, 339–40; *The
    Short Course of the History of the Communist
    Party,* 351, 352; subordination of all social
    priorities to struggle for communism,
    312 n.22
Bosnia-Herzegovina, 97, 131
Bowers v. Hardwick, 146, 146 n.31
Boyte, Harry, 178–79
Brain, David, xv
Brandeis, Louis D., 154 n, 190
Brasilia, 252–54
Brennan, William J., Jr., 145–46
Breytenbach, Breyten, 207–8
Brezhnev, Leonid, 313
brotherhood, 57–59
Brown, William J., 284
built environment, 237–67; built form and so-
    cial order, 240; representational qualities of,

248; shopping malls, 237, 238; social sig-
    nificance of, 246. *See also* architecture
Burke, Kenneth, 274
Burns, Scott, 215

Calhoun, Craig, xiii
Calvin, John, 354
capitalism: civil particularism of, 307; commer-
    cial society and, 45 n.6; factory system, 277,
    296; friendship in, 65, 65 n.54; laissez-faire,
    190, 191; late capitalism, 240, 245; legal-
    modern capitalism, 307; national integration
    encouraged by, 94; people's capitalism, 206;
    and the private sphere, 184–85, 307;
    public/private distinction in, 35; socializa-
    tion of production in industrial, 296; social
    life reorganized by industrial, 290; wealth
    distribution compared to Communism,
    313 n.25. *See also* market, the
Carey v. Population Services International, 145–
    46
Caudwell, Christopher, 43, 48
censorship, 192–93, 198–99
Central Control Commission (CCC), 345–46
Chandler, Alfred, 9
Chapman, Louisa, 286
chastnaia zhizn' (private life), 343–45, 355,
    356–57, 359–60
Chicago-school sociology, 239
Chikatilo, Andrei, 361
Chodorow, Nancy, 22 n.47
Chubarov Affair, 348–49
cities: Babylon, 26; Brasilia, 252–54; cosmopo-
    lis, 26, 99 n.45; dual character of, 26–27;
    edge cities, 238; Jacobs on the urban street,
    243; mechanistic approach of modernism,
    240; the modernist city, 252–55; new ur-
    banism, xv, 237, 257, 264; nineteenth-
    century views on, 240; the polis, 11, 26, 29,
    35 n, 64; as political communities, 238,
    239; the post-liberal city, 238; privatization
    of, 237; public life located in, 238–39; socia-
    bility in, 23–24, 238, 243; as *urbs* and *civi-
    tas,* 26, 239
citizenship, 10–16; agency of the citizen, 115–
    16; Aristotle's definition of, 12; community
    required for, 12–13; conformity as condi-
    tion for, 87; eclipse during Middle Ages, 13;
    equality and, 10, 13, 14; citizen as holder of
    legal powers in liberal theory, 103, 106–7;
    Hutcheson on, 129–30; absence in late

Communism, 327; Locke on, 125; modern Natural Law theory on, 122–23; popular sovereignty in, 79; in private communities, 261; the privatized citizen, 205; public life and, 10, 17; recovery in modernity, 14
civility, 23, 156, 176, 177
civil law, 308
civil particularism, xvi, 307, 315, 323, 324
civil religion, 199
civil society, 13; Arendt on, 35, 35 n; class basis of, 323 n.53; under Communism, 310–11; contemporary interest in, 196; contract theory of institution of, 109, 114; in former Communist countries, 303, 329; in fourfold typology of modernity, 308–9; friendship and strangership in, 43–74; Hutcheson on the state and, 127–28; in late Communism, 327–28; liberalism and, 13, 31; Natural Law theorists on, 110; as new public realm, 18; political society contrasted with, 14, 303 n; and the private, 30, 36, 306–7; the public sphere created out of for Habermas, 83; and Roman law, 14; as self-organized, 79; sympathy in, 54
Clark, Katerina, 340
Clark, Sarah Holmes, 283, 284, 288
codes of honor, 68–69
Cohen, Jean L., xiv, 15 n.29, 79 n, 192 n.27, 198
collectivity: Hobbes on collective action, 10; the homeland as a collective, 209; Hutcheson on maximizing collective pleasure, 126; the public and, 5; publics as collective, 197. See also society; state, the
commercial society. See market, the
Communism, 303–32; absolutism compared with, 310–11; basic institutional configuration of, 317; civil society under, 310–11; as classless, 326; Communist neotraditionalism, 315–16; demoralization of ruling elites in, 321; genealogy of social roles under, 321–27; goulash communism, 314, 315; hypertrophy of state sovereignty under, 312 n.22; independent public life suppressed under, 311–12; interest group model of Communist politics, 312 n.23; Kádárism, 320, 322; late Communism, 303, 310, 325 n.59, 327–29; legal codes as irrelevant under, 316; Leninism, 16 n, 305, 309, 310, 319; lumpenization under, 319, 319 n.42; Maoism, 16 n, 309; mono-organizational society in, 319;

national Communism, 314 n.26; new socialist man under, 311, 335; newspeak of, 326; the Party-state in, 303, 309–12, 317, 322, 326; personal life scorned under, 310; privacy under, 323–25, 336–37, 359–60; the private sphere under, 323–25, 325 n.57; privatization of social life under, xvi, 16 n.31, 303, 315, 322–25; the public elevated over the private in, 200; regimes as rotting away from within, 314–16; second economies under, 311, 315, 315 n.30; social atomization under, 326 n.61; socialist construction, 311; social personae under, 325 n.59; social realm of, 317–18, 325–27; state-engineered stratification and state dependence under, 319–21; state socialism, 16 n; totalitarianism of, 305–19; value orientations in, 318; wealth distribution compared to capitalism, 313 n.25. See also Bolshevism; Marxism; post-Communist society; Union of Soviet Socialist Republics
communitarianism, 13, 137–38, 144–58
community: citizenship requiring, 12–13; the city as political community, 238, 239; gemeinschaft, 13, 174; Hobbes on sovereign power creating from above, 306; the nation as political community, 78, 91; the people as political community, 78, 78 n.4; political community and identity-formation, 100; the public as political community, 76, 78, 100; sovereignty and political community, 88–94; the state and the political community, 75–79, 75 n.1; willed community, 13. See also private communities
community standards, 193
companionate marriage, 211
compromise, 179
confession, 341
Confino, Michel, 350
conformity, 87, 92, 93
Congrès Internationaux d'Architecture Moderne, 253
Conscience, Higher, 340, 342, 343
consent: in Locke's theory of legitimate power, 117; in master/servant relationship, 118; in Natural Law theory of institutions, 110; Pufendorf on, 112–13; in sexual activity, 194; by women in marriage, 113 n.21, 118, 141
conservatives. See right, the
consumerism, 226

contraceptives, 144–45

contract: in Locke's theory of legitimate power, 117; in marriage, 118, 119–21, 120 n.34, 141; between master and servant, 118–19; the right on regulation of private, 195

contract, social, 90, 106, 109, 114

Cooley, Charles Horton, 52 n.24, 68

Corbusier, Le, 240, 253

Corpus Juris Civilis, 12 n, 107, 306

cosmopolis, 26, 99 n.45

Costa, Lúcio, 253

Coult, Mary Giddings, 286

court rationality, 51–52

cult of true womanhood, 277

Darnton, Robert, 20

Davis, Mike, 238

Davis, Natalie, 20

Davis, Noah, 281

Davis, Robert, 257

Defoe, Daniel, 56

democracy: compromise in, 179; direct democracy, 130; identity politics as normal to, 88; in Locke, 90; and nationalism, xiii, 84, 100; plurality as basic to, 82; peoples as a given for, 91; the public as central to, 81, 135; property-owning democracy, 206; requirements for, 180; social isolation as threat to, 298

de Sade, Marquis, 360

descending theory of sovereignty, 88 n.21

design, 237–67; the discipline of, 247; gap between form and function in, 246–47; the logic of modernist, 248–52; mechanistic imagery of modernist, 240; in private communities, 258, 260; symbolic aspect of, 240. *See also* architecture

Dewey, John, 47

difference: civility embraced by the different, 177; Habermas's bracketing of, 83; nationalist repression of, 81–82, 87; personal privacy rights protecting, 153; public/private distinction and, 134; women's 161 n.67, 162

di Leonardo, Micaela, 287 n.53

direct democracy, 130

displacement of politics, 166–81; conditions for, 171; examples of, 171–78; identity politics as, 175–78

divorce rates, 222, 223 n

domestic sphere: feminism on, 27, 28; of modern middle class, 307; as private, 18, 37, 208–9, 294–95; in the Soviet Union, 311, 317, 319, 322, 324, 326–27, 329; treated as trivial, 28; as the woman's sphere, 28, 31, 277. *See also* family; home

domestic violence, 173–75

domination, 12

Douany, Andres, 257, 258

Douglas, Mary, 227

Downs, Anthony, 9

drinking of alcohol, 297

dual contract, 90

Dublin, Thomas, 275 n.21, 276 n.23

Duby, Georges, 2, 307 n

Dunham, Vera, 352–53

Durkheim, Emile, 7 n.12, 91–92, 196, 221

Dworkin, Ronald, 161

economy: household economy, 215; household goods, 215, 226; Keynesianism, 200; neoclassical economics, 8, 9, 44; physiocrats, 95; privatization, 108, 109, 304; property in Western economic discourse, 308; second economies under Communism, 311, 315, 315 n.30; self-service economy, 215, 219; visiting's economic function, 280, 285–87. *See also* capitalism; Communism; labor; market, the; public goods

edge cities, 238

education, 216–17

Eisenstadt v. Baird, 145, 192 n.27

electronic cottage, 219

Elias, Norbert, 20, 24, 51

Elshtain, Jean Bethke, xiv–xv, 30 n.61, 33, 34, 189 n.13

Elster, Jon, 9

empires: imperial rule and nationalism, 96–97; modern states contrasted with, 77; nation-state contrasted with, 99 n.45; relationship between state and people in, 76

Engels, Friedrich, 32

Enlightenment, Scottish. *See* Scottish Enlightenment

enlightenment universalism, 134

entertainment, home, 217–18, 220

entity privacy, 139, 141, 142, 143

equality: and citizenship, 10, 13, 14; Hutcheson's egalitarianism, 125–26; in liberal model of public sphere, 83; Locke on, 116, 117, 120, 121, 123, 124; Pufendorf on,

112, 114; of strangers, 53. *See also* inequality
ethnic minorities, 84, 87
exchange theory, 9, 51, 62
expression, freedom of, 192–93, 198, 199
extended family, 219, 286

factory system, 277, 296
Fainsod, Merle, 312 n.23
family, the: Arendt on, 212–14, 225; Ariès on, 209, 210–12, 210 n, 221, 225; as bulwark against modern society, 214; child-centered, 21; in Communist societies, 317; the contemporary family, 222–24; in decay of sociability, 25, 221, 225, 231; decline in twentieth century, 222–27; definition of, 223 n; emergence of the modern, 18–19; and entity privacy, 143; extended family, 219, 286; feminism on, 27–34, 211–12; in Habermas's account of public sphere, 83; the homeland modeled on, 208; individualism and, 19, 221–27; as island of domesticity, 18; law and regulation in, 229; Locke on husband's status in, 121; in mass society, 184; the medieval family, 209; new privacy doctrine as undermining, 147; in nineteenth century, 222; privatization of, 209; and private life, 18, 224; public/private distinction internal to, 192; as a quasi-public, 196; as residual category in Natural Law theory, 109; right to privacy in, 191–92; Soviet society to be run like, 359; the state taking over functions of, 214; triumph of, 21, 221; working at home strengthening, 219. *See also* domestic sphere; head of household; home; marriage; nuclear family
family values, 144
Fay, Brian, 168
feminism: on the family, 27–34, 211–12; on gender bias in Natural Law theory, 105, 108–10; on home, 204; as identity politics, 134; and Marxism, 30, 32, 35; on the personal as political, 136, 171–72, 295 n.66; on pornography, 193; privacy analysis criticized by, 140–44; on privacy in the family, 191; on the private, 136–37, 189; on private/public distinction, xiv, 27–34, 35, 134–37, 271–73; on public sphere, 27–34, 135–36; on separate spheres ideology, 278–79
Ferguson, Adam, 55, 57, 57 n.36, 66

feudalism, 13
Filmer, Robert, 116, 117, 120 n.34
Forster, E. M., 64
Foster, John Plummer, 283, 287–88, 289–90
Foucault, Michel, 20, 89, 188, 341
France: French Revolution, 92–93, 94, 308 n.11, 360; national integration in, 95; state smothering political life in, 16, 16 n
Fraser, Nancy, 34, 34 n.73, 295 n.67
freedom. *See* liberty
freedom of expression, 192–93, 198, 199
free-rider problem, 10
French Revolution, 92–93, 94, 308 n.11, 360
friendship, 43–74; anti-instrumental, 21, 45; in capitalism, 65, 65 n.54; classical liberalism on, 49–56, 59, 61; in commercial society, 56–67; exemplary significance of, 46–49; as historical survival, 44; Johnson's definition of, 59; marriage contrasted with, 46 n.8; modern ideals of, 69; as *necessitudo*, 50, 54, 59, 61, 67; noble ideals of, 56; as personal, 46, 48–49; in precommercial society, 59, 59 n; preferential, 60; as private, 46; Scottish Enlightenment on, 49–63, 67; as unprotected by law, 46
fundamentalism, religious, 134
Fustel de Coulanges, Numa Denis, 239 n.6

Gans, Herbert, 23
Garcelon, Marc, xvi
Gaus, Gerald F., 4 n, 64 n.51
gay liberation, 134, 175–78, 193–95
Geertz, Clifford, 6–7
Gellner, Ernest, 91
gemeinschaft, 13, 174
general will, 93
Germany, national integration in, 95
Gershuny, Jonathan, 215, 216
gesellschaft, 20–21, 22 n.46, 37, 51
Glendon, Mary Ann, 144–45, 146–50, 151, 156
Gobetti, Daniela, xiv
Goffman, Erving: on civility, 156; on interactional space, 16; on the public and the private, 2, 182–84, 185–88; on public behavior, 6 n.10; on territories of the self, 157, 159, 159 n.63
good, the, 126, 151
Gorbachev, Mikhail, 207, 321
goulash communism, 314, 315
government. *See* state, the

Great Retreat, 350, 353–54
Great Society, 47, 68
Greek polis, 11, 26, 29, 35 n, 64
Greenfeld, Liah, 90 n.27
Grimes, William, 288
Griswold v. Connecticut, 144–46, 144 n.25, 191
Grotius, 108, 117 n.27
group identity, 151, 153, 193, 198–99
Guenter, Klaus, 155 n.50

Habermas, Jürgen: Foucault contrasted with, 188; on identity-formation, 82, 86–87, 87 n.19; lifeworld distinguished from system by, 86 n.16; on the public and the private, 182, 184–88; on public sphere, 2, 14–15, 15 n.29, 81, 82–87, 82 n.11, 100, 135, 185–88
Halévy, Elie, 9 n.15
Hall, Mary, 286
Hamlet (Shakespeare), 65 n.55
Hankiss, Elemér, 311 n.20, 322
Hansen, Karen V., xv, 211 n.16
Hapsburgs, 96
harm (injury), 103–4, 103 n.1, 122 n.42, 124
hate speech, 192, 193, 198, 199
head of household: agency of, 122; Locke on, 31, 121, 122–23; Natural Law theorists on, 107, 110; Pufendorf on, 114–15
health care, 216, 217, 285–89
Hegel, Georg Wilhelm Friedrich, 13, 35, 79 n
Heimat (homeland), 204, 207–9
Henry IV of England, 78 n.5
Higher Conscience, 340, 342, 343
Hirschman, Albert O., 10, 49 n.16
Hobbes, Thomas: on collective action, 10; on legitimate sovereignty, 89–90, 90 n.25; Pufendorf influenced by, 112 n.20; on seditious ministers, 339; on social order problem, 9; on sovereign power creating the community from above, 306
Hobsbawm, Eric, 207, 208, 209
Holston, James, 253
home, 204–36; Ariès on, 209; Aristotle distinguishing household from polis, 29–30, 35, 104; as cut off from public realm, 231; education in, 216–17; entertainment in, 217–18, 220; etymology of term, 230; evolution of modern house, 209–10, 210 n; health care in, 216, 217; hearth as no longer center of, 227; home-centered society, 205, 206–7, 229; as homeland, 207–9; home

ownership, 205–6; hotel contrasted with, 227–31; household economy, 215; household goods, 215, 226; the individual in, 229; the left on, 206; limited privacy in, 227–28; as private, xv, 208–9; privatization of, 209; rediscovery of, 204–7; reevaluation of, 204–5; return to, 204, 207, 214–21; the right on, 206; single-person households, 222; technology in, 214–20, 230, 230 n.50; as under threat from mass society, 214; what and where is the home, 207–14; as woman's realm, 211 n.16; working at, 218–19; young people resisting embrace of, 220. *See also* domestic sphere; family; head of household
homeland (*Heimat*), 204, 207–9
home ownership, 205–6
homosexual (gay) liberation, 134, 175–78, 193–95
Honneth, Axel, 159 n.63
honor, codes of, 68–69
Hornius, Friedrich, 113 n.21
hotels, 227–31
household. *See* home
houses, 209–10, 210n
housing, public. *See* public housing
Huizinga, Johan, 19
Hume, David: on friendship, 50; on personal relations in commercial society, 45, 49; on two sorts of commerce, 49, 58, 66, 68
Hungary, 320–21, 322
Hunt, Lynn, 360
husband notification provisions, 142
Hutcheson, Francis, 125–29; on citizenship, 129–30; egalitarianism of, 125–26; on friendship, 60–61; on the good, 126; liberalism of, 57 n.36; on moral sense, 127; on rights, 127, 128–29; on woman's status, 126, 127 n.49

Iaroslavskii, Emelian, 346, 349
identity: the body as basic to, 159–62; group identity, 151, 153, 193, 198–99; identity absolutism, 177; individual identity, 151–54, 152 n.46; national identity, 88, 92; pregnancy and women's, 160; privacy and, 150–58; sexual identity, 177. *See also* identity-formation; identity politics; self
identity-formation: Habermas on, 82, 86–87, 87 n.19; in nationalist discourse, 91; as part of public life, 84; personal privacy rights

protecting, 162; political community and, 100

identity politics: dangers of, xiv–xv, 134; as displacement of politics, 175–78; gay liberation, 134, 175–78, 193–95; group identity as public and private, 198–99; left/right affinities influenced by, 189–90; as normal to democracy, 88; privacy issues affected by, 133, 134; public/private distinction as excluding the different, 134. *See also* feminism

imperial rule, 96–97

impersonal, the: in modern society, 48; the public as, 18, 20, 43–46

individual, the: affective individualism, 211, 224; agency in, 104–5; atomistic view of, 146–47; and civil society, 13; as embodied, 159; the family and, 19, 221–27; in the home, 229; individualism of Bolshevism and Puritanism, 336–37; the nation as dependent on, 93–94; Natural Law theorists on, 108; the private and, 5; in Roman law, 107; as situated, 147–48; sovereignty as complement of, 13; and the state, 8–9. *See also* self

individual identity, 151–54, 152 n.46

inequality: Aristotle on natural, 12, 29; Locke on, 123, 126; Pufendorf on, 114

informational privacy, 140, 144, 155

injury (harm), 103–4, 103 n.1, 122 n.42, 124

injustice, 168–69

interest: Ferguson on, 55, 57; in Hume's two sorts of commerce, 49, 49 n.16, 58; interest group model of Communist politics, 312 n.23; national interests, 93; Natural Law theorists on, 108; in Roman law, 107; in Smith's social theory, 52, 63; special interest, 5; at Versailles court, 64. *See also* public interest

interpretation, 129, 130

intimacy: and bioethics, 170; magic border between intimate life and public life, 172–73; modern society opposed by, 214; overinvestment in, 24–25; overloading the domain of, 22; as personal, 43; politics pervading intimate life, 171; and privacy, 138, 139, 140, 141, 143, 160; as private, 2, 27, 86, 136; privatization of the intimate, 18; the public contrasted with, 37; putting one's intimate life on display, 176; sexual acts, 194, 349; social station and, 65; split between the public and the intimate, 18, 20, 64; zone of intimacy, 140, 144–45

intimate relationships, 135, 142–43, 147

inviolate personality, principle of, 138, 139, 154, 158, 160, 162

Jacobinism, 16 n, 92, 310 n.17

Jacobs, Jane, 17, 23, 24, 231 n.52, 243–44

James, Samuel Shepard, 285

Johnson, Samuel, 59

Jowitt, Ken, 314 n.28, 349

judgment, 129, 130–31

justice, 147, 168–69

Kádárism, 320, 322

Kahn, Bonnie Menes, 26 n

Kerber, Linda, 278 n.32

Keynesianism, 200

Kharkhordin, Oleg, xvi

Khrushchev, Nikita, 313

King, Martin Luther, 178

Kluge, Alexander, 86

Kohn, Hans, 90 n.27

Konstan, David, 59 n

Korenkov, Konstantin, 333–35, 347

Kornai, Janos, 320

Krupskaia, Nadezhda, 354

kulturnost', 353

Kumar, Krishan, xv

Kundera, Milan, 172–73

labor (work): Arendt on praxis and, 82; Locke on ownership of our own, 117; Locke on servants' 119; and sociability in antebellum America, 280, 285–87; transformation of in nineteenth century, 276–77; working at home, 218–19

Laing, R. D., 212 n

laissez-faire, 190, 191

La Rochefoucauld, François, duc de, 65 n.54, 66

Larson, Margali Sarfatti, 256 n.41

Lasch, Christopher, 225, 225 n

late capitalism, 240, 245

late Communism, 303, 310, 325 n.59, 327–29

laundry, 289–90

law: civil law, 308; the family penetrated by, 229; friendship as unprotected by, 46; legal codes as irrelevant under Communism, 316; legal persons, 118, 149, 150, 156; public law, 308. *See also* Natural Law theory; Roman law

Le Corbusier, 240, 253

Lefort, Claude, 148 n.36

left, the: abortion supported by, 190; on the family as private, 192; on freedom of expression, 192–93; on the home, 206; identity politics affecting, 189–90; on the private, 190–91, 206; on the public, 188–89; on public health regulation, 193
legal persons, 118, 149, 150, 156
legitimacy, 78, 88–94
Lenin, 310 n.17, 312 n.22, 337–39, 342
Leninism, 16 n, 305, 309, 310, 319
Lewin, Moshe, 349, 351
liberalism: on agency, 104; Benn and Gaus on, 4 n; on citizenship, 12–13; and civil society, 13, 31; friendship in classical, 49–56, 59, 61; the ideal liberal commonwealth, 64; on justice, 147; on the market and the state, 8–10; model of the public sphere in, 83; nationalism in, 84; private and public agency at origins of, 103–32; public/private distinction in, xiii, 7–9, 63–64; utilitarian liberalism, 8–9, 8 n.14
liberals. See left, the
liberty: alienation of one's own, 114, 117; of domestic dependents, 115; freedom of expression, 192–93, 198, 199; *Lochner v. New York* and, 195; Mill on, 197; negative liberty, 178; positive liberty, 179
lichnaia zhizn' (personal life), 343–45, 354, 355–56
life, right to, 198
Littlejohn, Larry, 194
Lochner v. New York, 195
Locke, John: on equality, 116, 117, 120, 121, 123, 124; on harm as criterion of public/private distinction, 103 n.1, 122 n.42, 124; peoples as a given for, 91; political theory of, 90; on property and power, 116–25; on self-enslavement, 114, 123; on social order problem, 9
Lowenthal, Richard, 311 n.20
Luker, Kristin, 161 n.67
Lukes, Steven, 336
lumpenization, 319, 319 n.42
Luther, Martin, 166–67, 336
Lystra, Karen, 279

MacKinnon, Catharine, 33, 141
Maier, Charles, 2 n.4
manners, 352–53
Maoism, 16 n, 309
market, the: in antebellum New England, 296; and civil society, 13; in four-part model of

society, 293, 296; friendship in commercial society, 56–67; invisible hand of, 9; Leninism on, 310; liberalism on the state and, 8–10; marketization in post-Communist society, 304; personal life distinguished from, 20–21; as private, 5, 35, 36, 37–38, 306–8; private life as refuge from individualism of, 38; as public, 33, 35, 293; Scottish Enlightenment on personal relations and, 44–45; self-organization in, 79; social life reordered by nineteenth-century shifts in, 290; the state compared with, 37; traditional forms of authority displaced by, 307. *See also* capitalism
marriage: companionate marriage, 211; divorce rates, 222, 223 n; friendship contrasted with, 46 n.8; *Griswold v. Connecticut* on, 144–45; Hutcheson's egalitarian view of, 127 n.49; Locke on the marriage contract, 118, 119–21, 120 n.34; romantic marriage, 43, 46; Soviet emphasis on, 353–54; woman's consent in, 113 n.21, 118, 141. *See also* family, the
Mars, James, 288
Marshall, Alfred, 44
Marx, Karl, 125
Marxism: analytical Marxism, 9; Engels on the public, 32; and feminism, 30, 32, 35; on incompatibility of private and public, 44. *See also* Communism
mass society, 184, 214
master/servant relationship: Aristotle on natural inequality in, 12; Locke on, 118–19; Pufendorf on, 112, 114–15; in Roman law, 108
McAdam, Doug, 295 n.66
Mead, George Herbert, 196
Metcalf, Elizabeth, 270
Meyrowitz, Joshua, 230 n.50
Michnik, Adam, 327 n
microelectronics, 214–18
microwave ovens, 226–27
Mies van der Rohe, Ludwig, 249
Mikoyan, Anastas, 353
Miliukov, Pavel, 336
Mill, John Stuart, 5 n.7, 124, 197
minorities, ethnic, 84, 87
Mirzoev, 356
modernist architecture: Congrès Internationaux d'Architecture Moderne, 253; defined, 241; gap between professional and common views of architecture in, 248; Le Corbusier,

240, 253; lifeless urban spaces of, 244–45, 262–63; logic of modernist design, 248–52; mechanistic view of the city in, 240; Mies van der Rohe, 249; the modernist city, 252–55; Niemeyer, 253; public housing of the 1930s as, 241, 249–52; public/private distinction collapsed in, 262; standardization in, 251–52; vitality of public and private undermined by, 254–55

modernity (modern society): Arendt's tripartite model of, 35; citizenship and sovereignty in, 13–14; the family in, 18–19, 228–29; fourfold typology of public and private in, 308–9; friendship in, 69; impersonality of, 48; individualism in, 221; modernizing elites and nationalism, 98; the personal as private in, 43–46; public/private distinction in, xiii, 20–21; transition from medieval society to, 212. *See also* modernist architecture

Molière, 66 n.59

monarchy, 12, 14, 79, 89

Montaigne, Michel Eyquem de, 66, 66 n.58

Montesquieu, 93

Moore, Barrington, 324

moral sense, 127

Morgunov, 347–48

Morozov, Pavlik, 326, 326 n.62

Morrow, Glenn R., 52 n.24

Mudge, Mary, 281–82, 284, 286, 296

multiculturalism, 134

Nagel, Thomas, 105 n.4

Naiman, Eric, 348, 349

nation, the: empire contrasted with nation-state, 99 n.45; equivalence of national states, 98–99; formed from parts of empires, 96; the individual and, 93–94; as the relevant political community, 78; as political community, 91; and sovereignty, 88, 91–94; as unitary, 81–82, 94–100. *See also* nationalism

national Communism, 314 n.26

national identity, 88, 92

national interest, 93

nationalism, 75–102; in Austro-Hungarian Empire, 96; in the Balkans, 96–97; dangerous implications of, xiii; and democracy, xiii, 84, 100; difference repressed by, 81; English, 90, 90 n.27; French, 95; German, 95; Hobbes and, 90, 90 n.25; homelands desired by, 204, 207–9; as identity politics, 134; imperial rule encouraging, 97; and individualism, 93–94; in liberal political thought, 84;

modernizing elites and, 98; national unity stressed by, 94–100; the nation constituted in rhetoric of, 91–92; pan-Islamic, 96; as problematic, 80. *See also* nation, the

Natural Law theory: on agency, 104–5; on the citizen as holder of legal powers, 103, 106–7; class bias of, 105; on the family, 109; gender bias of, 105, 108–10; on harm as criterion of public/private distinction, 103–4, 103 n.1; on power, 107–11; on property, 107–11

necessitudo, 50, 54, 59, 61, 67

negative liberty, 178

Negt, Oscar, 86

Nelson, Benjamin, 56–57, 59, 60, 61, 66

neoclassical economics, 8, 9, 44

New England, antebellum: the market in, 296; private sphere in, 294–95; public sphere in, 295; the social in, 293. *See also* visiting in antebellum New England

new privacy doctrine, 144, 147, 148, 149, 157, 158

new socialist (Soviet) man, 311, 335

new social movements, 86 n.18, 88

newspeak, 326

new urbanism, xv, 237, 257, 264

Niemeyer, Oscar, 253

Nims, Brigham, 287, 290

nomenklatura, 317

nuclear family: antipsychiatry movement on, 212 n; and contraction of the family, 221; decline of, 224; the home and, 228; individualizing forces in rise of, 225; as one of many family forms, 223 n; as overburdened, 225–27, 229; as percentage of all families, 222; women in, 211, 212 n

oblichenie, 337–43

officialdom, 317

Olson, Mancur, 10

Ortner, Sherry, 30 n.63

Osterud, Nancy Grey, 278–79

Ostrander, Susan, 296

Othello (Shakespeare), 54

otherhood, 59–67

Ottoman Empire, 96

"our bodies, our selves," 160

paradox of privacy, 137–38

parental consent for abortion, 198

Park, Robert, 239 n.9

Parsons, Talcott, 9 n.15, 22 n.47, 214, 225 n

particularism, civil, xvi, 307, 315, 323, 324
Party Control Commission, 345
Pateman, Carole, 27, 30–31, 35 n, 105 n.6, 109
penance, 341
people, the: in empires, 76, 96; in modern states, 77, 77 n.2; as new notion of political community, 78, 78 n.4; popular will, 88; and sovereignty, 88–94
people's capitalism, 206
Perkins, William, 339
Perrot, Michelle, 360
personality, principle of inviolate, 138, 139, 154, 158, 160, 162
personal life: anti-instrumental ideals of, 67–68; calculative exchange in, 64; in commercial society, 44–45, 49, 67; Communist scorn for, 310; feminism on the personal as political, 136, 171–72, 295 n.66; in fourfold typology of modernity, 308–9; friendship as personal, 46, 48–49; *lichnaia zhizn'*, 343–45, 354, 355–56; market distinguished from, 20–21; overinvestment in, 25; as private, 18, 20–21, 37, 43–46, 307, 307 n; social realm of Communism contrasted with, 317. *See also* intimacy
personal privacy, 139–40, 142, 146, 153–56
persons, legal, 118, 149, 150, 156
physiocrats, 95
Pitkin, Hanna, 22 n.47, 359
planned communities. *See* private communities
Planned Parenthood v. Casey, 142
Plater-Zyberk, Elizabeth, 257
Plato, 55 n.32
plurality, 82
Poland, 303, 320, 321, 328
polis, 11, 26, 29, 35 n, 64
political correctness, 200
political society: civil society contrasted with, 14–16, 303 n; in fourfold typology of modernity, 308–9; as independent of civil society and the state, 15–16; in the public sphere, 14, 307; in Roman law, 14, 14 n.27
politics: accepted boundaries of lacking, 168–70; ambiguities in thinking about, 12; the city as political community, 238, 239; compromise in, 179; daily activity and, 269–70, 291; feminism on the personal as political, 295 n.66, 136, 171–72; Hutcheson on political rights, 128–29; interest group model of Communist politics, 312 n.23; public and

private in contemporary political practice, 188–94; the public and the political, 11–16, 36, 295, 305–6; public/private distinction in establishing boundary of the political, 2, 6–7, 8; sociability and the political, 24; as sociological problem, 79; sovereignty and political community, 88–94; the state and the political community, 75–79, 75 n.1. *See also* displacement of politics; identity politics; left, the; political society; right, the; state, the
popular will, 88
pornography, 192, 193, 198, 199
positive liberty, 179
Post, Robert, 156
post-Communist society: authoritarianism in, 329; civil society in, 303, 329; marketization in, 304; the public sphere in, 327–28; Solidarity movement, 303, 320, 328
postmodernist architecture: critiques of, 245; defined, 241; private communities exemplifying, 241, 257–61; public space in, 263–65; as reaction to modernism, 255–57; Venturi on, 255–57
power: Locke on, 116–25; in Natural Law theory, 107–11; Pufendorf on, 111–16, 112 n.19. *See also* sovereignty
praxis, 82
preferential friendship, 60
primary groups, 68
privacy: and the abortion controversy, xiv, 133–65; abortion justified on grounds of, xiv, 137–38, 150; and ambiguity of "public" and "private," 2; in antebellum New England, 294–95; as autonomy, 146–50; bodily integrity and, 158–62; Bolshevik individualism rejecting, 336–37; under Communism, 323–25, 359–60; communitarian critique of, 137–38, 144–58; the Constitution on right to, 144 n.25; entity privacy, 139, 141, 142, 143; in the family, 191–92; the family as island of, 18; feminist critique of privacy analysis, 140–44; and identity, 150–58; informational privacy, 140, 144, 155; as limited in the home, 227–28; as morally ambiguous, 186–87; new privacy doctrine, 144, 147, 148, 149, 157, 158; normative conception of, 155–58; paradox of, 137–38; personal privacy, 139–40, 142, 146, 153–56; in private life, 37; protection of, 134, 136; as public good, 187; relational

privacy, 143; right to be let alone, 139–40, 147, 153; triumph of in the West, 20; and visibility, 6

private, the. *See* private sphere

private communities: citizenship in, 261; competing interests in, 262; design in, 258, 260; fabricated vernacular in, 260; owners' associations, 260–61; as postmodern, 241, 257–61; public realm in, 263–64; Seaside, 257–58

private life: Arendt on, 213; *chastnaia zhizn'*, 343–45, 355, 356–57, 359–60; under Communism, 303; and displacement of politics, 171; as distinct from public world in liberalism, 64; as domain of personal relations, 37, 43; the family and, 18, 224; feminism on split between public life and, 27; friendship exemplifying, 61; in Habermas's account of public sphere, 83; the home in, 204–36; the left's indifference to, 206; preferred to public life, 205; as refuge from individualism of the market, 38; in Soviet Russia, 333–63; women belonging to, 30, 269, 271–72. *See also* personal life

private parts, 6

private property. *See* property

private sphere: as ambiguous, 2, 11–16, 80–81; in antebellum New England, 294–95; under capitalism, 184–85, 307; and civil society, 30, 36, 306–7; under Communism, 323–25, 325 n.57, 360; Communism preferring the public to, 200; in contemporary political practice, 188–94; in contemporary social theory, 182–88; different distinctions of, 85; domestic sphere as, 18, 37; expansion of, 125; feminism on, 27–34, 136–37, 189; in four-part model of society, 293, 294; friendship as, 46; Goffman on, 182–84, 185–88; Habermas on, 182, 184–88; the home as, xv, 208–9; Hutcheson on private rights, 128–29; the left on, 190–91; and the market, 5, 35, 36, 37–38; and the nonpolitical, 36, 305–6; as the not wholly revealed, 167; as the personal and the domestic, 18–19, 37, 43–46, 307, 307 n; preference for in immediate political future, 200; "private" having no unambiguous Russian equivalent, 304, 325 n.58; as realm of intimacy and emotionality, 20; the right on, 189–90; Roman origin of term, 11; sexual acts as private, 194; shrinking of in mass so-

ciety, 184; and the state, 15; in tripartite model of society, 35, 35 n, 196–201, 213–14, 274, 358–59; as woman's sphere, 28, 30, 31, 171, 269, 271–73, 277–79, 289–90, 291–92. *See also* domestic sphere; privacy; privatization; public/private distinction

privatization: and ambiguity of "public" and "private," 2; of the city, 237; in contemporary political theory, 133; of economic relations in Natural Law theory, 108, 109; of home and family, 209–10; of life under Communism, xvi, 303, 315, 322–25; marketization in post-Communist society, 304; the privatized worker and citizen, 205; of woman's sphere, 171

Prochazka, Jan, 173

promises, 49, 49 n.16

property: Arendt on, 212; as *dominium* in Roman law, 110–11; justification of private appropriation of, 110–11; the left's hostility to private, 188; Locke on, 116–25; in Natural Law theory, 107–11; and personal rights, 139; property-owning democracy, 206; public property, 308; Pufendorf on power and, 111–16; in Western economic discourse, 308

Protestant Reformation, 77

public, the. *See* public sphere

public affairs, 95

public goods: and ambiguity of "public" and "private," 2; economic definition of, 5; in Habermas's account of public sphere, 83; Hobbes on monarchy and, 89; limited privacy of the home as, 227; personal good contrasted with, 81; privacy as, 187

public health, 193–95

public housing: modernist projects of the 1930s, 241, 249–52; Public Works Administration guidelines for, 252

public interest: under Communism, 310; in international versus domestic affairs, 308; special interest contrasted with, 5

public law, 308

public life: as alienating, 206; and ambiguity of "public" and "private," 2; citizenship and, 10, 17; the city as location of, 238–39; of the old regime, 18; plurality as basic to, 82; and the political, 11; private life preferred to, 205; public space for, 17; as sociability, 2, 7, 16–25, 37; in an urban street, 243; the wealth of, 17, 22–23; women excluded from, 81, 105, 292

public opinion, 308, 346
public policy, 7, 188
public/private distinction: in architecture, 237,
247; Arendt on, 82, 212, 358–59; basic orientations to, 4–7; Berlin on, 179; in bioethics, 170; in built environment, 237–67; as
central concern of political theory, 133; and
citizenship, 106–7; in Communist and post-
Communist society, 303–32; conceptual limitations of, xii, xv–xiv, 15, 37, 269, 270,
291; contexts of occurrence of, xi–xii;
eighteenth-century and nineteenth-century
approaches to, 21 n.46; in establishing
boundary of the political, 2, 6–7, 8; as false
dichotomy, 196, 292; within the family,
192; feminism on, xiv, 27–34, 134–37,
271–73; in feudalism, 13; formal equivalence of states and, 99; four major ways of
drawing, xii–xiii, 7, 35; four-part models
for, 292–96, 308–9; gendering of, 276–79;
as grand dichotomy of Western thought, 1,
200; harm as criterion of, 103–4, 103 n.1,
122, 122 n.42, 124; implications of, 182–
203; and the individual and the state, 8–9;
in liberalism, 7–9, 63–64; Mill on, 197; as
misleading but necessary, 182; in modernity,
20–21; negotiating the boundaries of, 296–
97; neither term as wholly self-contained,
167–68; praxis linked to by Arendt, 82;
problematizing of, 80–88; as protean not
unitary, 2–3; in Roman law, 12, 107; shifting the debate on, 297–98; the social as mediating, 274, 298; terms as basic notions,
168; theory and politics of, 1–42; a trichotomy for, 35, 35 n, 196–201, 213–14, 274,
358–59; two families of approaches to, 36–
37; two kinds of imagery associated with,
4–6; varying in different spheres of discourse, 85; in visiting practices in antebellum New England, 268–302. See also private sphere; public sphere
public property, 308
public space: ambiguities in conception of,
238–39; Arendt's öffentliche Raum, 11; in
Brasilia, 254; dead public space, 24, 244; destruction of traditional, 237; the end of,
261; modernist spaces, 244–45, 262–63;
nineteenth-century views on, 240; patterns
of interaction in, 243; postmodern spaces,
263–65; private spaces' relation to, 244; the
problem of, 242–46; for public life, 17; requirements for a successful, 245–46; require-

ments for sociability in, 23–24; senses of
"public" blurred in, 242; as social and material, 245; transformations of, 237, 241; two
versions of, 25–26
public sphere: in absolutist period, 306; and
ambiguity of "public" and "private," 2, 11–
16, 80–81; in antebellum New England,
295; antidemocratic conceptualizations of,
81; Ariès's definition of, 17 n.35; as central
to democracy, 81; Communism's preference
for, 200; Communist suppression of independent, 311–12; conceived as homeland,
208; in contemporary political practice,
188–94; in contemporary social theory,
182–88; discursive conception of, 154–55;
feminism on, 27–34, 135–36; in four-part
model of society, 293, 295; Goffman on,
182–84, 185–88; Habermas on, 2, 14–15,
15 n.29, 81, 82–87, 82 n.11, 100, 135,
185–88; the home cut off from, 231; the
impersonal as, 43–46; the intimate split
from, 20; in late- and post-Communist societies, 327–29; Latin origin of "public," 11,
167; the left on, 188–89; liberal model of,
83; the literary public sphere, 86; and the
monarch for Hobbes, 89; multiplicity of
publics, 84–85, 196–97; nationalism and,
75–102; in nations formed from parts of
empires, 97; as paradoxical, 15; and the political, 11–16, 36, 295, 305–6; as a political
community, 76, 78, 100; and political society, 14, 307; in private communities, 263–
64; the private preferred to in immediate political future, 200; public arena of politics,
178–79; "public" having no unambiguous
Russian equivalent, 304, 318 n.39, 358; republicanism on, 306–7; res publica, 11,
81, 89; the right on, 190; in Roman law,
107, 306; Roman origin of term "public,"
11, 167; of sociability, 19, 24; as sphere
of publics, 100; the state associated with,
5, 8, 15, 37; supralocal, 95; in tripartite
model of society, 35, 35 n, 196–201, 213–
14, 274, 358–59. See also public
life; public/private distinction; public
space
Public Works Administration, 252
Pufendorf, Samuel: on equality, 112, 114;
Hobbes's influence on, 112 n.20; on ownership and power, 111–16, 112 n.19; on woman's consent, 113 n.21
Puritan Reformation, 336, 339–40, 351

quilting parties, 289

Raeff, Marc, 306, 310
rational choice theory, 9–10, 13
Rawls, John, 147
Reformation, Protestant, 77, 336, 339–40, 351
Reiter, Rayna, 32 n.66
Reitz, Edgar, 208
relational privacy, 143
relationships, intimate, 135, 142–43, 147
religion, civil, 199
religious fundamentalism, 134
republic, 11
republicanism, 77, 77 n.3, 107, 306–7
republican virtue, 12
res publica, 11, 81, 89
Rigby, T. H., 319
right, the: abortion opposed by, 190; on the family as private, 192; on freedom of expression, 192–93; on the home, 206; identity politics affecting, 189–90; on the private, 189–90; on the public, 190; on public regulation of private contracts, 195
rights, 127, 128–29, 139, 148, 148 n.36, 307–8, 316, 323
right to life, 198
Roe v. Wade: communitarian criticism of, 144; *Eisenstadt v. Baird* and, 145; MacKinnon's criticism of, 141–42; right to privacy as basis of, 137, 191–92, 198
Roman law: on citizenship, 107; *Corpus Juris Civilis,* 12n, 107, 306; Hobbes influenced by, 89; influence of, 11, 107; on property, 110–11; public/private distinction in, 12, 107; recovery of, 13, 13 n.26; on sovereign power creating the public, 306; Tocqueville on, 14
romantic marriage, 43, 46
Rome, ancient: friendship as *necessitudo,* 50, 61; "public" and "private" as Greco-Roman, 11, 167. *See also* Roman law
Rorty, Richard, 188
Rosaldo, Michelle Zimbalist, 28, 29 n.60
Rotundo, E. Anthony, 277–78
Rousseau, Jean-Jacques, 17, 65–66, 93, 214
Rubin, Gayle, 30 n.63
rules of civility, 156
Ruskin, John, 228
Russia. *See* Union of Soviet Socialist Republics
Ryan, Mary, 279, 294

Rybczynski, Witold, 238
Rykwert, Joseph, 230

Sacks, Karen, 33
Sade, Marquis de, 360
Saint-Evremond, Charles de, 64, 64 n
saints, 351
Sandel, Michael, 144–45, 146–50, 151
San Marino, 98
Saunders, Peter, 206–7, 206 n.5
Scarry, Elaine, 159 n.63
Schecter, Susan, 173 n.9
Scott, Joan, 295 n.66
Scottish Enlightenment: eighteenth-century approach to public/private distinction, 22 n.46; Ferguson, 55, 57, 57 n.36, 66; on friendship, 49–63, 67; on personal relations in market society, 44–45; on self-organization in the market, 79. *See also* Hume, David; Hutcheson, Francis; Smith, Adam
Scruton, Roger, 17, 242, 244
second economy, 311, 315, 315 n.30
secret ballot, 5, 5 n.7
self: atomistic conception of, 146–50; Bolshevism on, 340; as embodied, 159–62; modalities of presenting under Communism, 325; principle of inviolate personality, 138, 139, 154, 158, 160, 162; territories of the, 157, 159, 162. *See also* identity; individual, the
self-confidence, 159–60
self-enslavement, 114, 117, 123
self-service economy, 215, 219
Sennett, Richard, 2, 24, 244
servants: alienating their agency, 114–15; Locke on labor of, 119. *See also* master/servant relationship
sexual acts, 194, 349
sexual identity, 177
shame, 176
Shirk, Susan, 318
Shklar, Judith, 169
Shlapentokh, Vladimir, 322
shopping malls, 237, 238
Short Course of the History of the Communist Party, The, 351, 352
Shorter, Edward, 224
Silver, Allan, xiii, 21 nn.42, 46, 307 n
Simmel, Georg, 22 n.46, 48, 157 n.56, 211 n.16
single-person households, 222
Slater, Philip, 22, 22 n.47, 205 n.2, 225 n

Smidovich, Sofia, 334–35, 347–48
Smith, Adam: Adam Smith problem, 62–63, 63 n.50; on commercial society, 45 n.6; on friendship, 50–56, 61–62; on market society and personal relations, 45; on the moral order, 63; on *necessitudo*, 50, 54, 59, 61; on social order problem, 9; a supralocal public sphere assumed by, 95; on sympathy, 52, 52 n.24, 53 n.27, 55
sociability: area of in early modern house, 209–10; decay of, 24, 221, 225, 231, 231 n.52; gendered division of social work, 287–90; and the political, 24; privatization of social life under Communism, 303, 315, 322–25; public life as, 2, 7, 16–25, 37; public/private dichotomy as underestimating, 274; the public realm as realm of, 19; in public space, 23–24; the public sphere of, 24; Scottish Enlightenment model of, 66; urban, 23–24, 238, 243–44; visiting as, 281–84; and work in antebellum America, 280, 285–87
social, the: in antebellum New England, 293; in Arendt's tripartite model of society, 35, 35 n, 196–201, 213–14, 274 358, 359; in Communist societies, 317–18, 325–27; in four-part model of society, 292–96; genealogy of social roles under communism, 321–27; industrialization reordering, 290; as mediating public/private dichotomy, 274, 298; reframing social activity, 291–98; in Soviet life, 317–18, 358, 359; in visiting practices in antebellum New England, 268–302
social contract, 90, 106, 109, 114
social control school, 52 n.24
socialism, state, 16n
socialist construction, 311
socialist man (Soviet man), 311, 335
Socialist Realism, 340, 352
social order: built form and, 240; visual form and, 246, 261, 262
social order problem, 8–9
society: gesellschaft, 20–21, 22 n.46, 37, 51; home-centered society, 205, 206–7, 229; mass society, 184, 214; new social movements, 86 n.18, 88; social contract, 90, 106, 109, 114; social order problem, 8–9; Tocqueville on autonomous social organization versus the state, 308, 308 n.11. *See also* capitalism; civil society; collectivity; Communism; community; modernity; political soci-

ety; post-Communist society; sociability; social, the; social order
Solidarity movement, 303, 320, 328
Soltz, A. A., 342, 345–46, 359
Sorkin, Michael, 239
sovereignty, 11–12; ascending theory of, 78, 88 n.21; descending theory of, 88 n.21; eclipse of in Middle Ages, 13; hypertrophy of state sovereignty under Communism, 312 n.22; in modernity, 13; origin of term, 14 n.26; political community and, 88–94, 88 n.21; popular, 79, 91; in Roman law, 306
Soviet man (socialist man), 311, 335
Soviet Union. *See* Union of Soviet Socialist Republics
special interest, 5
speech codes, 192, 193, 198, 199
Stalin: explaining Marxism to workers, 339; in Great Retreat, 354; on Higher Conscience, 342; high totalitarianism under, 311, 312, 315, 326–27; *Short Course of the History of the Communist Party*, 351, 352; trappings of autocracy revived by, 313 n.26
standardization, 251–52, 256
Starr, Paul, 5 n.6
state, the: and the broader population, 77–79; commitment to under Communism, 318; Communist Party-state, 303, 309–12, 317, 322, 326; empire contrasted with nation-state, 99 n.45; equivalence of national states, 98–99; family functions taken over by, 214; in feminist critique of privacy analysis, 140, 141; in fourfold typology of modernity, 308–9; Hutcheson on civil society and, 127–28; hypertrophy of state sovereignty under communism, 312 n.22; the individual and, 8–9; legitimacy of, 78, 88–94; liberalism on, 8–10; the market compared with, 37; monarchy, 12, 14, 79, 89; national integration encouraged by, 94; the polis, 11, 26, 29, 35 n, 64; and the political community, 75–79, 75 n.1; the public and, 5, 8, 15, 37; public property as province of, 308; republicanism, 77, 77 n.3, 107, 306–7; republics, 11; Russian concept of, 314 n.26; separation of ethnicity and, 199; as specialized apparatus of rule, 76; state-engineered stratification and state dependence under Communism, 319–21; Tocqueville on autonomous social organization versus, 308, 308 n.11; welfare

state, 200, 229. *See also* absolutism; citizenship; democracy; empires; law; sovereignty; totalitarianism
state socialism, 16 n
Stone, Lawrence, 19
strangership, 43–74; in commercial society, 53; historical transformation of, 54; and sympathy, 52
Sunstein, Cass, 191
surety, 56
sympathy, 52, 52 n.24, 53 n.27, 55

Talmon, J. L., 310 n.17
taste, 247, 255, 262, 263
telebanking, 218
teleshopping, 218
temperance movement, 297
territories of the self, 157, 159, 162
Tertullian, 341
Thomas, Kendall, 160
Timasheff, Nicholas, 353, 354
Tocqueville, Alexis de: on French state smothering political life, 16, 16 n; on national unity eliminating diversity, 94; on political society, 14, 14 n.27, 15 n.28, 304 n; on the public, 306; on the state versus autonomous social organization, 308, 308 n.11
Toffler, Alvin, 218–19
Tönnies, Ferdinand, 20, 43, 51, 65, 65 n.54
total institutions, 186
totalitarianism: asylums as metaphor for, 183; in Communism, 305–19; high totalitarianism under Stalin, 16 n, 311, 312, 315, 326–27; origin of term, 305; retreat to privacy under, 16 n; self-censorship under, 172
Trask, Sarah, 284
Tribe, Lawrence, 195, 198
true womanhood, cult of, 277
Tuck, Richard, 110
Tucker, Robert C., 339

Union of Soviet Socialist Republics: authoritarian trappings revived in, 313 n.26, 314; Brezhnev, 313; as a comradely society, 357–60; Gorbachev, 207, 321; the Great Retreat, 350, 353–54; high totalitarianism under Stalin, 16 n, 311, 312, 315, 326–27; Khrushchev, 313; Lenin, 310 n.17, 312 n.22, 337–39, 342; Leninism, 16 n, 305, 309, 310, 319; manners campaign in, 352–53; middlebrow fiction in, 352; newspeak in, 326;
Party-state of, 303, 309–12, 317, 322, 326; period of stagnation under Brezhnev, 313; private life in, 333–63; routinization of partocratic oligarchy in, 313; second economy of, 311, 315, 315 n.30; Soviet man, 311, 335. *See also* Bolshevism; Communism; Stalin
United Nations, 98
universalism, enlightenment, 134
urbanism, new, xv, 237, 257, 264
urban planning, 237
USSR. *See* Union of Soviet Socialist Republics
utilitarianism, 126
utilitarian liberalism, 8–9, 8 n.14

Venturi, Robert, 255–57
violence against women, 173–75
virtuocracy, 318
visiting in antebellum New England, 268–302; economic function of, 280, 285–87; first-person accounts of, 279–81; as gender-integrated practice, 279, 283; industrialization constraining, 290; as ordered system of activity, 292; as primary mode of personal interaction, 274–75; sick visits, 285–87; as sociability, 281–84; visit defined, 279; women visiting more than men, 283
Vogel, Lise, 278 n.30
Vujacic, Velijko, 329

waiting period for abortion, 198
Wallas, Graham, 47
Walzer, Michael, 336, 337, 346
Warren, Samuel D., 154 n
washing clothes, 289–90
Watkins, Susan Cott, 95
Weber, Max, 306, 307
Weintraub, Jeff, xii–xiii, 200, 208–9, 210 n, 238, 242, 274 n.18, 294, 304 n, 306 n.6
welfare state, 200, 229
Wentworth, William, 58
Whyte, William Foote, 23
Whyte, William H., 23
willed community, 13
Williams, Patricia, 158 n.60
Williamson, Oliver, 9
Winiecki, Jan, 313 n.25
Wolfe, Alan, xv, 294
women: agency of impaired, 114–15; Aristotle on natural inequality of, 12; being female seen as a misfortune, 169;

women (*continued*) caring for the sick by, 287–89; citizenship accepted for, 87; consent of in marriage, 113 n.21, 118, 141; cult of true womanhood, 277; difference of, 161 n.67, 162; domestic sphere as sphere of, 28, 31, 277; exclusion from public life, 81, 105, 292; group identity of, 198; the home as realm of, 211 n.16; in household economy, 215; Hutcheson on status of, 126, 127 n.49; Locke on agency of, 120–21; Locke on the marriage contract, 118, 119–21, 120 n.34; in nuclear family, 211, 212 n; pregnancy and identity of, 160; in premodern household, 211; the private as the sphere of, 28, 30, 31, 171, 269, 271–73, 277–79, 289–90, 291–92; a public discourse of their own, 84; quilting parties, 289; special protection for, 162; violence against, 173–75; as visiting more than men, 283; work life in nineteenth century, 276–77. *See also* abortion; feminism

work. *See* labor

Yugoslavia, 96–97, 329

Zaretsky, Eli, 32
Zhdanov, Andrei, 356
zone of intimacy, 140, 144–45
Zukin, Sharon, 264 n.45